The Beatles

The Press Reports

1961 – 1970

By W. Fraser Sandercombe

We acknowledge the financial support of the Government of Canada through
the Book Publishing Industry Development Program for our publishing activities.
Published by Collector's Guide Publishing Inc., Box 62034, Burlington, Ontario, Canada, L7R 4K2
Printed and bound in Canada
THE BEATLES: THE PRESS REPORTS
W. Fraser Sandercombe
ISBN: 978-1-894959-61-2

The Beatles

The Press Reports

1961 – 1970

By W. Fraser Sandercombe

— Contents —

— Acknowledgments —

Thanks to the writers of all those Beatle articles in the music press, primarily *Mersey Beat*; *Record Mirror*; *Disc and Music Echo*; and *Melody Maker*:

Mike Adams; Neil Aspinall; Derek Boltwood; Caroline Boucher; Howie Casey; Bess Coleman; Ray Coleman; Bob Dawbarn; Jerry Dawson; Brian Epstein; Kenny Everett; Bob Farmer; Lon Goddard; Ren Grevatt; David Griffiths; Les Hall; June Harris; Bill Harry; Derek Harvey; Mike Hennessey; Laurie Henshaw; Frank Hilliger; David Hughes; Dick Hughes; Nigel Hunter; Jack Hutton; Bob Houston; David Hughes; Virginia Ironside; Peter Jay; Langley Johnson; Len Johnson; George Jones; Nick Jones; Peter Jones; Norman Jopling; Henry Kahn; John Kercher; Wesley Laine; Mike Ledgerwood; Jerry Leighton; Richard Lennox; Mike Martin; Keith Matthews; Brian Mulligan; Don Nicholl; Klaus Nicholson; Hugh Nolan; John Peel; Gavin Petrie; Harry Pules; Chris Roberts; Pierre Robin; Richard Robinson; Susan Shaw; Roy Shipston; Don Short; Anne Sims; Judy Sims; David Skan; Gillian Smart; Alan Smith; Ian Starrett; Alan Stinton; Derek Taylor; Peter Thomson; Penny Valentine; Virginia; Alan Walsh; Jeremy Walsh; Lu Walters; Jimmy Watson; Chris Welch; Richard Williams; Gillian Wilson; Tony Wilson; and Bob Wooler.

— Preface —

For my birthday in December 1963, my parents gave me a copy of this amazing new album by four guys from Liverpool, (where's that?) England. Across the top was the banner: *Beatlemania*. Below that: *With the Beatles*. The photo on the front, mostly black, showed the mysteriously shadowed faces of four unsmiling guys with interesting new hair styles. And the music... The music was fresh air and joy. All that Bobby rubbish that was happening round about then – you know, Bobby Vee, Bobby Rydell, Bobby Darin, Bobby Vinton – all that post-payola tripe just faded away... or so it seemed. This English group was IT!

She Loves You had been playing on the pop radio stations and it was exciting as hell. But this album, *Beatlemania: With The Beatles,* their first North American LP, went so far beyond anything ever before heard by a North American rock and roll fan that it opened up new worlds. (*Beatlemania: With The Beatles* was the Capitol Canada release; the album was released as *Meet The Beatles* by Capitol Records in the U.S.)

And the old world began to change. By the time the Beatles played the Ed Sullivan show in February 1964, enslaving, enthralling, enrapturing, and enchanting a generation, most of the guys I knew had washed the grease out of their hair and let the hair just flop. A few of my friends were actually expelled from school for their new hair styles – me too. And all around the city, groups were starting up, groups put together by guys who, prior to the Beatles, had had no thought of ever doing anything musically – guys who could not wait to skip music class at school because it was so god awful.

The Leach Organisation presents:–

St. PATRICK'S NIGHT
"ROCK ❧ GALA"❧

This Saturday 17th March 7:30-11:30 pm.
KNOTTY ASH HALL
(Junction Eaton Rd./East Prescot Rd.)

Starring

✳ *THE BEATLES*
✳ *RORY STORM & THE HURRICANES*

Hats ♦ Novelties ♦ Prizes   BUFFET

❧ Admission 5/- ❧
(at door)

An argument can be made that it was not the Beatles who started that social revolution way back in the 1960s. Some people think it started before that, with Jack Kerouac and the other beat writers, from jazz on into the folk movement. But it was the Beatles who launched all those 60s teenagers into uncharted seas of dreams, into unexplored realms of art and adventure. Not Kerouac or Ginsberg, not Bob Dylan, whose true impact would not be felt for a few years. It was the Beatles. Without a clue that it would happen, with nothing but the Dionysian energy of their music, their youth, and the brilliance of their untutored creativity, they changed the world.

They gave the kids something that they instinctively knew belonged to them and them alone. The Beatles were not owned by some recording company or some manager who cared only about the dollars. The Beatles belonged to themselves and, therefore, to their fans. Not only did the group sound original, they looked original, they approached the adult world with a certain originality and they were not, apparently, intimidated by that adult world. They exuded confidence. They made jokes with the press, laughed, made their music... and defied convention. They invented their own music. Sure, they played cover songs, but they also wrote their own. No Tin Pan Alley for this group. They had something they wanted to say and they said it. Thus began the rebellion, the revolution.

— 1957 —

On June 22, 1957, The Quarrymen played their first gig from the back of a coal lorry on Roseberry Street during the Empire Day Celebrations. Reminiscing, John said, *"We didn't get paid. We played at blokes' parties after that, or weddings, perhaps for a few bob. Mostly we just played for fun."* Such an ignominious beginning; such a stunning conclusion.

— Chapter One: 1961 —

July 6, 1961 – *Mersey Beat*, in their debut issue, published an article by John Lennon regarding the dubious origins of the Beatles. Once upon a time... three lads named John, George and Paul decided to get together and make music. Which they did. Since no one cared, they added another lad named Stuart Sutcliffe, whom they asked to buy a bass guitar. Reluctantly, he did that. But he could not play, and still no one was interested in their music. They worked with him until he could play... almost. But they needed a beat. Drums were the answer. The band needed a drummer.

Drummers came and went. The band came and went and played whatever gigs they could find.

Then they were invited to Hamburg to play... and to make money. They needed a full-time drummer. And they found Pete Best at the Casbah in West Derby and enlisted him to travel to Hamburg to play – and to make money – which they did.

July 20, 1961 – *Mersey Beat* **reported** that the Beatles had signed a recording contract with Bert Kaempfert and Polydor, in Germany, to make four records a year for the company.

At their first recording session, the band sang and played behind Tony Sheridan. They recorded *Why* which had been written by Sheridan, along with *My Bonny Lies Over the Ocean* and *The Saints Go Marching In*.

They also recorded two other songs on their own for Kaempfert. The first one was an instrumental written by George Harrison. It had not, as yet, been named but would likely be called *Cry for a Shadow*. The second one was *Ain't She Sweet*, sung by John Lennon. They sold the rights entirely to Polydor.

The band went back to England but Stuart Sutcliffe had decided to remain in Germany. He was studying art and would soon be marrying a German girl. The Beatles had decided to remain a quartet.

July 20, 1961 – *Mersey Beat*, **in a column called Mersey Roundabout, mentioned** that Richard Starkey, better known as Ringo Starr, of Rory Storm and The Hurricanes, was in Liverpool on July 8 to celebrate his birthday (he was 21) and also that Howie of Derry and The Seniors claimed that Paul MacArtrey (*sic*) of the Beatles could sing better than Cliff Richard.

August 17, 1961 – *Mersey Beat* **carried** a letter from Audrey McDowall of Lancashire. *"I've tried everywhere else and you seem to be my last resort. Please could you give me some gen on George Harrison, guitarist with the Beatles. I saw the Beatles at the Cavern on July 21st at the lunch-time session and I think George is the utmost, ginchiest, skizziest, craziest cool cat I've ever seen. Why don't*

the Beatles record The Hully Gully Song? I'm sure it would be a hit."

September 14, 1961 – *Mersey Beat*, **Virginia mentioned** that a Beatles fan club had been formed, due to open officially sometime soon.

September 14, 1961 – *Mersey Beat*, **Bob Wooler wondered** why the Beatles were so popular. Many people had asked him that question since Tuesday, December 27, 1960, at the Litherland Town Hall, when *"the impact of the act was first felt on this side of the river."*

Wooler had been associated with the launching of the Beatles that night. He was grateful for that, and grateful for the honour of presenting them to their wild and feverish audiences at nearly all of their subsequent appearances prior to their last stay in Hamburg.

He thought, perhaps, that his close association with the group induced people to believe that he might have enough inside information to be able to explain the Beatles' success.

He decided to try.

By the time the Beatles came along, rock and roll, music that had its roots with *"American negro singers,"* had been emasculated in Britain by Cliff Richard and the Shadows and their imitators. The drive, the power, had been removed from the music. Jungle music had been tamed.

But the Beatles came along full of energy and pounding rock rhythms, exploding on a tired, worn-out music scene, enchanting the crowds, infecting the audiences with their own enthusiasm and joy, letting the older ones relive the power of early rock, and letting the younger ones experience that power for the first time.

The Beatles symbolised rebellion. They were the real thing, five, then four, young men pounding out an irresistible beat, dynamic and powerful, as they turned back the clock to the roots of rock, all the while giving it a freshness that even the originals – Chuck Berry, Little Richard, Carl Perkins, the Coasters, and on and on – might have been hard pressed to equal. Scruffy, long-haired, loud, raucous – and romantic, the Beatles threw out their songs, bounced around on stage, and imprinted everything with their own touch and their own style, giving the crowds, whether in Liverpool or Hamburg, something that had not been heard or felt before.

Wooler thought the group was primarily a vocal act, rarely instrumental, playing whatever they liked for whatever the reason, their skills honed by a long gig at the Top Ten Club in Hamburg. Not only was

their music great, they had great personalities, and they looked great. They were a phenomenon. They were magic.

Their like would never be seen again.

October 5, 1961 – Bob Wooler, writing as Mr. Big Beat for *Mersey Beat*, said the Beatles were definitely number one amongst the Merseyside groups. On the same page, a reader, in a letter, asked why one of The Fabulous Beatles, the one who wore the dark glasses, had not been appearing with them lately. There were rumours that he had been killed in a car crash in Germany, and other rumours that he had married a German girl and had settled down. The paper reminded the reader that, in their second issue, they had announced that Stuart Sutcliffe intended to stay in Germany with a German girl.

December 14, 1961 – *Mersey Beat*, Bob Wooler said things were looking good for Liverpool groups. The Beatles' record for Polydor backing Tony Sheridan, *The Saints / My Bonnie,* was to be released soon in England thanks to the efforts of Brian Epstein of NEMS.

— Chapter Two: 1962 —

Virginia. In her column, Virginia wondered if Ringo Starr, the drummer with the Hurricanes, was planning to join the Seniors for a tour of one-night stands around Britain. She also mentioned that John and Paul of the Beatles had written over seventy original songs, she had seen the Beatles play at the Jacaranda Club, and Stuart Sutcliffe had returned to Liverpool for a visit and was now back in Hamburg.

March 22, 1962 – *Mersey Beat*, Bob Wooler said that the Beatles had had so much impact on the Merseyside beat scene that there was no stopping them. He suggested that Liverpool would be losing them soon, but only for a short time. On April 11, they would be leaving for Hamburg for seven weeks. Brian Epstein had assured Wooler that the group would be back in Liverpool in early June.

January 4, 1962 – *Mersey Beat* featured a photograph on page one of all four Beatles – John Lennon, George Harrison, Paul McArtrey (sic) and Pete Best – announcing that the Beatles had topped the Mersey Beat popularity poll; they were number one, the best group of 1961.

February 22, 1962 – *Mersey Beat* announced that the Beatles would be off to Germany again, this time for a seven-week gig at a new club in Hamburg. Before leaving for the continent, they would be doing shows in Southport, Chester, Liverpool and Gloucester. Also, they would be hosting a Beatles Fan Club night at the Cavern. Sometime later in the year, they would be recording in England; also, later in the year, it would be possible to hear the group on the radio.

He said their reputation would in no way be diminished by their absence. They would be better than ever, more mature, more professional, and more popular.

The Pavilion Theatre was holding box seats for a Beatles' show for the fan who could best explain why he/she liked the group.

April 19, 1962 – *Mersey Beat* reported that the Beatles' reception at the Star Club in Hamburg had been rapturous. A television producer had been in the audience and was so impressed that he was making arrangements for the group to appear on German TV.

On the same page was a photograph of the group, along with a shot of Rory Storm and the Hurricanes, with Ringo Starr on drums, and a brief good-bye for Stuart Sutcliffe. The news of his death had been shocking.

March 22, 1962 – *Mersey Beat* ran a photograph of the Beatles above the Mersey Roundabout column by

```
┌─────────────────────────────────┐
│ BEATLES at . . .                │
│ FRIDAY, 24th MARCH   WEDNESDAY, 28th MARCH │
│ FRIDAY, 30th MARCH   WEDNESDAY, 4th APRIL  │
│        . . . the CAVERN          │
└─────────────────────────────────┘
```

May 31, 1962 – *Mersey Beat* announced that Brian Epstein had secured a recording contract for the Beatles with EMI to make records on the Parlophone label. Their first disc was to be released in July. They invited readers to write in and say what songs the group should record first.

July 26, 1962 – *Mersey Beat* announced that the Beatles were to star at the Mersey Beat Ball at the Majestic in Birkinhead.

August 23, 1962 – *Mersey Beat* reported that the Beatles had changed their drummer, replacing Pete Best with Ringo Starr (formerly with Rory Storm and the Hurricanes).

"Pete left the group by mutual agreement. There were no arguments or difficulties, and this has been an entirely amicable decision," said The Beatles.

The article went on to say that the Beatles would be in London on September 4th to do some recording at the EMI Studios, where George Martin would produce them.

The directors of Whetstone Entertainment, who controlled the Plaza Ballroom in St. Helens where the Beatles had had phenomenal box office success on four Mondays nights in a row, had engaged the band to play four Thursday-night gigs at the Riverpark Ballroom in Chester. The engagement had started August 16th.

September 6, 1962 – *Mersey Beat* ran part one of an interview with Paul McArtney *(sic)* about the Beatles and Stuart Sutcliffe.

Said Paul, *"John, George, Stu and I used to play at a strip club in Upper Parliament Street, backing Janice the Stripper. At the time we wore little lilac jackets, or purple jackets, or something. Well, we played behind Janice and naturally, we looked at her, the audience looked at her, everybody looked at her, just sort of normal. At the end of the act, she would turn around and, well, we were all young lads, we'd never seen anything like it before, and all blushed, four blushing red-faced lads.*

"Janice brought sheets of music for us to play all her arrangements. She gave us a bit of Beethoven and The Spanish Fire Dance. *So in the end we said, 'We can't read music, sorry, but instead of* The Spanish Fire Dance, *we can play* The Harry Lime Cha-Cha, *which we've arranged ourselves, and instead of Beethoven, you can have* Moonglow *or* September Song, *take your pick. Instead of* The Sabre Dance, *we'll give you* Ramrod. *So that's what she got. She seemed quite satisfied anyway. The*

Strip Club wasn't an important chapter in our lives, but it was an interesting one."*

September 6, 1962 – *Mersey Beat* had a photograph of a smiling Ringo Starr. The caption said it was no wonder Ringo was smiling – he was now the drummer for the Beatles.

September 20, 1962 – *Mersey Beat* wrote that at 8:15 a.m. on September 4th the Beatles left Liverpool for London to record their first disc for Parlophone. George Martin and his assistant, Ron Richards, were awaiting their arrival, along with Neil Aspinall, who had trucked all their equipment down to the EMI studios in St. John's Wood.

For most of the day the group rehearsed six songs before two were selected.

They broke for dinner and George Martin took them to his favourite Italian restaurant where he regaled them with stories about recording Peter Sellers and Spike Milligan.

Then it was time for the final session, the recording. Fifteen takes were needed to finish *Love Me Do*. With everyone exhausted, the session ended at midnight. No one was certain, until the next day, whether or not the song was good enough. After one listen, Brian Epstein and George Martin had no doubt: it was great; it couldn't be better.

September 20, 1962 – *Mersey Beat* ran the rest of their interview with Paul McCartney *(finally getting his name right)*.

Said Paul, *"The first time we went to Hamburg we stayed four and a half months. It's a sort of blown up Blackpool, but with strip clubs instead of waxworks; thousands of strip clubs, bars and pick-up joints, not very picturesque.*

"The first time, it was pretty rough, but we all had a gear time. The pay wasn't too fab, the digs weren't much good, and we had to play for quite a long time. The club was a small place called the Indra and was owned by the proprietor of the Kaiser Keller, where we also played.

"One night, we played at the Top Ten Club and all the customers from the Kaiser Keller came along. Since the Top Ten was a much better club, we decided to accept the manager's offer and play there.

Naturally, the manager of the Kaiser Keller didn't like it. One night, prior to leaving his place, we accidentally singed a bit of cord on an old stone wall in the corridor, and he had the police on us. He'd told them that we'd tried to burn his place down, so they said, 'Leave please, thanks very much, but we don't want you to burn our German houses.' Funny, really, because we couldn't have burnt the place if we had gallons of petrol; it was made of stone.

"There was an article on the group in a German magazine. I didn't understand the article, but there was a large photograph of us in the middle page. In the same article, there was a photograph of a South African Negro pushing the jungle down. I still don't quite know what he has to do with us, but I suppose it has some significance."

October 4, 1962 – *Mersey Beat* ran a photograph of John Lennon and George Harrison. It had been taken at Rushworth's (record shop) as they received a pair of Gibson guitars, the only ones of their type in England. The instruments had been flown in from America. They also mentioned that the Beatles would be appearing at Dawson's Music Shop in Widnes on October 6th to sign copies of their record, which would be released on the 5th. They were to arrive at 4:00 p.m. and stay for an hour.

October 13, 1962 – *New Record Mirror* published a brief review of the Beatles first single, *Love Me Do / P.S. I Love You*. The reviewer wrote that *Love Me Do* began with a harmonica riff as a lead-in to the lyrics from this group with the peculiar name. He suggested the band's approach was quiet and included some unusual combinations for the vocals, but he claimed the song dragged through the middle, particularly during the harmonica lead. It was an okay song, he said, but he was not impressed with the B-side, calling it poorly arranged. The song was apparently a decent effort, but did not have enough happening to hold his interest.

October 18, 1962 – *Mersey Beat* announced that the Beatles would be playing at the Royal Lido in Prestatyn, and at the Empire, Lime Street, Liverpool, sometime soon. In response to a fan's inquiry, they said photographs of the Beatles could be had from NEMS Enterprises.

October 18, 1962 – *Mersey Beat* ran a hit chart that showed *Love Me Do* as the number one disc on Merseyside. The story of the Beatles' success had reached new heights with the release of their first British record. The writer reminded readers about their German Polydor recordings, and how *My Bonnie* had "soared" in the charts in Germany.

Love Me Do backed by *P.S. I Love You*, on the Parlophone label, was the best selling record on Merseyside. The writer thought *Love Me Do* was somewhat monotonous, but was the sort of song that would grow on you. He was disappointed the first time he heard it, but he was liking it more and more each time he played it, though he still preferred *P.S. I Love You*. He liked John Lennon's harmonica sounds.

October 27, 1962 – *New Record Mirror*, **Norman Jopling** wrote a piece inviting readers to meet the Beatles, saying that three weeks before the date of the article, most of the teenagers in England had not heard of them but that, even before their first record, they were sharing top billing on a tour with Bruce Channel.

They were the first new British vocal band to have a record in the charts in a very long time.

The band with the strange name, The Beatles, had been around for quite some time, known by every teenager in Liverpool, long before they had a record in the charts, long before they gained any recognition in the rest of Britain. The Beatles were the most celebrated band on the Mersey, where there was a proliferation of music groups, all trying to make it, hammering out their dreams on cheap guitars and drums.

The Beatles' style, the writer said, blended the best of skiffle, rhythm and blues, folk and rock and roll – with just a dash of the blues – an incredible combination that gained them fans from all around Liverpool and the northwest of England, and in Hamburg, Germany. The first of their three German visits was in 1960, and each subsequent gig was more successful and at a more important venue than the previous.

Their first recording was as a back-up band to Tony Sheridan's vocals, issued by Polydor. Their own first record, *Love Me Do / P.S. I Love You*, both sides written by John Lennon and Paul McCartney, was being called a hit, since it had made the top fifty. It featured John Lennon on rhythm guitar, harmonica and vocals; Paul McCartney on bass guitar and vocals; George Harrison on lead; and Ringo Starr on drums. He mentioned that Ringo went to school with Billy Fury and was the most recent member of the band.

According to a poll in *Mersey Beat Magazine*, the Beatles were the hottest act in the North West. That summer they pulled in the largest crowd ever at the Cavern Club in Liverpool, outdrawing both the Shadows and the Temperance Seven, who had set the previous records.

Liverpool disc jockey Bob Wooler said of the Beatles: *"The biggest thing to hit Liverpool for years. The hottest property any promoter could hope to encounter. Musically authoritative and physically magnetic, the Beatles are rhythmic revolutionaries with an act which is a succession of climaxes."* The writer suggested he might be right.

November 1, 1962 – *Mersey Beat*, **Alan Smith** said The Beatles had dropped by for a visit in London. He confessed he had never actually heard them play but he believed it when the group's fans said they were great. He mentioned that *Love Me Do* was now in the Top Thirty and that London fans were beginning to like it.

He asked the group what they thought of Londoners.

Said the Beatles, *"Not much. If they know you come from the North they don't want to know."*

They went on to tell him that they were going to have to play a lot of different venues if they wanted to be known beyond Merseyside.

Smith said it had been a pleasure meeting them.

The Beatles said, *"We've got wonderful fans, but some of them aren't buying our record because they don't want us to become famous. One girl said, 'Eh lads, if you have a hit record you'll go to London, then we won't see you any more. You've gorra stay in Liverpool. You're ours!'"*

November 15, 1962 – *Mersey Beat* **said** that Pete Best, former drummer for the Beatles, had joined a group called Lee Curtis and the All-Stars. They went on to say that the Beatles were still high in the Merseyside charts with *Love Me Do*.

November 15, 1962 – *Mersey Beat*, **Alan Smith wondered** if the Beatles would become national stars or if they would soon fade away, one-hit wonders. The competition to reach the top would be tremendous. He questioned whether or not the Beatles had what it would take.

The Beatles needed to escape being known as a Liverpool group in order to be widely accepted in Britain he said. Smith suggested their real fans would sympathise with that and cheer them on, their real fans knew that, in order for the group to truly make it, they would needed a much broader fan base than Liverpool could supply.

Smith believed the Beatles had great things ahead of them. They had actually made it into the charts with their very first record; they had a strange name that deejays would not be able to resist; and they had a brilliant recording manager in George Martin. Not to mention their sound!

He had spoken recently with Little Richard and Richard said, *"Man, those Beatles are fabulous. If I hadn't seen them I'd never have dreamed they were white. They have a real authentic Negro sound."*

November 24, 1962 – *New Record Mirror*, **Norman Jopling published** a story about the Beatles always

being certain of applause because they took their fans with them.

"When we played outside Liverpool, as often as not we would hire a couple of coaches and take an audience with us.

"On any dates we played outside the Liverpool area, we had to work hard to please our audience. Sometimes we couldn't do it. We either went down a treat or very badly," said Paul McCartney.

It was only recently that the Beatles were gaining acceptance outside their home area of Liverpool. *Love Me Do* had helped them attain their new popularity. But, the writer said, a lot of people really did not like the song.

"A lot of people," McCartney continued, *"still don't like our music; when we're performing we try to please the audience generally; if we find slow numbers aren't going down well we switch to fast ones. If they don't work, we might try something off-beat, like* Twist and Shout.

"They're the sort we like doing best – the Rhythm and Blues-y things. They go down well, we find." And he said the band started out *"more or less for the laugh."* They met at school and joined up to form a skiffle group.

McCartney said, *"I remember when we decided to play Twenty Flight Rock. I learned the chords and everything perfectly. I used to long to play it – it was my song, you know."*

He reminisced about their days at the Cavern in Liverpool, a back street club shaped like a railway tunnel.

"We love the Cavern. Surprisingly enough, groups from outside Liverpool don't like it. It's small and cramped, but we're at home there. We play the frantic beat numbers, and the R&B stuff, like Some Other Guy and If You Gotta Make a Fool of Somebody.

"We improvise on the original thing – not to improve it, but because we can't get the sound of the disc. Once we've performed it, it's kept in that same form. We won't change it at all."

The Cavern started out as a jazz club when Trad [traditional jazz] was all the rage in Liverpool, long before it became popular throughout Britain. But the Cavern-goers evolved into a rhythm and blues crowd, preferring the stuff the Beatles played. At the time, there were over three hundred bands in Liverpool, battling each other for gigs at the local clubs.

"The clubs in Liverpool are unique. Nothing like them anywhere else. The groups get their chances there, and in the ring of dance halls round Liverpool – well, two dance halls, if you can call that a ring."

The Beatles were not actually like any of the other groups. They did not label themselves with R&B or vocals or instrumentals. They were just a group. The writer suggested they did not actually know what they were.

When the Beatles returned to the Cavern from their last gig in Hamburg, the fans lined up from 7 a.m. to 6 p.m. waiting to see them. The attendance was nearly nine hundred, beating the previous attendance records set by the Temperance Seven and the Shadows.

The writer described the Beatles as an unusual team without pointed shoes, without greased-back hair. They had long hair and wore Chelsea boots and suede coats. In Hamburg, they were supremely popular with the art crowd.

Their next record was to be released soon. Paul McCartney was not sure what it would be but guessed that *Please Please Me* would be the one.

November 29, 1962 – **Mersey Beat** announced that when the Beatles returned from their fourteen-day gig in Hamburg – December 18th to 31st – they would do a five-day tour of Scotland. It was possible that they would be on Scottish TV. They went on to say the band would be back playing around Liverpool in January and that their next recording session in London was set up for January 16th.

December 15, 1962 – in Birkenhead, at the Majestic Ballroom on Conway Street, the Beatles took top honours as they played the **Mersey Beat Poll Awards** show.

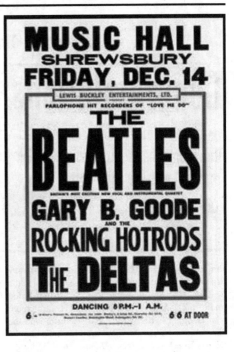

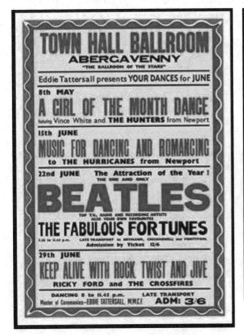

— Chapter Three: 1963 —

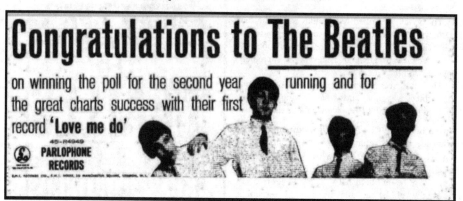

Congratulations to The Beatles on winning the poll for the second year running and for the great charts success with their first record 'Love me do'

45-R4949

PARLOPHONE RECORDS

January 3, 1963 – Alan Smith wrote for *Mersey Beat* about attending a recording session with the Beatles. The scene was EMI's St. John's Wood studio in London. Smith was in the control room with George Martin as the band set up around the microphones below. Martin waved his hand and the Beatles launched into *Please Please Me*.

Smith thought the song was destined to hit the top ten immediately. The beat was captivating, the harmonica magic, the vocals great.

John Lennon said, "*I tried to make it as simple as possible. Some of the stuff I've written has been a bit way out, but we did this one strictly for the hit parade. Now we're keeping our fingers crossed.*"

When *Please Please Me* was finished, they took a break for tea and George Martin said, "*The thing I like about the Beatles is their great sense of humour – and their talent, naturally. It's a real pleasure to work with them because they don't take themselves too seriously, as many groups do these days. You know the types: they think they're heaven's gift to the music business.*

"*The Beatles are different. They've got ability, but if they make mistakes, they can joke about it. I think they'll go a long way in show business.*"

Martin compared them to a male version of the Shirelles. Smith thought they were more like the Drifters.

After tea, the group went back into the studio to record the B side, *Ask Me Why*, another of their own compositions.

Smith mentioned that Ringo Starr was doing well. He was more relaxed during this session than a few months ago when the group was recording *Love Me Do*. The group also did another of their own songs, *The Tip of My Tongue*, which Martin had considered for the B side.

"*It's a great number*," he said, "*but we'll have to spend a bit of time giving it a new arrangement. I'm not too happy with it the way it is. Perhaps we can*

work it out when I come to Liverpool. I'm thinking of recording their first LP at the Cavern, but obviously I'm going to have to come to see the club before I make a decision.

"*If we can't get the right sound we might do the recording somewhere else in Liverpool, or bring an invited audience into the studio in London. They've told me they work better in front of an audience.*"

Martin thought the songs on the LP would all be originals, since the group had written more than a hundred numbers.

Added Martin, "*Another thing that's worrying us is the title. After all, LPs need a catchy name if they're going to stand out in the shop window.*"

January 17, 1963 – *Mersey Beat* said that the Beatles broke all attendance records during their first appearance on Merseyside, at the Grafton on January 10th, after their Hamburg gig. The reception had rarely been equaled.

January 31, 1963 – *Mersey Beat* said that the Beatles were number one again. *Please Please Me* had hit the top of the Merseyside chart. They went on to say that five hundred fans had been turned away from seeing the Beatles at the Majestic on January 7th – the room had been sold out. Manager Brian Marsden said he would get the group for two shows the next time, and clear the ballroom between shows so a new bunch could come in for the second set. He was certain the Beatles would be playing to two full houses.

A footnote mentioned that Andrew Oldham had taken over the publicity for the Beatles.

February 2, 1963 – *New Record Mirror*, Wesley Laine wrote a report on the Beatles, claiming that whether you liked them or not, the Beatles were hotter than anyone else on the British music scene. Even if you did not like their music, you supposedly liked their looks.

"A hip Temperance Seven," claimed Alma Cogan after seeing them play *Please Please Me* on Thank Your Lucky Stars.

"See you at the Palladium," said Frankie Vaughan after the same show.

The week before Thank Your Lucky Stars, as the Beatles were on their way to the BBC to do some recording, fans attacked their taxi.

And in Manchester, the fans refused to leave until the Beatles performed an encore. When they were finally able to leave, their cab was vandalised by rabid fans, mirrors and antenna pulled off, a widow shattered.

The writer suggested that it would not be long before the Beatles were accused of provoking violence. He went on to talk about the planned American release for *Please Please Me* on the Vee Jay label, which had presented a number of British hits, including *I Remember You* and *Lovesick Blues*.

On March 9, their new LP and single were to be released, while the band was on tour with Tommy Roe and Chris Montez. Then they were to do a series of ballroom dates until they went on a 12-day vacation on April 27. They had been working non-stop for months.

"Brian Epstein, our manager," said leader John Lennon, *"has decided that even if we were offered a tour of Moscow or Every Night at the London Palladium, we would still have a holiday."*

"One reason I think they'll succeed," offered Kenny Lynch, *"is because they manage to reproduce their record sound on stage. This is why the Shadows succeeded and this is why the Beatles will. Apart from that, their sound is so great they just can't miss."*

February 16, 1963 – *New Record Mirror*, **Norman Jopling talked** about the Beatles' proposed new album and single, saying there had been a lot of stuff justifiably written about the Beatles; they were that rarest of performers to chart a record – the British vocal group.

A few months previous, no British vocal groups would have been getting air play but, at the moment, perhaps thanks to the Beatles, there were a number of them: the Bachelors, the Vernons Girls, the Chucks.

The Beatles were making it on the crest of an oh-so-obviously-temporary wave. It was hoped that the Beatles would not be temporary because they were as popular for their personalities as for their music.

He said the Beatles were aware of that and played it up. They were currently touring with Helen Shapiro and Kenny Lynch, clad in suits with velvet collars and cuffs, backed by pink tab-collar shirts.

"It's all a big laugh," said the so-called leader, John Lennon. *"The girls scream over the Beatles the way they scream over any group of blokes who get up and sing, play the guitar or just shout."*

It was likely that the fans would still be screaming for the Beatles long after the other new bands had faded away because the Beatles were smart enough

fill an LP with material that was different from their stage act. Their two hits proved that. On stage, they would do stuff such as *Keep Your Hands Off My Baby* and *Chains*, but they did not release those as singles.

Plans for what would be included on the LP were indefinite. *Hold Me Tight, There's a Place*, and *My Misery* would be included for sure, along with *I Saw Her Standing There* – George Harrison to do the vocals.

"We want to try to make the LP something different," said John. *"You know, not just all somebody else's songs."*

The interviewer privately lamented that the title of the album was to be *Please Please Me*, suggesting that it was not a very original title.

The songs were also up in the air for the A and B sides of their next single, but one might be *Hold Me Tight*.

John Lennon said, *"There's a good catchy riff on that one."*

The writer was sure that regardless of what the band chose to release, it would be a hit.

March 30, 1963 – *New Record Mirror*, **Norman Jopling reviewed** the Beatles' new album, *Please Please Me*. He wrote that the Beatles, to date, had had two records released, *Love Me Do* and *Please Please Me*. Their third record was the LP *Please Please Me* with fourteen tracks. Four of those tracks had been released as the A and B sides of singles, *Ask Me Why / Please Please Me* and *Love Me Do / P.S. I Love You*, the other ten tracks were:

> *I Saw Her Standing There:* written by Lennon and McCartney, with a bluesy backing to a fast-paced tune, good enough to release as a single.
> *Misery:* a ballad originally written for Kenny Lynch. A melancholy tune with the group's signature backing.
> *Anna (Go to Him):* a song written by American Rhythm and Blues artist Arthur Alexander, a slow

bluesy atmospheric number with John Lennon singing the lead.

Chains: another cover song, one that was a major hit in the U.S. and a minor hit in Britain for the Cookies. The guitar work was good but, the reviewer said, the first play was a bit off because it was sung by men.

Boys: a rocker sung by Ringo, originally recorded by the Shirelles as the flip side to *Will You Love Me Tomorrow*. Polished and exciting, with Ringo show more raw blues power than any of the other guys in the band.

Baby It's You: another song from the Shirelles, a well-recorded faithful copy of the original with Lennon singing the lead.

Do You Want to Know a Secret: sung by George Harrison, original and slightly different, not great but pleasant.

A Taste of Honey: a lyric version of the Acker Bilk / Lenny Welch hit, tracked so Paul McCartney could sing a duet with himself; a sweet tune with good backing.

There's a Place: with Lennon on harmonica, John and Paul singing together – appealing but not great, according to the reviewer.

Twist and Shout: the Isley Brothers American hit from the previous summer, a frenzied rocking R&B song, powerful both vocally and instrumentally.

In summation, a remarkably good debut album with an excellent cover photograph and well done

sleeve notes; quite worthwhile.

April 13, 1963 – *New Record Mirror* carried a photograph on the Beatles on the front cover, mentioning their latest single *From Me to You*.

April 13, 1963 – *New Record Mirror* printed a shot of the Beatles in the hairdressing department of Hornes in Liverpool, along with barber James Cannon, accompanied by a story about Merseyside in general, and the Beatles in particular. The Beatles actually escorted the author on a tour of the scene, starting on a rainy Sunday night, their first appearance in Liverpool since the beginning of their international success. The gig was at the Empire Theatre for a crowd of six thousand, filling the place for two shows while hundreds more gathered in the streets outside, hoping for a glimpse of the band. One police officer showed the writer an autographed picture he had acquired from the band between shows.

May 25, 1963 – *New Record Mirror* ran a review of the record made by Tony Sheridan, with the Beatles playing backup. *My Bonnie / The Saints* – Polydor NH 66833. It was the very first Beatles recording, made in Germany and reissued by Polydor; well done but not very commercial. The reviewer mentioned that Tony Sheridan was no longer with the band.

June 1, 1963 – *New Record Mirror*, Peter Jones asked if the release of *My Bonnie* would hurt the Beatles. As *From Me to You* topped the British charts, Polydor, in Germany, released *My Bonnie*,

recorded three years earlier with the band backing Tony Sheridan. The writer wondered if such a record could harm their reputation.

The Beatles' press agent, Tony Barrow, said, *"My own view is that it can't possibly harm the boys' good name in the business. The shame is that this obviously inferior material should be available for the fans to put into their collections as a souvenir piece.*

"That's the only difficulty. The Beatles don't get a chance to do anything much, or anything particularly good, on the record. They were employed purely as a backing group for Tony Sheridan, and that's exactly what they did, with the limits – though to the best of their ability."

How this came about was simple enough. The Beatles, along with a number of other bands, were in Germany when Tony Sheridan was searching for a backup band, and he chose them. On the original record they were billed as the Beat Boys, because it was assumed that no one knew anything about the Beatles.

Pete Best was the drummer on the record; Ringo hadn't joined the band yet. But Ringo was in Germany at the time, playing with Rory Storm and the Hurricanes. Tony Sheridan had noticed him and later had him return to Germany to handle the percussion for his band.

Not long after that, the "new boy," Ringo, joined the Beatles.

It was decided that the release of *My Bonnie* could not possibly hurt the Beatles, that lots of fans would want it simply because it *was* the Beatles.

The Beatles were so good and so popular that nothing could damage their reputation. Their act was slick, polished and salted with humour, and the audience screamed non-stop during their performances. At one concert, Roy Orbison applauded along with the crowd and said, *"They really are very good."*

The writer went on to discuss the ethics of re-release and concluded that there was nothing wrong with the tactic, but suggested that the Beatles' actual name should replace the Beat Boys. The Beatles themselves, apparently, did not care one way or the other about the re-release of *My Bonnie*, but hoped their fans would realise that they were strictly the session musicians and had no control over the recording.

June 20, 1963 – *Mersey Beat*, Howie Casey of The Seniors wrote about seeing the Beatles for the first time at an audition held by Larry Parnes in Liverpool. Also on hand were Gerry and the Pacemakers and Bob Evans' Five Shillings. At the time, the group was called the Silver Beatles. Casey sat down to watch them, surprised to see Stuart Sutcliffe playing with his back to the audience. He later learned that was because Sutcliffe was self-conscious and quite uncertain about his musical ability.

Casey admitted to being unimpressed by the band. He remembered they had played some instrumental Shadow numbers, but had no

17

recollection at all of their singing voices from that particular day.

His own band was engaged to play the Kaiser Keller in Hamburg, and while they were over there, the Beatles did a gig at the Indra Club. The moment he heard them, Casey was impressed with their improvement. *"They were great!"* he said.

At first, they were still doing Shadow songs, but, gradually, their act evolved into Rhythm and Blues, songs such as Chuck Berry's *Roll Over Beethoven*.

On stage, they dressed in pointed shoes with mauve jackets and black shirts and trousers; also, they had belted brown jackets. Their hair was long at the back and causing some controversy.

When they were not working, the group hung out with Tony Sheridan at the Top Ten Club. Apparently, Sheridan helped them out and they learned a lot from him.

They were sleeping in the dressing room of a cinema and spent a lot of time practising their music.

Pete Best was a serious hit with the young ladies. Casey said Best was a great guy, the guy he liked the most of the five Beatles. But Best was quiet and did not fit in with the others.

Paul, he wrote, played a left-handed guitar and was quite talented.

At one point, the manager of the Kaiser Keller decided on continuous live music. He shut down the juke box that had been used between sets and split the Seniors into two groups, drafting Stuart Sutcliffe to play bass for the second unit, which included Casey on saxophone, Stan Foster on piano, and a German drummer. With Sutcliffe playing, all they could do was 12-bar blues, since that was all he could manage. When he was off stage, Sutcliffe used to sketch around the club. During that trip, he quit the band and stayed in Hamburg to attend art college.

The Beatles, of course, were a bit upset that Sutcliffe was playing with the Seniors. But when the cops closed down the Indra club because of the noise complaints, the group moved on to the Kaiser Keller and were reunited with Stuart.

Their act was pumped up, wild and raucous. The Seniors broke the stage one night and, when it was the Beatles turn to play, with the stage propped up by beer cases, they broke it again. Casey thought the group was *"really terrific in Germany."* And they were truly fabulous now, a credit to Merseyside.

June 20, 1963 – *Mersey Beat* wrote about the man who discovered the Beatles. A lot of people were looking for that glory, but it was generally accepted that the first promoter to believe in them was Brian Kelly.

Kelly said, *"I was organising a dance at Litherland Town Hall to be held on Boxing Day, 1960. But I was short of a group. On Christmas Day, I received a phone call from Bob Wooler, who said, 'I've found a group for you at the Jacaranda and they're free. They want eight pounds. Will they do?' 'Not at that price, they won't,' I said. 'A group won't increase my attendance enough to warrant that.' Bob told me that they were called the Silver Beatles and that they played at the Casbah, Heymans Green. We finally agreed to pay them six pounds.*

"On their first appearance, I was completely knocked out by them. They had a pounding, pulsating beat which I knew would be big box office. When they finished playing, I posted some bouncers on the door of their dressing room to prevent other promoters who were in the hall entering. I went inside and booked them solidly for months ahead.

"I had a huge poster made with 'The Beatles' written in large fluorescent lettering. The poster caused a certain amount of curiosity and I remember the first reaction to their name.

"Beatles – you've spelt it wrong mister. Beatles – where've you dragged them from? Beatles – who are they?

"The group went from strength to strength at Litherland, and built up a fantastic following. Even then, the song writing talents of Lennon and McCartney were evident. On stage, they'd say, 'Here's a song we've just written – if you don't like it you needn't clap.'

"The group went away to Germany. When they returned, we did reasonable business with them, but they had lost Stuart and seemed downhearted and had temporarily lost their lustre.

"They were the first really noisy group to appear on Merseyside, and amplifiers were insufficient to cope with their sound. I worked on the amplification for them, and received a great deal of business for Alpha Sound. Groups on Merseyside seemed to play wilder and louder and more and more of them approached me to help with their amplification."

June 22, 1963 – New Record Mirror, Peter Jones published ... Ugly rumours and the Beatles – Blindness, Death in the Family are just a Few of the Rumours Spread about the Boys... Now that they are well established, the sensational Beatles are getting the lot, unsubstantiated rumours started by shadow people, causing the boys some concern.

Paul's mother was supposedly dead, so one caller claimed.

John was going blind. He did not deny he could not see very far into the audience without his glasses, which he would never wear on stage. *"But I always know they're there."* But the impending-onset-of-

blindness story was traveling fast, phone calls to the band and their families compounding the rumour.

There were engagement rumours, and also the rumour that Ringo was married with two kids and heading for divorce court.

Peter Jones claimed that the Beatles were all free, unmarried and unengaged.

The Beatles were apparently philosophical about the gossip mongers, accepting it as part of being famous. Such events were more prevalent in the States, where it was rumoured that both Elvis and Ricky Nelson had only a short time to live due to some unknown fatal illness.

The article went on to quote Paul McCartney: "*The fans are fantastic. A line appeared in one of the papers that I used green toothpaste for shaving. It was really a gag about the fact that the shaving cream I do use happens to be green.*

"*Well, the inevitable happened. Fans sent me in tubes of green toothpaste just to keep me going.*

"*But that was nothing to the bloke who came up and said he couldn't understand how I managed to get a shave using toothpaste. He said he tried it and that it had left his face badly scraped...*"

John and George realised they had made a mistake when they announced that they liked "*jelly babies.*" Tons of candies began arriving in the mail; and even more began landing on the stage.

The Beatles were searching for a follow-up to *From Me to You*, and the author said that, no matter what they selected, it was guaranteed to be a hit; they could do no wrong.

Also rumoured was a tour of Bolivia.

Denied, of course.

The caption running with the picture that accompanied the article claimed that after a long run at the top of the charts, the Beatles had been overtaken by Gerry and the Pacemakers.

July 18, 1963 – *Mersey Beat*, Lu Walters of Rory Storm and The Hurricanes, reminisced about the days when Ringo played with the Hurricanes.

He had first met Ringo during Liverpool's skiffle days, when Ringo was with Rory Storm at the Mardi Gras club, clad in a black Teddy-boy suit. Later on, when the group was called the Raving Texans, Walters joined up to play bass, doing the circuit of clubs around Liverpool.

He said Ringo was not a very good drummer at the time but that, as the group got better, so did Ringo. Ringo was the laziest one in the band, sleeping late, awakening in a foul mood, refusing to even talk for the first hour of the day. But he was the life of any party they attended, well liked for his sense of humour.

Ringo took swimming lessons from one of the band members and seemed to be doing well, until he realised he was at the deep end of the pool. Then he sank. It took three other band members to drag him from the water. And the Hurricanes often went

horseback riding. Ringo went once. After the horse bit him, he walked back.

Round about the same time his drumming talents began to show, he also started singing. *Alley Oop*, sung by Ringo, was a crowd favourite.

When Rory Storm and the Hurricanes started to play in Germany, the crowds liked him there, too; so did Tony Sheridan, who asked Ringo to remain behind and drum for him when the group was heading back to England. He stayed for a few months, then rejoined the Hurricanes. When he left forever to play for the Beatles, the band knew what they had lost. He was still one of their closest friends, and one of the most famous drummers in Britain.

July 18, 1963 – *Mersey Beat*, John Lennon told the editor, "*I have been so misquoted by reporters. And I would appreciate it if you could clear up something that has been troubling me. I have been receiving letters condemning me for comments I made in a musical publication. Actually, it was all a misunderstanding.*

"*I had been discussing some charcoal drawings of members of the group which had been sent by a fan. I mentioned that Ringo Starr was ugly. I was, of course, only referring to the charcoal drawings and not Ringo himself.*

"*I would also like to point out to the people who say that Ringo is always kept in the background, this is not deliberate. Paul, George and I think Ringo is gear and have been trying to bring him forward in the act. However, Ringo is still rather shy and it will take a bit of time. In six months, Ringo will really be playing a major part in the act.*"

In a sidebar, Rita Mills, a Lennon fan, said, "*John Lennon's natural streak of wit really shone through recently on BBC TV's Juke Box Jury. He is so sincere and honest, let alone completely mad. Of course, this was obvious in the early days of Beatlehoop. At the Cavern, one could send all sorts of crazy requests and feel confident that they would read them out during their exhilarating act.*"

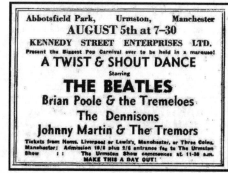

July 18, 1963 – *Melody Maker* wondered if wedding bells spelled disaster for big name pop acts. They opened by saying that Beatle John Lennon was married, that thousands of female fans knew, that there was no apparent harm to the Beatles' popularity. The writer suggested the fans' reaction might have been different had Lennon been a solo artist; many solo artists had avoided marriage while jealous female fans scrutinised their every move.

Fortunately for Lennon, Paul McCartney, George Harrison and Ringo Starr were still single – the fans could fixate on them and forgive John his transgression.

When asked about it, Lennon said, *"No comment."*

July 20, 1963 – New Record Mirror ran a short boxed piece about the Beatles EP featuring *Twist and Shout* and *Do You Want to Know a Secret.* By Tuesday of that week it had sold over 150,000 copies. Also, that week, their LP had topped the 100,000 mark.

August 1, 1963 – Mersey Beat showed before and after photographs of the Beatles. The "before" had them in black leather, the "after" revealed them in Mohair suits.

A section known as "Platter Patter" carried information about bands that had been recording songs written by John Lennon and Paul McCartney. They included Billy J. Kramer and the Dakotas and Tommy Quickly.

Talking about a song called *Do You Want To Know A Secret,* recorded by Kramer, Paul McCartney said, *"His phrasing has a wistful feeling about it and the sequences where he self-duets with his own voice have come out ideally."*

John and Paul Beatle were clearly Britain's newest and most popular team of songwriters.
August 1, 1963 – Mersey Beat carried an article about Pete Best, saying that just a year ago he was the most popular drummer around, at least with Merseyside's teenage girls. He was an attraction and credited with much of the Beatles popularity. Moody and quiet, with those James Dean looks, the girls loved him.

He was with the group through their early struggles, the mysterious one in the background. The Beatles were, according to Bob Wooler, physically magnetic… and Best the most magnetic of all. When John, Paul and George took the stage, the crowd was ecstatic. When Best followed them, the fans went wild. Girls were sleeping in his garden just to be near him.

Ron Appleby, a Southport promoter, said, *"He was definitely the big attraction with the group, and did much to establish their popularity during their early career."*

When it was announced a year ago that Pete Best had left the group, it became the number one topic for conversation around Merseyside. Pat Delaney, of the Cavern Club, said, *"Before the Beatles recorded, Pete was inclined to be more popular with the girls than any other member of the group. There were several reasons why I believe he was so popular. Girls were attracted by the fact that he wouldn't smile, even though they tried to make him. They also tried to attract his attention on stage but he wouldn't look at them. When he left the Beatles, there were exclamations of surprise. 'The Beatles will never be the same without him…' 'He was the Beatles…' 'They've taken away a vital part…' were comments I heard. When he left them, he was lost to the scene. When he joined the All Stars, the limelight he had with the Beatles seemed to go."*

Petitions were circulated, demanding that Best be reinstated with the band. He had been with them from the beginning, through their early struggles and hardships, traveling with them along that long, hard road from the days of dank basement clubs in Liverpool to the top of the Mersey Beat poll. The writer thought Best deserved to share in their success.

August 9, 1963 – New Musical Express published an interview with the Beatles by Alan Smith…
The interviewer asked if they had been changed by fame.

Said Paul, *"If anything, it's other people who are different. I can't quite explain it, but when I meet some of my old mates, they don't seem the same. They have a different attitude towards me. Perhaps they think we've all gone big-time since getting into the charts, I don't know. But they're so wrong. Mind you, I'm not knocking anybody. I suppose people can't help feeling we've changed. It's a natural reaction."*

He wondered how Paul had gotten started in the music business.

"I didn't start in a very spectacular way. I got my first guitar when I was fifteen, and I just used to fool about with it, more or less. As time went by, though, I got more interested. I was still fifteen when I met John Lennon at a village fête in Woolton, in Liverpool.

"He was playing with a couple of fellows and I asked if I could join in. That's how it started, really. I suppose we just went on from strength to strength – John, me, George and another lad named Pete Best, who's now with another group. You'd never dream the names we had: Johnny and the Moondogs, the Quarrymen and the Rainbows.

"We were called the last because we all had different coloured shirts and we couldn't afford any others! After that, somebody wanted to call us Long John Silver and the Pieces of Eight! We

weren't standing for that, but we did end up as the Silver Beetles for a while. After that, it became just the Beatles.

"I guess it's pure chance that I met John. You see, my mother was a district nurse until she died when I was fourteen, and we used to move from time to time because of her work. One move brought me into contact with John. Since then, I suppose John and I have written about 100 songs together, including Bad To Me for Billy J. Kramer. Fab about it doing so well, isn't it? I decided I'd like to enter art college if we flopped in show business. I got my GCE in art, and I'm still very interested in the subject. I often sketch when we're on tour – when I'm not writing or go-carting! That's the big rage for me these days, go-carting. We were doing some of it recently and now I'm thinking of taking it up in a big way. I'm not really interested in sport apart from that, except for swimming – but that's the thing these hot days, isn't it? It really cools you off."

Then he asked how the rest of them got along with Paul.

George said, "Oh fine. He hasn't changed a bit, you know. He's just the same old big-head we all got to know and love!

John added, "Funny habits? I'll say! Did you know he sleeps with his eyes open? We've actually watched him, dozing there with the whites of his eyes showing. And he won't believe us when we tell him. He's a good lad, really. We don't have much trouble with him, except that he gets a bit restless at feeding time. He's always good when we tell him, because he knows that if he isn't, we won't take him out for a walk on his chain!

Said Paul, "You have to laugh, don't you? If you don't live this life with a sense of humour, it could soon get you down. That's the way I look at it, anyway. Sometimes, you know, I feel as if there's nothing I'd like better than to get back to the kind of thing we were doing a year ago. Just playing The Cavern and some of the other places around Liverpool. I suppose the rest of the lads feel that way at times, too. You feel as if you'd like to turn back the clock. It's only a passing mood, though. Most of the time lately we've been living on top of the world. Everything has been going right for us! No, I haven't bought anything special for myself since everything happened. Perhaps I could get a cine-camera – then the lads could film me while I'm dozing, and I'd know if I really sleep with my eyes open!"

August 10, 1963 – New Record Mirror, Jimmy Watson announced that a new picture book had been published about the Beatles. The biggest impact on the record business during 1963 was, without doubt, made by the Beatles. Just a year ago, they were known only to a few fans in Liverpool and Germany. To everyone else at the time, Beatles (with a slightly different spelling) were black, shiny, skin-crawling things that scuttled through houses and

gardens. Now, they were a household name with best-selling records, endless TV and radio appearances, and countless concerts.

The writer was reasonably certain they had not, as yet, played the Palladium but assumed that even that venue would be behind them soon. And he went on to say that their most recent honour was the advent of the picture book, photographs by the top pop photographer, Dezo Hoffman. The book, titled *The Beatles*, listed at 2s 6d [2 shillings and 6 pence], was released the previous week and was nearly out of print already. It consisted of 77 candid photos, including two full-page and one double-page in full colour. The text was by Patrick Maugham, informative and informal.

The author accompanied Dezo Hoffmann on a number of the photo shoots and he reported that the Beatles' relaxed attitude and humour made for good sessions. He was surprised by the patience the band had for photographers, since they were constantly harassed by them.

Three periods with the Beatles stood out:

The night they returned to Liverpool to play the Empire Theatre, the numbers of the fans seem to knock them off balance, but what worried them most was being ordered by the police not to show themselves to the fans gathered in the rainy streets for fear of starting a riot. They insisted they had to greet the fans; they did not want anyone thinking they were getting big-headed.

His second fond memory was when they all went to visit Paul's family for tea the day after the Empire show. He was impressed by the down-to-earth attitudes of the family.

And his third memory was of traveling with the band to the Stow School in Buckinghamshire. This was an appearance they had scheduled long before their rise to fame; they were now being swamped with offers and huge financial promises and yet they insisted on doing the show and getting close to the fans. They were late and the crowd was getting ugly, but they made it.

He finished by saying the book was a must for Beatle fans.

August 15, 1963 – Mersey Beat spoke with Pete Best about his days with the Beatles.

Said Pete, "A few years ago, I used to sit in with various groups at the Casbah, and also had a trio called the Black Jacks. The Beatles used to play at the club and I got to know them there.

"They were auditioning for a drummer at the Wyvern Club, Seel Street (now The Blue Angel) and asked me to come along. They desperately needed at drummer at the time as they had to go to Germany within a few days' time. They asked me to join the group and two days later I was in Hamburg with them.

"We appeared at a club called the Kaiser Keller and remained there for five and half months. When the contract for the Kaiser Keller expired, we were *offered a job at the Top Ten Club, which was the top rock club in Hamburg at the time.*

"On our first night there, Paul was taken to the police station and later, I was taken too. We were accused of trying to burn down a cinema, and as we couldn't prove anything, the German police deported us. It was a frame-up, more or less, as we'd taken the Kaiser Keller's business to the Top Ten.

"When we got home, Paul and I cleared the charge we had against us by informing the Aliens Police in Hamburg. We told them what had happened and they replied saying that everything had been cleared up and we could return to Germany in future.

"We then started playing locally as the Beatles at the Casbah, Litherland Town Hall, Aintree Institute, the Cavern and other places, going from strength to strength. We were a little bewildered by the screams we were getting and the way people reacted to the group.

"During the next three months, we built up a huge following on Merseyside and then left for another season at the Top Ten Club. During our three months stay, we signed a Polydor recording contract for twelve months. We were to make four singles and an EP. We backed Tony Sheridan on My Bonnie *and made a couple of EPs with him. We heard that* My Bonnie *went to the top of the German charts; I'm not too sure whether it did, but I know it went to a very high position. We were paid a lump sum for the sessions and therefore didn't receive any royalties.*

"After three months, we came back to Liverpool and, after My Bonnie *had been released here, Brian Epstein approached the group and asked if he could be our manager.*

"After he'd taken us over, we started playing more and more out of town, and went on the BBC. On our third trip to Hamburg, we became the first group to play at a new venue, the Star Club. Whilst over there, we received a telegram saying we'd got a Parlophone contract.

"Just before the first release, I was told that I would have to leave the group. The news came as a big surprise to me as I had had no hint that it would happen and didn't even have the opportunity of discussing it with the rest of the group."

August 16, 1963 – *New Musical Express* **published an interview with George Harrison and Bob Wooler by Alan Smith...**

George said, *"You know, the Beatles have almost been my career. I had only one other job; lasted two months. I left Liverpool Institute when I was seventeen, then I worked for an electrician. Rewiring and that kind of thing. But I couldn't stick it. I liked music too much. Besides, I'd met Paul while I was at school and we both had this interest in guitars.*

"Paul actually had a trumpet at first; I remember we always used to be playing When The Saints Go Marching In. *On and on, always* The Saints! *Who knows, the Beatles might have had a Liverpool*

trumpet sound now if Paul could have sung and played at the same time! He got himself a guitar in the end, and then we met John. I didn't realise it until recently, but John and I both went to the same primary school, Dovedale Road. We never met until we were sixteen or seventeen.

"At one time I used to have a group of my own called the Rebels, or some such name. Later on, I appeared at British Legion halls and working men's clubs with the Quarrymen. They were John, Paul and myself. But it wasn't steady. I did a bit of freelancing for a while. In fact, at one stage I think I was in about three groups all at the same time! I remember when Paul and I used to play guitar, and John would just sing without any instrument. We were on a Buddy Holly kick in those days, with numbers like Think It Over *and* It's So Easy. *We certainly had some laughs.*

"We did a Carroll Levis Discoveries show in Manchester once, and Billy Fury was at the first audition. He was Ronald Wycherly then, and he did Margot *for his number. I think we were Johnny and the Moondogs at that particular time. You were judged by the audience applause, you know, but we had to catch a train home before the end. We never did find out if we'd won! But Billy passed his audition, I remember that.*

"It's funny, the Cavern is a home-from-home for us in Liverpool today, but they didn't used to be too keen on us a few years ago. That was when the place was mostly jazz and skiffle. We used to go on and play wild rockers like Whole Lotta Shakin', *and they'd pass notes up to the stage telling us to cool down! I think* No Other Baby *was the only Country and Western or skiffle number we knew, so we used to play it over and over again. It got so bad, they wouldn't book us! Nothing seemed to happen for a while. I think we broke up, then we got together with a lad named Stuart Sutcliffe. Stu left the group after one of our trips to Hamburg, because he wanted to stay in Germany, where I regret to say, he has since died.*

"I remember we had an audition for Larry Parnes once and he sent us to do a date in Scotland. We must have had about eight drum kits by then, because every time we had a new drummer he seemed to leave us with his gear! Paul even did a bit of drumming himself. After that we went to Germany. That must have been in August, 1960. I remember it well because the German police discovered I was underage to be working in the clubs, and they had me sent back home to Liverpool. A few days later the rest of the lads came home, but we didn't get together right away. In fact, it was a little while before we decided it was about time we got some work – and we owe it to Bob Wooler.

"I think Bob must know more about the Liverpool scene than anybody. He's now compere at the Cavern. Bob got us this job at a dance hall just after Christmas, 1960. It was funny; we'd spent so much

of our time in Germany, nobody knew us. We were billed as Direct *from Hamburg, and everybody thought we were German! One girl came up to me and said: 'Aye, don't you speak good English.'"*

Bob Wooler said, *"I'll tell you this about George – he's completely unaffected by stardom. I've written the lyrics to a number Billy J. Kramer has recorded for future release on an LP. I didn't think I'd hear the finished version for some time, but George got hold of a copy and drove four miles to let me hear it. That may not seem much, but what struck me was the way he went right out of his way to be helpful."*

George said, *"Well, you'd do the same for anybody, wouldn't you? I know what it's like when you want to hear how a disc has come out. After we recorded for Polydor in Germany, I didn't stop playing the disc for days. Actually, I've an idea we weren't called the Beatles when that German record was released. It was untranslatable, so on the label they called us the Beat Brothers.*

"Do I have any hobbies? Well, I'm lucky in that I actually like music. I'm always playing around with my guitar off stage. Or putting on records. Just lately we've all been having a bit of fun with a tape recorder. John writes down the words – you can't really call it poetry or verse – and then I read it out on the tape. It's weird stuff. I'm not sure that anybody else would know what it's all about! We had a gear time with the recorder a few weeks ago when we were with Gerry and the Pacemakers at Weston-Super-Mare. We were in a car and Gerry was wearing a big hat and dark glasses, asking people the way to the local golf course. We got some dead funny replies. Just like Candid Camera *it was, only in sound!*

"Then there's this idea we've got for a go-carting track. I was talking to Adam Faith a few weeks ago, and I think he's as keen on it as we are. We might be able to get a few more people interested. We've known each other for six or seven years. If we couldn't get along, we'd know it by now all right. I know I'm very happy. Ringo says I'm an irritable so-and-so, but I think he's just having me on. I think the future holds a lot. I'd like to invest money and perhaps branch out in different show business ventures.

"I suppose I've been a bit lucky when it comes to song writing. I haven't bothered in the same way as John and Paul, though I'd like to have a stab at it sooner or later. I did actually write one number, if you could call it 'writing.' It was in Hamburg just about the time the Shadows' Apache *came out. Somebody asked John and myself how the tune went, and we tried to demonstrate. The result wasn't a bit like* Apache, *but we liked it and we used it in the act for a while. We even called it* Cry for a Shadow! *Now it's on our Polydor EP.*

"I like parties and a bit of fun like anyone else, but there's nothing better, for me, than a bit of peace and quiet. Sitting round a big fire with your slippers

on and watching the telly. That's the life!"

August 24, 1963 – New Record Mirror wrote She Loves You was another number one for The Beatles. *She Loves You / I'll Get You*, the new Beatles disc, was rushing straight into the charts with an advance order of one quarter of a million copies. Two good sides, both songs written by Lennon and McCartney, cut with fine instrumentals and great vocal tracks. Headed for number one, no doubt at all.

August 31, 1963 – New Record Mirror, Langley Johnson said the Beatles were living the lives of hermits. The British police were beginning to see them as Public Nuisance Number One, near-riots breaking out whenever they were seen in public, forcing them to hide away.

They'd spent the last six days in Bournemouth, mostly hiding in their hotel. Arising around one in the afternoon, a simple appearance at the hotel window was enough to set the girls outside screaming.

The band could not leave the hotel without getting mobbed, so they were doing their best to relax, hang out in the hotel lounge, talk, take a few phone calls, chit-chat with the waitresses and hotel guests, or sign some autographs. Anything they wanted needed to be sent for – there was no chance that they could wander out to do a bit of shopping for themselves.

Nearing show time, they would rush to a car, lock the doors and head for the theatre, all movements based on surprise. During a sunny summer week in Bournemouth, there was no chance for a walk in the sun or a swim; they stayed inside, hidden away from the crowds. Their records were becoming the all-time bestsellers for EMI, even topping Cliff Richard; and advance orders for *She Loves You* had risen to 310,000.

The writer lamented that the hottest band in the UK beat scene rarely saw the light of day except through a window.

September 13, 1963 – *New Musical Express* reported that George hoped the airplane's exit doors would stay shut during his upcoming trip to America. They went on to say Beatle George Harrison was planning a trip to America for the holiday of a lifetime – but a previous plane trip that almost ended in disaster had him a little worried.

George said, *"We were taking off from Liverpool for one of our frequent flights across the country, when the plane suddenly came to a halt just as it was about to leave the ground. They gave me the jitters but what was to follow will make me sympathise with Elvis Presley's fear of flying for the rest of my days! As we made the proper takeoff, the emergency exits by which I was sitting suddenly flew open! I had heard stories about people being sucked out of aircraft, and I don't mind admitting I was pretty terrified. Our manager, Brian Epstein, who was sitting next to me, grabbed my arm and I yelled out for the air hostess – but she thought I was fooling, as we often do, since we fly in this plane so frequently."*

Crew members sealed the exit, but George was not to forget it soon. After completing their weekend gigs, the band was taking a sixteen-day holiday; George was planning to visit his sister in St. Louis. *"It's a trip I've always dreamed of and you can bet I'll make the most of it,"* he said. *"Mind you, I wouldn't like to stay there."*

John Lennon was planning to start his holiday in Paris. *"I intend to ramble through Europe just like we used to through England. Only difference is that this time I'll be able to pay my way."*

Hand bandaged from a burn, Ringo talked about his vacation plans with Paul McCartney, a trip to Greece. *"Partly,"* Ringo said, *"to look at the gear we've read about in the history books and partly because we feel we need a suntan after working under arc lights for so long."*

Paul mentioned that he and George had bought movie cameras and that he was planning to take one along on holiday, adding, *"Happily we've spent a lot of this year in front of television cameras. We've only just finished a film documentary for the BBC. Now George and I have got a yen to be on the other side*

of the camera and we aim to take movies of our fans in various parts of the country."*

September 26, 1963 – *Mersey Beat* ran a series of letters from fans, calling the section Mersey Beatle. Most of the letters moaned about the group's dearth of recent appearances in Liverpool.

October 19, 1963 – *New Record Mirror* reported that the Brooks Brothers were to join the Beatles and Peter Jay and the Jaywalkers on a four-week series of one-night stands. They also announced that the Beatles would headline a three-week show at the Astoria in London, starting on Christmas Eve. Joining the Beatles would be Billy J. Kramer and the Dakotas, Cilla Black, the Barron Knights with Duke D'Mond, Rolf Harris, Tommy Quickly, and the Fourmost.

October 19, 1963 – *New Record Mirror* mentioned that NEMS, Brian Epstein's company, would be moving to London, suggesting the move was inevitable since London had the main TV, radio and recording facilities. Under contract to NEMS were: the Beatles; Gerry and the Pacemakers; Billy J. Kramer and the Dakotas; the Fourmost; Cilla Black; Tommy Quickly; and others. Continuing, the writer stated that the Searchers' vocals were superior to the Beatles and went on to wonder when John Lennon would again appear on *Juke Box Jury*.

October 19, 1963 – *New Record Mirror* carried an article by Neil Aspinall about all that had happened in just a year. Aspinall started out by saying he was known as the Fifth Beatle but that his actual title was Road Manager. He was the one who had to wake up the Beatles and get them moving, the one who had to make sure they were fed, and the one who fended off the people that the band had no time to meet.

Aspinall had known George and Paul since schooldays, about ten years. He had associated with John Lennon for five years but had only just met Ringo when he joined the band. He said they were all wonderful people, but that he could not really say anything about them that had not already been said by others. He had been their road manager even before Brian Epstein signed on to manage them. In the early days, they could go anywhere they wanted, do anything they wished. Now, they were forced to stay indoors most of the time. Wherever they went, there was a crowd of fans. They couldn't appear anywhere without being mobbed.

On the road, having nowhere else to go, the group stayed in bed until the last possible moment, when Aspinall would get them up, arrange meals, whatever.

With regards to diet, he mentioned that they all liked steak, though Ringo hated onions; that they were somewhat revolted by tongue and/or ham because quite often that was only thing available at late-night hotels. He tried to procure chicken or cheese, but had to get the order in early.

Aspinall was also relegated to answering the phones for them, often non-stop calls, until it was arranged that no one got through without first identifying themselves and stating their business.

He also had to get them out of the hotel. Before the fans began to recognise him as being with the Beatles, it had been easier. He could simply go out, get the car and usher in the band. Now, he was forced to stay in the background while Mal Evans, the new road manager, went out for the car.

He stressed that the *boys* weren't trying to avoid the fans; they wanted to meet them all, but riot scenes made that impossible.

Most of their travel was by car, while the equipment went by van.

He ended by saying the biggest problem was getting the band out of their beds.

October 19, 1963 – *New Record Mirror*, Peter Jones wrote what had happened in just a year. He began by saying that it all started the week the Tornados topped the charts with Telstar. A record came out with only the slightest fuss, entering the charts at number 49; three months later it was still in the charts in the top twenty, and spent 18 weeks total in the *New Record Mirror* charts. But it, and the band, proceeded to ignite a fire that had rarely been seen in the music industry. The disc was *Love Me Do*, and Britain was beginning to recognise the Beatles. Four fabulous characters were embarking on an honour-studded career, four young men giving the music industry a boost that would never be forgotten.

The writer credited *New Mirror Record* with being the first newspaper to print a story about the Beatles, called them one of the hottest acts to come along in

many years, and continually sang their praises.

The Beatles had become a fixture in the British lifestyle, filmed, caricatured, photographed, and interviewed. They had headed the bill at the prestigious London Palladium, earned a gold record for *She Loves You*, and had had three number one hits. They had sold a quarter of a million copies of their first album and had packed the most important venues in the country.

All in just a year.

Before their first record, they had played around Liverpool, then in Hamburg, Germany to build their confidence. In Germany, they were urged to "make with the shout!"

Back in Liverpool and billed as being direct from Hamburg, they were somewhat surprised that all the locals thought they were German – though it was nice to be complemented on how well they spoke English. At that time, they were without a manager.

Enter Brian Epstein, who decided to seek them out after enough customers in his record store asked for the record the Beatles had recorded in Germany. He knew nothing about managing a band, but after he had seen them, he wanted to try. And The Beatles went from being unknowns to superstars in twelve months.

Said John Lennon, *"It's been fab. There's no other word for it. What can you say about the things that have happened to us? We're grateful to so many different people. To Brian Epstein; to our recording manager, George Martin; to our music publisher, Dick James; to Tony Barrow, who works all hours of the day and night on coping with the publicity calls; so many different people.*

"We believe in our fans. We appreciate the way they've stuck loyally to us and the help they've always given us. Sometimes we have to turn and run – but that's because we don't want to cause riots. But the fans have been so generous with their presents and their letters. Honestly, we love 'em all."

Regarding all the bands that have tried to copy them, they say *"In a way, it's flattering to be copied by somebody. But these other groups don't realise that they'd stand a much better chance if they created something for themselves."*

The writer was somewhat surprised to discover that the Beatles were actually four individuals, four separate people with four separate personalities, contributing equally to the band. A recent TV documentary provided insight into the Beatles' reaction to their own success. They knew the fame might not last, but Paul and John thought they would probably go on writing music, which, at that time, was just a sideline for them. Ringo suggested he might open a chain of hair salons. And George thought he might design guitars.

They might present themselves as relaxed and uncaring, but they had a serious regard for their music.

"Sometimes we're accused of getting away from Liverpool where we started," they said. *"It's not*

true. It's just that we have to reduce the time we can spend there. The Liverpool fans are still very near and dear to us."

Fame had not changed them, the writer observed. They were the same friendly guys they had been before all the fame, well-balanced and able to cope with all the changes in their lives.

In one year, they had achieved as much as one could expect to achieve in a life time, and they were not done yet.

The *New Record Mirror* congratulated them on the incredible impact they had made on the music industry.

October 24, 1963 – *Mersey Beat* said the stars of the recent BBC documentary *The Mersey Sound* had been the Beatles as they talked about the early days of their careers, fan letters, home life and ambitions. They were shown on stage at the Odeon Southport, playing, among others, *Love Me Do, Twist and Shout,* and their newest hit, *She Loves You.*

November 2, 1963 – *New Record Mirror* **reported** that Peter Jay and the Jaywalkers were so worried about touring with the Beatles that they insured themselves for thirty-five thousand quid. The tour itinerary:

November 2 – City Hall, Sheffield
November 23 – City hall, Newcastle-upon-Tyne
November 3 – Odeon theatre, Leeds
November 24 – ABC Cinema, Hull
November 6 – ABC Cinema, Northampton
November 26 – Regal Cinema, Cambridge
November 9 – Adelphi Cinema, Dublin
November 27 – Rialton Theatre, York
November 10 – Hippodrome Theatre, Birmingham
November 28 – ABC Cinema, Lincoln
November 13 – ABC Cinema, Plymouth
November 29 – ABC Cinema, Haddersfield
November 14 – ABC Cinema, Exeter
November 30 – Empire Theatre, Sunderland
November 16 – Winter Gardens, Bournemouth
December 1 – De Montfort Hall, Leicester
November 17 – Coventry Theatre, Coventry
December 3 – Guildhall, Portsmouth
November 19 – Gaumont Theatre, Wolverhampton
December 8 – Odeon Cinema, Lewisham, London
November 20 – ABC Cinema, Manchester
December 9 – Odeon Cinema, Southend-on-sea
November 21 – ABC Cinema, Carlisle
December 10 – Gaumont Cinema, Doncaster
November 22 – Globe Cinema, Stockton-on-Tees
December 11 – Furtuist Theatre, Scarborough

November 2, 1963 – *New Record Mirror* **announced** a free Beatles disc. The Beatles' next release would not reach the music charts – it was to be a special Christmas recording given to every member of the Beatles Fan Club who was enrolled by November 30.

The first pressing of this was thirty thousand and they were prepared to make more if necessary. It would contain a personal message from each of the Beatles, as well as their own rendition of *Good King Wenceslas*, with a running time of about five minutes. Apparently, fans were flocking to join the fan club, but the requests were difficult to manage, the delays long, and the club employees swamped. Anne Cunningham and four other full-time people were doing all they could to manage the applications.

"Everything possible is being done. We can only ask fans to be as patient as possible," said Anne Cunningham.

November 7, 1963 – *Mersey Beat* **talked** about George Harrison, introducing him as the lead guitarist for the Beatles, twenty years old, six feet tall with brown eyes and brown hair. He had a cheerful approach to life, and liked small blonde girls. Musically, he preferred the artists who did their own music, like Little Richard, Chuck Berry, Bo Diddley, and Duane Eddy. He was a modest man who had been through the difficult early days with the Beatles, when London had no interest in northern talent. But George had that "something" that would not allow him to give up. Along with the rest of the group, he worked hard and stayed at it. The results were becoming obvious to the world.

November 9, 1963 – **Peter Jay of the Jaywalkers wrote to** *New Record Mirror* **about** touring with the Beatles. Jay and the Jaywalkers loved the idea of touring with the Beatles, but they had no idea what they were getting into, Peter Jay mentioned that he was happy that they had taken out a thirty-five thousand pound insurance policy to cover the damages.

It started in Cheltenham, where thousands of fans were waiting outside the theatre by early afternoon. Peter Jay could not find a place to park and when he tried a nearby garage, the fans descended on his car and the garage owner told him to leave. He said getting into the theatre was not too bad because the fans were looking for Beatle haircuts. The Jaywalkers' reception was impressive, but nothing compared to what the Beatles received.

To get away later, he said the Beatles combed their hair back and were able to escape because the fans recognised them too late.

On to Sheffield and thousands of fans trying to break through the cordon of police. During the show, the screaming for the Beatles never let up, while the stage was pelted with jelly babies, dolls, autograph books, flowers, chocolate bars, you name it.

Next stop, Leeds, where the roads to the Odeon were blocked off with police cars, police dogs, mounted police, and police on foot. He compared it to a civil war and was surprised that no one was hurt. All the exits were surrounded.

He complemented the fans for being so good to the other acts on the tour, giving them a listen and tremendous applause, The Brook Brothers, the

Kestrels, the Vernons Girls, and of course, Jay and the Jaywalkers.

November 9, 1963 – *New Record Mirror* **reviewed** the new Beatles LP. The fantastic new album was released three weeks early, after an advance order of over 250,000 copies, the largest prerelease order for an album in British history. It was called *With the Beatles* and it meant that the four lads from Liverpool, in just one year, had total record sales of over 3,000,000.

The album contained fourteen songs, seven by Lennon and McCartney, one by George Harrison, the rest from assorted American R&B artists.

Side one opened with...

It Won't Be Long: a loud song with John singing the lead.

All I've Got to Do: with John once again singing lead, Paul harmonising.

All My Loving: Paul doing the lead vocals, backed by John and George. Somewhat ordinary, but punched up by George's lead guitar.

Don't Bother Me: George's debut as a songwriter; a rich song with George singing lead.

Little Child: featuring John on the harmonica and Paul on piano; the reviewer said it swings well.

Till There Was You: a haunting ballad from *The Music Man*, sung by Paul, while John and George play acoustic guitars.

Please Mister Postman: the final song on Side One, originally a hit for the Marvelettes, one that the Beatles usually performed live.

Roll Over Beethoven: opened side two, a Chuck Berry song with George singing the lead vocals. Chuck Berry fans probably wouldn't like it as much as the original.

Hold Me Tight: a lively song with Paul doing the lead vocals.

You Really Got a Hold on Me: a slow bluesy piece sung by John and George.

I Wanna be Your Man: a rocker written by the Beatles for the Rolling Stones; sung by Ringo.

Devil in Her Heart: originally a hit for the Donays, but with the lyrics somewhat changed; George doing the vocals.

Not A Second Time: John singing a dual-tracked lead.

Money: the closing song, originally by Barrett Strong, with John singing it raw and rough, Paul and George harmonising; a favourite from their stage act.

November 16, 1963 – *Record Mirror* [**no longer called *"New" Record Mirror*] featured a **photograph of the four Beatles on the cover, with a lengthy caption that praised them for their success in 1963, including being headliners on *Sunday Night at the London Palladium* and having a part in that show of shows, the *Royal Variety Performance*. *Record Mirror* mentioned how proud they were to be the first to give the Beatles a write-up in a national music paper.

November 16, 1963 – *Record Mirror* **wrote** about the Beatles' film deal, which was to be one of the biggest money-making attractions in years. Scriptwriter Alun Owen was said to be working closely with the band and Brian Epstein. On his way to Ireland to join the group, Owen said, *"It's most important to get to know the Beatles, to find out exactly what makes them tick. And also to ascertain which things cause those fantastic crowd receptions."*

The film was planned to be a 90-minute feature, production to start in February, based on the current lifestyle of the Beatles. Whether it would be fact or fiction was as yet undecided.

Meanwhile, Lennon and McCartney were said to be working on the score for the film, with plans for perhaps a dozen new songs.

And the latest Beatle news: following the release of *I Wanna Hold Your Hand* on November 29 the Beatles were to appear on the BBC's *Juke Box Jury*.

November 21, 1963 – *Mersey Beat* **said** one of the interesting things about the real Paul McCartney was the way he could change from singing a hard rocker to heart-rending ballad without losing the attention of the audience. He was adaptable. And he had gone from being a virtually unknown regular guy in a rock and roll band to being a national star without changing. He was the same person that was learning to play way back when the Silver Beatles were starting out.

His original work, penned with John Lennon, had a feel all it's own. McCartney's true self-expression came through his music.

He was remarkably attractive to girls, idolised by thousands all over Britain, and yet no one really knew him.

A footnote mentioned that the BBC was going to rerun *The Mersey Sound* and was already working on a sequel.

November 23, 1963 – *Record Mirror* reported it had been "the Year of the Beatles." Earlier that week, EMI Chairman Sir Joseph Lockwood had celebrated "B" day – "B" for Beatles – throwing a party as a tribute to the band. During his opening speech, he mentioned that the Beatles had sold more than 3,000,000 singles, LPs and EPs that year.

"They have created a disc success without parallel in these twelve months," he said.

The Beatles were given Silver Discs for sales of over a quarter of a million for each of their albums – *With the Beatles* had reached that sales mark without even being released, while their fifth single, slated for release on November 29, sold over 500,000 copies the day the release was announced and had topped the 700,000 mark by the following day. By then their first EP, *Twist and Shout*, had sold 650,000 copies.

Waitresses, reporters, disc jockeys and EMI employees gathered around the Beatles at the party, all requesting autographs.

November 23, 1963 – *Record Mirror* published Peter Jay of the Jaywalkers again reporting from the tour. He began by saying that it had always been difficult to visit the Beatles in their dressing room, but that it was even more difficult now because the band had bought a *Scalextric Model Racing Track* and were running races at every possible opportunity.

He mentioned that the Jaywalkers had their own set back home and were having it delivered to the tour so they could put the two sets together and race against the Beatles.

The tour itself was wilder than ever.

At East Ham, the Beatles sent out for food and they all watched from the windows as the food arrived with a police escort.

In Birmingham, the boys dressed up as cops to avoid being caught by their fans.

The stage was still being pelted with jelly babies, and now boxes of chocolates, which hurt.

He also mentioned that the flu was ripping through the tour, started by Paul McCartney.

November 30, 1963 – *Record Mirror*, Langley Johnson asked if the Beatles were bad for business. The opening paragraph theorised that, yes, the Beatles, the hottest pop act in years, *were* bad for business.

While there had never been anything quite like Beatlemania, with fans: sleeping outside theatres night after night to procure tickets; being fired from their jobs for having too much enthusiasm for the band; going without lunch to save money for concerts and records; forcing the police to lose most of their time off; it was bad for business. The Beatles could play different venues all day, every day, and still the theatres would be packed. There was a black market in ticket sales, and other bands on other tours were being shut out of the action. Other bands were reporting less-than-average ticket sales because the Beatles had either played nearby or were about to play nearby.

The unidentified leader of one big band said, *"You can see the difference all over the country. If our package show goes to a place where the Beatles are not expected, well, its business as usual for us. But if Beatlemania has hit an area, that's it. Sort of After the Lord Mayor's Show for us."*

Band managers were studying the Beatles' concert lists in order to plan dates that did not conflict with it for their own bands, making the Beatles play date list one of the most important documents in the British music industry. If someone put it in print, it would top the bestseller list.

It was a unique situation in the history of pop music and a remarkable tribute to the Beatles. Then the writer mentioned that the touring bands would be all right for a while, their shows well-attended, because the Beatles would not be on the road in Britain in the near future. They were planning to visit London for three weeks during the Christmas season – at Finsbury Park, doing their own show. Then they would be off the road for several more weeks while they made a movie. After that, in February 1964, they were headed to America for the *Ed Sullivan Show*, a few days' holiday in Florida, then back to New York to film another Sullivan show. Also, on December 7, they were taking over the panel of *Juke Box Jury* while fans held a convention in Liverpool. The BBC was planning to film the convention and air it that same evening.

American stars playing in England, Gene Pitney, Buddy Greco, the Shirelles, and Del Shannon, all claimed America was looking forward to the Beatles and unanimously predicted that the fab four would be just as popular in the U.S. as they were in Britain.

The writer wondered if the Yanks would be able to understand the Beatles' Liverpool accents. Apparently, American TV networks had cameramen in England filming the fans' manic reaction to the Beatles; also, *Life Magazine*, one of the most influential magazines in the world, had a slew of photographers following them around.

Thus, the scene was set for the Beatles to conquer America.

Beatlemania was infecting the entire world. That had to be good for business, regardless of what the sufferers were saying about it.

November 30, 1963 – *Record Mirror* published…

Dora Bryan said, *"Beatles, I haven't room for one, really!"* Dora Bryan, comedienne, was releasing a new record, *All I Want for Christmas is a Beatle*.

The interviewer asked how the song came about and she said, *"It was all a bit sudden, really. I went to see Jack Baverstock at Fontana to talk about a long-player I'm doing. And there was this office boy who said he'd written a song.*

"Well, Jack said 'Oh no, not now,' or something. I mean, everybody, but everybody, is writing songs, aren't they? Anyway, this chap actually had a tape of it. So we listened, without actually being hopeful. And it clicked. Jack said it was just right for me.

"Of course, I like the Beatles. But I don't really want one for Christmas. To be honest, we haven't got a spare bedroom at home.

"I'm very keen on their records. No, I don't actually buy them. I mean, you can hear them on the radio all the time, can't you? Or see them on Royal Variety Shows *and that kind of thing. But I really do like their kind of music.*

"I'm not like all the other fans, though. I don't actually LOVE them. I'm afraid I'm a bit too old for that kind of thing. But they are so exciting, aren't they – with all that rhythm and those haircuts and all."

During a show at the Adelphi Theatre in London, Bryan featured a skit about a group called the Cockroaches during her current review.

December 5, 1963 – *Mersey Beat* declared John Lennon the intellectual one. This aspect of his personality had been previously overlooked because so much was being made of his song writing and musical abilities. He had attended the Liverpool College of Art, where he had met and befriended Bill Harry. Harry later became the editor of *Mersey Beat*, where John's poetry and drawings had first appeared.

Perhaps if John had not pursued the music, he may have had success with his poetry and art.

It was considered unusual that John had as many fans as the rest of the group, because he was married.

He attacked a song the way you would attack an enemy, head on and hammering, a near-revolutionary event in the pop world. He was accepted as the leader of the band and his hair, his clothes, his looks, set new trends. His good looks were non-traditional, but he could get more response from an audience than anyone else in show business.

A footnote mentioned that the Beatles would be appearing in their own Christmas show at the Liverpool Empire on December 22nd.

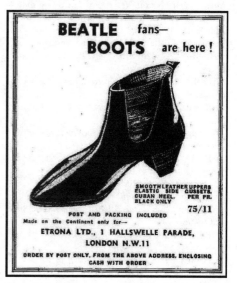

December 14, 1963 – *Record Mirror*, Peter Jones wrote a review of the Beatles' gig on *Juke Box Jury*. As host David Jacobs introduced each of the Beatles, screams erupted from the audience. They went right into the music.

First disc: *I Could Write a Book* by the Chants from Liverpool.

John: *"It's gear. Fabulous. Fab. It's it."*

Paul: *"I talked to the Chants recently about the disc. They said it was powerful. It is."*

Ringo: *"I'll buy it."*

George: *"It's great. Enough plugs and they've got a hit."*

David Jacobs added, *"Are they being too generous?"*

Second disc: *Kiss Me Quick* by Elvis Presley.

Paul: *"What I don't like about Elvis are his songs. I like his voice. This song reminds me of Blackpool on a sunny day."*

Ringo: *"Last two years, Elvis has been going down the nick."*

George: *"If he's going back to old tracks, why not release* My Baby Left Me? *It'd be a number one. Elvis is great. His songs are rubbish."*

John: *"It'll be a hit. I like those hats with* Kiss Me Quick *on them."*

Third disc: *Hippy Hippy Shake* by the Swinging Blue Jeans.

Ringo: *"Good... but not as good as the original by Chan Romero."*

George: *"It's a popular song around Liverpool. We used to do it. Could be a hit."*

John: *"The boys nearly made it before. I like Bill Harry's version as well."*

Paul: *"Doesn't matter about Chan Romero's disc. Nobody remembers it. It's as good as a new song."*

Fourth disc: *Did You Have a Happy Birthday* by Paul Anka.

All four Beatles panned that one, despising it.

Fifth disc: *The Nitty Gritty Song* by Shirley Ellis.

John liked it.

Paul: *"I like this kind of record, but it doesn't say anything."*

Ringo: *"We all like this sort of thing, but it won't be a hit."*

George: *"Won't be a hit in England. We haven't got around to that sort of thing yet."*

David Jacobs to George: *"You mean British teenagers are behind the Americans?"*

George: *"We've liked this type of thing for years, but it hasn't really caught on."*

Sixth disc: *I Can't Stop Talking About You* by Steve and Eydie.

Paul: *"People will whistle this one."*

Ringo: *"She carries him, actually."*

George: *"It could easily make the Twenty. So relaxed."*

John: *"They're relaxed 'cos they're getting on a bit. I don't like it."*

Seventh disc: *Do You Really Love Me* by Billy Fury.

Ringo: *"Not for me. I've never bought one of his records."*

George: *"O.K. But I wouldn't buy it. Guitar phrasing is like that on Cliff's latest."*

John: *"Tune's not bad but I don't like gallop tunes."*

Paul: *"I quite liked it."*

Eighth disc: *There I've Said it Again* by Bobby Vinton.

George thought it was nice enough.

John: *"Get an old song and everybody does it again at the same time."*

Paul: *"Secretly, teenagers don't want old songs brought back."*

Ringo: *"Nice and smooth. Specially if you're sitting in one night – and not alone."*

Ninth disc: *Love Hit Me* by The Orchids from Liverpool – who, unbeknownst to the group, were sitting in the audience.

John: *"Just a big cog – a pinch from the Crystals and the Ronettes."*

Paul: *"It's good for a British record."*

Ringo: *"It'll sell a few but not many."*

George: *"I'd rather have British groups pinch from the Crystals than the other stuff."*

When it was announced that the Orchids were present, John said: *"A lousy trick."*

With the **tenth disc**, *I Think of You* by the Merseybeats, there wasn't time for commentary, just the vote. All four voted it to be a hit.

The writer suggested the BBC should rerun the show as soon as possible.

December 21, 1963 – Record Mirror, Peter Jones announced: The Stars of the Year: The Beatles.

"Beatlemania," stated an unnamed university professor, *"is perhaps simply another word for entomology."*

The professor, of course, was talking about insects. But the millions of pop fans in Britain meant the Sensation of the Year.

The Beatles were so dominant on the British music scene in 1963 that no one else could even be considered as Star of the Year. The year began with *Love Me Do* at number twenty-four in the charts after hanging around for months, while the Beatles spent most of their time in Germany.

Beatlemania had not started yet; few outside of Liverpool knew them; the band called Brian Epstein daily to find out if their popularity was spreading; the reviews had been less than enthusiastic; some even suggested that the harmonica was too old fashioned.

But the next record did not linger long in the nether regions of the charts. *Please Please Me* hit the top three within a month. *From Me to You* raced up the charts even faster. And *She Loves You* broke land-speed records on its way up, while *I Want to Hold Your Hand* had more advance orders than any other British single – ever.

Also, there were three EPs: *Twist and Shout*; *Beatles' Hits*; and *Beatles No. 1*.

And the LPs: *Please Please Me* and *With the Beatles*. Busy boys!

All were huge hits, some selling so fast they were like singles.

That was the sort of music history that would never be repeated, Peter Jones said. There were political cartoons of the Prime Minister and Harold Wilson clad in Beatle clothes with Beatle hairstyles. The band had made headlines nationwide. And five national newspapers ran their biographies in time for the Royal Variety Show.

Even the upper classes were hooked on the Beatles. Fans all over Britain were changing their hairstyles. The members of British Parliament complained about police security and overtime hours for the cops wherever the Beatles played. Black market tickets were being scalped. Fans slept on sidewalks to procure tickets to their shows.

Paul McCartney compared it to a national disaster.

Every move they made was scrutinised and reported.

And the question most asked? – What were they really like?

John was quick to speak his mind, friendly if he knew you, smart and quick. Ringo seemed sad but was usually happy, dry-witted, and intense. Paul's humour could be devastating; he was knowledgeable, and at his most unserious when he appeared serious. George was the one who remembered the band's history, likable and with the longest hair.

As a band, they made a point of remembering people and had a lot of patience. The were generous, well-informed about the pop scene, and read a lot about it, particularly the American Rhythm and Blues scene.

The next question most often asked was whether or not stardom had changed them.

The answer: of course.

Jones went on to explain that handling the adulation and the fanatical fans had not actually changed them inside – but it had changed their lives and made them prisoners of fame, unable to do anything normal in public.

And the third most popular question was: How long will it last?

The Beatles, according to Jones, would never respond to that one. But he wondered if it mattered. Even if the group should disband, he thought they could go on individually for as long as they wished; that was how talented they were. And that was their main strength – they were all incredibly talented.

1963 had been an amazing year, and 1964 should be even more so, particularly after their film hit the silver screen.

Was it possible to predict where it would all end? No!

— Chapter Four: 1964 —

January 4, 1964 – *Melody Maker* **reported** that the Beatles had won the Melody Maker Press Awards for the Records of the Year. Journalists throughout Britain were invited to vote for the best single and the best LP of the year. And the Beatles took home the two trophies. The top single was *From Me to You*, just beating out *She Loves You*. The top album was *Please Please Me*. As the article was printed, *I Want to Hold Your Hand* was number one on the *Melody Maker* chart, and *She Loves You* was number three.

As a footnote, it was mentioned that the U.S. was getting ready for the Beatles' invasion. An American disc jockey had acquired a bootleg copy of *I Want to Hold Your Hand* and was giving it a lot of play.

January 11, 1964 – *Disc Weekly* **reported** that the Beatles had answered their American critics by selling, in just three days, a quarter of a million copies of *I Want to Hold Your Hand*. *She Loves You* had topped the charts previously. As a preface to their planned U.S. visit, the Beatles had a prefilmed trailer spot on *The Jack Parr Show* where they sang *She Loves You*. The *New York Daily News* claimed that these Beatles, these rock and rollers, were even worse than their American counterparts. And the *Journal American* said they were a throwback to the early Elvis.

January 2, 1964 – *Mersey Beat* **mentioned** that Richard Starkey had left Rory Storm and the Hurricanes in August 1962.

Said Rory, *"Ringo was with us for more than four years. When the group first started, only ourselves and the Blue Jeans were known on the Mersey Scene; we were the first rock group to do the rounds.*

"During the four or five years Ringo was with us, he really played the drums, he drove them. He sweated and swung and sang. Ringo sang about five numbers a night; he even had his own spot, it was called Ringo Starrtime. *Now, he's only a backing drummer. The Beatles' front line is so good, he doesn't have to do much. This is not the Ringo Starr who played with us.*

"When Ringo first joined the Hurricanes – we were called the Raving Texans then – he didn't have any rings and we just called him Ritchie. During our first year at Butlins, we all chose fancy stage names and that's when he became Ringo Starr."

Rory Storm and the Hurricanes had yet to find a drummer good enough to permanently replace Ringo.

January 4, 1964 – *Disc Weekly* **reviewed** the Beatles' Christmas show at the Astoria in Finsbury Park. A well-produced sell-out event, from the opening by Duke D'Mond and the Barron Knights to the final chords of the Beatles' finale, *Twist and Shout*.

During the Beatles' segment, as expected, fan screams were constant, girls and boys standing on seats, frantically waving their arms to be noticed, and unsuccessfully charging the stage. Also included on the bill was Rolf Harris – who asked the fans not to throw jelly babies because Paul had been hit in the eye with one, and remarkably, none were thrown – along with Billy J. Kramer and the Dakotas, the Fourmost, Tommy Quickly, and Cilla Black.

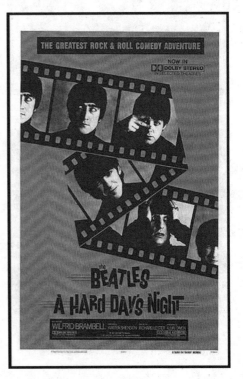

January 11, 1964 – *Disc Weekly*, **Pierre Robin said** the Beatles were all set to hit Paris as Olympia stars, ready to attack France as forcefully as they had attacked Britain. They were to do a 25-minute show at the Olympia, with French star Sylvie Vartan performing the warm-up for them. Posters were being pasted up all over Paris, complete with photographs and a list of the band's songs; France was going Beatle crazy. A French television crew was in England preparing a show about the Beatles, to be aired before their arrival. Papers and magazines were writing extensively about the band, again with scores of photographs. The *Paris Daily Aurore* praised them and featured a lengthy interview. And Beatle haircuts were appearing all over France.

Said Michel Etevenot, in charge of security for the show, "*When the Beatles step on to the Olympia stage on January 15, one hundred police will be waiting ready to deal with any fans who get out of hand. I know many British fans are coming over for the opening, but we don't anticipate any trouble from them.*"

In addition to the visible cops, there would be plain clothes officers mingling with the audience.

January 11, 1964 – *Melody Maker* **claimed** the States were going Beatle crazy. They began by talking about the Beatles' next appearance on the Palladium TV show "this" Sunday – at the end of their three-week Christmas show at the Finsbury Park Astoria, a show that broke all box office records – and only three weeks before their departure for the U.S., where American fans were already anticipating their arrival.

I Want to Hold Your Hand was getting fantastic air play on the U.S. radio stations. Capitol Records had been forced to release it after the fans' response to the radio play of the Parlophone original that had been smuggled into the country.

January 11, 1964 – *Melody Maker*, **Henry Kahn announced** that Beatlemania had hit Paris. The Beatles, not due in France until the following week, were already creating waves of excitement.

Photographs and posters were decorating the city; French TV was airing shows about them; the newspapers were publishing stories about them. One writer pointed out that the Beatles had shaken the "*phlegmatic British out of their phlegm.*" Then he went on to worry about the Beatle haircuts that were appearing all over France, but took comfort in the fact that the hair used in Beatle wigs was a French export.

They finished with the security arrangements, a hundred police ready to pounce on any fan showing too much Beatlemania, while plain clothes cops circulated in the music hall.

January 16, 1964 – *Mersey Beat* **printed** the first series of promotional photographs ever taken of the Beatles. They had been made by Peter Kaye, who said, "*A few years ago, Brian Epstein came to me and asked if I would take some photographs of the Beatles. I had not heard of the group at that time, but said I would take the photographs. However, Brian asked me to take the shots within a few hours of his calling me and I was not really satisfied. However, I undertook the sitting.*

"*When the Beatles came, they were very undisciplined and were jumping about and cracking jokes, with the result that the sitting was a dismal failure.*

"*I phoned Brian and told him that the sitting did not work out and would have to be redone. During the next few days, I had more time to think of ideas, and we took the Beatles on a very successful location job. No one ever did see any photographs of that first sitting and they have never been published before. However, as a special favour to* Mersey Beat, *I have allowed them to be printed as they may be of some historical interest to fans.*"

January 18, 1964 – *Disc Weekly* **declared** that the Beatles were headed for number one in the U.S. *I Want to Hold Your Hand* was on its way to the top spot in the U.S. pop charts, the record selling over a million copies in just three weeks. It seemed likely that the Beatles would be presented with a Gold Disc on the Ed Sullivan Show on February 9.

Capitol Records said *I Want to Hold Your Hand* was the fastest selling record ever, selling ten thousand copies an hour in New York City the previous Monday. Swan Records had just re-released *She Loves You*, originally launched with little fanfare the previous August. Vee Jay re-released *Please Please Me* and *From Me to You*, and they also put out the *Please Please Me* album, while Capitol, the previous week, released *With the Beatles* under a new title: *Meet the Beatles*.

The Music Corporation, while playing *I Want to Hold Your Hand* every half hour on their radio station, had sponsored a Beatles contest. A thousand winners were to receive copies of *I Want to hold Your Hand* while two "big prize" winners would receive $57.00 each.

The American public were rapidly getting to know the boys from Merseyside. *Time Magazine, Life Magazine, Look,* and *Newsweek* were all running articles about the fab four, while all the U.S. network news programs were featuring them. America would be theirs.

January 18, 1964 – *Melody Maker* published — Beatlemania U.S.A. — *I Want to Hold Your Hand* was flying up the U.S. charts and Brian Epstein was being bombarded with bids for the band to tour the U.S.

"I have had a stack of offers for tours, one-night stands, concerts and so on," said Epstein. *"I am not accepting any at present.*

"This is principally because we haven't got time, and also because I consider it better to concentrate on the American TV shows next month."

In the States, the Beatles were already the most talked about act since Elvis. Capitol Records announced that they'd sold a million copies of their single in one week, and it was rumoured that the disc was selling ten thousand copies an hour. *Meet the Beatles* had been rushed ahead for release and the orders were flooding in. Swan's re-release of *She Loves You* had sold 50,000 copies over the weekend. And Beatle wigs were showing up all over New York City.

The band was due in New York on February 7.

That very day (Thursday) the Beatles were opening at the Olympia Theatre in Paris for three weeks.

I Want to Hold Your Hand was number two in England that week, bumped out of number one by the Dave Clark Five's *Glad All Over. She Loves You* was number seven.

January 18, 1964 – *Melody Maker*, Henry Kahn reported that the Beatles were to open their first show at the Olympia in Paris that day. Even after a huge promotional build-up, stories in all the daily newspapers, and stories on the TV news, the Beatles' press officer, Brian Somerville, discovered there were still people in the city who had not heard of the fab four.

Odeon Records announced that thieves had lifted the empty Beatles' record sleeves with which they had decorated the Olympia lobby.

Somerville said the band was apprehensive about their Paris gig because French fans had a reputation for violence.

January 25, 1964 – *Disc Weekly* – a footnote mentioned that the band had two hits in the Australian top 15, while in Paris, **Henry Kahn wrote,** *"Les Beatles,"* the crowd cheered and chanted when the final curtain fell on their opening night at the Olympia.

Before the show, George Harrison had said, *"They don't know us. We hardly sell any records in France."*

But despite many problems, their debut was triumphant. There were too many cops – the Olympia was worried about violence. No one was allowed to approach the stage door or even walk down the street outside without a pass. There was a bit of a roughhouse with photographers in the Beatles' dressing room. And the mikes failed three times during the show, leaving the band to stand in silence while they waited for the problem to be fixed.

But, according to the writer, their superb talent carried them through.

After the show, George said, *"It was difficult, of course. But we couldn't see what was going on beyond the footlights – although I did catch sight of some waving hands."*

The Beatles played all their favourites, *I Want to Hold Your Hand, I Saw Her Standing There, Twist and Shout,* et cetera, to yet another frantic crowd. The French paper *Candide* announced that the Beatles were musicians and not amateurs. *Paris Soir* said the show was a knock-out success. *France Soir* mentioned that hands had never before clapped so hard at the Olympia. And *Le Figaro* mocked the boys' hair cuts, while ignoring their performance.

Prior to the show, there had been some speculation that the Beatles might change their program because three-quarters of the audience were the French "elite."

After the show, Paul McCartney said, *"We had no reason to change. We try to be original, and if we are, we want to stay that way."* He added, *"We have to produce six numbers for a film and we haven't written one yet. Now we are trying to get a piano into the hotel and get down to work."*

"I only wish they were here for six months," said Bruno Coquatrix, the manager of the Olympia. *"What a triumph."*

French fans Martine Destellian and Francoise Senard coined a new phrase that the Beatles were *"super-formid!"*

January 25, 1964 – *Disc Weekly*, **June Harris reported** that the Beatles were booked for Carnegie Hall.

There was no stopping the unbeatable fab Beatles. They had top billing for a Carnegie Hall concert. And Brian Epstein was being inundated with offers for U.S. tours. Beatlemania was taking the States by storm, the hysteria was building, and *I Want to Hold Your Hand* had sold a million and a half copies, number one on the Cash Box chart. The re-release of *She Loves You* was also on the way to the top.

And the story was the same in Canada. Brian Epstein said *She Loves You* was at the top of the Canadian charts and *Beatlemania* was at the top of the album charts. [*Please Please Me* was the Beatles' second album, but the first to be released in Canada, under the name *Beatlemania*.]

The Beatles were to give two performances at Carnegie Hall on February 12, one at 7:30 and one at 11:00. The shows were already sold out.

The Carnegie Hall gig was going to delay their Florida vacation; they were scheduled to leave New York on February 13 with a couple of days off before doing the Sullivan Show live from Miami on the 16th.

Not to be left out of the Beatles cash box, MGM released a single of *My Bonnie*, backed by *When the Saints Go Marching In*, the recording from Germany with Tony Sheridan.

A radio station in Fairfax, Virginia was running a series about the Beatles. The first one, an hour-long special called Beatles Bonanza, had aired the previous Saturday, featuring interviews with the various English folk found in the area, along with tips on where to buy Beatle wigs and other paraphernalia.

The Beatles were well on the way to conquering the country without even visiting. All that was left was to go there. One of the first things on the agenda was a meeting with the president of Capitol Records, who was planning to present them with Gold Discs for their huge record sales.

As a footnote, it was announced that a recent Beatles newsreel was available from Warner-Pathe on either 8 mm or 16 mm film, for 7 pounds 10 shillings in black and white with sound, or 12 pounds 10 shillings in colour with sound.

January 25, 1964 – *Record Mirror* **claimed** the Beatles were at the top in the U.S. The Beatles had hit number one in the charts with *I Want to Hold Your Hand* and were actually about to do battle with themselves – *She Loves You* was climbing rapidly. Also, *Please Please Me* and *From Me to You* were on their way up the charts, having been re-released by Vee Jay Records.

The Beatles were more than ready for their trip to the U.S. after their performances in France. It was their appearance with Jack Parr, doing *She Loves You*, that sparked the interest.

I Want to Hold Your Hand was Capitol Records' hottest single disc ever. In New York, everyone was talking about the Beatles, and the record was selling ten thousand copies a day.

A Beatles record had actually made the U.S. charts once before. *From Me to You* had cracked the top one hundred and fifty, but the cover version by Del Shannon had sold better.

January 25, 1964 – *Melody Maker* **reported** that *I Want to Hold Your Hand* was number three in the charts, *She Loves You* was number ten, and the French fans were chanting *"Beat-tles, Les Beat-tles!"*

The Beatles had finished an amazing two-year reign at the top of the pop scene by scoring yet another honour – top billing for two concerts at Carnegie Hall in New York, scheduled for February 12.

They were to fly to the U.S. on February 7 and, two days later, were to do the Ed Sullivan show live, to be broadcast coast to coast. On the 16th, from Miami, they were to do another live Sullivan show, then return two days later to London.

I Want to Hold Your Hand had been declared the fastest selling single in Capitol's history.

January 25, 1964 – *Melody Maker* **ran** the banner: *Vive Les Beat-tles!* **Ray Coleman reported** that, during a drive down the Champs Elysee, Paul McCartney said, *"They've all gone bloody mad. Never seen anything like this!"*

They left for France with some trepidation, never imagining that Paris would respond with such fervour. They had heard the stories of mayhem and havoc wreaked by the merciless French audiences.

"It's the greatest thing that ever happened to us," said George Harrison after the show, celebrating with bottles of Coke in their 50-pound-a-day hotel room. *"We're lost for words."*

Throughout their opening at the Versailles, a warm-up for the Olympia, the crowd was chanting *"Ye Ye Ye,"* and *"Oui Oui Oui,"* the vocals screamed by more men than women, more boys than girls.

During the flight to Paris, the writer had asked McCartney if he planned to make announcements in French and McCartney said, *"You're joking. The nearest I'll get to acting French is that I'll smell of garlic from the food. Haven't had time to do any practising. That's the story of my life."*

Fogbound in Liverpool, Ringo was not on the flight.

In Paris, scores of reporters fought for position and the three Beatles waved and descended the plane to yells of *"Ici, Ici"* from fans and reporters, record company executives and photographers, flashbulbs popping as John Lennon spoke his first words in France, *"Where's Brigitte* (Bardot) *then?"*

After a brief press conference, they headed for the George Cinq where John and Paul spent a quiet night indoors while George went out to visit the Eiffel Tower and a nightclub. When asked what he thought of the Tower, he said, *"It's tall."*

Back at the hotel room, where the phones were ringing non-stop, a girl demanded, *"I want to speak to a Beatle."*

Lennon got on the phone and she explained, *"I'm not a screaming fan. I just wanted to speak to a Beatle and I've done it. Thank you. Must go – I'm in a call box and haven't any more sixpences. Good luck!"*

On Wednesday morning, they attempted a walk down the Champs Elysees with a number of journalists. The French fans charged, chaos ensued, and the Beatles jumped into a taxi to return to the hotel while journalists climbed all over the car and refused to get off unless the band posed for more pictures.

"What a funny lot," George said. *"How do we feel about tonight? Well, you can only do your best. If they don't like it, they'll have to do the other thing. It's up to them."*

Ringo still had not arrived, but eventually the other members of the band were told he on his way. At the hotel, they waited for Ringo...

"I'd like to play some records," said John. *"We've got a record player but all the record company gave us in the way of records is a copy of every Beatle record ever made. They must be joking. I don't like any of 'em."*

Pale and worn, Ringo finally arrived.

"Where've you been you stupid git?" demanded George.

"Oh, I got lost in Liverpool," joked Ringo.

The warm-up acts were Trini Lopez and Sylvie Vartan, a sort of French answer to Cilla Black. The applause for Lopez was huge and an English fan said to the writer, *"Well, I wish them luck. They'll never follow that. Trini sings standards and gets the whole audience singing with him. They know these songs. But they've never heard of the Beatles stuff. I'm sorry to say it, but they're going to die a great big horrible death."*

The Beatles ripped into *Roll Over Beethoven* and the crowd erupted, quieting only slightly when they moved into *From Me to You.* They screamed for more basic rock and roll.

As they finished *From Me to You,* Lennon yelled, *"Gerrrarrt of it and shurrup!"*

I Saw Her Standing There; This Boy; Boys, with Ringo belting it out; *I Want to Hold Your Hand; Till There Was You...* and the crowd was almost theirs. After *She Loves You* and *Twist and Shout,* they owned the audience, fans and photographers rushing the stage, men screaming for the band, women quiet...

Encores were demanded with chants of *"Les Beat-tles!"*

Paul did *Long Tall Sally.* The crowd was sated.

Backstage, the reporters were ranting and demanding, bombarding them with questions.

"Well," said John, *"If they want things like Sally and Beethoven, we can do that standing on our ears. We might change the program for the Olympia tomorrow and put in some of the early rock numbers we used to do in Hamburg and at the Cavern, things like* Sweet Little Sixteen *and things, you know. Easy."*

"Funny thing," said Ringo on the way back to Paris, *"You get so many screams in England, you know, you can't hear a word we're singing or playing. Here, it's terrifying to be able to hear your voice for the first time in years at a live show!"*

They retired for an early night but, at three in the morning, Brian Epstein forced his way into their rooms with a telegram from New York, saying, *"You're number one in America with the record! Number one!"*

"I couldn't believe it," said Paul.

For a British act to make it to number one in America was virtually unheard of. The Beatles were stunned and did not manage to get back to sleep until the sun was rising two hours later, missing a lunch appointment with the manager of the Olympia, Bruce Coquatrix, and not getting up until late afternoon, when they ate cereal and rolls.

The writer asked John Lennon why he rarely had a proper meal and Lennon replied, *"Me, I believe eating is a waste of time. If I could arrange it, I'd have pills for everything. Pills that wash and dress you in the morning, pills that satisfy hunger, pills that make you need no sleep. Eating and sleeping are just time wasters – a sort of necessary nuisance."*

They went to the Olympia early on Thursday. In the dressing room, a reporter asked George about who cut their hair.

"Anybody can cut out hair – care to have a snip? But to say we have it cut is not very true. We have it diminished now and then, you know."

Five hundred cops were said to be on hand for the show. The streets around the theatre were sealed. And the audience was packed with celebrities, a few wearing Beatle wigs.

While the warm-up acts were playing, the crowd chanted for the Beatles, almost booing Sylvie Vartan off the stage. Three hours after the show's opening, the Beatles took the stage, launched into *Roll Over Beethoven...* and faded away as the power died.

"The power, the power, it's gone," yelled Paul.
"It's not our fault," declared Ringo.

The crowd turned on them, jeering, while Mal Evans fixed the electricity. They finished *Beethoven* and played *From Me to You* to a round of applause, then kicked into *I Saw Her Standing There*. The power died again and Lennon danced and clowned on stage to keep the crowd amused.

As the power resumed, they harmonised on *This Boy*, moved on into *Twist and Shout*, and started to own this audience made up of French society-types.

As they departed the stage, the screams for an encore were so loud that the Olympia management put on a Beatle record.

At the dressing room, cameramen were attempting to break in while the Beatles' press officer, Brian Sommerville, fought them off, fists and feet, a full-scale brawl broken up by the police, who arranged an escort back to the George V for the Beatles.

"In all my twenty-five years in Paris," said one bystander, *"I have never seen a foreign group get such a triumphant reception. The audiences here are never so enthusiastic and the fever is never so intense."*

"I didn't expect it from the French," said George, *"because, for one thing, they seem basically not pro-British and secondly, they didn't know us. When the electricity failed, we would have willingly died right there and then."*

The whisky flowed, smokes were lit, the phones start ringing and four happy Beatles tried to relax.

Vive les Beatles.

"Mersey bookoo," said McCartney.

January 30, 1964 – *Mersey Beat* **answered** the many fans who were worried about the rumours that Paul McCartney and Jane Asher were planning to marry by quoting Brian Epstein: *"Paul is definitely not engaged or married, and does not intend to become engaged or married."*

They went on to assure the fans, who worried about the impact of the Beatles forthcoming U.S. visit, that the group would be a huge success in the States. There was absolutely no doubt about it.

Next, they announced that John Lennon's *Beatcomber* column from Mersey Beat was about to be published as a book, *John Lennon In His Own Write*. It would be released by Jonathan Cape in about six weeks.

February 1, 1964 – *Disc Weekly*, **Henry Kahn wrote** a progress report on the Beatles in Paris, stating that the French fans were fiery and the second week was fabulous. Long queues and enthusiastic fans was the scene in Paris during the second week of the Beatles' Olympia gig. Since the problem-riddled opening night, the audience had changed from the French elite to the real fans, the young and the hungry, storming the theatre, wailing and screaming. Commenting on the difference, Ringo said, *"This is*

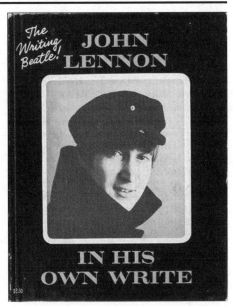

not the same thing at all. We are getting a splendid reception but, of course, the audience is different."

Some of the French newspapers were hostile, not so much towards the talent and the music of the Beatles, but more towards the fact that the Beatles were English and accomplishing something in France that French stars had never managed: they were making the fans hysterical, truly fanatical.

When they were not playing, the band spent most of their time sleeping, with occasional trips around Paris, recognised wherever they went but rarely attacked. *"A pleasure not to have our ties snatched off,"* said an unidentified Beatle.

In Montmartre, the band took pictures of the artists and the artists drew pictures of them.

At the Blues Club, where Memphis Slim was performing, they were invited to take the stage but declined.

And Beatle wigs were top-selling items around Paris, everyone, young and old, was buying them.

February 1, 1964 – *Disc Weekly*, **Laurie Henshaw announced** that Pete Best was about to make his own mark on the recording industry. Decca had planned to find a rival Liverpool sound, and was considering Pete Best's band, The Pete Best All Stars with Tony Waddington on lead guitar, Wayne Bickerton on bass, and Tommy McGuirk playing rhythm. They auditioned for Mike Smith at Decca in London.

"We did our own stuff," said Pete, *"then went back home and held our breath. Results came sooner than we ever dreamed. By express delivery came a contract. Now, all we're waiting for is to hear from Mike Smith when we can cut our first session."*

February 1, 1964 – *Record Mirror*, **Peter Jones reported** the Beatles news from America and Paris.

A hit in Paris; the biggest entertainment news in America; records topping the charts in Sweden, Australia, Norway, New Zealand, France and Canada; the Beatles were here, there and everywhere.

The mania had begun slowly in France, the mink-and-jewels opening night at the Olympia tending to drag things down a bit. But within a few days, the real fans, the French teenagers, had taken over the audience, leaping and bounding in the aisles, waving their arms, wailing, not screaming, but wailing for the Beatles like drooling Baptists at a revival.

The Beatles worked hard to conquer the Parisians, starting each day mid-afternoon with coffee at the George Cinq, then sitting for photo sessions and off to the theatre for two shows a night, three on Sundays. After a late meal, they would sit around the hotel room until dawn when they retired. George said, "*We miss the screams. But the audiences are great. Now its roll on America.*"

And America was announcing they were ready for the invasion. Newspapers discussed the Beatles endlessly; disc jockeys played their records hourly; some of them even called Paris to get live quotes from the Beatles. Cashbox declared the Beatles to be the hottest thing to hit the business in years, predicting that every group with long hair would soon be courted by the U.S. recording companies. They went on to suggest that the Beatles' success could change the thinking of American companies toward all things British. Until the Beatles, the British sound had been pretty much unsuccessful in the States.

Capitol had *I Want to Hold Your Hand*, Swan Records was pulling in the money with *She Loves You*, and MGM had come out with *My Bonnie*.

Behind the scenes was chaos. Capitol, Vee Jay and Swan were all suing each other for the music rights, while record distributors were getting telegrams from one or the other of the record companies, ordering them to stop selling the others' product.

The newly inaugurated Beatles' Fan Club was receiving two to three thousand letters a day.

The Beatles were Big Business.

In New York, one record store was offering to send customers to a barber shop next door for a free Beatles' hair cut if they bought a Beatles LP. And if they ended up with a real Beatles cut, the LP was free!

February 1, 1964 – *Record Mirror* carried a brief announcement that Brian Epstein's company, NEMS, had signed its first band that was not from Liverpool: Sounds Incorporated.

February 1, 1964 – *Melody Maker* ran a National Chart showing *I Want to Hold Your Hand* at number 6; *She Loves You* at number 13; *I Wanna Be Your Man*, the Stones song written by Lennon and McCartney, at number 21; the *Twist and Shout* EP at number 30; the *Beatles' Hits* EP and the *Beatles' Number 1* EP at 48 and 49 respectively; while the Top Ten LP chart had *With the Beatles* at number 1 and *Please Please Me* at number 2.

February 1, 1964 – *Melody Maker* updated this week's Beatlemania, mentioning that a helicopter salute was planned for the Beatles as they deplaned in New York on February 7th, and a reception was to take place in the VIP room at Kennedy International Airport. They had five records in the American charts and everyone wanted a piece of them.

Meanwhile, in Paris, they continued to fill the Olympia, long lines snaking away from the ticket office every day. The article mentioned that Beatles had stopped by the Blues Club to watch Memphis Slim perform but had declined when he invited them to take the stage. And Beatle wigs were still selling by the hundreds.

George Martin was in Paris to record a new single for the Beatles, as well as songs for their film.

And two British soldiers carried a 700-signature petition from Germany, presenting it to the Beatles, a plea for them to visit Germany, particularly Berlin: "*Berliners would rave as you are not unknown in the divided city,*" claimed the petition.

The Beatles promised to try to be there in May.

A P.S. from America mentioned that Capitol had released a joke song called *My Boy Friend Got a Beatle Haircut* by Donna Lynn.

February 1, 1964 – *Melody Maker*, Chris Roberts said Lennon and McCartney were going to tell the readers how to write a hit. If the band never played again, John Lennon and Paul McCartney would still be paid well every year as their song-writing royalties poured in. Both Beatles claimed they did not really know how to write hit songs.

Paul: "*We don't know how to write a hit. If we knew, we wouldn't tell you, and if we told you, Britain would have a great new industry, kind of hit factories all over the place.*"

Their early attempts to make a mark with their music were filled with crazy ideas – they were going to swim the Mersey as a publicity stunt; they were going to challenge the current British stars to musical duels at a big recording studios – a hundred off-the-wall ideas, some bordering on desperate.

Said John: *"And there we were with a big exercise book full of songs, wondering what the hell to do with them."*

How had they managed to write 100 songs between them without ever being in a recording studio? And how did they manage to structure the songs that would be sung everywhere, by factory workers and students, by office workers and other bands, all over Britain? Quite simply, how had they done it?

John said: *"It started in school holidays. I was about 15, I suppose. We knew each other, yes. I would've looked funny sitting in Paul's house without being introduced. At that time we did* Like Dreamers Do *followed by* Hello Little Girl *and* Love of the Loved *and* Please Please Me.

"The first song I ever wrote was called I Lost My Little Girl, *then* That's My Woman, *and we used to do one,* In Spite of All the Danger. *The bulk of the numbers were written between 1956 and 1961 when we were at the Cavern doing a lot of the songs. We'd do two together, then I'd do* Please Please Me *and Paul would do* I Saw Her Standing There *and* PS I Love You *all in a normal hour's program."*

Said Paul: *"We were influenced by Buddy Holly and the Everly Brothers and a lot of the numbers are Holly-ish. But when we came to do them at the club – we had hitherto only heard them with guitar or piano – the sound changed with the addition of bass and drums and they came out differently.*

"We both wrote words or music as we felt like, although we'd suggest changes to each other in different numbers.

"We don't think we write very hip words. We try to write words that we would like and not laugh at. Not moon and June stuff."

John said: *"What do you mean, moon and June? We had moonlight and Junelight in* I'll Be On My Way."

Paul: *"That's different. You know what I mean. Not corny."*

John: *"On the music side, as far as I was concerned, if I found a new chord, I'd write a song around it. I thought if there were a million chords I'd never run out. Sometimes the chords got to be an obsession and we started to put all unnecessary ones in."*

Paul: *"They started to get too complicated and chordy. No, not like modern jazz, but just dripping with chords that weren't supposed to be there anyway."*

John: *"We decided to keep them simple, and it's the best way. It might have sounded okay for us, but the extra chords wouldn't make other people like them any better. That's the way we've kept it all along."*

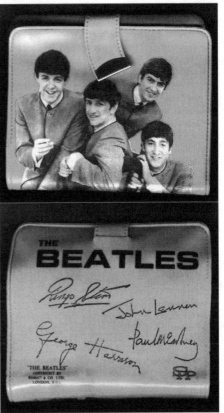

"We never consciously write B sides to records. We don't just sit down and say 'Right, let's whip off a B side,' just like that. Quite a few of our B sides could have been A sides, I suppose, but something has to go on the back, so we just choose."

Paul: *"The best time to write, I find, is sitting down. Seriously, sitting down on my own with a guitar or a piano. Smoking helps too. Why guitar all the time? Not always. Sometimes your ideas get blocked on guitar.*

"One night I was trying to write one, with a guitar, and I couldn't get it on the thing. I tried it with piano and it worked."

John: *"We don't sort of think of a catch phrase and write around it. It could be quite nice if a catch phrase comes to you, but it doesn't happen often."*

Paul: *"I don't think we write for this idiom of the moment or anything. All our numbers could be adapted, you know, to meet each style. Our arrangements are in this idiom, yes. But, for instance,* I Saw Her Standing There *could be a country and western thing with a big country sound. We don't write for any particular idiom. None of us read music. As far as I'm concerned, music is to be enjoyed and if we started studying, it wouldn't be."*

John: *"We have always done our songs and written them down in a weird sort of notation, using* chord names like A flat, C and Dm, and writing the notes separately. It would be much easier if I knew music, yes. After writing the words down and the chords in a night, you can generally remember the tune the next morning. There's more fun in that."

Paul: "Musically again, I don't think the stuff you do chordwise is quite as important as the tune and the words and the feel of the song. I heard two fellers in a club last night doing one of our numbers and in one place they did the wrong chord – but it didn't matter. The song was there."

John: "We thought From Me to You was too way out, although we have always had a fair bit of confidence in our own stuff, always thought it would make it somewhere."

Paul: "I played it on the piano and thought, 'No, no one's going to like this,' so I played it to my dad and he thought it was a lovely tune and that's how it was. You value other people's opinions.

"You know, we have always written for ourselves. We don't – we can't write it down. If we don't like the songs ourselves, how could we put up with them? People underestimate the intelligence of a lot of the record buyers. They're not so thick.

"Our lyrics aren't more intelligent than others have been, but we always try to say something different in the way a song should say it, you know."

February 8, 1964 – *Disc Weekly*, **June Harris** asked the Beatles if they were worried about their upcoming American Trip.

"My only problem," said George, "is wondering how I'm going to pack all my baggage into the 66-pound allowance! Worried about our American trip? Not at all! It's something to look forward to."

The next day was to be B-Day in New York City where the Beatles were Big Business. They were to arrive just after 1:30 p.m. to a huge reception at Kennedy International. As they stepped from the Pan-Am jet, Alan Livingston of Capitol Records was to greet them with a gold record each for the huge sales of I Want to Hold Your Hand. Brian Epstein was also to receive a disc. Then they would be off to the VIP Lounge for a press conference before getting into the limos for the ride into the city. The ten-day trip was to be packed full with interviews, photo shoots, press conferences and television shows. Carnegie Hall was sold out; and the Uline Hall in Washington D.C. was almost sold out.

John Lennon announced that they couldn't wait to get there. "It's going to be fab. I know we're not going to have much time to do anything, but I shall still buy stacks of records. None of us is nervous about our personal appearances or anything like that. The Americans are just going to get exactly the same thing as the British, French and all the rest of them."

Would there be a baggage problem?

George replied, "Not as far as our equipment is concerned. We're not taking our amplifiers, and

Ringo's not taking his drum kit. We've been promised the use of everything we need over there."

For the trip, they bought new suits. John said, "They're light grey. Four buttons and a funny kind of pleated back with velvet collars. But other than this, we haven't gone raving mad buying things for the trip. We just haven't had time!"

February 8, 1964 – *Disc Weekly* **mentioned** that the Beatles had six hits in the U.S. top 100. They had made chart history yet again as Cash Box reported they had six records in the Hot Hundred, including *My Bonnie*, the single made with Tony Sheridan in Germany when the band was made up of John, Paul, George, Pete Best and Stuart Sutcliffe. After only a fortnight on the charts, *Meet the Beatles* had reached number nine.

The six records were: *I Want to Hold Your Hand* – number 1; *She Loves You* – number 7; *Please Please Me* – number 55 in Cash Box and 57 in Billboard; *I Saw Her Standing There* – 100 in Cash Box, 68 in Billboard; *My Bonnie* – 80 and 107; and *From Me to You* at 74.

I Want to Hold Your Hand had just topped two million in sales, while the total record sales in the States were over three million.

February 8, 1964 – *Disc Weekly* **announced**… that Pye Records was about to release a *Beatlemania* album on their Top Six label, scheduled for February 11. The album was comprised of twelve songs by an assortment of anonymous recording artists, songs already recorded by the Beatles, including seven that had been penned by Lennon and McCartney.

Also on February 11, Cameo Parkway was to release *The Boy with the Beatle Hair* by the Swans, while Colpix was issuing a bit of similar drivel – *A Beatle I Want to Be* by Sonny Curtis.

February 8, 1964 – *Disc Weekly* **promised** coverage in the next issue of the Beatles in America, then went on to say that Germany's Polydor label was planning to issue previously unreleased recordings by the five original Beatles: John Lennon, Paul McCartney, George Harrison, Stu Sutcliffe and Pete Best.

"For its historical interest," said a spokesman for Polydor.

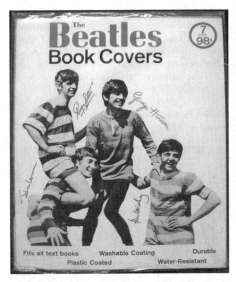

February 8, 1964 – *Melody Maker*'s **Top Ten Chart showed** *I Want to Hold Your Hand* at number 9 and *She Loves You* had slipped from the top ten.

February 8, 1964 – *Melody Maker* **said** American Beatlemania had landed in their offices that week.

"We want the group for an extra show at the eighteen thousand seat Madison Square Garden," demanded the assortment of impresarios and disc jockeys who called asking for help.

One American DJ called three times, assuming the paper could get the extra show done through Brian Epstein.

The producer of the Carnegie Hall show, Sid Bernstein, offered the Beatles fifteen thousand dollars if they would agree to a show at Madison Square Garden.

"All America wants to hear the Beatles and we want to satisfy the public," said Bernstein.

Epstein refused. This trip, he wanted the Beatles to do only major television shows and the Carnegie Hall show, The next trip would be all new venues.

After the festivities at the airport, the band were to be taken in limousines by police motorcycle escort to the Hotel Plaza. And after New York, they would fly to Miami and the Deauville Hotel, where the Ed Sullivan Show would be filmed live for Sunday the 16th.

February 13, 1964 – *Mersey Beat* **said** Ringo Starr had started his drumming career by pounding on tin cans. Today, he was on top of the world and taking America by storm. They spoke with his mother in Liverpool and she said, *"I don't see much of Ringo nowadays. Not half as much as I'd like to, but one thing you can say for the boys, they've never forgotten themselves. They're still the same as ever and quite sensible with all the money they're earning."*

They went on to talk about the Beatles in America and how they were making headlines in all the newspapers, and how all the glossy magazines were featuring them, and how the radio stations were constantly playing them.

And the legal battles. Capitol and Vee Jay were fighting for Beatle rights. Capitol had won the court case, but Vee Jay was still issuing Beatle records.

February 13, 1964 – *Mersey Beat*, Bill Harry spoke with George Harrison just before the Beatles left for America.

George said, *"No matter what happens in the States, we'll definitely be appearing in Liverpool again. We'll be here for an autumn tour and a Christmas show. In fact, we've got lots of dates open for things we may want to do. The Juke Box Jury was made specially for Liverpool fans, and the last Christmas show. We've been in Liverpool for twenty years and naturally we think of the people here.*

"We'd like to try and please our fans everywhere."

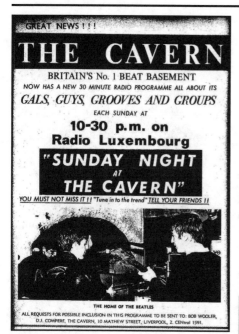

"We're number one and number three now. It's great being on top of the American charts, and our LP record topped the LP charts in two weeks. It's a funny thing, I Saw Her Standing There *is the B side of the single and it's on Capitol, and the same number is on the Vee Jay label on an LP which has also got into the charts.*

"I'm still interested in trying my hand at song writing and I've a couple of further numbers. Trouble is, I can't write lyrics. If I could write lyrics as easy as I could write melodies, I would be turning them out like Paul and John.

"I could write lyrics quick, but I would think them corny. I'd want to get them right, even if it took months to do. But we don't get a lot of time and it is not a necessity really; that is why I'm a bit lax. Still, with Don't Bother Me *I proved to myself I could write a song if I tried.*

"I almost did a number with Ringo. He was playing my guitar and I had the tape on, so we tried something. We played it back fast and we had a song.

We received a petition from Edinburgh with seven thousand names on it saying we'd never appeared there, with the result that we've now been booked to play there. This year has more or less been booked and contracted, so you won't see us staying in America.

"We still think of everybody. By the way, congratulations to the Searchers; you're doing a grand job.

"John's book isn't aimed at the fans, but I suppose a lot of them will buy it. The with-it people will get the gags, and there are some great ones; he's also got some weird sketches in the book.

"All four of us have got cameras and we take pictures all the time. When we get back from America, we'd like to publish a book of France and America as we see it. Don't know whether it will come out, though.

"There'll be a new book out on us by the fellow who took the photos for our new LP sleeve, Robert Freeman. He's just finished it and the photographs are a knock-out. He never posed a shot. The book will be called Beatles Limited, and he's going to America with us and doing a book for the Daily Mirror.

"He's a very good friend of ours. Through him we have all brought these cameras and ended up as budding photographers. But we don't use flash, though.

"By the way, there's a record out by the American Beatles... It's the Everly Brothers and the record's one of their old ones, Wake Up Little Susie. The excuse is that the Beatles used to call themselves the Four Everlys, but it's not true.

"When we get back from the States, we'll spend a whole week recording. Germany is the next biggest market after America and Britain, and we've recorded I Want To Hold Your Hand *in German. There had to be a literal translation and the nearest to the name was* Come Give Me Your Hand. *In German, the numbers are* Komm Gib Mir Deine Hand *and* Sie Liebt Dich."

A footnote mentioned that the market was flooded with Beatle buys – wigs, boots, stockings, talcum powder, wallpaper, caps, chewing gum, sweaters… The list was nearly endless.

February 15, 1964 – *Disc Weekly* devoted the front page to the Beatles – Yankee Doodle Beatles – and promised a four-page pull-out special section within.

February 15, 1964 – *Disc Weekly*, **in the Supplement, stated** that it was the weirdest welcome ever for the Beatles. The word *hysteria* did not even begin to describe the scene Friday afternoon when the group landed at Kennedy International Airport at 1:20 p.m. on Pan American Boeing 707 Jet Flight 101.

All week long, Beatlemania had been building. At the airport, the fans began to gather at 4 a.m., and by the time the Beatles landed, there were more than five thousand of them on hand, screaming, wailing, crying, all of them skipping school for the day to be there.

As the Beatles entered U.S. Customs, the fans began stomping their feet, and vibrations were felt throughout the building. And when the Beatles sat down for their first American press conference, there were more than two hundred photographers and reporters in a room with a legal capacity of fifty.

A woman reporter asked the band if they would sing for her.

"No, we need the money first," said a Beatle.

Another reporter asked if they were really for real. He was invited to, *"Come and feel for yourself."*

Asked if they actually bald, they all shouted, *"Yes!"* When asked if they ever got haircuts, one said, *"I got one yesterday. You should have seen me the day before."*

It was suggested that they were really just four Elvis Presleys, and one replied, *"Of course."*

The basically inane questioning went on for about twenty minutes before the band escaped to their limos and the ride to the Plaza.

February 15, 1964 – the *Disc Weekly* **Beatles Supplement declared** that five hits were rocking America: *All My Lovin', Till There Was You, She Loves You, I Saw Her Standing There,* and *I Want to Hold Your Hand.* The U.S. was going mad with Beatlemania.

The five songs performed by the Beatles on the Ed Sullivan Show had sent Americans into a frenzy that had been missing from the U.S music scene since Elvis Presley's early days.

Starting at mid-day, the fans began to gather in the streets around the CBS TV theatre at Broadway and 53rd. Long before the band showed up for the afternoon dress rehearsal, the fans, held behind police lines, many of them clad in Beatle wigs and waving Beatle banners, were dancing and screaming for their favourite Beatle. By 2:30, the streets were empty. Those few who had tickets were inside, the rest were gone.

Backstage, the press was jammed en mass into a space too small, while Cynthia Lennon, John's wife – known as Mrs. Beatle to the U.S. Press – and Louise Caldwell, George's sister, were confined to an outer hall of the rehearsal studio, along with the members of the press who were unable to get passes. The two ladies spent most of the rehearsal there.

A few hours later, to the usual screams and cheers, the Beatles took the stage.

They opened with *All My Lovin',* slid into *Till There Was You,* and finished their first set with *She Loves You.* At the end of the show, as the next-to-last act, they returned to do *I Saw Her Standing There* and *I Want to Hold Your Hand.*

And the crowd screamed right to the end.

Frank Sinatra said, *"I thought the Beatles would die in New York. I was very surprised by the reception they got. I guess I was wrong."*

And Elvis sent a telegram, congratulating the Beatles on their Sullivan appearance and their visit to the States.

The band was to appear on the Sullivan show the following Sunday from the Deauville Hotel in Miami. Sullivan announced that a further appearance on his show would be taped that day for a release later in the year.

Before the Sullivan show, the group hid out for a while at the Plaza and were available to talk to only a few selected disc jockeys – the Good Guys from WMCA and Murray the K Kaufman from WINS. Murray the K managed to get them to do his entire Saturday night show, each Beatle taking a turn selecting records and chatting about their choices. Meanwhile, the Good Guys from WMCA were phoning as often as possible, getting the Beatles to discuss music and to occasionally announce tunes about to be played.

Initially, they had planned a sight-seeing tour, but that had turned into a photo shoot in Central Park, across the road from the Plaza. Then it was on to the Twenty-One for dinner, though George stayed behind at the hotel with a sore throat. On Tuesday and Wednesday they were to play Washington and Carnegie Hall, a 25-minute show featuring ten songs. Immediately before the Carnegie Hall gig, WINS Radio intended to run a one-hour documentary about the Beatles.

A reporter from Nashville, Tennessee mentioned that people were even talking about the Beatles on the Grand Ole Opry radio show.

February 15, 1964 – again in the Supplement, Disc Weekly talked about the Beatles' arrival starting a disc jockey war such as has never been seen before. WMCA featured telephone interviews with the Beatles from London before their arrival and appeared to be winning the war until Murray the K Kaufman hit the press conference and more or less took it over, using a portable mike and firing a barrage of questions at the band, pushy and brash, elbowing out the other reporters, beating his way to the forefront. Kaufman had arranged with Brian Epstein to gain access to the Beatles' hotel room and he appeared there with the Ronettes. He conducted the only exclusive interview given by the group on their first day in New York.

February 15, 1964 – Disc Weekly said... Back in London, Brian Matthew, host of the Saturday Club on BBC, received a call from the Beatles in New York, which was recorded and aired. He thought it was marvelous that, with all the attention they were getting in the States, they still had time for their fans back home.

February 15, 1964 – Record Mirror carried a special cable from Sam Martin in New York. The Beatles had taken over America. They were the biggest sensation in the States since Elvis. People were talking about them everywhere; fans were wearing the wigs and the sweatshirts, buying the records, and singing the songs.

He mentioned that one New York radio station seemed to play only the Beatles. The reception at Kennedy International was so enthusiastic that a cop who had worked the airport beat for ten years said, "*I think the world has gone mad.*"

Five thousand truant teenagers were on hand to welcome the band, some screaming, some, to the tune of *I Want to Hold Your Hand*, singing, "*Don't say anything bad about the Beatles.*"

Chaos ensued as the plane landed. The crowd on the third floor observation deck screamed, "*We want the Beatles,*" while the fans inside the building went hysterical and rushed the police barrier.

After a few minutes for a photo session on the ramp, the band performed at their first American gig – the press conference. The room was small, and full of reporters and photographers, journalists and TV cameramen.

The writer suggested that the band looked tired and applauded them on their poise during the conference.

When asked if the Beatles wore wigs, Paul said, "*I've got to. I'm bald.*"

And when another reporter asked the Beatles for a song, John said, "*We only sing for money.*"

The reporters loved it.

From the airport, the band made its way to the Cadillac limos that were to take them to the Plaza Hotel. Fans broke through the barriers and mobbed the limousines.

More fans crowded the streets around the hotel, some of them screaming, "*Get a divorce, please, John!*"

That evening, after spending the afternoon with more reporters and cameramen, three members of the band headed down to Greenwich Village, leaving George behind with a sore throat.

February 15, 1964 – Melody Maker ran a chart showing America's Top Ten, with *I Want to Hold Your Hand* at number one. The front page was taken over by caricatures of the Beatles superimposed over a shot of New York City, with a box mentioning that the editor of *Melody Maker*, Jack Hutton, had flown to the States with the Beatles for on-the-spot coverage of their arrival.

February 15, 1964 – Melody Maker, Jack Hutton wrote that Beatle wigs were being promoted incessantly, and selling by the thousands, on the New York radio stations. Along with Beatle-everything-else, imitation records, jewelry, scarves, pajamas, pants and sweatshirts.

"*Sorry they're not in,*" was the normal Beatle reply to any telephone call that got through to their room at the Plaza.

Fifty to a hundred female fans stood vigil on the sidewalk outside the hotel, wailing Beatle songs and screaming every time a face appeared at a 12th floor window, one of them saying to the reporter, "*At the sight of them, I go absolutely ape!*"

Extra cops were hired for the CBS building when the Beatles were there to rehearse for the Sullivan show. And people close to the band were discussing the title for their forthcoming movie, perhaps "The Beatles" or "Beatlemania."

George Harrison was confined to the hotel room with a sore throat on Saturday, but was well enough for the TV appearance.

Local disc jockeys were at war with one another, one offering ordinary Beatle sweatshirts to call-in fans, the other offering Beatle sweatshirts if you traded in the one from the other station.

Broadway shops piped the music onto the sidewalks.

And disc jockeys were getting the Beatles' doctor to report on their health.

Some reporters had been asking snide questions of the band and George Harrison said, "*We don't mind on radio or TV because we can always give them the answer. But sometimes in a newspaper interview you give them a good answer and they use it out of context!*"

A reporter wondered what the Beatles would say if he told them he hated their music.

To which George replied, "*Hard luck. It's selling, isn't it?*"

Referring to the Carnegie Hall shows, George said, "*We'll probably do about 25 minutes, about 10 songs.*"

Paul McCartney added that they would not have any language difficulties the way they had in France. "*The only thing John could say,*" Paul went on, "*was 'I got up at 7:30 this morning' and that was a lie.*"

Ringo announced that his favourite Beatle song was *I Saw Her Standing There* while the other three nominated *This Boy*.

Transcript from the Kennedy Airport Interview, February 7, 1964:

Q: "*What do you think of Beethoven?*"
Ringo: "*Great. Especially his poems.*"
MC: "*There's a question here.*"
Q: "*Would you tell Murray the K to cut that crap out?*"
Beatles: "*Cut that crap out!*"
Paul: "*Hey, Murray!*"
Reporter: "*Is that a question?*"
MC: "*Will you be quiet, please.*"
Q: "*In Detroit, there's people handing out car stickers saying, 'Stamp Out The Beatles.'*"
Paul: "*Yeah, well, we're bringing out a Stamp Out Detroit campaign.*"
Q: "*What about the Stamp Out The Beatles campaign?*"
John: "*What about it?*"
Ringo: "*How big are they?*"
Q: "*What do you think of the comment that you're nothing but a bunch of British Elvis Presleys?*"
John: "*He must be blind.*"

Ringo: "*It's not true! It's not true!*"
Female fan: "*Would you please sing something?*"
Beatles: "*No!*"
Ringo: "*Sorry.*"
MC: "*Next question.*"
Q: "*There's some doubt that you Can sing.*"
John: "*No, we need money first.*"
Q: "*Does all that hair help you sing?*"
Paul: "*What?*"
Q: "*Does all that hair help you sing?*"
John: "*Definitely. Yeah.*"
Q: "*You feel like Sampson? If you lost your hair, you'd lose what you have? 'It'?*"
John: "*Don't know. I don't know.*"
Paul: "*Don't know.*"
MC: "*There's a question here.*"
Q: "*How many of you are bald, that you have to wear those wigs?*"
Ringo: "*All of us.*"
Paul: "*I'm bald.*"
Q: "*You're bald?*"
John: "*Oh, we're all bald, yeah.*"
Paul: "*Don't tell anyone, please.*"
John: "*And deaf and dumb, too.*"
MC: "*Quiet, please.*"
Q: "*Are you for real?*"
Paul: "*For real.*"
John: "*Come and have a feel.*"
Q: "*Listen, I got a question here. Are you going to get a haircut at all while you're here?*"
Beatles: "*No!*"
Ringo: "*Nope.*"
Paul: "*No, thanks.*"
George: "*I had one yesterday.*"
Ringo: "*And that's no lie, it's the truth.*"
Paul: "*It's the truth.*"
Q: "*You know, I think he missed some.*"
John: "*Nope.*"
George: "*No, he didn't. No.*"
Ringo: "*You should have seen him the day before.*"
Q: "*What do you think your music does for these people?*"
Paul: "*Uh...*"
John: "*Hmmm, well...*"
Ringo: "*I don't know. It pleases them, I think. Well, it must do, 'cause they're buying it.*"
Q: "*Why does it excite them so much?*"
Paul: "*We don't know. Really.*"
John: "*If we knew, we'd form another group and be managers.*"

February 15, Jack Hutton from *Melody Maker* reported that New York had gone insane, stark raving mad for the Beatles. John, Paul, George and Ringo all agreed that they had experienced the most uninhibited welcome yet. Five thousand truant feral fans went crazy as the band descended the plane at Kennedy Airport, some even carrying signs for whatever school they attended; one sign read *Ringo for Prime Minister* while many more said *Beatles we* *love you.* Hundreds of extra police were catching overtime hours, including, according to the Police Commissioner, *"Fifty of my top crime fighters."*

All day long, the radio stations had been telling their audience to go to the airport, all the while playing Beatles records and offering wigs and sweatshirts and books. Hutton mentioned that his coloured cab driver said, *"Man, those Beatles sure are a blast."*

After the wild welcome at Kennedy, they thought things might calm down, but things got even crazier. Reporters and TV interviewers fought each other in a feeding frenzy, trying to ask questions while the Beatles watched and talked unfazed, cameras and tape recorders shoved in their faces. It was bedlam. Before the cops could come in to break it up, the crowd settled into the scene, calmed by the Beatles' wisecracks.

When asked what his ambition was, Paul McCartney replied, *"To go to America."*

A woman reporter asked them to sing something. *"No!"* they all shouted. And John Lennon added, *"We need money first."*

What did they think of all the kids skipping school to see them?

Ringo asked, *"What? Isn't it a national holiday?"*

What did they have that made them so popular?

And George replied, *"A good press agent."*

When asked if they were for real, John said, *"Come and have a feel."*

"Me need a haircut?" said John. *"Had one yesterday. You should have seen me before that."*

Again, John said, *"If we knew what makes us a hit we'd form another group and become managers."*

When asked what they thought of the Detroit students who called for their demise, Paul replied, *"We have two answers for the Detroit students who want to stamp us out. We've started a Stamp Out Detroit campaign."*

Where did their ideas come from?

"From bananas and potatoes."

How did it happen that their music was both happy and negative?

"Because we're happy negative people."

Was there any social significance to their music? *"No!"*

"My main purpose in life?" said Paul. *"Saving up to become a rich tramp."*

"Why are we going to Miami Beach?" said John, echoing a reporter. *"To make sand castles."*

Patiently, they identified themselves, mentioning that John was married and had *"a little Beatle."*

"I'm not married," said George. *"I'm happy."*

"It's a dirty lie," was their response to the accusation that they had made a million each. And they were described as *"the hairy British quartet with the sheep dog hairdos."*

A phalanx of cops escorted them to the waiting limos and off they went to the Plaza Hotel.

Hutton interviewed fans at the airport and one said, *"When I arrived here I was normal. Now I'm all ripped up. I got George's autograph. They're wonderful. Fabulous."*

February 15, 1964 – Melody Maker continued with their special report… suggesting that the Beatles' appearance, finally, on the Ed Sullivan show was a bit of a let-down. The writer thought their final song, *I Want to Hold Your Hand* was slow and weak; and he was unhappy that the Beatles failed to close the show – that task was left to a writhing group of contortionists.

They did five songs: *All My Loving, Till There Was You, She Loves You, I Saw Her Standing There* and *I Want to Hold Your Hand.* The sound quality was poor, and the writer thought they should have closed with *Twist and Shout.*

The audience was mostly teenage girls, screaming for the band like the girls everywhere, the noise rising to a crescendo whenever one of the group would shake their hair. During their performance, the camera focused on each one individually, each close-up flashing the name of the band member.

The afternoon rehearsal had been tense, the CBS folks were caught off-guard by the full force of Beatlemania. George Harrison's sister and John Lennon's wife, along with dozens of reporters, had trouble getting in while cops on horseback prevented the crowds from rushing the Broadway studios. In summation, the writer said the Beatles' American debut was disappointing.

A footnote mentioned that Elvis and the Colonel had a sent a cable to band before the show, wishing them good luck.

February 15, 1964 – *Melody Maker* **reported** that Brian Epstein was booking a series of concerts called Pop's Alive! The shows would start on May 3 at the Prince of Wales Theatre. The Beatles' appearance, set for May 31, had sold out almost immediately.

February 22, 1964 – the *Disc Weekly* **Beatles Supplement featured** the Beatles in New York, Washington and Miami. Lesley Gore, with her song

You Don't Own Me placed at number 2 on the charts, sandwiched between two Beatle songs, sent a telegram that read: *"I'm in between you fellas. A girl likes to be squeezed but four against one? Congratulations and welcome to America."*

In Washington D.C., the Uline Arena was sold out. Even Frank Sinatra had not had the same impact as the Beatles.

The band played for 25 minutes and no one heard a note – the screams began as they took the stage and continued even after they were gone, screams so loud that the music was buried.

After the concert, the Beatles were escorted to the British Embassy for a party, hosted by Ambassador Sir David Ormsby-Gore. Then they spent the night at the Hotel Shoreham, returning to New York the following day to receive a gold record from Swan Records for *She Loves You*, their third gold record in a week, the first two being from Capitol.

They had the fastest selling single and LP in the history of the music business, declared Alan Livingston, Vice President of Capitol Records. *Meet the Beatles* had sold 800,000 copies in three weeks and *I Want to Hold Your Hand* had sold 1,800,000 in five weeks. During an interview after the Capitol presentation, the band was asked if they minded being compared to Elvis Presley.

"He's still the best," said Paul, *"whether you like it or not, so we think he's the best to be compared with."*

In a footnote, it was mentioned that Brian Epstein was being bombarded with offers for the band but that he would not be bringing the boys back to the United States until the autumn.

February 22, 1964 – Jonathan Clark wrote for *Disc Weekly* that the Beatles' Carnegie Hall appearance made an Elvis Presley concert look like a Sunday School picnic.

Clark was on stage with the band, along with five hundred other people, and mentioned that the group only had a small space for their setup. Somehow, the promoters had sold more tickets than there were seats in the hall – the extra fans were given seats on the stage.

The audience was a mixture of fans and celebrities, alive with cops and security guards who patrolled relentlessly.

Wooden barriers had been set up in the falling snow outside the Beatles' hotel to hold back fifteen thousand screaming, shrieking fans until they left for Carnegie Hall. Scalpers were flogging tickets, boys were carrying signs that read, "Go home Beatles, we want Liz" and "The Beatles are as crude as oil" and "Ringo, I wanna hold your nose." While the girls sang, "We love you Beatles."

They opened the Carnegie Hall show with *Roll Over Beethoven*, and chaos ensued. When they closed with *Twist and Shout* and *Long Tall Sally*, the entire crowd was out of their seats – or standing on their seats – dancing and cheering. But the band was

slightly disappointed, saying that their show had gone over better in Washington where it was videotaped to be shown on closed circuit TV.

February 22, 1964 – the *Disc Weekly* **Beatles Supplement continued** with a photo spread of the band in Miami, mentioning that this trip was the first time the band had been able to relax in months. They went for a cruise on a yacht, *the Southern Trail*, owned by millionaire manufacturer Bernard Castro, did the live Sullivan show from their hotel, and had an audience of seventy thousand viewers.

British Prime Minister Sir Alec Douglas-Home called the Beatles his *"Secret weapon."*

At one point, George said, *"We thought we had America with us after the welcome at Kennedy Airport, but that was nothing to what was waiting for us in Miami! The fans were breaking airport windows to get near us and eight cops on motor bikes took us right through red lights to escape the fans chasing us."*

Ringo added, *"We had seen Miami in movies, but it still takes some believing. Everybody's got a swimming pool, even if the sea is only a few yards away, and if you've only got one car, you're out. Some of the millionaires even have their own police force!"*

In a boxed caption, it was mentioned that the Beatles opened and closed the Miami Sullivan show, a better show than their first one. During the show, Richard Rogers sent a message that read, *"I am your most ardent admirer."*

New York had been wonderful and Washington fabulous, but Miami was the best of all. The band decided to stay on five more days and just relax. They were supposed to be home on Monday, but they put the return off until Friday, perhaps even over the weekend.

"It's a wonderful place and I guess we're just not ready to go home yet," said Paul.

After the Saturday rehearsal for the Sullivan show, they toured some of the Miami night clubs, including the Mau Mau Lounge where the Coasters were starring. They did a photo shoot on the beach, then made a trip to Fort Lauderdale for a private dinner by the ocean at the home of Bernard Castro, who invited them out on his yacht. They visited another private home, this one in Miami Beach, for a photo shoot arranged by *Life Magazine*, with the Beatles to be featured on the cover.

On Sunday, most of the day was given over to rehearsing for the Sullivan show, including a dress rehearsal which had just as many invited guests as the show itself.

More relaxed than they had been for the first Sullivan show, they opened with *She Loves You*, then moved into *This Boy* and *All My Lovin'*. They ended the show with *I Saw Her Standing There*, *From Me to You* (which they dedicated to Heavyweight Boxing Champ Sonny Liston and his challenger, Cassius Clay, who were both in the audience) and finally, *I Want to Hold Your Hand*.

And that wrapped up their first American appearances, though it was rumoured that a wealthy Texan had offered five thousand pounds Sterling if the band would play at his daughter's birthday party.

February 22, 1964 – the *Disc Weekly* Beatles Supplement finished with... It would have been the most monumental meeting in the history of rock and roll. Elvis Presley was to welcome the Beatles to Miami. He was a no-show, but the crowd, between six thousand and eight thousand fanatical, hysterical, window-shattering, fence-breaking fans, more than made up for it – all for a brief glimpse of the Beatles as they were rushed into limousines and spirited away to the Hotel Deauville in Miami Beach.

Mrs. Anne Stanley, a Vice President of National Airlines, said, *"I've seen Presidents and candidates for President come and go through the airport, but never has anything happened like this."*

And throughout it all, there was Murray the K Kaufman, continually taping the Beatles while taking credit for their appearances, night club visits and even a yacht trip, the self-declared fifth Beatle.

February 22, 1964 – Jack Hutton of *Melody Maker* declared that Beatlemania was truly international. The scenes in Washington and New York were no different than the scenes in Paris and London.

Outside Carnegie Hall, shouting teenagers filled the streets, herded by cops, held back by wooden barriers while hawkers flogged Beatle this and Beatle that, weaving amongst the screamers as police whistles blew.

Inside Carnegie was no different than The Olympia in Paris or The Finsbury Park Empire – bedlam.

We Love You – I Love Ringo – and *Beatles Forever* banners were draped from the balconies, while the girls wailed and wept, cried and screamed.

On stage, two or three hundred more sat on chairs, while the cops patrolled to discourage attacks on the fab four.

Preliminary rock acts were treated to constant screaming, but when the DJ host announced that the Beatles were changing into their stage clothes, the audience went berserk. And then they were there and the noise overwhelmed the music.

During introductions, the noise volume indicated that Ringo was the most popular, then Paul, then John and George in a tie.

They opened with *Roll Over Beethoven*, moved into *From Me to You*, shook their heads, evoked even more screams and stood beneath a barrage of jelly beans, one nailing George on the ear. *This Boy, Please Please Me, Till There Was You, She Loves You, I Want to Hold Your Hand, Twist and Shout...* and the noise rose to a crescendo. Fans charged down the aisles and bewildered cops looked nervous. And then it was over, the band was gone and the noise just faded away, a few bruises, a few broken teenage hearts, the heroes gone.

At the start of the show, a lady writer from Chicago told Hutton, *"They really are quite talentless."*

By the end of the show, the exuberance of the fans had enveloped her and she was clapping along with everyone else.

No one could explain the phenomena known as the Beatles.

February 22, 1964 – *Melody Maker* reported that the Beatles loved Miami. And Miami loved them. The mob scene at the Miami Airport was pretty much the same as the previous one at Kennedy in New York, though rougher and wilder.

Six to eight thousand girls – only a few boys – had shown up greet the band but, as John, Paul, George and Ringo stepped from the plane, the fans lost it, breaking windows, leaping over fencing. The cops hustled the band out of there as fast as they could.

The Beatles were enjoying Miami so much, they decided to postpone their departure.

At the Mau Mau Lounge to see the Coasters, George, Paul and Ringo had great-looking unnamed dates.

A Texas oil man offered the Beatles fifteen thousand dollars to play at his daughter's party, but it was doubtful they would agree.

After the band finished their Sullivan show from the Deauville, the writer congratulated CBS TV for being consistent in their presentation – both New York and Miami were equally bad. The sound was horrible.

February 22, 1964 – *Melody Maker* finished their weekly Beatles coverage. They pointed out that the Beatles had a heavier complement of guards than a touring show of the Crown Jewels would receive. Since the Kennedy assassination, American security had been beefed up.

The writer managed to get to the band, though, and announced that they were the same charming guys as ever, the same as they were before all the hangers-on, the parasites, the toadies, the press agents and the guards cluttered up the scene.

And they were thrilled with how well their record sales were going. In three weeks, *I Want to Hold Your Hand* and their album had sold 1,800,000 copies, verified by the Record Industries Association of America as the hottest selling discs in the history of American music.

They were not happy, though, with the way the Sullivan show had gone.

Paul said, *"One of the mikes wasn't working – John's – and it sounded weak on the air we're told. But the studio audience got it all right. Unfortunately we got one or two dodgy reviews and these are the ones that will get back to England, I suppose."*

But they were having a great time, as was John's wife.

"She's out spending now," grinned John.

When they mentioned not seeing many girls in New York, John said to Ringo, *"What about that one you were with last night?"*

Ringo had been dancing at the New York Playboy Club with a bunny.

Paul mentioned that their film was to start shooting at Pinewood Studios on March 2nd. The plan was to show a day in the life of the Beatles. The script was finished and the band was looking forward to making the film.

"We can't act but we'll have a go," said John. They were elated by the way Capitol was pushing their records. But John pointed out that the music had been released before, without fanfare, without publicity. "They just hoped someone would hear them as they passed by."

Lennon's book, John Lennon in His Own Write, was to be released in March. John mentioned that it had been rejected by three American publishers.

George had had the least American attention of the four band members, about which he said he did not care particularly, "As long as I get a quarter of the money."

Later on, American writers were allowed to interview the band. It seemed some of the Americans wanted to score points with them but to no avail.

One shapely lady asked them what subject they did not want to talk about.

"Your husband," said Ringo.

As sandwiches and coffee were served, a reporter apologised for questioning them while they were eating and asked what they would do if the furore ended tomorrow.

"We'd still be eating," John told him.

They were asked who selected their clothes.

"Obviously we do," said John.

The next question regarded what they were going to invest their money in and Ringo said, "Money."

When asked by one woman if he dated American girls, Paul said, "What are you doing tonight?"

And when they were asked if Liverpool was like Greenwich Village, George said, "No, it's more like the Bowery."

One reporter kept asking John about his wife and kid. John was patient but Paul ordered nicely, "Give up, will you?"

"We don't set examples," John said to a woman who told them they should not be smoking because it set a bad example for teenagers. "And we like smoking. Better than being alcoholics."

When a reporter announced being from Glamour Magazine, John waved a limp wrist and batted his eyes, saying in a lisp, "Oh reaaally."

Inanely, another reported inquired about why George was not dressed the same as the others, to which George replied, "Why aren't you wearing a hat?"

And on it went. They figured that it was the Royal Variety show that gave them national fame in Britain. And Ringo agreed that the band would not last forever, while John thought that he and Paul would probably end up writing songs together.

A reporter suggested that their sense of humour helped them through a lot of things.

And Paul agreed, "We're never serious." He pointed at Ringo who was sitting silently. "Just look at him. How could we be serious?"

February 29, 1964 – Disc Weekly declared it was fab to have them back; welcome home to those America-conquering Beatles.

They traveled up the Thames in a police cruiser, escorted by a flotilla of boats packed with film and newspaper people. The streets and the bridges were crowded and the ABC TV studio – their destination – was besieged – guarded by patrolling security guards and cops.

As the screams got closer and closer to the studio, the guards knew the Beatles were near. Then the boat was at the jetty and John, Paul, George and Ringo disembarked to meet the cast and crew of the show Big Night Out. Photographers and reporters crowded round as the band rushed to an awaiting antique Bentley for the two hundred yard ride to the studio where the show was to be filmed. Just as the car was leaving, a girl broke through crowd, dodged

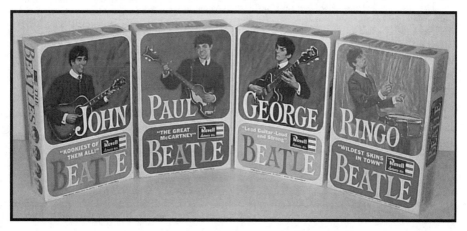

the guards, sprinted through the mob of press and TV people, and leapt at the moving Bentley, landing head first in Ringo's lap.

"We're very pleased to be back," said Ringo with a grin as Paul tried to calm the girl. *"In the rain and all. Quite fab."*

Asked what he had brought back from the States, Paul said, *"The Pan-American flying slippers you get to wear in the planes... Actually, we were given quite a lot of presents before we came home. We didn't do any shopping while we were there though; there wasn't time. Brought some records back with us, though, including some good rhythm and blues things."*

The TV show they were about to shoot was scheduled to air in the ITV broadcasting areas, except London, on the following Saturday at 6:35 p.m. Londoners would have to wait until the following Tuesday (March 3) at 8:00 p.m.

Their arrival at the studio by boat would be shown, and they were supposed to do some comedy sketches before they played. The play list included: *All My Lovin'*, *I Wanna Be Your Man*, *Till There Was You*, *Please Mr. Postman* and *Money*, while the finale, performed with the entire company, would be *I Want to Hold Your Hand*.

February 29, 1964 – *Disc Weekly* **reported** that the Beatles' next single would be released at the end of March, another Lennon and McCartney single, likely one they had written for their film *Beatlemania*.

They had started recording for the movie that week, and Brian Epstein said, *"They will make five or six recordings for the film and an LP will be released around August, when we expect the film to be showing."*

The band planned to spend the rest of the week recording. They were scheduled to start filming, for United Artists, on the following Monday. The location for the shoot was being kept secret to prevent the fans from trashing the event.

The movie, scripted by Alun Owen, was to be shot on black and white film.

Thirty bags of fan mail and twenty-five parcels were awaiting the Beatles on their return to England. And *She Loves You* had set a new longevity record by appearing in the music charts for twenty-seven consecutive weeks.

February 29, 1964 – the *Melody Maker* **music chart** showed a dearth of Beatles' music in the top ten.

The group was to decide on their new single that week, either one of the tracks cut by the band in Paris or a newer one from their most recent recording sessions.

George Martin said, *"It is likely the Beatles' new single will be a song from their new film. It will definitely be another John Lennon / Paul McCartney composition."*

The Beatles were to spend the week recording. The movie shoot would begin the following week at Pinewood Studios. The title, though, was still being

debated. A spokesman for NEMS denied that it would be called *Beatlemania*.

March 7, 1964 – Disc Weekly talked to Walter Shenson, the producer of the Beatles' movie. It was to be a day-and-a-half in the life of the group. It started shooting on the Monday of that week was scheduled to wrap in about eight weeks, due to be released sometime that summer. It was purported to show the Beatles, not as movie stars, but as they really were.

Shenson claimed his plan was to present the Beatles as you would like to see them, to take the viewer behind the scenes for a glimpse of how they worked and related and played.

He mentioned that they were such great personalities on their own that it was unnecessary to phony them up by turning them into actors.

They were not attempting to make a musical in any traditional sense of the word, but the film would not be a documentary, either, since it would have a plot and a story-line – and one fictional character: Paul's grandfather, played by Wilfred Brambell. Still, it was meant to be a vehicle for the band to present themselves as they were.

There would be no concessions to American audiences. It was irrelevant whether or not the U.S. viewers would understand every word, every nuance of the Liverpool accents, spoken by the Beatles. They would not compromise themselves to cater to the Americans.

The film was to be honest and true. The producer wanted that, the Beatles wanted that, and, Shenson was certain, the audience would want that, too.

March 7, 1964 – *Disc Weekly* **reported** that the Beatles were spending roughly eleven hours a day in a five-coach special train, provided by British Railways at six hundred pounds a day, while they shot assorted sequences for their United Artists film.

The train was traveling between Paddington Station and Minehead, fully equipped with everything needed and desired to make a movie, including a restaurant car and bar.

Producer Walter Shenson provided the Beatles with champagne to celebrate as shooting commenced; the band shared it with the crew. Everything was supplied by the film company. Publicity director Tony Howard said, *"Excellent menus have been prepared by the chefs on the train, and on Monday they were offered a varied choice of food, including roast pork and apple sauce, soup, ice cream melba, cheese and coffee.*

"The boys are real professionals and have taken their film directions in a willing and easy-going manner.

"They arrived at Paddington Station at eight a.m. and the filming on the train runs right through to seven p.m.

"Special suits have been made for the Beatles by the film company, and these train shots will give a

general picture of how they travel to and from their engagements.

"During some of the sequences, fans will see two girls on the train who realise that they are traveling with the Beatles, and who make eyes at them."

The Beatles would have the weekend off and be back at work the following Monday. It was unknown whether or not they would be on location or in a studio.

March 7, 1964 – Walter Shenson reported that he wanted to make the Beatles film as colourful as possible. He reckoned that should be easy since John, Paul, George and Ringo were such colourful characters.

He said if the film was successful in England, it would be successful everywhere, and, with regard to the music, it was international. He wanted to be present with a movie camera and sound equipment when the Beatles first heard themselves dubbed in Italian.

The movie would be shot on black and white film, no colour necessary since the Beatles were black and white characters themselves, Shenson claimed.

And there was no intention to feature one band member above the others. They were a team and would be presented as such.

Most definitely, the film was not a musical. There would only be six songs, all written by Lennon and McCartney.

Despite the secrecy involving shooting locations, scores of fans discovered the route of the train; the stations along the way were crowded with screamers.

Shenson mentioned that he had been asked time and again if the boys could act. He said they were naturals, particularly when delivering dialogue or ad libbing their own lines. It was important to maintain their own identities during filming since that quality was what helped them achieve such success. They were somewhat irreverent and definitely were not conformists. They shared a language with their fans. But their humour had a sort of universal appeal and had to be preserved for the film. They were well dressed, great looking kids, also an asset for film.

He predicted they would make a great movie. Just as they did during their first televised appearances, they were going to surprise a lot of people.

March 7, 1964 – Ray Coleman of *Melody Maker* posed the question: Could a Beatle go solo? And if so, who would it be? It was a thought that would horrify fans around the world but, it had happened before with other groups, with mixed success, sometimes the performer fading away into the abyss of wannabe stars; other times, the performer making it to the top.

Dusty Springfield had made it on her own after the Springfields died. Jet Harris and Tony Meehan had made it after abandoning the Shadows. Heinz had done well since leaving the Tornados. Lonnie Donegan had fled Chris Barber's Jazz Band to make it on his own. Adam Faith left Worried Men and

succeeded as a solo act. And Kennie Ball had trumpeted his way through a number of groups before forming his own band and making it big.

In the States, Ben E. King had left the Drifters and Dion Di Mucci had broken with the Belmonts, both to do well on their own.

The Beatles were the most famous act in the pop world, more talked about than anyone. As a group, they were stunningly powerful. And individually, each had his own following. What would happen if they separated?

Ringo had been the most popular in the States, but in the UK there was a more even split in the fan base. Lennon was considered the most intelligent Beatle and, for that reason, probably the least likely to succeed on his own with the teenage fans. McCartney and his baby face received the most screams. Harrison's fans loved his shyness. And Ringo was adored everywhere.

The question asked was: Could a Beatle go solo, and if one could, who would it be?

Tony Meehan, ex-Shadow drummer: *"The Beatles are so big right now that any one of them could leave and make a solo career. Probably John Lennon or Paul McCartney would be obvious choices because they are the singers.*

"I am not so sure that it would be a good move, though, for two reasons. People like the thought of the Beatles as four, regular stars, always together, and also, John Lennon needs the Beatles and the Beatles need John Lennon."

Mitch Murray, the writer of songs such as *I Like It* and *How Do You Do It*: *"I don't think it's time for any Beatle to go solo. I know this much – I'd like to write songs with John Lennon! But he's doing very well as he is. He would be a nut to leave. And if he left, I'd put in for the job."*

Disc Jockey Pete Murray: *"It would be a pity if any of them went solo. They are a team and I would like to see them remain like that. Their popularity among the fans is evenly split. But if anyone is more likely to go solo than any other, I'd say it's Paul McCartney."*

Kenny Lynch: *"If any member of the Beatles went solo, I reckon he'd be acting vain rather than sensible. The popularity of the group is guaranteed at this rate for at least two or three years. As a solo artist, whoever did it would more or less be starting all over again.*

"They help each other to shine. And anyway, a solo Beatle wouldn't make any more money than they're making individually now. No, stick together men!"

Tito Burns, agent for the Searchers: *"I'd say the two that could go solo are Paul or George. I go by my kids' opinions. They are a great yardstick and they know what's going on.*

"Judging by what my kids tell me, I'd put Paul out on tour with a lot of confidence. This isn't meant as

disrespectful to the other three because I think George could do it also.

"The only reason I don't mention Ringo is because I can't imagine him being a solo, as a drummer, because it's the wrong instrument."

Would he considering signing Paul or George on their own?

"The contract's waiting," Burns said.

What sort of money would they make as star attractions?

Burns answered, "Fairly comparable to our top solo artists."

Keith Goodwin, press agent to an assortment of stars, was asked if he would manage the press affairs for a solo Beatle: "Yes, I'd sign him, except for Ringo, because he isn't the experienced singer that the other three are. Without decrying the others, I'd say Paul is the most likely one. He has more teenage appeal than the others.

"Ringo is the obvious one to form a group of his own, like Tony Meehan.

"Yes, I would handle Paul's publicity if he went solo and I was offered the job."

Joe Brown: "I don't think the Beatles will ever part. They are such a fantastic team by themselves and have reached such a peak."

Alan Freeman of Pye Records: "No, I do not think the time is right for any one of them to go solo because they have done, and will still do, such great things for show business.

"And their personalities, though they are individual ones, blend as a group so there is one image. They have all got enormous followings but I don't know if they could get the magic over as solo artists."

Would he sign a solo Beatle to Pye?

"Of course. I'd jump at it like all the others. Nobody would turn down the chance. But I hope that doesn't happen."

March 12, 1964 – *Mersey Beat* said Bill Turner, a school friend of John Lennon, talked with them about Lennon and *The Daily Howl*.

Said Turner, "While we were at Quarry Bank School, I remember a book John produced called The Daily Howl. It was an exercise book filled with his stories, poems, drawings and cartoons. He used to show his work to a bloke called Pete Shotton before he let anyone else see it. Pete was his best mate at Quarry Bank and I think John wrote The Daily Howl mainly for him.

"I remember it was at the time Davy Crockett was the rage and one of the poems was The Story of Davy Crutch-Head. He also took a current hit song called Suddenly There Was A Valley and he incorporated this into a story.

"There were quick flashes in the book such as a weather report. He had an obsession for Wigan Pier, forever Wigan Pier kept cropping up, mainly in a story called A Carrot in a Potato Mine, and the mine was at the end of Wigan Pier.

"One of his favourite cartoons was a bus stop scene. I remember he wrote under the sign which said Bus Stop. And he had a flying pancake at the top of the cartoon and below it there was a blind man wearing sunglasses, leading along a blind dog, also wearing glasses.

"At one time, The Daily Howl was confiscated by one of the teachers and it went all round the staff before he got it back at the end of term.

"John and Pete formed a skiffle group which they named after the school, the Quarrymen. Also in the group was a chap called Colin on drums, another chap called Rod on banjo, and Len Garry on tea-chest bass. They used to practise in the bathroom at John's place.

"They played at Barnabus Hall and another early engagement was at Woolton Garden Fete. Paul joined the group after he'd seen them at St. Peter's Church Hall, Woolton, one night. He asked John if he could have a go on his guitar, and he's been with John ever since."

March 14, 1964 – *Disc Weekly* announced that Can't Buy Me Love was going to be the Beatles' biggest disc yet. Advance sales in Britain and the States had already topped two and half million, with more orders pouring in daily. It could easily hit the three million mark and earn them three gold records, even before its scheduled release date, March 20 in England, March 16 in America.

The Beatles were in a class of their own. Even Elvis Presley came nowhere near them. He had had two songs that cracked the million mark, Love Me Tender and Stuck on You. The Beatles had left him standing still.

On this day, March 14th, the new Beatles' song was to be played on the air. Juke Box Jury and Thank Your Lucky Stars would be using it. The following day, Alan Freeman would air it during his Pick of the Pops. Also, EMI planned to feature it on Radio Luxembourg, beginning the Sam Costa Show.

On the weekend before the record's release, the Beatles were to star in a 90-minute closed-circuit TV event that would be shown in 100 theatres around Britain. The Beach Boys and Lesley Gore were to play for fifteen minutes each; the Beatles would shine for an hour.

Roll Over Beethoven was initially planned as their next single release in the States, but *Can't Buy Me Love* was considered more typical of the band's current sound.

March 14, 1964 – *Don Nicholl* reported for Disc Weekly… that the Beatles' new single evolved in stages. In Paris, while they were playing The Olympia, they recorded the instrumentals for the B-side You Can't Do That; in Miami, Lennon and McCartney wrote Can't Buy Me Love; and, in London, on George Harrison's twenty-first birthday, they recorded both tracks.

Publisher Dick James said of George, *"He was really having a ball, too, because this was the first chance he'd had to record with the three hundred-pound twelve-string guitar which he bought in the States. He thoroughly enjoyed himself twanging and incorporating different effects."*

Finished with *Can't Buy Me Love*, they dubbed John's voice over the Paris recording of *You Can't Do That* to complete the package: *Can't Buy Me Love / You Can't Do That.*

Nicholl said *Can't Buy Me Love* was loud and pounding, Paul's lead vocal strong, George's twelve string guitar providing a new and exciting sound.

He thought John Lennon's singing on *You Can't Do That* was rough and interesting, but that the song was not up to the usual standards of Lennon and McCartney.

When you are successful, Nicholl suggested, people watch for you to falter. Enthusiastically, he said there was no indication here that they were faltering.

March 14, 1964 – *Record Mirror* published a story about the American Beatle-haters. In the States, they were still clearing the debris, sweeping up the mess left behind by the Beatles. The English takeover had left American business men moaning, *"the Beatles are bad for business."*

Apparently, the only ones not complaining were the ones who had Beatles' music for sale. When *I Want to Hold Your Hand* started its monumental race up the pop charts, most records that were not by the Beatles began to suffer. One record company executive said, *"the Beatles saturated air time. Some stations couldn't find time to plug more than a handful of our new releases, so the only thing we could do was not release anything remotely like Beatle music."*

Release dates were revised. All the huge American stars – Bobby Vinton, Trini Lopez, Jan and Dean, Brenda Lee, Ruby and the Romantics, and so on – were held back. The companies pushed all their non-rock discs instead, working the Country and Western circuit.

Even the big record dealers were staggered. One said, *"We could do huge business on Beatle discs, but nobody seemed interested in anything else. Sales on some of the established big-sellers have been way, way down in the past month."*

Some stores just surrendered and gave everything over to the Beatles, sticking up the pictures, displaying the advertising material, pushing the records, stashing the other new releases in a back room until the furore faded.

Cashbox, the American trade magazine, pointed out that the stations which concentrated on good music as opposed to rock and roll and rhythm and blues were doing a fine business, gaining larger audiences as people tired of the non-stop Beatles' saturation on the other stations. They went on to point out that the good music stations were helping

create hits for some of the old timers. Louis Armstrong had not had a hit in years, but *Hello Dolly* was tearing up the charts, thanks to people fleeing the great Beatles exposure.

That was small compensation, though, for the American stars who had to hold back their new releases rather than attempt to compete with this British invasion, this Beatlemania.

In Chicago, a recording by the Beatles of *Roll Over Beethoven* appeared from nowhere as if by magic. It was on a label no one knew – some suggested it was from Capitol Canada – and it was being played on a top Chicago radio station. It caused riots when fans discovered that they couldn't buy it in the record stores.

Regardless of whether or not the Beatles were bad for business, millions of American fans desperately awaited the return of the Liverpool mop-heads.

March 14, 1964 – *Melody Maker* again showed a dearth of Beatles in the top ten, but their new record, *Can't Buy Me Love*, was selling like crazy and wasn't scheduled for release until the following week. Ray Coleman of *Melody Maker* asked disc jockeys what they thought of the band's latest recording.

Alan Freeman: *"I don't think the new one is as strong as their other records. It has not the depth. But again, on this new one, we have the Beatles epitomising that life is a ball, the world's a lovely place. I don't think Paul McCartney sings extremely well on this record."*

Pete Murray: *"I don't think it is one of their best songs. It seems to me, whatever else may be said about them, they are very unselfish, because they're giving their best songs to other people, like Peter and Gordon. I have no doubt, however, that* Can't Buy Me Love *will top the chart."*

Jimmy Saville: *"You can't talk about Beatles records without thinking about the lads themselves. If ever I don't like anything of theirs at first – very rare – I always do twenty-four hours later – but as it happens, I like this one a lot after one play."*

Jimmy Young: *"It's a very fine single. They make a very fine noise. I think they have now set themselves a standard, and they always live up to it. I'm a Beatles fan. Who isn't?"*

March 14, 1964 – *Melody Maker* wondered how long could they last? In one year, the Beatles had become the top recording stars in the world. In a world of one-hit wonders, many artists fell back and faded away just as quickly as they reached the top.

The Beatles were something different, something unusual. Not only were they top act in the UK, they had a massive international following.

But could it last? Could they stay at the top of the pop scene? An assortment of show business folks were asked:

Harold Davison, impresario with years of show business experience: *"I'm not sure how long anyone* can last at the top in this business. *Frank Sinatra has been at the top for about twenty-five years, remember.*

"I think this present Beatle hysteria will last for as long as the teenagers of the present age group are around. By that, I'd give the present peak about eighteen months.

"That doesn't mean to say the Beatles won't be big in eighteen months. They'll still be very big, but the panic and the excitement will have died off. The fourteen-year-olds who are screaming for them now will have something else to think about."

Manfred Mann: *"Who knows? They can stay at their present peak until there is another really good thing to replace them. The pitch they were at about six months ago has fallen slightly, I think, but they are about the best pop group around.*

"A lot of groups are labeled as the answers to the Beatles. But personally and musically, in the pop scene, they are way out ahead. It would be foolish for me to give a period, or an estimate."

Mick Jagger of the Rolling Stones: *"Two years."*

Don Arden, promoter: *"If the present volume of publicity stays the same, the public must realise that no artists – and this is in no way detrimental to the Beatles – warrant such fame. No artists possess the talent to take over nationally, as the Beatles have done.*

"As soon as the public becomes aware of this – and it can't be far away – the Beatles will start to slide. If they are allowed to live normal lives, and quieten down the way Cliff Richard has done, they could last anything up to five years."

A number of other people refused to be quoted by name, though it was suggested that the Beatles were so well known it would be impossible to shatter their image.

Diz Disley, guitarist: *"The Beatles will last for a long, long time. Look at Gracie Fields."*

Norrie Paramor, EMI recording manager: *"They will last as long as they are popular. I can't see them dying out in the foreseeable future. They have set themselves a tremendously high goal and everybody is waiting to see what happens next."*

Julie Grant, singer: *"I think the Beatles will last for ages – for as long as they turn out good records like they do now."*

No one suggested that the Beatles would be falling from grace anytime soon.

March 21, 1964 – *Disc Weekly* **published** a story about being on the set of the Beatles' movie and chatting with George Harrison as he relaxed in a canvas chair with his name on the back.

"The boys have all got one," said George, referring to the chair as he sipped from a cup of tea. *"But I take mine everywhere I go."*

Ringo and Paul wandered around the set. John was relaxing on a sofa. Stage hands hammered, electricians shifted lights, and the director, Dick Lester, muttered quiet instructions. Red lights flashed on, the clapper-board clapped and another take was being filmed.

This was the second day of indoor shooting. The previous week, the train sequences had been shot.

"We traveled twenty-four hundred miles in all – I counted 'em," said George. *"But I didn't mind a bit. It's just this business of getting up early. Usually, after a job, we don't get up till around one p.m. We're really night owls. This early bit just about kills us!"*

March 21, 1964 – *Disc Weekly* **printed** a Western Union cable to the Beatles from Marvin Gaye, Stevie Wonder and Smokey Robinson and the Miracles. They expressed their regrets at not being able to meet the group during their recent U.S. visit. At the time, they had been touring Canada with Berry Gordy Junior's Motown Revue along with Mary Wells, the Temptations, the Contours, the Marvellettes and Martha and the Vandellas, who were also disappointed in not meeting the Beatles. They were overwhelmed when they heard that Smokey Robinson and the Miracles, Stevie Wonder and Marvin Gaye were the Beatles' favourite American artists. They hoped they might be able to visit England and meet the great Beatles then – perhaps even recording some albums together called *Friends Across the Sea.*

"Isn't that great?" said George. *"We were really knocked out."*

March 21, 1964 – *Melody Maker* **talked** about the Beatles' plans for their next U.S. tour. Advance orders for *Can't Buy Me Love* had hit 1,700,000 in the States and the band was ready for their next invasion.

In mid-August, they were to fly to Los Angeles to begin a month-long tour of twenty-five cities that would end in New York.

EMI reported in London that their advance orders for *Can't Buy Me Love* were at 1,000,000. The disc was due out the next day.

In the States, *I Want to Hold Your Hand* had passed 3,400,000 in sales, while in Germany, *She Loves You / I Want to Hold Your Hand,* together on a single disc, sung in German by the Beatles, was at the top of the chart.

March 26, 1964 – *Mersey Beat* **reviewed** *John Lennon In His Own Write* – introduction by Paul McCartney. Before this volume, only the readers of *Mersey Beat* had been familiar with John Lennon's drawings and tales. Now, the rest of the world would be able to experience them. Some would buy the book simply because it was by John Lennon; others would buy it for its quality. Regardless of the reason, it was destined to be a best seller.

March 28, 1964 – *Disc Weekly* **called** *John Lennon in His Own Write* "A Beatle in Wonderland." It had just been released by Jonathan Cape at 9s 6d. They said that the drawings and the writing were cute and crazy. Beside the review was a photograph of the Beatles holding what John Lennon called *Purple*

Hearts. They had been presented with Show Business Personality of 1963 awards from the Variety Club of Great Britain.

March 28, 1964 – *Disc Weekly* **reported** that those Kings of Popdom had made their long-awaited, long-anticipated visit to the TV show *Ready Steady Go.*

As they arrived outside the Kingsway studio, the cops fought back the crowds and the Beatles made it through the doors before the fans could do more than roar.

Inside, within minutes, they were set up in the studio and starting the rehearsal. Flawlessly, they played *It Won't Be Long, You Can't Do That* and *Can't Buy Me Love.*

They received a Billboard Special Achievement Award for owning the top three places on the Billboard Hot Hundred chart, and by the time the award was being presented, they actually owned the top *four* spots.

After the rehearsal, they retired to their dressing room.

The show itself went perfectly, and was played for *Ready Steady Go's* largest ever viewing audience.

A footnote mentioned that the Beatles would be starring on *Saturday Club*, April 4th, along with Gene Pitney, the Nashville Teens, Eden Kane and the Downbeats, Jerry Lee Lewis, and the Breakaways.

March 28, 1964 – *Disc Weekly* **said** the Beatles swept the boards in the Ivor Novello Awards. They were given a special award, along with their manager Brian Epstein and producer George Martin, for Outstanding Services to British Music. For *She Loves You* they were voted The Most Broadcast Work of the Year. Both *She Loves You* and *I Want to Hold Your Hand* shared The Highest Certified Record Sales. And *All My Loving* came in second for The Year's Outstanding Song, beaten by *If I Ruled the World.*

The Carl-Alan awards, presented by the Duke of Edinburgh, named the Beatles The Most Outstanding Beat Group of the Year while *She Loves You* was The Most Outstanding Vocal Record for Dancing.

A footnote mentioned that the Beatles held the top four places in the American Billboard Hot One Hundred Chart, while *Can't Buy Me Love* had entered the chart at number 27; *From Me to You* was number 50; *All My Loving* was at 71; *Roll Over Beethoven* at number 75; and *Do You Want to Know a Secret* at 78.

March 28, 1964 – *Melody Maker* **showed** *Can't Buy Me Love* at number 1, the *All My Loving* EP at number 24; and *I Want to Hold Your Hand* at number 37, while *With the Beatles* and *Please Please Me* held the top two places in the UK album chart. In the States, *She Loves You* was number 1, *I Want to Hold Your Hand* number 2, *Please Please Me* number 3 and *Twist and Shout* at number 9.

On the same page, they printed a lament for Pete Best. He was home in Liverpool, ready to play McIlroys Ballroom with his Original All Stars. As Best's band walked into the building, the group already on stage was playing *I Want to Hold Your Hand.*

They forgave him for feeling sad. The Beatles were playing chaotic crowds everywhere from The London Palladium to Carnegie Hall, while Peter Best and the Original All Stars were relegated to back country ballrooms in Chepstow, Chatham and North Wales.

Pete Best had provided the beat for the Beatles for two years, until August 1962 when he was replaced by Ringo Starr. Since then, he had been busy *"trying to clear my slurred name in Liverpool."* Was he bitter? Envious? Jealous?

"Nobody could have guessed in those days that they would be this big. But somehow, I – and a lot of other people up in Liverpool – knew they had hit potential.

"I had a feeling the Silver Beatles, as they were known then, would make it, nationally at any rate, but as for the other things that have happened to them – well, they have certainly been promoted, haven't they?"

The Silver Beatles had been formed before Best joined them.

"I went to Germany three times with them. I was with them until just before they got an EMI recording contract, just before they made Love Me Do.

"I felt bitter at first when I was told Ringo would join them. I was badly cut-up because I felt inside me that the group had a lot of potential. For a few weeks, I was really down in the dumps. Grew out of it though.

"I decided there was only one thing to do. Have another stab at making it with a new group. Now, things are going well. My group, well, we're not making so much money as the Beatles, but we're working all the time all over the country."

The Original All Stars featured Best on drums, of course, with Tony Waddington playing lead guitar and singing, Tommy McGurk on rhythm guitar and doing vocals, and Wayne Bickerton on bass guitar.

Waddington and McGurk were the All Stars' reply to Lennon and McCartney's song writing partnership.

"They are, I suppose, the answer," said Pete. *"They write a lot of original material for us. And it's good."*

When Best signed on with the Beatles, it was a five-man band. He continued, *"George Harrison was lead guitarist, John was on rhythm, and the bass guitarist was Stuart Sutcliffe, who died so tragically over in Germany. I was on drums. Paul was a sort of second rhythm guitarist. But when poor old Stuart died, Paul decided to take over bass as he was quite good at that time.*

"In any case, Stuart had decided to quit the group when we returned to England. Anyway, his terrible death cut the group down to four, and it stayed that way."

He was asked if he ever saw the Beatles these days. He replied, *"Yes, occasionally but we're all on the move so much we don't have a lot of time to talk."*

And in response to an inquiry about bad feelings when they meet, he said, *"No, none of that. I wish them the best of luck and I mean it. I don't know to this day why we parted company…"*

He mentioned that the Silver Beatles first met Ringo in the Kaiserkeller in Hamburg, 1960. *"That's when their friendship with Ringo began. Later on, Ken Brown played guitar with the Beatles at a club in Liverpool, but he seems to have disappeared since then. There was no drummer at one time. Oh, the club was The Casbah. That was where I met the Beatles."*

What was his opinion of their music?

"They have a good hit parade sound."

Did the Original All Stars try to sound like the Beatles?

"No."

Did they play any of the Beatles' songs?

"No."

Why?

"We have a different sound with the Original All Stars. And our harmony in singing is closer. We have a slightly heavier beat. I don't want to make the big time on the strength of being a former Silver Beatle. But I want to prove to all the people who made my name mud, a couple of years ago, that I have a good group. I want to forget the past and make it alone."

Peter Best and the Original All Stars had a recording contract with Decca, who were likely still trying to recover from rejecting the Beatles.

March 28, 1964 – *Melody Maker* **announced** that *Can't Buy Me Love* was closing in on two million sales in Britain alone. In America, it had already sold 1.5 million. The details of the Beatles' thirty-day U.S. tour had been made public. It would begin August 18th. They would fly to Los Angeles and would open the tour either there or in San Francisco. By September 13th, they would be closing the tour in New York.

Other cities on the tour would be Chicago, Minneapolis, Detroit, Cleveland, Pittsburgh and Philadelphia.

Approximately two million Americans had watched the band on TV the previous week and plans were being made to shoot another tele-record during their next U.S. visit.

In London earlier that week, John Lennon told *Melody Maker*, *"The people who call beat musicians non-musicians are bigots and idiots. If they have to be so narrow-minded, they ought to shut up and keep their opinions to themselves. From my experience, most beat musicians are musicianly – certainly more than some people think. To just lump them and say 'rubbish' is stupid."*

April 4, 1964 – *Disc Weekly* **reported** that after five weeks of filming, they were not ready for a career change; there were no plans to become full-time actors; music still came first.

John said, *"I like acting. It's a great kick. But I can't see myself being someone else. After all, we are playing ourselves in the film. I wouldn't want to try to adopt another personality entirely.*

"Anyway, we're not really acting in this film – we're just taking direction."

And Paul said, *"The corny answer to your question would be to 'say, yes I love acting and I want to be an actor.' But I love music much more. As kids, everyone has dressed up, put on funny hats and acted another part. But I wouldn't want to be someone else. And that's what serious acting would mean."*

"It might be okay if you were on your own," added Ringo. *"But there are four of us – and we work as a team."*

Producer Walter Shenson said, *"There's this one scene between John and Anna Quayle that is simply marvelous. It's where Anna Quayle stops to talk to John backstage during their TV sequence in the film. 'You look like him,' she says, thinking, and rightly, that she has met up with the great John Lennon in person. But John plays it cool, pretending that he just looks like John but that he really isn't a Beatle."* Shenson claims that it is one of the high spots in the film and adds, *"He came on the set absolutely word perfect."*

April 4, 1964 – Laurie Henshaw wrote for *Disc Weekly* **about** filming with the Beatles. Paul was wearing a dinner jacket and working through a dance routine step by step. Dick Lester was filming it one shot at a time, Paul moving just a little for each frame.

"They wanted us to dance," laughed George, *"But we're not dancers. The very idea is ridiculous. Lionel Blair and his girls do the dancing and we gag it up."*

Eating doughnuts and drinking with George and John in the Scala bar during a break, the writer asked about the music.

John replied, *"There are four I really go for. I like* Can't Buy Me Love *plus* If I Fell, I Should Have Known Better, *a song with harmonica we feature during the opening train sequence and* Tell Me Why, *a shuffle number that comes near the end of the film."*

Filming was a few days behind schedule. Completion was estimated for April 22nd with the premiere likely in July. The band might be flown to New York for the U.S. opening. Once that was over, they might start working on another film. Walter Shenson wanted to do one in period costume. The writer asked John what he thought.

"Could be. As a matter of fact, I have been reading a short story since I was about fourteen. It's in a book my aunt has. It would make a great film. I'm not telling anyone what it is in case they get the same idea, too. But it would make a great film. I get everyone to read it – and they scream their heads off."

Another Beatles film was a possibility. According to George, they had an option to do three.

April 4, 1964 – *Record Mirror* **talked** about the Beatles' planned Australian tour. They would be opening the festivities in Adelaide on June 12th. Australian newspapers were reporting that there had never been so much interest in a visiting attraction.

They held the top six spots in the Down Under charts with *I Saw Her Standing There*, *Love Me Do*, *Roll Over Beethoven*, the *All My Loving* EP, and *I Want to Hold Your Hand*. Local radio stations were playing the Beatles non-stop.

Records sales were still stunning. The U.S. *Meet the Beatles* album had sold half a million more copies than the single *I Want to Hold Your Hand*. A new album was planned for release in the next week or so. And their newest single, *Can't Buy Me Love*, had sold 2,700,000 copies so far just in the States.

BBC TV's Panorama show was to be devoted to Brian Epstein and his stable of stars this week. There would be interviews with Epstein and film clips of his various artists.

Also just confirmed, the Beatles were to do a television spectacular, directed by Jack Good.

Filming on the Beatles' movie was more or less on schedule. They had been at the Scala Theatre for the last few days, working on the interior sequences. Eighteen hundred extras had been hired to provide the cacophonous atmosphere required to truly show the band in their natural state.

April 4, 1964 – Peter Jones wrote in *Record Mirror* about John Lennon discussing his book, *John Lennon In His Own Write*, which was receiving favourable reviews and had been compared by various critics with the writing of James Thurber, Spike Milligan, Edward Lear and Stanley Unwin.

Kenneth Allsop, on BBC TV's Tonight program, asked Lennon about the things that made Lennon himself laugh.

"Lots of things. Apples and Derek Hart and that. Quite a few things. I used to like the Goons... and Stanley Unwin. Er, Nick McCutt."

Allsop wondered what made Lennon angry.

"Getting up makes me angry, you know, in the mornings. Apart from that, I'm quite quite healthy."

The interviewer asked if the approach to writing a song was the same as the approach to writing a book.

"No, it depends. Sometimes I just sort of sit and think of a lyric, the same as I do for those writties. But if I'm working with Paul, if he thinks of it first, well, we go from there."

Asked about money and such sudden success, Lennon said, *"It's great. It's good fun. If you can take it in your stride, I always say. It's good. I like it."*

How was Lennon coping with stardom?

"Well, I'm not cracking up, you know, but, I don't know about next year, but I'm all right now."

April 4, 1964 – *Melody Maker* carried a letter from American fan Mary Klein of South Pasadena. She wrote, *"I happen to be one of those screaming, swooning teenage girls whose heart does a double take very time I hear or see the Beatles.*

"I like the Beatles, not because I am rebelling against society... and not because I am a gullible adolescent who will swallow anything hook, line and sinker.

"I like the Beatles because they are a breath of fresh air in the murky climate the record industry has sprayed around the teenage population. Is it so wrong to like the Beatles?"

April 4, 1964 – Chris Roberts of *Melody Maker* wrote an exclusive with John Lennon. They were on the third floor of London's AR-TV House while rain soaked the fans in the streets below. Even wet and cold, they did not lose their enthusiasm as they wrestled with the police and screamed for their heroes, the normal pandemonium that accompanied the Beatles wherever they went, fans praying for just as glimpse of them as they inevitably fled the building.

Roberts mentioned how powerful the Beatles were and suggested that they were unaware of it. They were bigger than Elvis ever was; his public appearances were few as he hid away in one of his ivory towers. But the Beatles thrived in the limelight, a hard-boiled quartet able to hold their own with anyone.

He asked John Lennon, as half of the Lennon / McCartney team, which rock songs they would like to have written.

"Which songs? Well's there's so many of our favourites. I can't speak for all of us but Can I Get a Witness, *the Marvin Gaye number is one, I suppose.*

"Then there's some of the other stuff on Tamla-Motown we like.

"It's harder to write good twelve-bar numbers you know, because... well, because of so much being done before with them. We find that anyway.

"I'd rather write a song with chords all over the place. You can do different things on purpose. There's not much you can do different with twelve bars, is there?"

Lennon paused to request a drink, and then continued, *"We do all our main stuff in E. You get some nice big chords there.*

"When Paul and I started writing stuff, we did it in A because we thought that was the key Buddy Holly did all his songs in. Holly was a big thing then, an inspiration sort of. Anyway, later on, I found out he played in C and other keys, but it was too late and it didn't worry us anyway. It sounded okay in A, so that's the way we played it.

"Oh yeah, we keep up with all the keys – C, D, G, F – but that doesn't keep out B flat and that, it doesn't give you an artistic sound."

Roberts mentioned that John played the solo guitar on *You Can't Do That*. Lennon declined to comment on that but said, *"That's George with his twelve-string doing that bit at the end. Isn't it a great sound? Like a piano."*

Six months prior to this article, Lennon had loaned Roberts, to get repaired, his Hamburg-days Rickenbacker guitar.

"Remember that guitar?" John asked. *"Well, you've seen I've got a new one now. The arm on that old one wasn't bad, but we had the Rickenbacker people to see us in New York, they gave me a new one, and the neck is great!"*

Lennon had first seen a Rickenbacker in play by Toots Thielemanns, originally from the George Shearing Quintet.

"We met him in New York when we had the guitars. I was playing, and I did this slur on the strings. Toots Thielemanns said 'Man, don't play that stuff. I like blue stuff too much!'

"For the people who say we're not interested in music, we get the chance to meet a lot of great musicians and talk to them. This guy knocked us out.

"Yeah, I'd like to play this make of guitar I've got all the time. Oh, George only got his because he didn't want me to be the only one in the group with a Rickenbacker," he laughed.

As people began to gather round for autographs, someone asked Lennon how long he thought the Beatles would last.

"How the hell do I know? You can't tell, can you? It doesn't really worry us that much. If it all ended tomorrow, we'd be rich and out of work."

April 9, 1964 – *Mersey Beat* **mentioned** that ex-Beatle Pete Best flew to the U.S. in March to appear on a television show called I've Got A Secret. After the show, as he left the studio, he was mobbed by fans. Now back in Liverpool, he was waiting to hear from Decca about the release of his first record on that label.

April 9, 1964 – *Mersey Beat* **reviewed** a new book about the Beatles, *The True Story of The Beatles* by Billy Shepherd. Joining a list of at least two dozen books about the band, this one had a few inaccuracies, accompanied by some badly drawn illustrations and 32 pages of photographs. The best parts, the most interesting parts, were about the Hamburg days. But the book was definitely a must for any Beatles fan.

April 11, 1964 – *Disc Weekly* **carried an interview with George Harrison...**

"Trouble with the guitar," George began, *"You get serious about it. Really, I would like to take up classical guitar, but that would mean regular lessons. And it just wouldn't be possible, say, for me to arrange one at six p.m. on every Monday."*

The interviewer suggested that if he really wanted to, he could afford to retire.

"I suppose so but, you know, you could take a long holiday somewhere – and sure enough, you would want to get back into music. There's something about it that gets to you. And something about the whole of show business, too.

"But it is nice to know you have security. That, if you wanted to, you could pack up and open a tobacconists or something of the sort. Our parents

knew what it was when there was a depression around. That's why most parents want their kids to study – to make sure of the future.

"But all I wanted to do was play with a group. I just couldn't stand to work in an office.

"I suppose John could resume his art studies – but I don't think he would want to quit music either."

April 11, 1964 – Peter Sands of *Disc Weekly* **estimated** that the Beatles had another three weeks' work to put in on their movie, then they could take a brief holiday before starting their Australian tour. But during a short break in the filming, John Lennon explained, *"We'd like to get back on the road for awhile. We don't get the chance to play together much these days."*

The Beatles were pleased with the reception received by *Can't Buy Me Love*. When Sands mentioned that some critics were claiming the record failed to live up to previous Beatle standards, Lennon said, *"They must be joking. This is better than our other records. It's certainly the one we most enjoyed doing. This is a twelve bar number, which is what we've always wanted to do. You might say our other discs have led up to this one.*

"People think this twelve bar stuff is easy, but it isn't, and we really like this disc."

The interviewer mentioned how well the sales were going for *John Lennon In His Own Write* and wondered if there might be another book.

Said John, *"I haven't heard anything about doing another book, but I expect I will do one. I write whenever I get the time. I don't set out with any particular ideas, I just sit down and write."*

Ed Sullivan wanted the Beatles for three more appearances and Sands asked how the band felt about television and their American visits.

"We like America. We did three shows for Ed Sullivan the last time and I think we'll be going over for the American premiere of the picture in July, although they still haven't decided on a title for it yet.

"We want to keep our name out of the title because it will look ridiculous if we're in the title and the billing as well. They've had some titles over from the States but I don't know who will make the final decision on it. Walter Shenson, our producer, is a good bloke to work for so I expect we'll leave it up to him."

Later, at the Scala theatre, where a film sequence was being shot, the police were guarding every entrance to hold the fans at bay. The Beatles remained inside during the entire time, even having their food sent in.

"This is pretty typical for us," Lennon explained. *"Because we just can't get out on our own now. Occasionally one of us slips out on his own and we take a chance there because people think we travel in fours all the time. When they see us on our own they often don't recognise us.*

"People think fame and money bring freedom but they don't. We're more conscious now of the

limitations it places on us rather than the freedom.

"We still eat the same kind of food as we did before and have the same friends. You don't change things like that overnight. We can't even spend the allowance we get because there's nothing to spend it on.

"When you're on tour you exist in this kind of vacuum all the time. It's work, sleep, eat and work again. We work mad hours really, but none of us would have it any other way. When I look back, I can't remember a time when I wasn't in the business – it seems years for me now."

April 11, 1964 – *Melody Maker* showed *Can't Buy Me Love* still topping the chart. They went on to talk about the Beatles' plans for a tour of one-night stands throughout Britain in September, a tour that would coincide with a visit by the Miracles, the Contours, Marvin Gaye, Little Stevie Wonder, the Marvelettes, Mary Wells and the Temptations.

Lennon said, *"We're going out on tour about the same time that the Tamla-Motown artists come over. Hope we get some time to be with them."*

The Beatles' British concert tour was to come after their thirty-day American trip.

That week in the States, the Beatles held the top five spots in the hit parade: *Twist and Shout*, followed by *Can't Buy Me Love*, *She Loves You*, *I Want to Hold Your Hand* and *Please Please Me*.

On June 19th, they were to start their first Australian tour.

Their film was due to wrap in mid-April and would be premiered in London's West End sometime in July, with the band in attendance. After a show in Edinburgh and one in Glasgow the following night, they would take a month off.

On May 6th, their hour-long TV spectacular was due to be aired.

April 11, 1964 – Ray Coleman wrote for *Melody Maker* **about** attending a Beatles broadcast. He talked about George Harrison trying to eat a hot dog just before the red light flashed for he and Paul to do a fill in over Lennon's vocal solo for *You Can't Do That*. Mouth full of sausage, Harrison sang his vocal part over Lennon's playback. Formalities were forgotten at a Beatles radio session. The atmosphere was relaxed, casual. The stage was littered with debris. Only about ten people were present, including compere Brian Matthew and producer Bernie Andrews. The band was free to take their time, joke around, eat, drink, smoke and carry on.

When Bernie Andrews descended from the control booth to discuss their program, Lennon said, *"Don't forget, next time we're down I'm going to do some of that Bob Dylan stuff. You know,* Blowin' in the Wind *and that."*

Andrews agreed.

The group went through *Long Tall Sally*. Lennon was standing on a chair because his microphone could not be lowered. Paul McCartney sat on the

steps that led to the stage from the auditorium. Ringo sat silently out of sight. And George, with his back to the audience, said, *"I wish we could get a move on. I've got a knife and fork waiting for me at home."*

Lennon played the introductory riff to *Needles and Pins*, saying to Paul, *"Here, it's gear, that, eh? Great song. We ought to do it."*

Brian Matthew wanted the Beatles to read out the requests sent in by fans for The Saturday Club show. He waved a sheaf of request cards.

"Let Ringo announce one," said John.

"No, no, I can't do that; I'm the one who doesn't say anything," explained Ringo.

"Look," Paul told him, *"all you've got to do is read out what it says on the card. It's simple."*

"But I can't read either," joked Ringo, finally agreeing to read from the cards.

After ten minutes and a couple of takes, Andrews shouts, *"All right,"* and Matthew says, *"And the best of luck to the bloke who has to edit that lot."*

Next on the program was an interview between Matthew and McCartney about the Beatles' movie. While that was going on, Coleman spoke with John.

"Surprised at some of the reviews my book got. How's it selling? Marvelous – like a hit record. It's going like a bomb. Yes, I'll probably write another. I'll be writing things as a hobby, anyway, so they might as well put it out as a book, eh?"

Told that the band's favourite American stars were about to start touring Britain, the Miracles, et cetera, Lennon said, *"Yeah? When? Here, they're all coming over. Gear."*

After Ringo read the fans' requests, the group played *Can't Buy Me Love*.

"Ah, you see, we're not slipping," said John. *"Anyway, our popularity will never decline. It will recede!"* And he shook his hair to explain the joke.

While waiting for Mal Evans to repair a broken string on his twelve-string guitar, George said, *"It's so long since we played a proper date, like this, honest."*

"Shirrup. You're on the radio now," said John. The red light flashed and they recorded more songs. As they left the studio, shockingly, there were no crowds. Somehow, miraculously, the event had been kept secret.

April 18, 1964 – Don Nicholl of *Disc Weekly* **published** an article about the quality of John Lennon and Paul McCartney's song writing, wondering if someday they might be spoken of right along with Gershwin, Jerome Kern, Irving Berlin and Cole Porter. Could it be that they were creating the new standards?

In less than eighteen months, Lennon and McCartney had had thirty-two of their songs published and recorded.

Music publisher Dick James said, *"And of those, twenty-five are of the highest standard of songs that are being performed in the world today. The astonishing thing about John and Paul's work is not* the quantity but the quality. *Songs like* All My Loving, World Without Love, I Saw Her Standing There, Please Please Me, This Boy, I Want to Hold Your Hand *are going to be standards, all right."*

Their first two songs for Parlophone, *Love Me Do* and *P.S. I Love You*, were published by Ardmore and Beechwood. All subsequent songs were published by Northern Songs, in which they were partners.

Dick James said, "*John and Paul have changed the scene in pop composing because often they've changed the construction and tonal qualities of the pop song. Their most successful work has been somewhat unconventional.*

"*They do a demo on to tape, usually with a couple of guitars and maybe with Ringo bashing on a suitcase. Paul may be thumping piano to get a broadness of chord which they're trying to reflect in the composition. Both of them probably do a unison chant of the lyric.*

"*They will then write out the lyrics in longhand and where there are some special chords intended, they will explain this over the lyric."*

When that part is finished, Dick James takes the rough work to his arranger and copyist to get down cleanly on paper.

The songs were rarely written equally. Sometimes Lennon wrote most of it, sometimes McCartney. But they worked on them together and agreed to an equal split on the royalties.

It was estimated that at least another year would be by before Paul and John knew how much money they had made during those first eighteen months. The accountants were already stunned by the job ahead of them. The Beatles had had hits all around the world – Great Britain, Ireland, the States, Australia, Canada, New Zealand, South Africa, Japan, Hong Kong, Germany, Sweden, Belgium, France, Spain, Switzerland, Italy – tracking down the money would be a horrendous job.

The general consensus was that long after the Beatles had stopped performing, long after the Beatles were gone and forgotten, their songs would still be played and sung. The writer thought that was probably right, but believed John and Paul were nowhere near the status of Gershwin or Cole Porter or Rodgers and Hart. He went on to explain, though, that the Beatles were right for their time and place; this was what would turn their music into standards.

Nicholl said there was no sign that Lennon and McCartney would slow down. They had just written a song for Cilla Black, along with five new pieces for their film; and they were working on new songs for Billy J. Kramer and Peter and Gordon.

April 18, 1964 – *Disc Weekly* **quoted** Bob Hope: "*If the English really were our allies, they'd have sent the Beatles to Cuba instead of the buses."*

In the same column, they mentioned assorted Beatles facts: the Beatles were on the latest list of half-million album sellers in the U.S.; *She Loves You*

and *I Want to Hold Your Hand* were amongst the million-selling British singles in the States; Beatles' favourite Mary Wells had an instant hit with *My Guy*; and the Beatles topped Billboard's poll for the favourite foreign artists.

A few pages later, in the same issue, they mentioned that United Artists would be releasing the soundtrack from the Beatles' movie, and also that Ella Fitzgerald had recorded *Can't Buy Me Love* at EMI Studios in London. A brief note mentioned that the Beatles would be guest stars on ITV's Morecambe and Wise Show that week; also mentioned was that Murray the K Kaufman would be hosting the Beatles' television spectacular to be shown on May 6th. The show would be titled Around The Beatles. Filming would take place at the Wembley studios. Also on the show would be Long John Baldry; Cilla Black; the Vernons Girls; Sounds Incorporated; and J.P. Proby.

April 25, 1964 – *Disc Weekly* **wrote about** the police chase scene from the Beatles' film. Director Dick Lester said, "*We had an exciting time shooting the sequence. That chase scene with the police was tremendous. There were so many police around we couldn't tell ours from theirs! For instance, I saw one policeman with a huge beard. I said: 'We can't have that man in the scene. Move him out.' Trouble is, he turned out to be a real policeman!*

"*But the police were really wonderful. Their cooperation in controlling the crowd which sprang from nowhere, helped us to do the scene in two takes, right there in the street."*

April 25, 1964 – **Laurie Henshaw wrote for** *Disc Weekly* about Ed Sullivan flying in to meet the Beatles. He taped an interview to use back in New York, and arranged to get a trailer from their film, now known as *A Hard Day's Night*, to show on television.

The band and Sullivan met in the gardens of Les Ambassadeurs Club in London. Sullivan said, "*The girls want to know how you came to get those haircuts. Girls always want to know these things, it seems."*

Answered Paul, "*Well, it really started when we met a German photographer. We admired his haircut and wanted to get one like it. But ours came out like this."* He pointed at his hair.

Ed Sullivan said, "*Now, about that Mersey sound. A doctor friend of mine tells me quite seriously that it has something to do with that Liverpool climate. Can you tell me something about Liverpool, what sort of population it has?"*

"*They're partly Irish, Welsh and English up there. And we all talk through our noses. I suppose it's adenoids,"* joked John.

Laughter broke out, getting even louder as Walter Shenson, the producer of *A Hard Day's Night* came into the gardens wearing on his lapel a rather large button that read: I hate The Beatles. He asked, *"Can I get in this shot?"*

Sullivan said, *"We're all looking forward to your returning to America. I believe you're doing a tour of twenty-five American cities?"*

Replied John, *"Yeah, twenty-five cities in thirty days."*

As the interview wound down, Ed Sullivan said, *"All the correspondence I have had says that you are four thoroughly nice youngsters. I can say that that is the basis of your tremendous popularity."*

"Thanks for coming," said John. To the cameraman, he said, *"Cut."*

May 2, 1964 – *Disc Weekly* **mentioned** that the Beatles would gross roughly twenty thousand dollars for appearing at each show on their American tour. They were also to receive sixty percent of the box office receipts, and a percentage from program sales. In Sydney, Australia, seven thousand tickets were sold in the first hour after the box office opened for business.

Rumour had it that Ringo Starr and Dusty Springfield were engaged to be married.

And the Searchers were gearing up to chase the Beatles up the U.S. pop charts. They had three records in the Hot Hundred. Meanwhile, the Beatles still had seven discs in the top hundred with *Can't Buy Me Love* at number one and *Do You Want to Know A Secret* at number three.

George Harrison was to appear without the rest of the band on Juke Box Jury.

May 2, 1964 – Jack Good, producer of The Beatles TV show, wrote for *Disc Weekly*... The Beatles were the second Crazy Gang, natural successors. He had truly enjoyed working with them and they were, without doubt, the most exciting artists with whom he had ever worked.

He talked about the Shakespearean comedy sketch they were doing, a full-costume production of *A Midsummer Night's Dream* with John as Thisbe, George as Moonshine, Paul as Bottom and Ringo as The Lion.

The Beatles did not like it. *"Shakespeare's wet, Jack. It just won't be funny."*

Paul read the script and just said, *"No, no, no, no."* At lunch, they said, *"We'll never learn the lines. We can't even learn the lines for the film."*

But when it was time to film the sketch, after a few takes, they had it right. Their talent shone through.

May 2, 1964 – *Disc Weekly* **talked** about the Beatles' British tour, which was set for October. It was to be nationwide, taking in the major British towns, the dates to be set up by promoter Arthur Howes.

Brian Epstein's personal assistant, Derek Taylor, said, *"It will take in all the big centres – Manchester, Liverpool, Leeds, Leicester, and, of course, London."*

There were to be two shows nightly.

Regarding *A Hard Day's Night*, producer Walter Shenson said, *"We finished shooting on Friday and*

are now editing. But we still have to do the dubbing, which will take place the last week of June.

"When the film is completed, I hope to arrange a private showing for the boys and all the members of the cast, including the carpenters, electricians, and so on, in a small cinema in Soho. There's enough room to seat about a hundred people.

"It is always my policy on completion of a film to show the finished product to the cast as a matter of courtesy. I hope to do this with the Beatles' film."

A Hard Day's Night was set to be premiered at the London Pavilion on the 6th of July. Princess Margaret and Lord Snowdon were to attend.

May 2, 1964 – *Record Mirror* **announced** that the Beatles' film was finished. *A Hard Day's Night* was done, and countries all around the world were already clamouring for copies and pleading with the band to appear at their premieres.

The filming only ran a week longer than the estimated time and wrapped with a small party at pub near the Twickenham Studios. The various technicians were already leaking news about how great it was.

Supposedly, the Beatles came off as they really were, funny and unpredictable.

Director Dick Lester said, *"They're naturals. Sure they sometimes forgot their lines but they're completely professional all the time. And if they were asked to do something they regarded as being soft, well, they'd put up unanswerable arguments against it."*

Remarkably, even while shooting the movie, the band managed to carry on with other work. Television shows, radio programs, personal appearances. They were looking forward to a short holiday.

May 8, 1964 – George Jones wrote for *Mersey Beat* **about** a visit to the Beatles' film set and the filming of John Lennon's' bathtub scene. John and George asked Jones to convey a message to their fans in Liverpool: *"We want all our old friends to know we still think of them. The way things have happened... well, it's just sensational. But it would never have started if it wasn't for your loyalty and support. Lots of love, Liddypool!"*

Laughing, indicating his script, George Harrison added, *"You'd never believe half of this. It's ridiculous!"*

May 9, 1964 – Don Nicholl reported for *Disc Weekly*... a conversation between George Martin, John Lennon and Paul McCartney.

George Martin: *I've just been doing a disc session with Ella Fitzgerald.*

The Beatles: *Oh yes? That must have been interesting. What did she sing?*

George Martin: *Oh, a little thing called* Can't Buy Me Love.

The Beatles: *You're joking!*

It took some work to convince them that Ella Fitzgerald had recorded one of their songs. And

Martin said, *"Paul kicked me for not telling them about the session beforehand."*

When they heard the recording, they loved it. Fitzgerald had heard *Can't Buy Me Love* on the radio in the States and told Martin, *"I love it. And I'd like to record it. Seems to me to be such a good tune and it's almost a blues sequence."*

With Johnnie Spence, George Martin went for a big band sound. Fitzgerald loved it and hoped she would be able to come back to England to make an entire album with Martin.

Regarding the Beatles, she said, *"They're great songwriters. No mistake about that. This song's jazz sequence is so good, apart from the beat."*

The song was recorded with Fitzgerald at the mike and facing the band, moving in close to them, soaking up the mood and spirit of the music, going for a live sound.

George Martin said, *"Of course, being such a great technician, she can do this. Ella's never out of tune. And she's so wonderful to work with. Quiet, unassuming and supremely professional. Just stands there at the mike, shifting her weight from one foot to the other, pouring out the song."*

Publisher Dick James thought the Fitzgerald recording confirmed what he had believed all along: that Lennon and McCartney were writing standards. *"A good tune,"* he said, *"should take to almost any style and interpretation. Can't Buy Me Love has now been made Beatles-style, Fitzgerald-swinging style, and rather jazzily with piano and strings for George Martin's new album Off The Beatle Track."*

In a footnote, Peter Thomson remarked that the U.S. critics were not fond of John Lennon's book. And he pondered how strange it was that John Lennon and Paul McCartney had never written any songs for their friends from Liverpool.

May 9, 1964 – *Disc Weekly* **asked** the Beatles about the music they liked to listen to, saying that mainly they liked what was known as Rhythm and Blues, the big American coloured sound, though they hesitated to label it. *"I don't even know what R&B is,"* said John Lennon.

George:

Daddy Rolling Stone by Derak Martin.

"This is issued on the American Sue label and it's a marvelous R&B sound. The voice is great and so is the female backing. I also particularly liked the rhythm, particularly the drums."

Walk on By by Dionne Warwick.

"Dionne's a great artist and I love her voice on this one."

High Heel Sneakers by Tommy Tucker.

"Great guitar on this one. The voice and the organ are good, too. Nice bluesy feel."

What's Easy for Two Is So Hard for One by Mary Wells.

"Mary Wells is one of my all-time favourites. This is, perhaps, my favourite of all her numbers at the moment. Great voice, great song, great feel."

Hitch Hike by Marvin Gaye.

"I've never got Marvin Gaye discs off the record player. This one I play all the time. Marvin's voice is just right, the rhythm's fab and the backing is swinging."

Since I Fell For You by Lenny Welch.

"This isn't commercial but it's got a great big orchestra and good feel. I think it's catchy, with some nice pleasant notes in the tune."

You Might As Well Forget Him by Tommy Quickly.

"This is going to be a big hit for Tommy. We're all convinced it'll be his first big impression on the charts. Tommy Roe wrote it for Tommy and it's a very good song and a very good backing. Well done, Tommy!"

Dawn Go Away by The Four Seasons.

"This has a better melody than some of the others the Four Seasons have recorded. I like it."

Mocking Bird by Inez Foxx.

"This is just marvelous. She and her brother Charlie are great. The beat really gets me on this one."

I'll Be There by The Majors.

"It's really the trumpets which make me like this one. They trill along catchily. Very pleasant."

Ringo:

I Gotta Woman by Jimmy McGriff.

"This is just a great song and I like it a lot. Jimmy McGriff's one of my favourite artists. Like the organ, too."

What Kind of Fool by The Tams.

"This is one I think is really marvelous. It's a great song and the bass guitar sound in it is fabulous. I also like the way the voices harmonise and change during the number."

It's All Right by The Impressions.

"Apart from the backing on this one, which is great, I like the way different voices come in to take the lead. In particular, I like the falsetto lead which sings really high."

Monkey Time by Major Lance.

"This is about the only dance I learned to do in America and I think this is a great number to do it to. I like the sound as well."

Love is Blind by Emma Franklyn.

"Emma's a lovely singer. I dig her marvelous coloured voice, particularly on this one. She sings it slow with plenty of feeling."

Um Um Um Um Um by Major Lance.

"Another Major Lance, I know, but I think he's marvelous. This is one of his later releases here and although it wasn't a hit, I thought it was good."

Paul:

If You Want to Make a Fool of Somebody by James Ray.

"I like the oompah bass noise in this disc, which is great. I also love the voice and the overall sound."

World Without Love by Peter and Gordon.

"I hate the composers of this! But the way Peter and Gordon sing the number is gear."

Canastas by The Trio Athenai.

"This is a song that Ringo and I heard when we were on holiday in Greece last year. I think the

number is actually Spanish, though. It's a marvelous song and this trio sang it really well. The harmonies are marvelous."
Don't Let the Sun Catch You Crying by Ray Charles.
"This is my favourite Ray Charles number and it's obviously not the same number that Gerry Marsden wrote. It's the B side of Let the Good Times Roll and Ray sings it slow with a big orchestra."
Long Tall Sally by Little Richard.
"I love this. It's just fantastic the way Little Richard uses his voice. The disc generates a terrific beat and feeling and the whole thing swings like a bomb."
Pride and Joy by Marvin Gaye.
"I love anything Marvin Gaye does on record, but this one is a real knockout. It's my favourite number by Marvin. A gas."
I Keep Forgettin' by Chuck Jackson.
"Again, it's the voice I go for on this one. I think this artist is marvelous. I play this disc all the time."
Hitch Hike by Marvin Gaye.
"Sorry, but I always come back to Marvin. As I've said, he's one of my favourite recording artists and this one's never off my record player for long. Once again, I've got to say it's great."
John:
Can I Get a Witness by Marvin Gaye.
"This is the best Marvin Gaye record I've ever heard. It's marvelous. I love the voice; in fact I love everything about it."
Hey Little Girl by Major Lance.
"Anything by Major Lance is okay by me. This one stands out because of the arrangement."
Two Lovers by Mary Wells.
"This is a fine song and the way she sings it makes it even better. The beginning is really outstanding and the backing is particularly attractive."
Who's Loving You by the Miracles.
"They sing this dead slow and the singers do fantastic things with their voices. The tricks they do in this number are fantastic."
Please Please Please by James Brown.
"This is a medium-slow number with a high, almost screaming voice. This and the fab organ playing really knock me out."
Stay Awhile by Dusty Springfield.
"I like the way Dusty sings; she gets a real coloured sound in her voice. I like the song as well, I think it's just right for her."
Gonna Send You Back to Georgia by Tim Connor.
"I just like this one, for no particular reason except, I like the group and the guitar solo."

May 9, 1964 – the front page of Record Mirror carried photographs and a brief review of the Beatles doing Shakespeare's Midsummer's Night Dream the previous night on Rediffusion TV. Shakespeare Beatles-style, that is. The writer wondered if Shakespeare was twisting in his grave.

May 9, 1964 – Record Mirror mentioned that the Beatles' recording manager, George Martin, had put together a thirty-seven-piece band to record a dozen of the group's hits.
They went on to talk about the Beatles' planned visit to Copenhagen, Denmark, June 4th. A Danish newspaper reported that the police had seen a film of a Beatles' performance and "had misgivings," and were intending to ban the group from playing.
The Chief of Police considered the reaction of the teenagers to be hysterical. A Police Superintendent had been appalled and shocked. But the Minister of Justice of Denmark reversed the police decision, saying, "It is not for the police to consider the quality of concerts."
Still, one condition had to be met by the Beatles. They had planned to play two sets with only a very short break between them; they had to change the break to an hour-and-a-half, so that the first crowd could disperse before the second one arrived.

May 9, 1964 – Bob Dawbarn of Melody Maker claimed that the Beatles had beaten up Shakespeare. From a mock-up of the original Globe Theatre stage, they played A Midsummer Night's Dream, rehearsing for Rediffusion's TV spectacular Around The Beatles, the scene played to five hundred wailing teenagers.
He reported that few fans were waiting outside the Wembley Studios – but inside, two sets of five hundred kids attended each rehearsal, and another five hundred were invited to the final filming.
Producer Jack Good explained, "The set gives tremendous contact between the players and spectators. I am particularly keen on this idea because the relationship of the Beatles with their audience reminds me of the theatre as it was in the time of Shakespeare. It's a relationship that didn't occur again for about three hundred years."
Teenage hands pawed at the Beatles while they were on stage. A few girls were dragged from the front row while Good gave a lecture about teenage monsters.

May 16, 1964 – Disc Weekly reported that A Hard Day's Night was about thirty-six hours in the Beatles' life. They went on to give a short synopsis of the film, accompanied by photographs.

May 16, 1964 – Bob Houston wrote in his Beatletalk column for Melody Maker that George Harrison was the youngest Beatle at twenty-one years, the previous year and half of which were jammed with the excitement and the accolades that go with being a member of the number one group in the world.
He talked about being on the Scala Theatre set of A Hard Day's Night while the band was relaxing between takes. Combing his hair, glaring at a photographer who wanted a shot, Harrison said, "I'm only combing my hair, do you mind?" Then he joined Bob Houston for an interview.

Signing an autograph to someone named Janet, George said, *"I don't like the traveling on tour. It's a drag. On the last tour, it was wild every night. Places like the Manchester Apollo and Glasgow were really wild.*

"That twelve-string guitar was the first electric one to be used. When they first started using them, you know, after Walk Right In, *they were all the same. You know* (he hummed the introduction to *Walk Right In)* and I didn't fancy that. A lot of it was nothing like a twelve string and it was all sort of terrible. But I like it used our way. It's a great sound."

Tea and bread were delivered and George continued, *"Naturally, we aren't going to do anything unless we think it is good. When we do a number on stage, and the people like it, when we come to record it we may double track on it just to make the record that something extra. Anyway, we don't double track as much as some groups. In fact, it was only on our second LP that we did it. We just liked the idea. We just fancied it.*

"I like the other side of Can't Buy Me Love. *It's just about the best we've done. People don't think it's the best side when they hear it at first.*

"Yes, I know that You Can't Do That *and our other favourite,* This Boy, *were both B sides. It has to be that way because they weren't the sort of things people would like right off.*

"Despite the big rush to Liverpool in the beginning, there, only one group made it really big apart from us. That's the Searchers.

"Now groups are coming from all over the country, not just Liverpool, and the only standards are that those who make good records will have hits.

"I'm writing a couple of things myself. I'm hoping we'll do them on our next LP. We should be doing that shortly.

"The sort of things I like myself are stuff by Marvin Gaye, the Miracles, the Impressions, the Shirelles. And Timi Yuro, too.

"Buddy Holly and Eddie Cochran are really big favourites. It was through hearing them that I got really interested.

"But right in the very beginning there was just Lonnie Donegan. I suppose he really started most of the groups off. I suppose it was hearing him that made me want to play guitar, and then along came people like Buddy Holly and Eddie Cochran. They kept me going.

"Yes, Lonnie was a big idol of mine at that time."

May 16, 1964 – Chris Roberts wrote for *Melody Maker*: Hair flying, four Beatles charged out of an alleyway across the street from London's Scala Theatre. Chasing them was a gang of cops, while a crowd of girls set up their normal pandemonium at the sight of their idols, They were shooting a scene for *A Hard Day's Night*. Real cops mingled with actor cops. Fans hired as extras milled about. Tea was served. And the Beatles tried to relax amidst a clutter of empty cigarette packs, empty potato chip bags, ratty newspapers, used crockery, and butt-filled ashtrays. Chris Roberts asked John if he had heard the new Marvin Gaye tune, *You're a Wonderful One.*

And John said, *"New? We heard it months ago. Isn't it in the American charts or something? Yeah, I thought so."*

Smokes were lit by John and Ringo while Paul changed his jacket and muttered about having to be constantly on the move, never a chance to rest.

With a cup of tea and a cigarette, John said, *"At one time we got away, I mean the groups as a whole, got away from the sort of one singer, one group thing, and the music wasn't soft. But it's going back to that again now, I mean there's exactly the same thing happening as before. The music is still getting softer.*

"I don't mean we're the only ones who play hard or anything. Lots of groups do. But this old kind of pattern is starting up again.

"We will always continue to play the stuff we want, and that means there'll be a beat in it. I thought Ella Fitzgerald's version of Can't Buy Me Love *was great, and very musical and swinging and that.*

"Would we record with a big band? Ha! I don't know. You know, it's hard to say whether we'll ever have to or not. I don't know whether we would through choice. I don't suppose we'd mind having a go, strings as well, perhaps, one day."

Roberts asked a slightly controversial question: who did the real rhythm and blues, and inadvertently mentioned Carl Perkins along with Chuck Berry, Fats Domino, Jerry Lee Lewis and Little Richard.

John said, *"Carl Perkins? What's he doing in there? Anyway, why are you always asking questions like that? Carl Perkins is a country singer."*

The subject changed to guitars and amplifiers, on to newspapers and people. Then they broke for tea.

May 30, 1964 – *Disc Weekly* carried a short article about a recording the Beatles had made nearly three years ago while they were working in Germany, still playing with Pete Best. The songs were *Ain't She Sweet* and *If You Love Me Baby*. Executives at Polydor had forgotten about this recording. They were reminded of it in a recent newspaper article. And, of course, they rushed to release the record, which rapidly made it into the Top Twenty. The writer suspected the band would not be happy with this surfacing, no happier than they were when *My Bonnie* was released.

June 13, 1964 – *Disc Weekly* talked briefly about the Beatles' trip to Denmark with substitute drummer Jimmy Nicol. (There was no mention of *why* Nicol was there as a substitute. Ringo was back in Liverpool recovering from having his tonsils out, and he would join the band later in Australia). The shops in Copenhagen were spewing out Beatles paraphernalia, *Can't Buy Me Love* was at the top of the Danish charts, and a new single, *Long Tall Sally / Roll Over*

Beethoven, had been released to coincide with the Denmark visit. Six thousand teenagers were on hand to greet the band as they landed at Kastrup Airport.

One hundred and fifty photographers and journalists gathered at the Beatles' hotel for a press conference before the show. And five thousand fans gathered at the KB Hall for the first concert, the noise deafening as the group hit the stage.

From what little the writer could hear, he judged that Jimmy Nicol, of Georgie Fame and the Blue Flames, was a fine temporary substitute for Ringo.

June 13, 1964 – Nigel Hunter wrote about the Beatles' new single and album for *Disc Weekly*. The single, due out on July 3, was the title track from their film *A Hard Day's Night*. And the album, due to be released on July 10, was the film soundtrack. Hunter assumed both would garner astronomical advance orders and sales, becoming the next high spots in the band's stellar career. Regarding the album, George Martin said, *"There are seven new songs in it. Plus* Can't Buy Me Love. *The boys started writing them when they were in Paris and continued in America during their first visit."*

Ringo was the one who came up with the title for the movie.

Said George Martin, *"Everybody liked it right away. John went off and came back the next day with a song he'd written to go with the title."*

Martin went on to point out that the order of the titles on the album had not, as yet, been determined. Then he described the six new songs:

"Tell Me Why – *They all sing strident harmony for this one, over a shuffle rhythm which is almost Blue Beat.*

"And I Love Her – *This is a beautifully melodic ballad which Paul does solo in the same sort of mood as for Till There Was You. George has a very good solo on Spanish guitar during this one, too.*

"I Should Have Known Better – *This number is used during a luggage-van scene on the train in the film while the boys are laying cards.*

"If I Fell – *This one occurs when the boys are playing to an audience towards the end of the film. It's very much a Beatle song, with unusual harmony and voice placing.*

"I'm Happy Just to Dance With You – *A lively, up-tempo number with a definite Latin-American feel to it.*

"And I'll Cry Instead – *Originally* Can't Buy Me Love *was going to be featured twice during the film, but I thought a new song would be better for the second spot, and the boys came up with this. It's another good up-tempo number and features George on twelve string guitar."*

June 13, 1964 – *Disc Weekly* printed a cable from Gillian Wilson in Sydney, talking about the down under plans for B Day, when twenty thousand fans were expected at Sydney's Mascot Airport when the Beatles, still with Jimmy Nicol on drums, arrived for their Australian tour. She mentioned that regular Beatle drummer, Ringo Starr, would take over when the band played Melbourne.

Fifteen security experts were designing plans for B Day, led by George Inglis, the manager of the airport. He said, *"It really is up to the fans. We have no set blueprints as we would have with Royalty. Flexibility is the keynote with an operation of this size."*

The Beatles were to pass through Customs while they were still on the plane, then they would get into an open car and be driven past the herd of fans who would be penned up in a special enclosure and guarded by a gang of Sydney cops.

From there, the group was to proceed to a press conference.

Their Australian Fan Club, which received around four hundred letters at week at their Sydney headquarters, claimed to have a number of surprises in store for the Beatles.

Angela Letchford, who ran the fan club, said, *"Nearly the whole population of Sydney will be there to welcome them at Mascot. We are all excited about being able to see them as they step off the plane."* She went on to explain that the fan club would present the group with stuffed Koala bears, and that there would be a special present for Paul McCartney, who would be celebrating his twenty-second birthday in Sydney.

"We want to give them boomerangs as well," said Angela. *"So they'll come back."*

The band was to give three concerts in Sydney starting on June 18th.

June 13, 1964 – *Disc Weekly* went on with more details of the Australian plans, devised by the police and the public safety officials.

"I suppose we shouldn't admit this," said a high-ranking policeman, *"but this Beatles business will be the biggest thing to hit Sydney since the 1954 Royal Tour."*

Private detectives were to guard the band in their hotel; detectives were also to accompany them wherever they went. Guests at the hotel would have to have special passes to get beyond the guards to their own rooms, and twenty-four-hour patrols would triple the police strength in the Kings Cross area where the band would be staying.

The penthouse floor of a Kings Cross hotel had been reserved for them, complete with gold carpet, a cocktail bar, a television, and a sun balcony that gave sweeping views of the harbour.

The band was to arrive in Sydney on June 11th; play Adelaide on the 12th and 13th; Melbourne on the 15th, 16th and 17th (where Ringo would rejoin them); and Sydney on the 18th, 19th and 20th. Then it would be on to New Zealand to play Wellington on the 22nd and 23rd; Auckland on the 24th and 25th; Christchurch the 26th and 27th; and back to Australia for Brisbane on the 29th and 30th.

June 13, 1964 – *Record Mirror* reported that EMI executives met secretly to set their plans for the new Beatles album, *A Hard Day's Night.* Originally, it was planned to have an assortment of incidental tracks; now, they intended to have either six or eight songs from the movie along with four or six new tunes.

The *Long Tall Sally* EP was being rushed into release for June 19th.

Side One was to feature *Long Tall Sally* with Paul singing the lead vocals; and *I Call Your Name* featuring John, the only Lennon / McCartney composition on the disc. Side Two would have two songs recorded especially for the EP, *Slow Down* sung by John; and the Carl Perkins tune, *Matchbox*, by Ringo.

The band's next single, *A Hard Day's Night,* was due to be released on July 10, backed by *Things We Said Today*.

On the same page, *Record Mirror* wrote about their Pop Poll, saying that the Beatles and the Rolling Stones were almost tied as the best vocal group, the first hint of the more-or-less press-invented rivalry. Thousands of poll forms had been pouring into *Record Mirror's* offices for the past two weeks.

GEP 8913 (MONO EP)
PARLOPHONE 7"45rpm. EXTENDED PLAY RECORDS
E.M.I. RECORDS LTD., E.M.I. HOUSE, 20 MANCHESTER SQUARE, LONDON, W.1

June 20, 1964 – Gillian Smart, writing from Australia for *Disc Weekly*, said the Beatles were met by more than thirty thousand fans when they landed in Adelaide for their first concert on the Down Under tour. Lennon mentioned that that was the largest crowd ever to greet them. And the cops said it was one of the largest crowds in the city's history.

Fifteen hundred frantic fans forced their way through the police barriers when the band arrived at the town hall to be greeted by the mayor; the Beatles were trapped inside for over an hour.

Later, as the group took the stage, fans rushed them, battling with the cops who formed a barrier and ordered them to return to their seats if they actually wanted the show to go on. Moments later, they erupted in frenzy as the band opened with *I Saw Her Standing There*. The loudest screams were when George and Paul sang together, and another major explosion happened when John climbed on top of a piano.

Teenage girls wept as the group did *I Want to Hold Your Hand.*

Earlier, feeling slightly out of place, Jimmy Nicol had said, *"I'm using a lotion to make my hair grow."*

While most of the band was trapped in their hotel in Sydney, he had been able to escape the hotel to visit with family, later visiting a nightclub where he was recognised right away. He was asked to play the drums and did, accompanying Frances Faye, the American singer.

June 20, 1964 – *Melody Maker* reported that it was the Beatles versus the Rolling Stones, the battle ready to detonate, as the paper warmed up to report the casualties. The Beatles' new single, *A Hard Day's Night,* title song from their movie, was set for release. And the Stones new single, recorded in Chicago, was also ready to start up the charts.

Prior to this, the Beatles' and The Rolling Stones' singles had not been released simultaneously, each releasing a new tune as the other's last record was moving down the charts.

The Stones were touring the States; the Beatles were in Australia; and, in Britain, Polydor had just released an LP that featured eight tracks recorded in Hamburg with Tony Sheridan. The album had been named *The Beatles' First*. Release of their new single was to coincide with the film's premiere, July 10th in Liverpool, earlier in London. The album from the film, featuring seven new songs, was also due out on the tenth.

June 20, 1964 – Dick Hughes wrote from Australia for *Melody Maker*... Nothing like it had ever been seen in Adelaide. More than three hundred thousand fans were on hand to greet the Beatles when they arrived. Even the Royal Visit had not drawn that sort of crowd.

Teenagers flipped out; so did adults. A sixty-year-old woman dropped in her tracks, fatigued from waiting for them. Girls wept and clung to the band's getaway car, some being dragged along the street. Police and security guards fought off the fans, trying to keep them from the hotel where the Beatles were besieged, escaping only for their concerts, where they played almost inaudibly to wailing, screaming, shrieking fans. Plans to attend social gatherings in Adelaide were canceled. Carnival lunacy reigned.

Hughes went on to describe the Beatles' reception in Sydney when they first arrived in Australia. He said only four hundred fans had been waiting in the cold pouring rain. Four hundred cops had been on hand as well, expecting a much larger crowd. Security was tight; hotel guests where the Beatles were staying were issued special identity cards to prove they had business in the hotel. Girls climbed trees in an attempt to get in through the windows. Others had forged identity passes; one even tried to convince the guards that she was a special news correspondent for a Sydney paper.

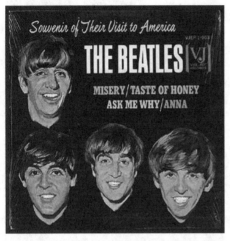

And the reception in Melbourne was even bigger than the one in Adelaide. Ringo had arrived and the fans went crazy.

Jimmy Nicol was to leave the group. And the fans cheered him wildly at Paul McCartney's request when he explained that Ringo would be on hand for their next concert.

June 27, 1964 – Gillian Smart wrote to *Disc Weekly* from Australia… The Beatles had spent most of their time on tour as prisoners in their various hotels, trapped and uncreative, unable to unwind.

"No song writing," said John. *"I have to wait for inspiration."*

During the celebration of his birthday, Paul said, *"Sure I like getting presents. Who doesn't? But I can't really think of anything I want. I don't expect the other boys will buy me anything. We don't exchange birthday presents. Most of what we want we buy for ourselves. I bought a gold watch in Hong Kong and I want to get all the usual Australian souvenirs."*

At a reception given by the Lord Mayor of Melbourne they tried out the traditional Australian musical instrument, the didgeridoo, and Paul played Chopin on the piano. As a parting gift, the Mayor gave each member of the band a boomerang and a lesson in how to throw one.

June 27, 1964 – Don Nicholl reviewed the new Beatles' single for *Disc Weekly*. To open *A Hard Day's Night,* George slammed a power chord on his

twelve-string guitar, suggesting that the song had been tailored for the film. That hard loud chord had to be heard over the screaming fans during the opening sequence of the movie. Even without the movie, though, the impact was effective.

The B-side, *Things We Said Today,* was a Lennon / McCartney song with Paul singing the lead vocal. It was a subdued ballad that would not be featured in the film, but would be used on the forthcoming album.

There was no doubt that *A Hard Day's Night* would be yet another major hit for the Beatles.

Nicholl went on to write about the group's new EP *Long Tall Sally.* Accompanying the title song were *I Call Your Name, Slow Down* and *Matchbox.* During *Long Tall Sally,* Paul screamed and squealed his way through the lyrics but, according to Nicholl, John was the best solo singer in the group. He proved it with *Slow Down* and *I Call Your Name,* the latter a Lennon and McCartney composition with the typical Beatle mix of beat and melody, the former a vintage rock tune by Larry Williams. The final song, *Matchbox,* a Carl Perkins number, gave Ringo a chance to shine.

The new Beatles album, *A Hard Day's Night,* was slated for release on July 10th. It contained the six new compositions from the movie.

June 27, 1964 – Jack Hutton wrote about the Beatles' new LP for *Melody Maker*. He had been at the EMI Abbey Road Studios with George Martin for a preview of the thirteen tracks that made up *A Hard Day's Night.*

Martin said, *"For a single, it's simple to have a rave, use a harmonica and yell your head off. But albums are another story. You've got to be different.*

"I know I'm biased, but I think this album stacks up against their previous discs."

Two of the cuts had been issued before, *Can't Buy Me Love* and *You Can't Do That.* They had been touched up for the album, voices and percussion added. And their new single, *A Hard Day's Night,* was the first song on the record, clearly the most commercial, and a great lead-in to the rest with George playing that hard-driving guitar.

I Should Have Known Better featured John singing and playing harmonica, with Ringo providing some powerful drumming.

If I Fell was a quiet non-commercial number.

I'm Happy Just to Dance With You had some of the best lyrics on the album, backed by the strange sound a special drum from the effects department.

And I Love Her had Paul singing the solo with the rest of the band coming in on the chorus. Ringo and George provided the unusual beat, playing bongos and claves.

Tell Me Why was the most polished Beatles tune ever, with John singing lead and others providing nice harmonies.

Can't Buy Me Love completed side one.
All the tunes from side one had been used in the movie; none of the tracks from side two were used, though some were written for it.
Any Time At All was exuberant.
I'll Cry Instead had been removed from the movie.
Things We Said Today seemed somewhat minor and folky.
When I Get Home had a fine melody and great lyrics.
You Can't Do That was polished for the album and much better than the version on the single.
I'll Be Back was a well-played slow number, demonstrating how much better the Beatles were musically than any of the other groups around.
Most of the songs had been completed after two or three takes. Nine of them had been recorded in three days.

June 27, 1964 – Dick Hughes reported for *Melody Maker* from Australia... The Beatles' Australian tour switched into high gear when they arrived in Melbourne. The Army and the Navy were brought in to help the police control the crowds. Frenzied demonstrations took place at the airport, at the hotel and outside the town hall where the band went for a reception.
Five thousand fans mobbed the airport. And more than two hundred thousand people were losing their minds outside the hotel. A club across the road was drafted as an emergency first-aid station. Over two hundred people were treated for minor wounds and major hysteria.
A teenage boy fell out of a tree when the branch broke beneath him. A sports car was crushed as kids climbed on it for a better view. A small girl hammered a large man over the head with a stiletto high heel because he was blocking her view. They pushed and shoved, screamed and fainted. Later, at a press conference, the band admitted the welcome was *"a little frightening."*
Ringo had rejoined the band in Melbourne. At the press conference, when asked what he considered the most objectionable question he had been asked since arriving in Australia, he said, *"How are you, John?"*
Traffic in Melbourne was grid-locked; streets were closed; fans slept on the sidewalk outside the hotel, girls screaming, *"We love you, Beatles."*
In Sydney, things had been relatively quiet, the reception at the airport somewhat subdued. The time and the weather were blamed – 6:30 a.m. in the cold pouring rain. But there had to be more to it than that. The Sydney concerts were not sold out; some three thousand tickets for each were unsold. And the crowds were much smaller, much better behaved. The fans who collected outside the Beatles' hotel, only five hundred or so, would disburse in the early evening and not gather again until late morning, unlike Melbourne where thousands of them lingered through the night.

No one understood why Sydney was so peaceful. No one understood how a city of 2,250,000 people could seem like a country town. Beatlemania failed to reign supreme.

June 27, 1964 – *Melody Maker* announced that the Beatles had won the Selmer Oscar, a silver trophy donated by Ben Davis, head of a musical instrument company in London, Henri Selmer. Thousands of *Melody Maker* readers had voted on what group had contributed the most to British music in the previous year.

July 4, 1964 – *Disc Weekly* reported that advance sales for the single and the album *A Hard Day's Night* had topped 700,000. Both were to be released on July 10th. LP orders were over 200,000, while the single had sold over half a million. Someone from EMI said, *"We confidently expect the single to hit the million mark soon."*

In a short piece on the same page, it was mentioned that Billy J. Kramer and the Dakotas' new single would released on July 17th, a Lennon and McCartney composition called *From a Window.*

July 4, 1964 – Dick Hughes reported to *Melody Maker* that ten thousand fans were waiting for the Beatles when they landed at Brisbane Airport just after midnight. The arrival began the same as always, a carnival of screaming, fainting teenagers and stressed-out cops. Then a small section of the crowd started throwing fruit and rotten eggs. This was the only anti-Beatle demonstration on the Australian tour, the first sign of serious hostility. There had been a few irate letters to newspapers about how the Beatles were a threat to the moral fibre of society; and one politician had claimed the young Australians would be better off in the national service rather than *"chasing these blinking Beatles all over the place."* But, until Brisbane, their reception had been overwhelmingly good.

They had arrived in Brisbane from New Zealand, where things had been quieter. Ringo claimed that the New Zealand visit was the first time on the tour that he could hear the other musicians.

However, New Zealand was not incident free. Staying at the same hotel as the band, a twenty-year-old girl slashed her wrists and was rushed to the hospital. In Wellington, a gang attempted to break into the Beatles' hotel to cut their hair, fleeing down a fire escape when they were discovered by a maid. In Auckland, the first show was nearly canceled because the police refused to provide an escort to the hall. One cop said, *"The Beatles are not royalty."* And as the group was getting set to fly to Dunedin, a bomb threat delayed their flight by forty minutes.

In a footnote, it was mentioned that ten thousand fans were at the Brisbane concert. Mostly, they were loud but well-behaved, only a few rushed the stage. The Beatles, still angry about being pelted with eggs and fruit, announced that all future public appearances would be made from behind plate glass windows. And, from London, manager Brian Epstein said the group would not cancel any shows because the flying food incident.

July 11, 1964 – *Disc Weekly*'s **Laurie Henshaw reviewed the film** *A Hard Day's Night...* It was a wild, funny, brilliant saga that covered thirty-six hours of Beatles life. *A Hard Day's Night* pretty much crowned the group as the Kings of the Pop Music World. The direction, the camera work, the music, the script, all were terrific, stupendous.

Said publisher Dick James, *"When that opening title song hit me, it was like an explosion. This is a marvelous musical documentary of the Beatles, a worthy record of their position in the entertainment world. I had a tremendous thrill in seeing the film."*

And disc-jockey David Gell said, *"It is a fabulous film. The boys are natural actors. I loved the scene* where Ringo dons an old raincoat. The film is such a refreshing change from all those pop cornball films we have suffered in the past."*

July 11, 1964 – two brief articles in *Disc Weekly* **related** that the Beatles would return home to Liverpool for a charity viewing of *A Hard Day's Night* at the Odeon Theatre. Afterwards, they would tour the city with a police escort, eventually ending up at the Town Hall for a reception hosted by Liverpool's Lord Mayor.

The second short piece talked about the capes the Beatles had been wearing when they flew in from Australia.

"We first saw them in Holland," George explained during an interview at the airport. *"We tried to get hold of them here, but couldn't, and eventually we had them copied in Hong Kong, where they'll do anything for money!"*

They bought very few things during the Australian tour, as John explained, *"Just a present or two each. We didn't have to buy anything there anyway. They gave us everything we wanted. It was great!"*

Ringo mentioned that he had returned with a ring and a watch. *"I didn't have to buy either."*

July 11, 1964 – *Disc Weekly* **reported** that the Beatles would be appearing live on the TV show *Lucky Stars.* To reach the Teddington Studios, to avoid being mobbed by crowds, they would travel by boat down the Thames just as they had for the show *Big Night Out.*

Also on hand would be Dusty Springfield, as the host, along with the Searchers, Sounds Incorporated and the Big Three.

The advance orders for the United Artists' American release of the *Hard Day's Night* album had reached one million. The company was expecting to have two million orders by the time the LP was shipped. They were considering the release of ten cuts from the album as singles.

The film *A Hard Day's Night* was to be premiered in the U.S. in August or September.

Ain't She Sweet, the Beatles / Tony Sheridan recording, had just been released in the States.

And in Britain, the film was getting great reviews from tough critics, while advance orders for the LP and the single were amazing the EMI executives.

"This group breaks every rule in the book on sales," explained an EMI spokesperson. *"At one time we thought the saturation point on a LP sale in Britain was five hundred thousand, but first Beatles album,* Please Please Me, *went to over half a million and their follow-up,* With the Beatles, *is already approaching the million mark. It wouldn't surprise us in the least if the* A Hard Day's Night *LP reached a million when the film makes its full impact."*

EMI expected the single from *A Hard Day's Night* to surpass the million mark very soon.

July 11, 1964 – *Disc Weekly* **wrote** that *A Hard Day's Night* was a sell-out in Toronto. Two months before the planned premiere, three thousand and twenty-eight seats sold as soon as the box office opened.

Stores in Florida and New York were reporting that the album *A Hard Day's Night* was outselling everything else in the stores by at least ten to one.

Vee-Jay had just released an EP featuring *Anna* and *A Taste of Honey*. And Atco had put out *Ain't She Sweet*, which was racing up the charts.

Radio stations were already playing individual tracks from the album *A Hard Day's Night*, thus creating a demand for more singles to be released on 45s.

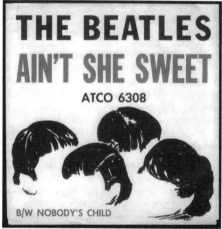

July 11, 1964 – **Chris Roberts interviewed ex-Beatles publicist, Brian Sommerville, for** *Melody Maker.* Roberts began by explaining that the Beatles were putting together a good collection of ex's. Ex-girl friends; an ex-hairdresser; an ex-drummer; ex-this and that. Their newest ex, an ex-publicity man, was Brian Sommerville.

Not wanting to be known as an ex-*Beatles* publicity man, he explained, *"I would like to be*

accepted in my professional capacity. Although my relations with the NEMS office are perfectly normal, I don't wish to be known as an ex-anything. It will help, of course, initially, but that's all."

Sommerville was planning to open his own publicity office so he could put together a stable of stars.

"The Beatles? Well, I believe again that they are leveling off in a way. Let's face it, yeah yeah and all that is a bit old hat now. They are changing their image and will broaden their appeal in the entertainment world. You have to have this; it must happen. I also believe that they have a tremendous amount of talent, much of it yet untapped, in the field of films, for instance."

Sommerville was upset about a report that he was one responsible for the Beatles' breakthrough. *"It said that when I took over, they were little-known outside Liverpool. Well, of course, this is ridiculous! They were already well on their way before I took over."*

Had he ever felt like quitting the job before?

"Yes, once in Paris, when I had a personal disagreement with one of the group. It was just unfortunate, but passed over soon enough."

Proudest accomplishment?

"Probably the American trip when I went over to see how the land lay and open the way a bit. It was a little embarrassing afterwards, because I had made myself known, and some people approached me on the business side. I received a letter from President Johnson, asking if the Beatles could lay a wreath on the Kennedy Memorial the next time they went there. And I was the one Montgomery approached in this country, when he wanted the group to visit his home."

Regarding the job he had done for the group, he said, *"It was a publicist's dream turned into a nightmare. A publicist's job, after all, is to make the artists approachable. After a while, I found myself doing exactly the opposite."*

July 11, 1964 – Ray Coleman wrote for *Melody Maker* **about** John Lennon's response to the reports about thrown eggs in Australia and New Zealand.

"It was a dirty lie," said John. *"Let's get the whole thing straight. There were six eggs, one in Brisbane, five in Sydney, two tomatoes and one lettuce. They were thrown by a group of students and we met them all later. They said they were idealists, but they didn't seem to me to have any ideals, and they said they didn't like us because we were materialistic, which we are.*

"Anyway, we shook hands and laughed at it. It was, well, just one of those things. But when I read the papers the next day, I thought we'd been battered."

Coleman found George Harrison through the smoky haze in the airport press room. George was obviously tired from the thirty-six-hour flight

"So, it's the Animals, is it? Good. They're good. Surprised they got there so quickly, though.

"Well, good to be back. It was quite an experience, but we all fell very out-of-touch after a month away. Australia was all right. But New Zealand, I don't know how to describe it. They're so old-fashioned. Nothing is up-to-date. The way of life is slow and funny. It's like I imagine England must have been in the eighteenth century."

Asked what was their most popular song on the tour, George replied, "The screams were the same, so it was impossible to know which song they screamed most for. The degree of screaming was just the same, some shows were smaller audiences than others, but the enthusiasm was just as great in comparison."

The interviewer found Cynthia Lennon, alone, mostly ignored. She had not, as yet, managed to even say hello to John.

"No I haven't had much time to be lonely," she explained. "I came down from Liverpool this week, I've been up there a lot of the time, with the family."

"It's good to see John back, and the others. I've been spending a lot of my time having driving lessons. Another dangerous woman driver to go on the road…"

Being married to a Beatle had its benefits – money, security, et cetera – but it was not problem-free.

Talking about their London home, Cynthia said, "We have a flat but you should see the outside of the house. It's been scrawled on by people with messages that can't be removed. They're engraved.

"I know, you expect people to find out where you're living, but it's a strange thing to want to do, unless they really are young kids. It's rather hard."

Asked how he was feeling after being hospitalised with tonsillitis, Ringo said, "I feel fine, but if you'd asked me that the day I flew out to rejoin them…"

Only about two hundred screamers were on hand to welcome the Beatles home from Australia. That was quite a difference, compared to the chaotic scenes that usually heralded a Beatles arrival, pointed out a reporter.

George asked, "Why shouldn't it level off? I think it was bound to, we can't expect huge crowds all the time. It's bound to quieten down. Couldn't have got much louder!

"I think that when we went over to America, and there were those fantastic scenes, it was a sort of reaction from the British fans generally, not necessarily Beatles fans. They thought: good old Britain, we'll show them Americans. Now, it's accepted that we've established things for Britain."

Paul McCartney added, "I think it's dropping off for everyone. It had to."

"I just need to get away and have some sleep," said George. "It's been a tiring flight."

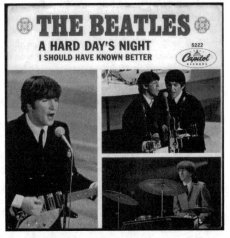

July 11, 1964 – *Melody Maker* posted a brief synopsis and review of *A Hard Day's Night*. The reviewer loved it, loved the wit and the impertinence, the take-it-or-leave-it attitude of the stars, loved everyone's but especially Ringo's performance, loved the music, loved everything about it. It was currently showing at the Pavilion in Leicester Square, London.

July 16, 1964 – *Mersey Beat* **reported** on the Beatles' brief return to Liverpool. Five cops on horseback and one hundred and eighty plain clothes officers and constables were on hand at the airport to control the crowd. The hysteria built slowly from around 5 p.m. until the plane arrived at 5:25. We Love the Beatles banners were flown; the fans milled about, pushing and shoving, already screaming. The screams rose to a crescendo when the plane arrived, going on and on and on until the group disembarked and made their way into the airport for a press conference.

Brian Epstein was on hand to welcome them, as was Paul McCartney's brother Mike McGear of the Scaffold, Ray McFall and Bob Wooler of the Cavern.

David Jacobs, who had made the flight up from London with the group, said, *"On the flight up the boys were obviously very thrilled to be coming home. They never stopped chattering the whole of the journey. When they saw the crowds waiting at the airport, they were really thrilled. Paul said to George, 'Look at those crowds. I never expected anything like this. It's absolutely fantastic.'"*

"It's really great to be home," said George Harrison. *"I just can't believe it. We never expected a reception like this."* George mentioned that he had occasionally stopped home to visit family. *"But I have to creep into our house about one in the morning to avoid the fans. The biggest hazard isn't the fans, though. It's the traveling. We all hate it. It's a real drag. It was worst in Australia, flying for hours on end is very boring. We eat corn flakes and drink tea."*

July 18, 1964 – Peter Thomson's Stop Pressings column in *Disc Weekly* **quoted** Colonel Tom Parker when he responded to a question about whether or not the Beatles could get as much money as Elvis for a film. *"There's no comparison because they have to split it four ways. Besides, they don't eat as much as Elvis."*

July 18, 1964 – *Disc Weekly* **carried an article about** *A Hard Day's Night* **by the producer, Walter Shenson.** Notices for the film had all been great. No one could have been happier than the producer. And he wanted to explain what the success meant in hard facts.

It proved to one and all that the popularity of the Beatles was not on the wane. He had never agreed with the people who were proclaiming that the Beatles were fading. He had worked closely with John, Paul, George and Ringo. He knew how great their talent was, not just for writing and performing great music, but for comedy as well.

When it was decided that they would make a movie starring the Beatles, they wondered how well the group would take direction. Now they knew. The boys were natural, unaffected, and their charm came across on film.

Any film starring the Beatles would have been a success. But the goal was not to make another insipid pop film, the goal was to do something new, something

that would present the group as they were, something that would not only capture Beatles fans, but non-Beatles fans as well… if such an entity existed.

Financially, in the U.S. alone, the album from the film sold more than a million copies in the first four days, already paying for the cost of the movie. A thousand prints of the film had been rushed to the States. In Britain, one hundred and sixty copies had been made, one hundred and ten more copies than any normal film.

Hong Kong was asking for prints of the film. And the British Foreign Office was to show *A Hard Day's Night* at a film festival in Prague, Czechoslovakia. There was a chance the band might attend. If they did, they would be the first British group to play beyond the Iron Curtain.

Already, they were considering the making of another film with the Beatles. John Lennon had some ideas that were being discussed. They wanted a stronger plot line for the next movie. That way, it would run on two levels, one showcasing the natural talent of the band, the other to run a story line.

For Shenson, one of the highlights in *A Hard Day's Night* was the scene where John played with toy boats in the bath. It had been an impromptu scene, so good they had to leave it in.

Some of the scenes had gone so smoothly that far less time was spent on them than expected. They had expected the scene where Ringo spreads his coat over a puddle for a girl to walk through to take an entire day. It was done in one morning.

Shenson's biggest thrill was the sequence near the end of the film, the TV show shot at the Scala Theatre, packed with real Beatle fans rather than actors. They had fought the union over that scene, and won.

Six cameramen wandered through the crowd with hand-held cameras, completely ignored by the kids.

Ringo came up with the title for the film. Late one evening, Shenson asked Lennon to write a title song. At 8:30 the following morning, John called and said that he and Paul had roughed one out on scraps of paper. They recorded it that night.

He was impressed with how professionally the band worked. As they were leaving for the U.S., he asked them to come back with six new songs.

And they did.

July 18, 1964 – *Disc Weekly* **briefly mentioned** that Freddie and the Dreamers were going to join the Beatles for their Christmas show at the Hammersmith Odeon, December 24th. They went on to talk about how the Beatles were already planning to make another movie, the shooting to start when the band was finished their Hammersmith Christmas Show.

A Hard Day's Night was breaking box office records. Harold Smith, manager of London's Pavilion Theatre, said, *"We have known nothing like it in all the London Pavilion's thirty-five years as a cinema. Since the film opened Tuesday of last week,*

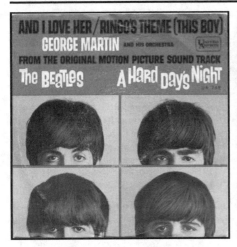

it has taken in eight thousand pounds and has been seen by twenty-three thousand people. It has broken all records for Saturday, Sunday and weekly figures."

Meanwhile, the group's records continued to burn up the international sales charts. *A Hard Day's Night,* the single, was number one on the Top Thirty chart, and had earned a Silver Disc award for sales in excess of a quarter of a million. American sales of the LP were around two million. The album had been released by United Artists in direct competition with the film, and Capitol had issued it as well. Both labels were selling.

George Harrison and Brian Epstein were going to appear on *Juke Box Jury.* And the band had agreed to appear for charity in *The Night of a 100 Stars* show at the London Palladium.

July 18, 1964 – Bob Wooler wrote for *Disc Weekly* about the Beatles' homecoming for the Liverpool premiere of *A Hard Day's Night.* Wooler was the disc jockey at the Cavern Club. He said the visit was a whirlwind of reporters, television interviewers, microphones, cameras and screaming fans. The group insisted Wooler join them at their table to chat and catch up on old times. Wooler had presented them at the Cavern two hundred and ninety-two times. He lamented that he could not have them back there again.

Six thousand fans cheered at Liverpool's Speke Airport. As the group was taken from the airport to the town hall, hundreds of thousands of flag-waving wailing fans lined the roads. They were on rooftops, up lampposts, waving from windows, throwing confetti, shrieking, a never ending clamour. It was eight miles of *Welcome Home, We Love You Beatles, Long Live the Beatles, The Beatles For Ever,* banners. And at the town hall, ten thousand more besieged the building like Wallace at Sterling Castle. Forty-seven people were hospitalised. Four hundred people fainted. Every cop in the city was on duty.

Five hundred applauding guests were on hand at the mayoral reception. Then it was on to the Odeon Theatre for the premiere, the streets still jammed, the fans still in a feeding frenzy.

At the theatre, the Liverpool City Police Band played Beatles tunes to a sellout crowd. As the lights went down, the curtain went up and the group took the stage to greet the audience. They goofed around on stage for a bit, then took their seats.

And the film began. The audience applauded every song. And just before the final credits, the Beatles departed the theatre through a side door and crawled by car through the crowded rainy streets to the airport, gone again after seven hours back home.

July 19, 1964 – Mike Ledgerwood wrote for *Disc Weekly* about the Beatles receiving yet another award, this one called the Getaway Trophy, presented in connection with the show *Battle for the Giants.* Ringo and Paul were on hand to receive the award from British and Empire Heavyweight Boxing Champ, Henry Cooper. Afterwards, Ledgerwood asked Ringo what he thought of *A Hard Day's Night.*

Ringo said, *"Well, we saw it on the Saturday before the premiere and I was a bit doubtful. But after the critics raved about it and we heard the audience response the other night, I knew we were all right.*

"I came past the cinema yesterday and saw people queuing and it made me feel good."

Ringo's twenty-fourth birthday had been the day after the premiere. He received a load of gifts from fans. *"I had scores of dolls and things. A couple of rather nice clocks and a bull ring. Not the place where they fight, the ring they put in the bull's nose!"*

Even though the first Getaway Trophy went to the Beatles, according to Ledgerwood, the actual favourite star was Elvis Presley, who beat them by over two thousand votes. A special award was shipped to Presley in California.

July 19, 1964 – *Record Mirror* stated that Elvis Presley was greater than the Beatles according to more than seven thousand Radio Luxembourg listeners who voted during the *Battle of the Stars* program.

Twenty-five thousand fans placed votes, seven thousand five hundred and ninety-nine of them voting for Elvis, five thousand seven hundred and forty of them for the Beatles. The Rolling Stones came third with one thousand eight hundred and ninety-five votes, Cliff Richard fourth with one thousand four hundred and two, and the Searchers fifth with nine hundred and thirty-one.

Paul McCartney and Ringo Starr were present at the Radio Luxembourg studios to receive their runner-up trophy from British and Empire Heavyweight Champion Henry Cooper. An award was also sent to Elvis Presley.

July 19, 1964 – *Record Mirror* **said** a ticker tape parade was planned for the Beatles when they flew to New York on August 17th. The American tour was due to open on the 19th at the Cow Palace in San Francisco. Other confirmed concert dates were: Las Vegas Convention Center – August 20th; Seattle Municipal Stadium – August 21st; Vancouver – August 22nd; Hollywood Bowl in Los Angeles – August 23rd; Denver Rock Stadium – August 26th; Cincinnati Gardens – August 27th; Forest Hills Stadium, New York – August 28th; Atlantic City – August 30th; Philadelphia Convention Hall – September 2nd; Chicago International Amphitheater – September 5th; Detroit Cobo Hall – September 6th; Toronto Maple Leaf Gardens – September 7th; Montreal Forum – September 8th; Jacksonville – September 11th; Boston – September 12th; Baltimore Civic Center – September 13th; Pittsburgh – September 14th; Cleveland – September 15th; New Orleans – September 16th; and Dallas – September 18th.

They were to be back in New York to finish the tour on September 30th.

The band was expected to earn twenty thousand dollars per show.

Footnotes mentioned first, that the Beatles had changed one of the dates for their autumn tour of Britain. On October 23rd, instead of playing the New Victoria Theatre in London, they would appear at a different London venue, the Kilburn State Gaumont. Next, the writer mentioned that the Beatles new LP, *A Hard Day's Night,* had sold more than a quarter of a million copies on the first day of its release.

July 18, 1964 – *Melody Maker* **showed** *A Hard Day's Night* at number one in the charts. And Ray Coleman declared that the Beatles were back and had done it again. *A Hard Day's Night* was number one, bumping the Stones' *It's All Over Now* into second place. The soundtrack from the film was number one on the album chart. And, speaking for EMI, an unnamed executive suggested their position in the charts ought to shut up the talk about the Beatles slipping in popularity.

He said, *"The single has sold six hundred thousand and the film soundtrack LP a quarter of a million. In America, we expect two million sales with the album. And the LP is selling very well in Britain. Record sales always slip a little at this time of the year, and considering that The Beatles are doing fantastically well. We are quite certain they are not slipping on this performance."*

The group was to head for Sweden on July 28th, the U.S. and Canada on August 15th, and their British tour was to open on October 9th. On Sunday the 19th of July, they were to star on the TV show *Blackpool Night Out.* And on July 25th, George was to appear on *Juke Box Jury.*

July 18, 1964 – Ray Coleman for *Melody Maker,* **reporting from Liverpool...** Ringo, if fan-appeal was any sort of guideline, was clearly the star of the group. Fans at Speke Airport were screaming, *"We want Ringo,"* as the Beatles arrived.

The return home was short, a mere five hours. But the reception was incredible, with thousands lining the streets, hundreds fainting, all screaming.

At the riotous press conference, George Harrison shouted, *"Where's me dad?"*

"It seems like years since we were here," said Paul McCartney.

"Didn't know it was so near London by plane," George said. *"But I hate flying. You don't stand a chance if the engine conks out."*

Ringo said, *"I wish we had time to stay here just for the night. The only time I get a decent breakfast is when I go home."*

Responding to being told he was the star of the film, Ringo said, *"It's nice to read, but I don't believe it. I think John is funnier than me."*

After the press conference, they went by limousine to the town hall where Liverpool's Lord Mayor held a reception for them. Commenting on the size of the crowds that were cheering for them, John Lennon said, *"It's just fab. The best thing that's happened to us."*

After the reception, it was on to the theatre for the premiere of *A Hard Day's Night.*

"In a few moments," said David Jacobs, the host for the evening, *"I'll be able to introduce you to four young boys who will probably have something to say, which will be nice. I mean, the Rolling Stones had nothing to say.*

"Do you know, I was chatting to this bird up at the TV centre the other Saturday and I was getting on famously and I thought how lucky I was. Then, it turned out to be a boy."

Finally, the Beatles were on stage and the crowd, of course, erupted.

George said, *"All my people are here!"*

John asked, *"What happened to all my relations at the town hall?"*

And Ringo announced, *"What you did for us this afternoon was marvelous and we appreciate it. People kept coming down to London saying 'You're finished in Liverpool.' But we proved them wrong, didn't we, kids?"*

After the premiere, the group was gone, flying back to London to appear on *Lucky Stars.* Ray McFall, manager of the Cavern, said, *"They're just the same as they ever were. Just as friendly and pleasant. I think they'd have liked to visit the Cavern and play a session there. Gerry* (Marsden) *did this recently and he really enjoyed turning the clock back. I reckon if the Beatles played the Cavern again, they'd enjoy playing* Long Tall Sally *and* Twist and Shout *as much as they did in 1961."*

Bob Wooler, the Cavern disc-jockey, said, *"Success has not spoiled the boys. It never will."*

And Paul McCartney summed up the Liverpool visit by saying, *"It meant more to us than any other. We will never forget it."*

July 19, 1964 – *Melody Maker* **announced** that Paul McCartney had criticised Elvis Presley during a Radio Luxembourg recording in London. *Battle of the Giants* was the show. The Beatles were given an award for being the most successful artists, but Presley had beaten them by two thousand votes as the most popular artist.

Paul said, *"He did much better stuff in the early days when the songs did not come from films. In fact, we all liked him much better then. The songs were good, and we all used to think he was great.*

"I still like Elvis' singing. His voice is good and he does the songs well. But the songs are not very good, in my opinion. I wish he would come away from the films for his records. Then, I think things would be much better.

"I'm not knocking Presley's singing, just the choice of material. I don't rate it at all since he got so involved with the film songs. I even heard the other day that Elvis was planning to have all his singles from films in the future.

"What a drag."

July 23, 1964 – Les Hall wrote for *Mersey Beat* that he had found out, while chatting with George Harrison, the true story of the jelly baby barrage.

"It all started of course," said George, *"when one of the others, Paul, I think, said in a TV interview that I liked jelly babies. After that fans sent tons of the sweets to me and started to throw them at us on stage.*

"But it was dangerous. I've almost been hit in the eye a few times. Thanks goodness they don't throw them as much as before. It was even worse in America because they have jelly beans not jelly babies there and they are very hard!"

George also talked about the eggs that were thrown in Australia. He said, *"A lot of publicity has been given to this incident, but I'd like everyone to know the true facts. It was four students out of an audience of* six thousand, who threw the eggs and we looked them up afterwards and had a chat with them. After about half an hour they agreed it was a stupid and childish thing to do and we all parted the best of friends."*

July 23, 1964 – *Mersey Beat* **published** a short piece about the success of the records and the film *A Hard Day's Night.* The Beatles were back on top and had not slipped at all, despite the predictions of some gloomy critics.

July 23, 1964 – *Mersey Beat* **printed** a photograph of Ringo and Wilfred Brambell in a scene from *A Hard Day's Night,* mentioning that the film had been brilliantly directed with some particularly stunning camera work. Writer Alun Owen had captured the group well. But it was Ringo Starr and John Lennon who truly shone in the film, particularly Ringo. His part engaged the sympathy of the audience.

Over seven hundred prints of the film had been ordered in America.

On the same page, a photograph of Paul waving from the limo as the band drove through Liverpool carried a caption mentioning that the group had proved beyond any doubt that they were still loved in Liverpool, regardless of predictions to the contrary.

July 25, 1964 – *Disc Weekly* **announced** that the Beatles were millionaires. Their movie was to open in eighteen theatres in New York on the 11th of August, along with another fifty dates across the country. The *Hard Day's Night* album had hit the top of the charts in just ten days and had already sold a million copies. Three singles from the film's sound track, along with George Martin's *Ringo's Theme* and *Ain't She Sweet,* were all climbing the charts. And every concert date for their U.S. tour was sold out.

The Beatles were expected to pull in somewhere around four million dollars on the tour, including extra record sales.

The LP was the fastest selling record United Artists had ever released.

The three singles were available on the Capitol label, *A Hard Day's Night / I Should Have Known Better, I'll Cry Instead / I'm Happy Just to Dance with You* and *And I Love Her / If I Fell.*

Security arrangements for the tour were tighter than ever. No one would be able to reach the Beatles directly without prior approval. Each city on the tour would have extra police and special traffic arrangements to accommodate the band.

July 25, 1964 – *Disc Weekly* **carried** a short piece mentioning that Ringo Starr had been booked for *Juke Box Jury.*

Ringo said, *"It will be fun to be on the show. It's a good panel, and I am looking forward to it as much as the multiple panel we did last year. It should be good for a laugh."*

July 25, 1964 – *Disc Weekly* **reported** that the Beatles had been invited to appear on Ready Steady

Go's New Year's Eve party. Elkan Allan, of Rediffusion, said, *"I talked to Brian Epstein on Ready Steady Go on Friday. I said I would like to have the Beatles on our New Year's Eve Show and he said he would see what he could do."*

The article went on to talk about how *A Hard Day's Night* was breaking all records during its prerelease showing around the country.

A spokesman for United Artists said, *"Money wise, this is the greatest cinema we've ever had."*

Producer Walter Shenson said, *"In many places it has beaten* From Russia with Love, *which was an all-time high. The great thing is that we have beaten the weather. A temperature in the eighties is usually bad for business. It just proves that when people want to see a film, then they'll go see it."*

The film was expected to repeat its success in the States. It was given three preview showings at the Beacon Theatre on Broadway. Shenson said, *"It was seen by a cross-section of American audiences, ranging from children to adults. Although there were over two thousand seats at each show, the demand for tickets far exceeded the seating capacity, the first time this theatre has ever been filled to capacity for three screenings.*

"I have had a cable from the States which says that the reaction to the film was absolutely electric."

Shenson mentioned they were going ahead with the next Beatles' film. *"Dick Lester [director of A Hard Day's Night] and I want to talk with the boys before I fly out to New York for the premiere. Dick is shortly going on holiday so we want to get things started as soon as possible."*

A footnote added that the Beatles were returning to Stockholm to play four concerts on July 28th and 29th.

July 25, 1964 – Nigel Hunter reported for *Disc Weekly...* He had been at the BBC's Paris Cinema radio station in Lower Regent Street to watch the Beatles record their *Light Programme August Bank Holiday Monday* show – *From Us to You*.

Bearing a carton of cokes, Paul was the first to arrive, saying, *"Phew. Isn't it hot? It's a drag working on days like this. Still, at least it's a good excuse to wear some crazy casual clothes."*

Hunter asked him what he thought about the reaction to *A Hard Day's Night.*

"Fabulous. I thought it might be regarded as a load of rubbish by the critics. I enjoyed doing the picture – we all did – but I never expected everyone else would enjoy it too. You can say I'm surprised and delighted."

As John Lennon made his entrance, Hunter asked him about a second film.

"Dunno yet," said John. *"We're still talking about it. It will be done by United Artists again, and Walter Shenson and Dick Lester will be handling the production and direction.*

"It's a bit difficult about what we can do, isn't it? We can't do another Beatle-type thing like the first

really, *and we can't take the parts of total strangers if we're going to sing together. I'm looking at a book at the moment which might be okay to adapt into a film."*

Production for the holiday show got under way. First, they recorded *Long Tall Sally* featuring Paul on vocals; next was *Things We Said Today*. Ringo left his drum kit, grabbed his coat and wrapped the coat around his snare drum.

Paul said, *"Here's a story for* Disc, *then. Ringo's playing his coat. Improvisation and all that."*

Ringo explained that he was not doing it to prevent his coat from catching cold. *"It's for contrast. Helps deaden the sound a bit, and comes close to the effect we got in the studio when we recorded the number. I should use a cloth on the drum really, but I forgot it."*

Next, George sang *I'm Happy Just to Dance With You.* Unhappy with the performance, he said, *"Sorry. We haven't got much idea about this one yet. If I knew the chords, I could read the words, or if I knew the words, I could read the chords."*

They worked hard through the hot afternoon, joking around but keeping the music tight, getting each number down in as few takes as possible.

Hunter left the session, certain that the show would be great. He ended with a footnote about the possibility of the Beatles meeting Frank Sinatra. There was a chance that Sinatra would be flying in to appear on the *Night of a Hundred Stars* charity show, along with the Beatles.

July 25, 1964 – Record Mirror asked the burning question... Have Paul McCartney and Jane Asher broken up? They also mentioned that Cilla Black had recorded a new Lennon / McCartney composition, *It's For Me.*

July 30, 1964 – Mersey Beat published a piece about the rehearsals for the TV show Blackpool Night Out. Paul was singing *Long Tall Sally* as the writer arrived. The band played for about an hour, watched by the other members of the cast.

Later, John said, *"I wish we could have mimed during rehearsals. We've been rehearsing for hours."*

As well as playing a number of songs, the group was featured in some of the comedy sketches.

July 30, 1964 – Mersey Beat published a round-up of Beatle news, starting off with Ringo's appearance on Juke Box Jury. They talked about how the band was looking forward to their American tour, which was promising to earn them around four million dollars. The tour was to run for twenty-seven shows, each one a sell-out. Mention was also made of the Mike Cotton Sound joining the Beatles for their Christmas Show, due to open on December 24th at the Gaumont, Hammersmith.

John, Paul and George's families had all moved into new homes, but Ringo's mother, Elsie Starkey, intended to remain where she was, saying, *"We are perfectly happy living in Admiral Grove."*

The Beatles next visit to Liverpool was for an appearance at The Empire on November 8th.

July 30, 1964 – *Mersey Beat* **talked** with George Harrison about the new Beatles film.

He said, *"We'll be making another film in February, but I've no idea what it will be about. I hope there are no songs in it. It was all right getting songs in the last one because we had an excuse; they worked into the film all right. But I don't like these films where everyone bursts into song for no reason and you have a full orchestra blasting out of nowhere. Yes, I'd prefer to make a film without any singing."*

When the conversation turned to song writing, George said, *"I have written a couple of numbers since* Don't Bother Me, *but I don't think they are all that good."*

Still, his instrumental *Cry for a Shadow* had reached number one in Australia, and Gregory Phillips had recorded *Don't Bother Me.*

They moved on to discuss the possibility of a new book by John Lennon. Brian Epstein said it was unlikely that he would have a new one this year. *"But I am sure he'll have another book ready by next year."*

Lennon himself said, *"I just haven't got the time."* Then he told the writer that he had lost his copy of a story called *Small Stan*, which had been published in *Mersey Beat*. They sent him one to include in his next book.

Also at the meeting with John Lennon was Rod Murray, a former art school pal of John's. Murray mentioned he had found *The Daily Howl* which John had lost.

Lennon had searched for it for years. He said, *"I even went back to Gambier Terrace to see if I could find it."*

The Daily Howl was the exercise book in which he had written many of his early stories and poems. *"I wrote most of the stuff years ago and most of it isn't very good, but it means a lot to me. I spent years filling that book up.*

"You can print any of the items in Mersey Beat, *but explain that they were written a long time ago."*

He also mentioned two poems *Mersey Beat* had found for him that year, saying, *"I'd appreciate it if you can trace where the poems came from as there may be some more of my writings there."*

July 30, 1964 – *Mersey Beat* **published** an editorial wondering why so many people were suggesting that the Beatles were falling from grace. People seemed to think the band had said and done everything there was to do and say – that they had little life left as entertainers.

He predicted that their next trip to America would be even more successful than the last; that their one-night-stand tour of Britain would be met with Beatlemania as powerful has it had ever been; that their next movie would be better than *A Hard Day's Night*; and that they would continue to break box office records.

He thought they were the greatest entertainers the world had ever known; suggested that John had more books to write; Paul and John had more songs to write; Ringo had more photographs to make; and George would continue on his path to becoming a great guitarist.

No other group would ever reach the same heights as the Beatles.

July 30, 1964 – *Mersey Beat* **wrote about** Beatles buying new houses, pointing out that Ringo was the only Beatle who had not purchased a new home. They spoke with John Lennon about the new twenty-thousand pound house he had bought in Surrey.

Lennon said, *"From the reports in the papers, people think we've already moved into it. But there are still people living there. When they move out we've got to get it furnished and decorated."* He explained that the main reason he had bought it was for privacy. *"We don't get any privacy in our flat. People seem to be hanging around outside all day."*

George Harrison had also bought a twenty-thousand pound house in Surrey.

And Paul had just bought one in the country, fifteen miles from Liverpool. Fans had already discovered his new address.

The Beatles had virtually no privacy in their caged lives. On the road, they stayed indoors most of the time and, even in London, there were few places they could go to relax.

Living in the new house with Paul were his father, Jim, and his younger brother, Mike, who used the name Mike McGear and was a member of the group the Scaffold.

July 30, 1964 – *Mersey Beat* **talked with George Harrison and Ringo Starr about** photography, asking how things were going with their picture-taking.

George said, *"We've all got Pentax cameras. They look good. They're black. We take pictures of anything.*

"I have some good photos but most of them are nothing. I've also got a fish-eye lens on my camera.

"Ringo's having a book of photos published. He takes pictures of anyone and anything, anyone who's around. I think the book is just being published in America."

Regarding the book, Ringo said, *"I hope the book's out before we get to the States, then I'll be able to plug it.*

"They're mostly photographs of the boys. When we were making the film I had my own Pentax and I just kept clicking all the time."

The writer asked about the camera that fell in the river during the filming of *A Hard Day's Night*.

"Well, although I used a real camera in the rest of the film, we had a dummy one in the river sequence made up of old Pentax parts."

August 1, 1964 – *Disc Weekly* **wrote about** Cilla Black's new record, the Lennon and McCartney tune *It's For You*. She knew the disc was okay because the Beatles had told her so. And she said, *"Paul himself came along to the session and contributed a few ideas about how it should be done. But actually there were very few changes made to George Martin's fabulous arrangement.*

"Paul stayed to the end and said he thought it sounded great."

The same day that Cilla Black was cutting *It's For You*, the Naturals were recording *I Should Have Known Better*, overseen by Brian Epstein. The song was John and Paul's fiftieth published tune. It was said that Lennon and McCartney did not want to release their own recording as a single because it would clash with their current release.

August 1, 1964 – Laurie Henshaw reported for *Disc Weekly* **about** Ringo's appearance on Juke Box Jury. The writer had attended the recording and promised audiences that they were in for a treat. Ringo stole the show.

He admitted being nervous about appearing on the panel, but when the time came to roll the film, he presented himself with poise and assurance. He was outspoken and knowledgeable. George Harrison had accompanied him to the show.

Ringo said, *"I wish we could have been together on the same panel but George was booked some time ago and I came in at the last minute. We would all like to be together on occasions like this. We work so much better as a team. Frankly, I feel lost on my own.*

"I only had shredded wheat for lunch. And look, I'm drinking milk. I'm quite a bit upset in my stomach."

Henshaw would not reproduce any of the comments Ringo made during the show, but hinted that his opinion of one song in particular would upset a lot of fans.

The writer also spoke with George Harrison about this new twenty-thousand pound home in Surrey. George had hired a gardener to look after the grounds.

"I'm not much of a hand at gardening," Harrison said. *"The lawn had grown pretty long before I took the place over, and it first of all needs a rotor scythe to get it trim. But I am taking a big interest in the furnishing and decoration.*

"It's all very modern. The place was built about ten years ago, but parts are just a couple of years old. There are five bedrooms, but I shall only use three.

"I'm putting in lots of teak furniture in the dining room, and I have got some very modern lampshades, those big ones like pumpkins.

"A couple of the bedrooms are separated by built-in wardrobes. I'm having them knocked into one room, where I can fit in my hi-fi equipment, tape-recorder and stuff like that.

"I shall also have a projection room. I took some films with John in Tahiti. We were fooling around playing natives. They should be worth a few laughs."

August 8, 1964 – Mike Ledgerwood reported for *Disc Weekly* from backstage at the Gaumont cinema in Bournemouth. Earlier, when the Beatles had arrived at the rear exit, the doors were locked. They were trapped by fans for a few minutes.

"It was quite terrifying," said John. *"We didn't stand a chance. I suppose it was only a matter of seconds really before the doors were opened, but it felt like about ten minutes."*

Ledgerwood asked John if it were true that he was buying a Rolls Royce.

"That's right. But it's not really for me. It's for my wife and child. I don't drive anyway. I was getting fed up with taxis and hiring cars to go out in the evening, so I asked my accountant what I should get and he suggested a Rolls."

George Harrison said he was considering a change from his Jaguar to a Bentley or a Rolls.

When Paul arrived in the dressing room, salads and steaks were brought in for the band.

Teasing their chauffeur, Big Bill Corbett, Ringo asked, *"Why did it take three and a half hours for the two-hour journey from town?"*

"Order me a Bentley tomorrow, will you?" said George.

"He can't," John explained. *"It's a bank holiday tomorrow."*

"So what? I'm not buying it from a bank."

More seriously, John said, *"Do you know that some newspaper in the States had got hold of a story that I'm taking my old Ford over there to sell. They say I'll get more for it because it belongs to a Beatle. That's a laugh. I've never had a Ford in my life. I've never had a car before, at all."*

Outside, the fans were screaming. While John was tucking in his shirt, another wave of screams rolled through the dressing room. *"They can't see in here, can they?"* he asked.

Trying to get his hair to cooperate with his comb, Paul asked, *"What are we playing? Anybody know?"*

"You got my list on the drums?" asked Ringo.

In a short article, *Disc Weekly* mentioned that *John, Paul and All That Jazz* had just been released on the Swan label in the States. It was an album of twelve Lennon / McCartney songs played in a jazz-style by Roger Webb and His Trio. The album had been produced in Britain by Mickie Most.

Said Most, *"The album will be released in Britain on Parlophone the first week in September."*

Disc writer, Laurie Henshaw, said, *"It proves, if proof were needed, that the Beatles are writing tomorrow's standards. Just, in fact, as Disc critic Don Nicholl said in our issue April 18th. These jazz stylings by pianist Roger Webb and His Trio are going to bring the Beatles' numbers to a whole new audience of jazz fans. If you like Ella Fitzgerald's swinging version of*

Can't Buy Me Love, *then you'll go for these great instrumental treatments by Roger Webb."*

August 15, 1964 – June Harris wrote from New York for *Disc Weekly*... It was one continuous Beatle Day throughout the land. The group's return visit promised to be the most amazing that the States had ever experienced. Final arrangements were being made for the tour.

The band was due to arrive in San Francisco on Tuesday the 18th and set to open at the Cow Palace the following night. Press coverage would take place at the airport, followed by a ticker tape welcome. Waiting at the airport would be the vice president of General Artists, Norman Weiss; general company manager, Ira Sidelle; and NEMS American Press agent, Bess Coleman; along with executives from Capitol Records and representatives from all the leading radio and TV stations in America.

A private chartered airplane was to take the Beatles to their concerts, with a fairly loose takeoff and landing schedule to accommodate the expected mob scenes.

Each individual concert promoter was responsible for press and security arrangements, but the band would be well guarded at all times.

There would be a press conference before every concert, and a welcome at every airport, but the only other official gathering was scheduled for when they opened in New York on August 28th.

All concerts were sold out, but black market tickets were available. Harris lamented the exorbitant prices the scalpers were charging – twenty dollars and up – while the average box office ticket was seven-fifty.

The Beatles would have little time to enjoy the country, but they were planning to attend a party after their Hollywood Bowl appearance on August 23rd. The party was a charitable event, all would pay to attend. And the band had one other charity concert, heading an all-star show at the Paramount in New York on September 20th, proceeds to go to the Cerebral Palsy Fund.

Magazines had been packed with Beatles tales for weeks, scores of Beatle books were on sale, and all the fan papers had declared August to be Beatle Month.

Beatle records were playing non-stop on the radio and a number of the stations were running contests to give away concert and movie tickets.

The band would not have time to do three shows for Ed Sullivan. Sullivan was planning to rerun the three appearances they made during their last visit to the U.S.

August 15, 1964 – *Melody Maker*'s Chris Roberts pondered the future for the Beatles. He began by pointing out that there was little more to be said about the Beatles, for or against, as so much had already been said. In spite of all that had been said, no one had figured out how they managed to stay on

top for so long. Song after song, all selling in the millions; sold-out shows; *A Hard Day's Night*; the whole world at their feet. When would it level off? When would it peak?

Paul McCartney said, *"Don't ask us. We thought a number one was the top, then a million seller, then the American tour, then the film. If there's more to do, we'll do it."*

Roberts suggested that the rest of the year for the band was predictable. They would receive the same accolades on their new American tour as they had received on their last one. There had been no cooling of Beatlemania in the States. The *Hard Day's Night* single was at the top of the charts, and all the other singles released from the album were on their way up.

After their American tour, they were scheduled to play a series of one-night stands all over Britain. Roberts said it would be business as usual, riotous receptions, hundreds of hours of overtime for the cops and the ambulance crews.

Before the end of the year, their next single, whatever it was, would be number one. It would be different from the others, yet pure Beatles. And their Christmas show would be sold out for three solid weeks.

After that, they had no plans... except for a Spring Tour, another American tour, and more and more and more records.

He pointed out that it was all speculation, but he believed the Beatles could do all these things, with ease.

Answering the suggestion that, in films, the band would have to stick to Three Stooges-type comedy, Brian Epstein said, *"Not at all. The Beatles are the Beatles. They do what they want to do and they aren't really influenced by anyone. If they feel like doing something different in films, I'm sure they can do it."*

Roberts wondered about the future. Next year. The year after that. Some people still believed the Beatles were just a passing fad, doomed to die away as soon as the public tired of them. He wondered if that would ever happen. Their achievements were stunningly huge; they handled them with aplomb, staying level-headed through it all.

Certain writers pointed out the laws of gravity: what goes up must come down. Roberts thought that, aside from the possible step up into Knighthood, they would just level off and become part of the British way of life, like the Queen.

He thought it was becoming fashionable for the press to attempt to tear the Beatles from their lofty perch. But no one around the band was very concerned about it.

Brian Epstein said, "*This happens every now and then. Thank goodness it hasn't made any difference so far. They still go on becoming more popular.*"

Even if the interest in their records faded, Lennon and McCartney had a rich future as songwriters. And the Beatles could make it truly big in movies. *A Hard Day's Night* proved they had whatever it took to do that; and no one ever said other comedy teams were finished, were has-beens, after their first films.

Roberts believed that, in the long run, films were their future.

August 20, 1964 – *Mersey Beat* wrote about a Beatle named George, born February 25, 1943, a date that should be of great significance to teenage girls all over the world. Born to Mr. and Mrs. Harold Harrison of Chestnut Grove in Wavertree, Liverpool, he grew up to be a member of the most successful rock and roll band the world had ever seen.

Apparently, he was a normal kid living with his family in a normal house. His mother, Mrs. Louise Harrison, said, "*George was good as a child. He was no trouble at all and was never a naughty boy. Lots of people think that maybe I say this because he's famous now, but he was good, so it would be unfair to say he was a naughty boy!*

"*George was very eager to start school. He was a bright, intelligent child and very independent. He used to travel to school in Mossley Hill alone even when he was small. He's always been very independent.*

"*His hair changed colour. He was quite blond as a child. He and his brother, Pete, were always together, and as a very small child, George would look at photographs of Pete and think it was himself.*"

She continued, "*He never played about the house or the streets as a child. He used to like swimming, and he always found something to do in his spare time.*"

At eleven, in 1954, George went on to Liverpool Institute High School for Boys, the same school as Paul McCartney.

George's mother said, "*George seemed to enjoy school, but he didn't want to stay on to take his G.C.E. He said that life in an office would bore him,*

and when he asked if we minded him leaving school, we said 'No.'"

Talking about George and Paul, she said, "*They were always together. And George met John Lennon through Paul. I think they all met in a chip shop one night after school, and Paul introduced George to John.*

"*I honestly never heard them argue. They fooled about, but I've never heard a nasty word between them. They shared everything, shirts, jackets, and money too.*

"*I've often thought it odd that the three boys, who were quite small when they met, grew up to be the same height, and with the same colour hair and eyes.*"

George left school to apprentice as an electrician.

"*But we could tell that he wanted to make the group, then called the Silver Beatles, his life.*"

When he was seventeen, the group headed for Hamburg.

"*But they were only there a short time before George had to come home. Over in Germany, teenagers under the age of eighteen have to be home by ten p.m. and the authorities suddenly realised that George was only seventeen and playing in a night club until the early hours of the morning.*"

The band went back, of course, when George was old enough to stay. Enough said.

August 20, 1964 – Les Hall wrote for *Mersey Beat*... being the mother of a Beatle had its ups and downs. He spoke with Mrs. Louise Harrison, George's mother, about what it was like. She said she looked after all of George's fan mail. "*Quite a job but we felt that if the fans have taken the trouble to write to George, then they deserve a reply. We couldn't possibly keep all the letters for George to see, he's only managed to get home twice in the past seven months, but we do our best to answer the fans' queries ourselves.*"

The day Les Hall dropped by to visit, the postman had already been there to drop off stacks of postcards, cards and letters.

"*The postman is very good, never a complaint,*" said Mr. Harrison.

"*Many of the letters are very interesting,*" added Mrs. Harrison. "*And they often enclose drawings, newspaper clippings from abroad and even small dolls.*"

Privacy, though, was something to be remembered these days, seldom experienced.

"*I had to build a screen to put in front of the window to stop fans from peering in,*" explained George's father. "*We've had people from America here quite recently. One American family, off on a continental tour, even flew up from London especially to come and see George's home.*"

George was now living in Surrey and calling home every day. Said Mrs. Harrison, "*He's been having a few days holiday before the Beatles' American tour. And he told us that he's really enjoying relaxing for a short while. George's brother, Harry, and his wife and two children have been down to the bungalow for a few days, too, and thoroughly enjoyed themselves. We stayed there when we down for the London premier of the film A Hard Day's Night, but our home is here in Liverpool and this is where we'll stay."*

August 22, 1964 – *Disc Weekly* reported that the Beatles were to be recorded at the Hollywood Bowl for a live album to be released by Capitol. George Martin was to fly to Los Angeles for the event. Being an outdoor event, it was believed that most of the screams and shrieks of the fans would dissipate into the air without affecting the recording.

George Martin said, *"We're doing it on spec. If it comes off successfully, I think Capitol will make it a souvenir album for the American market only. It will consist of old numbers already familiar here, so I doubt whether it will get a British release."*

Martin was to fly to New York after the Hollywood Bowl concert to work on promotion for his *Off the Beatle Track* orchestral album. Also, he was planning an EP of orchestral versions from the sound track of *A Hard Day's Night*.

The excitement in the U.S. was building. Prior to the Beatles' arrival, one Florida radio station had broadcast Beatle records for twenty-four hours and had made a link-up with the Cavern Club in Liverpool.

The full bill for the Beatles' Christmas Show was set. It would include Freddie and the Dreamers, the Yardbirds, Sounds Incorporated, Mike Haslam, Jimmy Savile, the Mike Cotton Sound, Elkie Brooks, and host, Ray Fell. On Christmas Eve, there would be a single show, two shows daily after that.

August 22, 1964 – *Record Mirror* claimed the U.S. film reviewers had gone overboard for *A Hard Day's Night*. It was receiving rave notices everywhere, critics unanimously agreeing the film was funny and well-done.

They went on to say that members of the Beatle Fan Club, in San Francisco, had put on BB armbands and helped the police in their attempts to keep the crowds orderly at the airport for the band's arrival. As expected, though, chaos ensued.

Management of the Hilton Hotel in San Francisco had invited four teenage girls, including Fan Club president, Helena Rand, to a meeting to discuss behaviour. Rand promised that Fan Club members would be *"if not models of decorum, at least somewhat civilised."* From that had grown the idea of Fan Club volunteers helping out the cops and security guards.

A special Beatleville area had been set up at the airport. The band was to be taken there immediately "so that the fans can look at them and scream and faint to their hearts' content without disrupting airport operations."

August 22, 1964 – *Melody Maker* reported that the Beatles were due to arrive in San Francisco to a ticker tape welcome, the sort of reception normally reserved for presidents and national heroes.

It was estimated that more than a quarter of a million fans would see the band during their twenty-four sold out shows. The tour launched in San Francisco the previous evening, then would move on to Las Vegas, Seattle, Vancouver, Los Angeles, Denver, Cincinnati, New York, Atlantic City, Philadelphia, Indianapolis, Milwaukee, Chicago, Detroit, Toronto, Montreal, Jacksonville, Boston, Baltimore, Pittsburgh, Cleveland, New Orleans, and Dallas, finishing in New York for a charity show on September 20th.

The band and their entourage would tour in a chartered plane, expected to travel around fifteen thousand miles.

Radio and television stations all around the country devoted themselves to the Beatles. Often, Beatle records were played for twenty-four hours at a time. And George Harrison's sister, Louise Caldwell, was interviewed by a Florida radio station.

In Blackpool, before the American tour, Jerry Dawson talked to Paul McCartney.

Dawson wondered how the Beatles felt about their upcoming trip to the U.S.

McCartney told him, *"If I said we were not excited about the trip, I'd be lying. But I am wondering how we will feel when we get halfway through the tour.*

"Sure, we enjoy tours, seeing new places, new people. But we soon get homesick. I am sure that after a couple of weeks we shall be counting the days to the end of the trip.

"This will be the longest period we have been away from Britain, almost five weeks. We know things are bound to be hectic. We are certain to get fed up and a little homesick.

"But there are lots of kicks, such as the news, and we have no reason to doubt it, that Frank Sinatra and Dean Martin tried to get tickets for our Hollywood Bowl concert and had to be refused!

"We prefer being at home but if we have to go abroad I would rather it were America than anywhere else.

"The audiences are great, and when we are not working or flying to the next town, there is always radio and TV to relax with, whatever the hour of the day or night.

"We are great TV addicts, even watch News in Welsh and the Epilogue. Great!"

As Paul spoke, the other three members of the group were watching TV in the next room.

Paul continued, *"It's a pity we don't have a little more time to see America itself. Last time we were there we played only two live shows. The rest of the time was taken up with TV.*

"This time we are visiting large and small centres but most of them have huge auditoriums, some holding as many as eighteen to twenty thousand. I hope someone turns up."

"Seriously, we have few problems, from an organising point of view. Last time it was obvious that over there arrangements are carefully planned down to the last detail."

August 22, 1964 – *Melody Maker* **mentioned** that America was raving over the Beatles film. Beatlemania hit New York all over again when the film opened. It would appear that America had decided the Beatles were here to stay.

A Hard Day's Night opened in twenty-two sold-out New York theatres simultaneously. A *New York Times* critic said, *"The new film with those incredible chaps, the Beatles, is a whale of a comedy. I wouldn't believe it either if I hadn't seen it with my own astonished eyes, which have long since become accustomed to seeing disasters happen when newly-fledged pop singing sensations are hastily rushed to the screen."*

August 27, 1964 – *Mersey Beat***'s Bill Harry wrote** about the Florida radio station, WROD, the one that called the Cavern to tape a show that would broadcast widely around the States. The group assembled included Mr. and Mrs. Harrison; Mrs. Starkey; Freda Kelly, Northern Area Secretary of the Beatles Fan Club; Arthur Ballard, one of John Lennon's former art teachers; Ray McFall, the owner of the Cavern; Bob Wooler, the Cavern DJ; Alan Williams, former manager of the Beatles; Kathy Baldwin, a Liverpool fan; and, of course, the writer himself.

Bob Wooler answered the phone when the call came through. First, he introduced Ringo's mum. She talked about when Ringo was with Rory Storm and the Hurricanes, and how he had his own spot with them called Ringo Starrtime; she mentioned that he was her only son and that he had been singing for a long time; and that he was romantically unattached. She finished by saying, *"I'd like to go to America. I believe it is a lovely place you have there."*

Ray McFall was next. He spoke about the early days of the Cavern, saying, *"It was a cellar which used to stock wines and spirits."*

George's mother was next. She mentioned noticing George's talent for music when he was just fourteen. *"I bought him a guitar then and, later on, I bought him an electric guitar. He wouldn't put it down."*

Art teacher Ballard said, *"I read John's book, and the drawings are the same as those he did when he was a student – unofficially. He draws naturally, as he talks in that way. As a conventional art student he was not very good but as an artist, which is very much more important, he was very talented."*

When asked if he thought Lennon would take up art again, Arthur Ballard replied, *"He's in the happy state of being a dilettante now."*

Introducing Alan Williams, Bob Wooler said, *"His name means so much on this scene. He's the owner of the Jacaranda and the Blue Angel. And once he had a strip club where the Beatles played."*

"How's the weather over there?" asked Alan Williams. Talking about the music scene of a few years ago, he said, *"They were the golden years of Liverpool. It was all jazz then, but now its so accepted that even the debutantes are dancing to beat music."* He went on to talk about how the Beatles had gained their first wide acceptance when they played the London Palladium and the Royal Command Show. He also mentioned that the Beatles' closest competitors were the Rolling Stones and that the Dave Clark Five was fairly insignificant in Britain.

George's father mentioned that he had to leave soon; he had to get home to answer *"the correspondence, which is arriving in hundreds at the house. George used to say 'you help me when I'm famous and I'll see you all right.' All the boys have really helped their parents and they are good boys in every sense of the word."*

He went on to talk about the group's early days and how they were now prisoners wherever they went, unable to go out for fear of being mobbed by fans.

Bill Harry asked the American disc jockey about Ringo's book and was told it had been published in the U.S. and would be reviewed on the program.

Freda Kelly talked about the history of the fan club and spoke about various Beatle interests, saying, *"They watch TV a lot; spend a lot of time sleeping; Ringo reads a lot of outer space books; they all like American groups, especially the Miracles and Shirelles; John's favourite record is* Can I Get a Witness." She went on to talk about mail. *"We get a lot from America. The girls ask what size socks they wear, what coloured pajamas, request fingernail clippings and want to know what kind of girls they like."*

Kathy Baldwin talked about Beatlemania in the UK, explaining, *"It's been in Liverpool for four years."*

And Bob Wooler said, *"The group have played at the Cavern two hundred and ninety-two times between January 1961 until August last year. We are absolutely knocked out by this foursome."* He went on to describe the stage: *"It's only three foot high and the audience sit right up to it, but it's never invaded. There's a homely atmosphere and when a performer goes on he is really appreciated. The club is the busiest beat club in Britain and we look forward to the time when the Beatles can appear here again."*

Ray McFall closed the show by saying that the Beatles were *"very sincere, enjoy their music and one another's company. I've never seen them fighting amongst themselves or having a cross word and I think they have succeeded so much because they are sincere."*

August 27, 1964 – Ian Starrett wrote for *Mersey Beat* **about** the Beatles' recent visit to Northern Ireland for two shows at the King's Hall.

Fog made their landing an hour late, and when they arrived Aldergrove airport, security cocooned them as they headed for Belfast.

Many of the fans on hand were soldiers of the 1st Battalion the King's Regiment – from Liverpool. The Beatles had hoped to visit the soldiers earlier in Berlin; instead, they sent three hundred free tickets for the concert in Belfast.

Normal Beatles chaos reigned at the hall. Maniacal teenage girls did a striptease for the band while others fainted and were hauled from the hall.

Seventeen thousand and five hundred fans made this the largest audience ever assembled in Britain for a rock show, just another record to add the group's list of accomplishments.

August 29, 1964 – *Record Mirror* **described** the pandemonium that was greeting the Beatles wherever they went on their American tour. American teenagers were experiencing those carnival scenes of frenzied feeling yet again, everywhere the band played. And everywhere the band went, even when certain venues were not truly sold out, they experienced the same terrifying, sometimes violent, riots of madness, idolatry and hero worship.

The most recent riot had been the Empire Stadium in Vancouver, Canada, when thousands of fans charged across the field, crushing hundreds against the fence that protected the stage. Some with broken ribs, some suffering from emotional breakdowns and hysteria, hundreds crowded around the first aid station.

Around the Hollywood Bowl, where the Beatles had played after Vancouver, police and firemen set up road blocks.

In Seattle, Washington, the car that was to convey the band was so damaged by fans that it could not be used; the Beatles made their getaway after the concert in an ambulance.

During the opening concert at the Cow Palace in San Francisco, two were arrested, fifty were injured, and fifty more were forcibly restrained from climbing up on the stage. At the end of that show, after a barrage of jelly beans and stuffed animals, the band dropped their instruments, fled through the back door, gone before the fans knew the show was over.

At their hotel in San Francisco, girls dressed as maids tried to gain access to their rooms, while the police rounded up dozens of other girls who were wandering in the corridors.

In Las Vegas, the group had two slot machines hauled up to their room – it was not safe for them to appear in a casino. During the show at the Vegas Convention Center, they were pelted with peanuts. Fans later gathered up the fragments as souvenirs.

Everywhere, the noise of the crowds was so loud that few actually heard the music.

Policemen were going to join the band on stage for their next show, the one at the Cincinnati Arena. And,

according to *Record Mirror*, an extra date had been added to the tour, a single performance in Kansas City for one hundred and fifty thousand dollars.

Variety, the American show business newspaper, was reporting that the Beatles would make as much as a million dollars for the tour. American ticket sales to *A Hard Day's Night* had already grossed more than a million and a half dollars.

August 29, 1964 – June Harris wrote to *Disc Weekly* **from New York…** American fans had lost their minds over the Beatles. And so had American stars. Pat Boone and Connie Francis had been at the Las Vegas show; and half the stars in Hollywood had been at the cocktail party thrown by Alan Livingstone, President of Capitol Records. Tickets for the bash were twenty-five dollars each, the proceeds going to charity. Bing Crosby and Dean Martin were amongst the partygoers.

New York's International Hotel had canceled the group's reservations, forcing them to stay at the Lincoln Center Motor Inn.

In San Francisco, when their hotel reservations were canceled, they rented a private home for two days.

The Cow Palace opening concert broke all box office records, taking in $92,000.00, $40,000.00 more than the previous record set by Chubby Checker.

Thursday's crowd in Las Vegas was to capacity. And from Vegas, they went to Seattle and another sell-out concert.

In Vancouver, the group played to twenty thousand people. Some who could not get in broke down a fence outside.

At the Hollywood Bowl concert, which was recorded by George Martin, the place was sealed off and filled with hundreds of cops, ready for the evening show.

August 29, 1964 – *Disc Weekly* **reported that** the Beatles were about to receive one thousand pounds a minute for the extra date added to their American tour. The show would take place at the Kansas City Baseball Stadium, 17th September; the band would play for less than an hour.

The 17th had originally been planned as a day of rest, and they had turned down an earlier offer of twenty-five thousand pounds for the same place. But when the offer was doubled, they acquiesced.

George Martin and a crew from Capitol Records recorded the Hollywood Bowl concert, but it was doubtful the tapes would be usable. The crowd had been too loud.

The group had a day off, then did the Red Rock Stadium in Denver. Next, they were to appear in Cincinnati, then Forest Hills.

August 29, 1964 – a brief article in *Disc Weekly* **announced that** the Beatles had arrived in San Francisco. The city's cops had been expecting between fifty and one hundred thousand fans at the airport, but only nine thousand showed up. Still,

Beatlemania was felt around the city. Fans protested at City Hall when they discovered that Mayor John Shelley had no intention of holding a ceremony for the group. Also, several of the hotels on the tour where the Beatles had reservations had canceled.

The writer was planning to attend the Forest Hills concert on August 27th. He had heard the group would be deposited on stage by helicopter.

A footnote mentioned that the Beatles' tour had heralded the beginning of a new British invasion. Also planning to tour the U.S. in the near future were Dusty Springfield, the Animals, the Searchers, the Bachelors, Gerry and the Pacemakers, Billy J. Kramer and the Dakotas, Cilla Black; the Rolling Stones, and the Dave Clark Five.

August 29, 1964 – Brian Epstein wrote to *Melody Maker*... He hoped no one would ever again say to him that the Beatles were slipping, or that some new group was a threat to them. Their triumph in America was so total, so complete, that he doubted the group's impact would ever be matched again.

Everywhere they went, in a country that had seen it all, he was told, *"There has never been anything like this."*

For the Beatles, and for Epstein himself, it had been the most exciting week of their lives. There had been many thrills, of course: the first record, the first show at the London Palladium, their first trip to the U.S., but there had never been anything quite like this tour.

The San Francisco show, with an audience of seventeen thousand, celebrated their reentry into the States and released a lot of tension. The band was great, facing their largest and wildest audience ever.

One hundred cops guarded the stage, some of them rough, if not actually violent. From San Francisco, they flew to Las Vegas, arriving at 3 a.m. The group bedded down at the Sahara Hotel while Epstein wandered the neon Strip. During the Las Vegas show, the house lights were on for security reasons. The Beatles truly faced their audience for that one.

The sound equipment was the best ever. Both concerts were truly wonderful.

It was in Las Vegas, Epstein explained, that he realised the Beatles were the greatest attraction in the world. They were magnificent performers.

They had attempted to plan the tour to take in a variety of locale. From the Nevada desert, they went to Seattle's raincoast, then on to Vancouver.

Seattle fans were wilder than anyone had ever seen and, for the first time, the band's getaway plans went awry. The limousine that was to take them away went to the wrong door; fans destroyed it. Many of the fans were injured; the first aid station looked like a wartime casualty post. And the Beatles were trapped until an ambulance was backed up to the stage door.

In Vancouver, the fans were even wilder. Authorities wanted to stop the show. The Beatles

refused, finished the concert, and fled Canada for Los Angeles and the Hollywood Bowl. For Epstein, the sight of those four lads on that vast stage seemed simply right, as it should be. The Beatles had made history.

August 29, 1964 – Ren Grevatt wrote for *Melody Maker* **about** the Beatles landing in Hollywood in their chartered Lockheed Elektra after four days of fantastic adventure. Two of the biggest events of the tour were coming up, the concert at the Hollywood Bowl and the cocktail party that was being thrown by Alan Livingston, President of Capitol Records. The charity party was to raise money for the Haemophilia Foundation. Some of the expected guests were Carol Baker, Leslie Caron, Richard Chamberlain, Bing Crosby, Nanette Fabray, Zsa Zsa Gabor, Van Johnson, Burt Lancaster, Jack Lemmon, Dean Martin, Jack Palance, Edward G. Robinson, Andy Williams, Eva Marie Saint, Los Angeles Mayor Sam Yorty, and many more, most of whom were bringing children, each to have his or her photograph taken with the Beatles.

The Hollywood Bowl had been occupied by hundreds of police in order to secure the place for the Sunday night concert.

George Martin had gone to the Bowl early in the day to set up for recording the concert.

After the Hollywood Ambassador Hotel canceled the group's reservations, the Beatles were secured in a private home in West L.A. for two days. Even limousines were difficult to obtain – the fate of some of those vehicles was no secret.

In San Francisco, the Fairmont Hotel had canceled the Beatles' reservations and they had moved on to the Hilton. While the first waves of hysteria were rolling through the streets, one of the Hilton's guests surprised a burglar in her room. She was shot and killed and the murder was overlooked for seven hours. A maid who had heard the screams and shots was certain it was all part of the fans reaction to the band.

During their opening show at the Cow Palace, they broke the venue's previous sales record of $52,000 set by Chubby Checker. The Beatles grossed $92,000.

In Las Vegas, they were mobbed constantly, never getting near a casino. A prisoner in the Hotel Sahara, Ringo said, *"What kind of life is this?"*

For the first time in its history, the Sahara was fully occupied, the rooms sold out.

The air temperature in Vegas was one hundred and ten degrees.

And Brian Epstein said the two Las Vegas shows were the best concerts the Beatles had ever given.

Even Pat Boone was getting into the Beatle business. He had arranged for a series of paintings of each member of the group, as well as one that featured the entire band. He had announced this new business venture on television, at the same time claiming to be throwing a party for the Beatles after their Las Vegas show.

He settled into the Beachcomber's Bar in the Sahara with some of his friends, Ed Burns and Connie Stevens, among others. But someone forgot to tell the band they were invited.

Brian Epstein heard about it late and squelched the deal.

From Vegas, the group went to Seattle for another sold out show. A gang of kids chased their limo through the streets and some were hurt as they bounced on the pavement, trying to keep up with the car.

On to Vancouver for another sell-out, twenty thousand wild teenagers, with more bashing down a fence to get in.

Then it was off to Los Angeles.

At every concert, identified flying objects were a serious peril. Jelly beans and girls' underwear, peanuts and stuffed animals, even a fountain pen that hit Ringo on the nose in Las Vegas.

September 3, 1964 – *Mersey Beat* **wrote** about the most famous drummer in the world. Freda Kelly, secretary of The Beatles northern fan club, went to Ringo Starr's parents' house every Wednesday to answer Ringo's mail. She said, *"Elsie opens it and reads it. I answer it. And Harry writes out the addresses on the envelopes."*

Mrs. Elsie Starkey invited the writer to join Freda Kelly in her home one Wednesday. It was a nicely decorated house in Admiral Grove, Dingle, Liverpool. Mrs. Starkey began by showing him a fifty-foot long chain of chewing-gum wrappers that had arrived in that morning's post. She said, *"There are over eleven hundred different wrappers in the chain. And the fan must have spent a great deal of time making it."* Then she revealed a sketch of Ringo that another fan had drawn. She was flattered and proud of the fans who wrote and sent gifts.

She said, *"I keep everything that's sent in. I don't like doing away with any of them. I still have all the birthday cards and get well cards sent to Ritchie, and I'd like to say thank you to all the people who sent them."*

The room was decorated with stuff mailed in by fans, including Beatle cushions and Ringo dolls. *"If I keep on receiving so many gifts, I'll have to move into another house."*

Regarding Ringo's early career, she said, *"When he was very, very young he always wanted to make a noise on something, empty boxes, suchlike. The first kit of drums he had we bought from some friends of ours. He used it for a little bit then went on to better things.*

"He used to practice in the back room, but only for half an hour a night. That was all he was allowed because of the noise."

"Ritchie joined the Eddie Clayton Skiffle Group with Ed Mills, the boy who lived next door. Roy Trafford and Johnny Dougherty, they all worked together in the same place. Eddie used to take his guitar to work every day. He was a smashing fellow,

if ever a lad should have got somewhere, he should have. I believe he's with Hank Walters and His Dusty Road Ramblers now."

Mrs. Starkey had not followed Ringo's time with Rory Storm and the Hurricanes. She said, *"The first time I saw them was at New Brighton Pier and I thought they were very good.*

"I always thought Ritchie would make a career for himself as a musician because he was so very keen, but I didn't think it would be like this. I thought he would eventually find a place for himself in an ordinary dance band."

Reminiscing, she continued, *"Ringo was at Butlin's when George came up to the house – I hadn't met him before – and asked if Ritchie was home. I told him he wasn't and he said, 'Tell him we're trying to get him to join us.'"*

She missed having the boys around and, most particularly, she missed Ringo. *"Ritchie can't get home to see us as often as he'd like to. When he was home at Christmas, we had a wonderful time. And he had his camera and was taking lots of photographs of us."*

Ringo was the oldest Beatle, and the last to join the band. He was also the shortest. He had an ambition to open a chain of hairdressing salons. At school, he was in the same class as Billy Fury.

Ringo, as well as being a great drummer, was adept at the electric organ and was also a fine photographer. His first book of photographs was climbing the bestseller lists in the States.

While having no regular girlfriend, his name had been romantically linked with Maureen Cox, a local hairdresser.

September 4, 1964 – *Record Mirror* **said** the Beatles may die today, Thursday September 3rd, 1964. Their Lockheed Electra chartered plane would crash and burn in Indiana U.S.A. as it carried the band to their concert in Denver, Colorado. Three Beatles would perish and a fourth would be maimed for life.

The prediction had been made by Jeane Dixon, the self-proclaimed prophetess who had predicted the assassination of John F. Kennedy.

The Beatles were reportedly unworried. From NEMS London headquarters, publicist Tony Barrow said, *"We're not taking it seriously at all."*

They went on to mention that Brian Epstein, however, was no longer traveling with the band. He had returned to London. The last concert Epstein had attended was in Atlantic City, when the crowd was nineteen thousand. Five ambulances had gathered to treat the casualties, including one police officer who fainted from exhaustion.

The night before that, helicopters and vehicle decoys were employed to take the band to the Forest Hills Stadium. Back at their hotel, police had erected barricades to control the crowds.

During the press conference at the Delmonico Hotel, John Lennon said, *"I don't mind not being as popular as Ringo or George or Paul because if the group is popular, that's what matters."*

When asked if they ever rehearse, Lennon said, *"Why should we? We wrote the songs and we play the same music every night."*

Prior to New York, they had been in Cincinnati, where dozens of the fans fainted, one even going into convulsions. And before that, in Denver, apparently not dead or maimed from Jeane Dixon's plane crash, they set a new box office record.

In Hollywood, they attended a party where guests paid to see them, the money going to charity.

And in Los Angeles, teenagers had been arrested for breaking the city's 10 p.m. curfew.

A footnote added that Elvis Presley had sent the Beatles cowboy outfits and six-shooters. They supposedly dressed up in the Western gear and played cowboys and Indians around the grounds of the estate they were renting.

September 5, 1964 – *Melody Maker* published another cable from Brian Epstein in America. He talked about the Beatles having two days off after the great Hollywood Bowl show, lounging about their rented Bel-Air estate, while Epstein himself met with an assortment of film, record and television executives, one of whom was Jack Good, who had produced Six Five Special and had recently been in London to produce *Around The Beatles*. Good had landed a contract to do a new network show for ABC called Shindig and he was hoping to secure appearances from a number of Epstein's artists.

Good would be flying to London in October to tele-record the Beatles. Brian was certain that would become the most important TV show in the world.

He mentioned that the most special time for him during the stay in Hollywood, though, was meeting Elvis's manager, Colonel Tom Parker. He thought Parker was warm, shrewd and generous. They spoke about managing stars. And they spoke about the early days, the publicity schemes, the show gigs. Epstein wondered if, like Parker, he would have been happier just managing one act.

The following day, he took the Colonel and his wife to meet the Beatles.

He talked about the charity garden party where famous fathers paid twenty-five dollars a head for their children to be photographed with the Beatles, and mentioned that the Beatles were gracious throughout the event.

They flew from Los Angeles with happy memories, on to Denver, Colorado. The show had been at Red Rock Stadium, about eight miles outside Denver, perhaps the most beautiful setting ever for a rock and roll concert. A long way from a cellarful of noise at the Cavern Club in Liverpool.

In New York, Epstein had to find a new hotel for the band. Four times on this trip, reservations had been canceled because the hotel proprietors were afraid of the consequences of having Beatles on hand.

During their stay at the Delmonico in New York, the hotel switchboard was flooded with over one hundred thousand phone calls. But the Beatles were happy to be back in New York amongst familiar faces.

They were delivered by helicopter to Forest Hills Stadium to a horrendous uproar.

Epstein was on his way back to London to find out what his other eleven acts were doing, planning to rejoin the Beatles before tour's end.

September 5, 1964 – Ren Grevatt reported for *Melody Maker* from New York. The Beatles hit New York with a force almost equal to hurricane Cleo, which, as the band arrived, was chewing up the South Florida coast.

In an attempt to keep the madness to a minimum, they landed in New York at three in the morning. But New York disc jockeys had broadcast the time of their expected arrival. Three thousand fans were waiting at the airport. They flipped as soon as the Beatles arrived, one sixteen-year-old girl attacking Ringo, tearing at his shirt. As the band was whisked away, Ringo discovered his St. Christopher's medal was missing.

When an appeal for its return was broadcast on the radio, one hundred and sixty girls responded, including the one who actually had it. She was invited to visit with Ringo, returned his medallion and received hugs and kisses while the flashbulbs popped.

A spokesman for the Delmonico Hotel, where the band was staying, said, *"We welcome the Beatles. We used to be dowdy, but now we swing."*

Fans tried all the usual ploys to gain access to the group at the hotel, dressing up as maids or nurses, trying to bribe newspaper men for their credentials, all busted by the cops for their efforts.

The two shows at Forest Hills were packed, highlighted by the band's arrival and escape in helicopters. Five hundred police attended the first show and controlled the crowd well in spite of the Beatles being an hour late.

After the press conference, a disgusted George Harrison said, *"They asked one question eight different times."*

Regarding the Animals, soon due in New York, Paul McCartney said, *"The Animals and the Beatles are very good friends."*

September 12, 1964 – Bess Coleman spoke to *Disc Weekly* about the Beatles reception at Maple Leaf Gardens in Toronto. A crowd of fifteen thousand had filled the place and there seemed to be almost as many cops.

"It's two a.m. on Tuesday morning as I am putting in this call to Disc. *But who cares about sleep, anyway? I've forgotten what it's like on this fabulous, hectic and wonderful tour. And so have the Beatles.*

"When we arrived here in our private charter plane, there were thousands of youngsters at the

airport to greet us. And this despite the unearthly hour of one a.m.

"And those kids lined the eighteen-mile route all the way to the Beatles hotel – the King Edward in Toronto. They crammed the lobby and absolutely besieged the hotel. Ringo was mobbed, despite the security precautions, and all the boys had a job to get through safely.

"There wasn't any sleep for anyone. All night, the kids were chanting outside the hotel: 'We love you Ringo – oh yes we do!'

"And Ringo, bless him, waved to the crowds from his window at five a.m.

"Frankly, I had fears for the Beatles' safety when we reached Detroit on Sunday. The security corps had dropped off at the county line, and there were hardly any police to escort the boys along in the limousines. It was all a bit frightening.

"The only time we have had any peace is on the charter plane, which is really fun for all concerned. The Beatles are marvelous company on the plane and keep everyone in fits with their cracks.

"When they do have time to relax, which isn't often, out come the cards. The big game at the moment is Monopoly. Jackie de Shannon started it all when she bought a Monopoly board. George said he hadn't played since he was seven, but now all the boys have gone Monopoly crazy.

"Any untoward incidents? Only when John was taken ill with a sore throat in Milwaukee. A doctor was called in, and we all had a shot of antibiotics just to be on the safe side.

"But John was soon fit again. It just meant that instead of opening with Twist and Shout, the Beatles started with I Saw Her Standing There to save John's throat.

"Of course Twist and Shout always breaks up the crowds, they really go wild over this opener. And Ringo's vocal spot always brings the house down.

"Just to give you an idea of how tight the schedule has been, the Beatles didn't even have a chance to risk a buck on the coin machines when they hit Las Vegas, America's world famous gambling spot.

"But somehow, John did manage to slip out to buy a check jacket with a fur collar while he was in Los Angeles for three days. And George went out for a dinner date – in a police car.

"The only complaint the boys have, and it's a mild one, is that they always seem to be eating steaks and American salads. 'I wish I could get some good old mashed potatoes,' moaned John. 'I'm sick of these French fried.'

"But John did manage to get some roast beef for a change on one occasion. I think they miss the English style of cooking, though.

"The boys asked me to send greetings to all their fans back home. It won't be long before you see them again. Meanwhile, they're having a tremendous trip, their popularity could never be higher. And they never want to forget what they owe to the fans."

September 12, 1964 – June Harris wrote for *Disc Weekly* **about** the Beatles' past week on tour, starting with three days in Atlantic city and ending in Toronto.

They spent their time in Atlantic City swimming in the pool, listening to records, and playing cards with reporters.

Fans were actually dipping pop bottles full of water from the pool where the group had been swimming. Some were selling it as Holy water for a dollar a bottle.

Until barbed wire was strung along the wall that surrounded the Lafayette Motor Inn, fans had tried climbing in.

On Wednesday, they were in Philadelphia, easily one of the most successful concerts. Fans pelted them with an array of souvenirs. Something crashed into George's picking hand and stopped the music for a moment. Sandwiches, cakes, milk, and the usual assortment of stuff was tossed at their feet.

In Indianapolis, the cops insisted that *they* would need to usurp half the hotel rooms that were originally slated for Beatle use, forcing some of the entourage into somewhat lesser accommodations a few miles away.

The crowd in Milwaukee was hysterical throughout the show, throwing everything from sirloin steaks to plaster of Paris hands.

They reached Detroit in the middle of the night. Unescorted, they rode into town at high speed, dogged by hot-rodders who raced alongside, trying to get a glimpse of the Beatles.

After the Toronto show, they were to move on to Montreal, followed by a three-day break before the next show in Jacksonville, Florida.

September 12, 1964 – *Disc Weekly* **carried a short note mentioning** that the Beatles had been lined up for Jack Good's American TV show Shindig. Good was to arrive in England in October to record the Beatles. They went on to say that tickets for the Beatles' Christmas show at the Odeon, Hammersmith, had gone on sale on Monday. Despite the fact that there would be one hundred and fifty thousand tickets available for the three-week show, fans had started lining up around eleven o'clock the night before, the queue over five hundred yards long by morning and throughout the morning. Tickets were already growing scarce.

September 12, 1964 – Penny Valentine wrote for *Disc Weekly...* Top priority for the Beatles when they returned from the U.S. tour was to get into the recording studio. They wanted a new LP and single out before Christmas.

She spoke with George Martin, who said, *"The problem is finding material for them to record. They are literally living hand-to-mouth because anything they write is snapped up by other people. It's not easy to write good material all the time and they won't record anything they don't think comes up to standard.*

"The LP will be of songs they have written themselves and more standard material, rather like the first two albums.

"It certainly isn't going to be a Christmas album. I hardly think that's their cup of tea."

Martin had spent two days in Hollywood with the band, and also traveled to Denver with them. He said, *"We were talking shop quite a lot. They are hoping to use some of the time out there to write songs.*

"It's been very difficult because there has never been a piano where they've been staying."

The main purpose of Martin's visit to the States had been to record the Hollywood Bowl concert for a live album.

September 12, 1964 – *Melody Maker* showed *A Hard Day's Night* still at number one on the album chart. **Ren Grevatt** cabled from the U.S. explaining that the problems on this tour had people asking, *"Will there ever be another Beatles visit to America?"*

The hailstorm of junk being thrown at them on stage was becoming increasingly hazardous. One of the group commented, *"It used to be jelly beans, now it's the works."*

The worst problem, though, was the exuberance of the police. Their new policy was to keep the Beatles completely screened from their fans. And the cities on the tour were hoping the band would simply play and then get out of town, do not pass Go, do not collect two hundred dollars and, whatever else you do, do not linger long, do not expect a hotel room.

It was frustrating. And irritating.

After three relaxing days in Atlantic City, they were on the road again. In Philadelphia, the junk rain continued: cake, sandwiches, milk cartons, food of all kinds, lipstick tubes, purses, combs, even binoculars. George was hit on the hand and shaken up.

Prior to the show, they had decided not to stay over in Philadelphia; recent race riots suggested that moving on to Indianapolis would be prudent. But at Indianapolis, radio correspondent Art Schreiber said, *"That's where our troubles really got bad. There were twelve rooms reserved for the party at the Speedway Motor Inn in Indianapolis. But the police decided they needed five of those rooms to carry out their job of guarding the Beatles. We press fellows were herded off to an athletic club about five miles away and had to sleep in a locker room. That was the biggest fiasco of the trip."*

In Milwaukee, things got worse. Schreiber said, *"There, the police decided to keep the Beatles from seeing their fans and vice versa. And they separated them from the press guys completely. We've been kicked around in just about every important city of the United States in the last two weeks and we're all getting pretty sick of it.*

"The press people had a meeting this morning and laid it right on the line with the Beatles' road people – Bess Coleman of the NEMS office, Derek Taylor, their press man, and Ed Loeffler from GAC.

We told them if we can't stay close to the boys, to hell with it. We're all leaving the tour. It's up to them to see that this is all worked out. But we're fed up."

The Beatles, too, were getting fed up. Paul McCartney said, *"In Milwaukee here the police are protecting us to a ridiculous extent. I think they're a bit off, I really do. It's a great big drag. If we are not allowed to see our fans, it puts us right on the spot. We feel like heels."*

While that was going on, official order from the city of Chicago canceled their previous sleeping arrangements.

"We don't want them here," said one of Mayor Richard Daley's assistants to the Beatles' road manager, Ed Loeffler.

They flew into Chicago, performed, and immediately flew on to Detroit. McCartney, referring to the events in Chicago, said, *"Maybe we can get on radio or television there somehow. We want to explain to our fans what has happened. We're sorry. It's not our fault."*

The downside in the Saga of the Beatles: Fans gather for hours for a glimpse of their heroes, only to be denied by heavy-handed cops and photo-op politicians. Four rock and roll superstars are herded about like sheep. Four guys, with a million dollars in the bank, cannot get a hotel room. They are pushed and shoved around like stone idols on moving day. They are not quite human, not quite real.

Only in America.

As Schreiber explained, *"Put it this way. Nobody likes them but people. And the very ones who shove them around the most, who get the most officious, are the ones who are always climbing aboard the plane, always hanging around their rooms with their hand out with an autograph pad and a pencil. It's a funny world."*

September 19, 1964 – June Harris wrote to *Disc Weekly* **from New York…** The Beatles had finished off their week with a four-hour jam session in a tiny Key West bar, a week that had been one long confrontation with the cops from Toronto and Montreal to Jacksonville and Boston. In Boston, Derek Taylor was slammed in the gut with a billy club as he argued with the police who surrounded the Beatles' plane when it landed at four in the morning. Fifty or so people, fans and press, had been waiting to greet the band. Taylor was upset that the cops were refusing to let the Beatles meet them.

Demanding tight security no matter what, the cops hustled the group into limos and sent them on their way.

Earlier, in Jacksonville, Florida, their plane was hammered by the gale winds left over from Hurricane Dora, the first hurricane on record to hit North Florida. Exiting the plane, the group was hustled to a motorcade which had just delivered President Johnson to the airport; he had been there earlier to inspect the storm damage.

The band was taken to the Gator Bowl and a crowd of twenty-three thousand hysterical fans. Derek Taylor mounted the stage and told the audience that the Beatles would not go on until all the TV and newsreel cameramen were escorted from the stadium.

The stage shook in the high winds as the group took the stage. When the show was over, they were hustled to the airport for the night flight to Boston.

It had been planned that, after Jacksonville, the Beatles would have a few days off, they would go to sea on a private yacht. Since Hurricane Dora made that somewhat unrealistic, they tried to get hotel reservations in Miami, New Orleans and Las Vegas. In each city, they were refused clearances for an airport landing.

They decided on Key West, five hundred miles south of Hurricane Dora, the southernmost city in the U.S. Once word spread of their arrival in the Keys, hotels in Miami offered to accommodate them. Jackie Gleason said they could have an entire floor at the Miami Beach Hotel. But the band decided to remain in Key West, staying at the Key Wester Motel. They played cards, swam, played Monopoly, slept… and played a jam session at the Key Wester bar, a small room with a capacity of fifty. They made music, along with the Bill Black Combo, until four in the morning when the police broke up the party.

From Boston, they had gone to Baltimore for two sell-out concerts. They had planned to stay in Baltimore overnight, then move on to Pittsburgh. Overnight in Baltimore worked out fine. Pittsburgh refused them accommodations so they flew on to Cleveland to stay at the Sheraton.

The final concert, the benefit at the Grand Old Paramount Theatre in New York, would happen on the following Sunday night. No one knew where they would be staying in New York. The Delmonico, the place that had claimed "We used to be dowdy, but now we swing" had refused to put them up, thus avoiding the misery that would entail.

September 19, 1964 – Ren Grevatt cabled *Melody Maker* from New York. With the tour wrapping up, the Beatles were to fly home to London on the following Monday, due to land at 9:35 p.m. Their Boeing 707 was to be taxied to the Queen's Building at London Airport where the roof garden had been reserved for fans.

Bettina Rose and Anne Collingham, secretaries of the Beatles' Fan Club, were to play Beatles records through the airport's PA system for two hours before the band's arrival. The music would be spliced with updates on their flight's progress, kinda like Santa Claus' Christmas Eve journey.

The epic tour of the States was laced with storms and controversy. Who would blame the group if they thought America a police state? Security arrangements of a sort reserved for Presidents enveloped them wherever they went. In some cities,

they were refused a place to stay, the enthusiasm of Beatles' fans terrifying the hoteliers.

In Montreal, the Queen Elizabeth Hotel shut them out. After the concert at the Montreal Forum, they went directly to their chartered plane.

In Miami, Las Vegas and New Orleans, the airports refused to give them landing clearance. They went to Key West, Florida, instead, holidaying at the Key Western Motel where they jammed with the Bill Black Combo, Clarence 'Frogman' Henry and the Exciters in the motel bar, playing until four in the morning, when the cops shut them down.

In Jacksonville, buffeted by high winds as they landed, they used the motorcade left over from President Johnson's visit.

In Boston, when they landed, security officials outnumbered the fans. Derek Taylor, Press Officer, was hit in the stomach after an argument with a cop; he was left stranded at the airport.

Rumour had it that the Beatles refused to play the Jacksonville show until they received assurances that the crowd was not segregated.

September 26, 1964 – *Record Mirror* reported that the Beatles were home at last, after the most punishing tour of their career. They arrived at London Airport on Monday night to a huge welcome by fans, some of who had been waiting on the roof of the Queen's Building since early in the morning.

Constant Beatle music and flight progress reports through the Airport loudspeakers kept the fans somewhat pacified during the long day and into the evening. As the Boeing 707 came to a stop below the waiting fans, The Beatles knew they were still number one in Britain; they knew the month in the States had not harmed their popularity.

A million pounds richer, home from the wars, home to rest and recuperate, they descended the gangway, climbed into a waiting car, and fled the airport.

The tour had been a dream… and a nightmare. Battles had been won and lost. The whirlwind was fading and the Americans were still trying to figure out what it was that hit them.

Promoters were counting their profits. Cops were comparing wounds. And the fans were cherishing their souvenirs.

Peanuts and jelly beans, ground underfoot on stage, had been gathered up by fans after each concert, small treasures. Dirt trod upon by Beatles had been collected.

Girls had grazed on grass where the band had walked. Said Ringo in Dallas, "I hope they don't get indigestion."

After Cleveland, fans had tried to buy the sheets from the beds where Beatles had slept, but the hotel refused, declaring the concept to be in bad taste.

One businessman attempted to buy some carpet where Beatles had walked, hoping to cut it into one-inch squares to be sold for one dollar each. "The kids are dying for some sort of souvenir. They're bugging radio stations for crushed jelly beans the Beatles might have walked on, or a piece of dirt they may have stepped on. What I was offering was a nice, clean souvenir."

He was refused.

In Kansas City, the hotel where the group stayed did, indeed, sell their bed linen, sixteen sheets and eight pillowcases, to a Chicago businessman for seven hundred and fifty dollars.

Kids gathered up cigarette butts, one even secured the gnawed remains of a slice of watermelon.

The final concert in New York, played to a gathering of society types and serious fans, raised money for the United Cerebral Palsy of New York City and for the retarded infants services. Three thousand eight hundred and sixty-two seats were sold, a sell-out show.

At the end of the show, the Beatles were given a scroll as the chairman of the charity declared, *"The Beatles have brought an excitement to the entertainment capital of the world and have given of their time and talent to bring help and hope to the handicapped children of America."*

September 26, 1964 – *Disc Weekly* **carried Laurie Henshaw's interview** with Walter Shenson, the producer of *A Hard Day's Night,* the producer-to-be of the Beatles' next film. Shenson outlined his plans to truly turn the Beatles into movie stars. He revealed that their next film was in production and outlined his ten-point strategic guidelines.

"Shooting should start the second week of February. The film will be made in Britain. It will not be a pop musical. It will be quite different from A Hard Day's Night. *The Beatles will not be playing in period costume. The Beatles will write at least six new songs for the film. Director Dick Lester and cameraman Gilbert Taylor will both work on the film – and so will the Beatles, as scriptwriters. The film will be a zany comedy. It may be shot in colour, unlike* A Hard Day's Night. *And the boys will not be involved in any romantic love interest."*

Shenson continued, *"My main talk with the boys about a new film took place on the fifteenth floor of the Hilton Hotel when they opened their American tour in San Francisco.*

"First, we decided that the new film would be an out-and-out zany comedy. One that would give us an opportunity to introduce the type of comedy the Beatles excel at.

"They will, of course, still play themselves. That's why we discarded an original idea to have them portrayed in a period role. Working so closely with the Beatles convinced me that they have such a distinctive brand of hip modern humour, it would be a mistake to put them in anything other than a modern setting.

"But the new film will not be a pop musical. We shall find a new and exciting way of introducing their

songs, and something quite different from A Hard Day's Night.

"We shall feature a much stronger plot line than the first film. We all agreed we do not want to do an extension of A Hard Day's Night. *We don't want to flog this formula to death.*

"We have not ruled out the possibility of shooting the film in colour. But whether it is in black and white or colour will depend on the final story.

"We are all striving to make a hilarious comedy. One that will start with a laugh that continues right through. The Beatles have a wonderful sense of fun and we want to make the most of this.

"They are all very keen – particularly John who, as you know from his book, has a way-out sense of humour. I know we can make use of the boys' comedy talents in the script sense, and who knows, may even bring a new dimension to their work.

"Unfortunately, their heavy commitments on the forthcoming British tour and their Christmas show will make big inroads on their time. And then there are the new film songs to write. But I am sure we can all work something out.

"I shall want to use at least six new songs. And probably some more that have already been published.

"The film will probably be made in Britain with a British crew. It will be an entirely fictional story, but the possibility of foreign location is not ruled out.

"As in A Hard Day's Night, *we want to have lots of pretty girls in the new film. But we don't think the Beatles should have any romantic involvement at all.*

"Many youngsters from all over the world have written to me asking that there should be no love story in a Beatles film and this backed up my opinion in the first place.

"We hope to start shooting in the second week of February, depending on whether the Beatles get a chance for a holiday break before their Christmas show."

September 26, 1964 – *Melody Maker* **cheered** for the Beatles home from the wars, home from America, after setting new records for travel, crowds and money.

They survived being manhandled and mishandled; praised and damned, they were banned and embraced; hotels rejected them, others courted them; con men and idiots, fanatics and friends, the greedy and the foolish, all besieged them; pelted with food and junk; threatened with bombs... And they endured it all, mostly with poise, with aplomb.

The writer outlined the plans of the group, now that they were home.

First, they would be recording a new single and a new album, although no dates were set. For certain, though, whatever they recorded would be out for Christmas.

TV producer Jack Good was in London, hoping the get the Beatles for his new American show Shindig.

The American tour had taken them on the road for five weeks, twenty-five thousand miles and four bomb threats. And more than four thousand bawling, shrieking fans had gathered for their farewell concert at New York's Paramount Theatre.

In Dallas, Texas, there had been two bomb threats and one serious injury. The cops barely showed for the Beatles' arrival. The band was mobbed at the airport and mobbed at their motel, where Ringo was jumped by a fan. At the motel, fans shattered a plate glass window. One teenage girl was seriously injured, and three more need emergency care.

The Beatle tour had been one of the most extraordinary and significant events in the history of American show business. For the energy alone, it was awesome.

October 1, 1964 – Brian Epstein reported for *Mersey Beat*... there had never been anything like it, not even in the States. The American tour had been unique. The group invaded twenty-five cities in thirty-two days, played to more than half a million people and flew roughly forty thousand miles.

They even got to sleep now and then, and went swimming as often as they could. John Lennon even managed to sneak out for a few shopping trips without being recognised.

It was difficult to select a highlight. There was the show at the Hollywood Bowl; the one at Red Rock Stadium in the Colorado mountains; the State Fair Coliseum in Indianapolis. These were great shows, but Epstein reckoned that his happiest time was on September 19th, his thirtieth birthday, spent in the Ozark Hills in Missouri, the day before their final New York Concert.

From Dallas, they had flown to a deserted Missouri airstrip, the Beatles, Derek Taylor, Neil Aspinall, and Epstein. They stayed at a millionaire's secluded ranch that night and all of Saturday, horseback riding, fishing, and lounging about in the sunshine. Though novices, the group enjoyed the riding, stuck with it for about three somewhat painful hours and, the following morning, McCartney went out on horseback again for an even more painful attempt.

During the flight from Dallas, Paul McCartney had commandeered the airplane's intercom, singing Happy Birthday, before presenting Epstein with his gifts.

The tour had been an outstanding success, playing to mostly capacity audiences, and breaking virtually every show business record. No one, not even Elvis, had had larger crowds.

Epstein mentioned there were a few controversial incidents but refused to go into detail. He did say that travel difficulties forced them to fly mainly at night, often during severe climate conditions. For example, from the cold rain of Montreal to the hot sunburned sands and humidity of Key West.

The tour had been a great adventure for all concerned, including the promoters. No one was

disappointed with the outcome.

He considered the most thrilling moment to be landing home at London Airport to be greeted by thousands of loyal British fans. But a moment in Detroit almost equaled the homecoming, when four girls from Liverpool held up a banner that read, "We are from Tuebrook. We are proud of you."

Epstein concluded by saying that no matter how much distance they put between themselves and the Cavern, Liverpool would always be home.

October 1, 1964 – *Mersey Beat* **published** a brief review of a new book about the Beatles, calling it tedious and suggesting that books devoted to the band had reached the saturation point. Fresh ideas, original ideas, were a thing of the past.

It was called *Here Come the Beatles*, published by Four Square Books at 3s 6d. It boasted one hundred new pictures. Unfortunately, most of the pictures were not new but had been printed in so many other publications that it was hard to imagine someone who had not seen them all. Even worse, not all of the pictures were of the Beatles. There were many photos of fans, along with shots of Robert Morley, Marlon Brando, Tarzan, South Pacific girls, Peter Sellers, Brigitte Bardot, and even more shots of fans. Accompanying the photographs were comic book balloons that had the Beatles spouting mindless tripe. And the accompanying text was equally insipid.

October 10, 1964 – *Record Mirror* **carried a story about** the Beatles at the Top Ten Club in Hamburg. The club owner, Peter Eckhorn, had been in London on a hunt for new British talent, when *Record Mirror* spoke with him. He had not seen the Beatles since they had become superstars, but he spoke about his first meetings with them.

"They were working at the Kaiserkeller in Hamburg at the time, but they didn't like it there and so they came to see me and ask if there was any work to be had at the Top Ten. To show what they could do, they played a couple of numbers for me. I liked them. I said okay, I'd give them a job, but before I could hire them, the owners of the Kaiserkeller made a complaint about the boys to the police, saying they'd tried to set fire to the club. It wasn't true, of course, but the complaint had the desired effect: the Beatles were deported. It took seven months to get them back again.

"They stayed three months and were very popular, not so much for their music – which wasn't so different from the other groups – but for their personalities. Nobody in particular shone out, they were all well-liked, John Lennon, Stuart Sutcliffe, Paul McCartney, George Harrison and Pete Best."

After their time at the Top Ten, the group returned to Liverpool, leaving Stuart Sutcliffe behind to study art in Hamburg. He died about three months later.

The reporter wondered if Peter Eckhorn had met Ringo Starr.

"Yes, when I went to Liverpool a few months later, looking for a drummer to back Tony Sheridan. Gerry's [Marsden] brother Fred recommended Ringo, took me over to his home and he packed his kit and came straight back with me. He was extremely pleasant and very quiet-natured, rather shy, in those days."

In January, 1962, Eckhorn had been hunting for new talent in Liverpool. He visited the Cavern and saw the band.

"I also met Brian Epstein, who was just in the process of signing them up. We had a merry night, drinking rum out of cups. But there was one thing worrying the boys – they had a recording test coming up. It was making them nervous. George asked me if I had a tranquiliser to help them do a swinging test."

That was the audition when Decca rejected them.

When asked if he would like the group to play the Top Ten Club again, Eckhorn said, *"Sure, I'll find a spot on the bill for them any time. Might even be able to give them a little raise."*

Their original contract had been four pounds for each seven-hour night per man.

He added, *"To be a little more practical, I must say they deserve their success and I'm proud to have had them at the Top Ten."*

October 10, 1964 – *Melody Maker***, Ray Coleman reported** about the beginning of the Beatles new tour. It was to capacity audiences all the way. All records would be broken.

He spoke with George Harrison, who said, *"We're all looking forward to this tour for a special reason: it'll be a change to be in England for one after America and all that. It seems we haven't done this country for ages."*

Did he think the smaller British audiences would be anti-climactic?

"We have never been worried about scenes and anything like that, and we haven't ever had anything to worry about regarding to and from theatres with safety.

"We are used to that sort of difficulty now. When you look back to American trips, and audiences and crowds of between twenty and thirty thousand at a time, Britain is going to seem a bit different. I don't think this one will be as frantic as the last one. But it ought to be a good show, and we're particularly glad to have people like Sounds and Mary Wells with us this time."

What songs would they play for this tour?

"Funnily enough, we haven't yet sat down to plan it, although we've had odd conversations on the lines of 'Oh, we ought to do so-and-so on the tour.' This week we want to get down to rehearsals and map it out properly. We will probably do a couple from the film – If I Fell and maybe I Should Have Known Better.

"Here's one interesting thing people might like to hear about: John has one of those things that fits around his neck now, making it possible for him to blow harmonica and play rhythm guitar at the same

time. So he may be doing that, in fact, I hope he does, and even though he does look a bit odd, it ought to be quite a sight.

"Other numbers will probably be A Hard Day's Night *and of course the songs that everybody wants to hear. The usuals and a few new ones, maybe, when we've discussed it fully."*

Did the Beatles resent the way the screamers drowned out their music whenever they were on stage?

"We like screams. We have never really minded the screamers. Because they do pay money, don't they? And the fans who come have probably got the records anyway, and all they want to do is see us. If they didn't scream, they wouldn't enjoy it, and nor would we.

"So scream louder and louder as far as we're concerned!"

Some people theorised that the screaming, the pandemonium, was morally bad and dangerous. What did he think of that?

"Oh, I thought psychiatrists gave up trying to work it all out a long time ago. They tried to work it all out in America. We think psychiatrists should see a psychiatrist. I think there's nothing wrong with screaming at all, considering the same thing with football matches where you get soft men shouting and punching each other. Especially if it's a cup match. I don't see any difference between that sort of behaviour and our fans, except our fans are naturally younger and behave in a different way. Is that wrong? I don't think so."

George then spoke about music and recordings.

"We're just recording things as fast as John and Paul write them. We have been dissatisfied with our last three LPs. We thought they were okay at the time, but on hearing them over and over we noticed where we could get things better here and there.

"So this time, we want to take it easy with the LP. We've done about six tracks already. We're not recording anything specially for the next single just yet: we're just recording a lot of numbers and then we'll see what happens, what they sound like."

Asked about the Rolling Stones challenging the Beatles for popularity, George said, *"As far as I can remember, it was Brian Poole with* Twist and Shout *who first became the Beatles' challenger as people call them. Then it was Dave Clark, I think. Now it's the Stones. The whole thing's getting ridiculous. New groups get to number one in the chart and so people say the Beatles are slipping, oh dear, or dear, and all that. There are bound to be other groups who get very popular and it's a good thing. But I reckon the way it's played up is sometimes nothing but a farce.*

"The Stones are very popular. I know that. But our records have sold a lot. Our film's doing well. So really, who cares? You know, our record sales are now almost a hundred million round the world. Can't be bad. I doubt if the Stones have sold two

million. Have they? Whatever it is, we know we're doing all right.

"*I believe our tickets have gone okay for this tour, too.*"

October 10, 1964 – Ray Coleman reviewed Brian Epstein's autobiography for *Melody Maker.* It was called *A Cellarful of Noise* – Souvenir Press, 15s. He suggested Epstein was somewhat immodest for writing an autobiography when he was a mere thirty years old. But he believed Epstein was an important man. He had revolutionised the pop charts, the thought processes in the pop world, and conversations of the world. The book was fascinating and Epstein told all.

"*I have never actually made a star*," said Epstein. "*The material is woven when I buy it over a sixpenny stamp on a contract. But I am a demon for balancing the careers of my artists.*"

He set the record straight about the so-called crowd of teenagers asking for Beatles' records at his music store. There had been three requests only, for a record called *My Bonnie.* But those three requests inspired him to visit the Cavern, where he first saw the band. Epstein had never seen anything quite like them. They were messy and not very clean. On stage, they smoked and ate and talked and fooled about; they turned their backs to the crowd, made private jokes, yelled at the audience.

But they had something, and Epstein wanted to harness it. He signed them up and made the rounds of record companies with a demo tape and a lot of persistence.

Regarding Pete Best, Epstein said George Martin had been unhappy with Best's drumming and the Beatles had decided his sound was all wrong for their music. Sooner or later, Best would have to go. It turned out to be sooner.

Epstein was frank about money, saying he took twenty-five percent off the top. Some people accused him of being greedy. Some thought him a hard businessman. He claimed to be neither; claimed he was deeply concerned about his artists.

Coleman pointed out that the British pop scene had been virtually a monopoly before Epstein came along to shake things up. He was more than just another money-grubbing businessman – he made things happen.

October 17, 1964 – *Disc Weekly* **reported** that the Beatles' received a screaming welcome at Bradford Gaumont Theatre to kick off their new tour. Six thousand people attended the two shows.

The early show had a few empty seats but it was still the biggest reception ever given by a West Riding audience.

It opened with all the usual hysteria, the fainting wailers, fans rushing the stage, the shower of flying objects – jelly babies, autograph books and anything else easily found and portable.

One fan, in honour of John Lennon's twenty-fourth birthday, threw a Teddy Bear at him.

The loudest screams were reserved for Ringo when he sang and played *I Wanna Be Your Man.*

John Lennon mastered playing the harmonica and guitar at the same time; and George Harrison's guitarwork was the backbone of the music.

Others on the bill were Mary Wells, Sounds Incorporated, Tommy Quickly, the Remo Four, Michael Haslem, and the Rusticks.

October 17, 1964 – *Melody Maker* **reported** that the Duke of Edinburgh had said the Beatles were "on the wane."

Paul replied, "*I bet the Duke's book hasn't sold so much as our records. And I bet it didn't sell so many as John's book.*"

"*The bloke's getting no money for his playing fields from me,*" said John.

Added George, "*And tell him I'm withdrawing from his award scheme. Here, I bet he buys our next LP.*"

Paul continued, "*Tell the Duke we want our autographs back, those we signed specially for the Royal Family.*

"*What they mean when they say we're slipping is that we're leveling off. That's true, I suppose.*"

George said, "*Yeah, but until somebody else manages to get the first half-dozen places in the American hit parade, then where are we slipping from?*"

And Ringo said, "*Something's bound to change. You can't keep it up forever, whether your name's John Lennon or the Duke of Edinburgh.*"

"*If you ask me,*" Paul said, "*it's all part of a secret plot.*"

"*By who?*" John asked. "*Jagger?*"

Shortly after that, the Duke of Edinburgh sent a telegram to Brian Epstein explaining that he had said The Beatles were "away" not "on the wane."

Declared George, "*It's good to know what he really said.*"

"*I'm glad we're back in business,*" said John.

October 17, 1964 – *Melody Maker* **reported from the Beatles' tour.**

Mary Wells said, "*I really do dig the Beatles a lot. So far, I haven't had the chance to talk to the Beatles properly, although I played Paul my next record,* Ain't It the Truth, *and he helped me decide to make that the A side and put* Taking Me For Granted *on the back.*"

Opening night, every artist was tense, nervous. But the supporting acts realised they were involved in something special. It was an important tour. And the audiences would be huge.

The Beatles opened and closed with *Twist and Shout,* their signature tune. In spite of all the shrieks and screams, the music seemed to be more audible on this tour than the previous one. Perhaps the audiences actually wanted to hear the band.

From *Twist and Shout* they moved into *Money, Can't Buy Me Love, Things We Said Today, I'm Happy Just to Dance With You, If I Fell,* and *I Wanna Be Your*

Man – sung by Ringo, and finishing with *A Hard Day's Night*, *Long Tall Sally*, and *Twist and Shout*.

They held the stage for half an hour, their presence tighter than ever. John stood arrogant and mildly disinterested, Paul moved from mike to mike, George moved very little, and Ringo rocked.

The most popular song in the line-up seemed to be *A Hard Day's Night*, Lennon's cutting vocal at its best.

The other acts were good; it was a well-balanced show.

October 17, 1964 – *Melody Maker*, **Ray Coleman, traveling with the tour, wrote** in Leicester, as the Beatles' limousine pulled up at the police station to gather up their escorts, a group of cops wandered over to the car with autograph books. One said, *"I see you have the same car as when you came here last year. Money tight, then?"*

After a few seconds of silence, John replied *"Yeah. And you've got the same bloody uniform on that you wore last year. How about that?"*

The cop disappeared and Coleman pointed out that the band was sharp, musically and verbally.

He said moving the band around Britain was a major operation, cleverly devised. Even a stop at a traffic light could be a dangerous event, people screaming, mobbing the car. Traveling with the group, Coleman realised that they truly liked each other. They would have occasional disagreements but never fought. Joking around, they talked about the pylons scattered around the countryside. Paul thought they improved the rural scenery by breaking up all that rustic beauty. They smoked and chatted about their American tour, the conversation getting into black artists.

"I hate singing Twist and Shout *when we have coloured artists on the bill,"* said John Lennon. *"Seems to be their music and I feel sort of embarrassed. Makes me curl up."*

"I don't care about that," George said. *"If someone like us has made a hit out of a coloured song, then it's up to us to show them how to sing it."*

"Yeah, but these coloured acts CAN sing," answered John. *"They do these songs so much better than us. When we started, we did songs like* Money; *they were nothing like the songs we write now. We never used to sing our own songs, always others."*

"I suppose that was when we really became the Beatles. This is very interesting, really. Because now, we are looking for old songs we used to know and sing, because we're running out of good stuff to put on LPs. Material's becoming a hell of a problem."

Paul said, *"We spend a lot of time trying to write a real rocker. Something like* Long Tall Sally. *It's very difficult. I* Saw Her Standing There *was the nearest we got to it. We're still trying to compose a Little Richard song."*

George said, *"I was thinking, how about something like Richard's* Bama Lama Bama Loo."

"You just write daft things, George," replied Paul. *"As I was saying, about writing a rocker. I'd liken it*

to abstract painting. People think of *Long Tall Sally* and say it sounds so easy to write. It's the most difficult thing we've attempted, isn't it, John?"*

Lennon agreed. *"Like at art school, I maintained abstract painting was easy and chucked paint everywhere, and they all said it was rubbish. I said 'Prove it,' and they did."*

"Writing a three chord song that's clever is not easy," added Paul.

"We used to write a lot in the back of a coach," explained John. *"We did* Bad To Me *in the back of a van, and* From Me To You *on a coach, then* She Loves You *was half-written in a coach."*

Ringo interrupted, asking, *"Where do we stop for lunch, Neil?"*

"Leave it to me," replied Neil Aspinall.

Reflecting, Paul said, *"Back home in Liverpool, we used to sing over some of our songs to relatives, I did to my Dad and my aunties. My Dad would look at me disappointed.*

"'I don't know, young Paul,' he'd say. 'I try to get you to speak properly and you drop your aitches. Why sing Yeah Yeah when you mean Yes Yes.'

"I tried to explain this was the whole point of the song."

John asked, *"Anyone ever heard someone from Liverpool singing Yes? It's Yeah."*

"Well," Paul went on, *"we just laughed. My Dad gave us some of the worst advice ever. He said this music thing will never last. It's all right on the side, he'd say, 'but, Paul, it will never last.'"*

"Remember," said George, *"he always wanted us to sing* Stairway to Paradise?"*

And John added, *"My auntie said, 'Ah, this is all very well but you'll never earn a living at it. Finish your education, get your GCEs. Then you can play your banjos. You need something to fall back on...'"*

"They'd probably have been right if it wasn't for a fluke," said Paul.

John agreed that if they had not been so popular, the Beatles would have ended up playing gigs in London nightclubs and sweating about the future.

"Then people would say, 'Here, you don't want to see so-and-so in the hit parade and not you.' Then we'd feel rotten. But we'd be playing the gen stuff, and the people'd put the word around, go and see the Beatles. They play the real stuff."

In Nottingham, they stopped for lunch. On to Leicester and the crowd of waiting policemen.

"Yeah, he's definitely got a daughter," said John, eyeing one of the cops. *"Look, look. His hand's going to the autograph book in his pocket. Wait for it."*

The officer strolled over, asking for an autograph.

Autographs collected, he began to leave and Lennon said, *"'ere, you've forgotten your pen."* When the man was gone, he added, *"That's fantastic. Policemen always demand their pen back. They've got that sort of mentality."*

On to the theatre and the final preparations. After yet another great show, they head for the M1 and the journey back to London.

"Tired?" said John. *"No, we're just numb."*

October 17, 1964 – *Melody Maker* **published** a series of remarks in the column Beatletalk.

John Lennon: *"No interview for whites. Only coloured press allowed. We're on a Charlie Mingus kick."*

Ringo Starr claimed he had two thousand seven hundred and sixty-one rings. *"I only wear four because I can't get these off my hands."*

George Harrison, regarding Mary Wells' song *Time After Time*: *"It's a cabaret song, not right for her."*

Mary Wells' drummer, Melvin Terrell to a fan: *"We've not been introduced. My name's Ringo – suntanned, of course."*

Paul McCartney: *"Mike Haslam looks like Pete Best."*

Mary Wells, on hearing the Beatles play live for the first time: *"That's one hell of a sound."*

May Hampton, Mary Wells' secretary: *"England's a drag. Full of antique rooms and cars from the twenties."*

October 24, 1964 – *Disc Weekly***, Alan Walsh reported** spending some time with Paul McCartney in the Beatles' dressing room in Ardwick, Manchester.

Paul said, *"We're hoping to have our next single out by November 27th. We're due to release a new one soon and this it the date which has been provisionally set for its release."*

It was the fifth day of the Beatles' tour; Walsh found them cheerful, feeling fine in spite of all the hard work over the last nine months.

Lighting a smoke, exhaling heavily, Paul said, *"We recorded five or six tracks before this tour started, but we all seem to be keen on different ones.*

"I think the one we'll probably settle for is one which has a big and really distinctive intro. We wanted to do a number which had a start as distinctive as the chord at the beginning of A Hard Day's Night *and we decided to do a fast drum roll with a guitar phrase over it.*

"When we did it in the studio, we kept doing the roll wrong and we'll probably re-record this bit before the disc comes out."

The close of November was chosen so the band could promote the song on TV shows before starting their new Christmas event at the Hammersmith Odeon. The Beatles were looking forward to the Christmas Show. Also on hand would be Freddie and the Dreamers; the Yardbirds; Sounds Incorporated; the Mike Cotton Sound; Elkie Brooks; comedian Ray Fell; and disc jockey Jimmy Savile.

George Harrison said, *"It'll be along the lines of last year's show at the Finsbury Park Astoria, but there'll be more production. We'll probably be doing sketches again like last year, although the script hasn't been worked out yet."*

The group wanted to stay home as long as possible this time, giving their British fans a chance to see them, giving themselves some time to relax before starting their next feature film in February.

Said Paul, *"This will probably be in colour and will have more of a story. We'll have to be ourselves in it, because we don't kid ourselves we can act. But it'll definitely have a plot."*

Walsh asked George Harrison about the problem of being recognised every time he went out.

"I find it's not such a problem. I go out all the time. In London, for instance, we often go out to a number of clubs where we aren't bothered and I sometimes ring up a restaurant, tell them who it is and ask for a table out of the way. I'm not bothered then.

"Of course, this isn't the case abroad, particularly in America. It was just impossible to go out all the five weeks we were in the States. We realised that it would be like that before we went, though, so it didn't bother us too much.

"The problem isn't too great, here, though. After all," George finished, joking, *"everyone looks like us now anyway!"*

October 24, 1964 – Ray Coleman interviewed John Lennon for *Melody Maker***.** The Beatles were in their dressing room. Lennon was applying powder to his face, prior to going on stage, and he said, *"I wish I could paint a smile on. Don't think I'll manage one tonight. Sometimes I wonder how the hell we keep it up."*

Somewhat taken aback, Coleman pondered that statement. It was honest. It was remarkable. But then, John Lennon was honest… and remarkable. He hated the phonies and he refused to buy into the whole star cult mythology.

"Almost suicidally frank," Ray Coleman wrote. The Beatles collected hangers-on, parasites, the way a car wreck draws a crowd. And John was the least tolerant of the group when it came to idiots and fools. When it was time to tell someone off, Lennon could be devastatingly cruel. Anytime anyone insulted the Beatles, Lennon would lash out at him or her. Never at a loss for words, he won more arguments than he ever lost. And he knew every con imaginable whenever someone wanted personal contact with a Beatle.

When the group stopped at a restaurant for an unscheduled lunch, a waiter approached the table saying, *"Personal call for Mister Lennon from Liverpool."*

"Rubbish," said John. *"No one knows we're here. It's a con. We've gone."*

Coleman said Lennon had the most powerful personality in the band.

Kidding around, Paul McCartney once said, *"Two things I hate in life, y'know: racial discrimination and coloured people."*

And Lennon told him, *"People who talk like that really don't like coloured people, otherwise they wouldn't think that way at all. I've heard it all before."* Mocking the broad Lancashire accent, he added, *"Aye, theer all reet but they're so dirty and they bring down the value of property."*

Both Lennon and McCartney loathed racism.

Lennon was independent; no one was allowed to tell him what to do. But Coleman wanted his readers to understand that Lennon was not big-headed about things. The conversation began with the questions: Where do the Beatles go now? How did John see his future? It had been reported that John had once made the comment that he would be *"out of it in a few years, anyway."*

Replied John, *"I said that during a conversation with Mick Jagger. I was talking about when I was thirty. I don't want to be fiddling round the world singing* It's Been a Hard Day's Night *on one-nighters when I'm thirty, do I?*

"If the films work out well, I'll like that.

"People say that's where the Beatles are heading for, and I suppose it makes sense. I also like A and R-ing records. Haven't done much of it, but from what I've done and from what I see, I'd like to try more.

"I'd like to continue writing for other people, and I hope we'll still make records.

"Mind you, I still enjoy playing. I get slightly less kick out of things now compared with some time ago, but that's natural.

"I enjoy playing, really, but in America it was spoiled for me because of all the crap there. You know, meeting people we don't want to meet. It spoils things for me because I suppose I'm a bit intolerant.

"But is it any wonder I got fed up? When they kept sending in autograph books and we signed them only to find they belonged to officials, promoters, police, and the rest of that lot? The real fans, they'd waited for hours, days, well, they were treated like half-wits because they wanted out autographs. But the cops made sure they got theirs.

"I bet every policeman's daughter in Britain's got our autograph. Half of them aren't our fans, I bet, but what can you do? It's bloody unfair on the kids who really want them."

Paul interrupted then, saying, *"Hey, I've had enough of you blasting off, John."*

John replied, *"You say what you want to say and I'll say what I want to say, okay?"*

"You're bad for my image," Paul told him.

"You're soft. Shirrup and watch the telly like a good boy," John said.

John continued speaking to Ray Coleman, lamenting the lack of new Beatles material, lamenting the lack of time in which to create more.

"We might have got some good ideas if we hadn't got stupid people to contend with. You know, we got about four hundred records in the States, and they might have had something on them for us, but we couldn't get them through customs here. They asked four thousand pounds for them. Must think we're mad.

"Anyway, we got it down to two hundred pounds and then we still refused to pay that amount, so they're still there, waiting, as far as we know. It's costing the authorities more to keep sending them backwards and forwards from America to London than it would to hand them over."

Asked what he thought about the theories that the Beatles' popularity was being surpassed by the Rolling Stones, John said, *"We-e-e-l, there comes a point where the only thing left to do to a group like us is to knock.*

"I get on all right with Jagger – I'll call him that because he always refers to me as '—— Lennon.' But ask him where the hell's their new record? They need one out now. I'd know what to say. I get fed up with the whole crazy scene sometimes. 'The Beatles are slipping.' 'The Beatles have had it.' What the hell's it all amount to?

"I think there probably was a moment a few weeks ago when the Stones had it over us just a bit. Jagger's the one, of course. He is the Stones, isn't he?

"Well, about the time everybody went potty for Jagger, that's when it could have meant something about them taking over. But I don't know now. I just don't know."

Did John think he might one day write a book about the Beatles?

"I don't know, don't think so, really. It would be too much like writing an essay at school for me to write a book. I'm more interested in making things up than in documentaries. Anyway, I've got a lousy memory, really. I can never remember anything, what city we're in, where we're going, what hall we're at. It's just a sea of faces, then back in the car.

"I'm not a man of detail. I'm not forgetful about the house. I can remember things I am interested in very clearly, but other things are just a jumble in my mind.

"For instance, you know Cyn and I have moved into this new house in Surrey? Well, the other night the chauffeur was taking me home and he said, 'Where to?' I hadn't a clue, even though we've been living there a month. Couldn't remember where I lived.

"We drove around for three hours before we got from London to my home. So you can imagine the sort of mind I'd have for writing a book and remembering all the things that've happened to us!"

Regarding the genre labels for music and the controversy raging in the *Melody Maker* letter columns, John said, *"We were pop when we started. Now you get Mary Wells and Bo Diddley saying they are pop. What's it all amount to anyway? When Bo Diddley says he's pop, you might as well pack it in.*

"It makes all those letters on the back pages ridiculous. He's R and B to me. But it's such a ridiculous subject, anyway. People get so heated about it and it amounts to a lot of rubbish."

It was almost show time. The group dressed for the stage and John sat fingering his guitar, strumming a few licks. He said, "*It's fantastic, really, how all this happened. I mean, we're lucky sods, aren't we?*"

October 24, 1964 – *Melody Maker* **published** a series of questions and answers with John Lennon.

Did he practice the guitar these days?

"*I never did practice. I never practiced because I only learned to play to back myself. In the old days we all used to sing. Originally, I'd sing one, then Paul'd do one, then George and so on. So you didn't need to be a genius of a guitarist to back yourself.*"

He was asked if he could read music, and, if not, was it a problem?

"*It's not essential for what I'm doing to read music. And no, I've never found it a handicap. These dance bands that play pop on the BBC, they sound all right at that, because they can read it off music sheets, but have you heard some of them playing rock? It's rotten.*

"*If I wanted to read music, I'd pack all this in and start from scratch. Sometimes I think I'd like to but I'm a cheat. I can't play finger style. I just manage to do something that makes it sound like I can. I started with a banjo when I was fifteen, when my mother taught me some banjo chords. I played the guitar when I was young like a banjo, with the sixth string hanging loose! I always thought Lonnie and Elvis were great, and all I ever wanted to do was vamp. I got some banjo things off okay, then George and Paul came along and taught me other things. My first guitar cost me ten pounds, it was one of those advertised in a paper you send away for.*

"*Why did I get it? Oh, the usual kid's desire to get up on stage, I suppose. And also my mother said she could play any stringed instrument. She did teach me a bit.*"

He went on to discuss his musical role in the group. "*The job of the normal group rhythm guitarist is to back the solo guitarist like the left hand does on a piano. Unless the lead guitarist is very good and can back himself like finger-style guitarists can, he needs someone else to help fill out. Most of our stuff in the early days was twelve-bar stuff. I'd play boogie and George would play lead. I'd vamp like Bruch Welch does, in that style of rhythm.*

"*We always have someone playing rhythm in the set style all the time, although it's too thin for records so we just both go full-out.*

"*I'd find it a drag to play just rhythm all the time, so I always work myself out something interesting to play, the best example I can think of is like I did on* You Can't Do That. *There wasn't really a lead guitarist and a rhythm guitarist on that because, well, as I say rhythm guitar's too thin for records. It'd drive me potty to play chunk-chunk rhythm all the time. I never play anything George couldn't do better, but I like it. So I do it.*"

October 31, 1964 – *Disc Weekly* **reported** that a new Beatles' single and a new LP would be out for Christmas. The single was slated for release on November 27th, both sides written by John Lennon and Paul McCartney. Side one was *I Feel Fine* and the flip side was *She's a Woman*.

The new album would be called *Beatles For Sale*, due for release on December 4th. There would be fourteen songs, all new recordings and excluding the latest single. Nine of the tunes were Lennon / McCartney compositions.

October 31, 1964 – *Disc Weekly* **said** Paul McCartney held up a cigarette lighter, saying, "*See this? It hit me on the head at our concert in Leeds last night. That's how excited the audience was getting! They were throwing all sorts of things at us in their enthusiasm. I've got so many bumps on my head from being hit by flying objects that I feel more like a prize fighter.*"

He was speaking during a press conference before taking the stage at the Gaumont State Theatre in Kilburn.

The reporter asked Paul what he thought about the Tamla-Motown bands.

"*They're great... and will continue to go down well here. They're all exciting entertainers, as those Supremes showed during their trip.*

"*The odd thing is though that these coloured singers aren't really appreciated by white people in the States, they come over to Britain and are knocked out by the reception they get. It seems it's only their own kind that likes them back home.*"

October 31, 1964 – *Melody Maker*, **Ray Coleman spoke** with Paul McCartney.

Said Paul, "*I don't believe we should push our luck too much by releasing too many records. We're aiming for about three a year at the moment. If you put out too many, you bore people, and, anyway, when we had about five in the British top twenty, people came up to us accusing us of flooding the market and edging everybody else out. What do we do for the best?*"

Regarding his guitar-playing, he said, "*I won't talk technically about bass playing because I can't read music, for a kick off. I know little about bass guitar, really, and all I do is what sounds right, what suits the song. Millions of people know more about bass guitar than me, and that's a fact.*

"*Still, you can get your own thing going. Acker Bilk plays clarinet better than a lot of people who read music.*

"*I find the best bass I can play in some songs is two-in-a-bar. Lots of people would be disgusted with that, but for my money it can be the most effective bass ever. Like on those early Little Richard records, those records still move like hell.*

"*My policy's straight forward enough, really; I always keep in with what Ringo's doing on his bass drum. If he does one-in-the-bar, I do.*"

Mentioning that he considered John Lennon the cynical Beatle, Ray Coleman described Paul McCartney as the one with instant mass appeal. Wherever they were, Paul was usually the one to welcome newcomers, handling strangers with ease. He was also good at getting rid of the ones who needed to go, tactfully and with tolerance, but sending them away just the same.

During an after-the-show meal at their hotel, round about 1 a.m., a few young ladies arrived with autograph books.

To the other three Beatles, Paul said, *"Oh, let 'em come in, eh? It's just the usual, they just want to check up and see that we're real."*

Autographs signed, Paul said, *"Aye, well, that's it then, all right? Unless there's any more out there who'd like to come and see the grotto, you can collect your programs on the way out."*

They assumed he was joking but left just the same.

Coleman wondered where the Beatles stood today.

Said Paul, *"I don't think we realise, never have and never will do, at least not for a long time, how big we are. We know we get big hits with records round the world, and we know we earn quite a lot of money. But sitting here, just the four of us always together when we're playing, you just can't get the impression the public gets of the extent to which we've made it, can you?*

"Course we know what's being said now. People say it's changing and the Beatles are sliding. But are we? You see, we came into this business professionally, into the hit parade scene, that is, as a recording group. We came into this business to sell records of the music we like. We're basically a recording group.

"Now, if you look at who's generally leading the sales in that field, right now, I mean, not a few months ago, the answer, from whichever way you try to analyse it, has got to be us.

"I mean, we've sold eighty-five million records altogether now, and for all I know, more. It's fantastic! Fantastic! I can hardly believe it.

"You get people saying so-and-so is chasing the Beatles, and they may be, in some ways. But I'd like to get this on record now, so we make our position clear: we've only ever gone by record sales. When we stop selling records, we'll probably pack it in.

"We came into this business like we are now to sell records, and we're selling records, I'm glad to say. I hope a lot of others are doing well, too, you know. But from where I'm sitting, the Beatles look to be doing okay, slipping or not."

Coleman wondered if McCartney missed the freedom he had had when he was unknown.

"Until I was nineteen, I had every bit of freedom any teenager has. Then this lot came along and, of course, there's a considerable lack of privacy. But let's face it. There are bound to be some

disadvantages when you are earning money. Any job that gives you good pay has disadvantages.

"So you come to accept that you have to think twice before you can move around in our position. Mind you, we've got it all worked out nicely now; we all move around London quite easily.

"We can do what we like most of the time, not like ordinary people though. For instance, when we go to the pictures, instead of going in when the lights are up, we sneak in just as the lights go down and the main film's about to start. We have to arrange that sort of thing with the cinemas before we go. It's just the bother of thinking before we do thing like that. But if you work things out, you can do almost anything without getting huge crowds.

"But I'm not daft. I know for a fact that one day, interest in us is bound to die down. Then we'll be able to sit back with privacy. Then the big laugh will be that we've got the cash. The hard fact is that one has to go through this sort of thing to get the cash.

"You know, we hear a lot of people think we don't work for our money and all that goes with it. They are just thick. I had two jobs before I came into this lot. Once I was in coil-winding and the other job I was in was as second man on a lorry. Well, I'd say they're about as average jobs as anybody could get, aren't they? Both those jobs were ten times easier than this one. This job I've got now, it's like teaching. You never stop. Or a vicar's. Only instead of planning sermons, we're writing songs and singing them.

"Mind you, we love it. I remember in the early days we never dreamed we'd earn the big money doing what we're doing now. I suppose we were just lucky.

"There were hundreds of groups that could have made it like we did. We just happened to be coming up at the right place at the right time.

"And to think, people still come up to us, you know, and say, 'Was it worth it? All the trouble?' They do, you know.

"Of course it's worth it. We thought we had something and we've proved it. But I'll never forget this much: You need about seventy-five per cent luck."

November 7, 1964 – *Disc Weekly* **reported** that the Beatles new single *I Feel Fine / She's A Woman* and their new LP, *Beatles For Sale*, had each reached advance orders of over half a million.

The single was to be released on November 27th, the LP shortly afterwards. A spokesman for EMI said the orders were increasing, that this was just the initial reaction to the announcement that the discs would be available.

The group was set to play Thank Your Lucky Stars and Top of the Pops to tie in with the new releases. Also, it was confirmed that they would head the bill on the Boxing Day edition of Saturday Club.

Music publisher Dick James had recorded a selection of Lennon / McCartney songs, scheduled to be released on the same day as *I Feel Fine*.

And Walter Shenson, producer of *A Hard Day's Night*, announced there would be six to eight new songs in the Beatles' second movie, scheduled to start filming on February 22nd.

"*I don't think we shall be using any Beatle songs that have been published,*" Shenson said. "*The film will be in colour, and it will be a wild comedy with the boys playing themselves, of course. A script is now being prepared, and will take about two months to complete.*"

November 7, 1964 – *Melody Maker* **announced** that the Beatles had officially arrived on the map, literally. A mountain in Canada had been named after them, to be identified on maps as Beatle Mountain.

George Harrison said, "*It's just outside Toronto. When we were on our American tour they wanted us to fly over it and drop bottles of champagne over the peak, but we didn't get the time. So we did a phone interview with somebody, accepting the title. It'll be good seeing our name on the maps, won't it?*"

November 7, 1964 – Ray Coleman wrote for *Melody Maker*... about *I Feel Fine*, written by John and Paul and due for release on November 27th.

Paul said, "*Don't be put off by the opening noise. It was a laugh. John was playing his Jumbo guitar as we did the final run-through before recording, and when the red light came on for the actual session he played it, unintentionally. The result's a sound of feedback, and after a bit of thought we decided to leave it in. It's the biggest gimmick thing we've ever used.*"

"*Yeah,*" added John. "*I'm interested to see who gets it for review in* Blind Date, *because I don't reckon they'll guess who it is for some time till it gets started.*"

Lennon sang alone on *I Feel Fine*, double-tracking the harmonies. He said, "*The selling part of the song, commercially, is the phrase I Feel Fine and the guitar run that follows it. George and I play the same bit on guitar together on the record. I suppose it has a bit of a country-and-western feel about it, but then so have a lot of our songs. The middle-eight is the most tuneful part, to me, because it's a typical Beatles bit.*"

Paul thought the phrase 'I'm in love with her and I feel fine' would be the catch phrase, the selling point.

Mockingly, Lennon said, "*Ah, that's the bit that'll set your feet a tapping, as the reviews say.*"

"*We like the B side a lot,* She's A Woman," Paul said. "*This is the first real rocker we've written, and we're glad. We played it to Mary Wells and said to her 'Listen, it's the coloured sound.'*"

John said, "*We're really pleased with the record, and with the new LP. There was a lousy period when we didn't seem to have any material for the LP and didn't have a single. Now we're clear of things and they're due out, it's a bit of a relief.*"

November 7, 1964 – *Melody Maker*, **Ray Coleman interviewed George Harrison.** Coleman called George the reluctant Beatle, the one who did not expect fame, the one who had found it bewildering when it came. He was also the most easy-going of the group, friendly and honest. And, like John, he abhorred the star treatment.

Young girls wanted to mother him. Parents liked him best because he was quiet and seemed the most respectable member of the group. He had a huge personal following, and he liked to follow the money, needed to know what was happening to it, where it was going, who had it.

He was conscientious about signing autographs, considering it fair play for the fans. He would go out of his way to accommodate them.

And he was painfully honest.

"*That boy George, he's very quiet but he's cute,*" said Mary Wells.

Coleman pointed out that Harrison was only quiet until he was annoyed. Then he was anything but. He asked George how he felt about putting their success into perspective.

"*I dunno. I don't feel any difference now from when it all started. See, although success is good and I enjoy everything it means, I feel exactly the same about the group, the music and the audiences, in fact life generally, as I did when we sweating away in Hamburg.*

"*Apart from the obvious differences, of course, like money. But let's face it; physically, I'm the same bloke.*

"*I'll say this much: I feel odd when people look up and point at me on stage, like they do with all of us now. It seems odd to think we are the centre of attraction because, you know, we've gone through so much to get where we are.*

"*None of us look upon ourselves as stars. It's the other people who say we're the stars, we don't. All we wanted when we started was to have hits and top bills and go on TV and make money. I never thought this sort of situation would ever develop, like everybody knows who we are and all that.*

"*It all happened so quickly, though, that I didn't get any chance to turn back; none of us did. It's a good job we all had the right sort of mentality to hold ourselves from going mad, with everything going on round us like it did.*

"*But it's been great, what else can you say about this sort of thing when it happens to you? It's like winning the pools!*"

Ray Coleman wondered how George viewed the future.

"*We are going to make two more films at least under this present contract; one starts next February, you know. I'd like to make more films, and I think we're all agreed we want to carry on making records.*

"*Personally, I'm a bit fed up with touring. Not so much in England, but particularly in America, for instance. I feel sure we wouldn't do another tour of* the States for as long as five weeks ever again. It's so exhausting and not really that satisfying for us like that. And that's about it, as far as I can see, films, records, a bit of TV. I like doing TV. But I'd like to get some little business going on the side. Something completely away from this business that'd give me another interest. I haven't had much luck, though.

"People think we have worked out everything perfectly, been everywhere and done everything at exactly the right time so ourselves where we are. That's ridiculous. It's been luck most of the way. For instance, before we made our first film, we were offered some scripts and told that this was exactly the right time we should be making one. But none of us liked the films we were offered at first, so we didn't make one until we did.

"See, we were determined never to make a film where we'd be stuck in for five minutes, like so many artists are on these rubbishy film spectaculars with millions of names. They're awful.

"That sort of thing would either be damaging or a complete waste of time. Probably both."

Paul interrupted, saying, "That's it, George. You tell 'im. I can see the headline now – 'Beatle Hits Out at Film Phonies!'"

"Okay," George said, continuing. "From the beginning we've always met the right people. Before we got wise to the business, we heard and experienced so many sharks who were raking in the loot and paying the groups nothing. It's still going on, but the whole scene's become so big that more people are wise to it now. But this is where I can give an example of our luck. We were lucky to meet Brian Epstein.

"Then we got George Martin, lucky again, because there are so many bad A and R men. Same with the film. It made all the difference to work with Walter Shenson and Dick Lester. They have the perfect natures for us."

The subject changed to music and George discussed other guitar players.

"Jim Sullivan, he's a knockout. I wish he'd show me how he does it. I've never met him and I'd like to one day. Then, the guitarist in the Remo Four, Colin Manley, is good. He used to go to school with Paul and me, and he's always been great.

"No, not reading music's no handicap. It might be if I played with say, Joe Loss."

George mentioned that his first guitar cost two pounds ten shillings. "I was fourteen. That was in Slim Whitman days. Donegan was my great hero. Then came Buddy Holly and Eddie Cochran."

Did he have any advice for would-be rock and roll guitarists?

"Practice is the most important thing. I don't do it as much as I used to, mainly because we're on stage so much that when you come off you want to forget it a bit and relax. But I still have a good, solid practice occasionally."

"I'd like to make that point strongly about our luck. We've always dealt on the level with people. I'll tell you this much about the people who have given us phony deals: We'll never forget them."

November 12, 1964 – Bill Harry wrote for Mersey Beat... The Beatles' British tour had ended, and was a huge success. At the Empire in Liverpool, it was obvious that the Beatles were still at the top. Huge crowds had gathered outside the theatre. Harry was there in the afternoon for a special press conference. He chatted with the band briefly and George said to him, "You'll be coming in the dressing room later?"

Paul talked about their next film, pointing out, "No, John isn't writing the script."

National newsmen were asking how often they got home and Paul said, "I get home more often than people think, usually it's in the early hours of the morning."

Later, settling into the dressing room, Harry asked McCartney about song writing.

Paul said, "Mary Wells has told us she will be recording an LP of our numbers, and she asked which would be most suitable for her. I'm not sure of all the titles she'll be doing, but she said she'll record Do You Want To Know A Secret and Ask Me Why.

"John and I write numbers whenever we've got time to and our latest numbers are the ones we wrote for our next LP and single. We only finished writing for the LP the day before the recording session, and we finished our single two days before we recorded the number.

"For the film we'll probably write six numbers. We've written a lot of numbers during the last year. And John and I have written more numbers since we started recording than in the early days. But there are still one or two of our very early numbers which are worth recording. One of them, I'll Follow The Sun, is on the LP. But a lot of the other early stuff is not very good. But every now and then we remember one of the good ones we wrote in the early days, and a lot of numbers have been used, Love Me Do, World Without Love, Loved of the Loved and a number of others.

"I think there are about six hundred and forty versions of our numbers around the world including songs we've recorded ourselves on LPs, singles, and in the film, and numbers recorded by the Fourmost, Billy J. Kramer, Cilla, Tommy Quickly and other artists."

Old friends began to crowd into the dressing room, Ray McFall and Bob Wooler, John's cousins, Paul's brother and father, Bessie Braddock.

Later, Harry heard from John about his forthcoming book; and he arranged to help John find some of his early work. John went with Bill Harry later to visit with Stuart Sutcliffe's parents.

Sutcliffe had been a very close friend; John was overjoyed to be allowed to look at Sutcliffe's paintings at his parents' home. Mrs. Sutcliffe gave Lennon some early Beatles' news clippings, along with a book John had won in school and loaned to Stuart, a book about how to draw horses.

They talked about old times, old friends. And before John departed, Mrs. Sutcliffe asked him to select a painting. He examined the canvases, saying "*I remember him doing that one*," and "*That's the one he had in the John Moore's Exhibition.*" Finally, he selected a blue abstract that Stuart had done early on in Hamburg. "*This will take a place of pride in my living room*," he told Mrs. Sutcliffe.

November 14, 1964 – Keith Matthews interviewed Ringo Starr for *Record Mirror*. In spite of being continually misquoted and misinterpreted, the Beatles really did not worry about what was said about them…

"*Providing it's nice*," said Ringo.

Nor were they worried that all would end suddenly.

"*We've had one helluva time.*"

On stage, they played their hearts out, giving each song everything they could possibly give it at the time, no matter that few could hear the music.

"*It's a fact that it's definitely reached the stage where you cannot really hear us and to be quite frank, we find it a job to hear each other! But as we know each others' movements so well, we sort of cue in at the right time*," Ringo explained. "*Well, we hope we do, anyway…*"

Matthews asked Ringo about Elvis Presley and the success he was having with the re-release of his older songs, about how the Beatles had predicted the outcome of Presley's venture. He wondered if they were becoming prophets.

"*Not really*," Ringo said. "*It's just a case of plain and accurate, logical if you like, thinking. It stands to reason with all the beat floating around at present, and successfully, surely El is one of the best people around to sell it. After all, he did have something to do with starting it.*"

"*People are continually comparing us to him on actual sales of discs. But a lot of them seem to forget that we haven't been around as long as him to sell as many. But we haven't done too badly considering the length of time we have been in.*"

"*On our last visit to the States, it was sheer bad luck we couldn't meet him, though we had an invitation from him personally. But we managed to keep in touch with his manager, Colonel Parker, and Paul had a nice talk with him. He is well aware of us, just as we are of him, but that doesn't mean we can't be friends because so-and-so thinks we shouldn't.*"

"*Though we haven't met, we consider ourselves good friends, and appreciate what each of us is doing. El and his manager were very generous to us, showering us with presents and keepsakes. These include some very expensive silver guns and holsters which the four of us and our manager Brian received.*"

Matthews wondered about loyalty to the fans.

Ringo answered, "*We owe them everything, but when they go to our own houses or flats, it gets ridiculous. They should leave us alone once we get home. They are entitled to know a certain amount about you, that is essentially their due, because they made you. But some of them go to extremes by following you all over the place, bothering you and trying to pry into your private affairs.*"

He asked if the group had been inspired by anyone in particular.

"*Not exactly. We just listened to people like Elvis and Bo Diddley and a few other singers, were influenced by these greats but didn't copy them. Of course we wanted to do well, but didn't expect all this!*"

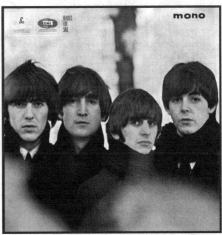

November 14, 1964 – *Disc Weekly*, Nigel Hunter spoke with Paul McCartney about the Beatles new album. *Beatles For Sale*, the group's fourth LP, was to be released on December 4th. There were fourteen tracks, eight of them new songs by John Lennon and Paul McCartney.

Said Paul, "*We got fourteen tracks into the record, which is about as much as you can fit in. We're pleased about this because we don't like to give short measure and we felt a bit bad about the* Hard Day's Night *album only having thirteen numbers.*"

Hunter asked if Paul and the others had any favourites among the new songs.

"*We like them all. If there was something we weren't keen on after we'd recorded it, we would scrap it and do something else.*"

The six songs that had not been written by Lennon and McCartney were all numbers they had played during their Cavern days.

"*We think there are some interesting sounds on the LP*," said Paul. McCartney then proceeded to review each song in order.

No Reply: "*John sings this one and I do the vocal harmony. We tried to give it different moods, starting off quietly with a sort of vaguely bossa* nova tempo, building up to a straight beat crescendo in the middle, and then tailing off quietly again."

I'm a Loser: "I reckon the best way to describe this one is a folk song gone pop. John and I both sing, but John does most of it. He also plays some nice harmonicas, too."

Baby's in Black: "I better explain what John and I meant by this title, hadn't I? The story is about a girl who's wearing black because the bloke she loves has gone away forever. The feller singing the song fancies her, too, but he's getting nowhere. We wrote it originally in a waltz style, but it finished as a mixture of waltz and beat."

Rock 'n' Roll Music: "This is an old Chuck Berry thing which we used to do at the Cavern, and we've tried for that old-type clipped down-in-the-valley echo on it. There's some piano going, too. George Martin, John and I on the keyboard all at once."

I'll Follow the Sun: "John and I wrote this one some while ago, but we changed the middle eight bars before we actually recorded it. John and I sing it, and Ringo played the top of a packing case instead of his drums this time. Just for a change, you know."

Mister Moonlight: "This is the second one we didn't write. It was originally the B side of Dr. Feelgood and one of the numbers we played at the Cavern. I play a bit of organ softly in the background, and John and I do the singing. Ringo got hold of a horn-shaped sort of conga drum for this with good effect."

Kansas City: "Another old Cavern thing of ours, which we've been asked to record. I mean, it's one we used to play there, not one we wrote. I do most of the singing this time and some piano playing, and John and George join in on the vocal bit."

Eight Days a Week: "I got the title for this once when I was being driven over to visit John. The chauffeur was talking away to me, saying how hard his boss worked the staff, so hard they seemed to do eight days a week. We've altered the plot a bit for the song, of course. The bloke loves the girl for eight days a week. John and I do the singing."

Words of Love: "This isn't ours. It's an old Buddy Holly specialty which we used to do again at the Cavern. There was a fabulous guitar bit on the Holly disc, sounding almost like bells. George took the same riff and double-tracked it, and sounds just as good."

Honey Don't: We didn't write this one, either. It's Ringo's solo piece, a simple and sweet piece which he handles as well vocally as he does his drum kit. Yes, he's singing! Again it's another Cavern item of ours, only John used to sing it in those days."

Every Little Thing: "John and I got this one written in Atlantic City during our last tour of the

States. John does the guitar riff for this one, and George is on acoustic. Ringo bashes some timpani drums for the big noise you'll hear."

I Don't Want to Spoil the Party: "We went after a real country and western flavour when we wrote this one. John and I do the singing in that style and George takes a real country solo on guitar."

What You're Doing: "We wrote this one in Atlantic City like Every Little Thing. It's not that Atlantic City is particularly inspiring, it's just that we happened to have a day off the tour there. Ringo does a nice bit of drumming decoration in the introduction and I double track on the vocal as well as playing some piano."

Everybody's Trying to Be My Baby: "This is another Cavern thing, an old Carl Perkins number. We've got that clipped tape echo effect for it again. It's a swinging end to the album, and George has a good solo again."

Hunter considered this album their best yet. After hearing Paul's description of each number, he enjoyed it even more. The album has much variety and contrast; and it had a nice range of tempos.

November 14, 1964 – *Melody Maker*, Ray Coleman interviewed Ringo Starr. On their way to a concert the previous week, the band stopped in Devon, walked into a confectionery and bought some sweets. That may sound sort of ordinary, but not for the Beatles.

Ringo said, "*It was like jumping school, doing something that wasn't on the schedule. Pleasing yourself with what you do at a certain moment, instead of being hemmed in, and timed to do everything at a given minute.*

"*The majority of people would go into a shop and buy sweets without thinking. To us, it's a very big thing. I'm telling you, it was a very funny feeling to be free again. We enjoyed those sweets more than many a big, lavish, expensive meal.*"

In a barren dressing room in Plymouth, Ringo was in a reflective mood. He talked about the size of his nose, his individual popularity, his name; he talked about his home and his car; he talked about how people thought the Beatles were millionaires. He was not truly "the quiet one." That was just an act. He was thoughtful and confident. And he considered himself lucky to have been chosen over Pete Best just when the Beatles were about to conquer the world.

He spoke freely and modestly, with humour and intelligence. Coleman wanted to know why he had taken so long to publicly express himself; why had he taken so long to reveal his true nature?

Ringo said, "*It's all simple, really. When we started people kept asking questions about the early days of the Beatles, how it started, what stuff we played. I wasn't in a position to talk about it. I hadn't been with them long enough. I knew the story pretty well because I'd been on the Liverpool scene with Rory Storm, but I didn't want to make any* mistakes in my early days when the press kept asking questions. I was the new boy. I felt a bit out of it. It was like joining a new class at school where everybody knew everybody except me.

"And then there was the nose. It put everybody off and they might have thought I was a freak or something. I thought about this a long time. I wondered why it was they couldn't be bothered with me, as some of those early press conferences. Okay, so I decided what to do. I was shy, more than I am now, so I thought, 'Right. They don't want to talk to me, and I don't particularly want to talk about Beatles history I know little about. So keep your mouth shut and you'll be all right. Play it nice and safe.' But now, I'll talk about anything you like."

How did he feel about being voted the most popular Beatle in America?

"It knocked me right out because I know for a fact I'm not the most popular Beatle in Britain. Paul is. Throughout the world, Paul's the most popular of us four. The eligible, handsome bachelor and all that. He's the one the birds want.

"But in the States I know I went over well. It knocked me out to see and hear the kids waving for me. I couldn't believe it, because usually a drummer is the odd one out. His face isn't at the front enough, you know. And I don't reckon any drummer should be at the front. It's bad for the group sound and bad for the overall look. It drowns guitars and basses. That's why I was so pleased about my American reception. I'd made it as a personality. Who wouldn't be flattered?"

How much did his nose contribute to the wealth amassed by the Beatles?

"A lot. People talked about it. They joked about it and laughed about it."

Did he have a complex about it?

"If I hadn't been the sort of bloke who can take it, I could have done. At first, I disliked all the talk. I hated it. People shouted rude things at some places. I remember once looking into a mirror and saying to meself, 'Ere, it's not that big, is it?'

"Now? I'm used to anything you'd say about it. You could say I've to terms with my own nose. It's the talking point when people discuss me. I have a laugh, and it goes, er, up one nostril and out the other."

Had he considered surgery?

"The only time I'd consider that is if I had a car smash, or something. I suppose I might say to the doctor, if they had to patch my face up, 'While you're about it, mate, take it off a bit, eh?' I've got no complex now. Can't hide it. I don't fancy walking around with my hand in front of my face, either. Anyway, I get more pleasure smelling things than you do. And another thing, Schnozzle Durante didn't do so badly out of his. So why worry?"

When asked about money, Ringo said, "You can never say it doesn't matter. I've never been broke. Even when I was on the dole I had a bit of money. We have no idea how much we're making and that's the truth."

November 21, 1964 – *Disc Weekly* **announced** that the Beatles had been booked for Ready Steady Go on November 27th, the date when their newest single, *I Feel Fine*, would be released. For the show, they were expected to play *I Feel Fine* and the B side, *She's A Woman*, and possibly another track from their new LP, *Beatles For Sale*. They would not actually be in RSG studios but would pre-record their appearance.

Advance orders for the new records had paused at 700,000 for the single, 600,000 for the album. The next surge in ordering was expected when the distributors and the wholesalers received their copies and placed fresh orders based on what they heard.

With the Beatles had now topped 980,000 copies in Britain alone and seemed destined to be the first album to ever sell a million copies in the UK.

Also, the Beatles were set to play the Light Programme's Top Gear show on November 26th.

November 28, 1964 – *Melody Maker* **announced** that advance orders for the Beatles' new single had reached 750,000.

Ray Coleman spoke with John and Paul about the big beat boom and if it was on the way out, was the group sound losing its popularity?

John said, "Clashing tours on the road are the only thing that could kill the concert scene."

Paul added, "Anyway, if groups are going to die, they will all die happy. However, I don't think so. I can't see where the beat situation is sliding."

"The trouble," John said, "has been the small promoters who were responsible for killing tours. The shows that are not making money now wouldn't have made money a year ago, either. It's a question of who's appearing most of the time."

Wryly, he added, "Ah, but what will be the next trend, chaps? I'll tell you, girls are coming back! I notice how everybody's saying that right now. It's very easy to say it now, especially with about eighty girls in the hit parade. Everybody in the business seems wise to the next trend, as soon as it starts."

November 28, 1964 – Mick Jagger said to *Melody Maker…* "*I like* I Feel Fine. *I like the backing more than anything, I reckon they must have spent eight days of the week working that out because it's very good. I don't like the lyrics all that much. But the backing is excellent. I dare say I'll buy it. There's nothing very striking about* She's A Woman, *but I like the way Paul sings it. The tune is not that much, but like all their records, you can play the other side as much as the A side and like it."*

December 5, 1964 – *Disc Weekly* **announced** that the Beatles had won a Silver Disc for sales in excess of 250,000 of *I Feel Fine*. The award, of course, was no surprise. *I Feel Fine* had been released the previous Friday with advance orders of more than 750,000. 50,000 more copies were sold over the weekend. This was the ninth Silver Disc awarded to the Beatles.

December 5, 1964 – *Melody Maker* said *I Feel Fine* had hit the top of the charts the moment it was released. Ringo had been in the *Melody Maker* offices for the final countdown as the record climbed the chart.

It was the day before Ringo was to go into London's University College Hospital for a tonsils operation. He said, "*I feel fine. In fact, I'm made up!*"

At *Melody Maker*, it was Operation Beatles Day as they rushed to gather reports from record shop managers throughout the country in order to quickly assess the impact of *I Feel Fine*.

The results were in. It was number one.

December 5, 1964 – *Melody Maker* printed a letter from a reader, Andrew Beeman of Lancing, Sussex. Beeman suggested the Beatles were famous more for their sex appeal than their music. He used the advance orders figures to support this theory. He said three-quarters of a million advance orders of an unheard song meant their appearance mattered more than their sound.

December 12, 1964 – *Disc Weekly* said Ringo Starr was due to be discharged from University College Hospital that morning after having his tonsils out. Throughout the week, NEMS had been bombarded with telegrams, letters, get well cards and telephone calls from people concerned with Ringo's health.

Ringo was expected to convalesce at his flat in London until rehearsals began for The Beatles Christmas Show.

I Feel Fine had sold 65,000 copies on Monday of that week and had just passed the 900,000 mark in total sales in Britain alone, assuring the band of yet another million-seller.

Beatles For Sale had sold 715,000 copies so far.

December 12, 1964 – *Disc Weekly* gathered an assortment of personalities together to get humorous stories about the Beatles on their way to the top.

Brian Epstein said, "*When John was guest of honour at a Foyle's lunch to mark the success of his book, he made no speech. In answer to the toast, he stood, held the microphone, and said, 'Thank you all very much. You've got a lucky face.'*

"*Here John was behaving like a Beatle. He wasn't prepared to do something which was not only unnatural to him, but also something he might have done badly. He was not going to fail.*

"*After the luncheon he commented, 'Give me another fifteen years, I might make a speech. Not yet.'*

"*I rely on John's instinct and, in fact, on the instinct of all the Beatles, not only on music, but in matters of taste and style and general behaviour.*"

Said George Martin, "*There are so many endearing moments connected with the Beatles. But one I remember best was when the Beatles were staying at the King George Cinq Hotel in Paris. I was flying over to record them there, but for the German market. They were going to sing* I Want To Hold Your Hand *and* She Loves You *in German. But it transpired that they did not like the German lyrics. So they failed to turn up at the recording studio on the outskirts of Paris. And I had the German recording man there with me.*

"*When they explained over the phone that they would not be turning up for the session, I was absolutely furious. I wasn't going to argue over the phone so I said, 'I'll see you all later at the hotel.'*

"*When I arrived, I stormed in, with the German recording man. And there were the Beatles, all seated around a long table with Jane Asher pouring out tea. With her long hair, it looked just like The Mad Hatter's Tea Party from Alice in Wonderland. The boys all disappeared in a flash, and took refuge behind sofas and chairs, putting cushions over their heads. Finally, they began to emerge, one by one.*

"'*I think you owe this gentleman an apology,*' *I said. Sheepishly, they said, 'Gee, we're sorry, George. Really we are.'*

"*After that, I just couldn't be angry with them. And I am happy to say they agreed to make the recordings after all.*"

Dick James, song publisher said, "*Paul McCartney was going to lunch with me and George Martin and some other people were due to join our table later. Altogether, it would be a party of five. Paul and I got to the restaurant early, and sat down for an aperitif when the waiter came up and asked if we would like to order. So I said, 'We have some other joining us so I think we had better soft pedal for a while.'*

"*At which point, Paul looked up, beckoned to the waiter and said, 'Can we have five soft pedals, please?'*

"*That's absolutely typical of the Beatles' humour. It's just one instance that you can multiply by four. So many times one has a diabolical laugh over the dozens of funny things all of them say. But I'm biased. I love 'em.*"

Walter Shenson, film producer said, "*The funniest incident I remember was in* A Hard Day's Night *when John did that bath scene.*

"*The original idea was to put the comedy emphasis on George, where he squirts the shaving cream on the mirror. But at the last minute, I thought we should include John in the scene, and when he came in wearing three hats and clutching a handful of toy boats, everybody broke up.*

"*And it was absolutely hysterical the way he ad-libbed the part of the German U-boat commander while in that bath. It was entirely unrehearsed, and typified John's great sense of humour.*"

"We were fortunate that director Dick Lester captured the scene so beautifully. Of course, there are always lots of laughs when the Beatles are around, but I always get hilarious when I recall this particular incident."

Bess Coleman, former New York representative of Brian Epstein explained, "During their last American trip, on the long flight from Montreal to Key West, Florida, Ringo started a pillow fight. Within seconds everyone in the party was hurling seat cushions at each other. Outside, a hurricane was raging!

"Suddenly, over the intercom a voice commanded, 'Sit down everybody. You're all behaving like idiots. You ought to know better. This aircraft's in danger of crashing. Return to your seats and fasten your safety belts please.'

"We all scampered to our seats and did as we were told when Paul appeared from the flight deck, grinning all over his face. It had been him using the intercom."

Brian Matthew said, "We were recording the Beatles part of Thank Your Lucky Stars at Teddington a week or two ago. We were using stand-ins for them at the rehearsals and run-throughs. Then when everything was ready for the tele-recording, we could only find George. John, Paul and Ringo had vanished and George didn't know where. Everybody went potty trying to find them. The whole place was in an uproar searching for them. Then somebody found out that they'd gone off with one of the carpenters.

"At that moment, they came back and seemed bewildered by the fuss and bother over them. 'We've just been playing billiards,' they said with such wide-eyed innocence that everybody burst out laughing. Equally funny was George's reply when we told him he'd have to go on by himself if the others didn't show up in time. He looked horrified and said, 'I'll retire first.'"

Alan Freeman added, "I was visiting New York at the same time as the boys, and I took some private letters addressed to George with me, intending to pass them on in person when I met up with him.

"There's a famous American columnist called Alec Freeman, and he was in New York at that time. When I rang George's hotel, getting through at the third attempt, the operator asked who was calling him and I said, 'Alan Freeman of the BBC.'

"'Oh yeah,' she exclaimed, and pulled the plug out of the board.

"You see, a whole lot of Americans had been ringing the hotel, and using English accents to try and get through to the boys. I ended up spending five days trying to contact George, and I never made it."

Dick Lester, director said, "It was Ringo who related one of those incidents that pinpoint the Beatles' marvelous sense of humour. It happened early last year, when the Beatles were entertained at dinner at Oxford, where they were supposed to meet Mr. Harold Macmillan. Ringo said, 'All those teachers were there, what do you call them? When we were at school we called them warders!' He meant the Oxford Dons. And you can imagine the reaction of this distinguished company when, during the dinner, John and Paul kept asking for their favourite dish, jam butties."

December 19, 1964 – *Disc Weekly,* Anne Sims reported that it took about five minutes from a quiet Surrey town to get to George Harrison's twenty-thousand pound house, but without directions from Harrison you would never find it.

The house was on a beautiful property five miles from the home of John and Cynthia Lennon, hidden from the world by a tall wall and trees. Perfect privacy for a Beatle. George had invited Sims to spend an evening.

He rang her up and asked, "Have you got a car? You'll need one!"

She did; they arranged to meet in the parking lot of a nearby hotel.

Pulling into the lot in his E-type Jaguar, Harrison said, "Right. Follow me, and don't lose me or you've had it. No hanging around either, or there'll be crowds."

Stopped at a red light, George was recognised. Deciding not to encourage them, he ignored the people who were pointing and staring, and led Sims off through a series of country lanes. Three minutes later, they arrived at his home.

"We're here," George said. "Welcome to the Harrison pad. You'll never find it again."

They went in through the kitchen of a well-appointed house. In the lounge, George asked, "Would you like a meal, or coffee or biscuits or just a drink? No, first sit yourself over there." He pointed to a large black leather settee. "I've just bought it and it needs breaking in."

He returned from the kitchen with a pot of coffee, biscuits, and a bottle of red wine. Sims noticed a sunset picture on the wall and George said, "The answer is that I took it in Tahiti on holiday. It's a huge blow-up from a tiny snapshot. Isn't it fantastic how they kept the detail in, in such a big blow-up? What I like about it is that it isn't one of those typically corny sunset pictures. And believe it or not, I took it on a one-second exposure."

He put his own LP of The Beatles Live at the Hollywood Bowl on his stereo as Sims asked him about the bungalow.

"I'll show you around very soon. I'm lucky, really, because this bungalow was occupied by somebody before me, so all I had to do was change it to my taste, whereas poor old John with his place, well, he had to start right from scratch. They're still building parts of it. He had builders there when he moved in and as far as I know, he's still got them.

"You see all those lights, though? They're going. I can't stand them and I'm having them taken out. I'm also having hi-fi equipment built in. Funny how your ideas change once you're in a place."

He pointed at the twenty-one-inch TV set and said, *"It's too big. I'm getting a smaller one built into a cupboard along the wall."* And he mentioned that he was not fond of the studio couch on which he was sitting. *"I like that black leather one you're on. That's staying."*

The walls were white and the furniture, Scandinavian. There was a fireplace, and flowers, mainly white chrysanthemums, were in abundance.

George said, *"I might have that fireplace knocked down. It's useless."* He glanced around the room, lit a smoke, and continued, *"And those curtains, too. Out. I want much more modern things than that."*

The curtains were old-fashioned, brown brocade, unsuitable for the room.

"Come on," George said after playing a few records, talking about the Beatles and how a hospitalised Ringo was feeling. *"I'll show you the rest of the place."*

She was impressed by the size of his bedroom, and by how tidy everything was.

"It's really like a good hotel suite, this part, isn't it? I like comfort, generally I go for modern things all the time."

He continued, *"I have a couple of spare bedrooms, and another rocking chair in the other one. I like 'em a lot. In one of the built-in wardrobes, in the other one, there's my own collection of tape recordings and reels of film from shots we're always taking. You know, we're all camera happy."*

Next, Harrison showed her into a room which featured a large portrait of himself. He said, *"I want to make this a sort of playroom. I'm gonna have it decorated and it will be good to have my projector out here all the time for when people come round. I also keep a lot of things like gold and Silver Discs here, out of the way and safe."*

Back in the kitchen, she asked him if he cooked much.

"No, I have a man in to do things like that. I'm too lazy and I haven't the time to cook. When I do eat here, it's roast lamb or pork. Anything plain, and it can be stored for months in the deep-freeze."

They returned to lounge to play more records, George complaining about the noise from airplanes.

December 19, 1964 – *Melody Maker* showed *I Feel Fine* at number one on the Top Fifty chart, and also at number one in the charts in the States while *Beatles For Sale* was the number one album.

Ray Coleman said not all pop stars would be having a good Christmas. The Prophets of Doom were saying the groups were dying out, their heyday was over. He said the Beatles had exploded on to a fading, spiritless music scene two years previously

and had gone on to conquer the world. But that was the Beatles. The British Prime Minister at the time had called them his secret weapon; and Royalty welcomed them. Old ladies fainted at the sight of them, even as far away as Australia. They had broken records for success everywhere.

The day their first serious hit, *Please Please Me*, made it to number one, rockers saw a bright horizon. What was overlooked was the personalities in the group, four talents that went well beyond making records. The Beatles were now established film stars, song writers of incredible originality, and symbols for a generation. They were probably millionaires, too.

People could talk about the end of beat music.

But the Beatles were looking forward to 1965 with the same optimism they had had when they hit the big city to record *Love Me Do*.

Of course, there was less for them to achieve in 1965. America had been conquered, fans had screamed worldwide, and they had ravished the pop charts throughout the world. Even as film stars, they were the talk of the town.

What was left?

Would there be any satisfaction in simply repeating their former success?

John Lennon said, *"Yes. We still get a terrific sort of pride out of reaching number one first go with anything. When I Feel Fine got there first go, we were glad, you know. But the next year will be hard, because it's obvious for people to expect us to top everything we've ever done, and that's ridiculous.*

"The way I see it, the only way we can top everything we've done before is by either making better films, or by all dying!"

What was the most memorable moment in 1964?

Said John, *"I suppose the film was the main thing."*

Why? Because it showed that the Beatles could more do than sing pop songs?

"I know what you mean, and in a way, yes. But we don't ever want to be established by other people as people who aren't pop stars any longer. We started as the Beatles, pop stars, and we want to stay that way.

"We don't want to be Beatles at ninety and everybody saying we're great film stars. That's not the plan. We want to be out of it all at ninety. The only way I imagine we can keep up the pace next year is by making a film better than A Hard Day's Night*."*

The new film was due to start shooting in February. John said, *"We're all resigned to something happening record-wise. I don't honestly see how the hell we can keep on getting number ones every time at the first go, though it would be great if we could, and we'll always try.*

"With I Feel Fine we were ready to get to number five at first go, and I suppose if we'd done that we'd have been written off. Nobody would have remembered that the Beatles had had six numbers

ones on the trot before I Feel Fine. *We've got to accept that sort of thing. Yeah, when we start slipping with records, it will be a hard slide, I suppose.*

"*But there's nothing you can do about that. If our next record doesn't get to number one, there'll be plenty of rough rides. It's bound to happen eventually, so the big thing for us I think is the film. We've got a long way to go in that business and we're all keen on doing well.*"

Paul agreed that *A Hard Day's Night* was their most important landmark in 1964.

Coleman asked John if he and Paul had considered writing a musical.

John replied, "*Well, if we find ourselves with a lot of time, we'd like to have a go at writing something like that, yeah. As a matter of fact, a couple of people have offered to work on a sort of musical show with us, but you can say that if we did a musical, we'd do it alone.*

"*We don't think it would work out for us to work with anybody else on that sort of thing.*"

Would they tour the States again?

"*We'd never go for as long as five weeks again. That was just bloody hell, what with all the rubbish that went on over there. But if Brian* [Epstein] *said we ought to go for a couple of weeks, we'd go okay. It's up to him.*"

When Ringo was asked for his views regarding 1964, he said, "*There's been so much, such a lot. I wouldn't know where to start. Coming in at number one with* I Feel Fine *was great because, well, we weren't sure we'd do it. Then the Palladium TV was important. But to me, going down so big in the States was probably the biggest thing to happen in the last year.*

"*That's a very big country, and for a group to go over there and win was ridiculous. That's my big sort of memory of 1964, and if we do half as well in the next year, we'll be doing okay.*"

Coleman suggested there would likely be three new singles from the group in 1965. And the new film. 1965 would be as challenging as 1964 had been. And new groups would come along to battle for the Beatles' popularity. But they would continue to be incredibly successful, he knew that. They had

survived John's marriage and the publicised affairs of the other three; survived the romance stories; survived the overexposure of film and TV and the print media, the kind of exposure that would have destroyed other performers. The Beatles were still there, still at the top, because genuine talent would always win out.

December 26, 1964 – *Disc Weekly*, **Mike Martin wrote** about the adventures of the Beatles during Christmas shopping. Clearly, they could not wander around London, dashing in and out of shops. George was in the Bahamas on holiday. Ringo explained how he and John and Paul solved the shopping problem.

He said, "*We decided the only way we could get down to buying the presents was to sort of hire a store for a couple of hours.*"

They arranged it with a Knightsbridge department store, Woollands, not far from Ringo's flat.

"*We got to the store at six thirty in the evening, and there were five assistants, three girls and two men, to serve just John, Paul and me while the store was closed.*"

What did you buy?

"*Not telling you! Can't have things like that in the papers, it would spoil the surprise for my relatives. I prefer getting my relations and pals a few little things instead of one big thing. It's more fun and more of a surprise that way.*"

Did he get anything for himself?

"*No, I can't be bothered.*"

Would the Beatles exchange gifts?

"*I haven't bought them anything yet, and I'm not really thinking about it, to tell you the truth. I suppose we might get each other some kind of zany present, something funny, that's for sure.*"

No money passed hands in the store. The bills were sent to the band's London office. And no one had to carry the parcels through the streets.

"*They're delivering them,*" Ringo said. "*It was a great way of doing the shopping, and good fun. We were there from six thirty until eight thirty. First time I'd shopped in a closed shop, though!*"

— Chapter Five: 1965 —

January 2, 1965 – *Disc Weekly*, **Mike Martin wrote** about the benefits and penalties of being a Beatle. He spoke with Ringo Starr in Starr's Knightsbridge flat. Martin wondered how he dealt with the ordinary trappings of life: laundry, groceries, cleaning windows, getting fish and chips…

Ringo said, *"Well, I'm lucky. The porter's wife in this block of flats is really nice and she goes to no end of trouble for me. I've only got to say to her that I need some food and she'll go round the corner and do the shopping. Don't even tell her what I need. She knows by now that if I cook myself, and that's not too often, all I can manage is to fix some corn flakes, egg and bacon and frozen fish fingers and instant chips.*

"I hate cooking, and what's worse, I just can't stand washing the dishes. I'm awful like that.

"What I do is this: I use up all the dishes in the flat, then go downstairs and knock for the porter's wife and she comes up and washes the whole lot of them for me. Then I'm okay for another week. She also makes the bed for me."

According to Martin, Ringo was very organised when it came to laundry and the milk. The porter dealt with the laundry; and Ringo paid for the milk delivery himself, two bottles a day.

Ringo said, *"I often say to the porter, 'Would you mind asking your wife to get me some biscuits and easy things to cook?' And she goes and gets it."*

He had first known how helpful she would be when he and George first rented the flat – George had since moved out to his house in Surrey.

Ringo explained, *"We got here at night and one of the nicest things that happened was that she came up and said did we want anything? Were we short of anything? We said we'd like a little bit of food because we hadn't got any in yet. She went back down and reappeared soon afterwards with two plates of eggs and chips. That was a lovely welcome for two blokes who were staring in their new flat on the first night."*

She also baked bread and tidied up the flat from time to time; a regular cleaner came into for the actual cleaning. The flat was large, with eight rooms.

"Let's see," said Ringo. *"Three bedrooms, two bathrooms, a kitchen, a lounge which is also the living room, and a dressing room. Not that I use the dressing room, I get dressed in the bedroom like any normal bloke. Use the dressing room for my guns and targets."*

Alone in the flat, Ringo either listened to music, watched TV or fired off his guns. He loved guns and displayed his collection and his bullet-holed targets.

"I've got two BB guns and they fire ball-bearings, but I want to get a twenty-two rifle now. I've got these targets and they're okay because I stack them on top of high boxes when I shoot. But I'm getting a six-foot high target specially made, then I'll really be able to practise shooting properly."

He also liked to spend his time making models, the plastic ship kind. He said, *"This sort of thing, as well as the odd game of cards, roulette, and also the fact that Brian [Epstein] lives underneath me in the same block, means I'm never bored. Brian sometimes pops up out of the blue."*

That was the picture of Ringo – Domestic Beatle. There was only one problem: he had to move. Until the fans discovered where he lived, it was quiet and private. Now, they gathered outside. The other tenants had signed a petition to force Ringo to move. He was house hunting.

While explaining that he was not anti-fan, he said, *"I wish some of them would realise that we must have some peace sometime, especially in the place we live. It's simply because of the behaviour of some of them that I've got to leave this place, which I like."*

He was in the process of packing. The flat had been furnished when he rented it but he had gathered a few things, the TV, the radio, et cetera. He said he would miss the porter's wife.

"And I'll always miss going to the pub for a drink, or going for a walk round town."

January 2, 1965 – *Melody Maker* **ran a Beatles quiz,** twenty questions with the answers inverted in the lower left corner of the page.
The Questions:

1. Name the Beatles singles that topped the Pop 50 in 1964.
2. *Please Please Me* was the first Beatles record to top the chart – when was that?
3. Name the Beatles EP that was the first ever to enter the Top 10 at the same time as a single.
4. Name the year in which each Beatle was born.
5. While they were in Germany, the Beatles played several times at a famous club. What was the club and when did they first play there?
6. Polydor, in February, released an early instrumental by the group. Name the title, the song writer, and the drummer.
7. What was Ringo's real name and John Lennon's middle name?
8. Lennon and McCartney music had been used for a ballet. Name the ballet.
9. Who wrote the script for *A Hard Day's Night*?
10. How many LPs has the band made for Parlophone and what are the titles?
11. Which Beatle went to school with Billy Fury; which one led a band called the Rebels; and which one was an art student?
12. Name the drummer who filled in for Ringo while he was ill last summer.

13. Who sang the lead on *I Feel Fine*?
14. What song were the Beatles considering for release before they launched *I Feel Fine*?
15. What was the name of the singer for whom the Beatles once provided backing?
16. Name the band's recording manager. What instrument does he play on some of the records?
17. On which single did George Harrison first play the 12-string guitar?
18. What was the Beatles' first record to hit the pop charts?
19. Which one drives which car: an E-type Jaguar; a Rolls Royce; an Aston Martin; and a Facel-Vega?
20. Who were the five original Beatles?

The Answers:
1. *I Want to Hold Your Hand; Can't Buy Me Love; A Hard Day's Night;* and *I Feel Fine.*
2. February 1963.
3. *Twist and Shout.*
4. George Harrison 1943; John Lennon 1940; Paul McCartney 1942; Ringo Starr 1940.
5. Star Club, Hamburg – 1960.
6. *Cry for a Shadow* by George Harrison and John Lennon, Pete Best on drums.
7. Richard Starkey – Winston.
8. Mods and Rockers.
9. Alun Owen.
10. Four: *Please Please Me; With the Beatles; A Hard Day's Night;* and *Beatles For Sale.*
11. Ringo Starr; George Harrison; John Lennon.
12. Jimmy Nichol.
13. John Lennon.
14. *I'm a Loser.*
15. Tony Sheridan.
16. George Martin – piano.
17. *You Can't Do That.*
18. *Love Me Do.*
19. George Harrison; John Lennon; Paul McCartney; Ringo Starr.
20. George Harrison; John Lennon; Paul McCartney; Stuart Sutcliffe; Pete Best.

January 9, 1965 – Mike Ledgerwood wrote for *Disc Weekly...* They were backstage at the Hammersmith Odeon, moments before taking the stage for their Christmas show, jotting down telephone numbers and addresses for assorted New Year's parties.

Lennon, sitting beside Cynthia, asked, *"What's that number again? What's this party going to be like? Who's going to be there that we haven't met already?"*

All but Ringo decided to attend the party at EMI's Norman Newell's West End flat.

"What do we have to wear? We don't need a flower in our button-hole or anything like that, do we?" asked John.

"Three minutes to go!" shouted someone.

Ringo butted his smoke and struggled into a gigantic wool sweater that had been designed to fit the entire band, a gift from a Swedish fan. They all wore it on stage, did a brief appearance, and returned to the dressing room a few minutes later, smoking, sipping cokes and lemonade, preparing for the next sketch.

Pulling on a large pair of Eskimo boots, Ringo started humming Cilla Black's new release, *You've Lost That Lovin' Feelin'.* Before long, the other three joined in, all of them putting on Eskimo boots, Paul donning an Arctic parka and explaining he had made it to Liverpool in three hours in his Aston Martin. *"Did a hundred and forty miles an hour at times up the M1!"*

Ledgerwood asked Cynthia Lennon how they had spent Christmas and she replied, *"Oh, quietly. At home. It was just a nice family Christmas."*

What had she bought for John?

"Nothing spectacular. More novelty things than anything."

Jimmy Savile showed up, clad grotesquely as an abominable snowman.

Asked George, *"Are those your own teeth?"*

As they headed for the stage to do the Eskimo sketch, George said to Ledgerwood, *"Before you say anything, we think it's dreadfully unfunny, but there you are!"*

Ledgerwood watched from the wings. He thought their antics were hysterically funny.

January 9, 1965 – Mike Ledgerwood again for *Disc Weekly...* John Lennon wanted to set the record straight regarding his appearance on the BBC-2 show Not Only...But Also. He was to read some his poems from *John Lennon in His Own Write.*

"I'd like to stress that I was invited," John said. *"All the papers have said that I asked to be allowed to appear. That's entirely untrue. They asked me. There wasn't much to it. I just read some of my poems, assisted by Dudley Moore and Norman Rossington.*

"The readings are really just dramatised versions of my poems. One I read on my own and the others are read in conjunction with Dudley and Norman, each of us speaking a different part."

With regards to any plans he might have to do other television programs, John said, *"I might do. Originally, I only agreed to do this one because I thought it would be a good plug for my book, at the time. But they didn't actually record it until the end of November. Of course, not many people will see the showing anyway. Only those who have BBC-2."*

January 16, 1965 – Laurie Henshaw wrote for *Disc Weekly...* The Beatles' new movie was taking them on the road, to the Bahamas, Austria, and around England, being chased by villains, and the band outwitting them all along the way. Fun and thrills and pretty girls, the long-awaited successor to *A Hard Day's Night* was planned for release in the fall.

Henshaw conducted an exclusive interview with producer Walter Shenson. The director and the scriptwriter were ready to go. Shooting was to begin in five weeks, on February 22nd, in the Caribbean.

Said Shenson, *"The Beatles will be there for two or three weeks, and then fly to the Continent for snow sequences, probably filmed in Austria. We shall be there about a week, and then return to England for six weeks' studio work. Altogether, shooting should take around ten weeks.*

"The film will have a very spectacular look about it. And we aim to make it even more exciting visually than A Hard Day's Night. *And I would just add that this film has been mentioned in* Variety, *the American show business paper, as a possible contender for six Academy Award nominations.*

"They are for the Best Black and White Photography, in two categories: the Best Black and White Art Direction; Best Picture; Best Direction; and Best Song written specially for a film – the title song.

"This is a tremendous tribute to director Dick Lester, the crew, the Beatles, and myself. Now, we have a real challenge to meet with this new one. I have already had talks with the Beatles on three separate occasions. One meeting was in my office with John and Paul, who sat on that settee where you are sitting right now. Unfortunately, Ringo was in hospital for his tonsils operation at the time. And George had just flown to the Bahamas on holiday.

"But I know John and Paul filled them in later on the broad outlines we had discussed over a cup of coffee. Dick Lester, who directed A Hard Day's Night, *is very excited about the prospect of filming in the tropics and in the Alps. The colour of the Bahamas and the snow in the Alps will provide a wonderful background for the Beatles and the action of the film.*

"And there will be a good deal of action in this one. For one thing, it will be much more 'plotty.' That's why we have signed Marc Behm, an American who lives in Paris, to write the script. Marc has already drafted an outline script, and one of the things we discussed with John and Paul was how the story line should be developed, and how we can translate the comedy into the special Beatles brand of humour.

"We are in no way attempting to do another Hard Day's Night, *but the Beatles will again play themselves. And there will be even more opportunities for them to show their natural acting talent as they get unwittingly involved in the intrigue and find themselves pressurised by big things from the mysterious East.*

"Basically, the film is a chase with the Beatles running away from trouble. But it always turns up, in the Bahamas, on the Continent and in Britain. And one of John, George and Paul's major problems will be to protect Ringo from the crooks.

"Songs? Most important, of course. Immediately after their Christmas Show at Hammersmith, the boys will take a holiday. But John and Paul will be working even then, on the six new songs we plan for the film. There may even be a couple more. Then, during the week of February 15th, they will record the new songs. This may or may not include the title song, but a single from the film will almost certainly be issued around Easter, with the album being released in the autumn, when the film is due for release.

"The songs will be worked into the film to complement the story line and the action. The Beatles will not play them on a stage, or in a television studio, before screaming fans. We have already captured the fan fever in A Hard Day's Night, *which was intended to be a kind of documentary of a day in the life of the Beatles.*

"The locations we are choosing are colourful, and there will be lots of picturesque scenes and pretty girls. But I can assure the fans that, again, no love interest will be allowed to intrude!

"The title of the film? That's always a big problem. John is writing a new book, and maybe with his permission, we could use something from that, if it turned out to fit the situation. But Ringo came up with such a perfect one last time, it became a catchword of 1964; we may again rely on the Beatles' spontaneity to do the trick."

January 16, 1965 – *Melody Maker,* **Ray Coleman talked** with Brian Epstein. He mentioned that Epstein had been mobbed by autograph hunters after a Beatles concert in Bradford the previous October, an incident that established him as a star, not just one of the most successful show biz managers in the world. The Beatles had topped the world for two years; and Epstein's other acts were also successful, Cilla Black, Gerry and the Pacemakers, Billy J. Kramer, and others.

Coleman wondered if Epstein thought the beat music boom was fading.

Brian Epstein said, *"The theory that beat music is dead is nonsense. How can anyone say it is dead when you consider the current number one record? But if you are implying that vocal-instrumental four-man groups are not having such success as, say, this time last year, well it is obvious that there are not going to be so many of these around, successfully. Some will stay, and do well, and others will filter out. The ones that are going to filter out are the ones inspired by the Beatles. By that, I mean Beatles copyists. And that is not meant nastily. It is flattering to the Beatles that they have had copyists. But remember a solo artist is not necessarily non-beat. Georgie Fame is recognised as a soloist, but he performs beat. So does Cliff Bennett."*

Have the Beatles peaked?

"No. They are unique because they will continue to make brilliant records, one hopes. And I don't think their style will ever go out because they have a

personal style and sound that is recognised and which will be acceptable for as long as they want to make records."

How long can they keep up this tremendous pace?

"I think they will maintain strong teenage appeal for two or three years. After that, maybe they will become really established film stars. They have the talent to make brilliant film stars. They are unique in this respect: they are capable of making films, they have a long way to go in films, and I see their future in films being quite remarkable, something very few people expected."

Are they worried about their futures?

"I think they would only get restless if their work, and interest in their work, was not allowed to develop properly. They're as much pleasure-loving as anyone else. At the same time, like anybody else, they have no desire to give up and do nothing simply because they have made some money. They want to carry on creating for a long, long time."

Do you discuss their long-term future with them?

"Of course. They are worried no more and no less than anyone else. I hope they never get to the state where they think they are slipping. The last month or so has been marvelous for them, topping the single and LP charts in Britain and America. Can you call that slipping? As I said, the Beatles are sensible people and I am convinced of their great future in films."

January 23, 1965 – Disc Weekly reported that the Beatles would be doing a short tour of the States during the summer. Brian Epstein was in the U.S. making arrangements.

It would be the group's third trip to America, their second tour. It was planned that this tour would be shorter than the last one.

January 23, 1965 – Disc Weekly reported... the new film was the hot topic for conversation. The writer spoke with the Beatles just before they left for individual holidays. Paul insisted, for the snow scenes in Austria, he would need a bright red ski suit. *"If I could have that red ski suit, I wouldn't even ask for a big part in the film, mind, I don't want to look conspicuous though."*

George said he would like an Eskimo outfit similar to the one he wore for the Christmas Show at Hammersmith. John, however, had little interest in the film: he was studying the proofs for the cover of his latest book *A Spaniard in the Works*, due to be published by Jonathan Cape for a spring release. The cover showed him dressed as a Spaniard. And Ringo was sitting alone in a corner, trying to decide if he should get a new ring for the film.

February 20, 1965 – Disc Weekly suggested that the Beatles' new film would be called *Beatles Two*. The film was due to begin shooting in six days. The crew, plus the Beatles, were flying to the Bahamas the

following Monday. After a day of rest, the first footage would be shot on the Wednesday.

They were to spend sixteen days in the islands, staying at a cottage near Cable Beach, Nassau, then returning to England to shoot a number of local sequences before flying to Austria on March 13th.

Beatles Two was only the working title for the movie; producer Walter Shenson was hoping Ringo would come up with a good title, as he had with *A Hard Day's Night*.

Marc Behm, author of the original story *Charade*, had delivered the script. The synopsis suggested that the Beatles would have another runaway hit. The film was scheduled to be released in July.

February 20, 1965 – Disc Weekly asked twenty-five questions of a newly married Beatle... Ringo, that is.

1. Where would he live?
   I don't mind, as long as it's with Maureen. We went back to my place in London after the honeymoon.
2. How long had he known Maureen?
   It was about two and half years.
3. Where did they meet?
   At the Cavern in Liverpool.
4. When did he ask her to marry him?
   I proposed about three weeks ago, in the Ad Lib Club.
5. Was it tough to keep the marriage a secret?
   We tried to keep it a bit secret. Weddings aren't stage shows, and we tried to keep the honeymoon secret, too.
6. Will Maureen still work?
   She'll carry on as usual.
7. Children?
   Well, we don't know, do we? Maureen wants some. I want to or three, but Maureen hasn't made her mind up.
8. What did her parents think?
   I asked her dad for permission to marry her and he agreed, so I suppose he must like me.
9. Who was your best man?
   My manager, Brian Epstein.
10. Was there a lengthy official engagement?
    No, but we'd been going steady for three months.
11. Did you get her an engagement ring?
    No, we didn't have time, but I gave her a wide gold wedding ring with a criss-cross design.
12. Did she get you one?
    My ring is a plain band of gold. It was my grandfather's. He gave it to me three years ago, before he died. I always reckoned I'd wear it when I got married.
13. Can Maureen cook?
    No, she can't. I can cook corn flakes!
14. Does she want you to get your hair cut shorter?
    I haven't been told to get my hair cut, yet. Maureen wouldn't cut it for me, anyway!

15. Did you get any wedding presents from the other Beatles?
    We haven't had any yet. I know the others have got some, but they couldn't give them to us in time.
16. What presents did you get?
    Brian Epstein gave us a dinner service. He brought a plate down to Hove to see if we liked the pattern.
17. Why did you pick that Register Office?
    Caxton Hall just happened to be the Register Office for the area where I lived.
18. Will Maureen ever go on the road with you and the band?
    I doubt it. She says she wants to keep out of the limelight. She doesn't like publicity.
19. Did the rest of the group know you were getting married?
    George and John didn't know until the Wednesday afternoon. Brian Epstein just told them: 'Ringo's getting married tomorrow. Come along if you want to – if it's not too early for you.' Paul was away on holiday. He couldn't be reached.
20. Are you going on a honeymoon?
    Well, we hoped we'd be alone in Hove! I went back to work this week. I reckon we'll have to go to Vietnam to be alone!
21. Are you going to live in the South or will you go back up North?
    We don't mind.
22. Do you worry that your marriage might have a bad effect on your fans?
    I don't think it will hurt at all. After all, John's married, isn't he?
23. Is her real name Maureen?
    No, it's really Mary, but she's always been known as Maureen.
24. Who were the official witnesses at the ceremony?
    John and George.
25. Why did you have it so early in the morning?
    We had to. It was the only way to make sure that the fans didn't spot us.

February 20, 1965 – Ray Coleman wrote for Melody Maker, wondering how Ringo's marriage would affect the group. A number of show business folk, on hearing the news, declared, *"That's the beginning of the end for the Beatles."*

It was a popular belief, that marriage would ruin pop stars.

Coleman asked what difference Ringo's marriage would make.

John Lennon said, *"I don't think Ringo's marriage will affect Beatles popularity, really. But there might be a shuffling of fans from one Beatle to another, at least, that's what happened when news that I was married was 'revealed,' as they said.*

Would fans desert them?

"You're bound to lose a few, the ones who believe that one day they might marry you. But I think most of them are quite sensible."

Did John consider fan reaction when he first heard the news that Ringo and Maureen had been married?

"No, no. First thing I thought was, what a sneaky thing to do, before I'm back from holiday. But still, it was good. He's joined the club."

Were there any changes in the sort of fan mail John received when news of his marriage was announced?

"Yeah, they all say they love your wife and son as well as you. Fan mail does change a bit, for a start, but now they all seem to carry on as if I'm not married."

George Harrison talked about the wedding and it's possible effects.

"I stayed at John's the night before. During the night we were going over songs for the new film and we started writing lyrics. Well, it was four thirty in the morning when we got to bed, and we had to be up at six thirty; what a fantastic time.

"I don't honestly know what to think about what the fans will say. Naturally, from Ringo's point of view and from our reactions, it's great. I mean, I like the idea of him being married because Maureen's a nice girl and he's a good bloke.

"I realise the news of Ringo's marriage must be shattering for the pop fans around the world. You know, in America, we've all been married off about twenty times in various magazines, so I suppose when this news gets over there they'll go pretty mad. At least they'll all know it's definite now!

"I suppose a lot of kids around the thirteen and fourteen age might have thought to themselves, 'I stand a chance of getting Ringo,' but over that age group, they've passed the stage of believing that.

"I suppose that people will start saying, 'Ah, well, I always did like Paul best.'"

He went on to say that Ringo was lucky *"to have no fuss at the wedding. When you've got a steady girlfriend, people are waiting for it and looking out for it. That's why Ringo was clever to keep it secret. If it was a public wedding, half of America would have come across."*

Asked what he intended to give the happy couple, Lennon said, *"If anybody's got any ideas, we'd like to hear. It's a problem."*

Did George plan to get married?

"I don't think so," he said. *"Not for a long time. At least, if I am, I know nothing about it."*

February 27, 1965 – Nigel Hunter reported for Disc Weekly that the Beatles had been at the EMI studios to record the songs that would be featured in the new film.

George Martin said, *"We're hoping to get twelve in the can before they leave. This will make up the film album. We want to get them done before the* boys go so that they can take the results with them for the location work.

Most of the new songs had been written by John Lennon and Paul McCartney for their Northern Songs Ltd. Publishing company, which had gone public the previous week, a very successful debut in the London Stock Exchange. But...

"*George Harrison has written a couple for the film, too,*" George Martin explained. "*And they're both very good.*"

As before, it would probably be up to Martin to arrange the musical segments and background sounds for the film.

February 27, 1965 – *Disc Weekly*, Laurie Henshaw reported... The Beatles had flown off to paradise, an island in the Bahamas. George had once said he would like to retire to some place like that, "*If I ever gave up music, which is highly unlikely.*"

They were in Nassau, where the shooting for *Beatles Two* – working title only – had begun. Said Walter Shenson, producer, "*We shall be in Nassau until March 10, then we'll come back to London for a few days before leaving for Salzburg, Austria, on March 13th, where we remain until March 22nd. Then it is back to London, again.*"

Meanwhile, the Beatles got to play in the sun for awhile before heading back to winter and the snow scenes in Austria. The locales for the shooting seemed to be as colourful as the script.

After leaving a recording session at EMI studios the previous week, Dick Lester, director, said to Henshaw, "*That recording session? The Beatles recorded the numbers they had specially written for the film.*"

In the Bahamas, aside from working, what would the group be doing? Swimming, cycling, sailing, golfing... Deep sea fishing?

Lester said, "*I believe George Harrison did some last time he was there, and caught something pretty big.*

"*Exactly what we shall be shooting each day depends on what is being arranged. Scenes we shoot depend on the equipment that will be ready first.*

"*Frankly, the boys won't have much time for leisure activities. We shall work until the sun goes down, and I shouldn't imagine they would want to stay on the beaches after that.*

"*After all, it's going to be a pretty strenuous day, every day. I should think the boys would have to be up by about seven a.m. They will have to go to make-up, which, as we are shooting in colour, will take a little longer.*

"*We want to start shooting around eight thirty a.m. and run through to about six p.m. There will be a break for lunch, of course, but whether this will be taken in a restaurant or brought out to us depends upon the location we are working in at the time.*"

And what would the Beatles mostly eat?

Lester said, "*Well, the food is sort of American. Then there are the traditional dishes like local sea fish and local fruits. Probably, we shall have to rely on a lot of packed lunches. These things have to be flexible, so many things crop up that you can't predict.*"

He was aware of the possibility of fan interruptions and said, "*We have chosen places that are a little more isolated than most so I should think we should be able to keep to ourselves. To go from Britain into the sun is marvelous. And that's one thing you can guarantee in the Bahamas.*"

Everyone involved in the film would be staying at the Balmoral Club on Cable Beach, a couple of miles of white sand, five miles from Nassau.

Lester said, "*I have worked and stayed at this hotel twice now. The colonial cottages have six to eight rooms each and a central lounge. There is a main dining room with a small orchestra, and a patio overlooking the ocean where lunches are served. The swimming pool is delightful.*

"*It is ideal for a swim before breakfast, so if the boys want to splash about first thing in the morning, then they have plenty of opportunity to do so. I bathed all the time and I am sure the boys will want to do so as well.*"

Thousands of local fans had been on hand to greet the Beatles as their flight landed at Nassau's Windsor Field. No police escort had been planned for the Beatles, but the cops were standing by just in case.

Shortly after their arrival, the group went swimming in the Atlantic by moonlight.

Press Officer Tony Howard said, "*It was a pretty tiring flight. But the boys were all in good spirits, cracking jokes and taking turns to move around the plane to sit with various members of the crew unit. They got through a big quantity of Cokes on ice on the trip. Our first stop was Kennedy Airport in New York. We were able to stretch our legs, but the Beatles had to be locked in the plane, there were so many fans there to welcome them.*

"*There were also scores of photographers and fans present when we arrived at Nassau. The Beatles held a press conference, then went straight to the lovely Georgian house that had been reserved for them in the grounds of the Balmoral Club. They didn't even have time for a meal.*

"*But before retiring for the night, they did take a dip in the sea. It is wonderfully warm here.*"

February 27, 1965 – *Melody Maker*, Ray Coleman reported that few rock stars ever thought beyond their latest hit recording, but John Lennon did. He was the mastermind behind the band, the skeptical one, the cynic who would wonder why things seem to be going so smoothly.

The bond of friendship amongst the group was indestructible. But John Lennon was the most thoughtful one, with the sharpest wit, and with the plans for the future.

He was a millionaire, of course, but not flashy about it. He rarely carried money and was always bumming smokes that he lit with matches instead of an expensive lighter. He was more interested in cracking jokes or lancing someone verbally than in any sort of physical activity. And, above all else, he was into the music. During a break at a recording session in London, while Paul played a piano and Ringo and George listened to a playback of a song they had just recorded, John talked about his personal plans and about the future of the Beatles.

Was the day coming when the Beatles would cease to be pop stars?

John said, *"No. We'll still be pop stars as long as we continue making records. And we intend to go on doing that."*

Was making movies a serious business for them or just a bit of light relief?

"Yes, we regard filming as a bit of a giggle. We regard recording as a bit of a giggle, as well. So we're film stars and pop stars, we hope."

There were rumours that they were done, that they would soon disband. What about that?

"I don't see why these things are even considered, the supposition that just because we've done well we might as well pack it in. The much more sensible thing for anybody to say is that we'll never pack it up completely because we've made so much money and we are still making it.

"People talk a load of rubbish about us. We have no plans to break up. We might be interested in doing other things as well as make records and films, but the Beatles will still be the Beatles.

What plans did he have for the future?

"Well, I'll tell you exactly what I'm involved in right now. I'm definitely going to do some A and R work. I want to be an independent record producer. I'd like to find someone as good as, say, Tom Jones, and record them. Probably Paul and me, actually, working together. Until now, there's never been time. But there might be now.

"I was going to have a recording studio built at my house. But I gave up the idea. I've decided I

couldn't work it. Good God, I can't even work a bloody tape recorder, so I can't see myself doing the big equipment bit!"

How did he plan to make records?

"Well, I'm getting this shed built at the back of the house. That's for practice. I'll discover people and then hire a studio to record them. It won't be for some time yet, so I don't want hundreds of people imagining that I'm walking around with a big cigar and open to offers."

What sort of acts did he have in mind?

"I've been thinking about this. I reckon there's nobody in the world equivalent in popularity, I suppose you'd say, to Presley or us. I mean, a girl singer. That's who I'd like to discover. Someone with the looks of Bardot and the voice of Dionne Warwick. Do I like Dionne that much? Well, her voice is okay. I'm not exactly crazy about her, but that's the sort of combination I'm thinking of. A big sex symbol. A girl who looks great and sings wild. She's got to be somewhere. There's never been anybody like that as I can remember. The sort of girl I'd be interested in for this would be someone with such a voice that all the fellas would queue up to see what she looks like. And when they see what she looks like…"

Since he was so interested in producing a solo act, did that mean he thought the group scene was fading?

"All I can see in that way is that, this year, the record companies won't be signing up all the crappy groups like they did last year. There was a time when the companies signed up anybody who made a noise like four men with guitars. They got lumbered and they deserved to get lumbered."

Did he think that hurt the British music scene?

"I don't know. And I couldn't care less. It's just true, they signed up rubbish and when they didn't get hits, they started running. Can't blame 'em, but they should have been more sensible."

George asked, *"Who should have been more sensible, John?"*

"What do you want?" Lennon demanded.

"What are you talking about?" George asked.

"Mind your own bloody business. Got a ciggie?"

John grabbed the pack from Harrison's pocket before George could reply. George wandered off. And John said he enjoyed recording more than anything else the Beatles did.

Was it still as much fun to make records?

"Yeah, much more, really. When we started recording, I didn't know much about it, what to do, what sounds to expect in the end. But now we know little bits about it, it makes it much more interesting. I get a great kick from recording. You never know what's going to happen."

Was the band considering new musical directions?

"If that happened, it would happen accidentally. We've never had policies or anything. We're just a group."

What about the influence of Bob Dylan's work?

"I just started doing it because it was different and I like it. I'm not going over to it permanently, just now and then, when I feel like it. I just felt like going that way a bit, y'know. If I'd not heard Dylan, it might have been that I'd have written stuff and it sung it like Dominic Behan, or somebody like that."

What did he see the Beatles doing in five years?

"Don't know. Who can answer that? Even if we retired we wouldn't split from each other altogether. Anyway, who wants to talk about retiring now? It would be a drag. None of us could stick it."

February 27, 1965 – Ray Coleman wrote for *Melody Maker*... that the Beatles considered the success of *A Hard Day's Night* to be somewhat of a handicap because it meant that people would be watching carefully for failure in the second film.

To sum it up, Ringo said, *"It's just like doing your first one, only worse. People will be watching us and expecting better. We can only do our worst. I mean, best."*

"It's much worse this time," said John. *"Having something to live up to. I suppose if nobody likes it, that's it."*

Until late the previous week, Paul had not yet read the script. He had been late getting back from his holiday in Tunisia.

"I don't know a lot about it," he said. Kidding, he added, *"I believe it's provisionally titled* All Aboard For Fun*."*

As in *A Hard Day's Night*, Ringo was again the focal point. The theme was a chase for Ringo's ring.

Ringo said, *"I hate the idea of being the central figure again this time. I didn't want to be anything special in the last one, and nor in this one. But I didn't have any say in it. I suppose if they'd been chasing a boot in the film's story, it might have been one of the others who had this part. But it's obvious if it's rings, they choose Ringo. Drag, in a way."*

Was he not happy with the acclaim he received for the first film?

"It didn't do me any harm. When we made that, people got the idea we could act. But let's get this sorted out before the new one comes: that one film doesn't make us actors. We'll do our best again, and if it works, it's great. If it doesn't, then good-bye, Beatle people."

Not all the recordings made the previous week would necessarily appear in the film.

"They haven't been tailored to the film or anything," explained John. *"They're just songs. If they fit the story and the sequences, some of them will be in. It's up to the film bosses, not us. We've just concentrated this week on making records. There are a couple of obvious songs for the film, at least we think so, but nothing's been decided. We haven't written anything with the film in mind. If you do that, it restricts the story line."*

All of them laughed when they were asked if they had memorised all their lines and if they new the full story.

February 27, 1965 – Ray Coleman for *Melody Maker*... The group had just finished recording, George was passing around the smokes, and Ringo had left the room to talk with George Martin.

John said, *"Look, what are we going to get him as a bloody wedding present? Let's get it sorted out right now."*

Paul said, *"I don't know what you're worried about. I've brought him back something from Tunisia."*

"What?" demanded John.

"A silver apple, nice, Arabic thing. Very unusual."

"What's your game then?" George asked. *"You're sucking up to Ringo a bit, aren't you?"*

And John asked, *"What are you after, Paul, a job in Ringo's group when we give him the push? I reckon somebody should go out tomorrow and buy him and Maureen a bloody big gold clock. The biggest gold clock there is. Didn't you realise we waited for you to come back from holiday before deciding what to buy him from all of us? Listen, somebody go out and spend a lot of money on this lovely gold clock. Then we'll send him a note saying he's out of the group."*

It was a joke, a rough joke entirely in keeping with their sense of humour, the sort of joke that flew constantly whenever they were together. They had spent four days in the studio and had recorded six new Lennon / McCartney songs and two by George Harrison.

"We're on our way out, John and me," said Paul. *"George is moving him. Him and Ray Davies* (of the Kinks) *are taking over. Folks, they are the new hit writers."*

Some of the songs would be for the film, the rest would be for stock. No one was sure what they had or how it would be used.

Said John, *"We've just been getting plenty of stuff recorded and we'll decide what to do with it later."*

The band enjoyed recording more than anything else. Laughter flowed, barbed jokes flew. As they completed a song that featured Ringo on vocals, John said, *"I wrote it. It's the funniest thing I've ever done, listen to the words."*

Ringo sang, *"You've gone soft in the head."*

John laughed, *"I didn't expect anybody to want to record it."*

And George Martin said, *"Right, Ringo. That sounded okay. Let's try it for taping properly, now."*

The song had a slight Bo Diddley rhythm. Ringo sang. And when it was done, George Martin joked, *"Okay. John and Paul played awfully but Ringo was very good. Have your food."*

They broke to eat as a man arrived with a tray of food – pork, chicken, drinks – Ringo saying to Neil Aspinall, *"I can afford real chicken, y'know. This looks bloody horrible."*

Aspinall replied, *"But you asked for chicken sandwiches."*

And Ringo said, *"I know. But if this is the best sandwich there is, get me a whole chicken next time. I've never seen imitation chicken before tonight."*

Ringo wandered back to his drum kit, cursing chicken sandwiches. And Paul said, *"He's never been the same since he got married. Still, I don't think it will harm his career. It will mature him as a man!"*

As George played back what they had just recorded, John said, *"Hey, listen. Hear that play by Paul? He's been doing quite a bit of lead guitar work this week. Gear. I reckon he's moving in. Listen. On that one, George and Paul are playing the same break exactly, both playing in different octaves."*

Paul thought the sound was one of the best ever and John mentioned they were still searching for the best sound. *"I don't know if we'll ever find it. We still haven't made the sort of sound we want to, and we don't even know what we're after."*

Lennon had done another record with some Dylan influence. *"Well,"* he explained, *"it's not pure Dylan, really. Just a folky song which I try to sing in Dylan's style. I don't want to overdo it, but I like it. Out of the eight songs we've done so far, I've written three, Paul's written three, and George had done two. What did I say? George has written two? He'll have to go!"*

Continuing, John said, *"It's not easy to write songs like Bob's. 'Ere, who's seen that bloke Donovan on TV?"*

George answered, *"I have. All that bit about 'This Machine Kills' on his guitar."*

And John said, *"I think I'll have 'This Machine Smells' on mine."*

Then it was back to work, a further two and half hours, with George Martin singing along as they worked out the arrangements. When it was time to record, George Harrison laid down his guitar and played a drumstick and a piece of wood while Ringo, not on the recording, wandered off.

As the music stopped, George Martin said, *"Let's have one more go at the backing, then we'll record your voices separately. This time, we'll get it exactly right."*

"Why?" Paul asked. *"What exactly was wrong?"*

"The tuning sounded wrong. And you, George, should be coming in on the second beat every time instead of every fourth beat."

"Oh, I see," said Harrison.

The music started.

George Martin said, *"Stop. Somebody played a wrong note."*

One more try and all went well. As the final note faded, Lennon said to Harrison, *"Give us a ciggy, quick!"*

Playing back their recording again, John asked, *"Have you heard George Martin's orchestral version of* I Feel Fine*?"*

"Gear," said Paul.

Then they recorded John and Paul's vocals, then added Ringo on maracas and John on tambourine.

"We want the Mexican effect," said John.

The song went on and on as they tried it time again before they were satisfied with the sound.

As the evening wound down, with Paul playing electric piano, John shouted at roadie Mal Evans, *"I like electric pianos, Mal. Buy me one tomorrow."*

Ringo was on his way to a ball at Albert Hall. As he was changing his trousers, in walked a lady with a tea tray. Ringo dashed behind a screen, still trying to put on his pants without removing his boots while John sang a few bars of *I'm A Loser.*

Paul declared it had been an enjoyable night, then asked George Martin if they could try a new song tomorrow, one he had just finished a few hours earlier.

George Harrison announced that America was a lunatic country and wondered what it would be like when they stopped there on their way to the Bahamas, *"with all the deejays going potty."*

John said he could not care less.

And they left the studio, the fans outside getting a brief glimpse of their heroes. On the floor behind them was a cable from the States, wedding congratulations for Ringo. Leaving, he said, *"See, they still care."*

March 6, 1965 – *Melody Maker* **announced** that the Beatles deserved to be nationally honoured. They had broken all rock records, had become the biggest phenomenon ever and deserved to be celebrated for that. Millions of British records had been selling around the world. The Beatles' success had inspired hundreds of other groups and solo acts. The sales of musical instruments had soared, making huge profits for the makers and distributors. The Beatles had brought glory to not only the British music scene, but to Britain as well.

And *Melody Maker* was demanding that they be honoured. They were not certain that knighthoods were in order, but Britain should definitely show its gratitude. National Beatles Day? Or perhaps the group should be feted at Buckingham Palace. They invited the readers to make suggestions.

March 6, 1965 – *Melody Maker,* **Ray Coleman spoke** with Ringo and George on the telephone from the Bahamas.

Said Ringo, *"We've been up just one hour, and it's twenty past twelve in the afternoon. Last night was George's birthday and we had a party. It was good, we all had a great time."*

Through a crackling phone line, Ringo said, *"Yeah, we're all okay and it's been fun so far. We have to get up at a quarter to seven every morning, except this morning. The first couple of days were the worst. We've done a few shots. There was this part where we were all being filmed cycling round the island and it was very hot. It went off all right. We could have kept it up for a long time, actually, we were enjoying it.*

"Eleanor Bron's a knockout. We haven't been involved in working with her yet, but she is great company. There are about seventy of us in the whole film company, that's including technicians."

George Harrison, talking about the actual filming, said, "We've done quite a bit, really. More than you'd expect. I know this must be difficult to follow, but we come out of this sort of hole in a tent and emerge into a swimming pool, all in our clothes. What do you mean you don't understand it?"

He explained that the shooting was disjointed, saying, "You can't connect the pieces we've done. We did this bit in a quarry, too. We had these sports cars we'd hired, as well, that was marvelous, great fun.

"It's been quite hot and we've done a little bit of swimming, but right now it's rather chilly. No, we've not had a lot of leisure time. We enjoy working here, it's all new, different, and we've got something different to tackle all the time. Who wants leisure time?"

Was the group being bothered by American deejays and journalists?

Ringo answered, "It's not been that bad. Not so far, anyway. There've been a few in here from Miami. A few of the disc jockeys have been making a bit of noise, they're a fantastic crowd, really. They stand on the other side of the road while we're filming, for instance, and shout, 'Hey, Ringo!'

"I don't know what I'm supposed to shout back because I don't know 'em. They probably just want me to look that way to have my picture taken. But I'm afraid I can only sort of ignore them. When you're filming, you've got to concentrate, haven't you?"

The police were trying hard to control the invaders, explained Ringo, but, "We're not worried. This is such a great place that you can't get bad tempered with anybody."

March 13, 1965 – *Disc Weekly*, **Laurie Henshaw spoke** on the phone with George Harrison from the Bahamas.

"We've only just got up," George said. "I'm in the little villa we have rented here. Paul is in the middle of breakfast at this very moment.

"This has been our first morning off. We've been working every day on the film, including Sundays. We've been up most days at seven. And yesterday, we got up at six. We haven't had much time for leisure. And we've been pretty tired anyway after the day's filming."

Had they gathered any souvenirs, conch shells, whatever?

"Not really. There isn't much to buy out here, anyway. And they tell me those shells smell quite a bit.

"The filming has been fun, though. We dived into the sea with all our clothes on. And some of the sequences were shot through a glass-bottomed boat. Some of the filming has been done on an island off here called Paradise Island. It's easily the nicest one of all and is practically deserted.

"Birthday presents? Brian Epstein gave me a lovely pair of chunky white gold cuff-links. The other boys are giving me a present when we get back to Britain."

George said he had some good stunts in the film. "I leap off the back of a car, and in another scene, I dive through a window."

The Beatles were due back in England from the Bahamas soon, then off to Salzburg, Austria.

George said, "I hope it's not too cold in Austria."

March 13, 1965 – *Melody Maker*, **Ray Coleman spoke** with Paul McCartney about accusations that the Beatles had been rude to journalists while they were in the Bahamas, exhibiting bad manners and foul language.

Speaking from Nassau, Paul said, "Anyone who doesn't realise by now that we are not clean-living little angels must be mad. We don't pretend to be anything like that. We also swear, and I thought that most people who were interested in us knew that already. But we have not been rude or anything to anybody particularly.

"It's simply that certain people struck us as more friendly than others, and so I suppose we might have appeared more friendly to some people than we were to others. But that's normal human behaviour, isn't it? We have not been any more rude than we normally are."

With regards to the filming, Paul said everything was on schedule; they were enjoying the Bahamas.

"John and Ringo were working this morning, they had something to do with smoke bombs, and Ringo nearly got smoked to death. They thought he was acting, but he wasn't. We are not finding that some of the shots begin to link up and make sense. But sometimes, we'll start making a piece of the film out of sequence and they'll explain that it goes in before the thing we shot yesterday. Interesting, but peculiar, when you can't follow properly what's happening."

He said the film was, as yet, untitled, but they had some possibilities. "We're leaving it for a while to see if anything better turns up. We've had rushes of what we've made put on locally, and the colour is marvelous. Dick Lester is controlling us well. The film's on schedule, apart from one afternoon thing when a piece of machinery went wrong and that put the thing out.

"Apart from that, it's fine. It's been boiling hot and we've had a good time. Also, the press out here has been very good."

March 20, 1965 – *Disc Weekly* **reported** that the Beatles were having problems with more than just the title of their new film. Fans were mobbing the locations in the Austrian Alps.

Publicity officer, Tony Howard, explained, "The Beatles are filming in public places. We can't keep the people away. Many of them come down on skies during filming and others crowd around, making it very difficult to complete the shooting.

"But gradually, the people are getting to see they are making it very difficult for us under these conditions and are keeping back."

The group had been hard at work since arriving in Salzburg. They were only scheduled for a ten-day shoot; they worked entire days and often into the night.

Road manager, Neil Aspinall, said, "All they have been able to do is work, sleep and eat. They went down to a bar the other night for drinks and it was their first time out."

They were doing some tobogganing and skiing for the film, but there were stand-ins for the trickier work, all locals in Beatle haircuts.

There had been an avalanche on a nearby mountain peak. Aspinall said, "It was pretty frightening. None of us would have like to be caught in it."

March 20, 1965 – *Melody Maker* **reported** on the Beatles' new single, due out on April 9th. It was *Ticket to Ride*, backed by *Yes It Is*. Both were Lennon / McCartney songs, with John singing lead on the A side and Paul playing lead guitar. The selection was made by the group and Brian Epstein while flying over the Alps on their way to Salzburg, Austria.

Regarding the record, Paul said, "Ticket to Ride *is quite different from anything we have done. It is pretty slow and we are all very pleased with it because we felt we have got some good vocal harmonies going on with John's lead voice. I suppose it has a bit of an Arabian rhythm going on.*"

John said, "It's the slowest B side we've put out. But it has a beat."

"We did it in one morning," continued Paul. "We finished Ticket then went on to another number and when we heard the play-back in the evening we all thought it sounded very weird. It's so unusual for us."

Ticket To Ride was about a girl who was leaving her boyfriend. The group said it was very difficult to chose between *Ticket to Ride* and *Yes It Is* for the A Side.

John agreed that *Ticket to Ride* was a very "far out title" for a song by the Beatles.

"But you see," he explained. "We are very far out people."

March 20, 1965 – *Melody Maker*, **Ray Coleman recalled…** how someone had predicted that the Beatles would die in a plane crash in America the previous year. The group remembered it well and Paul talked about it on the way to Austria for filming.

"We were very worried. I remember we didn't talk too much about it during the flight and we all wore St. Christopher medals. We took it very seriously because everybody was talking about it and frightening us. There was only one thing to do, we had some drinks and forgot about it."

The group did not enjoy flying, merely tolerating it, although George said he absolutely hated it. "My stomach somersaults."

As they were leaving London, the airport was crowded with fans and a banner was flown: "Misery Until You Come Home."

Ringo said, "It's marvelous. We never expected this sort of thing all the time, but when it does happen, it's a knock-out. It shows the fans are still with us."

The group sat together in their cabin at the back of the plane, John drinking brandy and saying, "They've run out of wine on this bloody airplane. And somebody told me to just drink wine because it keeps the weight down. So wine is my drink now."

Said a stewardess, "We had wine here, Mr. Lennon, but you drunk it all."

John said, "That's a lie, a dirty rotten lie."

He moved to sit with Paul, and Paul said, "There's a new record out by an American girl called Little Esther Phillips. It's And I Love Him. Best version of anything of ours I have ever heard."

"'Ere," said John, "Do you remember when you used to sing this in the old days, Paul?" Singing falsetto, John sang a few lines from *He's in Town*. They fooled around, sang a bit, moved into a version of *Blue Moon* that made Ringo cringe. As the pilot came over the intercom, Ringo said, "This is your captain bailing out."

A stewardess told Paul she thought *She's a Woman* was the best record ever made and Paul replied, "You have taste."

Later, Paul said, "The worst thing about flying is taking off and landing."

They were arriving in Salzburg.

"Hey," Ringo said. "All that snow and mountains. Do people live here?"

As the plane touched down, Paul said, "Marvelous landing."

"No such thing," said George.

Fans, photographers and journalists were all gathered at the airport to cheer the Beatles' arrival.

"Why are the press so soft on the continent?" asked Ringo. "They push and shove and argue and, in the end, nobody gets anywhere."

March 20, 1965 – Ray Coleman wrote for *Melody Maker…* about how there was once a sleepy village in the Austrian Alps called Obertauern, a hundred miles from Salzburg, where no one cared much about anything except skiing… until four lads named John, Paul, George and Ringo arrived. Then it woke up, fans gathered around to clutter up the scene, while the Beatles cavorted in the snow for the winter scenes in the new film.

Warned of avalanches, they spent the first night at the Hotel Edelweiss, signing autographs, making jokes, dining and drinking. John talked about Bob Dylan and Donovan, and said the Rolling Stones were winners; Paul mentioned being a fan of Patrick

Campbell; Ringo said he had no idea what Lennon was talking about; and George said very little. They were in their rooms by 11:30 p.m. and up again at 6:30 a.m. for the first day of the Austrian shoot.

In the make-up room, they learned what they were to wear for the day and discovered that the black trousers were too tight. Said Lennon, *"It's no good complaining. Tailors always excuse themselves by saying you have gained weight."*

Wearing a cape and a top hat, George said, *"Shazam! I'm Captain Marvel."*

The first shot of the day took nearly four hours to complete because so many fans were getting in the way, blocking the cameras, waving autograph books. During the final shot, Paul split his pants and wandered off to get a new pair. That was it. They broke for lunch.

Coleman said the film was costing around seven hundred thousand pounds, while *A Hard Day's Night* had only cost one hundred and ninety thousand pounds.

From somewhere up the mountain, John Lennon shouted, *"Mal, I want some tea."*

Mal Evans made his way up with four cups of tea. Then Neil Aspinall was sent off to get some sunglasses, falling in snow up to his waist, cursing loudly.

They shot some more snow scenes and George mentioned that that part of the film was to have a song put in. *"But God knows how."*

After a meal up the mountain, the group began jumping around in the snow and director Dick Lester demanded that they stop, explaining, *"I need that virgin snow for some shots!"*

George replied, *"Lay off. It's as much my bloody snow as yours."*

They filmed until the sun went down. Sunburned and tired, they returned to the village for a few hours of eating and drinking.

Paul was asked by a local what he thought of the snow and he said, *"It's very soft."*

George said, *"It's gear."*

March 27, 1965 – *Melody Maker,* **Ray Coleman interviewed** Paul McCartney. During the group's stay in Austria, John Lennon was angered by the crowds who flocked to the set, ruining assorted shots; and he let them know it, loudly, most definitely, and often crudely. Charm was not one of his major personality quirks. That was more Paul than anyone else in the group. George was funny, Ringo was a comedian, John was abrasive, and Paul was confident and often charming, perhaps more conscious of the press than the others. Not that he courted publicity. He was simply more thoughtful. Over dinner at the Hotel Edelweiss in Obertauern, Austria, he spoke with Coleman.

Asked Coleman, *"Do you think you have some sort of responsibility to your fans? Do they look up to you?"*

"No, it would probably be a nicer answer if I said yes, we have a responsibility to fans. But I can't be noble for the sake of it. The answer's no. I don't believe we have any responsibility, frankly, and it takes a bit of saying. It's insulting the intelligence of a lot of young people to say we have.

"We used to get requests from people, asking us if we'd go to a meeting and tell loads of people they shouldn't drink. What do they take us for? We'd get laughed at if we said the youth of Britain shouldn't drink. It'd be bloody impertinent. I haven't the right to interfere with anybody else's life.

"Do you think just because a Beatle said, 'Don't go beating people up,' the crime figures would go down? They wouldn't. And it's a cheek to expect us to do it. And I'd feel a right nit saying 'Thou shalt not drink.'"

Is the image of the Beatles changing?

"Yes, I think it is. At least, I do feel it is switching a bit now. Let's get one thing clear, though. It's other people looking at us that creates the image. We can't create it. We can just notice it and sort of say, 'Ah, well...' I think it is good that it's changing, as well. You ask how is it changing? I'd hesitate to use the word maturing. That word has certain connotations. People who are mature are respectable, ordinary, and I think dull. They use the word mature when what they mean is that people are in a rut. I hope we're not mature.

"My feeling about our changing image is this: Everybody goes through certain stages of growing up. For us, this is one of them. People are simply realising that we're growing up."

How will you feel, how will you react, if *A Ticket to Ride* does not go immediately to number one?

"It would be a terrible drag and then I'll really pay attention to the knockers who say the Beatles are slipping. I mean, think of those horrible quotes we'd have to give people. 'Proves there's room for everybody,' we'd say, if it goes in the chart at number fifteen.

"Seriously, if it doesn't get to the top first go, I'd say damn and blast it, because as you know I never swear. I might say flipping heck! Come off it. Truthfully, I'd feel very depressed and I'd be in a disappointed mood."

Do you expect it will hit number one immediately?

"It's not a questing of expecting, but hoping. It's always hope rather than expectancy. Once you start expecting success you get blasé. We'll never get to the stage of releasing rubbish because we know people will buy it. Disaster.

"We've always been terrified with each new release and we're the same now. We like it, but people might hate it, and that's their right. This business of singles has always been a real worry for us, and I mean this, because every time we've tried for something different and we have done it this time.

"Not that we've got The Black Dyke Mills Band backing us! The worst attitude anybody in the chart can have is: 'The last one did okay so this one will.' All I can say is, let us pray."

Are The Beatles knockers moving in?

"One thing on this subject has always struck me as stupid. You get people who say things like: 'A bit of criticism is always good for you. Being taken down a peg and getting advice never hurt anyone.' It's a load of rubbish. I've never met anyone yet who liked being criticised, even when the criticism was meant as advice.

"Let's face it, our knockers aren't interested in helping us, or giving us advice. They're simply malicious. Another thing I hate is where somebody tells you his opinion after the event, you know the sort, 'Well, if you want my honest opinion, I didn't like it in the first place.' We've had a lot of that and we hate it. It's cowardly.

"We've always been worried about knockers. Isn't everyone? If somebody walked up to another person in the street and said, 'That's a lousy jacket you're wearing,' he'd be a knocker. And the bloke wearing the jacket would hate it; so do we. If the knockers are moving in now, we don't like it. We don't like Clever Henry's."

What are your feelings about invasion of privacy?

"Mainly, yes, we resent it a bit. It depends on my mood. If I'm away on holiday and photographers start chasing, I get fed up. But if the photographer's okay and asks if I'd pose for a picture or something, and he's reasonable about it, I'm not annoyed.

"After all, you've got to face the fact the press is after you, haven't you? It's when people start sneaking pictures and wrecking a private holiday that I get temperamental."

What do you think of John's idea about becoming a record producer in partnership with you?

"I don't mind the idea, as long as he let me set up the mikes for him. Just to keep my hand in, like. Seriously, I'd love it. It'd be a challenge."

What do you dislike about show business?

"Shaving. Right, I'll answer that properly. Those daft people who go backstage after an opening night and say, 'Dahling, you were super.' Women in show business who swear like troopers to make everybody know they are in show business. Show biz women who act like men. I hate this type. All the 'oh dahling' types. Horrible.

"Also people who talk around, calling each other 'love.' Not the 'luv' that shop assistants in the North mean, but the show biz 'love.' This type is often the floor manager on a TV show. It is so affected.

"They think these affectations make them individual. Actually, they are following every known rule in the book, and falling into every possible show biz trap that makes them UN-individual. To me, this is one of the drags of show business."

John interrupted, saying, *"That's it, Paul. Have a bash. Have a go."*

How aware are you of personal images?

"I used to panic about images, because I'm very easily influenced, impressionable, truthfully. I used to worry about whether we should smoke on photographs. Then I realised it would be daft not to.

"I used to panic about being seen anywhere with Jane, because I used to have this old-fashioned idea that recording people were never seen out with girl friends. Now, I don't care much. No, these things don't matter to me or any of us, because we don't really believe in images. We never talk about them, except to send-up the word image."

How would you define a hanger-on?

"There are various kinds of hangers on, we find. Some hang on because they can tell their friends they've met the Beatles. Big deal. Some hang on because it's their job to do so. The very worst kind of hanger-on is the one you discover was a hanger-on three weeks after he's left your company."

Do you think anyone will ever have greater success than the Beatles?

"Yes. I think they might easily. Nobody thought Elvis's successes could ever be surpassed, but I think we might have surpassed one or two of his, haven't we?"

Would you ever leave Britain to live abroad?

"No, definitely not. Out of everywhere I've been, I like England best."

And George added, *"Leave England? Never. Best country in the world to live in."*

How would you like to be remembered?

Paul said, *"With a smile."*

John replied, *"I won't be interested in being remembered. I'll be in a mental home and* Melody Maker *will run articles saying, 'Now, direct from the mental home, we present John Lennon in Blind Date.' No, I'd like to be remembered as the one with the twinkle in his eye."*

George said, *"I just don't care."*

And Ringo added, *"I'd like to be remembered as Mrs. Starkey's little boy."*

March 27, 1965 – *Melody Maker* **reminded** people that Ringo had come up with the title for *A Hard Day's Night*, and that he had named the new film *Eight Arms to Hold You*.

Producer Walter Shenson said, *"Ringo's the surprising man of the Beatles; quiet for days, then suddenly he'll come up with something, like the title, that takes everybody off guard and proves he's as sharp as the rest."*

Since Ringo had announced the title, Lennon and McCartney would be writing a song to go with it.

Most of the music for the film was already finished. Hearing the songs, the writer pointed out that one could only be awed yet again by their talent and skill. *Ticket to Ride* had a slower tempo and more blues than any other Beatles' A side record; *Yes*

It Is, on the B side, was a ballad equal to *This Boy*, charming and memorable.

About *Yes It Is*, George said, *"I prefer this one; it should have been the A side, really."*

And Paul said, *"No, but I know what you mean. I probably prefer it, too, but you mustn't confuse what you prefer with what's the best A side. They're two totally different things."*

April 10, 1965 – Susan Shaw wrote for *Disc Weekly* **about** the Beatles' new film. She was on hand for some of the filming and she talked about the fabulous flat shared by the band in the movie, and about the scaled-down version of the theatre organ that Paul had learned to play with some proficiency.

The flat was meant to be completely self-contained so that no one had to go outside for anything.

As they took a tea break, John spoke with her about his new Ferrari, saying, *"I haven't had any accidents in it yet, but there is a dent in the bumper. I backed it into George's garage the other day!"*

Paul wandered over in search of Ringo. He was found later playing chess with Neil Aspinall, the road manager.

April 10, 1965 – *Melody Maker* **asked** John Lennon about his style of rhythm guitar playing.

"I've never been a conventional rhythm guitar player. It seems the most impossible thing in the world to try explaining how to play rhythm guitar and what I do. For a start, although I've always been tagged the rhythm guitarist, that position is shared between all of us. I like doing the odd bit of lead playing to relieve the monotony and I expect George likes switching with me as well. In the beginning, I never sat down and said I wanted to play rhythm guitar. It was simply that George was better than me, so he nobbled lead and I got lumbered. Now then, the way I make sure I get a fair chance to do lead sometimes is by writing a tune. Naturally, I'll write the guitar solo, too, in my mind, so it's obvious I'm going to play my own tune solos, usually anyway. Advice: don't clash with the lead guitar and then you can do what you like. Fill in nicely and try to add to what the lead guitar's doing all the time. The bass guitarist should never stop playing and always be there, but the same can almost be said for rhythm, in a way."

April 10, 1965 – *Melody Maker*, **Ray Coleman wrote** about life with the Lennons. As they left the Twickenham film studios in a Rolls Royce, the car was mobbed by fans, hammering on the doors and bumpers, screaming for John as they damaged the vehicle in their enthusiasm.

John said, *"The way I see it is that they bought the car, so they've got a right to smash it up."*

Coleman dined with the Lennons, then watched a film, then moved on to the Ad Lib Club in London.

"We're going to see The Ipcress File," said John. *"We hire the cinema in town quite often."*

During the drive, he talked about music, about the charts and the Beatles' prospects with *Ticket to Ride*. Then he said, *"First time I saw Donovan on TV I fell off my chair. I couldn't believe it. We'd got back from Austria and I thought, Good God, Dylan's in Britain. I still can't believe it.*

"Yeah, great to see Dylan doing so well. I never thought he's so much with this single. Hope we get the chance to get together again when he comes over. I'll have him out to the house if he'll come."

He said it would not surprise him if *Ticket to Ride* did not hit the top of the pop charts. *"It's got to happen sometime, so it might as well be now."*

Arriving home, Lennon said, *"This is it. Let's go and play some records."*

The twenty-thousand pound country house was comfortable but not ostentatious. Lennon's new Ferrari sat outside the front door.

"Marvelous car," John said. *"George and I ran it in the other night down the road, in one burst of a hundred and twenty miles an hour."*

Inside, he greeted his wife and introduced his son, Julian. *"He's two, I think."*

Lennon put Dylan's *Subterranean Homesick Blues* on the record player, saying, *"Great. Very Chuck Berry-ish."*

After that, he brought dozens of albums into the lounge, while Cynthia announced that the cook was ready to serve supper. Over the meal, Lennon talked:

"The scene's in a funny position at the moment. It goes up and down a lot. It came up with Proby, then went down, and up again with Tom Jones. It's gone a bit thin at the moment, with corny songs in the chart and so on.

"There are some good things around, like the Yardbirds and the Who, but I keep thinking how much better made their records could have been. Then there's this folk thing. I mean, if Donovan thinks he's a folk singer, what about Count Basie? LP Winner!"

Coleman then explained that Lennon was playing a sort of game. He would make an outrageous statement and then declare: *"LP Winner!"* as a joke about *Melody Maker*'s Mailbag writers, the ones who spent so much time analysing what was folk music and what was not, and were awarded LPs for the best letter. Lennon thought they were amusing.

All through the meal, John was up and down from the table, into the lounge, changing records. Finally, Cynthia said, *"For goodness sake sit down. You're giving me indigestion."*

Said John, *"I think* [Bernard] *Levin* [Not So Much a Programme, More a Way of Life] *was a bit soft saying that bloke's an imbecile. He's been waiting for people to have a big go at him for a long time. Now it's happened. Well, if he thinks he can get away with it like Proby did, he can't. What about R and B? Signed Al Saxon, Stoke-on-Trent. LP Winner!*

"I like the pop shows on TV. Even enjoy seeing the rubbish. I like plays as well. There have been

some good ones lately. I like pop shows first, plays second. I watch Not So Much a Programme.

"I like that bloke Patrick Campbell and Harvey Orkin. But sometimes they get terrible drags on the panel. Altogether, it's a bit of a loser program.

"I was asked to go on it but I turned it down. I'd only go on if they had people on the panel I like, otherwise it would just be a nasty night. They'd probably carve me up and if that happened, I'd get bloody rude."

With regards to growing old, Lennon said, *"It's very difficult to imagine. I sometimes try to look into the future, and stop myself doing it because it's such a drag thought. Thinking about an old Beatle, or a gray-haired Beatle, or a spastic Beatle.*

"But the thought of somebody coming up and saying, 'How old are you?' and me saying 'Fifty' is a bit off-putting. You know what I hate about the thought of growing old? When I was sixteen or seventeen, people kept saying to me, 'Wait till you're twenty or twenty-four, and you'll laugh at how you looked and behaved at sixteen.' And bloody hell, they're right.

"If I grow old and miserable, I'll paint myself green and red and have balloons popping out of my earholes."

Cynthia glanced at him as he she was sure he was talking rubbish.

Would everything be boring after so much Beatles success?

"I want no more from being a record star. I'm not disinterested, but there is more now than to make good records and sell them. I'd like to see us making better and better films. That's very difficult, and unlike pop music, it allows you to grow up as a person. I'm not craving for any more Gold Discs, even though they're a nice boost. That's all over. I just want to be an all-round spastic. LP Winner!"

Why do you talk so much about spastics?

"I mean nothing nasty, honest. I don't think I'd know a spastic from a Polaroid lens. I'm not hung up about them. When I use the word 'spastic' in general conversation, I don't mean to say it literally. I feel terrible sympathy for these people, it seems the end of the world when you see deformed spastics, and we've had quite a lot of them in our travels.

"In the States, they were bringing hundreds of 'em along backstage and it was fantastic. I can't stand looking at 'em. I have to turn away. I have to laugh, or I'd just collapse from hate.

"Listen, in the States, they lined 'em up and you got the impression the Beatles were being treated as bloody faith healers. It was sickening. I use the word spastic as slang. It's old fashioned to say 'he's got a leg missing.' If you talk about spastics, at least you're modern."

Cynthia glared at him.

"Enjoying your dinner?" John asked.

John had a reputation for being outspoken and vicious. Did he like it?

"It's been very useful. A lot of slimy little reporter types seem to have got to fear me. It's fantastic. I didn't work for the title of the Vicious Beatle, the Biting Beatle, the one with the rapier wit. It's a load of crap.

"It's handy being tagged like this. When I meet intelligent and hip people, I have to be on my toes not to disillusion them. The people who have fallen for my image and publicity go to Paul, which I think's funnier still.

"Paul can be very cynical and much more biting than me when he's driven to it. Course, he's got more patience. But he can carve people up in no time at all, when he's pushed. He hits the nail right on the head and doesn't beat about the bush, does Paul. LP Winner!"

Cynthia mentioned it was time to get ready to go out. John played a few more records, showed Coleman around the house – one room had eleven guitars – and introduced his dog Nigel. *"He's soft so I bought him to protect me."*

They departed for a West End basement theatre as a record by Bobby Goldsboro came on the radio. Lennon said, *"'Ere, that's the bloke who turned me on to contact lenses during the Orbison show. He used to be Orbison's guitarist."*

The next song on the radio was the Beatles' *I'll Follow The Sun.* John said, *"I suppose they think that's folk so they might as well plug it. Paul wrote that when he was ten. So how can it be folk? LP Winner!"*

A show band came on next and John said, *"We played opposite one on our first public appearance in a theatre, at the Pavilion, Liverpool, year's ago. We all fell about with laughter. It was so funny, I can't believe they're taking themselves seriously.*

"They were old fashioned then and they're the same today. I haven't anything against them personally, but their music is quite incredible; lousy, I mean. It's like watching a long, long talent contest. All the musicians are about twenty-eight or thirty and they look so bloody soft leaping and dancing about and singing about stupid things. Surely they can't get very big?"

At the cinema, they were joined by Ringo and Maureen, George and Patti Boyd, Paul and Jane Asher, roadies Neil Aspinall and Mal Evans, and film producer Walter Shenson.

John sang *Goldfinger* to the tune of *The Ipcress File.* After the show, he said the picture started slow but was not bad.

At the Ad Lib Club, they drank whisky and cokes. And John said, *"Notice the place fill up after we arrived?"*

He spent some time talking with Alan Price of the Animals, and with Dionne Warwick. At 4:30 a.m., it was time to go. Cynthia slept in the car on the way home. John had to be at work on the film the next morning at 8 a.m. and, as they passed Twickenham, he said, *"I might as well sleep in a chair at the studio."*

During the ride, though, he was awake, joking, philosophising.

"I bet you won't be joking in a couple of hours," Cynthia said. *"He's terrible first thing."*

John sang a few bars from *A Hard Day's Night*.

April 17, 1965 – Nigel Hunter spoke with music publisher Dick James for *Disc Weekly*.

"I sat with Paul in the stalls watching some of the other acts," Dick James said, recalling a time four months previously, during the rehearsals for the Beatles' Christmas show at the Hammersmith Odeon. *"Then Paul sang a few snatches of melody to me which he and John had in mind for future songs."*

Shortly afterwards, John went through the same tunes, saying to James, *"There's a sort of title I've got in my mind which I can't get rid of:* She's Got a Ticket to Ride."

Dick James liked the sound of it, liked the originality of it, and encouraged Lennon and McCartney to continue with it. In early February, George Martin was with John in Switzerland on a ski holiday. After a day on the slopes, John borrowed a guitar and played a new song for Martin.

"I liked it straight away," Martin said. *"And John said he'd get together with Paul as soon as he got back to London and finish it off. It went in with the rest of the songs the boys had lined up for their forthcoming film, and it was one of the first we recorded during the week in the studios before they went off to the Bahamas on location."*

Dick James was on hand for the recording sessions at the St. John's Wood studios. He liked to keep in touch with the progress of their music.

"As usual," he said, *"I received a rough acetate of* Ticket to Ride *when it had been cut. Exactly as it was without any technical treatment."*

The number was then registered with the British Museum, as is everything ever published in Britain, and a copy filed. After that, the song was filed with the Performing Rights Society, a contract drawn up with John and Paul, copyright protected.

Dick James said Lennon and McCartney's enthusiasm was the reason for all their success. *"They really work at their song writing. A lot of their ideas and groundwork happen in hotels, dressing rooms and while traveling, and often George and Ringo help out, too. When they've got something definite which needs to be finished, then John and Paul will lock themselves away and get on with it until it's completed to their satisfaction."*

The evolution of a song: a few words that Lennon could not forget; a rough melody worked out with Paul; a run-through for George Martin; off to the studio to polish and record it; and then off to register the copyright. All that was left was to release the single.

April 17, 1965 – *Melody Maker* led with the headline: Beatles Crush Knockers. *Ticket to Ride* hit number one, shutting up the critics who believed they couldn't do it again. The group was told the news on the set at Twickenham. And Paul said, *"John and I wrote it in the middle of doing some other stuff for the film at his house one afternoon. It's great news – what more can we say?"*

George added, *"We are always worried with each record. With this one we were even more worried. There's bound to be a time when we come in at nineteen. But this number one business doesn't seem to stop; great while it lasts, but now we'll have to start all over again and people will start predicting funny things for the next one."*

Ringo said, *"I'm glad it's top; quite honestly I didn't expect it. Of course, it makes it even more difficult for the next single. The knockers can't have a go at us just yet, but I suppose their day is bound to come eventually. It's got to stop somewhere, hasn't it?"*

Ticket to Ride was the Beatles' eighth single to top the charts. They were due to finish the film *Eight Arms to Hold You* in a month or so.

In a footnote, Bob Houston predicted that the Beatles' stay at number one would be short, suggesting that either the Supremes or the Animals would take over from them quickly.

April 17, 1965 – *Melody Maker*, Ray Coleman wrote that the Beatles were considering their future more now than at any other time. They had gone the fame and fortune, route but there must be more to life...

Ringo, sitting in his flat with Coleman, said, *"It bothers me, sometimes, when I sit wondering about what's going to happen. You can't sort anything out. It's impossible to say that if we stop being the Beatles in two years, we'll split up. We've come too far to split away from each other. We couldn't ever go our separate ways, never seeing each other again.*

"But the funny thing right now is that we're in a corner. A to B is a straight line, but there's no straight line for us. I'd love to know how all this will end. It would be stupid to pack it up while things are like they are. None of us wants to, anyway. At the moment, everything's great.

"But if we carry on playing and wait for the records to start slipping, as they're bound to one day, people will say we're packing it all in because we've had it. I'd hate that.

"Then I look at Elvis, who's thirty, and I wonder how he keeps on. John and I often have a laugh and say to each other, 'I'm not going on stage when I'm thirty.' You know, I wouldn't go on tour as a rock-n-roll drummer with a group if I was thirty. I'd feel so old and out of it. I feel old now, man. When I get on the stage and see the audience I think to myself, 'Good God, they're sixteen and I'm twenty-four.' It doesn't seem right.

"I suppose the best thing to do is roll along and say, 'Well, let it happen as it does.' But I've been thinking and wondering where it's all going. I want our end as the Beatles to be a good one, man. I mean, some of the rockers of the late fifties thought they were the living end at the time, then one day the public didn't want to know and they were finished. They got to be mentally washed up, as well. It finished them. We don't want that to happen to us. And it could.

"One day, when we're going to have to stop, and I only hope everything's nice when we do stop. I hope the films work out good. We all like filming. I hope I'm not giving the impression it's nearly all over. That's not true. But there comes a moment when you start thinking about where the whole thing's going.

"But I've always been a bit of an optimist. Things worked out great on the way up, and I hope it's as smooth the other way, really. I've always said that if you've got a pain, don't dwell on it. Think to yourself, 'Well, one day it's going to go.' And it does."

Ringo was spending one of his rare days at home, during a break in the filming. He said, "This is more of a home than the other flat. And being married is great, man. I hope we'll be able to live here for a nice long time. I only hope I don't get thrown out of this place like I did the last one because of the behaviour of fans, if they can be called fans.

"They're a lot of scrubbers and exhibitionists who hang around, shout outside all day and night, ring the bells and all that. It's enough to drive me mad. They can't be fans. Real fans don't behave like that.

"I can't understand why people don't let me lead a reasonably normal life when I come home from work. If I get out of the car and refuse to sign autographs, they shout four letter words at me and everybody near here hears it. It's not very nice.

"I've tried it every way. I've tried saying please be quiet but they won't. I've tried signing autographs but they stay shouting at the door. It's a shame because if any genuine fan finds out where I live and comes down, they suffer because of the others."

Ringo put on a record, a Woody Guthrie album, and talked about a letter that had been printed in *Melody Maker*, one that requested the Beatles have Ringo sing more songs. Coleman asked if he would want to.

"It doesn't bother me. I'm quite happy with my one little track on each album. I enjoy singing the odd number or so, and I wouldn't like to do it too much. I don't see myself as the lead singer, and certainly not as the best singer. Still, I'd like to thank that reader – Mark Radford – for writing such a nice letter. Why wasn't he an LP winner? It was a lovely letter.

"Tell him I'd like to buy him an LP for writing it. Tell him to send the bill to *Melody Maker* and I'll pay it."

They spoke about fatherhood…

Ringo said, "I'm made up, out of my mind with happiness, and Maureen's so thrilled. The baby's only the size of a sixpence, so let's not get that carried away. As far as the baby's future life's concerned, well, I didn't have the best education in the world. I attended secondary modern and I've not done badly out of it. If the kid passes exams, he or she can go to university or college, but I'll never push it. And I'll never be the sort of dad who say, 'You won't get your bike unless you pass your exams.' I hate that, man."

Would he want his kid to be a musician? Would the kid have to live with the Beatles image?

"If I had a ten-year-old son or daughter right now, yes. He'd probably be lumbered with being described as my kid. But by the time he's grown up, I won't be playing rock-n-roll drums, will I? It will be very funny. I can imagine him playing all our records and saying, "Come off it, dad. Why did you play all that old-fashioned rubbish. Listen to this sound, man.'

"I don't care if he's a musician or not. Let them make their own mistakes, says Ringo Starr. When I was sixteen, they tried to get me in a trade, which is a good thing if you're an ordinary person. I suppose I wasn't an ordinary person. I took a chance and I think I've been lucky.

"I met Maureen three days, exactly, after I'd joined the Beatles, and from then on it's been a knockout all the way. We met at the Cavern. Doesn't everybody?"

At that point, Ringo's dog, a poodle, dashed about the room. Laughing, Ringo said, "Very intelligent dog. Much more intelligent than John's. John's dog is just dim. Tiger isn't, poodles are very brainy. You know, there are times when I'd give all my earnings to hear this dog speak."

He thought about that and added, "Well, a week's earnings."

May 1, 1965 – Walter Shenson wrote for *Disc Weekly*... The Beatles performed their own stunts for the new movie. They considered using doubles for the more dangerous scenes, but they were determined to do those sequences themselves. Jumping on and off moving vehicles, diving through windows, falling through trapdoors, hung from ropes, The Beatles did it all.

Shenson worried about the ski scenes in Austria, and experienced skiers were used for some of the long shots, but the group did ski in the film. Throughout the time there, injured people were carried from the slopes daily. There was good reason to worry about the Beatles on skies. But it all worked out well.

He reported that the shooting was going well, the film was on schedule and should be done by May 14th. The London premiere was set for the end of July or the beginning of August. He promised the film was being played for laughs, that it would be a *"feast of fun"* when it hit the big screens.

Lennon and McCartney had penned six new songs for the movie, one of which, *Ticket to Ride*, was already number one in the country. Another single would be released to coincide with the film's premiere, the title song.

As yet, they did not have a title as good as *A Hard Day's Night*. To date, they had been going with *Eight Arms to Hold You* and, more recently, *Help*. He thought *Help* would be the final choice, but it wasn't final yet.

Since the beginning of shooting this new film, people had been asking Shenson if he planned to do another movie with the Beatles. He said he had an option on a third one and mentioned that the Beatles wanted to do a movie called *A Talent For Loving*, a Western.

He was not sure about that one, but he was certain he would like to make another picture with *the boys*. Not more than one a year, of course.

The boys had had a great time making this newest film. Shenson, Dick Lester, and the entire production staff, hoped the audiences would have as much fun when the movie was finally released.

May 1, 1965 – *Melody Maker*'s **Ray Coleman wrote** about Beatle money.

George Harrison was the one most concerned with the cash. When John, Paul and Ringo were asked about money, inevitably they would say, *"Ask George. He's the one who asks the questions and finds out where it's going."*

Harrison said, *"I'm not really the most interested money Beatle. Just the only one interested in what's happening to it. I like to know exactly where it's going.*

"Actually, I can quite understand why the others aren't so bothered. We sit at accountants' meetings and are told we've got two per cent of this and four-and-a-half per cent of that. It's confusing and boring, and just like being back in school.

"Well, after a year or so of the Beatles making records and doing well, I started trying to find out what was happening, where was it going? John and Paul and Ringo were equally interested. But they gave in. I didn't. It's easy to get blasé and think we're making plenty and somebody's taking care of it. But I like to know how much is coming in; where it's being put; how much I can spend. I'm no more money-mad than the others. I've just persevered and found out.

"We all have some private investments. Believe it or not, we still haven't got a terrific amount of money in real capital. There are a lot of group investments in the name of Beatles Ltd., obviously because that's a very safe thing. There are lump sums in bank deposit accounts in the names of all four of us, I believe. There isn't a million pounds in cash or anything like that. It's mostly investments.

"Ringo has got this brick-building company, and John and I have got a supermarket somewhere, I don't know where it is exactly.

"I don't know about Paul. But I'm sure he has got some good investments as well. That's how it's been done, anyway, we've been partnered up for investments. I remember being told something about two per cent in some building society, but there are so many details to remember you just give in in the end. It's a very complicated business, money.

"I wouldn't like to say that I or Ringo was a millionaire in any way. I'd say there's a fair chance John and Paul are because of all the money they've earned through Northern Songs. I think it would be very hard for all four of us to be real millionaires, anyway.

"Let's say for example that a big pop star in Britain is earning two thousand pounds a night. Then say for example the Beatles earn four thousand pounds a night. That solo star's got the two thousand pounds for himself. With us, it's got to be split four times for a performance. That makes, on paper, one thousand pounds for each show. We just don't do that many real shows. And for us to be millionaires, every one of us, would mean the Beatles would have to gross four million pounds altogether for a four-part split of the money.

"And don't forget, there's a tax fee to be paid, plus Eppy's percentages. So I'm sure Ringo and I can't be millionaires. With John and Paul, it's different because of their song writing.

"Hey, it sounds like I'm talking myself into being broke! It's not that bad. I know I'm okay. If I've got five hundred thousand pounds, I'm not really bothered about the other half million. For half a million, you can buy the sort of house you want, furnish it, and the sort of car you want. The millionaire business is just status. There's a limit to how much you want to spend, in my opinion."

The Beatles met with their accountant every three months to find out what was going on with their money.

"I ask most of the questions, that's why the others say, 'Ask George.' Also, I often have a private chat with the accountant about my own affairs."

The Beatles were not obsessed with money, not on any day-to-day basis. They rarely carried much cash. And large purchases were paid through their office.

Ringo said, *"I just don't find anything to spend money on if I've got it. Sometimes, I haven't got any money on me at all and I have to borrow from Neil or Mal,"* (Roadies Neil Aspinall and Malcolm Evans).

Coleman wondered if they ever thought about how comparatively broke they used to be? Did they miss not being able to go shopping without being crushed by fans?

George replied, *"We've never really thought that much about what we've done and what we've earned and how well off we are. That's one reason we've kept our heads. Everything still knocks us out, we're just not the types to say, 'We've earned plenty, that's enough.' When we hear we've sold another million,*

or something, we still go out of our minds thinking how great it is, and what an achievement.

"It wasn't for the money in the first place. We never sat down and said we wanted to be rich and all that. The money's nice, naturally. But it was getting somewhere that mattered, pride.

"I thought recently it would be nice to walk down a street without people saying, 'That's George Harrison.' But then you see, I probably wouldn't be in that street and able to buy from the shops there if they weren't saying that, would I?

"People say, 'Don't you miss going for a bus ride like any normal bloke?' The answer's no. What? Get some dirty old man breathing down my neck? And anyway, you can never get on buses when you want. I used to stand in bus queues and think how great it would be to have a car, especially when they put the chain across the bus and the conductor said, 'Sorry, full.' I never liked buses and I hate them now, because they get in the way of my posh car!"

Coleman mentioned that John Lennon had four cars, a Rolls Royce, a Volkswagen, a Ferrari, and a Mini – and a twenty thousand pound house. Paul McCartney had an Aston Martin DB5 and a Mini. George Harrison had a twenty thousand pound Surrey bungalow, an Aston Martin DB5 and a Mini. And Ringo Starr had a Facel Vega and a Mini… and rarely carried much cash.

May 15, 1965 – *Record Mirror,* **Norman Jopling reported** that until the Beatles turned up to see Bob Dylan, it was a quiet evening at London's Savoy Hotel. In the restaurant, they all ordered Porridge and Pea Sandwiches… and received them. When one of the group noticed Owls Legs on the menu, that was ordered as well.

"But we wouldn't have known if they hadn't been Owls Legs," Paul explained.

It was rare for the group to have a night out. Their lives were mostly self-contained, insulated, and devoted to self-entertainment.

Said Paul, *"We've all bought sixteen mm film projectors with sound and everything. And we hire loads of films, it's surprising but you can get some of the really latest top films. For instance, I've got* Topkapi *and* Tom Jones. *And we hire some of Elvis's films too. I like them in the same way that I like* Double Your Money.

"The projectors cost a lot of money, about two hundred quid, I think. But they're worthwhile, to us at least, because we don't get a chance to get out and see these films. John is the really keen one. He has it all organised, showing two films a night now. It's just like the cinema round his place. We all sit there eyes glued to the screen. And he doesn't start showing them until late, well, after television has finished and none of us get to bed until fantastically late hours. We sit all bleary-eyed in front of the screen making signs with our hands on the screen, little animals and all that.

"So far we haven't got a copy of A Hard Day's Night. *Not that it bothers me. I didn't like the film anyway. Seriously, I mean that. The original novelty of seeing yourself on screen wears off. You know, like home movies of yourself at the seaside. The good thing is that at least you can come out with anecdotes every ten seconds about what happened behind the scenes."*

He switched subjects to their next film, *Help.*

"I like this one better. It has been great filming it. But all the residents of the Bahamas hated us. Really. They're so rich there and they were so rude to us that we just didn't care. We all rented Triumph Spitfires and drove them around the island. They didn't like that, either. But there are some good scenes from the film. There are shots of us in a disused quarry, using it as a race track. We found it when we were waiting for the technicians. We were screeching around it like mad. Well, they filmed it slyly and put it in the film, just like that.

"There are no speeded up shots, like in A Hard Day's Night, *but there are some visual gimmicks. Like standing on a rock in the middle of the ocean playing our instruments. And the next shot with us up to our necks in water, still playing. And one of Ringo, lying on his stomach on the beach swimming in the sand."*

Paul sang the Beatles' next single, *Help,* maintaining it was much better than *Ticket to Ride.*

He said, *"Can't say I liked* Ticket *much. But his new one is, in my opinion, good. I hope I don't sound big-headed. But I like it, it's certainly the fastest record we've made and it's very different. It's a bit like the middle eight in* It Won't Be Long.

"I think that John and I are writing different sort of songs to what we were a couple of years back. I can't say whether they're better or worse, but they're certainly different. And that is okay by us because we wouldn't want to stand still, to stagnate musically…"

Jopling doubted that would ever happen.

May 29, 1965 – *Melody Maker* **reported** that once again the British press was declaring that the Beatles were finished.

Said John Lennon, *"It's a load of crap, there's just nothing to it. Until we don't get number one hits, or something near the number one position, there can't be anything in any claims that we're slipping or finished. The whole bit about 'Beatles slipping,' 'Beatles finished' and all that, bores us all. People who say that's what's happening have usually got a bee in their bonnet. The same old stuff all over again, someone says it every couple of weeks, anyway. 'The Beatles are ill-mannered,' 'The Beatles have had it,' 'The Beatles are all over,' – let 'em say it if they want to. We just couldn't care less."*

Ringo snapped, *"Not again. If we are going down, so what?"*

And George Harrison said, *"For a kick-off,* Ticket to Ride *got to number one, and as far as I'm*

concerned, that means it sold more records than any other single at the time. A number one record's good enough proof to me that we're fairly popular still.

"Fans going off us? We still must have millions because if we hadn't they wouldn't have sent us to number one. We wouldn't sell out shows, either. People who attack us like this really do talk crap. As Brian Epstein said on TV last Sunday, we're still apparently big enough to be talked about.

"I'd like to make one point especially, if people are going to knock the Beatles, would they please come and do it to our faces? Let's have it out direct."

June 19, 1965 – *Disc Weekly***, Laurie Henshaw spoke** with Walter Shenson. The final touches were being put on the Beatles' new picture, *Help!*, which was to premiere on July 29th at the London Pavilion. Princess Margaret and Lord Snowden were to attend as, of course, were the Beatles.

The group was doing a post-sync session. And Walter Shenson, producer of *Help!* and *A Hard Day's Night* explained what that meant.

"It's merely re-recording some lines and words that were not audible when we were shooting on location in Nassau and the Alps. Obviously, extraneous noises, such as an airplane passing overhead, can blot out the odd word. And then, of course, you can't always keep all the people around absolutely quiet. So the boys will be re-doing the words that are not clearly recorded.

"This is absolutely normal filming procedure."

Henshaw said the Beatles' next single would be the title song from the movie, due out on July 23rd. The B side would also be a Lennon / McCartney composition, but not one from the film. And two weeks after that, an album of the film soundtrack would be released. It was to include all seven of the songs that were featured in the picture, along with other new stuff written by the Beatles.

Shenson thought *Help!* was one of the best Beatle songs ever. He also singled out *The Night Before,* heard during a film sequence that had been shot on Salisbury Plain.

Shenson said, *"One thing we were all determined upon, and that was not to make* Help! *anything like* A Hard Day's Night. *The Beatles had very strong feelings about that, too. I can tell you that* Help! *is pure entertainment, and the colour is absolutely wonderful."*

June 19, 1965 – *Disc Weekly* **reported** there had been considerable controversy about the Beatles being awarded the MBE. The writer asked other entertainers what they thought about it.

Graham Nash of the Hollies: *"Wonderful news. They've done so much for British pop music all over the world. It's an honour really deserved."*

Athol Guy of the Seekers: *"This is just great. It shows the awareness of pop music that exists in the world today. It's an honour not only for the Beatles but for pop music as a whole."*

Dusty Springfield: *"They've done so much for the business and there's no doubting that they really are the stand-out people on today's pop scene."*

Ken Lewis of Ivy League: *"We're knocked out. There's bound to be criticism from some quarters but certainly not from us. Let's not forget that such an award reflects great credit on the entire younger generation."*

Gene Pitney: *"That's great! Think of it. Ringo Starr MBE, what a gas! Seriously though, they deserve it for the work they've done in pop and the way they've handled themselves all over the world."*

Tom Jones: *"Well done! Good luck! Over here* [New York] *all the papers were headlined 'Beatles Get MBE for Putting Britain on the Map.'"*

Francois Hardy: *"I think it's great and very normal. They've done very much good for England."*

The Shadows: *"Congratulations."*

Cliff Bennett: *"They deserve it, if anybody's going to get it in the music business."*

Marianne Faithful: *"That's great. I think it's very funny and I'd like to hear what John Lennon has to say about it. I don't think it will upset their popularity."*

And finally, Paul's girl friend, Jane Asher: *"I'm delighted. Absolutely thrilled."*

June 19, 1965 – *Disc Weekly,* **Laurie Henshaw spoke** with George Harrison about the Beatles receiving the MBE.

"I was at home when I heard it was definite," George said. *"But it was while we filming six weeks ago that we had the forms from the Prime Minster's secretary. We found them in the dressing room. The day after they'd been put there.*

"Paul opened his first. He looked amazed and said, 'Here, look at this!' We looked and saw the forms and a letter saying, 'Your name has been put forward for The Queen's Birthday Honours for the MBE.' It added how it was all in confidence and he was not to say a word.

"We asked Paul whether we had similar letters. We thought he'd just got one on his own. That would have been a laugh. All we had to do was fill in our names and addresses, send the form back and just wait. We didn't really find out until the same time as the Press that it was definite."

His reaction to it?

"There's nothing really to say apart from it's great. And it wasn't expected at all."

How had George and the rest of the Beatles been spending their time since finishing the movie?

"I went up to my parents' in Liverpool over the weekend. Otherwise, I've just been lazing about. But I've been out a lot around the clubs like the Ad Lib.

"Paul was the only one who went away. He stayed in one of those flats in Portugal owned by Cliff, the Shadows and Frank Ifield. They've all got flats adjoining each other.

"John, Ringo and myself stayed in England. I've just had my swimming pool at home finished and

John and I have been swimming. The pool is about forty feet long. It's the ideal size for a private pool. Not too small and not too big. Just right."*

He mentioned that he was looking forward to the group's trip to Paris on the weekend. *"This will be my third visit. I've got a couple of friends there, French people, and it makes it much easier. They know all the places to take people. The first time we were a bit lost, wandering around. We didn't really know what was happening."*

Had he learned any French?

"Not really. I'm a bit lazy about languages. It took me so long at school, and I didn't even manage to pick up much German during the twelve months we were there. So I couldn't be bothered staring again with French... If they can't speak English, hard luck!"

Henshaw asked who would get married first, George or Paul.

"I've no idea at all. We'll have to wait and see what happens. I've nothing planned yet."

June 19, 1965 – *Melody Maker* **wrote** the facts about the Beatles and the MBE. They reminded everyone that four months previously, they had started their *Honour the Beatles* campaign. March 6, 1965, to be exact. And then, last weekend, the MBE was awarded to Ringo Starr, George Harrison, Paul McCartney and John Lennon.

Then the critics started knocking and the complaints began. Two MBE awardees declared they would return their medals. The Beatles were attacked up and down the country by reactionary clowns who should have known better.

Melody Maker reiterated: the Beatles deserved a national honour.

In the past two years, they had contributed far more to British exports than any of the folks who were complaining about the Beatles being honoured for their achievements. They had *"waved the British flag"* all over the world. And the standards for rock music would never be the same again. Thousands of teenagers had taken up music making. Even adults had been thrilled and entertained by them, even the ones who supposedly loathed pop music.

Melody Maker made one simple declarative statement regarding its feelings about the Beatles and the MBE:

"We are knocked out with delight."

The writer wondered if *Melody Maker* had influenced Premier Harold Wilson into suggesting that the Queen make the award.

"It was a nice idea, the campaign," said Ringo. *"We didn't really take it seriously at the time because we never dreamed anything like this was possible. But now it could have influenced the decision."*

Congratulations, Beatles, from *Melody Maker,* the magazine that leads.

June 19, 1965 – *Melody Maker* **declared** again that it was the first British voice to suggest national honours for the Beatles. And so, they were. John Lennon, Paul McCartney, George Harrison and Ringo Starr were each accorded the right to follow their names with the letters MBE – Members of the British Empire.

Melody Maker was thrilled that their campaign to honour the Beatles ended with such positive results. They were delighted that the Beatles had been feted. They had brought glory to Britain and had rejuvenated an entire country; no honour was more greatly deserved, no group of people more deserving than John, Paul, George and Ringo – Members of the British Empire.

June 19, 1965 – *Melody Maker* spoke with John Lennon and George Harrison about the Beatles' planned European tour.

Said John, *"As far as we're concerned, touring Europe is just about the same as starting all over again. It should be interesting because everything's so much more different over there. There's less Beatlemania on the Continent than in many other parts of the world, mainly because their sort of music is different. So I suppose we'll give them plain, hard rock and roll numbers, especially in places like France and Italy.*

"We're not blasé about it. We're approaching it more with interest than confidence, and every show we're doing, I believe, all over the Continent, is being televised. It'll be good in Paris, with all these lads chasing us about again. They seem to lock their women away over there, they're not allowed out at night, or something."

George said, *"We haven't had really big hits in Spain, France or Italy. The whole idea of going there is to get them interested in the film. I'm not expecting anything very big. They're so far behind there with the music, anyway. I suppose we're reasonably okay in Paris; when we played a three-week season there it was a complete sell-out, so we're not exactly flops, are we. Even the biggest artists in Paris don't sell a lot of records. What this European tour will give us, more than anything to us, is the chance to play. We just like playing, y'know."*

The tour was to include Paris, Lyons, Milan, Genoa, Rome, Nice, Madrid and Barcelona. They were to return to England on July 4th.

June 19, 1965 – *Melody Maker*, Mike Hennessey wrote from Paris… that France was probably the least Beatle-mad country in the world aside from, perhaps, certainly up-country regions in central Asia. Their previous visit, while successful, was not the incredible triumph they had experienced in other countries. The Stones, the Kinks, the Animals, had all received better receptions. *A Hard Day's Night*, dubbed in French, did not do very well. Their records sold, of course, but no figures were available.

After saying all that, he pointed out that both concerts at the Palais des Sports were pretty much sold out. Paris was festooned with advertising posters for the shows, both of which would be filmed and broadcast on French TV as well as being recorded for the radio.

Apparently, the latest Beatles EP was selling well, though no one could find copies of *Ticket to Ride*. Another EP was planned for the following month, including songs from *Help!*

He spoke with Henri Leproux, operator of the rock club *Le Golf Drouot*, perhaps the number one authority in Paris on Beatles fans. Said Leproux, *"The kids rate the Beatles tops musically, but they are disappointed that they cannot make any personal contact with them. The Stones, the Kinks, the Animals, they have all visited the club and circulated freely among the fans.*

"There is no mobbing here. French kids aren't like that. I think the kids realise it is not the fault of the Beatles themselves, but of the people who over-protect them."

Hennessey suggested though that, for all the lack of Beatlemania, the concerts would be a riot. Literally. Sunday was the best day in Paris for a concert and the Palais des Sports was well-known for it's sports riots. Every rock and roller and every available cop would be there. Six thousands teenagers in a place known for riots could be quite interesting.

As a footnote, he added that hotel rooms for the Beatles had been difficult to find. Finally, five rooms had been booked at the Relais Bisson on the Left Bank, not far from Notre Dame.

June 26, 1965 – *Record Mirror*, Chris Denning of Radio Luxembourg, reported on the Beatles in Paris. A young French reporter asked John Lennon, *"How many times are you doing here in Paris?"*

Stone-faced, Lennon replied, *"We're here about two days. I suppose that's about eight times…"*

The group's reception at the George Cinq Hotel had been quiet, only about fifty people on hand to greet them. But the show as a huge success, the evening appearance even wilder than the matinee. Playing to an audience made up of more boys than girls, the Beatles opened with *Twist and Shout* and the cheers grew louder. Cops were everywhere but they allowed fans to break through their cordon and hang out by the Beatles dressing room door; however, they refused to let Brian Epstein through with his camera.

Denning suggested that if the reception in Paris was any indication of how they would fare during the rest of the tour, then the tour would be incredibly successful.

June 26, 1965 – *Disc Weekly* published a letter from Morris Rowland of Warrington, Lancashire: Isn't it now time for the Beatles to retire? Pack away their drums and guitars and find employment in other branches of entertainment?

Lennon and McCartney were, of course, all set for a future as prolific songwriters. Harrison, failing the former occupation, could be an excellent session man, or retire completely with a steady income from Northern Songs. And Ringo? Well, he's Ringo, the most popular Beatle of them all. He could find immediate employment in films or television.

But NOW is the time for the four to decide – and not let the public 'get wise' to the fact that they have left their teens. The signs are evident in America, where their latest disc made Number One for one week only. Let them quit at the top.

Disc went on to ask its readers what they thought – should the group retire, is their popularity fading, or would they continue to pump out number one hits? *Disc* also wanted to know what its readers thought about the Beatles receiving the MBE. The best writer would be… an LP Winner!

June 26, 1965 – *Disc Weekly*, **Laurie Henshaw reviewed** John Lennon's book *A Spaniard In The Works,* suggesting the entire thing was done tongue-in-cheek, from the pose on the cover to the last word of this ninety-page volume. Sardonically giving a clear picture of Lennon's thoughts on people, attitudes, politics, religion, hypocrisy and newspapermen, this is John being, at times, cruel, and always grotesquely humorous.

June 26, 1965 – *Melody Maker*, **Mike Hennessy wrote** from Paris, the last holdout against the worldwide Beatlemania epidemic. The city finally surrendered to the inevitable. The Beatles conquered, with two sold out shows at the Palais des Sports. The reception was superb. But, by French standards, it was astounding. Hennessy said MBE stood for Massive Beatle Enthusiasm – in Paris.

He applauded the group for receiving their MBEs, and quoted Brian Epstein, *"How can they bloody well say they didn't deserve them?"*

Of course they deserved them.

With the MBE controversy out of the way, Hennessey suggested that the opening of the European tour could not have been more successful. With Paris in ruins, they were ready to storm through the rest of Europe. Lyons had been a sell-out show; Milan – eighteen thousand seats – was a sell-out show, as was Genoa.

Looking further ahead, Brian Epstein told him that every ticket had been sold, fifty-five thousand seats, for the Beatles' show at Shea Stadium in New York City in August. It would be the largest audience the band had ever faced.

In Paris, Hennessy said the sight was unforgettable, the audience, a mass of swirling colour, leaping and screaming, waving their arms and yelling for the Beatles. At the end of the second show, he said, the gendarmes and the security guards did everything they could to start a riot but that there were only a few overturned seats, no real damage, no

serious trouble. The endless security precautions, cops with fire hoses at the ready, leaflets warning fans they would be tossed from the stadium, proved unnecessary.

The over-caution started as the group landed at Orly Airport. The cops refused to allow a press conference for fear of a riot. Since there were only about fifty people on hand to greet them, including a number of British girls who had stayed overnight on the roof of the airport, the gendarmes' fear seemed somewhat unnecessary. At one point, they even refused Brian Epstein entrance to the Palais.

Said John Lennon, *"These coppers think they're okay while De Gaulle's in charge, but just wait till Eppy takes over. The trouble is, they read in the papers about all this Beatlemania crap – sorry, for the* Melody Maker *I have to say rubbish – and then they panic."*

Before the show, the band was a bit nervous. They had not played to an audience in a few weeks and felt themselves out of touch. There was some pre-show confusion, John discovering he had packed two left boots, the skin on Ringo's snare drum split, no one could find the small amps that the band used for tuning their guitars…

"We'll have to be folk," said John. *"And tune up on stage."*

But when they hit the stage, the confusion vanished, professionalism took over, and they literally attacked the audience with sound while Paul announced the numbers in French… sort of. They closed the second show with *Ticket to Ride.* The audience, not expecting an encore, started to leave their seats. And the Beatles re-took the stage to finish off with *Long Tall Sally.*

The fans charged the stage, the cops plowed into them to keep them back. Hennessy saw a young girl punched in the face by a cop, saw others slashed with police capes. He saw three young boys in John Lennon caps and red shirts with *"We love you Beatles"* stenciled on their backs, have their Beatle-decorated umbrella grabbed and smashed by the police during the cop-inspired chaos.

Back in the dressing room, John said, *"You don't get any time to breathe."*

June 26, 1965 – *Melody Maker* **said** if anyone attempted to catalogue the British export trade during the past few years, he would have quite a task simply trying to sort out the effects of one simple force: The Beatles.

The international lunacy, the waves of worldwide publicity, tended to mask the simple fact that the Beatles had contributed incredibly to the world music scene. More than merely selling records and sheet music, they had inspired huge sales of musical instruments, particularly guitars.

Music publisher Dick James said, *"At last count there were one thousand nine hundred and twenty round-the-world cover versions of Beatles songs –*

songs written by Lennon and McCartney. Without the Beatles, the whole trend of popular music in the last few years just wouldn't be.

"They fired the imagination of every back-room guitarist. They drew the map and marked the path. Thousands and thousands of groups followed, all round the world.

"Music took on a new lease on life as a result of their effect. They should be honoured to mark the gratitude of many, many people all over the world."

In Japan, and even behind the Iron Curtain, the Beatles had hit records, while in England, the explosion of Merseyside musicians led the way. The Beat Boom was the largest pop movement ever, still going strong in an active music scene.

And the Beatles started it all, whipping up a frenzy everywhere. One record, *I Want To Hold Your Hand*, sold 4,900,000 copies in the U.S., another 10,000,000 worldwide.

Said George Harrison, *"What amazed us has been the sales in places like Japan. You expect that if you're going to be internationally successful, you should make it in the States. But you don't really expect the Far East. We've also had terrific success in places like Peru, the Argentine and the Philippines. Somehow, you don't expect them to be twisting and shouting so much, over in those places."*

It was more than just the music industry that was to benefit from the Beatles. Merchandising of epic proportions was happening everywhere, Beatle shirts, Beatle skirts, Beatle bubble gum cards, Beatle shoes, Beatle jewelry, Beatle lunch boxes, Beatle juke boxes, Beatle record players, Beatle dishes and glassware, not to mention Beatle wigs, Beatle hair gunk, Beatle buttons and badges, Beatle posters, Beatle coin purses, Beatle bath curtains, Beatle plastic dashboard Jesus figurines, Beatle everything…

And it all grew from four young guys who basically started with music as a hobby and ended up conquering the world. In 1966, they were slated to be listed in Who's Who as a group and as individuals.

It seemed appropriate.

July 3, 1965 – *Melody Maker* **wrote** about the Beatles in Europe. A young Italian girl screamed for the group as they entered a hotel in Milan. Immediately, the kid's mother *"belted the hell out of her,"* said Paul McCartney. *"That's the sort of attitude there is from some of the adults here. Some of these parents, the big fat Italian mamas, think it's a disgrace for their kids to scream for the Beatles. We just think it's a bloody shame."*

They had no idea how they would be received as they entered Italy.

"But really," Paul said, *"it's been a knockout. There have been some reports, I believe, that the Beatles were a flop in Milan. Well, there were ten thousand at the first show and twenty-two thousand at the second. I didn't think that was too bad."*

"We've been enjoying it quite a lot. Working one day, resting the next. Officially, the second day is supposed to be for traveling, but that hasn't been too rough."

With regards to their doubts before starting the tour, Paul said, *"We thought they wouldn't know anything about us here. We expected it to be just like it was in Paris on our first trip, very cold from the outset. Well, it hasn't been, and there have been some fantastic scenes. I think the reason is that they have found out much more about the international music scene in the last year or so.*

"We've made a film, Hard Day's Night, that's been reasonably popular, and I think they simply have more knowledge about us now than we feared."

Talking about Italian journalists, Paul said, *"There is a corps of these little fellows on scooters, Italian photographers, I think they call them paparazzi, who never seem to stop taking pictures every time we step out. We'll probably be very fed up with it by the time we get to Rome.*

"I walked down from my room to the car and I'll swear there were thirty pictures taken in the second I ran from the door to the car. It's fantastic."

Asked what were their most popular songs in Italy, he replied, *"Ticket to Ride was very popular, lately, it has been getting quite a bit of airplay. Things like A Hard Day's Night and Rock and Roll Music have always been good for the Continent. Long Tall Sally as well, straight rockers are the most popular.*

"It's all going well but we're all a bit nervous, still. Big crowds have always scared us."

July 10, 1965 – *Record Mirror* **announced** that the Beatles were to headline the TV show Blackpool Night Out on August 1st. They went on to talk about the Beatles' new LP, which contained fourteen tracks, the majority of them Lennon / McCartney songs, including *Help*. The record was due to be released on August 6th by Parlophone. *Record Mirror* was predicting huge advance sales. The songs were:

Help: sung by John with George and Paul harmonising.

The Night Before: featuring Paul, with John and George singing back-up. The electric piano was played by John.

You've Got to Hide Your Love Away: John sang the lead, accompanied by flutes.

I Need You: written by George and featuring him as the lead vocal, accompanied by Paul and John.

Another Girl: with Paul singing the lead vocal and playing lead guitar, backed by John and George.

You're Going to Lose That Girl: John singing lead.

Ticket to Ride: the end of side one, sung by John and Paul, Paul also playing a guitar solo.

Act Naturally: Ringo sang the lead.

It's Only Love: John's vocals.

You Like Me Too Much: another Harrison composition with George singing, John playing electric piano, George Martin and Paul on Steinway pianos.

Tell Me What You See: sung by John and Paul with John again on electric piano.

I've Just Seen a Face: Paul took the solo.

Yesterday: Paul sang the lead and played the guitar solo, backed by a string quartet.

Dizzy Miss Lizzy: a rocker sung by John.

They finished with a footnote mentioning that an excerpt from *Help!* would be televised during the 200th episode of Lucky Stars.

July 17, 1965 – *Disc Weekly* reported where the new Beatles film could be seen. *Help!* was to premiere at the London Pavilion July 29th. Also on July 29th, it would be opening at the following Odeon theatres: Brighton, Worthing, Canterbury, Ramsgate, Folkestone, Dover, Deal, Lowestoft, Clacton, Grimsby, Morecambe, Llandudno, Rhyl, Southend, Gaumont Weymouth, and Drake Plymouth.

On August 1st, it would be released in forty-four theatres throughout North London, and commencing August 8th, thirty-three theatres in South London.

Also on August 1st, the Liverpool Gaumont and the Manchester Odeon would have the movie.

The group was to appear live on Blackpool Night Out on August 1st.

On August 13th, they were leaving for the States.

July 17, 1965 – *Disc Weekly* announced that Paul McCartney had been on hand for a Variety Club luncheon at the Savoy Hotel in London to receive Ivor Novello awards for: Outstanding Theme for Radio TV or Film: *A Hard Day's Night*; the Highest Selling A-side: *Can't Buy Me Love*; and the Most Performed Record of the Year: *Can't Buy Me Love*.

July 17, 1965 – *Disc Weekly*, Ray Coleman spoke with George Harrison. The single *Help!* was due to be released on July 23rd.

George said, "*I'm not presuming we will go straight to the top or anything like that. But I hope we'll get up there even if we don't go there straight away. As far as the chart's concerned, there are only two or three really strong movers and I can't see why the Stones shouldn't be the group to knock us off the top if we make it.*"

Satisfaction, by the Stones, was due to be released at the end of August.

Said George, "*I like the Stones' thing. It's the best one they've done, I think, and I wouldn't mind being knocked off the top by it.*"

Talking about *Help!*, George said, "*It's quite involved, a bit more involved than others we've done because it has a counter-melody going as well as the main melody. It features John singing the lead lines, with Paul and me doing counter-melody in between. There's a repeating line in each chorus. Again, I think it's a grower, the sort of song people will have to hear a few times before they realise what it's all about.*

"*Ticket to Ride was probably one of the hardest singles, for others to get used to, that is, because of the strange lines. It's roughly the same with this, people will have to hear it a few times before they get the gist of it.*

"*We all think it's the best single we've had out for a long time. We are all really pleased with it.*"

Coleman asked if George could compare it with any other Beatles record.

"*It's a bit like It Won't Be Long, that's the only one it is anything like.*"

Coleman asked about a Lennon / McCartney song on the B side, *I'm Down*.

"*It's a rocker and Paul takes the lead vocal. John is on Hammond organ. It's pretty wild. Wild because it has Paul's wild voice, it's either his best singing voice or his worst, depending on which you like. I suppose he did it with his Little Richard-type voice. It's that sort of number, anyway.*"

The group had always strived for some good solid rock. Coleman said they preferred *I'm Down* as a song, though perhaps not commercially.

George told him, "Help! *is an A-side song, and the natural main side. But John and I wanted to have* I'm Down *as the A-side, if there wasn't a film to consider. We think it would have been good to have parts one and two for* I'm Down*, but looking back on that, it was just a crazy, wild idea.*

"It's a funny thing about B-sides. Fans often say they prefer them to the A-sides, but I imagine that's because they've heard the A so much, and suddenly they realise the B is a good song as well. Then what happens is that they grow to like it more because they don't get so exposed to it on TV and radio."

After listening to the Stones' *Satisfaction* again, George said, "*I like it. But the guitar bit's very much like* Nowhere To Run. *It'll be funny if they do knock us off the top of the chart.*

"The headline writers can get busy with things like 'Stones taking over from Beatles!'"

July 24, 1965 – Chris Welch wrote for *Melody Maker* that he had just heard the Beatles' new LP. He thought it was good and predicted the rest of the bands in Britain would be crying for Help in order to produce something equally good. He reviewed the album track by track, enthusiastically until he reached the final song, *Dizzy Miss Lizzy*. He thought it was a let-down and somewhat unconvincing after following *Yesterday*. The beauty of the Beatles' music was that they knew how to communicate. They had good, original ideas and set them down so people understood what they were talking about. He pictured them as medieval minstrels, performing beneath some lady's window.

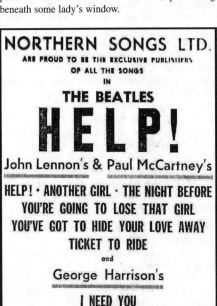

NORTHERN SONGS LTD.
ARE PROUD TO BE THE EXCLUSIVE PUBLISHERS
OF ALL THE SONGS
IN
THE BEATLES
HELP!
John Lennon's & Paul McCartney's
HELP! · ANOTHER GIRL · THE NIGHT BEFORE
YOU'RE GOING TO LOSE THAT GIRL
YOU'VE GOT TO HIDE YOUR LOVE AWAY
TICKET TO RIDE
and
George Harrison's
I NEED YOU
NORTHERN SONGS LTD., James House, 71-75 New Oxford St.
London, W.C.1. Tel.: Temple Bar 1687.

July 31, 1965 – *Disc Weekly* **announced that** *Help!* had gone straight to the top of the charts. They ran the opening lyrics and asked John how it had been written.

He said, "*We wrote it in my house. I had little bit of a song which I'd played around at writing, called something like* Keep Your Hands Off My Babe. *Anyway, it was floating around for a long time, and when Paul came over we decided to sort of adapt it. We wrote* Help! *after we'd been told of the film title. We never write to fit in with the story line. This one seemed to fit okay.*"

July 31, 1965 – Ray Coleman wrote for *Disc Weekly...* Five years ago, Ringo Starr had been considering emigration. Had he gone through with it...

Said Ringo, "*I was on the dole when I was twenty. There wasn't anything for me to stick around for. So a mate and I decided we'd emigrate to Houston in Texas, because Lightnin' Hopkins lived there and we liked his stuff. We even went as far as getting the emigration forms to fill in. But we took one look at the things they wanted to know and packed in the whole idea.*

"Questions like 'Was your grandma's uncle's best friend a whatever?' We just laughed and packed it in."

The leap from collecting the dole in Liverpool to being a member of the most important rock band in the world was stunning, dizzying. Shyly, Ringo said, "*I've seen the picture, we all went to the American embassy to see it. They can go ahead and release it, I'm not ashamed of it or anything. I hope the fans like it, really. If they liked* A Hard Day's Night*, they ought to find this one hundred per cent better. As a picture, it's much better made, although this is fantasy compared with* A Hard Day's Night *being documentary.*

"We're quite prepared for a knocking. We've had a hell of a lot of it lately, what with the MBE business. When you get popular, you must expect it. Look at Georgie Fame. When he played club dates at the Flamingo, they said he was great. Suddenly, he made a hit and laid himself wide open for knocking.

"Everyone wants to be a David Frost because it's so easy to knock big names."

The Beatles had been relaxing lately, just waiting for the storm when *Help!* was released.

Ringo said, "*We need it. In the last two years we have worked so hard, and we couldn't carry on at this pace. We'd die. Two or three tours of Britain, American and the Continent, plus all the TVs and other things, it was enough to kill anybody.*

"We had a conference with Brian and it was decided to ease off a little bit. I reckon it was the sensible thing."

Regarding *Help!* he said, "*I hate being put in the front of anything. And I don't want anybody to think the film hangs on me. But it's all about a ring, and it* would have been soft if Paul, for instance, had been chosen as the central figure, it would have been daft."

He talked about buying a house near John Lennon.

"With the baby coming I need some more space than I've got in this flat. And how could we put a baby outside the front door in a pram? Somebody might pinch it and raffle it off. Win Ringo's baby or something."

About the Stones' new song, *Satisfaction,* which he and the rest of the band liked a lot: *"Watch out, Matt Monro. It's a good record."*

And his Rolls Royce, which he bought from John Lennon: *"Compared with his new one, it's just a mini."*

July 31, 1965 – *Disc Weekly* declared National Beatles Week, saying the group was back with a bang. *Help!* the single was at the top of the charts. And they would soon be facing the verdict on their new movie.

Said Ringo, *"We've done our bit. Now it's up to the public, they're entitled to hate it. But we're quite pleased with the result."*

Disc told their readers to forget about *A Hard Day's Night* when they went to see the new film. They were nothing alike. *Help!* was a full-colour flight into fantasy, brilliantly filmed, the comedy a cross between the Marx Brothers and *It's a Mad Mad Mad Mad World,* inspired flashes of humour, slapstick and otherwise, and great music.

They went on to mention that Eleanor Bron would not be attending the premiere since she was on the road with a repertory company. She had been worried about accepting the part in *Help!* and said, *"I needn't have worried. They were very kind, and made me feel at home. They've all got a marvelous sense of humour and are wonderful company. I became very fond of them all. I suppose it's silly, but you can't help being a little in awe of them. They don't like this at all, and hate people keeping their distance."*

Describing *Help!,* Walter Shenson, producer, said, *"A comic strip vividly brought to life and packed with colour, thrills and that distinctive Beatles humour, that's how I would sum up* Help!*, the film we have now brought to you, the Beatles fans, after months' of hard work.*

"But it's a different kind of magic, this time. Instead of depicting a day in the life of the Beatles, we show their adventurers through a whole series of days. Adventures that take them from England to the Alps, where you'll see breathtaking scenery and wonderful skiing sequences, to Salisbury Plain, and then to the Bahamas. But, apart from the scenery, there are plenty of thrills."

The Beatles' *Help!* LP proved beyond all doubt that the Beatles were not losing their touch. George Martin said, *"When sessions begin, my heart's usually in my mouth. I wonder sometimes whether they can keep it up time after time, but they do. They're terribly workmanlike in the studio. I don't*

mean that they're deadly serious and sombre. They're always full of fun."

Delighted with George Harrison's song writing, he said, "I Need You *worked out very well. George got a bit discouraged some time ago when none of us liked something he'd written. He has got something to say as a songwriter and I hope he'll keep at it."*

You've Got To Hide Your Love Away clearly showed the influence of Bob Dylan and Martin said, *"I asked him not to sound too much like Dylan. He wasn't doing it deliberately. It was subconscious more than anything."*

July 31, 1965 – *Melody Maker* said that the Beatles had gone directly to the top of the charts – on release day – for the sixth time. *Help!* was a huge hit, their ninth number one song.

"We are delighted and surprised, we always are surprised when it happens," said the Beatles.

The next event for the group would be the premier of *Help!* at the London Pavilion, a royal occasion featuring Princess Margaret and Lord Snowdon.

July 31, 1965 – *Melody Maker* reviewed *Help!*

"Not nearly enough of the Beatles," said a young girl after the press viewing two days prior to the World Premiere. And she was right. In spite of the fact that the Beatles were in every long scene, they did not talk enough, no chit chat, no quips and quotables. The reviewer thought the other actors, Roy Kinnear, Patrick Cargill, Eleanor Bron, Victor Spinetti and Peter Copley, were on screen far too often.

There was far too much buffoonery. The very best sequences were when the Beatles were simply being the Beatles, skiing, hanging out in their flat, playing cards in the palace. The writer suggested that sometimes, their humour went by so fast that it was missed completely, but it was always better than the lines from the pros, which often seemed mistimed and awkward.

The songs were great, some of the best ever written by Lennon and McCartney. *Help!, You're Gonna Lose That Girl, The Night Before...* all were brilliant.

Dick Lester's direction was beautiful. And of the Beatles, Ringo again stole the show. In summation, it was great entertainment. But in the future, lose the supporting cast. They were not needed.

August 7, 1965 – *Disc Weekly*, Ray Coleman suggested that the Beatles' new movie, according to the bad reviews, was not successful. Ironically, *Help!* was being panned at a time when it was said that the Beatles needed to be knocked down a peg or two. Using the new film, the reviewers were attempting to do just that.

But the Beatles could take care of themselves.

Paul McCartney said, *"The big mistake too many people make, including me, is in believing that all they read in certain newspapers is true. After all our* time in reading what the writers say about us, I think what happened was this: some of them went along with preconceived ideas about the film and wanted some sort of headline like: Beatles Flop!

"Then I imagine they saw the film and couldn't honestly say that, because it isn't a flop. They had to get something to justify their ideas so they found little things to niggle about. I would like to have seen what they said about it if this was our first film and Hard Day's Night the second.

"Most of the critics had to say it would be a big hit, and that was their get-out, I think. They decided that after they'd admitted that it would make money, they might as well have a go. Fair enough, I suppose, if they wanted to. But we know enough about the attitude of critics now to understand what's happening, it wouldn't have been so newsy and such a talking-point for the public if they'd all said it was the second film and much better than the first, would it?

"What really makes us laugh about the whole business of being criticised is that some of the people who knock actually believe in what they're saying. They think what they write is the truth, the whole truth, and nothing but the truth. It's just one big laugh if they do believe it, because we know different."

He went on to say that the danger in criticism was that the public might actually believe it, rather than making up their own minds and doing their own thinking.

"The world's just not got used to realising, as we do, that it's just one man's opinion against another's. And also, it's a question of the mood a person goes to see the film in. I know if it was my job to go and see a picture and comment on it, I might well be in a lousy mood when I saw it. And the result might easily be a bad review."

Coleman wanted to know if the Beatles were developing an immunity to the knockers.

"The knocking hasn't had any real overall effect on us. It's like if somebody comes up and says, 'that's a nice jacket you're wearing.' You think: Great.

"If somebody comes up and says, 'You were lousy on Blackpool Night Out,' of course we're not pleased. But we don't brood on it, or anything. It's just depressing at the time.

"People are entitled to their own tastes. If I said Elizabeth Taylor was the best looking actress in the world, and somebody else argued that Bardot was, it wouldn't make me right and him wrong. It's taste, that's all. We don't mind the knocks, really. We try to ignore them. It's much nicer to read nice things about us than nasty things. But you've all got to remember one thing all the time – even knockers are human, aren't they?"

As a footnote, Disc printed eight letters from "fans." The score was: Great Film 5, Bad Film 3.

August 7, 1965 – Dave Clark of the Dave Clark Five wrote for Disc Weekly, answering the critics who regarded Help! a flop. Theatre queues were stretching around the blocks hours before the

theatres were to open. How could that be considered a flop?

Clark mentioned that if he had not liked the film, he would be willing to say so. Some critics suggested that the Beatles were trying to be the Marx Brothers but simply were not good enough. Dave Clark maintained they were not trying to be anyone other than Beatles, at which they were very good. He loved Lennon's wit, which shone throughout the film. And he enjoyed the slapstick sequences, even though some folks were inclined to sneer at that sort of comedy.

As for the music, all the songs were great. The more you listened, the more you would like them.

The photography was stunning, the scenery brilliant. The film makers deserved much credit for what they had done.

The film was a success.

And the critics approached it, first, with a preconceived idea of what it should be, what they wanted it to be. Help! was funny… and commercial. And the reviewers were hardened critics seeking to find fault, looking for something to knock. They derided it for being pop. But, really, what was bigger than pop? What was bigger than the Beatles and their MBEs?

The Beatles may be taking a few knocks from hard-nosed critics. But certainly not from their fans. And most definitely not from Dave Clark.

August 7, 1965 – Disc Weekly spoke with John Lennon about that week's Top 30 Chart which featured Help! at number one.

"Can't think of anything I'd rather see at the top," said Lennon. "The Fortunes isn't a bad song, and I suppose it's a well-deserved hit. Their song was written by two of the Kestrels and they used to tour with us. They're writing good material like the Fourmosts's Everything In The Garden as well."

Disc asked what would knock the Beatles off the top.

"…so all those headlines can scream, 'Beatles slipping!' It might be Jonathan King [Everyone's Gone to the Moon]. It's very commercial but not the sort of stuff I like. I want to be knocked off the top by the Stones' Satisfaction. Either that or the new Kinks, See My Friends. It's great, the best they've done. Hope Ray Davies' finger gets better.

"All the daft ones are coming up and all the good ones are going down. It must be the summer. It always happens like this in the summer. Can't stand all those crappy Walks in the Black Forest [Horst Jankowski] and all that.

"I've always thought P.J. Proby [Let the Water Run Down] could be very big, but I never thought much of his latest song. He's got a good voice, but he needs a Lennon / McCartney song to get away.

"Quite like the Zorba's Dance [Marcello Minerbi], but only when I'm high.

"Dave Clark up to five? [Catch Us if You Can] Good luck Dave.

"The Joan Biased thing [There But for Fortune] *is a bit ancient and anyway, she's made much better records than that. It's quite nice, but I never expected it to get so high.*

"I like the Animals but I'm not keen on the intro to Gotta Get Out of This Place. *But I like most of their stuff. Fab gear, whack.*

"Brian Poole's [I Want Candy] *got a good commercial sound going, it's the only one of his I've ever enjoyed.*

"Definitely the White Priest.

"Altogether, I think the chart's a bit weedy. Even though we are in it. Something funny's happened, but even so, it's not so bad as I thought it might be.

"We've got the new Kinks coming out, and the Stones, Byrds, and Sonny and Cher. Sonny and Cher are almost crap, but not quite, and that's what makes them good. It's corn, I suppose.

"It's a bit weedy now, but it might brighten up. If it doesn't brighten up, the scene's had it."

August 7, 1965 – *Melody Maker,* **Jerry Dawson wrote** that it had been an exciting day in the ABC theatre in Blackpool. As the filming of the show ended, a girl dashed to the edge of the balcony, waving a scarf, screaming for Paul, nearly flipping over the edge, saved by an attendant who caught her before she fell.

The afternoon rehearsals had been as crowded as the evening show. John, Paul and George were there early, sitting in front row seats, chatting as photographers popped flash bulbs all around them. Ringo's flight from London had been delayed. When he arrived, they began a two-hour rehearsal of the five songs they were doing for the show. After that, they filmed a short promotional piece that was to be shown as a trailer. The Beatles finished it with a humorous rendition of *I Do Like to be Beside the Seaside.*

At five o'clock, the photographers were asked to leave. Reporters chatted awhile longer, then came the dress rehearsal.

At eight o'clock, the fans were allowed in, walking a gauntlet of managers and commissionaires.

The show was aired live.

Afterwards, George spoke about *Help!*

"We're a bit baffled that some of the critics should knock Help! *I must confess that when we first saw the completed film, we were knocked out. But obviously, some people weren't. Let's face it, the whole thing is a fast moving comic strip. Just a string of events. There must be a thousand and one ways of editing it and whichever way it has been done, the result would have been the same. What did the critics expect? A* Cleopatra *or* King of Kings?*"*

Ringo said, *"I don't know just what to say about some of the reviews of* Help! *Some of the critics seemed to be going out of their way to knock it, or us. Even the fact that the single has already passed the half million in sales doesn't seem to keep them quiet.*

I've come to the conclusion that it wouldn't have had the raves even if it had been noticeably better than it was, or better than Hard Day's Night.

"When we first saw the completed film we all turned to Walter Shenson with one remark, 'You can release it now, Wal,' that's how pleased we were.

"I'm afraid that many people just didn't dig Dick Lester, the director. Just didn't rumble what he had set out to do, I think he did a great job for me, he is just fantastic.

"I'm very happy about the record, too. We took the best part of a day to make it, and we just set out to make a good record. We also hoped to hit the top of the chart, of course, but there's always that nagging doubt. I suppose one day it just won't happen, we obviously can't go on forever.

"But for the time being, we shall just carry on as usual, films, records, personal appearances. I can assure you I am not worrying about the future, that's the way to get ulcers.

"By the way, we taped the single Help! *while we were making an LP. It's far and away the best we've made, has a lot of variety.*

"I'm looking forward to the trip to America. It has a different atmosphere to anywhere else in the world and I love television over there. It's great! Mind you, I wouldn't like to live there permanently, but it's a great country to visit."

Paul McCartney said the reason for all the criticism was obvious. *"*Hard Day's Night *was so much better than they all expected. But it was hopeless to expect* Help! *to live up to it.*

"The single? I'm chuffed, naturally. I suppose that one day one of them won't make it, but we'll wait until that happens."

Was he looking forward to flying to America?

"None of us likes flying. Let's face it, if anything does go wrong up there, you're helpless, aren't you? I don't blame Alan Price one bit for revolting against it. I know exactly how he feels."

August 7, 1965 – *Melody Maker* **announced** that the Beatles might film a worldwide Christmas TV show during their planned American tour. Brian Epstein was intending to shoot the show at Shea Stadium in New York, a sell-out of fifty-five thousand seats.

Touring with the Beatles would be King Curtis, Brenda Holloway, Cannibal and the Headhunters, and the Discotheque Dancers, along with Sounds Incorporated. And Cilla Black would be joining them on the Ed Sullivan show, August 15th.

August 14, 1965 – Ray Coleman wrote for *Disc Weekly…* The Beatles were to leave for their U.S. tour on Friday the 13th. And they were not fond of flying.

Said John Lennon, *"The only thing we can do is get stoned for all the flights and try not to notice it. Friday the 13th, that's all we need."*

The tour was already a sell-out. And it involved thousands of air miles. It would be worth it. Even

after three years of hard work, the group still enjoyed playing to live audiences.

John said, *"That's what makes it worthwhile. Just playing. It still knocks us out, just playing and having a good time.*

"If we're playing to audiences of fifty-five thousand, which is the size of the crowd on the opening show in New York, there are bound to be some wild scenes. Even if the crowd was watching a display of ping-pong, there'd be a scene because of the size of the crowd."

Did the group enjoy the idea of going to the U.S. again?

"It's a drag going away from home, but if you have got to go anywhere, it might as well be America. It's one of the best places there is, I'd sooner be off there than go to Indonesia.

"We're really looking forward to playing to that size of crowd. It's still amazing to hear the row they make, it's exciting."

What songs were they planning to play?

"We'll do I'm Down, Help, Ticket to Ride, I Feel Fine *and one of George's, probably* I Need You. *Also probably Ringo's thing,* Act Naturally, *and a couple from the LP before last."* [Beatles For Sale]

Before leaving for the States, the group enjoyed the night life in London, most particularly the Scotch of St. James club off Piccadilly. Lennon said, *"We wanted to pack in as much as we could of the scene before we vanished."*

The group, except for Ringo, were in the studio helping record a single by one of Brian Epstein's bands, the Silkie. John was the recording manager. *"It was my first job as an A and R man, great! We enjoy all recording sessions and it was great working with them."*

He predicted that the Silkie would have a hit with the song. They had recorded the Lennon / McCartney song *You've Got to Hide Your Love Away.*

George had joined with the tambourine while Paul played guitar.

Said John, *"It was the Silkie and it sounded very silky. If the fact that it's on our LP doesn't mar it, it ought to get away okay. It's coming out in two*

weeks, so it ought to be right for a hit. I enjoy other people's recording sessions.

"It's good commercial folk, which seems to be happening right now. The record's not typical Silkie, but it's a good record."

August 14, 1965 – *Disc Weekly* **asked** Paul McCartney what advice he would give to autograph-seeking fans.

"Try to collect autographs where people are working and not where the artists live! The most successful Beatles autograph collectors are the ones who have managed, by some devious means, to get in the places where we are working.

"Alternatively, send your books to a theatre with a stamped addressed envelope. Ninety per cent of these will be returned to the sender with the artist's autographs.

"Another trick is to find out the name of the compere on the tour and send him a fan letter telling him he's marvelous. Then you can say 'P.S. Can you please get me so-and-so's autograph?'

"The last resort is to send an artist a fan letter asking for an autograph and saying, 'Enclosed is my picture.' But make sure the picture is of Brigitte Bardot!"

August 14, 1965 – *Disc Weekly* **spoke** with Paul McCartney about that week's Top 30 Chart, which still featured *Help!* at number one.

"Contrary to what John said last week, I don't think it's a bad chart at all. It's a very commercial chart. They may not be songs people in the business get knocked out by. But what I like is that most of the songs are obvious hits.

"There doesn't seem to be any rubbish to me. It's a much better chart than five years ago. Everyone's getting so purist these days, they forget what the scene was like. We've got loads of variety today, and I enjoy dead commercial songs.

"Like the Dave Clark thing [Catch Us If You Can]. *I'm not mad keen on the record but it's such an obvious hit I get my enjoyment out of thinking about that aspect of it. 'Is it commercial?' I ask myself, and if the answer's 'Yes,' then that's good. It was the same with the Hollies'* Stay *a few months ago. I preferred the original version, but really, the Hollies' was such a commercial record I had to like it because it would be an obvious hit.*

"John wasn't all that keen on either the new Fortunes record [You've Got Your Troubles] *or the Animals hit, but I like both a lot. The chorus on* Gotta Get Out of This Place *is marvelous. Eric's voice is dead commercial. Especially when he takes it up an octave on the second time through. The funny thing is that Eric gets more sick of the Animals' records quicker than we do ours.*

"I love the way the lead singer sings on Mister Tambourine Man [the Byrds]. *What's his name, Jim McGuinness? It's a lovely song. Same with the Ivy League. They sing it well, and it's a nice song.*

"Don't like the Joan Baez. [There But For Fortune] *I like the guitar chords in it, but I'm afraid she sounds too unnatural for me. It bothers me the way she hangs on the notes. She sings like she's trying to show everybody she's got a good voice. I know she has, but that's the whole impression I get and I don't care for it much.*

"Marianne's [Faithfull] [Summer Nights] *completely different, and I like her because she's natural. Like the backing and production of her record, as well.*

"Isn't the Jonathan King [Everyone's Gone to the Moon] *thing a funny record? I listened to the lyrics properly the other night and somebody said to me in a club, 'It's going to be a big hit.' I said it wouldn't, but now I can see how commercial it is.*

"Not keen on Billy Fury's In Thoughts of You. *It's easy to see how* Walk in the Black Forest [Horst Jankowski] *is a hit, although I don't like it much. It's catchy, like* Happy Days are Here Again.

"I love Zorba's Dance [Marcello Minerbi] *mainly because I've been to Greece and had a go at it. I know it's daft, but it's nice.*

"Another daft one is Wooly Bully [Sam the Sham] *but it's great because it is daft, real corny, out-and-out rocker. The Shadows'* Don't Make My Baby Blue *is great, and Hank is a good singer."*

August 21, 1965 – *Disc Weekly* **talked** about the Beatles' new U.S. tour. In New York, the group stayed at the Warwick Hotel. U.S. reporters claimed the only reason they were allowed in there was because the hotel was redecorating.

While the group had been planning the tour, music publisher Dick James had been in the States distributing sheet music to music shops in every city on the tour.

Disc spoke with George Harrison on the phone from New York. Said George, *"The others are asleep. I've just got up and I'm playing Nina Simone records. Quite a few friends have been up to see us. Dylan came to our hotel last night, and Mick, Keith and Andrew of the Stones have been up, too. They came to see the show.*

"Everything's going okay and we're all fine. I'm the only one who seems to have gone out. That was last night. I went to a club called Arthur, the one run by Sybil Burton. It's trying hard to be an Ad Lib.

"I went out by the back door. The crowds are very big outside the hotel all the time, but I went out by the back and came back very, very late and managed to get through okay.

"Tonight we're off. It's a bit difficult for us to move about properly so I suppose a few friends will come up."

Regarding the Shea Stadium concert, George said, *"It was marvelous, one of the most fantastic experiences we've ever had. We expected it to be pretty wild, with a crowd of fifty-five thousand, but not that wild."*

Show promoter Sid Bernstein had made an offer of one hundred and twenty-two thousand five hundred pounds if the Beatles would return to New York next summer. Epstein said they would if they could.

August 21, 1965 – June Harris reported to *Disc Weekly* **from New York.** The Beatles' Shea Stadium concert, both financially and in terms of audience, was the biggest show they had ever done.

The group landed by helicopter at the World's Fair grounds, one hundred yards from the stadium, then entered Shea in a Wells Fargo armoured car. The fans were so loud they drowned out the noise of the airplanes leaving Kennedy and La Guardia airports.

After the show, back at the Warwick Hotel, John Lennon said, *"It was great. I suppose you could call it our fave rave. You couldn't hear a thing. I heard one jet taking off and thought it was one of our amplifiers blowing up. I got quite scared.*

"We couldn't hear ourselves sing. All we could hear were our guitars, which were turned up and going full blast.

"I must say it was a good show. We weren't there in time to hear the rest of the acts, but it was a great line-up. Sounds Incorporated were doing well, and the other acts were Cannibal and the Head Hunters, Brenda Holloway, the King Curtis Band, and the Discotheque Dancers."

Harris said this year's Beatles tour had inspired three times the Beatlemania as the last one. Ten thousand people were on hand at the Warwick Hotel. The cops had blockaded two square blocks around the hotel while twenty-four police and security guards protected the front doors and the main lobby.

The 5 p.m. press conference was chaos, questions flooding over the band, replies snapped back just as fast. Afterwards, in their hotel room, the group ordered scores of Cokes and tried to relax. They decided it would be unwise to go out and, instead, invited up a number of friends, including Bob Dylan and the Exciters.

Said Lennon, *"It was great seeing the Exciters. They were with us on the tour last year and their mother came too and brought us all Southern Fried Chicken!"*

On the Saturday, they recorded the Ed Sullivan show with Cilla Black.

Lennon told Harris, *"We did six numbers on the Sullivan show. I played organ on* I'm Down. *I can't really play but I treated them to an elbow exercise with one hand and did a few chords with the other.*

"The other songs we did were Ticket to Ride, I Feel Fine, Yesterday, *which Paul sang straight with three violins,* Act Naturally, *Ringo's C and W number, and* Help!

"We didn't go out after the show. But we just played around in the hotel. We thought of going on to see Cilla's closing night at the Persian Room but it was impossible to get out."

Talking about the cops throughout the hotel, and just outside the door of their room, John said, "*You'd think there was a Presidential election, the way all this security is being handled.*"

Harris closed by saying the Shea Stadium concert would be televised at Christmas.

August 21, 1965 – *Disc Weekly***, in an assortment of miscellaneous columns, asked** if the Beatles should tour Britain again. Of course, the overwhelming response was a resounding yes! They went on to talk about how Ringo would like to stay at home, now that he was married and Maureen was expecting a baby.

They also announced that Paul McCartney and Jane Asher were planning to get married. The news had been broken in New York. That would only leave George and Patti Boyd unwed.

As soon as the world new that Ringo and Maureen were married, speculation began, what difference would it make to the band? Apparently, it made no difference at all. The Beatles were too good, too big, too brilliant, to be affected by something so trivial.

August 21, 1965 – Don Short wrote for *Melody Maker***, saying…** The Shea Stadium concert, with 55,600 in attendance, was the most fantastic of all the Beatles' shows he had ever seen. The stadium had been sold out months in advance, not a single seat was available. A blimp floated overhead, festooned with Beatle slogans. And over three hundred cops were on hand to control the enormous crowd.

The group was flown from their hotel by helicopter, soaring over the stadium to land at the World's Fair grounds, then taken to Shea by car. As they emerged from baseball players' tunnel, flashbulbs flashed, screamers screamed, and the Beatles were clearly overwhelmed by it all.

Afterwards, at their hotel, they threw a party. Mick Jagger and Keith Richards were there, along with Andrew Oldham and the Supremes. The party broke up at 5 a.m.

At the press conference, there were disc jockeys wearing headbands with aerials attached; one in particular had three aerials and John exclaimed, "*He's from Mars!*"

A deejay said to Ringo, "*Are you still as popular as before?*"

"*You wouldn't be here if we weren't,*" Ringo replied.

Fans had sent fruit, pounds and pounds of it. Looking at twenty pounds of grapes, George said, "*We feel like fruit pickers.*"

Squads of security guards had been assigned to the hotel day and night. One girl masqueraded as Jane Asher but was stopped from entering because she had no luggage. Four kids with long hair posed as the Beatles and made it as far as the second floor before they were stopped. They were actually a local band called the Teddy Bears.

Gifts and fan mail were arriving by the ton, delivered hourly. The penthouse suite was nearly full to the ceiling. A chambermaid named Anne Lennon was appointed the job of going through it all. Interestingly, her husband's name was John. Her story was featured in the New York newspapers.

So enamoured with the idea of the Beatles receiving MBEs, U.S. radio stations were also awarding them medals. One was Citizens and Heroes of America.

The group was due to have a free day before flying to Toronto for their only Canadian show on the tour.

August 21, 1965 – *Melody Maker***, Ren Grevatt wrote…** about the fans swarming the Warwick Hotel, ten thousand of them waiting for their heroes to arrive. The group came in from the west, going the wrong way along 54th Street, getting into the hotel with very little difficulty. They took over an entire floor, one donated by the Warwick owner, Larry Tisch. The press conference, an hour later, was so crowded, it seemed as if the entire street had been allowed in, reporters and deejays jammed in shoulder to shoulder, hip to hip, firing questions…

"*Ringo, what are you going to name your baby?*"

Said John Lennon, "*How about naming him Lyndon?*"

"*Have you added anything to your act for Shea Stadium?*"

Replied Paul, "*Yes, we're going to do a good bit of juggling between takes.*"

When asked if a quote reported last year had been accurate, that they never wanted to tour America again, Paul answered, "*We love it here and I'm sure we'll be coming again as long as they want us.*"

Ringo said they would all like to be able to leave the hotel. "*We'd like to see Cilla, and the Supremes at the Copa, and I'd like to even go to Nashville, and to Harlem especially. The other fellows, the Stones and the Animals, who've got up there, say it's a good scene but we really can't get out. It's too much of a problem.*"

On Friday night, Bob Dylan dropped in for a visit. On Saturday, the band spent ten hours getting things ready for the Sullivan show. By mid-afternoon, they had recorded six songs and were watching the playback unhappily. They did them all again and got back to the hotel around ten while the crowds continued to swarm the streets outside.

August 28, 1965 – *Disc Weekly***, June Harris wrote from New York…** Riots broke out at the airport in Houston, Texas as the Beatles arrived for their two shows at the Sam Houston Coliseum. Only a thin rope, no cops, separated the group from the crowds. A gang of kids charged through the rope and climbed on the wings and tail of the plane, throwing things through one of the open exits. They were within feet of the group by the time the police arrived to haul them away.

Later, the Houston Police Chief said Texans would never behave that way. Lennon, outspoken as ever, shot a few barbs at the Texas cops which were printed the next day in Chicago papers.

The Houston concerts were judged only fair, certainly not the best they could do. The group themselves had enjoyed the Maple Leaf Gardens show in Toronto, Canada, and the one at the New Ballpark in Atlanta, Georgia.

The Maple Leaf Gardens shows, complete with thousands of wailing fans, were sold out and wonderful. But at the New Ballpark, the band played through the best acoustics they had ever experienced. They were the first British act to play there.

So impressed by the sound system, Lennon made announcements before each song, something he rarely did. Normally, no one could hear the announcements anyway.

The crowds at the airports on this tour were smaller than on the previous tour, while at the hotels, the crowds were larger. And each of the venues had a greater capacity than the previous tour so the audiences were much larger.

In Chicago, still a bit shaken by the events in Houston, they played weakly to a near-capacity concert at Comiskey Park. Still, the show went well and the fans were happy.

Next was Minneapolis, then on to California where the band planned to visit with Joan Baez in Monterey.

In California, they would have a few days off, even a few days away from their entourage, as guests at a Hollywood home.

September 4, 1965 – *Disc Weekly* led with the meeting between Elvis and the Beatles.

"*He was exactly as I thought he would be,*" said George Harrison. "*Very friendly, very hospitable, easy, relaxed and very interested in us and our music. A real star in every sense of the word.*"

Finally, it had happened: the inevitable meeting between the biggest rock and roll stars ever. In Elvis's Bel-Air mansion, they chatted and joked, played and sang, at a get-together arranged by Presley's manager, Colonel Tom Parker. They were together for three short hours. At one point, Elvis passed around some guitars for a jam session. They played along with Cilla Black's record *You're My World* with Elvis on bass and Paul McCartney on piano. The Colonel and Brian Epstein joined them as they played and talked.

September 4, 1965 – *Melody Maker*, Don Short reported on the historic meeting between the Beatles and Elvis.

On the way to Bel-Air, Lennon said, "*I expect we'll find he's just like one of us.*"

"*I hope so,*" said Harrison. "*Some people are a let down.*"

Fans were gathered outside Elvis Presley's mansion as the security guards checked the Beatles

through in their limousine. As they met with Elvis, John said, "*Oh, there you are.*" And the ice was broken. With a record player blasting out Beatles and Elvis songs, they gathered in the lounge, along with Colonel Tom Parker and Brian Epstein.

Sitting with Paul and John, quietly in a corner, while Ringo shot pool and George sat at a roulette table, Elvis asked, "*How many hits have you penned now?*"

Paul and John started counting and John asked, "*Why don't you go back to your old style of discs?*"

"*It's my film schedule,*" explained Elvis. "*It's so tight but, I might just do one more for kicks.*"

"*Then we'll buy it,*" laughed John.

Elvis joined the crowd at the billiards table and John sat with George at the roulette table. Somewhat later, Elvis brought out a bass guitar which he was just learning to play. Cilla Black's record *You're My World* was played on the record player. John, Paul and George were handed guitars and the four of them played along. Then Elvis played bass along with *I Feel Fine.*

"*Coming along quite promising on bass, Elvis,*" said Paul.

Later, the five them sat around talking. The subject of fanatical fans came up and Ringo said, "*They were just as bad in your day, man.*"

Elvis agreed. "*There were plenty of thump-ups. It got so bad one time that I decided to learn karate.*"

"*Well,*" said Paul, "*That's not happened to us. Maybe they don't like taking on four at time.*"

And that was that, the historic meeting drawing to a close, handshakes all around.

Later, Paul said, "*The best bit about it all was that there was no big publicity bit. It was just an informal domestic affair. Elvis? Great man.*"

Added Ringo, "*It was no big show business thing. I mean, he was just like us when it came down to it. Quite normal.*"

The next morning, a parcel arrived from Elvis, a collection of all his old albums, accompanied by a note inviting them to his "*real home in Memphis. Come any time.*"

A footnote announced that P.J. Proby's next record would be *That Means A Lot,* a Beatles composition.

September 11, 1965 – *Disc Weekly* announced, in an article by Ray Coleman… that the Beatles were planning a tour of Britain that fall, a relief to many fans who had believed the rumours that, when they returned from their U.S. tour, the group was "*going to do a bit of a Presley.*" That was, retreat from the world, hide from the public.

Said George Harrison, "*We are doing fewer things than we used to. I agree, mainly because we think we are entitled to. I think the public has seen quite enough of us, for a little time, anyway. They'd get sick and tired if we kept on pushing ourselves around to too many places. You can't carry on at the same pace all the time and, anyway, we want a holiday.*"

Their plans until the November tour were to make a new album and release a new single, receive their MBEs at Buckingham Palace, and make their own TV special, something similar to *Around The Beatles.*

George said, *"I suppose you could say we're doing a bit of a Presley. But it's not really planned that way."*

He talked about the group's meeting with Elvis, saying, *"He was nicer than I expected him to be; to be honest, I expected him to be the sort of bloke who talks about buying a house for his folks, somebody with the non-smoking, non-drinking image. But he was much more natural. We all had a good laugh and he had got all our records."*

Did they ask him if he was planning a trip to the UK?

"No, why should he particularly come to England, anyway, when he is known all over the world? He doesn't even do tours in his own country, so I don't see why he should especially make it to Britain. I don't really blame him for not doing tours, especially now it's ten years since he's been called the King.

"If he came to England his image would probably be shattered. Right now, instead of having the normal pop star image, he appears rather like a James Dean thing. He'd wreck all that if he came. And he probably wouldn't sell so many records afterwards, either."

With regards to the Beatles new tour of Britain, George said, *"I don't think it was ever said we were not doing the tour. I just don't understand what all the fuss is about, we toured America last year, and this year we did our first real tour of the Continent. We didn't say we weren't doing a British one at all. I know this is a short tour we're lined up for, but at least it's covering all the main places. Some people will feel left out of it, but when you're on the other side organising it, you see it differently.*

"You can't win, wherever you play!"

About the U.S. tour, he said, *"It was much better than last time. Last year, they weren't quite sure what was going to happen. This year, they knew exactly and so the security was very much better. Travel arrangements were better and we didn't fly so much."*

The MBE: *"We still don't know when we're going to receive the medals. Even if we get only three or four days' notice, we'll have a chance to have a suit knocked up. Yes, we'll wear whatever we're supposed to wear, I think."*

September 11, 1965 – *Melody Maker* said the Beatles were resting after their American tour but would be touring Britain later in the year. The tour, in November or December, was to hit seven cities: Glasgow, Newcastle, Liverpool, Manchester, Sheffield, Birmingham and London.

Before Christmas, the band was set to record a new LP and single. There were plans for them to be in the recording studio during the next two months. During the recording sessions, they would not be making any public appearances but they would be getting together with Walter Shenson to discuss future film projects. Something in a different style, something without Dick Lester. They were talking with Dick Condon, author of *A Talent for Loving*, the basis for the film. Plans were afoot for them to spend three or four months in 1966, working on location in Spain and Britain.

Also, they were hoping to tour the U.S. again in 1966, perhaps South America as well.

In October, perhaps November, they were to film a TV special for Granada Television, along with Cilla Black, the show to be produced by Johnny Hamp.

The film from the group's Shea Stadium concert was said to be brilliant. American TV had already bought it, British television had not.

September 18, 1965 – *Melody Maker* ran the results of their Pop Poll. The Beatles were declared Britain's most popular group; *Ticket to Ride* won the honours as Best British Vocal Disc of the year.

September 25, 1965 – *Disc Weekly* spoke with Ringo about his new son, Zak.

Would Ringo allow his son to be a musician?

"Yes, as long as he doesn't want to play drums. It's just a drag playing drums, and I wouldn't advise him to start it, at least, not as a job."

What would he want Zak to be?

"I don't care what he does, as long as he's happy. I haven't anything in mind yet. It's too early. I'd just like him to make a success of whatever he settles down to. He may turn out to be a lazy bum, anyway. I think I would mind that. If fact, if that happened, I'd probably kick him out and tell him to get a job."

Would he be a tough father?

"Don't think so. Not as I see it at the moment, anyway. But only time can tell.

"He'll have an ordinary education, just like any normal person. He won't go to a public school because I just don't like what they stand for."

Hundreds of congratulatory cards and telegrams had poured in and Ringo said, *"A lot of them have come from groups, the Pretty Things, the Kinks, and a lot of others. It's ridiculous... and a knockout... to get them all."*

Maureen was do to leave the hospital that day.

Ringo joked, *"I believe Ed Sullivan has got the orchestra ready and Colonel Tom Parker has got the contract ready. Only pity, Zak's got a nose just like mine."*

October 2, 1965 – *Disc Weekly*, Ray Coleman spoke with John Lennon. Part One:

England was gearing up for another round of Beatlemania and a new wave of knockers was demanding to know how long the group could keep it up, the same question that had been asked ever since the group first gained recognition. Now that the Beatles had been awarded MBEs, they were members of the Establishment. Clearly, they were on their way down, with nothing left to achieve. They were old now, John and Ringo both 25, Paul 23 and George 22, and on the way out.

John began, "*I only think about age if somebody reminds me. I don't like thinking about it very much. I ought to start by saying we felt old when we started, that is, when Brian Epstein found us. We thought we'd had it and we'd left it too late to make it.*

"*But I reckon this: years don't affect your mind, really. They can give your face wrinkles, but it's your attitude and outlook that counts.*

"*According to the rules of the pop world, we are too old. But we don't look any older than the Stones, do we? And we don't act any older either. We only look older than, say, the Who, and I've seen them looking about thirty some nights.*

"*The most important thing about all this is that I've known people of thirty who aren't thirty in mentality. The law says they've lived thirty years. But although age can give you experience, some people aren't capable of using the experience.*

"*I'm twenty-six next year. The rules say I'm a fully-grown man, settled down and all that. But I'm not, I've still got a young outlook, I hope.*

"*Age can give you a lot if you want to use what it offers. That's what I want to do with my age and experience. Use it.*

"*Thirty years doesn't necessarily mean intelligence, you know. I've met some right old nits of forty…*"

As the band aged, were they still hoping to draw in new fans? Were they targeting an older audience?

"*You can never satisfy them all. There was a time when we seemed to be doing everything at once, getting older people interested in what we were doing as well as younger people. But to try to satisfy everybody is hopeless. This tour we're doing, for example. We can't cover the whole country with it unless we do a very long tour. So because I don't feel like dropping dead from overwork just yet, not even if I am twenty-five, there's bound to be people writing in from Umbo-on-Sea saying, 'Why aren't the Beatles coming here?'*

"*It's the whole attitude to fans that we've got to think about. I think we've got it all sorted out in our own minds, but it's hard to try to make people understand. The* Help! *single sold much better than the two before it,* I Feel Fine *and* Ticket to Ride. *But there were still a lot of fans who didn't like* Help! *They said, 'The Beatles are dropping us. This isn't as good as* A Hard Day's Night.' *So you can't win. Trying to please everybody is impossible, if you did that, you'd end up in the middle with nobody liking you. You've just got to make the decision about what you think is your best, and do it.*

"*People think of us as machines. They pay us for a record and we have to do what they say, like a jack-*in-the-box. I don't like that side of it much. Some people have got it all wrong.

"*We produce something, say a record, and if they like it, they get it. The onus isn't on us to produce something great every time. The onus is on the public to decide whether they like it or not. It's annoying when people turn round and say, 'But we made you, you ungrateful swines.' I know they did in a way, but there's a limit to what we're bound to live up to, as if it's a duty.*

"*When I had black windows put in my Roll Royce, somebody said, 'Lennon's turning his back and running away from the people who made him. Hiding.' Rubbish! If I go to a shop down the road and buy a bunch of roses, I don't expect the bloke to be so grateful that he spends his life bowing and scraping. I like the roses, so I buy them, and that's that.*

"*I don't want to sound as if we don't like being liked. We appreciate it. But we can't spend our lives being dictated to. Think about Kellogg's corn flakes. If you buy corn flakes, do you expect Mr. Kellogg to spend his life being told how to do everything and how to behave? No. And if you buy a loaf of bread and it's lousy, just don't buy it again. It's not all that much different with us. We make a record and, if you like it, you buy it. If you don't, you don't buy it. It's up to the public to decide.*"

Talking about *Help!*, he said, "*We went wrong with the picture, somehow. I think we went just slightly the wrong way with it.* Help! *as a film was like* Eight Days a Week *as a record, for us. A lot of people like the film, and a lot of people liked the record. But neither was what we really wanted, we knew they weren't really us. We weren't ashamed of the film. But close friends know that the picture and* Eight Days *as a record, weren't our best.*

"*They were both a bit manufactured. The film won't harm us, but we weren't in full control. We're not sure what comes next in the way of a film, it isn't definite that the next will be* Talent For Loving. *Nothing's certain about it. We just want to make sure we do better than* Help!"

October 2, 1965 – *Melody Maker*, **Jack Hutton talked** with Paul McCartney about what he thought of the protest song movement in pop.

Paul said, "*Well, the songs are getting a bit silly, aren't they? I mean, Sonny's even on about protests on the length of his hair! Paul, of Peter Paul and Mary, said* I'm A Loser *was a protest song. Well, John wrote most of it. Did he think he was protesting? Don't be daft!*

"*You know, if you think about it,* Don't Stand on My Blue Suede Shoes *is a protest song. So are thinks like* I Love You Baby But You Don't Love Me. *Seriously, I don't like* Eve of Destruction *very much. It seems to be cashing in on a trend. Somebody like Bob Dylan comes up and people say, 'Let's copy him, he's good.' And then the whole market gets saturated.*

"Protest songs make me concentrate too much on the lyric which I don't like. These labels like 'protest' become ridiculous. Most of them are made by newspapers. It reaches the stage where, one week, you meet a character who knows the scene and you joke, 'Yeah, it's folk this week.' Next week you meet him and you say, 'Yeah, it's protest this week.' Own up.

"It reminds me about all the nonsense written about the Mersey Beat. Everyone was jumping on the bandwagon."

October 9, 1965 – *Disc Weekly*, Ray Coleman spoke with John Lennon. Part Two:

The Beatles were horrified by the thought of being named all-round entertainers. The were not fond of the traditional show business. And they were a bit uneasy being embraced by adults, the ones who had originally decided they were one-hit wonders. Coleman wondered if John would be worried about having too many mums and dads in the audience.

"If that's what it looks like out front, I reckon I'll be off. I couldn't stand it if the audiences were too old."

He mentioned not really liking their London Christmas shows because the audiences were considerably older than the crowds at their concerts.

"It doesn't seem natural to see older people out there looking at us like that. It's nice to see anybody, but I always think old people should be at home, doing the knitting, or something."

Were the Beatles happy with the success they had achieved? Or would they have preferred a situation where they could live quieter lives?

"No, I'm glad things got as big as they did, because when we got nearly big, people started saying to us, 'You're the biggest thing since...' I got fed up hearing that we were the biggest thing since. I wanted the Beatles to just be the biggest thing. It's like gold, the more you get the more you want."

He mentioned that the volume of fan mail had dropped recently.

"I'm talking about the stuff I get myself, now. American fan mail has built up. Paul's had a lot every day. Mine fluctuates, goes up when we've got a new record out. Since our European tour, we've been getting plenty of mail from Yugoslavia, Italy and, for some reason, Japan."

What about marriage for pop stars?

"I don't think two of us being married has had any bad results on our popularity. Remember that when it was announced Ringo and I were both married, there hadn't been anybody in such a position who had got married.

"It was Silver Disc people as opposed to Gold Disc people, who'd got married before us. People who relied mainly on the fact that they wiggled, all sexy, in their act. We didn't rely on wiggling and we still don't. We were never dependent on fans being in love with us so much as others are."

With regards to the current state of British pop, he said, *"It's got a little boring. The same names are*

coming up in the hit parade all over and over again. We could do with something new. I listen to Radio London most of the time when I'm not doing anything because, although they even get a bit boring by playing little other than the hit parade, it's the best thing there is on the air for pop."*

Would he like to be a deejay?

"I wouldn't mind it, but I'd only play records I like. It would be a drag if I had to play records I didn't like."

Talking about Bob Dylan, he mentioned that the reason Dylan first liked the Beatles' music was because, when he first heard *I Want to Hold Your Hand*, he believed one of the lines in it was, "I get high... I get high." In fact, though, the line was, "I can't hide, I can't hide."

"How could you not dig a bloke like that?" John asked.

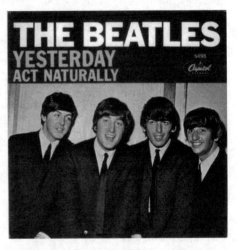

October 9, 1965 – *Disc Weekly*, Nigel Hunter talked about the Beatles' song *Yesterday* and Paul's solo vocal. Dick James explained the evolution of the song. During the filming of *Help!*, he heard from George Martin that Lennon and McCartney had a new song, one with a gorgeous melody. Music for the movie was finished, but James went to the studio anyway, wanting to hear it.

He said, *"I got Paul to run through it for me during a break in the filming. He played it on the organ they had in their strange flat with the four front doors in the film. At that stage, he and John hadn't put the finishing touches to it, and hadn't decided on a title. So instead of* Yesterday, *he was singing* Scrambled Eggs *when he played it to me."*

Finishing the song, Paul looked at Dick James for approval.

James said, *"For God's sake, finish it! And they did."*

Shortly afterwards, it was renamed *Scrambled Eggs*. James explained, *"George Martin had another orchestral album of Beatle tunes due for rush release in the States. There weren't enough* songs in the actual film to make up the album, and there weren't enough non-film ones available to complete it without Yesterday. *But if* Yesterday *had been released in the States on the album under that title, anyone over there who wanted to cover it could have done so, and they could have done it in advance of the single by Paul being issued there.*

"Naturally, we didn't want that to happen, so we called George's orchestral version Scrambled Eggs. *No one would dream of investigating a tune with a title like that as a potential vocal, would they?"*

And, of course, no one did. The tune already had the cover versions piling up. Dick James thought it would be the song of the year.

October 9, 1965 – *Melody Maker* reported that the single release of *Yesterday* in the U.S. had hit number one almost immediately. The Beatles received full credit for it, but it featured only Paul's solo.

McCartney said, *"We didn't know at first whether to release the number as a single or not. So I was very relieved indeed when I heard it had gone to number one. It's really marvelous!"*

Tony Barrow, NEMS Press Officer, said, *"This track and* Act Naturally, *which features Ringo singing a country and western number, were not included on the* Help! *LP released in the States, and that is why it was decided to release them as a single. There are no plans at all to release* Yesterday *as a single in Britain. It is, of course, available on the LP and will also be included when the LP is broken down for EP release in the future."*

October 30, 1965 – *Disc Weekly* reported it was honours week for the Beatles. They had received their MBEs from Queen Elizabeth at Buckingham Palace. Also, John and Paul had been awarded Silver Quill awards from *Disc Weekly* to celebrate the upwards of two hundred and fifty thousand sales of *Ticket to Ride* and *Help!*

Said George about the MBE investiture, *"It was a much better do than I expected. Everyone at the Palace was very nice and any bad feeling we expected, or feared, from other people getting medals wasn't there. We were all glad about that.*

"The Queen was great, I'm a big Queen fan now. It was obvious she was doing her best to make everyone feel relaxed and not nervous. When she gave me my medal, she said, 'It's a pleasure to present you with this.' I said, 'Thank you.'

"The Queen said to John, 'Have you been working hard lately?' He forgot to tell her we'd been making an LP and said, 'No, we've been on holiday.'

"She said to Paul, 'How long have you been together?' and Paul said, 'Many years. Forty years.'

"And when she said to Ringo, 'Did you start the group?' he replied, 'No, they did out there.' He was pointing towards the crowds and said, 'I was the last one to join.'"

November 6, 1965 – *Disc Weekly*, Penny Valentine talked about the Beatles' TV special, filmed in Studio 6 at Granada TV in Manchester. A cast of more than eighty people had gathered, surrounded by heavy security, to take part in a show that was pure Beatles.

Esther Phillips flew in from the U.S. to join the show and sing her cover version of *And I Love Her – And I Love Him. "I would have come further,"* she said. *"It would have been worth it for a show like this."*

Peter Sellers recorded himself singing *A Hard Day's Night.* Also on hand were Richard Anthony, arriving from Paris to perform *All My Loving.* George Martin was there with an orchestra. Henri Mancini was there by special invitation. Also there to sing Beatle songs were Peter and Gordon, Lulu, Marianne Faithful, Billy J. Kramer and Cilla Black.

The set was composed of more than one mile of scaffolding, a mile of gauze, and more than one thousand square feet of sheet metal. Everyone involved was there because the Beatles had chosen them.

Said Paul, *"We had talks with Johnny Hamp, the producer, about two months ago. We had a list and we chose most of the people ourselves. There were some, like Ella Fitzgerald, who couldn't make it, but we're still hoping that she might be able to tape something in America in time for the show.*

"In form, the show will be rather like Around The Beatles *in that it will be fast moving. Nobody sings more than one number, except us. We're doing two numbers that we've just written. One's* Day Tripper, *the other's* We Can Work It Out.

"They'll probably be going on the new LP."

To date, the new album was without title. John and Paul kicked around a few ideas, sitting in their dressing room at the studio. *It's The Bloody Beatles Again* and *Eight Feet Away* were two of the suggestions.

Lennon and McCartney were at the studio early, arriving through a crowd of schoolgirls, gathered with their backs to the high winds and hail.

McCartney said they would not be doing any comedy for the show, just a few *"weak jokes."*

He explained, *"One is where we introduce Henry Mancini, saying, 'And now our favourite composer, Henry Mancini, known to his friends as Hank.' Then I turn to him and say in a deadpan voice, 'Well, Henry?'*

"Originally, John and I weren't going to introduce everyone as we are now. We were just going to come on at the end or the beginning or half-way through and say, 'Thanks everyone for doing all our songs – and making us money!'"

A footnote talked about John Lennon and Paul McCartney receiving their Silver Quills for *Help!* and *Ticket to Ride,* presented by Dick James.

The Beatles were considering an extra concert during their tour. The tour was to begin in Glasgow on December 3rd and they were to have a day off on the

6th, but fans were clamouring for more. There was talk of adding a show in either Leicester, Bristol or Leeds. So far, tickets were sold out for three of the concerts.

November 6, 1965 – *Melody Maker* **spoke** with Paul McCartney about the Beatles' next LP.

Said Paul, *"We are in the midst of recording sixteen tracks. We have no idea yet what our next single will be. When they are all completed, we will decide which to release as a single and which to use on the new LP.*

"I've no idea how much money we'll get. It takes all our time to write and record songs and make whatever public appearances we have to make. If we try and deal with the business side as well, it would be ridiculous."

George Martin said, *"The new LP is our first objective. We already have ten numbers on tape. We need sixteen more and hope to record them on Wednesday and Thursday this week. We hope to get at least one single out of the sixteen. We may release more than one as singles in America. The Beatles need singles over there much more than they do in Britain."*

Regarding the group's TV spectacular, Martin said, *"In this television show the Beatles are doing two new numbers. They are* We Can Work It Out *and* Day Tripper. *These two might be the next single. On the other hand, they might not."*

November 13, 1965 – *Disc Weekly*, **Frank Hilliger analysed** the Beatles' handwriting.

According to Hilliger, Lennon's handwriting revealed he had a good imagination, that he was musically original. As a socialite, he obviously liked getting together with all sorts of people; also, he enjoyed traveling. His sense of colour was well-developed, balanced with an equally well-developed sense of rhythm. At work, he was patient. He loved children. And he could see all points of view at once.

McCartney was ambitious and enthusiastic but could easily experience physical fatigue. Support from the three other band members, however, would help him through. His musical sense of melody and rhythm was wonderful. He was imaginative, colourful and creative.

Ringo was inwardly sensitive and often inhibited but liked to project an air of relaxation and enjoyment, particularly during public performances. His success was the result of hard work. He was self-disciplined, able to surmount obstacles and solve problems. His mind was logical and perceptive. He had a good sense of fun but his sense of humour was a bit thin when it came to jokes about himself.

George Harrison was independent, with a well-developed outlook on life. Creative, original and unusually clever in rhythm and melody. He was organised and seldom upset. His patience was nearly infinite, his endurance and physical strength above average.

November 13, 1965 – *Melody Maker*, **Jerry Dawson spoke with** John Lennon.

Said John, *"Beat music has been with us for so long, it is stupid to say that it won't last, at least in some form or other. It has proved that it was not, and still is not, merely a craze. It can't disappear just like that.*

"I personally haven't a clue as to how the scene will progress, what, if anything, will replace it. In any case, I don't like predictions, they are always vague and invariably wrong. If I knew, I could make a fortune...

"I find that predictions are usually made up by someone with a phony group that they want to get away from. If anyone wants to know what the future holds, why not ask Maurice Woodruff?

"If there is anything I hate it is labels such as this. The 'protest' label in particular means absolutely nothing, it's just something that the press has latched on to, and as usual, is flogged to death. Some of the songs which appear to come under this heading are simply good songs, some are not. But personally, I have no time for the Eve of Destruction *songs.*

"In any case, the label is so wide. I just don't believe in it, it's too wide even to consider. Just like the original Merseybeat label. That one even included the Rolling Stones and the Dave Clark Five. How stupid can you get!"

At that point, Paul interjected, *"I'm writing a protest song... about John!"*

Lennon continued, talking about *Yesterday*, *"This song was around for months and months before we finally completed it. Paul wrote nearly all of it but we just couldn't find the right title. Every time we got together to write songs or for a recording session, this would come up. We called it* Scrambled Eggs, *and it became a joke between us. We almost had it finished, we had made up our minds that only a one word title would suit, and believe it or not, we just couldn't find the right one.*

"Then one morning Paul woke up, and the song and the title were both there, completed. I know it sounds like a fairy tale, but it is the plain truth.

"I was sorry, in a way, we had so many laughs about it. And it has now been issued in America as an orchestral piece by George Martin, called Scrambled Egg. *This was after our version of* Yesterday, *something to do with copyright. Now we are getting letters from fans telling us they've heard a number called* Scrambled Egg *that's a dead copy of* Yesterday."

Regarding the new tour, Lennon said, *"Some people are complaining that the tour is too short, and we would have liked a longer tour ourselves. It's good for us, make no mistake, and half the time we can get home nights, not like touring America.*

"But originally, we didn't have a British tour scheduled for this year, we just hadn't the time. We should have started our third film, which was to be a cowboy epic. The nearest location for the outdoor

scenes was Spain, but it got so late in the year we couldn't risk the weather, so it was postponed till the spring. Which left us with just enough time before Christmas to play the dates that are lined up.

"I'm glad to hear that the tickets are going well. We always worry, who wouldn't, with all the knockers around?

"On our last tour, when we got to one Yorkshire town, we were shaken to find there were some empty seats. Then we discovered that the Mayor or somebody had stopped the fans from queuing for seats and insisted on postal bookings only.

"I suppose a lot of fans thought they would be wasting their time writing. I personally always have that fear, that perhaps they think the queues would be too big and they wouldn't stand a chance of getting tickets, and they would stand even less chance if they wrote. If they all thought this way, we might conceivably get no one there! Then it would be said that we were slipping. But that's my excuse anyway!"

In a footnote, Esther Phillips talked about working with the Beatles on their TV special. "It was a wonderful surprise. We never met in the States. The first time I saw them was at the TV studios. They are beautiful. Apparently, they heard my version of And I Love Him and said it was the best version of all their songs on record."

November 13, 1965 – Melody Maker talked about Brian Epstein visiting the U.S. to stop the release of two Beatles songs on the Capitol label. The numbers were Kansas City and Boys. Capitol had already released the disc to record stores and radio stations, but they were forced to call them back. Epstein said the songs were not current enough, not what the group was doing these days.

They closed by mentioning that all the tickets, thus far on sale, for the Beatles' tour, were gone, snapped up by fans.

November 20, 1965 – Disc Weekly said the planned release date for The Beatles' next single, Day Tripper / We Can Work It Out, was December 3rd, the day the new tour was to begin. At roughly the same time, their new LP, Rubber Soul, would also be out.

The band was pumped about the new disc, considering it their best ever. Said George Harrison, "We're all made up about it."

Day Tripper was a rock and roll song with some good guitar work. John double-tracked his lead vocals while Paul and George sang in the background.

The new record was considered a double A-side. But George said, "After a lot of talk, we decided Day Tripper is really the top track. This is what we wanted all along."

Did they plan the release so they could have a number one hit at Christmas?

"Not especially, but it would be nice if we made it."

The Rubber Soul album contained all new Beatles' compositions, two by George, the remainder by John and Paul. One song featured Ringo singing, a five-year-old country and western song, What Goes On, written by Paul.

The Hollies were planning to record one of George's songs from the album, If I Needed Someone.

Said George, "We've finished all our LP tracks, fourteen songs altogether. We're very pleased with the way everything's turned out. We all think it's just about our best LP. I can't wait for it to come out. The sleeve's finished, too, and the picture on the front is pretty good."

November 20, 1965 – Melody Maker said the Beatles were coming back with a new assault on the hit parade. Their new single would be released on December 3rd. We Can Work It Out / Day Tripper, both written by John Lennon and Paul McCartney, with Paul singing on We Can Work It Out, John singing doubled-tracked on the other.

Their new album, Rubber Soul, would also be released in early December. All the compositions were by the Beatles, two by George, the rest by John and Paul.

November 27, 1965 – Disc Weekly announced that Paul McCartney won their poll for favourite Beatle. Fans said, "He's charming and is never big-headed. They're all fab but Paul is the best-looking. Paul looks just like the boy next door, nothing has gone to his head. It hasn't gone to the others' heads either, but Paul, well, he's just smashing. He's such a warm person..."

November 27, 1965 – Disc Weekly, Penny Valentine reviewed the new single. We Can Work It Out was arresting, wonderfully made, and obviously destined to hit number one. Day Tripper was aggressive and very much John Lennon, the one getting all the radio plugs. She thought it was very masculine... and somewhat disappointing.

November 27, 1965 – *Disc Weekly*, **Ray Coleman reviewed** the Beatles' new album *Rubber Soul*. He thought it was a new Beatles' sound, tighter, better, more harmonious. He pointed out that the group had improved with each new album, but that this one showed the greatest improvement yet.

Think For Yourself by George Harrison, featuring George on the lead vocal with Paul and John harmonising. It had a great beat and a wild finish, the best song ever written by George.

If I Needed Someone, again by George, also released by the Hollies as a single. Coleman said it was Harrison's tribute to the Byrds, an excellent song.

Drive My Car with John and Paul singing the lead, Paul playing lead guitar, a Chuck Berry-type song, very catchy.

This Bird Has Flown (Norwegian Wood) was a Lennon effort, poetic and Dylanesque. The guitar was haunting, the lyrics funny, a beautiful song.

Nowhere Man featuring John, Paul and George singing on one of the best tracks on the album. Very tight new Beatles' sound, with Lennon and Harrison playing the same guitar riffs together.

Run For Your Life with John singing the lead vocal, Paul and George backing. A happy-sounding tune.

The Word was an angry song with Paul on piano, George Martin on harmonium, and Paul and George singing lead.

Michelle with Paul singing solo, very catchy with a French sound to it.

Girl with John singing the lead, a soft and lilting tune.

I'm Looking Through You with Paul singing the lead vocal, another rocker.

In My Life had the feel of a ballad, sung by John, Paul backing. A pretty song.

You Won't See Me, another hard-driving song with Paul playing the piano and singing the lead.

What Goes On with Ringo singing, a country and western number written by Paul.

Clearly, the Beatles' best LP, brilliantly played and sung.

In a footnote, *Disc* announced a new contest was forthcoming, the prizes to be the new Beatles LP, the new Beatles single... and all the top thirty hits in the country. Details the following week.

Also, the Beatles were about to launch their new tour. The appearance places and dates were: Glasgow Odeon, December 3rd; Newcastle City Hall, December 4th; Liverpool Empire, December 5th; Manchester Apollo, December 7th; Sheffield City Hall, December 8th; Birmingham Odeon, December 9th; Hammersmith Odeon, December 10th; London's Finsbury Park Astoria, December 11th; and the Cardiff Capitol, December 12th.

November 27, 1965 – *Melody Maker*, **Chris Welch reviewed** the Beatles' new single, saying it lacked spontaneity. *Day Tripper* and *We Can Work It Out*

were obviously the product of a lot of hard work, but did not have the volatile closeness, the lyrical importance of songs such as *Yesterday* and *She Love You,* songs so wonderfully complete they could never be improved upon.

He thought *We Can Work It Out* was the most satisfying song but that *Day Tripper* would probably be the number one hit.

Melody Maker provided a track-by-track description of *Rubber Soul* and announced that it would be released on December 10th.

December 4, 1965 – *Record Mirror* **announced** that the Beatles' new LP, *Rubber Soul,* would soon be released to large advance orders. They provided a track by track summary of the album and wondered how the group could continue to produce such a marvelous stream of melodies. Their creative output was impressive, fantastic.

December 4, 1965 – *Disc Weekly* **declared** it was Beatles Week in the UK. *Day Tripper / We Can Work It Out* was being released at the beginning of the week, and half-a-million copies had already been ordered by records stores for the Christmas rush.

On the same day that the recording was being released, the group was starting their new tour, reported to be a total sell-out.

And the Beatles' new album, *Rubber Soul*, was also being released. The advance orders were rapidly approaching the half-million mark. Also, they would be appearing on Top of the Pops and Lucky Stars.

Definitely, it was Beatles Week in Britain.

December 4, 1965 – *Disc Weekly*, **Derek Taylor wrote** from Hollywood about what an exciting week it was – because there were two new Beatles songs. Capitol Records had demanded that no radio stations play the songs until November 29th. Deejays around the country were desperate to get advance copies, and those who had them were desperate to play them, each waiting for another to break the deal with Capitol. WFUN in Miami did just that, playing *We Can Work It Out* on November 23rd.

Stations around the country followed suit – and Capitol bowed to the inevitable, releasing all of the one thousand American rock and roll radio stations from their bargain. *Day Tripper* and *We Can Work It Out* were instant hits.

December 11, 1965 – *Disc Weekly* **announced** that *Day Tripper / We Can Work It Out* had gone straight to the top of the charts.

Said George Harrison, *"We were a bit worried about this one, mainly because of the business about split A-sides. Even after all that's happened to us, we still get a terrific kick out of being number one."*

Regarding their sold-out tour, the group described the fans' reactions as *"organised mania."*

George said, *"There's just the same amount of mania as always. The reason there isn't the degree of riots is that they seem to have trebled the number of attendants everywhere. As soon as things look a bit dodgy, the fans are held back by more attendants than ever."*

Disc reporter Mike Ledgerwood had been dragged out of the Newcastle City Hall when he tried to get in to interview the Beatles. The cops threatened him with a night in jail if he persisted in trying to get backstage. But Ledgerwood prevailed...

December 11, 1965 – *Disc Weekly*, Mike Ledgerwood wrote that it was always an exciting experience, seeing the Beatles on stage. As the band took the stage, the crowd screams rose to a crescendo, the debris began to fly, a constant barrage of candies and autograph books and an assortment of UFOs.

The Beatles started with a bang and a crash, pounding out *I Feel Fine*, sliding into *She's A Woman* as a red jelly baby hit John on the head.

The screams rose and fell in waves, each wave cresting higher than the last until the final chords of *I'm Down* were struck. The show was over and the group had mesmerised an audience yet again.

Ledgerwood had managed to get backstage where, he said, the Beatles were watching *The Avengers* on a large-screen television, all dressed in black, waiting as much as watching.

"Come on in and watch the telly," said Paul.

"Have you seen the show?" asked George. Ledgerwood explained that getting in to see them was like trying to rob a bank.

"Oh well," George said, grinning, pulling up a chair for the reporter. *"Have a ciggie then."*

Nodding to the television, Harrison said, *"I'm not really interested in this."* He and Ledgerwood talked about the tour.

George said, *"We do still get the butterflies before a first night. You always find yourself wound up a bit before the curtain goes up. But it soon goes.*

"First house at Glasgow last night was a bit dodgy. My amps went dead after the first three numbers. It takes awhile to get the feel of things on a tour again. The lighting, the mikes, you know.

"One thing we've noticed is that although the noise from the kids is the same, the difference is that they don't get a chance to express themselves like they used to. There are too many attendants about. It's more organised mania this time. They don't get a chance to go mad."

George, sucking hard on a cigarette, alleged that the group was good for many more tours, saying, *"It's only on things like America that we get a bit bored. I suppose we could go on an ever-lasting tour here and still not please everyone. We're always getting letters asking when we're going to be at this place or that. It's a shame. We do the best we can in the time available."*

The reporter asked what they did after each show and Harrison said, *"Nothing. Just go back to the*

hotel and play records and eat. If we went out any place, we'd spend all our time signing autographs.

"Traveling is hard this time. Through all the snow. Makes the journeys much longer."

What about having the Moody Blues on the tour?

"We've always been good friends. We seem to get on well with them. I don't think we specifically asked for them, but I know we all agreed when the name was mentioned. They go down well with the kids. Their style's different to ours but they follow the same trends."

There were complaints that the group was failing to do enough plugs for *Day Tripper / We Can Work It Out* to satisfy the fans. George explained that they were doing exactly the same amount as they had done for *Help!*

"This is the crucial record, I think," he said. *"It's difficult having two A-sides. I prefer* We Can Work It Out, *but, obviously,* Day Tripper *has words which are more easily remembered."*

Regarding the group's career in general, George said, *"We've enjoyed making records and writing and playing songs one hundred per cent more this year than we did last. And we feel it'll go on like this."*

December 11, 1965 – *Disc Weekly* reported that the opening of the new tour in Glasgow went as smoothly as possible. Prior to the show, George Chantrey, manager of the theatre, had been hit with scores of job applications, girl fans all wanting to work as usherettes. All the applications were refused, and extra bouncers were hired for the show.

Chantrey said, *"The NEMS organisation control the show as soon as they arrive. They secure themselves backstage with the artists and our only contact with them is by intercom."*

More than two hundred cops were engaged to control the crowds, six thousand fans waiting to get into the theatre, thousands more, ticketless, trying to see their heroes. One hundred and thirty ambulance and first-aid workers were on hand to deal with hysterical girls. During the first performance, sixty-five girls fainted and five of them were hospitalised. Another seventy dropped during the next set.

Sandra Shields, one of the fainters, said, *"I couldn't bear it any longer. I wanted to rush closer to the stage. I was crying so much that I couldn't see properly and I can only remember staggering into the aisle with one thought in mind, to get closer."*

Forty bus loads of teenagers came to Glasgow from all over Scotland, to see the band, to hear the band, to experience the band.

Beatles' Press Officer, Tony Barrow, said, *"We make all our own security arrangements. Our overnight stays in top class hotels are left to the discretion of the managers, and they know as well as we do the standard of protection and service we require..."*

In Liverpool, ambulance workers said there were only seventeen cases of hysteria needing treatment.

The crowds were more orderly than ever, the double-performance at the Empire a complete sell-out.

In the audience were Ringo, George and Paul's parents.

But there was bad news. The Cavern was being closed by the City Council unless the drainage system was repaired – a three thousand pound repair job.

Two girls, Susan Hall and Josephine McQuaid, were handing out *Save the Cavern* handbills when Paul saw them. He invited them into the dressing room for a chat, then sent someone out to get them seats for the show.

Said Paul, *"The City Council should regard the Cavern as a tourist attraction, not just an old warehouse. They come from all over the world to see it."*

Ringo said, *"It's been the greatest club in the country for two or three years."*

George added, *"Until tonight, we have not been approached about the club but we cannot commit ourselves."*

And John, *"Although we owe it nothing physically, we have a great allegiance to it."*

December 11, 1965 – *Melody Maker* **said** that for the first time in the last few years, a Beatles single has failed to hit the top of the charts the moment it was released. *Day Tripper / We Can Work It Out,* released on Friday, was sitting at number three, behind the Seekers and the Who.

Somewhat angry at this state of affairs, Brian Epstein said, *"The chart must be made up of returns from inferior shops, fish shops and the like."*

Ringo said, *"Coming into the* Melody Maker *at number three is quite something. And in any case, the main thing is that people seem to like both sides of the record."*

Melody Maker made spot checks at record stores around England. A Brantford shop said the Seekers' *The Carnival is Over* was outselling the Beatles by around ten per cent, but, of course, the Seeker's song had been out and selling for over a week, the Beatles' record had only been selling for two days.

Another shopkeeper said in two days he had sold twenty-nine copies of the Beatles record, fifty copies of the Seekers disc over the entire week. Another shop reported selling eighteen copies of the Seekers, fifteen of the Beatles.

The last six singles from the Beatles, *I Want To Hold Your Hand, Can't Buy Me Love, A Hard Day's Night, I Feel Fine, Ticket to Ride* and *Help,* all went immediately to the top of the charts. But the new Beatles record would likely hit number one the following week.

December 11, 1965 – Alan Walsh reported from Glasgow for *Melody Maker***...** Backstage, trimming his own hair, easily the longest hair of any of the group, John Lennon said, *"It's always the same at the start of a tour. We've done it hundreds of times but we are always nervous just the same. It's funny*

because, once we're on stage, it all goes. It will be the same at Liverpool on Sunday. Liverpool's home, and they all know us, and we're sort of expected to do well and we get nervous."

Ringo said, *"I'm nervous now, sort of worked up inside. I can't explain it, I'm just nervous inside."*

George, who was examining the ruins of a guitar that had fallen off the back of a limousine, said, *"It's mangled. It's one of my best guitars, too."*

And Paul, talking about the new single, said, *"Do you think the single will be another hit? You can never tell, you know. You can just never tell."*

It had taken the band two days to get to Glasgow. Lennon explained, *"We don't like flying. If we can go by road, we do. We've done so much flying without really any incidents that the more we do, the more we worry. I suppose we think that sooner or later, something might happen. Anyway, we weren't in a hurry as long as we got there on time."*

They had spent a night in Berwick, moving on to Glasgow the next day. In the dressing room at the theatre, with the TV going and screaming fans in the distance, Lennon said to Mal Evans, driver and road manager, *"Give us the scissors, Mal. I'm going to chop it* [his hair] *and prove I've got ears on this tour."* He did that.

Walsh asked Ringo if he was happy to be back on tour.

"I wouldn't say that."

Walsh was unsure whether or not Ringo was joking. Starr continued, *"Tours are good for us, though I enjoy playing, too. I never get to the stage where I don't, of course."*

John talked about the use of profanities, saying, *"I swear sometimes but I hate to hear women swear or for men to swear in front of women. Cyn has heard me swear when I'm angry, but she wouldn't like it if anyone started trying to butter her. If they apologised afterwards, she would like them for respecting her, though she wouldn't like the swearing.*

"What I can't stand are those old show business lesbians who swear all the time for effect. They think they're embarrassing you by swearing, but you're really only embarrassed for them."

George cried out for food, saying, *"Can we have some tea and scones? We haven't eaten all day. We're having a meal at the hotel later but I can't wait till then."*

But when they saw the time, they headed downstairs to watch the Moody Blues take the stage.

Afterwards, they returned to dressing room to get ready for their own show.

"There's some new make-up here," said Paul. *"It covers up the beard but doesn't make you red-faced."*

"Where are our Beatle boots?" asked Ringo. *"We're the only people in the world who don't wear Beatle boots other than on stage."*

Agreed George, *"We never wear them now."*

Dressed, they were almost ready. Paul slapped on a little more make-up, saying, *"Got to get that rosy-cheeked look, you know."*

And then they were on the stage, hammering into their first chords as the curtain rose and the audience wailed.

The first show in Glasgow was certainly not the best performance ever. Seconds into the gig, George's amp crashed, beyond repair – not that anyone in the audience could have heard it.

December 18, 1965 – *Disc Weekly* **reported** that this Christmas was to be the first one in five years during which the Beatles would not be working.

Ringo said, *"The best thing about it this year is that it's the first Christmas we'll be able to spend properly. I mean, we've always had Christmas Day off, but this time it's going to be a nice long rest. Me? I'm just going to sit around and have a good time."*

John mentioned he would be *"Staying in to unwind. We'll probably all get together at some time. I like Christmas, well, it's just a holiday. I never plan anything for holidays, anyway. I haven't a clue what's going to happen at my house this year. All I know is I'll wake up and it'll be Christmas.*

"The rest of it's up to Cyn. It's a woman's time of year, anyway."

Presents for his son?

"I bought him a slide but he's got it already. He goes up and down on it but I'm always buying him things anyway. There are a few things stuffed away in the attic which he'll get. But Cyn takes care of it all.

"The main thing is, we'll take it easy. No, I haven't the slightest idea what we're having for Christmas dinner. I don't have anything to do with it. I just eat it."

George Harrison said, *"I'll probably go up to Liverpool part of the time, maybe just before the real holiday, and the rest of the time I'll just spend here. We'll probably get together for a few nights, and there are a few other parties I don't intend to miss.*

"This week I shall have to spend buying some more presents. That day we spent at Harrods was okay but we bought a lot of stuff that wasn't exactly for Christmas. I love Christmas. I got a bit fed up with it when I was around eighteen, but then we never really had a proper Christmas when we were away."

And Paul said he would be spending Christmas in London, too.

Ringo was expecting to be in his new home in Weybridge by Christmas. He said he would get his son Zak some toys, adding, *"He's too young, really, to get much else for him."*

Carol singers would not be welcome at Lennon's house. He said, *"The gates are being locked. I used to be a carol singer myself, but I don't like them now, especially when I remember what a cheat and a robber I was."*

December 18, 1965 – *Melody Maker* **said** it was unlikely that the Beatles' next film would be Richard

Condon's western, *A Talent For Loving*. Rumour had it that the band was unimpressed by the script.

A NEMS spokesman said, *"It's virtually certain that the Beatles will not now make the film. Producer Walter Shenson is looking for a new script."*

They went on to talk about the Beatles TV spectacular that was due to air that week. Along with the Beatles would be Marianne Faithful, Esther Phillips, Peter Sellers, Peter and Gordon and Fritz Spiegel.

The 1965 tour had ended in Cardiff after selling out in all nine venues. The band had no plans for another tour in 1966.

December 18, 1965 – *Melody Maker* **reported** that the Hollies were hitting back at George Harrison. George, the composer, had called their new single rubbish, claiming it sounded like session musicians together for the first time.

Said Graham Nash, *"It's that bit about the session men that really annoyed us. We did the record off our own bat even though most people were against us doing it. You can't please everyone, we know, but if it's a hit, it'll mean two or three thousand pounds for George.*

"The Beatles are always having a go at us quietly. But I'd back any of our boys against any of the Beatles musically any time."

December 25, 1965 – *Record Mirror*, **Mike Adams quoted** Paul McCartney, *"It's been great, really great."*

Paul was talking about their recent tour. Adams told him that he had heard the Rolling Stones were more popular than the Beatles in America.

And Paul said, *"Are they? I don't think so. I wouldn't like to say who's more popular. The Stones have got their publicity agent and we've got ours. It's up to you who you believe.*

"I mean, some people say one minute that the Hollies are more popular than us, and the next it's Herman or someone else. If the Stones are, good luck to them... No,

I don't think they are. I remember reading in some musical paper that the Stones were more popular and had a better reception than us in Boston. I don't even remember us being in Boston. It may be true, but did they play to fifty thousand odd in New York?

"Mind you, all this chat is fine, but I don't want people to think that it'll come to us sticking our tongues out at each other like school kids. No, the Stones are good lads."

Adams asked Paul for some personal comments on the national music scene and Paul said, *"Oh, it's a lot better than when we started, I think. It was all false before. Mind you, rubbish still gets in."*

Would he like to be more specific?

"No, I don't think so. It might hurt someone."

At the time of the interview, there was some speculation that the Beatles' next movie would be a western but Paul said, *"We're not really sure."* Since that statement, of course, the group had rejected the film and wanted producer Walter Shenson to find something else.

What about marriage?

"Oh yeah, marriage. Yes, I think it's fine, a great institution."

Was he planning to get married?

"I just don't know. I fancy it but I've got no idea when." Or who?

"You know who. Yes, you do know – Audrey Hepburn." McCartney grinned and said, *"No, I suppose I will marry Jane eventually. We've been going together for three years."*

Someone else in the room made a comment about the show, about the UFOs, the flying jelly babies, flying money, flying everything. Paul said, *"This throwing business is a lark. Although I think most of the teenagers realise that even jelly babies can hurt when they're really traveling, some do it when they get carried away."*

Regarding audiences: *"They are about the same, although I suppose it depends on the place, the geographical position. That doesn't half make a difference."*

About the tour again: *"The whole tour was a gas, but the best four shows were in London when we played at two theatres. The other shows we've done haven't been far below. All great, in fact."*

Then they were gone. The group dashed out the doors, into a car, and headed off with a police escort.

December 25, 1965 – *Melody Maker* held a pop think-in with Brian Epstein. They asked, he answered.

Juke Box Jury: *"I love playing it because it's a television show that I can do. I seldom watch it and I don't think it's a good program. It's quite meaningless. I probably won't be doing it again because they won't be asking me after that, will they?"*

John: Lennon. *"Great mind, great person. One of the best people I've ever met. He's an interesting character to watch develop."*

Red wine: *"I like to drink red wine and nothing else alcoholwise. But this doesn't seem to work out."*

Semi-detached houses: *"If I say something nasty I'll get little letters because I said something nasty about semi-detached houses before. But I'd rather have a hut on its own."*

George: *"Harrison. I always think of George as a friend. Somewhat inconsistent person. Can be difficult. Never has been with me. Great personal charm, but this goes for any Beatle. Any faults the Beatles are supposed to have are never apparent individually. Any faults they have probably only come when they are together as a group. When there is too much talent in one room."*

Love: *"A good word in pop songs."*

Pop writers: *"Rather intelligent, as journalists go. The dearth of pop knowledge is quite incredible amongst non-musical journalists."*

Clive Epstein: *"I'd like him to come into the entertainment business."*

Ringo: *"Ringo's coming into the group was one of the Beatles' most brilliant doings. It was something they wanted and that I carried out. It was for so many reasons a quite brilliant move."*

Public schools: *"Difficult, because I went to a few. If I had a son I don't know whether I would send him to one or not."*

Paul: *"Probably the most changed Beatle. He's mellowed in character and thought. A fascinating character and a very loyal person. Doesn't like changes very much. He, probably more than the others, finds it more difficult to accept that he is playing to a cross section of the public and not just to teenagers, or sub-teenagers, whom he feels are the Beatles' audience."*

R.A.D.A.: *"Didn't like it. Don't believe in acting schools. I believe in acting experience."*

Success: *"I'm told I'm successful but I really don't believe it."*

Failure: *"I'd much rather be conscious of my own failures than successes. What good do compliments do?"*

Larry Parnes: *"Fascinating! I often wondered if I'd go the same way, but knowing him as I do now, I know I won't because we're two very different people."*

Old age: *"Don't mind. I like getting older because I know more about things."*

Money: *"Still scarce."*

Palais bands: *"Hush. Silence."*

Elkan Allan: *"He wouldn't be the producer I would choose to direct a spectacular for me. A lucky man, I think."*

Liars: *"Almost everyone."*

Gossip columns: *"The greatest. I love them."*

Christmas: *"I quite like Christmas. I don't mind the trappings."*

Music publishers: *"Very boring people. They've forgotten what a good song is."*

Beatles' next film: "*No comment yet. Still shrouded in secrecy. There are no announced plans. There will be a new single record in April or May.*"

Smoking: "*I'm not frightened of it.*"

Drinking: "*I haven't touched spirits for three weeks. It's a new sensation. I may keep off for a long time.*"

Freemasonry: "*Not for me.*"

The name 'Eppy': "*I quite like it but I don't like it being used to my face. I don't mind the Beatles using it. I know they do.*"

Blunt northerners: "*Splendid, but they're a bit conscious of their interesting bluntness.*"

Anti-Semitism: "*I'm not so conscious of it. Jews who are conscious of it should remember if they had green hair people would stop and stare and sneer and snigger. Particularly if they were famous. I don't think people in this country particularly dislike people with long noses.*"

Ken Dodd: "*I admire him. Where does he go from here? The challenge is whether he could make it out of this country.*"

Millionaires: "*Usually disappointing.*"

Blackpool: "*Quite like Blackpool, but I shouldn't want to do a season there, personally.*"

Seekers: "*Don't know much about them. I met one the other night, quite pleasant.*"

Traditional folk music: "*On the whole I find it boring.*"

Being disliked: "*I suppose I'm conscious of it. It can't be helped.*"

Andrew Oldham: "*An incredible person. He was with us for six months. I had no idea he had creative ability. It taught me not to underestimate people.*"

West End theatres: "*A sad business but I'm not disillusioned with my first year's activities. It's not going to be of tremendous interest to me until I can bring into the theatre a broader section of the public.*"

Rumoured closing of the Cavern: "*This shouldn't be so, but it's nonsense to make it into some sort of charity. It has had a lot of help from people like the Beatles. If it's not successful now, nobody's going to cry over it being closed.*

Labour Party: "*I'm a socialist at heart.*"

Summer seasons: "*They are good for an artist. Can be depressing.*"

Wigs: "*Splendid.*"

Butlins: "*I'd like to go there. Better than a semi-detached house.*"

Dogs: "*Terrified of dogs. Almost put me off people.*"

Marriage: "*I'd like the state of marriage five days a week.*"

P.J. Proby: "*I should have managed him.*"

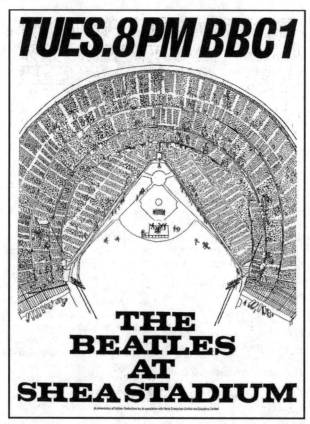

— Chapter Six: 1966 —

January 1, 1966 – *Disc Weekly* **spoke** with Paul McCartney about the 1965 pop scene and asked him to look forward to 1966.

"I think it was a pretty good year, altogether. The Who are my own favourites and I really think they were the best thing to happen because they brought something different, a fresh sort of sound and new ideas. But it really wouldn't have mattered if I didn't like what they were doing. I still think they were good for the scene because they gave it a lot of punch.

"1965 was also Donovan's year. Once you realised what he was doing and that he wasn't doing a straight copy of Dylan, it was okay and he took his place nicely in the year.

"The thing that strikes me more than anything is that there's such a big opening on the British pop scene at the moment for a single solo singer with a good voice. It sticks out like a sore thumb. I suppose it could happen in 1966. Maybe we've got to the same state we were in just after Elvis happened, nobody quite knew what would happen then.

"And now the group thing has happened, nobody quite knows what's coming. My name's not Maurice Woodruff so I can't say for sure.

"The most obvious commercial thing to come up would be a new singer with a great voice. Someone who has everything and who writes good stuff himself. Donovan might have been it, but I don't think folk music was right for a really big breakthrough."

McCartney was asked about the Beatles' year and said, *"The most satisfying thing for me was Yesterday. And I was knocked out that it was so successful. I'd choose that mainly because it was such a change for us. Also the new LP,* Rubber Soul. *I think it's the best we've done."*

Would he predict any big names for 1966?

"Hmmm, I thought perhaps Eric Clapton (ex-Yardbird) might make it. He's a knockout guitar player and he's got some good ideas. Given the right kind of number, he could do something. Same with Chris Farlowe and a lot of other groups.

"But there are a lot of excellent musicians around who never make it and nobody seems to know why. But I wouldn't be surprised if these groups make it. After all, a lot of people once thought the Stones were just a little cult, and look what happened to them."

And which stars showed the most improvement over the year?

"The Beatles," said Paul. *"We think so, anyway."*

January 1, 1966 – *Disc Weekly* **spoke** with Ringo Starr about country life. Before Christmas, he had moved his family to a country mansion at Weybridge, Surrey, neighbours with John and Cynthia Lennon. Said Ringo, *"I never really wanted to leave town.*

But we needed a lot more space when the baby arrived. And anyway, with the number of fans who had discovered where we lived in town, it was becoming impossible to lead an ordinary life."

This was Ringo's third residence since joining the Beatles. First he had shared a Knightsbridge flat with George Harrison. Both of them were forced from those digs by fans mobbing the place day and night, even crawling in through the windows. That was when George moved to his house in Surrey and Ringo found a flat in London's West End.

Now, he was the third Beatle to become a country squire. Paul was the last Beatle left in London.

In a footnote, *Disc* mentioned that the most pleasant shock of the previous year had been when the Beatles had been awarded their MBEs. They went on to remind readers that Paul had won a poll last November as the most popular Beatle, but that Ringo's popularity clearly rivaled it, judging by the number of baby gifts that had been arriving for Zak.

January 1, 1966 – *Melody Maker* **conducted their pop think-in** with Paul McCartney, asking about…

Glamour Girls: *"Most are so unglamorous, it's true. Girls with Brillo hair who shouldn't be seen."*

String Basses: *"They hurt your fingers, especially if you're a two-pound weakling like me."*

Eppy: *"Someone who's learned a lot in a very short time and is as straight as they come."*

Tito Burns: *"While Rome fiddles."*

Ciggies: *"I seem to smoke them all the time and get great pleasure from it, so there."*

George Martin: *"Great fellow who's very good at his job."*

Photographers: *"They've got a hell of a job because if the editor says go and get a picture of someone in his bath, they have to do it. They probably realise it's a dirty trick but they do it just the same. It's a good thing they realise it's a low trick, but they still have to do it.*

Psychiatry: *"It helps but it's not the whole answer."*

Dressing gowns: *"I like them. I like the backing. Good to dance to."*

Liverpool: *"Home."*

Cars: *"I like them, but mainly because they get you from place to place."*

Rhodesia: *"Colour prejudice, I suppose."*

Dogs: *"The only ones I don't like are those without a sense of proportion."*

Cats: *"I like them but my dad hates them because they pee on the lavender."*

Italy: *"I like Rome. It's another fantastic looking place. It's one of the greatest looking cities in the world."*

De Gaulle: *"De Gerrier!"*

Cowboys: *"I don't like them but I liked pretending to be one in America last year."*

Children: "*Up to a certain age, I love all of them. After that, some of them get wrecked, mainly by parents.*"

Count Basie: "*I haven't heard enough of him to know if I like him or not.*"

Tooth paste: "*Fab. Gear. Madison. Twist. Crazy. Dig. Most.*"

January 1, 1966 – *Melody Maker* mentioned that the Beatles were the top pop name, according to a poll run by Billboard, the U.S. music paper. Based on total sales, they were also named as America's top album recording stars.

January 8, 1966 – *Disc Weekly* spoke with Dick James, the Beatles' music publisher, about *Michelle*.

Said James, "*Already, there are over twenty different versions of the song recorded by artists in all parts of the world, France, Germany, Spain, America, and Britain. And right now, a battle royal is waging in the American charts between Britain's David and Jonathan, in Billboard's Hot One Hundred at ninety-eight, and America's Billy Vaughn, in at ninety-six. Other stars are also jumping on the band wagon.*

"*I'll go on record in predicting that* Michelle *will be every bit as big as* Yesterday, *undoubtedly the outstanding song of the Old Year.*

"*No one was more surprised than Paul McCartney that* Yesterday *was such a smash hit. When it was issued as a single by the Beatles in the States, it shot right to the top. And the LP track also became a tremendous hit here, plus the single versions by Matt Monro and Marianne Faithfull.*

"*Now, the same pattern is repeating itself with* Michelle. *And there isn't the time lag with this that there was with* Yesterday. *Although the Rubber Soul album was only released on December 10th, people are rushing to record* Michelle. *It has already been recorded on new British singles by David and Jonathan and the Overlanders.*

"*At this stage, there's no knowing what the final total of recordings will be. That's why I'm confident that* Michelle *will be every bit as big as* Yesterday. *Maybe even bigger.*"

January 8, 1966 – *Melody Maker* conducted their pop think-in with Ringo Starr, asking about…

Christmas: "*Happy times. Food and drink. It doesn't mean anything religious to me. This year, it meant a holiday.*"

Chris Farlowe: "*I enjoyed him on Ready Steady Go but I've never seen him live in a club.*"

Birth control: "*Each to his own ideas.*"

Clean-up TV campaign: "*It's a load of rubbish. Those people are living in the past.*"

Jagger: "*Mick Jagger? A friend. A good fellow. Britain's best ballad singer.*"

Oldham: "*Andrew Loog! He's trying, I think. One of the few A and R men who are trying to do something different. God rest Phil Spector.*"

Pop art: "*I like the Who. It doesn't interest me. It's okay, I suppose. I don't buy all the clothes. Half of them are rubbish.*"

Millionaires: "*I'd like to be one. The only thing I've got against them is, they've got more money than me.*"

Obscene lyrics: "*Never heard any. It's an individual thing. You can read obscene lyrics into any song.*"

Folk: "*I like folk.*"

Public schools: "*I don't like them. They're against any upbringing I've ever had. A bad thing for me and my family.*"

Jimmy Clitheroe: "*I wish he'd get a pair of long pants. Not one of my favourite comedians.*"

Murray the K: "*Fastest talker I've ever met. He knows what's happening in radio. I wish we had someone like him here.*"

Communism: "*I don't like Communism. We're restricted enough as it is. If they got in it'd be last. Nothing would happen.*"

Elvis: "*I liked his early records. Don't like what he's doing now. Met him. He's okay.*"

Middle-aged autograph hunters: "*Silly people. Because they hate to admit they like you, too. They think it's wrong.*"

Cliff: "*Ballad singer. Never bought one of his records in my life.*"

Godfrey Winn: "*Journalist… of sorts. Only met him once.*"

James Bond: "*Best comedian on the scene today.*"

God: "*Somebody must like him.*"

P.J. Proby: "*Good singer. Someone who is silly to himself.*"

Zoot Money: "*Organ. Nice fellow. I think it's too late for him to make it very big now.*"

Policemen: "*A regiment of ants in blue uniforms.*"

Scrubbers: "*I hate them. They come round to the flat and shout and scream and annoy everyone.*"

January 22, 1966 – *Disc Weekly* ran a photograph of bearded Beatles. The one of Ringo was legitimate. He had been on holiday and had not shaved. The other three were an artist's mock-up created for *Disc*. They were wondering how the Beatles would look if their faces were as hairy as their heads.

January 22, 1966 – *Melody Maker* conducted their pop think-in with George Harrison, asking about…

Christmas: "*Fun and twinkling lights. Nothing religious for me, really.*"

Chris Farlowe: "*Great voice and nice lad.*"

Birth control: "*Nothing. I don't think about it.*"

Clean-up TV campaign: "*Rubbish. Stupid. The more true-to-life TV the better.*"

Jagger: "*Mick. The singer with the Stones.*"

Oldham: "*Andrew. I think a lot of Andrew as an A and R man. I agree with his ideas about recording pop music.*"

Pop art: "*I haven't seen enough to form an opinion.*"

Millionaires: *"Anyone who can be a millionaire in this country with the government taking most of it is a real winner. We're not millionaires.*

Obscene lyrics: *"Haven't heard any yet. It's more a case of obscene minds listening to them."*

Hamburg: *"Yeah, yeah, yeah."*

Ewan MacColl: *"I only heard him for the first time when he moaned about Dylan."*

Folk: *"Good folk is great, but there's too much bad folk which people say is great."*

Public schools: *"They are a case of trying to buy brains for thick kids."*

Murray the K: *"He's smart, because he's always the first one around with anything."*

Debs: *"I don't get them at all. Debs are something that've passed. Some people wish they hadn't."*

Eppy: *"An amazing businessman and our pal."*

Communism: *"It's terrible. I only know a little bit about it but what I know is off."*

Elvis: *"Well done."*

Middle-aged autograph hunters: *"Depends on their attitude. They are not bad on their own."*

Carnaby Street: *"I haven't been there. It's a nice street, I believe."*

Cliff: *"Looking rather undernourished."*

Father: *"Which art in heaven."*

James Bond: *"Overdone."*

God: *"The Naz."*

Private Eye: *"Not as funny as they think it is, but quite nice."*

P.J. Proby: *"A bit foolish but great to have around."*

Boxing: *"A violent sport."*

The Who: *"Great ideas."*

Zoot Money: *"Big voice and big smile."*

Punch-ups: *"To be avoided."*

A Talent for Loving: *"A good book. A western but different to others."*

Policemen: *"A bit simple and not understanding."*

Germany: *"Good fun and laughs."*

Scrubbers: *"Need scrubbing."*

Hipsters: *"Great, I like hipsters. As trousers, not as people."*

January 29, 1966 – *Disc Weekly* **talked** about the marriage of George Harrison and Pattie Boyd, and about plans for a honeymoon.

Said George, *"Maybe we'll push off in about a fortnight. Fans have been great, and I'd like to thank everybody for messages and telegrams and things."*

They were married at the register office in Epsom, Surrey, the previous Friday with Paul McCartney and Brian Epstein standing in as joint best men.

George said, *"We decided to marry two days before Christmas. Although I'd asked Pattie to marry me a week after I met her on the set of* A Hard Day's Night*. She refused. It was very embarrassing at the time. That was two years ago."*

Pattie added, *"I turned him down because I didn't think he was serious."*

"Well, I wanted to make sure I kept her," George said.

John and Ringo were on holiday, plans that were made before George had set the wedding date. Paul gave them an Oriental head carved from mahogany, inlaid with ivory. Brian gave them an antique table. Pattie presented George with silver wine goblets.

Sandra Cohen, the volunteer secretary of the Beatles' fan club, quit her job, stating she was greatly disappointed when she heard about Harrison's wedding.

The telegram from the Lennons and the Starrs said, *"Welcome to the club."*

February 5, 1966 – *Disc Weekly* **spoke** with George Harrison about his marriage.

Said George, *"Marriage is great. The strangest thing about it really is trying to realise all the time that you are actually married. It's difficult to explain. But I feel great and so does Pattie. It's marvelous, an interesting new side to life, and we're glad we're married."*

Apparently, George's marriage to twenty-one-year-old model Pattie Boyd broke a million hearts. At a press conference, the day after they signed the papers, George said, *"I haven't had enough time to make a decision on married life yet. Come back and ask me in a week."*

A week later, *Disc* spoke with him again – he and Pattie had been decorating their home.

George said, *"The house seems like a home now. Before, it was more like a flat, just a place where I lived. It means such a lot more now.*

"I've always liked it here, but now it really seems as if we belong.

"Pattie's a good cook, and she cooks quite a lot. Am I hard to please with food? No, not really. I like all meats and she can cook them all. Lamb, steak, veal, pork, great.

"She doesn't really do anything spectacular with cooking, well, a few things. But she's finding out how to do more with the help of her big cookery book.

"We knew each other's character properly [before the wedding] *so we haven't really had any big shocks. I think all people who get married should really make a point of really knowing all about their future husband or wife. I mean, getting married is a pretty final thing. You should know all about each other's peculiarities, and Pattie and I did.*

"You tend to forget you're married sometimes, even now. Every now and then I have to remind myself that Pattie's my wife now, not my girlfriend."

Said Pattie, *"We are getting a bit more used to it. It's still a little difficult to believe we are actually husband and wife. But it's nice. There's a lot to be done in the house and it's fun."*

How did she feel about breaking all those hearts?

"I hope I didn't, but anyway, I never think of George as a Beatle when we are together here at

home. I think of him as, well, just George." She went on to say he was not difficult to please. "I knew roughly what he liked and didn't like."

Beatle fans had not reared up against the marriage. Hundreds of congratulatory messages were coming in from all over the world. A spokesman from the Beatles' office said, "We have had no angry letters at all. It was the same with Ringo and Maureen's marriage. Stacks of letters, cables, telegrams and phone calls of congratulation."

February 5, 1966 – *Melody Maker* **talked** about rumours that Brian Epstein was getting involved with managing Elvis Presley. Tony Barrow, NEMS press officer, said, "We know nothing at all on these lines. These rumours have circulated before, but when I asked Brian Epstein about them, I was answered by a laugh."

It was suggested that Colonel Tom Parker, Elvis's manager, was intending to retire.

Elvis's response was, "You could have knocked me over with a Beatle when I heard of it."

Presley called Parker; Parker denied having any plans to retire unless the Beatles had enough money to buy both he and Elvis.

A spokesman for RCA Victor said, "Even the Beatles don't have that kind of money."

February 19, 1966 – *Disc Weekly* **said** the Beatles were still officially on holiday. People were wondering about their next film and their next single.

John Lennon said, "I haven't a clue about the new single. I don't suppose we'll start thinking about it very seriously until we're told we're due to record it. We usually work like that, anyway."

Asked what the Beatles were doing, Ringo said, "Well, the telly doesn't start till late in the afternoon, so we get up about two o'clock, and John comes to my house one day, I go to his the next. I find it's better to go to his house because he's got all the toys there, tape recorders and things, which we like playing about with."

"You see, man," John joked. "We're trying to create his new sound. Create, man, create."

How did Ringo like being a father?

"It's wonderful. Every little thing he does gives Maureen and me a kick. When he smiles and laughs especially."

John said, "He doesn't have spasms."

"No," echoed Ringo, "no spasms. It's lovely having a son, you get that feeling like when you are first married."

March 5, 1966 – *Disc Weekly* **announced** that the Beatles would be touring the UK again that year, also that they would be playing short tours in Japan and Germany, possibly even a return concert at Shea Stadium in New York.

A spokesman for NEMS Enterprises said, "Dates for all these concerts, including the British tour, are held up pending the next Beatles' film, scripts of which are being considered.

"The Beatles were offered two return concerts the same evening at Shea Stadium, but Brian Epstein said it was out of the question. He would, however, consider one."

No one had yet made a decision about the group's next single.

March 5, 1966 – *Disc Weekly***, Ray Coleman talked** about the Shea Stadium TV show, saying the Beatles had finally had a successful TV documentary. The Beatles at Shea Stadium had been shown on British TV the previous Tuesday.

He thought the program fell slightly short of its possibilities but that it was good, capturing the true reality of Beatlemania in a way that it had never been done before.

It was not the best the Beatles could do musically; nor was the photography the best it could be. There could have been less time devoted to the dancers and to Brenda Holloway and Sounds Incorporated. But the show had an immediacy, a sense of life, a sense of the full fifty-six thousand-member audience. And George Harrison's comments at the end rounded out the best Beatles' TV appearance to date.

Coleman lamented the lack of interviews with cops and fans and first-aid workers. He suggested that would have made for a far better documentary. But he liked it – it was spectacular.

Fans were invited to send in postcards, no more than fifty words, expressing their opinions of the Beatles at Shea Stadium.

March 11, 1966 – *New Musical Express***, Chris Hutchins interviewed** John Lennon at a cafe in Soho, London…

He'd been quoted as saying he did not want to be playing in a rock and roll band when he was thirty. He was now twenty-six and the only gig the Beatles have set for 1966 was, apparently, the NME Poll Winners concert in May. Had retirement begun?

Said Lennon: "No. We're going to Germany, America and Japan this year. It's an accident that we're not working now; we should have just had two weeks holiday after Christmas and then started on the next film, but it isn't ready and won't be for months.

"We want to work and we've got plenty to do: writing songs, taping things and so on. Paul and I ought to get down to writing some songs for the new LP next week. I hope he and Jane aren't going away or God knows when we'll be ready to record. George thought we'd written them and were all ready – that's why he came dashing back from his honeymoon and we hadn't got a thing ready. We'll have to get started, there's been too much messing round. But I feel we've only just finished Rubber Soul and I keep looking for the reviews, then I realise we did it months ago. We're obviously not going to work harder than we want to now, but you get a bit fed up of doing nothing."

Now that the Beatles were all rich, does he ever feel like doing something different?

"*I've had one or two things up my sleeve, I was going to make recordings of some of my poetry. But I'm not high-powered. I just sort of stand there and let things happen to me. I should have finished a new book – it's supposed to be out this month but I've only done one page! I thought why should I break me back getting books out like records?*"

Was he worried that he might not have enough money to last the rest of his life?

"*Yes! I get fits of worrying about that. I get visions of being one of those fools who do it all in by the time they're thirty. Then I imagine writing a series for the people saying 'I was going to spend, spend, spend...' I thought about this a while back and decided I'd been a bit extravagant and bought too many cars, so I put the Ferrari and the Mini up for sale.*

"*Then one of the accountants said I was all right, so I got the cars back. It's the old story of never knowing how much we've got. I've tried to find out but with income tax to be deducted and the money coming in from all over the place, the sums get too complicated for me, I can't even do my times table. Every now and again the accountant clears some money of tax and puts it into my account saying: 'That's there and it's all yours but don't spend it all at once!' The thing I've learned is that if I'm spending ten thousand pounds, I say to myself: 'You've had to earn thirty thousand pounds before tax to get that.'*"

What sort of people dropped by his house?

"*We entertain very few. Proby was there one night and George Martin another, I think those are the only two we've specifically said 'Come to dinner' to and made preparations. Normally I like people to drop round on the off chance. It cuts out all that formal entertaining business. We've just had Ivan and Jean down for a weekend – they're old friends from Liverpool – and Pete Shotton, the fellow who runs my supermarket came round on Saturday.*"

Was the Weybridge house his permanent home?

"*No it's not. I'm dying to move into town but I'm waiting to see how Paul gets on when he goes into his town house. If he gets by all right then I'll sell the place at Weybridge. Probably to some American who'll pay a fortune for it! I was thinking the other night though that it might not be easy to find a buyer. How do you sell somebody a pink, green and purple house? We've had purple velvet put up on the dining room walls – it sets of the old scrubbed table we eat on. Then there's the 'funny' room upstairs. I painted that all colours changing from one to another as I emptied each can of paint. How do you show somebody that when they come to look the place over? And there's the plants in the bath... I suppose I could have a flat in town but I don't want to spend another twenty thousand just to have somewhere to stay overnight when I've had too much bevy to drive home.*"

What did he watch on TV?

"*The Power Game is my favourite. I love that. And next to it Danger Man and The Rat Catchers – did you see that episode the other night when that spy, the clever one, shot a nun by mistake? I love that and I was so glad it happened to the clever one.*"

What would happen during the Beatles' next recording studio sessions?

"*Literally anything. Electronic music, jokes... one thing's for sure – the next LP is going to be very different. We wanted to have it so that there was no space between the tracks – just continuous. But they wouldn't hear of it. Paul and I are very keen on this electronic music. You make it clinking a couple of glasses together or with bleeps from the radio, then you loop the tape to repeat the noises at intervals. Some people build up whole symphonies from it. It would have been better than the background music we had for the last film. All those silly bands. Never again!*"

March 26, 1966 – *Disc Weekly*, **Ray Coleman talked** with John Lennon about personal possessions, things found in and around his home. Lennon cared little for material items. Coleman asked about...

First Rickenbacker guitar: "*It's a bit hammered now. I just keep it for kicks, really. I bought it in Germany on the HP, I remember that whatever it cost, it was a hell of a lot of money to me, at the time.*"

Three cars: "*A Rolls, Mini and a Ferrari – the Mini for pottering about in, the Rolls for relaxing in, and the Ferrari for zoom. I do very little driving, I'm not a very good driver.*"

Swimming pool: "*It's been in my garden for four months but we haven't been in it yet, it's been too cold.*"

Two pictures: "*...drawn by Stuart Sutcliffe, our old bass player. I'll always keep these, for sentimental reasons.*"

A lump of stone: "*We found it on the doorstep and somebody said it was prehistoric. I've since been enlightened and I believe it's a load of crap.*"

An outsize boot: "*This is the one from the film* Help! *I keep it in the garden, as a sort of mascot.*

A stone frog: "*I like to see this in the fireplace near the TV set. I just like it, sitting there looking at us all.*"

About twenty suits: "*Well, yeah, but only wear about two, both black. I've got an evening dress but I only wear it when I have to because it's so uncomfortable. I get my clothes from Dougie Millings.*"

The singing postman's record: "*It's all right but you wouldn't exactly have it on hour after hour. Just part of my record collection, I've got everything. Electronic, Indian, classical and modern jazz.*"

An office: '*Part of the house. I use it for getting a few things written. It's just got a desk and a grandfather clock.*"

Pin table, football game table and fruit machine: "*In my den here at home. Just for a laugh.*"

Juke Box: "*I never did get round to seeing how it worked properly. It's got forty-eight records, I keep it mainly for standards,* Be Bop A Lula *and* Some Other Guy."

Four car number plates: "*...pinned to the wall of the playroom. Also a model race track, Julian will probably have it when he grows up.*"

A studio: "*...which contains two very good tape recorders from which you can make your own records. And a bath full of plants. And twelve guitars, some of which are wrecked.*"

Aldous Huxley: "*...books. I've just started reading him because he's the new guvnor, it seems to me.*"

April 2, 1966 – *Disc Weekly***, Ray Coleman spoke** with John Lennon about politics.

"*The trouble with government as it is,*" said John, "*is that it doesn't represent the people. It controls them. All they seem to want to do, the people who run the country, is keep themselves in power and stop us knowing what's going on.*

"*The motto seems to be: Keep the people happy with a few fags and beer and they won't ask questions. I always wondered what it was about politics and government that was wrong. Now, since reading some books by Aldous Huxley, I've suddenly found out what it's all about.*

"*I'm not saying politicians are all terrible men. It's just the system of government that I don't like. It's been going on for hundreds of years, and it'll be hard to change. I'm not an anarchist and I don't want to appear one. But it would be good if more people started realising the difference between political propaganda and the truth.*

"*The only possible reason they have had so many TV election broadcasts is because they've got to force the public to watch them. Otherwise, people couldn't care less, because at the back of their minds, most thinking people know there's something wrong with the present form of government.*

"*We're being conned into thinking everything's okay, but all these bloody politicians seem the same to me. All they can talk about is the economy and that, what about people and freedom? These things that matter more don't seem to worry them.*"

Lennon pointed out that the politicians believed that if everyone had a television, a place to sleep, a car to drive, smokes to smoke and beer to drink, they could keep the people quiet.

"*But what can you do about it?*"

From across the room, Ringo said, "*He's right, you just can't win...*"

Said John, "*There's nothing you can do about it, it's too big. What I would really like to see is people generally getting more say in what goes on. From what you hear, none of the politicians has any intention of giving ordinary people complete freedom. Just keep them down, that's all they want.*

"*I'm not suggesting I know what the answer is, I just know there's something wrong with the present* way of governing the country, and the more people like us realise it, at least we are on the way to changing it.*

"*What I don't like is this bit, politicians aren't politicians because they genuinely want to do the people good. They're politicians because they want power. What we need to change things is a bloody revolution.*

"*I'm bored by politics because the three of them, Harold, Ted and Jo, all seem the same to me. They know all the tricks. It's a drag but I can't see the way out.*"

April 9, 1966 – *Melody Maker* **talked** about the Beatles' new single, which was to be released within six to eight weeks. For the last few weeks, the group had been working on fifteen new songs, preparing to record after Easter. The single would be one of those, their first follow-up to We Can Work It Out / Day Tripper, which started in the charts at number eighteen and quickly moved to number one, holding that spot for four weeks.

After the single was selected and released, the remainder of the tracks would be used for the band's next album, guaranteed to carry on from where Rubber Soul left off, with strange instruments and unusual instrumental effects.

April 16, 1966 – *Disc Weekly***, Derek Taylor, in his Hollywood column, said** the Beatles had hit number one in the Record World national charts, but failed to reach number one in Cash Box and Billboard.

April 16, 1966 – *Disc Weekly* **talked** about Beatle plans and activities. The group was in the recording studio, preparing their next single and album, the single due out in four to six weeks.

Dates had been set and announced for their next tour of the States. And plans were being made for trips to Japan and Germany.

If their next film was shot from September through November, then their next UK tour would be in December. Music publisher Dick James told *Disc* that he was getting constant requests for Beatles music in the U.S., Germany and Japan.

"*Although the Beatles' story started in Hamburg,*" James said, "*the Germans were slow starters on the Beatles' scene, but now their own writers find it more profitable to write lyrics in English rather than in German.*"

He went on to explain that special Beatles' albums would be released in the States to coincide with the next tour. Once again, a trailer full of Beatles records would precede the group, traveling from venue to venue with copies of the record.

The U.S. tour dates were: August 13th, Amphitheatre, Chicago; August 14th, Fairground Stadium, Louisville; August 15th, Washington Stadium; August 16th, Philadelphia Stadium; August 17th, Maple Leaf Gardens, Toronto; August 18th, Fenway Park, Boston; August 19th, Memphis

Coliseum; August 20th, Crosby Field, Cincinnati; August 21st, Busch Stadium, St. Louis; August 23rd, Shea Stadium, New York; August 25th, Seattle; August 28th, Los Angeles; and August 29th, San Francisco.

In June, they were to tour Germany; in July, Japan.

April 16, 1966 – *Melody Maker* talked about the Beatles' planned U.S. tour, saying fourteen concerts had been set, including one at a stadium that would hold one hundred and three thousand people. Also planned was a return to Shea Stadium.

Six outdoor sports stadiums, each holding more than forty thousand people, were on the tour, which was to open in Chicago on August 12th – twenty thousand seats. Also planned: August 13th, Detroit Olympia Hockey Stadium; August 14th, State Fair Grounds, Louisville, Kentucky; August 15th, Washington DC Stadium – fifty thousand capacity; August 16th, Philadelphia Municipal Stadium – one hundred and three thousand capacity; August 17th, Toronto Maple Leaf Gardens; August 18th, Fenway Park, Boston; August 19th, Memphis Coliseum; August 20th, Cincinnati Crosley Field; August 21st, St. Louis Busch Stadium; August 23rd, New York Shea Stadium; August 25th, Seattle; and August 28th, Los Angeles. They were also expecting to play San Francisco but there was, as yet, no confirmation.

Plans to record in Memphis had fallen through.

April 23, 1966 – *Disc and Music Echo* (no longer *Disc Weekly*) talked about the Beatles' plans for Germany and Japan. The group intended to do six shows in Germany and three in Tokyo. They would appear first in Munich on June 24th at the Circus Corner; then Essen Grugahalle on June 25th; and Hamburg Ersst Merck Halle on June 26th. Two concerts were planned for each venue.

On June 27th, they were due to arrive in Tokyo for three shows at the Budo Kan on June 30th, July 1st and July 2nd.

April 23, 1966 – *Disc and Music Echo* mentioned that being a Beatle presented few new problems, but that some of the old ones got worse. Fans had discovered Lennon's house in Weybridge, and were invading the grounds weekends on some sort of pop pilgrimage.

Said Lennon, "*I'm fed up with it, some weekends it gets so bad we go away somewhere to get away from the people who come to gawp. You'd think it was a holiday camp or something. They come with babies, sandwiches, flasks of tea, the lot! What do they think it is here, a national park?*

"*These people aren't fans. They can't be. I reckon there's something wrong with people who just come to look. If they were young people who came to look where a Beatles lives, I suppose it would be understandable. But it's adults. They seem to think I'm on stage every minute!*

"*I went out and told them to get away once because they started camping and having picnics in the grounds. We all know we've got to expect to have the public chasing us a lot. But this is where I live and I reckon it's unbelievable to have the house treated as some kind of park.*

"*This happens most weekends. Sometimes it's worse than others. But it shouldn't really happen at all. People have got a cheek. I just can't understand what gets into their minds.*

"*There's another reason why I find it a big drag. I'd like to think people were doing something better with spare time than coming gawping round here.*"

May 7, 1966 – *Disc and Music Echo*, announced that the Beatles' new single was due out on June 10th. It would be *Paperback Writer* backed by *Rain*, both written by John Lennon and Paul McCartney.

Paperback Writer had Paul singing the lead with John and George backing him on harmonies. The lyrics were written in a letter format. Paul's lead vocals were double-tracked. It was an up-beat rock and roll tune, described by George as a "*joggety-rogalong song.*"

Said George Martin, "*Of several numbers recorded, these two titles were the obvious and immediate choices for the new single. The rest will go on the new Beatles LP.*"

Rain was a slower tune, featuring John on double-tracked lead vocals.

The American release date was to be June 6th.

In a footnote, *Disc* reminded readers about the prediction made a few years ago, during the Beatles' first long tour of America, the prediction that their airplane would crash on the way to Indianapolis, killing or maiming the group and all aboard. That did not happen, obviously, but that very same airplane had just crashed in Oklahoma. More than eighty soldiers were killed.

May 7, 1966 – *Melody Maker* talked about the new Beatles' record, their first single since *Day Tripper / We Can Work It Out*. It was *Paperback Writer* backed by *Rain*. It would be released on June 10th in the UK, June 6th on Capitol Records in the States. Both songs were Lennon / McCartney compositions. Unusual musical instruments, such as the sitar on Norwegian Wood, were not featured on either track.

The A side, *Paperback Writer*, was the story of a man trying to get a paperback novel published. The point behind *Rain*, the B side, according to the reviewer, was simply that, whatever the weather, someone will complain.

As yet, no TV or radio shows had been planned by the Beatles to promote the new disc.

May 7, 1966 – *Melody Maker*, Alan Walsh spoke with Walter Shenson, wondering what had happened to the plans for the next Beatles movie. Originally, they had intended to shoot Richard Condon's novel *A*

Talent For Loving. The plans had gone awry and Walsh wondered where things stood regarding the group's third movie.

Shenson said, *"Well, it's so difficult to find a suitable script because we are all demanding a very high standard. It's not enough to make a frivolous film or trade on the success of the Beatles generally. We don't have to make a film at this moment and we are all agreed that it's better to make no film at all than make a bad one. We have to be very careful. The Beatles have always been first at everything they've done; Hollywood are now copying* Hard Day's Night, *and* Help! *was a beautifully visual pop-art film, and they never do what's expected of them. We want this film to be unexpected as well.*

How did he envision the script?

"We are more or less agreed this time, that the Beatles would not play the Beatles, as they did in the first two. They will have to play four leading characters who look, think and talk like the Beatles but are different characters. This has been the fault with most of the scripts and ideas so far submitted, they've followed the first two and written a film about the Beatles. To find a good enough story line, which had four leading men, is very difficult. The fault with the things submitted hasn't been bad writing, but ignorance of what we are looking for. The script must be a strong story line, with four leading characters, and different from the first two, forgetting that the Beatles are to play the characters, and visualising a story line that would suit John, Paul, George and Ringo."

Would there be music?

"This time, we'd like to have a script from which the Beatles can write the songs, and we'll have to find a way of including six or seven songs. But, of course, if in the script they don't play a group, this will have to be done some other way than in the first two films, although we did dub the music over the sequences in both of them, so have set this precedent."

How many scripts had he seen?

"I've seen everything from single page ideas to shooting scripts, I'd say about forty in all, from America, Great Britain and the Continent."

From what sort of people had the scripts come?

"We've had ideas or scripts from fans, from professional writers, from novelists, from screenwriters, and even from journalists, some of them quite well known. We've even interviewed writers to see what they could come up with."

Who rejected the scripts?

"I turn down the obviously useless ones. The ones with some worth are put up to Brian and the boys. So far, I've never been disappointed by them not liking a script. They know what they want, they are, after all, the best judges of themselves, and there's been no script that I've wanted them to do that they've turned down. It would be easy for us to

do the same as Elvis does, Elvis in the Army and that sort of thing. Even when he uses a different name in the film, it's basically the same Elvis character. The same with Cliff Richard, on holiday, et cetera. That wouldn't work with the Beatles. They know it."*

As a producer, what were his ideas for a workable script?

"The Beatles, first of all, don't want to do a period story. It has to be a modern story, set in Britain, though short location trips would be all right. They don't want to compromise. The script will have to have a good story line, a well worked out plot, and not be a plotless cashing-in on the Beatles reputation."

Would he separate them and make a film with one or the other?

"No, that wouldn't work. But if we could find the right story, the character and personality of each of the four could be brought out in one film."

What was so important about this third film?

"Because the succeeding films will be affected if it's a bad film. And the boys themselves don't want to do anything bad. There will be such a gap between Help! *and this one that it will have to be good. Also, as the boys say, if they make a bad record, they can throw the tapes away. But if half a million is spent on a film, good or bad, it has to go on release."*

What if another producer came up with a story before he did?

"Well, I have a contract to make another film, but I wouldn't stand in the way if the Beatles wanted to do something that someone else offered. We'd come to some arrangement. But we work well together and I don't think anyone could walk in and con the Beatles into doing something that's bad for them."

Were they all playing down the idea of the Beatles as film stars?

"No, but they don't want to appeal to any specific age group or country, and they are aware, as I have said, that at all costs they must make good films, or their film career will come to an end."

Was the search for a script frustrating?

"Yes, it is frustrating, but it's necessary to be sure."

Was it rewarding to be associated with the Beatles?

"Yes, both financially and by the fact that they are so stimulating because of their talent and the fact that they are so in tune with modern times."

How successful were the first two films?

"They were extremely successful. They were big-grossing films and, because they weren't too costly to make, they reaped good profits as well."

May 14, 1966 – *Melody Maker* **said** the Beatles were hard at work on a new album, the follow-up to their hit *Rubber Soul* album. They spent the week at EMI studios, cutting new tracks.

Brian Epstein was in Denmark the week before, accepting two awards from a Danish magazine on behalf of the group. The awards were for best foreign song, *Michelle*, and best foreign group. Also, in Denmark, he was presented by EMI with five Gold Discs, one each for himself and the Beatles, for selling more than a million records in Denmark.

The Beatles were the first recording artists to ever sell more than a million records in Denmark – population four million.

May 21, 1966 – *Disc and Music Echo* reported that the Beatles were to make a guest appearance, June 4th, on Saturday Club, to be interviewed by Brian Matthew.

In the Far East, so many people were applying for tickets that extra shows were being planned. They were to do two shows at the National Football Stadium in Manila on July 4th. They were also going to do afternoon performances on July 1st and 2nd in Tokyo, as well as their scheduled evening gigs.

Cliff Bennett and the Rebel Rousers and Peter and Gordon had signed on to tour Germany with the Beatles.

May 28, 1966 – *Melody Maker* said the Beatles had been to Chiswick House in London the previous week, playing on the grounds for TV cameras. Brian Epstein's Subafilms was making shorts in colour and in black and white for British and American television shows.

Top of the Pops would be showing one of Epstein's new films on June 9th, featuring the Beatles performing their new single, *Paperback Writer / Rain*.

The group had also filmed a colour piece for the Ed Sullivan Show, along with a series of interviews.

June 4, 1966 – *Disc and Music Echo* spoke with their readers to get the verdict on the new Beatles single *Paperback Writer / Rain*. The consensus was that most fans liked the A side and were not fond of *Rain*. Also, most fans did not believe it was the group's best work.

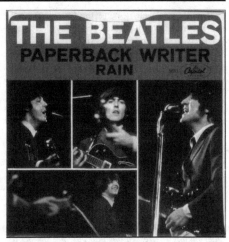

Penny Valentine pointed out that if anyone else had done the record, people would have loved it but, since it was the Beatles, fans wanted something more. Without a doubt, there was a new Beatles' sound evolving. It would grow on some fans and be lost on others.

June 4, 1966 – *Melody Maker* mentioned that the Beatles were to headline the 400th Saturday Club show that week. They went on to talk about a mystery interview that had fired up some controversy in the U.S. Supposedly, it was a telephone interview. A Pittsburgh deejay ran it on the air, an interview wherein the Beatles slammed the huge Barry Sadler hit, *The Ballad of the Green Berets,* calling it rubbish.

A wave of anti-Beatle protest rolled across the country. Capitol Records were deluged with requests that Beatles refrain from that sort of talk. Retailers reported that fans were threatening to boycott their stores if they did not remove the Beatle records from the shelves. And, in London, the Beatles denied giving any such interview to an American disc jockey.

A footnote added that the film clip of the Beatles performing *Paperback Writer* was to be shown on Top of the Pops.

June 4, 1966 – *Melody Maker* reviewed the Beatles new single, *Paperback Writer / Rain,* the brand new record written by John Lennon and Paul McCartney. They applauded producer George Martin for getting such a powerful sound and such a nice mix of wailing harmonies and driving bass. It was completely up to the Beatles' standards and sure to be a hit.

June 10, 1966 – *New Musical Express* announced that the Beatles had recorded their first ever jazz tune. They had secured the backing from five of the UK's top jazz men, trumpet players Ian Hamer, Les Condon and Eddie Thornton, and tenor players Peter Coe and Alan Branscombe.

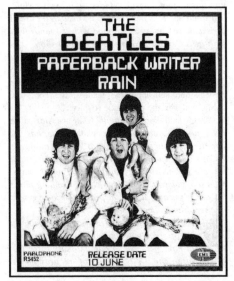

The Beatles were leaving for Germany a day earlier than originally planned. Four days later, they would fly from Hamburg to Tokyo for three nights in Japan. After a concert in Manila, they were to return to London.

June 11, 1966 – *Disc and Music Echo* declared it was Beatles Week again. Their new single was due out the following day. But they wondered about the jacket photograph of the group draped in raw meat, the most controversial shot ever of the Beatles.

They spoke with the photographer, Bob Whitaker, who said, "*I wanted to do a real experiment. People will jump to the wrong conclusions about it being sick. But the whole thing is based on simplicity, linking four very real people with something real.*

"*I got George to knock some nails into John's head, and took some sausages along to get some other pictures. Dressed them up in white smocks as butchers, and this is the result, the use of the camera as a means of creating situations.*"

After the session, Paul McCartney said, "*Very tasty meat.*"

Said George Harrison, "*We won't come to any more of your sick picture sessions.*"

John Lennon said, "*Oh, we don't mind doing anything.*"

And Ringo announced, "*We haven't done pictures like* this *before…*"

Disc put out the call to their readers, asking for their opinions, sick or super?

In a footnote, they reported that the Beatles departure for Munich, the beginning of their Germany / Japan tour, had been moved forward a day. After Munich, Essen and Hamburg, they were to fly to Tokyo, then home via Manila. Less than a month later, they would be leaving for their U.S. tour.

June 11, 1966 – *Disc and Music Echo*, Ray Coleman conducted a two-part interview with Paul McCartney. **Part One:** Coleman started by saying with the arrival of the Beatles on the pop scene, everything changed. Prime ministers and royalty wanted to be seen with pop stars. And four incredible rock and rollers rose to the top of the world, rich, with MBEs, hot cars and very nice homes. John Lennon penned a pair of books and gained literary status. Ringo emerged from *A Hard Day's Night* and *Help!* as a movie star. And George went Indian, sipping Indian tea, burning incense, and learning to play the sitar. But to the fans, Paul appeared to be the same boyishly charming guy, polite, well-groomed, still unmarried, still just Paul McCartney of Liverpool.

But, Coleman pointed out, McCartney had changed considerably. More worldly, more confident, more thoughtful, poised and polished.

As he joined Coleman for lunch, his thumb was dripping blood. And he said, "*I gashed it when I was shaving. Drag.*"

The new Beatles single was due out that weekend and fans were criticising it as being a bit ordinary. The Beatles worried about criticism. And Coleman asked if the early fire had left them?

Said Paul, "*Has the battle left the Beatles, folks? No, not in that sense. I suppose when we started we had this rebel image and long hair and people thought that was part of our battle for getting on. But the Stones, and us, and a lot of others, we get bored by this rebel business.*

"*It was all right when we were trying to make it, but those rebel days have gone. There's so much more to do now than sit and think about battles and rebel images. We just want to make good records and do good shows. We've grown out of all that image thing now.*

"*The scene's changed so much, and it's changed for the better. Long hair and gimmicks don't always make it, there's a very good chart all the time these days, and images don't come into it much. You don't get that business of 'Look at us, we've got long hair' any more. Both the Stones and us had got fed up with it. Rather than try to be controversial and look kinky and use all these fab gear words and act like kinky people, we'd rather concentrate on being musicians. I don't want to sound big-headed but we've all gone through that phase.*

"*I'll say this much at the risk of sounding big-headed: however much we might have been presented to the press and elsewhere as gimmicks, we always knew in our own minds where it was all leading. I'm not really sure that's the case with some of the people who've come up…*

"*Generally, it's the people who have nothing else to offer who lean on gimmicks and things. Masters of the bloody trivial. That sort of person makes me sick. I mean, some of them actually get good ideas, but if an idea's good, you don't have to gimmick it up. Just present it as a good idea. If it's worthwhile, it'll stand up on its own, there's no need to try to sell it ridiculously as 'gear fab mod with-it sounds with built-in polka dot rhythms' and all that crap. You can't talk down to people, it shows.*"

They chatted a bit about the in-crowds, the pop parasites, the self-important with-it crowds, the gossips and self-appointed leaders, the cool, the publicly clever, the pop-circle royalty…

"*Yes,*" said Paul, "*I think what we started in 1962, and that attitude to the whole scene, has got into the wrong hands. For me, as soon as a thing is 'in,' it's 'out.' In-crowds. Big drag. I've always felt terribly embarrassed by in-things. Protest songs, Madison, calypso. There's always something that's 'in' and it's nearly always the product of some genius of a recording manager.*

"*That was never what we wanted, especially when we got stuck with this 'Mersey Beat' thing. We might have believed in our publicity for a few weeks after the first couple of records made* number one, but we soon realised what was going on. We soon hated being called pioneers of Mersey Beat.

Pointing out that nothing was really 'in' at the moment, McCartney said, *"I hope the whole pop thing stays wide open and nothing ever comes to be 'in.' What these trendy pounds / shilling types don't realise is that by going along with trends, all they're doing is behaving like parasites and bastards, there's so much copying, and so much lack of originality going on, it's fantastic.*

"A lot of people have got ideas, but for every person who's got an original musical thought in his head, there is another who's wanting to ride to the top on his back. They look so lame, and they stand out a mile. 'My bell bottoms are bigger than yours!'

"I suppose people like the Stones and us are lucky now, because we don't have to do a thing if it is bad, just because it sounds commercial and because it might help us get away. But some terrible things happen and I can't understand them. How did Nancy Sinatra have the nerve to follow-up that number one hit with a song that sounded exactly the same?

"Fantastic. And now we've had time to sit and think, I've realised that it's the people who act intelligently and think about where they're going, these are the people who get on.

"Barbra Streisand. I personally don't like her singing, but she obviously made it because she tackled what she wanted to do properly and intelligently. Frank Sinatra, the same, and Brook Benton, people like that. So many people think 'Pop music? Huh, easy.' It's not that easy to do it well and do it successfully."

Now that the controversy over the Beatles receiving their MBEs had faded a bit, how did he feel about it?

Said Paul, *"I've forgotten about the MBE. It doesn't mean anything to me now. It's nice, but just something that happened on the way. I've probably lost my insignia, maybe it's in a cupboard somewhere. The only time I'd think of wearing it is when I go to the pictures, do you think they'd let me in for nine pence?"*

The Beatles were their own toughest critics but, at the moment, they were excited about their new album.

McCartney said, *"It will be the best we've done. We'll lose some fans with it, but we'll also gain some. The fans we'll probably lose will be the ones who like the things about us that we never liked anyway, and those we'll gain are the ones who want to hear us breaking into new things. Every track on the LP has something special. I'm not saying they're all good. But this rest period of the last few months gave us all a chance to think.*

"George wanted to get his Indian stuff on the record. I wanted to do some new electronic things, and John even had a song in which his inspiration was the Tibetan Book of the Dead.

"The people I talked about earlier, the people whose only idea is to copy, always remind me of a long queue, with the people with original thoughts at the top and the rest of the queue all in a line, following the people at the top. I once wrote an essay on this at school. Well, for this new album, we got off the queue for a bit… Already, we think there are better things on the album than the new single. But they're LP songs."

When all was said and done, how would he like the group to be remembered?

"I'd hate us to be remembered for one or two things we seem to be getting remembered for now, I don't like our American image, for instance. I'd hate the Beatles to be remembered as four jovial mop tops, four silly little puppets, which is what Americans tend to think of us sometimes. If it's possible, I'd like us to be remembered, when we're dead, as four people who made music that stands up to being remembered.

"I don't want to be thought of as four-men-who-made-a-few-hits-and-now-I'm-buying-a-house-for-me-dear-old-mum-in-Stepney.

"I can't imagine the Beatles as we are, when we're all thirty. People say, 'Don't worry, Jock, there's always songwriting to fall back on.' But that's not the answer, and I think we're all, well, not worried exactly, but thinking and wondering which way everything's going to go for us.

"The future could be very interesting, there's so many things to try. We've been lucky, so lucky. We've had some great experiences, and now it's something like a school-leaver wondering what career to choose, something new to break into."

Did money loom large in his thoughts?

"It's like winning the pools, except that we've been able to do everything on a much more sensible level than pools winners, who often just go mad and spend, spend, spend.

"I've not gone mad with money, in fact I felt bloody poor last night. I was driving off to meet somebody for dinner, and on the way I ran out of petrol. I felt a real idiot. I hadn't got a penny on me!

"Well, one of the advantages in being who we are is that people will always help us. I got out of the car and conned a bloke into lending me five bob for a gallon, and I wrote down his name and address. I'll send him the money back."

June 11, 1966 – *Disc and Music Echo,* **spoke** with George Harrison about the sitar, the Indian instrument which he had first played on *Norwegian Wood.* Ravi Shankar, the Indian sitar master, had given a concert at the Royal Festival Hall in London; the musical instrument was now 'in.'

Said George, he was fed up with the way the *"Indian sitar thing has become just another bandwagon gimmick, with everybody leaping aboard just to be 'in.' A lot of people will probably be saying that I'm to blame anyway, for making the sitar commercial and popular. But I'm sick of the whole thing now because I really started doing it because I want to learn music properly and take it seriously.*

"Now, people are treating it as a bandwagon and when that happens, it loses its original path. I'm genuinely interested in the sitar and I hate all this sort of crap being blown up.

"The audience at Ravi Shankar's show was full of mods and rockers who, more likely than not, just went there to be seen at the Ravi Shankar show. The big shame is that there are some people who are really interested in the sitar. Jim Sullivan, for example, has been playing it for quite a while."

After the show, the Merseys' Bill Kinsley said, *"We're fans of Shankar's now. Perhaps it's true to say that if George Harrison and Brian Jones hadn't brought him to our notice, we wouldn't be interested. But so what! If Bill Haley hadn't started rock and roll, probably no one would be playing that now!"*

June 11, 1966 – *Melody Maker* **declared** it was John, Paul, George and Ringo week. *Paperback Writer* was due out the following day. And the Beatles had recorded their new album with the top jazz musicians in Britain. Georgie Fame had advised the group on the best jazz guys around who would "think Beatle." In the studio with the group were: Ian Hamer, Les Condon and Eddie Thornton (trumpet players) along with Alan Branscome and Peter Coe (tenors).

Melody Maker spoke with Les Condon about working with the Beatles.

He said, *"Interesting and unusual, I've never done a session quite like it before. The tune was a rhythm-and-bluesish sort of thing, we were only on one number, which they had recorded previously.*

"Apparently, they felt it needed something extra. That's why we were all there. The arrangement? Well, they didn't have a thing written down. We just listened to what they'd done and got an idea of what they wanted. Then we went ahead from there and gradually built up an arrangement. We tried a few things, and Paul McCartney, he's really the prime mover who gets everyone at it, and recording manager George Martin, decided between them what would be used.

"But most of it went right the first time. Ian and I jotted down some voicings but everybody chipped in and credit for the arrangement must be evenly divided. I suggested something for the trumpets for an ending, and we dubbed that on. They didn't think it was quite strong enough, so we dubbed it on with the three trumpets again. You'll really be hearing six trumpets in that coda.

"It was the most relaxed session I've ever been on. The Beatles all seemed very nice fellows. And do you know what? They didn't tell us any thing. They kept asking things."

Melody Maker inquired at record stores around the country about the demand for the new Beatles single. In London, they were told the demand was no more than usual, perhaps a bit less because people were on holiday. In Manchester, there was a big demand, though public reaction could have been better. And in Birmingham, the demand was as strong as ever. EMI claimed there were advance orders for over 300,000 copies.

June 18, 1966 – *Disc and Music Echo*, Ray Coleman conducted a two-part interview with Paul McCartney. Part Two: Paul mentioned that he regretted only one thing about being so famous – messages had been painted on the front door of his new house in London, messages from fans, from admirers.

Said Paul, *"Who do they think we are, mugs? I don't think the people who take liberties and do things like this can really be fans. They're trouble makers, and we can do without them. Because they are just not decent people.*

"People explain it all away by saying, 'Ah well, Paul, if you're in business as a big star and you like the limelight, you've got to take all that goes with it.' That's a load of crap. I've never believed that we have to put up with this sort of treatment, and we wouldn't, whoever we were. I've got a new house and, like anybody with a new house, I take pride in it. I don't expect people to come up there day and night and daub paint all over it.

"I expect they thought: 'Ha, ha, isn't it cute, painting the front door pink for Paul?' Well, it depends on the shade of pink! Fans should realise that we are normal human beings who occasionally like to get away from it all. I don't have any time for the wreckers, because they just can't be fans if they treat us like fools."

On to autograph hunters and being hounded by them...

"They think, 'Oh, he's hanging round doing nothing. He'll sign this for me.' The trouble is that if you sign a few one day, the fans who got them that day will be back later with a dozen of their friends, and the thing snowballs like mad.

"Surely people can realise that we like a bit of time off. Some of them must wonder why we run away and won't sign autographs, but it's not a question of being lousy, or tight, or difficult. We've just got to protect ourselves from being invaded all the time, every day.

"That's why pop stars don't talk to fans as much as they'd like to. The fans don't make it easy. I still love meeting fans, but if I went up to a fan and started talking, it'd just make things impossible for myself.

"Why do you think the Walkers don't talk to people very freely? It's just the same, fans go mad and make stars' lives hell.

"Do you know, Joan Baez never gives autographs. We were with her once in the States and when somebody went up to her and asked her to sign, she said, 'Sorry, I don't sign autographs, but I'll shake your hand.'"

Still, Paul thought, Beatle life was well worth the problems.

"Sometimes, I wonder about it all. We have to go through all this business with the so-called fans, but for every dozen who are wreckers and fools, there are about a thousand real fans. And we never get tired of them. They make it all worthwhile!"

June 18, 1966 – *Disc and Music Echo* **declared** that Beatles fans were slamming the 'sick' picture. Of the nine letters printed, three fans loved the picture, the rest thought it twisted. Footnotes mentioned that Paul McCartney was about to turn twenty-four; Freddie Lennon, John's father, was planning to remarry; and *Daily Sketch* declared the Beatles' meat cover to be sick.

June 24, 1966 – *New Musical Express* **announced** the opening of a new discotheque in London, Sybillas, partly owned by George Harrison and disc jockey Alan Freeman.

June 25, 1966 – *Record Mirror* **said** the Beatles were earning yet another gold record, this one for *Paperback Writer*, which had just passed the million-sales mark. 750,000 copies sold in the U.S., more than 500,000 in Britain. Both Billboard and Cashbox were showing the song at number one.

The group was leaving London that day for Germany and the Circus Krone in Munich where their show would be videotaped for German television. When they arrived in Tokyo, NTV planned to televise an hour-long Beatles special.

June 25, 1966 – *Disc and Music Echo* **announced** that the Beatles new single, *Paperback Writer*, had topped the million sales mark worldwide. They went on to say the group was leaving for Germany that day, on BEA Flight BE 502 at 11:05 a.m., to film a concert for German TV, and also that NTV Japan would be on hand to film a one-hour Beatles special.

June 25, 1966 – *Disc and Music Echo*, **Mike Ledgerwood spoke** with George Harrison in Dressing Room 45 at the BBC's Top of the Pops studio. The Beatles were to make their first live appearance on the show. Ledgerwood was one a few specially-invited reporters, on hand to write about the event.

He said the group was looking good, in fine form, happy to answer questions. They had been out of the spotlight for quite a while and reporters were wondering why, after so long, they decided to make a live appearance. Were they worried that their popularity was waning?

Said George, *"We've done this* Top of the Pops *because Brian* [Epstein] *asked us. I believe there have been loads of requests to the BBC. I know we've had a lot at the office. So here we are.*

"We know we've been out of the public eye for a long time and there has been a lot of criticism. But personally, I don't care what anybody thinks of us. If we do too much TV or radio, people start complaining. If we do too little, they do the same.

"You know, the Beatles are just a little part of me. And I like to keep it that way. We've changed a hell of a lot in the last two years. It used to be Beatles, Beatles, Beatles, all the time!

"We have got to live, just like everybody else. So that's what we're doing. After all, the whole idea of working is so that you can one day sit back and do what you want. Anyone who makes money and doesn't take time off to enjoy it is mad."

How did he feel about the publicity that was generated by every thing the Beatles said or did?

"I'm sick of publicity from nothing. If you go to the pictures, somebody leaps up and takes your photograph. You know it probably won't be printed. But they have to take them because it's us.

"Same with interviews. As you know, we'll always do interviews, aside from Press conferences like this. Provided people have something definite to ask us. We know as well as the next person that nearly everything that could be written about the Beatles has been done. But we tire of being asked what we had for breakfast or what time we get up.

"I don't care if they never write another word about me. As I said, the Beatles are just a small part of my life now and I want to keep it that way."

June 25, 1966 – *Disc and Music Echo*, **Derek Taylor wrote** from Hollywood about the new Beatles' album jacket, the lumps of wet red meat draped everywhere. Capitol Records had called back as many of the covers as they could get and supposedly destroyed them, making that jacket an instant collectors' item.

Unfortunately for Capitol, they had sent out review copies to all the fan clubs, radio stations and record reviewers before they decided a more suitable photograph was necessary.

By that time, the controversy had begun. No album art had ever provoked such a reaction. The general reaction was shock. The four mop tops were not quite so cute after all. Capitol had to recover half a million albums at a cost of around seventy-five thousand dollars.

Taylor went on to talk about an interview with Paul McCartney he had recently read. He considered McCartney the best Beatle interview, suggesting Lennon could be better if he tried a little harder. His favourite quote from the interview was Paul's observation of the people who rely on gimmicks, *"Masters of the bloody trivial."*

A footnote mentioned that the Fourmost were likely to record their next single from the Beatles new LP.

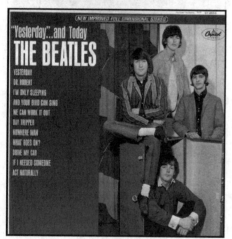

June 25, 1966 – *Melody Maker* **declared** it was Beatles Action Week. The group was on its way to Germany and the Far East for their first concert gigs since the previous December. First, they would be in Munich where they would hold a press conference at the Beyerischer Hof Hotel; the following day, they would be doing two shows at the Circus Kroner. Two

of their concerts, one in Germany and one in Tokyo, would be filmed for TV.

The Beatles had finished recording their new album that week. A spokesman for the band said, *"They completed the last track of their 14-track LP on Tuesday. They had hoped to have it finished before leaving for their dates in Germany and the Far East."*

Tentatively, the album was scheduled to be released in August.

Paperback Writer had passed the million sales mark, 750,000 in America, another 500,000 in Britain.

June 25, *Melody Maker,* **Alan Walsh spoke** with George Harrison, suggesting George was the most independent of the Beatles. The interview was during the rehearsals for Top of the Pops.

George said, *"I've changed a lot over the past two years. I've realised that the Beatle bit is only a small part of myself and I try to keep it in perspective. I've increasingly become aware that there are other things in life than being a Beatle.*

"I'm not fed up at being a Beatle, far from it. But I am fed up with all the trivial things that go with it. For instance, at one time, you could never go to the pictures or for a meal without some idiot taking a photograph of you. No one uses the photographs, so he's wasting my time and his own for nothing.

"I suppose I have consciously been backing away from this side of Beatle life. In fact, it wouldn't worry me at all if nobody ever took my photograph again."

Did his marriage to Patti Boyd influence this new attitude?

"No, I got married because I'd changed. Marriage didn't bring this about. I'd already changed."

What did he think of the fans complaining that the Beatles were neglecting them?

"I don't think we neglect them. Whenever we are doing something, like the new single, we do appearances. They can still see us. People still write articles about us and so they can still read about us."

He wanted his life to be more low key these days, less publicised and scrutinised. He said, *"For one thing, it means we can move about a lot more freely. London has always been better than anywhere else, because its bigger and there are more places to get lost in. We've found it better these last few months that we've been out of the public eye. I prefer to be out of the public eye anyway.*

"After all, what's the use of making money and becoming successful if you don't have any time to yourself? Anyone who's successful likes to have time off to relax. You may think we have more than most. But that's up to us."

What did he think of the group's musical progress?

"Musically, we're only just starting. We've realised for ourselves that as far as recording is

concerned, most of the things that recording men have said were impossible for the last thirty-nine years are, in fact, very possible. In the past, we've thought that the recording people knew what they were talking about. We believed them when they said we couldn't do this, or we couldn't do that. Now we know we can, and it's opening up a wide new field for us.

"In the Beatles, we're fortunate because each of us has something different going. I've been going for the Indian thing in a big way, John and Paul have their own thing going, and there are also things Ringo likes. Paul likes classical music, at least, I think he does from what I've been able to make out watching him, and he contributes things like Yesterday and Michelle, while John does things like Norwegian Wood.

"This means there's no single influence, such as there is with Brian Wilson, in the Beach Boys. We have a wide range of things available to us, which makes it exciting.

"For instance, we have a number on the new LP called Eleanor Rigby, which is Paul's. It's a bit like Yesterday, though not the same. On this we used four violins, two violas and two cellos to get the sound we wanted."

If they continue to move into more complicated studio music, how will they be able to play it on stage?

"On Paperback Writer there are no electronic sounds as such, just some recording techniques which are used in recording all the time. We'll be able to reproduce any of our records. If we get to the stage of doing some of the things on our LP on stage, I suppose we'll go on with a couple of tape recorders!"

Prior to speaking with George, Walsh had entered the journalist scrum in the group's dressing room, asking if the Beatles planned to go nostalgic and visit some of their old Hamburg haunts.

"I hope not," answered John. "Brian Epstein won't get out of Hamburg alive as it is. We might just make it to the plane for the eight-nine hour flight to Japan. Is Hamburg the last date before Tokyo? Oh well, that kills visiting the clubs then."

Were they planning any special numbers for the concerts?

"Before we go, we get a list of the hits in any particular country, so we include them," John explained. "But we haven't decided what we are doing in Germany or Japan, yet."

Regarding the outrage in the States over their draped-meat album cover, Paul said it was all, "a bit soft. We were asked to do the picture with some meat and a broken doll. It was just a picture. It didn't mean anything. All this means is that we're being a bit more careful about the sort of picture we do. I liked it, myself."

John added, "Anyway, it's as valid as Vietnam!"

After they finished with Top of the Pops, the Beatles were heading back into the recording studio to work on the final song for the new album, which they wanted to have completed before leaving for Germany.

Said John, "I've got something going. About three lines so far."

"Have you?" Paul said. "That's good."

Walsh asked what the group thought about the anti-British pop comments made by Len Barry the previous week.

John said, "He must be after publicity or something. I thought he had something going, but when he started talking about Freddie and Herman, it was a joke. And we've never even met him!"

Straight faced, Paul added, "I suppose he's entitled to his opinion. He's a good artist, if rather repetitive. In fact, he's the best artist we've never worked with!"

June 25, 1966 – Melody Maker had been sent out questionnaires to one hundred and thirty fans around Britain, asking how they felt about the Beatles these days.

The fans were generally happy that the Beatles were progressing, experimenting with sounds.

They were unhappy with number of recent public appearances in Britain, wanting more, of course.

No one seemed to be put out about the long wait for the group's next movie.

More than half the fans believed Beatlemania had passed its peak.

The opinion was split on whether or not Paperback Writer was up to the group's usual standards.

And finally, Paul received the most votes for favourite Beatle.

July 2, 1966 – Disc and Music Echo, Ray Coleman wrote about the Beatles in Germany.

"Please don't fly to Tokyo. Your career is in danger," read the anonymous telegram, arriving at the band's dressing-room in Hamburg just before their last German concert.

George was the only one who worried about it. He said, "It makes you think. We've got a lot of enemies as well as friends."

The concerts in Munich, Essen and Hamburg had been sensational, thirty thousand screaming fans, Beatlemania raging, a triumphant return to the country where they had developed their skills, honed their art. Strangely enough, it was the German boys more than the girls who clamoured for the Beatles. And the German police had a field day, pounding the hell out of overly enthusiastic fans, brutal and savage, damaging many, seriously wounding a few.

And the barrage of press conference questions…

What's your opinion of the anti-baby pill?

Paul said, "It is good, of course."

Do you speak German well?

"Like the natives," said Paul.

Who's the greatest, you or Cassius Clay?

Ringo answered, "It's a toss-up."

Do you wear long pants in wintertime?

"No, hipsters," replied George.

What do you dream about when you're sleeping?

"Same as anyone else," said John. *"We're the same as you, you know, only we're rich."*

Why are you such horrible snobbies?

"It's only in your mind," said George.

Asked John, *"Because we're not flattering you?"*

Said Paul, *"We're just natural and we don't pose like some people."*

It was a whirlwind tour, crossing Germany by train, maniacal receptions everywhere. The songs they played were: *Rock and Roll Music, If I Needed Someone, Day Tripper, She's a Woman, Baby's in Black, Yesterday, I Wanna Be Your Man, Nowhere Man, I Feel Fine, Paperback Writer,* and *I'm Down.* In Hamburg, John lost his voice shortly into the program. Lemon and honey was sent for. And John explained, *"It was the comeback after a ten-month layoff. That cracked it. We should never have come out of retirement."*

Yet more questions:

Do you polish your MBE medal?

Said Ringo, *"Every week without fail... we don't."*

How rich are you?

"Not as rich as Harold Wilson," replied George.

What's the best beat band in the world?

"Freddie," said Paul.

Would you be a Beatle fan if you were not a Beatle?

Said John, *"No."*

What is the time?

"Time you were in bed," answered Ringo.

In their hotel room, they played the tape of their newest, as yet untitled, album. The sound quality of the machine they used was hopeless. John said, *"It brings me down, listening to things that sound so bad on rotten machines."*

Regardless of the sound quality, Coleman was impressed. *Good Day Sunshine, We All Live in a Yellow Submarine, Love You To, I Want to Tell You, For No One, Tomorrow Never Knows, Tax Man, Eleanor Rigby, Doctor Robert...* *"It's all about a queer,"* explained John. Great music, all of it.

And a great tour, Germans going crazy over the British Beatles.

July 2, 1966 – *Melody Maker* **led with headline: Brutality at Beatles Shows. Alan Walsh wrote** the story. Fanatical German fans and iron-fisted ferocious German police added an extra ingredient to the Beatlemania – violence. It started slowly in Munich, flowed over into Essen, and turned into a storm-trooping all-out battle in Hamburg, the brutality of the cops changing the cheerful fan mood into something dark, something ugly, something vicious.

The tour began quietly, with only about a hundred fans on the London Airport roof to see them off, subdued, un-Beatlemaniac. They flew first class to Germany and as the plane landed, the first hint of the lunacy to come presented itself. Hundreds of autograph seekers, photographers, film cameramen,

television cameramen and journalists jostled and thumped each other, mobbing the Beatles as they attempted to depart the plane.

At the hotel, hundreds of fans waited, held back by the cops, as the Beatles arrived with a police escort.

From the hotel room, Ringo looked out the window and said, *"It's starting all over again."*

Said John, *"We're always nervous before a show and the first night is worse still. As well as that, we haven't played a live show for ages, so we're a bit rusty."*

They were still working out the concert program. Lennon said, *"The songs that are hits here are different in some cases to Britain. The old ones we've almost forgotten, and we'll have to rehearse tonight to learn the words and that."*

Talking about their new LP, still trying to find a title, kicking around a few ideas, Paul said, *"Let's call it* Rock and Roll Hits of '66. *That'll solve it."*

Backstage at the Circus Krone, road manager Neil Aspinall said, *"I always look forward to them* [tours]. *When I'm on them, they're always a drag."*

The momentary calm, Paul and Ringo relaxing with a drink, John and George discussing music... Then it was time to hit the stage. The bouncers went to work immediately, throwing back the fans who tried to climb onto the six-foot stage. The boys were losing it, screaming, singing along with the band, fighting, worshipping, at one point down on their knees and bowing as if to Mecca.

After the show, the Beatles were out of the hall and back to their hotel before the fans were on the street. The next day, it was on to Essen by train, all of them half-an-hour late for train time. But it was their train; it had to wait.

As they left the train at Essen, they were forced to fight their way through the crowds of fans, who were loose in the train station, virtually unpoliced. At the concert venue, though, the police made up for their lack of presence at the train station – jack-booted cops with guns and dogs, beating back the fans.

Later, Walsh asked Ringo what the group thought of the violence, wondered if they were actually aware of it.

"We know about it and we hate it," said Ringo. *"It's happened in other places, too. We get really mad and, once, John even jumped off the stage to try to stop it. But you can't. They don't take any notice."*

After Essen, it was back on the train and off to Hamburg, a quiet ride, meals eaten, cards played.

The Hamburg concerts were held in Ernst Marck Halle. Backstage, old friends were re-met, Astrid, the former girl-friend of Stuart Sutcliffe, Bettina from the Star Club, Gibson of Paddy Klaus and Gibson, Bert Kampfaert and his wife, Lee Curtis, a Liverpool singer working in Germany...

Outside, fans who could not get into the concert were fighting with the cops – chanting, swinging clubs, tear gas thrown during running battles, chaos ruling, the danger thick, the violence going on long after the show...

Did the group intend to visit the Star Club while they were in town?

Said George, "*We haven't planned to. But I can't see us getting out of this town without going.*"

July 2, 1966 – Melody Maker, Gene Pitney explained what he thought of the Beatles' new single, *Paperback Writer*. "*I'll try and put into words what I think of the Beatles' latest. For me, a song is essentially about romance, there must be a romantic element in it. I think the Beatles have written better songs than this. A song must be related to an area of romance. On that score, this doesn't appeal.*"

July 2, 1966 – Melody Maker, reviewed the Beatles' German concerts, explaining that they used the same formula they had used before, some hard driving rock and roll, broken up by softer songs that sent the fans into spasms. The only hint of the new Beatles was *Paperback Writer*, which they played at every show.

At first, their harmonies were off, but they steadily improved. The writer wondered what the group would do if they ever had to play live some of their more inventive, intricate songs.

Still, Paul was singing well, and George and Ringo performed beautifully. John was having trouble with his voice. But the fans loved it all, *Rock and Roll Music, She's a Woman, If I Needed Someone, Day Tripper, Baby's in Black, I Feel Fine, Yesterday, Nowhere Man, I Wanna Be Your Man, Paperback Writer, I'm Down...* Paul and John screamed out the finale while the crowd went berserk.

July 9, 1966 – Disc and Music Echo, Len Johnson, the only reporter traveling with the Beatles to Japan, wrote... thirty-five thousand cops were on hand to protect the band. Most people believed the reason for so many police officers was to keep the Beatles and their fans apart. But the truth was, there had been threats from extremist right wingers who declared the Beatles were not going to be allowed to defile the sacred Nippon Budo-Kan venue by corrupting it, by sullying it, with a rock show.

Outside their hotel, protesters in military gear distributed pamphlets and flashed signs that read "Go Home!"

Some broke through the police cordon but were arrested before they could do any damage to the Beatles, who were ensconced in a presidential suite on the tenth floor of the Hilton Hotel.

In Germany, most of the questions asked at press conferences were trivial, insipid, spit out by journalists in a feeding frenzy. In Tokyo, the questions were put formally through a translator, low-keyed, cold and precise.

What were the incentives which made you devise your present hair style?

Said George, "*We were too poor to afford a haircut.*"

Unfortunately, the translations fell flat. The sarcasm, the wit, failed to translate. And the conference ended awkwardly as an Englishmen,

representing the foreign correspondents association of Japan, asked, "*What will you do when you grow up?*"

"*What will you do?*" snapped Ringo.

And John said, "*If that was meant to be a joke, it wasn't funny. You look too old to ask soft questions like that.*"

Thousands of cops lined the route to the Budo-Kan, clearing the roads of rush-hour traffic. At the hall, twenty-five hundred cops kept the peace.

The audience did not display the wildness that was normal for a Beatles' concert. But the handkerchief waving and the screams were constant.

After the show, back at the Hilton, John went to bed, the other three went to the Hilton's bathhouse to sample Japanese massage bathing.

Said George, "*It just relaxes you completely, it's like being in your own fantasy world.*"

Paul said, "*I felt great afterwards but the massage hurts sometimes. I was waiting for the knee-in-your-back-bit and it came. When the girl pressed her thumbs into the back of my neck it was like pushing stuffing into a broken teddy bear.*"

On Friday morning, Lennon and McCartney made an escape from the hotel. Lennon went to an ivory shop with Neil Aspinall. He bought an antique snuff-box and said later, "*They had dozens of these great things called Happy Gods but I just bought a small one and a big fat Buddha thing. I saw one ivory ornament and asked how much. The man replied, 'I don't know. Nobody ever asked to buy it before.'*"

Paul went out with Mal Evans, but at the Imperial Palace they picked up a police escort, figured that would attract too much attention, and returned to the hotel without shopping.

After that, local merchants were invited to flog their wares in the suite at the Hilton. The president of the local fan club, a fifty-year-old named Tetsusaburo Shimoyama, presented them each with the newest hottest transistor radios. The Beatles created a painting for him, each putting their signatures to it.

July 9, 1966 – Melody Maker, Alan Walsh put ten questions to John and Ringo.

Do you ever wish you were just another unknown beat group again?

John: "*I don't ever wish I was in an unknown beat group again. Just that I was an unknown person.*"

Ringo: "*Not any more.*"

Do you like the seclusion of living in the country?

John: "*At the moment, I'm quite happy in the country, because I know I'm not there forever.*"

Ringo: "*It's great. I love it. I never thought I'd like the country and I was a bit worried before we moved into the house. But we had to move because of the baby. Now I really enjoy it.*"

Were you happy to be returning to Hamburg?

John: "*No.*"

Ringo: "*No more than anywhere else.*"

What's going on with Bob Dylan? They booed him on his last visit to England; he seemed to be on the way out. Was he?

John: *"All that stuff about Dylan being booed has been exaggerated. I saw the London concerts and about five or six people booed. That's all, and everyone else in the audience were shutting them up. The newspaper writers got it completely wrong. They didn't know what they were talking about."*

Ringo: *"When he started, the fans turned to him because he was doing something new. Perhaps now, they've turned to someone else. Perhaps that's what's happened to him."*

Are you too old to be a Beatle?

John: *"I don't think I'm too old to be a Beatle. I never think about being a Beatle until I'm on tour or something. The rest of the time I'm just me."*

Ringo: *"I sometimes do. I think I'm a bit old to be going on stage doing this. Then I look around at all the other people doing the same and I don't feel so bad."*

Do you have stock answers for the reporters these days?

John: *"No. We just answer them as they come."*

Ringo: *"Not really. You get the same questions in each place, so you give the same answers."*

Could the Beatles stop touring and just make records?

John: *"Not the way the fans keep moaning about not seeing us all the time."*

Ringo: *"No."*

Your newest LP has taken longer to record than any other. Can you put in that much time and effort every time you want to record?

John: *"I can't even visualise the next one. I really can't. I can hardly remember parts of the new one. I'm not even thinking about the next one."*

Ringo: *"It can only get harder. I think we've achieved a high standard and done the best we can do. But we've spent so long on it because we insisted on having the time to do what we wanted to do. As we're quite big with EMI at the moment, they don't argue. There's none of this bit about doing an LP in ten hours the way we did when we first made it. Now we take the time we want. The important thing is to get it right."*

Have you been influenced by the Beach Boys recording techniques?

John: *"I can see that people think we're traveling along the same lines. But it's coincidental. When people are working on similar things a long way apart, they often seem to be following each other. We're not following them."*

Ringo: *"No. It's a natural step to try to make the next thing better than the last. The Beach Boys do the same."*

Do the Beatles have limited potential for a film career?

John: *"No one's come up with the right script yet, that's why we've been so long."*

Ringo: *"Being a group of four people didn't limit the Marx Brothers. Why should it limit us?"*

July 9, 1966 – *Melody Maker* **wrote about** the Beatles' new album, saying the group was about to change the pop scene. Their new LP would change the direction of pop music. The fourteen tracks displayed and distilled a wide range of influences. Eleven of the fourteen tracks had been released to reviewers.

Good Day Sunshine: A Lennon / McCartney composition with a street band sound to it.

Yellow Submarine: A children's song written by John and Paul and sung by Ringo.

Love You To: Written by George.

I Want to Tell You: Another one by George, featuring Paul on piano. About this song, George said, *"It's regularly irregular. But I didn't realise this until the others told me."*

For No One: By Paul and John with a very nice French horn passage.

Eleanor Rigby: This featured Paul's classical sound, the one established with *Yesterday* and *Michelle*.

Tomorrow Never Knows: This featured electronic sounds and was supposedly the Beatles' favourite.

The other tracks were *Doctor Robert*, featuring John; *Tax Man*, another George Harrison composition; *And Your Bird Can Sing*; and *I'm Only Sleeping*.

Were the Beatles taking a new direction? Were they redefining pop music? Had the group found the way to remove themselves from the pop scene into a scene of their very own?

Paul said, *"They'll never be able to copy this."*

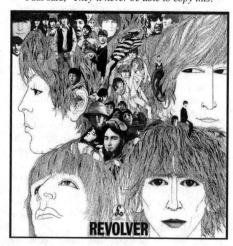

July 9, 1966 – *Melody Maker* **said** the marines had been called out, two full battalions with bayonets, machine guns and tear gas, to guard he Beatles as they arrived in the Philippines. More than fifty thousand fans had gathered at the airport to meet the band, who were taken directly from airport to naval headquarters. None of hotels in Manila were considered safe enough, so the group stayed on board a ship in Manila Bay.

July 16, 1966 – Disc and Music Echo, Richard Lennox quoted John Lennon with regards to the Manila affair. Said John, *"No plane's going to go through the Philippines with me on it. I wouldn't even fly over it."*

During the press conference as they arrived back in Britain, the group said Manila had been the most terrifying event in their career. At the Manila airport, they had walked a gauntlet of outraged Filipinos, outraged because they believed the Beatles had insulted their President's wife by refusing to attend a reception she had thrown for them. But, as the group explained, no one had actually invited them to the party.

Paul explained, *"There were about thirty of these thugs, some of them with guns, waiting for us, and it was very obvious they were trying to get us. They were pushing us around, and our chauffeur, Alf Bicknell, was pushed over on his back.*

"I was frightened, and sad. I thought, 'Why are you doing this, you idiots?' Because we hadn't done anything wrong to deserve it. But it was no good saying that, or smack!

"It was very cowardly because there were thirty of them and only ten of us. The police didn't do anything and the promoters' men guarding us left us.

"The President has sent us a telegram saying he was sorry this happened. He's like us, just some poor fellow in the middle of it all. It was a big misunderstanding, and we tried to clear it up with the people concerned.

"I was shopping in Manila when suddenly I was told we were supposed to have been at this reception. There was never an invitation for us. The promoters got the invitation and thought we were bound to want to go and see the President, not thinking of our time schedule. I can't believe we got involved in political things. What interest have I got in the politics of Manila?"

Said John, *"All along the route to the airport there were people waving at us, but I could see a few old men booing us. When they started on us at the airport, I was petrified.*

"I thought I was going to get hurt, so I headed for three nuns and two monks, thinking that might stop them. As far as I know, I was just pushed around but I could have been kicked and not known it."

Added George, *"They were waiting for us to retaliate so that they could finish us off. I was terrified. It was very bad. These thirty funny-looking fellows with guns had obviously arranged to give us the worst time possible. They were like the Gestapo and looking for a fight."*

Ringo said, *"Manila was the roughest reception we've ever had. Being booed by thirty people out*

of two thousand isn't too bad, but they really had it in for us."

And Paul said, *"And we just went there to sing."*

July 16, 1966 – Melody Maker spoke with the Beatles about their approach to song writing, which was somewhat loose, unstructured, lyrics written on scraps of paper, melodies recorded on cheap tape recorders. The writer asked about their approach to the fourteen tracks for the new album.

Said John, *"The first thing that happened with the new album was that Paul and I decided we'd have to get together. We'd been seeing each other socially, but we decided we'd have to get down to some serious work. Getting together is the first step, and it's not always the easiest.*

"Then when we've got together either at my place or at Paul's house, we starting thinking about the songs. One of us usually thinks of a musical phrase or part of a tune in our heads, like Paul did with Paperback Writer. *He thought that out in the car on his way to my house."*

The Beatles' new LP, *Revolver*, was recorded over eleven or twelve weeks, John and Paul tossing around ideas, then going into the studio with George and Ringo to work things out. For this album, George, too, was emerging as a creative force. Three of the songs were his.

He said, *"I've been writing songs all the time. But when you're competing against John and Paul, you have to be very good to even get into the same league. How do I write a song now? I turn on a tape recorder and play or sing phrases into it for perhaps an hour. Then I play it all back and may get three or four usable phrases or runs from it. When I just had one tape recorder, I'd finish a song and put it onto the tape recorder. Then I'd often throw it away because I thought it sounded awful. Since I've bought all the taping and mixing equipment, I can add things and do a lot more. So what seemed on one machine to be a waste of time, sounds possible when mixed and re-recorded and perhaps dubbed."*

And the lyrics?

"This is the hardest part for me. I write them slowly, a word or phrase at a time, changing them about until I get what I want, or as near to it as I can. When the thing is finished, I'm usually happy with some parts of it and unhappy with others. So I then show it to John and Paul, whose opinion I respect.

"They usually like the part I don't like. But think that the other part is wrong."

John Lennon said, *"There comes a time when you've got to stop fiddling about with the song. If you didn't, you'd never get a record out at all.*

"Later, you think of things you could have done with it, but unless you call a halt, you'd spend a whole year doing just one track.

"I write things that I like. But you have to consider the commercial aspect. It's no good writing stuff that no one wants to listen to."

July 23, 1966 – Ray Coleman wrote for *Disc and Music Echo* that it had not taken the Beatles long to shed that cute and cuddly mop-head image. Their intelligence was almost immediately obvious. Their sophistication grew as time went by. They became more worldly, more aware of the world around them.

McCartney had discovered that war concerned him. After seeing the movie *The War Game*, he went home angry, saying, *"Does this world really want to blow itself up?*

"There are hundreds of films about which people say to you: 'You've got to see it!' Often, it's just a passing moment. But if anyone ever says this to you about The War Game, *take them seriously. This picture is not just important, it's terrifying and urgent.*

"I always used to think that CND meant marching, Trafalgar Square, Ban the Bomb posters and Paul Jones. After seeing The War Game, *I reckon I knew what they were on about after all, although I still believe CND people are unsuccessful because they've failed to get the message across.*

"But if the world was forcibly made to see The War Game, *maybe they'd understand why some people think they've got to do something, sit down and squat, protest, shout, write to the papers, anything!*

"The War Game is a film that shows what could happen in the event of a nuclear war, a fictitious documentary which made me shudder. It was the most terrifying experience I've ever had, watching the film. But it's so important to the world that everyone of the right age should be made to watch it.

"They should put it on TV, for a start. Okay, so there are some squeamish people who'd object. But they could warn the viewers before it appeared.

"At no point in the film do they categorically say, 'This is what's going to happen.' But the message came across pretty strongly to me. Obviously, it could happen.

"And we seem so badly prepared…

"The War Game should be compulsory viewing, it's so important. When a thing is as terrible as this, it's idiotic worrying about people's nerves. If they don't know what's possible, they won't have any nerves left anyway…"

A footnote mentioned that the title of the Beatles new album, *Revolver*, had been Paul's idea.

July 30, 1966 – *Disc and Music Echo* **led with a headline which announced** that the Beatles were splitting… to do some solo film work. Said Brian Epstein, *"I am only prepared to say at the moment that they might make films separately."*

Paul was the most likely candidate to start off in the solo-film business, but not until after the group did their next film, which was to begin shooting in January.

July 30, 1966 – *Disc and Music Echo* **said** Ringo Starr was the featured singer on the Beatles' surprise new single, due out the following week, *Yellow Submarine / Eleanor Rigby*, both cuts from the new

Revolver LP. It was the first time Ringo had been the singer on a British single, and the first time the Beatles had released a pair of album songs as a single.

A footnote mentioned that the Beatles had turned down a South African tour. Rumour had it that they were refusing to go on racial grounds, but this was denied by NEMS Enterprises.

July 30, 1966 – *Disc and Music Echo* **spoke with** Ray Davies, singer / songwriter of the Kinks, about the Beatles' new album, *Revolver*. Apparently, the Beatles were so excited about the record that they were releasing the *Yellow Submarine / Eleanor Rigby* single on the same day as the album. They asked Davies his opinion and he suggested the Beatles were making a huge mistake. He believed *Eleanor Rigby* was dedicated to Lennon and McCartney's music teacher back in primary school and that *Yellow Submarine* should be pitched in the garbage.

Said Davies, *"It's a load of rubbish, really."*

Davies went on to give *Disc* his thoughts on the album, track by track.

Taxman: By George Harrison, George singing the lead.

"It sounds like a cross between the Who and Batman. It's a bit limited, but the Beatles get over this by the sexy double-tracking. It's surprising how sexy double-tracking makes a voice sound."

Eleanor Rigby: By John Lennon and Paul McCartney, with Paul singing the lead.

"I bought a Haydn LP the other day and this sounds just like it. It's all sort of quartet stuff and it sounds like they're out to please music teachers in primary schools. I can imagine John saying, 'I'm going to write this for my old schoolmistress.' Still, it's very commercial."

I'm Only Sleeping: By John Lennon and Paul McCartney, with John singing lead.

"It's a most beautiful song, much prettier than Eleanor Rigby. A jolly old thing, really, and definitely the best track on the album."

Love You To: By George Harrison, George singing lead.

"George wrote this, he must have quite a big influence on the group now. This sort of song I was doing two years ago, now I'm doing what the Beatles were doing two years ago. It's not a bad song, it's well performed, which is always true of a Beatles track."

Here There and Everywhere: By John Lennon and Paul McCartney, with Paul singing the lead.

"This proves the Beatles have got good memories, because there are a lot of busy chords in it. It's nice, like one instrument with the voice and guitar merging. Third best track on the album."

Yellow Submarine: By John Lennon and Paul McCartney with Ringo singing the lead.

"This is a load of rubbish, really. I take the mickey out of myself on the piano and play stuff just like this. I think they know it's not that good."

She Said She Said: By John Lennon and Paul McCartney, John singing the lead.

"This song is in to restore confidence in the old Beatles sound. That's all."

Good Day Sunshine: By John Lennon and Paul McCartney with Paul singing lead.

"This'll be a giant. It doesn't force itself on you, but it stands out like I'm Only Sleeping. *This is back to the real old Beatles. I just don't think the fans like the newer electronic stuff. The Beatles are supposed to be like the boy next door only better."*

And Your Bird Can Sing: By John Lennon and Paul McCartney, John singing the lead.

"Don't like this. The song's too predictable. It's not a Beatles song at all."

For No One: By John Lennon and Paul McCartney, Paul singing the lead.

"This will get covered, but it won't be a hit. It's really better than Eleanor Rigby *and the French horn is a nice effect."*

Dr. Robert: By John Lennon and Paul McCartney, John singing the lead.

"It's good. There's a twelve-bar beat and bits in it that are clever. Not my sort of thing, though."

I Want to Tell You: By George Harrison, George singing lead.

"This helps the LP through. It's not up to Beatles standard."

Got To Get You Into My Life: By John Lennon and Paul McCartney, Paul singing lead.

"Jazz backing, and it just goes to prove that Britain's jazz musicians can't swing. Paul's singing better jazz than the musicians are playing which makes nonsense of people saying jazz and pop are very different. Paul sounds like Little Richard. Really, it's the most vintage Beatles track on the LP."

Tomorrow Never Knows: By John Lennon and Paul McCartney, John singing the lead.

"Listen to all those crazy sounds. It'll be popular in discotheques. I can imagine they had George Martin tied to a totem pole when they did this."

In conclusion, Davies said, *"This is the first Beatles LP I've really listened to in its entirety but I must say there were better songs on* Rubber Soul. *Still,* I'm Only Sleeping *is a standout.* Good Day Sunshine *is second best and I also like* Here There and Everywhere.

"But I don't want to be harsh about the others. The balance and recording technique are as good as ever."

July 30, 1966 – *Disc and Music Echo*, **Mike Ledgerwood** reported that the Cavern Club was going to be reopened, renovated and redecorated. On hand for the ceremonies were Prime Minister Harold Wilson, Jimmy Savile, Ken Dodd, Bessie Braddock, and many others. Conspicuous by their absence were the Beatles. But they sent a telegram congratulating the club, as did Brian Epstein.

July 30, 1966 – *Melody Maker* **talked about** the new Beatles' single *Yellow Submarine / Eleanor Rigby*, saying it had been rush-released and pointing out that it was the first time the group had ever released LP songs as a single in Britain. They suggested this was to prevent any other groups from having a hit with *Eleanor Rigby* by releasing a cover. *Rigby* was being called a classic, in the same class as *Yesterday* and *Michelle*, both of which had been covered by other singers, preventing the Beatles from having a hit with either.

A footnote mentioned that the Beatles were to leave in August for their next U.S. tour.

July 30, 1966 – *Melody Maker* **held a pop think-in with** John Lennon, asking about:

Marriage – *"Just a name."*
Billy J. Kramer – *"Where?"*
Chelsea – *"So what?"*
In crowds – *"Do me a favour."*
Reeperbahn – *"Yeah."*
War – *"Terrible. No excuse for it."*
Harold Wilson – *"Like the rest of 'em."*
Power – *"I haven't used mine fully yet."*
Clothes – *"Useful for taking off."*
God – *"Where? You point him out. See marriage."*
Russia – *"I like."*
Television – *"Love it. Sometimes great, sometimes a joke, but I like it."*
Weybridge – *"See marriage."*
Death – *"The end, daddy-o."*
Hair styles – *"See marriage and God."*
Gimmicks – *"I don't know what they are unless they work. I've never employed a gimmick in my life. Next."*
Paul McCartney – *"Just Paul. Just our Paul."*
Animals – *"I love."*
Swimming – *"Keeps you clean."*
Sky – *"That's where I belong, baby.*
Paul Jones – *"Nice ideas but he puts them over stupidly and so he doesn't impress anyone, especially me. What the CND crowd believe in is right, but how they communicate themselves lays them open to ridicule."*
Journalists – *"Fruitcake."*
Help! film – *"Crap."*
Milk – *"Okay."*
Politicians – *"Losers."*
P.S. I Love You – *"It was a period."*
Electronic – *"Music. I've heard a bit and some is crap. Some's okay."*
Brian Epstein – *"Our manager."*
Drunkenness – *"Often."*
Dylan – *"Good."*
Police – *"See politicians. They're a necessary evil. No, a necessary very evil."*
Sex – *"Life."*
Fans – *"Harmless."*
Ray Davies – *"He's the Kinks."*
Cigarettes – *"Cancer."*

Hangers-on – "*Useful sometimes. Not all are drags. They're people and it's up to us to separate the good ones from the drags.*"

President Johnson – "*No.*"

Flying – "*No thanks.*"

Vegetarianism – "*I've not come across it. If people want to eat nuts that's okay with me. I wish I could do it, the way I feel about animals.*"

The bomb – "*Should be bombed.*"

Wine – "*And women.*"

Jagger – "*A good nut.*"

America – "*Great possibilities.*"

Life and death – "*Time I was on stage.*"

August 6, 1966 – *Disc and Music Echo***, Ray Coleman spoke** with George Harrison about the government's plan to ban all the pirate radio stations… among other things.

Said George, "*I can't understand their attitude. Why don't they make the crummy BBC illegal as well, it doesn't give the public the service it wants, otherwise the pirates wouldn't be here to fill the gap. The Government makes me sick. This is becoming a Police State. They should leave the pirates alone. At least they've had a go, which is more than the BBC had done.*"

Coleman wondered why the Beatles had broken their own rule about not releasing singles from albums, in particular *Eleanor Rigby*.

George said, "*We just thought we may as well put it out instead of sitting back and seeing dozens of cover versions all getting hits. Well, we might as well cop the hit as well as anybody else. I believe there are about ninety-three versions of* Good Day Sunshine *being put out!*

"*Apart from that, well all think it's a good commercial single. I like them both.* Yellow Submarine *will appeal to old-age pensioners and that kind of mob, whereas* Eleanor Rigby *will probably only appeal to Ray Davies-types…*"

George was referring to the Davies review of *Revolver* that *Disc* had published the previous week.

Said George, "*He's entitled to his opinion. But I think if Ray Davies met us, he might change his tune. I'm sure he's more like us, and thinks more alike, than he thinks. I think Ray Davies and the Beatles would have plenty in common.*"

Upcoming plans for the Beatles?

"*Not doing much,*" George told him. "*We've got to go and get beaten up in America in a fortnight. I'm not looking forward to it much, except for California, which comes at the end of the tour. There, at least, we can swim and get a bite to eat.*"

A music scene wrap-up column mentioned that Paul McCartney's father's horse, Drake's Drum, had won again the previous Friday.

August 6, 1966 – *Melody Maker* **announced** that the Beatles would most definitely begin work on their next film at the end of January. They would write the entire score, including the incidental music.

The story is from an idea by Owen Holder who was working on the script. Again, the film would be produced by Walter Shenson in colour. As yet, a title had not been found, nor had a director, but United Artists was lined up as the distributor.

The group would begin working on the music after their American tour, which was to start in Chicago on the 12th of August.

Also, a British tour before Christmas was a possibility.

August 13, 1966 – *Disc and Music Echo* **said** the Beatles were off to America, flying into the storm of an anti-Beatle campaign. The anti-Beatle movement started with a John Lennon interview in the *London Evening Standard*. Journalist Maureen Cleave quoted Lennon as saying, "*Christianity will go. It will vanish and shrink, we're more popular than Jesus now. I don't know which will go first, rock and roll or Christianity.*"

The article was subsequently quoted in a U.S. magazine called *Datebook*. After that, Tommy Charles, disc jockey from WAQY in Birmingham, Alabama, started a *Ban-the-Beatles* movement. Other American deejays followed him, calling for public bonfires of Beatle records and memorabilia.

When all that started, Brian Epstein flew to New York for a television appearance, claiming that Lennon's comments had been "*misinterpreted out of context.*"

Epstein's damage control was ineffectual. The furore spread. Tommy Charles said, "*You can't compare Christianity with the top ten.*"

The Ku Klux Klan accused John Lennon of being brainwashed by communists.

Other American radio stations were against the "Burn and Ban the Beatles" craze, claiming it was all a publicity stunt, while Epstein said he would leave it up to the concert promoters, whether or not they still wanted the Beatles to appear. Despite the lunacy, the tour would go on.

The first public burning event was in Starke, Florida. Three hundred teenagers ignited Beatles records, shirts and memorabilia.

British vicar the Rev. Bill Shergold of St. Mary's, Paddington, London, claimed Lennon was, "*Getting his own back on Cliff Richard for his religious comments. The Beatles are very good at off-the-cuff remarks like that and very witty usually. But I feel this one just may have just slipped out, and is not really John Lennon's considered opinion on religion.*

"*I think it may have been his reaction to Cliff Richard's coming out on the side of the angels.*"

Disc said they were free to reveal that Lennon had a deep interest in religion and had been studying it. What he said was not a *boast* that the Beatles were more popular than Jesus, but a *lament* that it was so, a lament that the Church of England had suffered such a decline in interest, a lament that a rock group could be more popular than Christianity.

America may have been losing its collective mind about some misinterpreted Lennon comments. But Britain had bought enough Beatle records that week to place *Yellow Submarine / Eleanor Rigby* at number four in the charts. Still, it was the second time in a row that a Beatle single had not gone immediately to number one. *Paperback Writer* had failed to enter the charts at number one as well, coming in at number two before moving into the top spot.

August 13, 1966 – *Disc and Music Echo* announced they had been correct three weeks previously when they claimed the Beatles would be pursuing individual film careers. John Lennon has accepted the roll of Private Gripeweede *(sic)* in *How I Won the War,* directed by Dick Lester, who had directed both *A Hard Day's Night* and *Help!* His part would be a supporting role; the star was Michael Crawford. It was to be a World War Two comedy, planned for release in the summer of 1967.

Also, they mentioned that a number of the tracks from *Revolver* had already found cover artists. She Trinity had released *Yellow Submarine*. Glen Dale, the Tremeloes, and the Eyes had all released their own versions of *Good Day Sunshine*. *Here There and Everywhere* had been put out by Brian Withers, the Fourmost, and Episode Six. Cliff Bennett had covered *Got to Get You Into My Life. Tax Man* was out by the Loose Ends. And *For No One* had been done by Marc Reid.

August 13, 1966 – Bob Farmer of *Disc and Music Echo* spoke with Brian Epstein.

Regarding the Beatles' new album, Epstein said, *"I doubt whether they realise what an explosive LP* Revolver *really is. They've covered such new and important territory. While they are creating albums like* Revolver, *how can the public expect much more of them?*

"Live appearances have got to simmer down. They like playing and singing to the public, but they've become open to so much misinterpretation, such as the appalling debacle in Manila, that the enjoyment and pleasure, let alone the finance, is taken away."

If Paul were to get married, would it change things for them?

"It's certainly never been a preconceived plan that one of them, Paul as it turned out, should stay single to keep the fans happy. I wouldn't consider such a suggestion for Paul as a friend as much as a client. I don't think that even if he did marry the effect would be harmful to any important degree.

"The Beatles have all matured and improved in every possible way from when I first met them. They were always intelligent people, but they're more perceptive, generous and sympathetic today. People probably wouldn't believe that, but it's dead true. Although they say they rely on me, none of them are fools."

August 13, 1966 – *Disc and Music Echo* wondered, with regards to the Beatles' new single *Yellow Submarine / Eleanor Rigby,* if it had been launched from panic or genius. They asked a number of celebrities to judge…

Georgie Fame: *"*Eleanor Rigby *is a serious number. They're going out on a limb but that doesn't matter because they are streets ahead of everyone else. The only effect it will have is to confuse the groups who try to copy them.* Yellow Submarine? *Ha ha. Very clever, but hilarious. I won't say any more."*

Dave Berry: *"*Yellow Submarine *is fabulous. It's a very good, funny record, and since they obviously did it for a laugh, I'm sure they're pleased with it.* Eleanor Rigby *is the best record they've ever made. The words are fantastic. I think everyone who hears them feels a little sad, but then there's a little sadness in us all."*

Chris Farlowe: *"I really think* Yellow Submarine *is fabulous. If it had been released at Christmas it would have sold five million. And I'm convinced that's the Goons in the background.* Eleanor *is very good, and very different. Both sides of this single manage to cover a wide audience range. It's great!"*

Lulu: *"*Eleanor Rigby *is absolutely sensational. The Beatles still really knock me out.* Paperback Writer *didn't impress me as much as some of their other ones, but* Eleanor Rigby *makes up for it.* Submarine *is fantastic. It's so funny.*

Gary Leeds: *"*Eleanor Rigby *is a song I could just listen to all day. It's beautiful. Personally, I can't* understand why the Beatles took either track off the LP. I would have kept this as a single and not put it on the LP in the first place. Yellow Submarine is the sort of record I would like people to play to me. It's really refreshing and a change from anything else that's in the chart at the moment. Extra special."

Billy Fury: "I'm afraid I haven't heard Eleanor Rigby yet. But Yellow Submarine is marvelous. People have been telling me that this is a terrible record for the Beatles, and I've been saying, 'Hang on. Listen to it carefully before you decide.' That's what you have to do. The song is almost nursery rhyme-ish and tremendously commercial."

Alan Price: "I'm glad they issued Eleanor as a single. Anyone else would have made an abomination of it. It's all Paul, isn't it? It's as near as they'll get to making solo records. Submarine is a wise move. It's a kiddies song, and old people's. 'Good old Beatles!' they'll be saying."

Alan Freeman: "I like the elegance of Eleanor Rigby, it's artistic. Yellow Submarine is a great big giggle. A wonderful change from their recorded image. It's going to be a great big number one smash, I'm sure."

Jonathan King: "This record will go down in Beatle history as their one of their top three creations. Yellow Submarine is unbelievably catchy, it rings of youthful nursery rhymes and other simple melodic structures. The entire treatment, tongue-in-cheek and send-up as it is, manages to be original, amusing and inventive without stooping to frivolous gimmickry. Eleanor Rigby is beautiful, plaintive, though perhaps not quite so unusual as the other side, and it cannot even be compared to the wonderful For No One on the album. It's interesting to see that, for the first time, both sides of a Beatle single employ session musicians. If they have ventured so far to augment the basic four-man rhythm sound, they can go as far as they like. Can we visualise a future Beatles track incorporating a full orchestra?"

Manfred Mann: "I think they're both great songs. Yellow Submarine is the most commercial thing I've heard in ages. They've done a very childrensy kind of song and it's also an absolutely gas track. Eleanor Rigby is also great and obviously it's the song that will last over the years."

Spencer Davis: "Without doubt, Eleanor Rigby is the best side. It's an absolutely marvelous song, a cert. number one and far better than Yesterday. I can't really see that there's a fantastic amount in Yellow Submarine, it's a bit of a joke, actually, and the boys just seem to be having a rave-up."

Mindbender Bob Lang: "The Beatles are great to come up with something like Yellow Submarine, it's so cute and catchy. I haven't heard Eleanor Rigby many times yet, but it's obviously a lovely song."

Steve Marriott: "Yellow Submarine is the sort of song grandmas will be singing in pubs a hundred

years from now. It could become another Bull and Bush. Eleanor Rigby is the stronger side, though, and is a great number."

Hollies Allan Clarke and Tony Hicks: "Beautiful!"

Graham Nash: "I must be the only pop star who hasn't heard Eleanor Rigby yet. I have heard Submarine. It's effective in its simplicity. But I think this is all part of their plan to gradually disappear from the scene. They've done as much as they can."

August 13, 1966 – *Melody Maker* **wrote** that the Beatles were off to America... to stand up to the outrage over John Lennon's alleged comments about Christianity. The writer was bemused by the hysteria caused by Lennon's religious views... three months after they were published in Britain. He reckoned the Beatles fans were as surprised as the Beatles themselves.

Melody Maker believed Lennon had a right to say whatever he wanted on any subject at all. His belief that the Beatles were a hotter act than Jesus Christ was possibly a shocking truth. But time would be better spent trying to figure out why it would be so, rather than burning Beatle records and memorabilia.

They went on to point out that the Christian cause could not truly be helped by some of its anti-Beatle proponents, in particular the Ku Klux Klan. Still, burning records was probably a nice change from arranging lynchings.

In South Africa, Dr. Verwoerd had banned the Beatles, though a little late, since the group had already said they would never go there as long as apartheid was in effect.

They defended Lennon's statement that some of Christ's followers were "a bit thick," claiming the outcry tended to prove that.

The writer regarded Lennon as a remarkably intelligent person, regardless of whether or not people agreed with whatever he had to say. Most of the reactions to his out-of-context comments were neither bright nor Christian. His attackers, it was suggested, had probably done more damage to the Christian cause than any of Lennon's alleged remarks.

Brian Epstein said, "If any promoter wants to cancel, I will not stand in his way."

But, as it turned out, none of the concert dates were canceled, not even in the American south. The Ku Klux Klan and a number of radio stations did their best, but fans still wanted to see the Beatles.

Deejay Tommy Charles and colleagues Jim Cooper and Doug Layton of WAQY in Birmingham, Alabama, deep in the belly of the Bible Belt, claimed they were going to rent a wood-chipper to destroy every Beatle record they could acquire. They intended to present the ruined records to the group when they arrived in Memphis for their gig there.

A footnote mentioned that the new single, *Eleanor Rigby / Yellow Submarine* had leapt to number four in the charts at the moment of its release. *Revolver* was topping the album charts.

As of press time, this year's Shea Stadium Concert was only half-booked. Some thirty thousand tickets were still available.

August 13, 1966 – Ren Grevatt cabled *Melody Maker* that there was no serious Ban-the-Beatles campaign in the States. He went on to talk about the press conference held by Brian Epstein, in advance of the concert tour, to explain that Lennon's remarks about Christianity had been taken out of context by the teen fan magazine *Date Book*.

Epstein, Grevatt claimed, was very concerned about the misunderstanding. Lennon's comments had been made three months previously, to journalist Maureen Cleave of the *London Evening Standard*. Epstein explained that Lennon's remarks referred to his *"astonishment at the fact that in the last fifty years the Church of England had declined so much in England."* Brian added, *"John Lennon is deeply concerned about the publication of his remarks out of context in America and regrets any offense to people with certain religious beliefs."*

August 19, 1966 – *New Music Review* announced that the film of the Beatles' Shea Stadium concert was going to be rerun on BBC-1. The film had been seen on the BBC in March but had not, as yet, been shown in America. They mentioned that the Beatles would be at Shea Stadium again this year, but that the concert was not sold out.

August 20, 1966 – *Disc and Music Echo*, Jerry Leighton, chief disc jockey of Radio Caroline North, wrote... Five thousand fans in Cleveland, Ohio tore down the barricades at the Beatles concert. Halfway through their second set, the fans tried to get on the stage. The cops were helpless. The group was rushed to safety, taking refuge in a caravan.

Half an hour later, the police and the security guards restored order and the Beatles returned to the stage to finish the show without any further interruptions... until the end. They just managed to get to their cars as thousands of fans charged them again.

Leighton said badges stating, "We still love you, Beatles!" were selling by the thousands and that, so far, the concerts – Chicago, Detroit and Cleveland – had been incredibly successful, although the South was still waiting.

After Lennon's press conference in Chicago, Disc jockey Tommy Charles had called off his plan to hold Beatle-bonfires.

Lennon said, *"I wasn't saying the Beatles are better than God or Jesus. I was using the word Beatles because it's naturally easy for me to talk about Beatles. I could have said TV or cinema or anything popular."*

Leighton guessed this tour would be as successful as any of the others the Beatles had played.

August 20, 1966 – Jerry Leighton wrote again for *Disc and Music Echo*... "We still love you,

Beatles!" That was the prevailing mood amongst most American fans. Large badges bearing that slogan were selling by the thousands at half-a-dollar each. Huge arenas in Chicago, Detroit and Cleveland were packed and overflowing... but the south was still waiting.

In Cleveland, it was raining and Leighton wondered what would happen in that open-air arena.

Said John Lennon, *"Oh, we won't get wet because we're covered in. We might get blown up, though..."*

The manager of Olympia Stadium in Detroit claimed the Beatles were still the biggest draw to ever appear there, outselling the Rolling Stones by two-to-one, and the Animals / Herman's Hermits by three-to-one.

Leighton found it surprising that the Beatles had never actually seen America.

Said John Lennon, *"We dare not go out on the streets. We just stay in the hotel room until the car or coach calls to take us to the show. We miss an awful lot, but I suppose we will see it one day."*

They traveled to Chicago from Detroit by coach and, round about one in the morning, got out to stroll around an empty parking lot, *"Stopping off at the Rose and Crown,"* as Ringo put it, stretching their legs, breathing fresh air, the first, perhaps, in a long time. He said they looked pale, permanent indoor dwellers.

Said Paul, *"We feel all right, though. You can't really tell by looking at us because sometimes we look terrible and feel great, and other times it's the opposite."*

He talked about the Chicago press conference, saying Lennon spoke intelligently, acquitted himself brilliantly.

He talked with George about Indian music...

"To me," said George, *"it is the only really great music now, and it makes Western three-or-four beat type stuff seem somehow dead. You can get so much more out of it if you are prepared really to concentrate and listen. I hope more people will try to dig it."*

George was planning a trip to India sometime in the near future to study the music in depth.

Speaking with John, Leighton wondered if his solo excursion into film meant he was quitting the Beatles.

Said John, *"No, it's just a bit of practice while we have nothing to do for a bit."*

What type of film was it?

"Well, a sort of war comedy. I just play a Scouse batman. It should be a good experience."

Following Leighton's article were the on-air comments made by deejay Russ Reardon of WPEG radio in Winston Salem, North Carolina.

Reardon said, *"Beware! Your reactions and actions in judging the Beatles could give yourself away for what you really are. Only a Christian knows John Lennon is right: the Beatles are more popular than Jesus Christ.*

"Seven days a week, Beatle records are broadcast and adored; Beatle concert attendances overflow. One day a week, Jesus asks to be adored. Church attendance is off forty per cent less than it was.

"A non-Christian arrogantly demands an apology for his statement. A Christian is ashamed and embarrassed to know that the Beatles know of his apathy."

Reardon spoke about Nazis burning bibles and compared it to the great Beatle-burning of 1966. He ended by saying, *"A Christian will thank John Lennon for shocking him into proper perspective. John is a very perceptive student of human nature. It will be most interesting to watch your reaction and actions in judging the Beatles. Beware! You could give yourself away for what you really are."*

August 20, 1966 – *Disc and Music Echo*, Derek Taylor wrote from Hollywood... America was unsettled. It was violent, crazy, paranoid. It was no time, it was a dangerous time, for the Beatles to visit.

Eight nurses had just been butchered in Chicago. Fourteen people had been shot down in Austin, Texas. And all over the country, other lunatics were emulating these mass murders.

And all across the country, people were hating John Lennon for daring to speak his mind. Brian Epstein had told Taylor that the group was not comfortable with the forthcoming tour. He was worried about the Beatles being a target for the crazies, and did not understand how they could go from bringing such joy to millions with their music, to being labeled as evil by so many harmful people.

Still, many good people in America were responding to the hatred with an outpouring of love. Radio stations that had never before bothered with the Beatles were playing their records for hours on end. And the true fans were a loyal and loving as ever.

He thought the tour would bring fresh honours to the band, unless some cracker tried to pull a Jack Ruby.

August 20, 1966 – *Melody Maker* asked an assortment of British celebrities what they thought about John Lennon's Christianity remarks.

Jonathan of David and Jonathan: *"I think it was a stupid lapse on John Lennon's part. If anyone else said it, though, it would never have been given the publicity it has. And as for South Africa banning Beatle records, that's the biggest piece of hypocritical nonsense I've ever heard."*

Alan Price: *"Lennon's got every right to say what he likes. But it's only because he's a Beatle that it's been picked up the way it has. If I'd said it, no one would have taken a blind bit of notice. I think they're making a mountain out of a molehill. They should ask Cliff Richard what he thinks."*

Athol Guy of the Seekers: *"In America they are always rather hell-bent on sensationalism and at last they have got their hands on something they can throw up at the Beatles. People have been waiting for the chance. Considering the length of time they*

have been the world's top attraction, the Beatles have carried the weight on their shoulders very well. If it were sincerely religious people who had been offended it would be fair enough. But the way this had been handled, I can't see how it can be. The whole thing has got way out of proportion."

Donovan: *"John Lennon is a beautiful character and I think this whole thing has been blown up out of all proportion. My own view? That's a matter between myself and my conscience."*

Ken Lewis of the Ivy League: *"If you think about it, I suppose what Lennon said was true. Let's face it, given the chance of going to church or going to watch the Beatles, I'm sure seven out of ten young people would plump for the Beatles every time. It's a shame that so much has been drummed up by one small comment. John is entitled to his opinion and at least he has the guts to air them in public."*

Reg King of the Action: *"Everyone is entitled to say what they like. I don't really think it will affect the Beatles' popularity but when he says the disciples were a bit thick, I disagree. By following Jesus, they were constantly scorned by the rest of the people and they had firm and intelligent minds."*

Jimmy James: *"I'm a Catholic by religion and I don't stand by what John says. But to be fair, he is entitled to his opinion and I think, I certainly hope, that this won't affect the group's popularity. But when he says that Jesus Christ's followers were thick, that strikes me as funny because Beatles' followers, the name today is fans, can also be somewhat on the dim side."*

Barry Fantoni: *"In the absence of Jesus Christ, it's impossible to know what to say. Put it this way, if the Beatles were at the London Palladium the same night as Jesus was topping the bill at the Talk of the Town, we would soon know who was more popular. And, in all honesty, I think Jesus would prove to be by far the biggest box office draw."*

Pete Quaife of the Kinks: *"The drag is it looks as though what he said is true. This is a typically hysterical let's-cash-in make-a-lot-of-money show-them-we-are-the-best American attitude. What I'd like to know is what the other Beatles think about it."*

Graham Nash of the Hollies: *"I, personally, don't believe the Beatles are too upset by the whole thing. I have the impression they are trying to cool things down for themselves, they want to be more independent and live a more comfortable life. Not that I think they started this row on purpose. Anyway, the way it has all been handled is hysterical and ridiculous."*

Dave Berry: *"Lennon probably said all that for a laugh and didn't expect it to be taken so seriously. Anyway, people ought to look at the facts because what he said is probably true. As far as the people in the Bible Belt of the Southern States of America are concerned, and they seem to be making all the fuss, that is the biggest laugh of all. They are nothing but bloody hypocrites. They ought to straighten out their own house before they start blasting other people."*

Carl Wayne of the Move: *"The reason for the uproar is that what John says is possibly true. However, his remarks have created an impossible situation. It's all too exaggerated now to be looked at objectively. But I don't think it will affect the Beatles' popularity."*

Plonk Laine of the Small Faces: *"Somebody had to tell the Americans the world was round, and they wouldn't believe that."*

Zoot Money: *"I'm buying a John Lennon tee-shirt. He's my hero. If he opens a church, I'll be the first in."*

Melody Maker also asked the readers what they thought. The opinions were mixed... John Lennon was not boasting but condemning a society in which the Beatles can outshine religion... The Beatles should be sent to Sunday School so they can grow up... Considering the history of Alabama, how popular would Jesus be if he was there today... The hypocrisy of the Ku Klux Klan is beyond belief... Lennon was right, the Beatles are more popular than Christ... *The Ballad of the Green Berets* was the most un-Christian record ever produced and it sold by the millions in America... These protests come from the worst areas of racial conflict in the world... Some Christians... Other pop stars are in court on drug charges and paternity suits while the Beatles are being dragged through the world courts for nothing at all... American teenagers... If those people burning Beatle records went to Church instead, they might be able to do themselves some good...

August 20, 1966 – Kenny Everett wrote for *Melody Maker*... The Beatles still provoked incredible excitement. In Cleveland, two thousand fans broke through the barricades to charge the stage. The band was playing for an audience of twenty-five thousand. The stage was in the centre of the grassy field. And as the group hit the first chords of *Day Tripper*, the crowd exploded. The Beatles hid out in a trailer behind the stage until order was more-or-less restored, then went to finish the show. The fans were reasonably well-behaved until the end, when again they charged the group.

In Boston, when they arrived from London, hundreds of kids were waiting at the airport for them, the normal Beatlemania scream-fest.

In Chicago, there were capacity crowds at each performance. Prior to the Beatles going on stage, the warm-up act, the Cyrkle, played their hit *Red Rubber Ball*. A publicity stunt had armed the audience with small red rubber balls, obviously to celebrate the song. But the balls were saved for the Beatles, peppering the stage along with the usual shower of jelly babies.

Posters and placards everywhere read, "We love John Lennon and God."

At a press conference in Chicago, John apologised about the whole religion thing, lamenting that his remarks had been misunderstood, explaining that he certainly was not anti-religious.

I Love John Lennon badges were outselling, by ten-to-one, the ones that read, "I Love Paul," "I Love George" and "I Love Ringo."

After the show in Detroit, they stopped a small cafe where the Beatles hung around the roadside eating hamburgers. People walked by without recognising them and Everett wondered what would have happened if they had been recognised.

Every hotel where they stayed was surrounded by fans.

In Cleveland, en route to Washington DC, their plane was delayed and John Lennon said, *"Tell Lyndon we'll be late for tea."*

In Washington, thirty thousand fans crammed the stadium. The Beatles were protected by patrolling cops. No riots occurred.

The Ban-the-Beatles campaign was a non-event. No incidents touched the group, though the Ku Klux Klan was demonstrating in other States. The Beatles had not, apparently, lost any fans over Lennon's religious gaffe. Sometimes, it seemed quite the opposite.

August 20, 1966 – *Melody Maker*, **Ren Grevatt wrote** about the Cleveland riot, about the Beatles hiding out in a trailer while the cops and the security guards restored order. After a thirty-three minute delay, they finished the concert and fled the scene in Cadillac limousines.

Back at the hotel, they spent the night playing Dylan's new album, *Blonde on Blonde*.

In the Chicago press conference, even while apologising for the connotation put on his Christianity remarks, Lennon did not back down from his opinion about the decline in religion in Britain.

Airport security had been good, though, Grevatt said, the airport crowds on this tour were smaller than on the other tours. There was, however, no decline in the Beatles' sales power. *Yellow Submarine / Eleanor Rigby* was a smash hit for Capitol Records. Radio stations were playing *Rigby* more than *Submarine*. Radio stations were ignoring the demands that they ban the Beatles, a campaign that began in Birmingham, Alabama, at one of the weakest stations in the city.

He mentioned that it was quite obvious George Harrison was a truly serious fan of Indian music. He was carrying around a small tape recorder and playing as much off-beat material as he could find.

Forthcoming concerts were to be in Philadelphia, Toronto, Boston, Memphis and St. Louis, and New York's Shea Stadium. After that, it was on to the West Coast.

SID BERNSTEIN
Presents the

BEATLES

IN PERSON

PLUS **ALL STAR SHOW**
SHEA STADIUM
TUES. 7:30 P.M. AUG. 23

ALL SEATS RESERVED $450 500 575 phone 265-2280 FOR INFORMATION
TICKETS NOW AT
SINGER SHOP RECORD DEPT. Rockefeller Center Promenade 49th 50th Sts on Fifth Ave

August 27, 1966 – *Disc and Music Echo*, **Jerry Leighton of Radio Caroline North wrote** that the Beatles' American tour was more than half over. The question being asked everywhere was: Are the Beatles still as popular as ever in America?

Box office receipts, according to Brian Epstein, proved that more people were out to see them this year than last.

That was answer enough.

Money talks. The knockers were knocked.

The show in Cincinnati was rained out. Kids stood in the rain for four hours waiting while the equipment on the stage was left uncovered. By the time the rain stopped, the equipment was impossible to use, dangerous to use, and the show was postponed until noon the next day.

The threats that had been made by the Bible Belt crowd prior to the group's arrival in Memphis had not materialised. A huge and enthusiastic crowd was on hand the greet the Beatles.

The police and the fans made the group feel at home, welcomed and loved. A religious get-together was held at the same time as the Beatles concert. The attendees prayed for forgiveness for the Beatles and their audience.

In New York, the security was tight. The hundreds of fans gathered round the hotel for a glimpse of their heroes were disappointed.

Said George, *"We come out here to do shows, and if we show our faces outside our room, we would be torn apart, so it has to be this way. After all, the main thing we want to do is stay alive."*

Paul explained that the decision to release *Yellow Submarine / Eleanor Rigby* had been made by Brian Epstein so the Beatles could reap the benefits before any other artist had an opportunity to record a cover. With the tour and the new record sales, Epstein expected the group to bring home more than one million dollars.

On the plane from St. Louis to New York, Lennon joked with Leighton, telling him that he had heard Radio Caroline was the number one station in Britain. They discussed the major difficulties confronting radio stations while George worked on some sort of flowery doodle.

The band explained they were looking forward to Los Angeles and a short holiday before they headed home to England.

August 27, 1966 – *Disc and Music Echo* **announced** that Paul McCartney had told New Yorkers he would probably marry Jane Asher. But the date had not been set.

August 27, 1966 – *Melody Maker*, **Kenny Everett reported** from the States. In New York, two girls had threatened to jump from the twenty-first floor of the Hotel Americana unless they got to see the Beatles. They sat on the ledge, legs dangling in the air, promising they would not jump if the cops would get a message to Paul McCartney.

One cop got down on his knees and begged them to come in. Crying, the girls did that.

Later, Paul said, *"I don't understand it, it's so silly."*

Apart from that, though, Everett explained, the tour had been much quieter this year. Not because the Beatles were less popular, but because the fans were a little older, a little more aware, a little more interested in the music.

There was less screaming and wailing, more listening.

It was being reported that this tour was less successful than the others, but Brian Epstein said the gate receipts were higher than ever.

There was some bad weather; with a rain-out in Cincinnati, the show canceled until the next day, when thousands of joyful fans turned out for the show.

The Beatles were apparently enjoying the tour, though wished they could get out and about.

The press conference in New York was the best yet. It was filmed and televised.

Everett thought George was getting thoughtfully deeper and deeper, wondered if the Beatle might end up a bald monk hiding on a mountain somewhere.

John was his normal sarcastic self.

Paul was chatty and friendly.

August 27, 1966 – *Melody Maker*, **Ren Grevatt announced** two Beatle firsts: In Cincinnati, the first ever rain-out for a concert; and in New York, the first time the group threw a press conference for their teen-aged fans.

After the regular session with the press, the Beatles entertained a crowd of one hundred and fifty fans, most of them shrieking girls. Tony Barrow, press officer, hollered at them until they quieted. And for half an hour, they were allowed to ask questions. At one point, Paul McCartney said, *"I will probably marry Jane Asher this year."*

What do you think of mini-skirts?

Said Paul, *"I like mini-skirts and they'll probably go higher."*

What about Vietnam?

John answered, *"The war in Vietnam is wrong all the way and you know it is, but that's all we'll say in America about it. We could give our opinions in England but not here. America, being larger than Britain, has more bigots who tend to twist everything you say."*

The Saturday night show in Cincinnati had to be canceled. Even though the rain had stopped, the equipment had been soaked. One of the roadies was electrically bounced across the stage when he attempted to hook up an amp.

Only about twelve thousand fans showed up for the Philadelphia show… but they were as enthusiastic as ever.

Three girls had forged some Brian Epstein stationary and wrote a letter, ostensibly from Epstein, authorising them to have a personal audience with the Beatles in their dressing room. Tony Barrow knew the letter was phony but the Beatles were so impressed by the girls creativity that they had them brought in.

In New York, forty-four thousand seats had been sold, so far, for the Shea Stadium concert.

September 3, 1966 – *Melody Maker***, Kenny Everett of Radio London said** it was difficult to sum up this most recent Beatles concert tour. It had been hectic, wild, crazy… total madness in a whirlwind dash.

The final concert had been in Los Angeles, where more than a thousand fans crashed the barriers and were stopped on the brink of assaulting the group by the L.A. cop shock troopers, out in full force.

After the concert, the Beatles and entourage retired to a rented mansion to relax a bit… and to throw some parties, hundreds of guests rocking and rolling in the hills outside L.A.

Everett noted that the group had seemed a bit depressed when they were leaving England to do this tour. Now he understood why. There was little pleasure on a tour, just hard work, discomfort, adrenaline, isolation, and endless repetition of the same old songs. He thought the Beatles were somewhat jaded by it all and were seeking something new, something fresh, something to fire up all their creativity again.

September 3, 1966 – Ren Grevatt interviewed the Beatles for *Melody Maker***.**

He started by wondering if the Beatles would ever try legitimate musical theatre if the group suddenly fell from the top.

Said John Lennon, *"Most of legitimate theatre is just a load of rubbish as far as we're concerned. We would never want to be like Rodgers and Hammerstein or anyone who preceded us. If we did anything, it would be a musical of today, not the twenties like the* Hello Dolly *thing."*

Paul McCartney did not like the term *legitimate*. He said, *"That puts it all in a slot, like* Funny Girl *and a lot of others. We'd never be able to write that way because we wouldn't feel that kind of show. I don't mind that type and I quite like seeing them, but we'd have to put far more into it.*

"Lionel Bart once told us that the easiest way to do a show is to write twelve songs and give them to a great producer like Joan Littlewood and have her build the whole show around the songs. I don't think we could work that way. It would be harder for us because we would have to put much more into it. I don't like that term legitimate*. I guess if we ever do a show, we'll have to call it an illegitimate show."*

"I never lie awake," John said, *"thinking of what I'll be writing next year, or about show business for that matter, because I probably won't be in it at some point. Show business we never really ever see. That business is a little bunch of red nosed people who live together and call themselves show business. We know some people in that club but we don't belong to it."*

Grevatt asked John about the future of rock… and about Americans.

Lennon answered, *"I'm no soothsayer on music and where it's going. I just hope it continues to get better, that it progresses and doesn't step back. I think, for instance, that Brian Wilson is great, he's doing some very good things. We like the Beach Boys, the Byrds, the Mamas and Papas, a lot of them. They make sounds we like. You know? And we listen to everything we can.*

"With Americans, well, I don't like to generalise, but I think we showed some people here that not all Englishmen are like John Bull or a happy go lucky Cockney. Well, once I thought Americans were all loud mouths with big ties and lots of cameras. Well, they're not.

"I hope I get to see more of America because it's the kind of place that might blow up some day, by itself, or with the help of some other country."

He wondered if there would an ultimate downfall for the Beatles.

Said Paul, *"There'll be no downfall for us. We're not worried. We don't dread it. When we get sick of all the hocus pocus and the press and the screaming, we'll just take a fat holiday on our fat wallets."*

September 17, 1966 – *Disc and Music Echo***, Penny Valentine wrote** that Tuesday, September 6th was a day that would forever be recorded in history. It was the day John Lennon had all his hair chopped off. It was a shocking day. A nasty sign of the times.

The Beatles had been the first long-haired rockers. Parents were outraged. And everyone copied whatever they did. Now, one was shorn. Could the rest of the rock world be far behind? Would this signal a return to the days of short back and sides?

She spoke with other pop stars, asking what they thought about Lennon's new look, asking if they would follow along.

Wayne Fontana, with hair down to his shoulders: *"Good for him! Mine's just about scheduled for a cut anyway, under strict instructions from the management. I don't think I'll go to the extremes he's had to go to, although I suppose if a good part came up in a film like this and I wanted to do it badly enough, I'd even have a Yul Brynner."*

Eric Stewart of the Mindbenders: *"It's okay as long as he doesn't want a part in the remake of* The Robe.*"*

Tony Hicks of the Hollies said he was stunned when he saw the *after* pictures: *"Mainly because I always thought that with John, this hair thing was a matter of principle. I was really surprised to see he'd had so much taken off. I don't think I'd go to such lengths, but then, of course, you never know. If the right part came along, I suppose I'd do the same thing."*

Ray Davies of the Kinks: *"I think John is all right as long as he doesn't start wearing Brylcreem."*

Dave Dee said, *"It's great. Of course, if the long-haired boom wasn't in, nobody would have known the difference anyway."*

The Troggs were all in favour of it. *"From the pictures we've seen it looks as though this film part is going to establish him as an actor. And in this case, that's well worth his while having every bit of hair off if he felt like it."*

Tony Crane of the Merseys: *"I was staggered to see how much they'd cut off. I couldn't believe it. When they first announced that John would have to have it cut, I thought they'd just adapt the Beatles style. Really, only John could get away with this. If it was Paul, it would ruin his image. Would I do it? Well, if I was as big as the Beatles, of course I would. They don't really have to worry, they can do exactly what they want. But you've got to be established, really, to get away with such a drastic step."*

September 24, 1966 – *Melody Maker* **ran an ad for** *Music Maker***, quoting John Lennon…**

"I can't stand listening to most of our early stuff. Songs like Eight Days a Week *and* She Loves You *sound like big drags to me now. I turn the radio off if they're ever on."*

October 15, 1966 – *Disc and Music Echo* **announced** that another Beatle was going solo. Rumour had it that Paul McCartney would be doing something on his own.

Said Brian Epstein, *"All I will say is that a solo project is planned for one of the Beatles which will be announced soon."*

Another rumour suggested it would be a solo album of Indian music by George Harrison, who had been in India for the last month studying the sitar.

October 22, 1966 – *Disc and Music Echo* **said** the rumours that the Beatles would break up before Christmas were unfounded.

A Beatles spokesman said, *"The Beatles are NOT splitting up. They'll be writing material for their next film the usual way."*

Still, the group was pursuing individual activities. Lennon was shooting a film on location in Spain. Ringo and Maureen were holidaying in Spain. George Harrison was in Bombay learning the sitar. And Paul was only member of the band still in London.

Lennon and McCartney had contracted to score the next Boulting Brothers' movie *All In Good Time*, starring Hayley Mills. After watching the finished film with Brian Epstein, Paul agreed on behalf of himself and John to do the music.

A footnote mentioned that the London Jazz Four had recorded jazz versions of a number of Beatles songs.

October 29, 1966 – *Disc and Music Echo* **wondered** if it was time for the Beatles to retire. With Lennon in Spain working on a film, Ringo and Maureen holidaying in Spain, George studying sitar in India, and Paul all alone in London, they had clearly gone their separate ways. They had no plans for their next single, and no plans for a tour of the UK. Should they retire? Should they pack it in now, rest on their laurels, leave the world to remember when there was nothing like the Beatles? Or should they carry on? They asked a few celebrities…

Cliff Richard: *"Retirement is a personal thing. One day I'm going to retire to take up teaching. But as far as the Beatles are concerned, I would say no. Why retire? Unless they have definite ideas about what they are going to do. If they came into the business with the idea of making a smash and getting out, then that's fair enough.*

"Fact is, they'll never always be on top. Really, there's no answer to the question, 'Should they retire?' If they want to retire at the top of their careers, then get out now. If they want to stay big in show biz, then they should continue as they are."

Hank Marvin of the Shadows: *"I'm one of the never say die people, actually. Whether the Beatles can get any higher than they are now, no one knows. If I was them, I wouldn't pack it in unless I was really cheesed off. But if it was a case of personal happiness, then I would. I think they have a lot to offer, both musically and entertainment-wise. But they have to face up to it, they're not going to be teenage idols all their lives."*

Brian Epstein: *"There's no real question of the Beatles retiring. Let's face it, what is happening at the moment is that they're simmering down. Making films, writing music, making records… that's their future."*

"While I know live appearances are of permanent importance to many people, the Beatles find themselves open to so much misinterpretation… like that appalling debacle in Manila and the comments about Christ.

"Be sure the Beatles themselves like singing and playing to a public, but it's become so difficult and so tense that their enjoyment and pleasure, let alone finance, is taken away.

"Still, while they are creating albums like Revolver, *I doubt if the public are entitled to expect much more of them. Their future together really lies as far as the moon. I'm not thinking of theatres, but a big record buying market. With this, and more good films, they can only continue developing. I know the main contention of their critics is that they have become too flippant as far as their fans are concerned. But I don't think many of the fans really feel this. And those that do just don't consider the difficulties that the Beatles encounter through being who they are."*

Derek Taylor: *"No, the Beatles shouldn't retire… Well, it all depends what you mean by retire. The Beatles clearly shouldn't, won't and can't retire from writing music. No one ever retires from writing. Some become written-out. But the evidence is that McCartney and Lennon are only just now on the threshold of profoundly great words and music.*

"Their success has so compounded their confidence, their experiences as world-traveled, brutally exposed star-giants have so heightened their perception, and their increasing maturity is so deepening their lyrical and melodic resources, that hundreds of songs may tumble from their heads if John and Paul wish it so.

"So John and Paul will continue to record. And so too, one assumes, will Ringo and George whose creative contribution, though, on paper, smaller, is too closely attuned musically and spiritually to be lightly replaced. George, of course, is settling with determination to writing and when it becomes less of an effort for him, we may see some fine music.

"Next, should the Beatles retire from performing? This, I suppose, means should they retire from personal appearances, from concerts on television, from in-public appearances as a foursome, at presentations and so on. We're now getting into the heart of the matter because to give up collective appearances is the nearest they could reasonably get to retiring.

"It might be a very good idea if the Beatles gave up touring at the end of this year. I'm thinking only of their prestige, because I know they enjoy many of their concerts, more, much more, than they did a couple of years ago.

"But I don't want to witness any furtively gleeful derision if there are empty seats at auditoriums. I don't want their detractors to be given the satisfaction of detecting the slightest whiff of failure.

I don't want to see the level of excitement dwindle, nor the aura grow stale.

"I used to suggest to the Beatles that the logical end to it all was for all four Beatles to die in an air crash in front of ten thousand fans at Liverpool airport after playing a final retirement concert at Wembley Stadium. They would have, I put it to them, a memorial service at Westminster Abbey, or St. Paul's, which somehow is more them, and a massive funeral procession to Liverpool Cathedral. But there were certain drawbacks to this proposal and it may well be that there is no rational end to the Beatles."

November 12, 1966 – *Disc and Music Echo* **wondered** if it was the end of the road for the Beatles. That week, fans had marched and picketed outside the home of Brian Epstein, demanding to know what the Beatles were doing, begging for news, praying for information. Were they going to tour? Were they making records. Were they quitting?

The fans were demanding another tour of Britain. And Brian Epstein said, *"Nothing has been decided."*

Disc then quoted an earlier interview with Epstein: *"The Beatles like singing and playing to a public, but it's become so difficult and so tense that their enjoyment and pleasure, let alone finance, is taken away. Making films, writing music, making records, that's their future."*

With regards to the demonstrating fans, he said, *"I was out at the time, at the Prince of Wales theatre and then at the Beach Boys concert to see Sounds Incorporated, but I was told some fans did come round to complain."*

British Beatles tour manager, Arthur Howe, said, *"I'm beginning to believe the rumours myself. We've been inundated with requests by fans for another tour and there used to be petitions, too. But now I think a lot of them are giving up hope."*

Disc then ran a series of letters from fans… If the Beatles are planning to retire, they should do one final tour of Britain… The Beatles should not retire, should not stop touring… So many people would be disappointed if they retired… They've peaked… Maybe they are getting stale… They should develop their individual talents… Touring doesn't matter… If they keep making records, they have to make personal appearances… It has been ages since they toured Britain, the fans have a right to complain… They should not, should not, should not retire…

November 12, 1966 – *Melody Maker* **said** the Beatles would have a new single out for the Christmas rush. EMI expected the group to be in the studio before the end of the month.

They only had one song recorded, *Bad Boy*, but that was likely for a future album. Lennon was back in England after *How I Won the War* wrapped. George was also back. And Ringo would be home soon.

Their new film was due to start in January. But a spokesman for producer Walter Shenson said, "*The script has not been finished yet. We are waiting to see it before we can arrange a tentative starting date or even a title for the film.*"

Rumour had it that the Beatles would make no more personal appearances.

And Brian Epstein said that no decisions had, as yet, been made about whether or not the band would perform together in public again.

The rumours about the group breaking up were gaining momentum, becoming, for many people, truth.

NEMS press officer, Tony Barrow, said, "*We have nothing more to add at the moment to what has already been said.*"

November 19, 1966 – *Disc and Music Echo* reported that no British Beatles tour was foreseeable. Fans were again demonstrating for Brian Epstein, this time in the streets around the Saville Theatre in London where Epstein was presenting the Four Tops.

A new single was in the works but would not be released until after Christmas.

And a NEMS spokesman said, "*The new Beatles film has been delayed owing to the problem of finding a suitable script. No tour or major commitments can be undertaken until the film is scheduled. But when Paul comes back from holiday later this month, the Beatles will make a new single, if not before Christmas, early in January.*"

A new Beatles album was due out on December 9th. It was to be called *Oldies*, a sixteen-track LP from Parlophone, planned to include fifteen old Beatle songs along with *Bad Boy*, which had been released by Capitol in 1965 on the album *Beatles VI*.

Along with *Bad Boy*, the Parlophone release was to include: *She Loves You, From Me to You, We Can Work It Out, Help, Michelle, Yesterday, I Feel Fine, Yellow Submarine, Can't Buy Me Love, Day Tripper, A Hard Day's Night, Ticket to Ride, Paperback Writer, Eleanor Rigby* and *I Want to Hold Your Hand*.

As a footnote, *Disc* mentioned that Brian Epstein had told interviewer David Frost, "*The Beatles think of what's already happened to them as a little beginning. What is left for them to do? There are masses of things for them. But I can't forecast how their careers will go.*"

November 26, 1966 – Derek Taylor reminisced for *Melody Maker*... He had always had difficulty writing about the Beatles because he had always felt they were watching him closely, sort of like God when a little childhood thievery was in progress.

It had been three years since he had first spoken in depth with George Harrison, after a few earlier meetings at press conferences.

Recalling the press conferences, at the first one he had accused the group of selling out their teenage fans by appearing on the Royal Variety Show. He

realised now the question had been nonsense, but he appreciated the way the group handled it.

Lennon had said, "*Eppy decides.*"

Ringo had added, "*I wouldn't mind playing drums for the Queen Mother.*"

George and Paul had asked who else was on the show.

In the early spring of 1964, he had joined them as a publicist. At the time, he had known only what they revealed to journalists. But as time went by their personalities had emerged. George could be moody and miserable. Ringo was very human... and very witty. John, hiding behind a wall of acid and bite, was actually very thoughtful, a man loyal to his family. Paul, disguised by a rough Liverpool accent, was quite sophisticated and had a great appreciation for fine things.

1964 had been a wild year. They were the heart of show business, sought by journalists and royalty, presidents and fans. Gradually, they drew back. The erstwhile easy access granted to photographers and journalists was being withdrawn. And the tours were already starting to drag them down. Records, though, were beginning to receive the studio work, the care and attention required.

At the end of 1964, Taylor had left to go to the U.S. and did not see them again until February, 1965, in the Bahamas during the filming of *Help!* Interviewing them for an American radio station was somehow embarrassing both for Taylor and the Beatles.

They were different people, now. Still four Beatles, but more relaxed, more sure of themselves, more creative.

He met them again a year later, in Los Angeles at the end of a concert tour. This time they were not present as Beatles but as four individuals with different attitudes and different motivations. They were no longer four guys as one. Now they had their own plan, John to film in Spain, George into Indian music and Ravi Shankar; Ringo the family man, Paul, content and confident, getting set to write a film score.

Three months later, Taylor was with them again, well, except for Paul, who was on holiday after completing the music for the film. John was back from Spain. Ringo was home. And George talked about Bombay and dressed in Indian clothing... because that was what he wanted to do and needed no approval from anyone.

Now, they knew who their real friends were.

They denied rumours that they were about to end their relationship with Brian Epstein.

They said not a word about any future tours.

They were un-rushed, un-frantic, un-harassed. Calm. Unworried.

They were all now aware that they could have individual lives independent of each other. They were free to pursue their individual interests.

If the Beatles were dead... Long live The Beatles!

December 10, 1966 – *Record Mirror*, **Derek Harvey said** the Beach Boys had been voted more popular than the Beatles… deservedly. While the Beatles were doing *Yellow Submarine*, the Beach Boys were recording *God Only Knows*, and, more recently, perhaps the finest record ever made, *Good Vibrations*. It was time for the Beatles to wake up.

December 17, 1966 – *Disc and Music Echo* **said** sixty thousand Beatle fans would be receiving the newest Beatle record… free. There would be no new record in the music shops, but the members of the Beatles fan club would still be getting their free Christmas gift from the group. It was called *Pantomime – Everywhere It's Christmas*.

This fourth Christmas giveaway was thoughtful and well-produced. It was a pantomime, drifting through a vaudeville chorus sing-along, banter and jokes, a situation comedy, and a fairy tale spoken by Paul and John, Podgy the Bear and Jasper.

The tracks were: *Everywhere It's Christmas*, *Orowayna*, *A Rare Cheese*, *The Feast*, *The Loyal Toast*, *Podgy the Bear and Jasper*, *Felpin Mansions*, *Please Don't Bring Your Banjo Back*, followed by a reprise of *Everywhere It's Christmas*.

The disc was not for sale. The writer thought it was surprising that more stars were not following the Beatles' lead here and giving out Christmas gifts to their fans, but then, the Beatles always were ahead of everyone else.

— Chapter Seven: 1967 —

January 14, 1967 – *Disc and Music Echo* **ran a photograph** of John, Paul and George costumed for a fancy dress party in Kensington, London. John was clad in priest's cassock and hat, along with a dog collar; George was wearing Regency gear; and Paul was dressed as a U.S. Confederate Army officer.

January 28, 1967 – *Melody Maker* **printed** a footnote that mentioned that the Not Only But Also show that featured John Lennon as a washroom attendant was to be rerun on BBC-1. Another footnote mentioned that George Harrison was still on his "Indian kick."

February 4, 1967 – *Disc and Music Echo* **reported** that the Beatles were due to appear on Top of the Pops on February 18th to promote their new double-A-side single, *Strawberry Fields Forever / Penny Lane*. Brian Epstein told reporters that "the boys" had spent some time filming around the countryside in Kent for Peter Goldmann, a Swedish TV producer. Some of the footage was to be shown on Top of the Pops; other clips would be released in the U.S.

A new Beatles TV special was to focus on their next LP.

A footnote mentioned that John and Paul had joined Brian Epstein at London's Saville Theatre to see Jimi Hendrix and the Who.

February 11, 1967 – *Record Mirror* **mentioned** that the Beatles had a new single out on Parlophone, *Penny Lane / Strawberry Fields Forever*. A film clip of the group performing *Penny Lane* was to have been shown on Juke Box Jury, but the Beatles canceled the showing because the BBC would not play the entire film. Clips of the group performing both songs would be shown on Top of the Pops.

Regional TV stations around Britain were currently negotiating for the rights to show the films (of what are amongst the first rock and roll *videos* ever made).

EMI Records told the world they had resigned the Beatles for nine more years, the contract signed by Sir Joseph Lockwood and Brian Epstein.

In October 1962, the Beatles released their first record, *Love Me Do*. It sold 100,000 copies. Since then, total world sales had reached 180,000,000 (this figure was arrived at by converting each LP to half-a-dozen singles and each EP as four singles). The contract announcement tied in with the release of *Penny Lane / Strawberry Fields Forever*, the group's first single of 1967.

February 11, 1967 – *Disc and Music Echo* **announced** that the Beatles had signed a nine-year contract with EMI Records, the deal signed by Brian Epstein and Sir Joseph Lockwood.

EMI had released the first Beatles record, *Love Me Do*, in 1962. It sold 100,000 copies. Total world sales had now reached 180,000,000.

The Beatles first record of 1967, *Penny Lane / Strawberry Fields Forever*, was due to be released on Friday, February 17th.

As a footnote, *Disc* mentioned that by the time the new contract expired in 1976, Ringo and John would be thirty-five, George and Paul, thirty-three.

Another footnote said that Phillip Solomon of Radio Caroline had banned the new Beatles single until it hit the charts. He explained, *"The Beatles single has to suffer, just like all other EMI records not already in the chart, because of the strongly anti-pirate attitude of EMI's chairman, Sir Joseph Lockwood."*

Solomon said Lockwood was suing Radio Caroline for airing EMI's records without permission. In retaliation, Radio Caroline, with the largest audience amongst the pirate radio stations, was refusing to give advance promotion to any of EMI's records.

February 11, 1967 – *Disc and Music Echo* **said** a new Beatles' record was on the way. With Monkeemania raging throughout Britain and with the Rolling Stones buried in controversy, the Beatles were again poised to regain their crown at the top of the rock and roll heap.

Strawberry Fields Forever / Penny Lane, both Lennon and McCartney compositions, made up the double-sided single that was due out on the 17th. It was their fourteenth release since *Love Me Do* in October 1962. Their last single, also double-sided, *Eleanor Rigby / Yellow Submarine*, sat at number one in the charts for a month. *Disc* wondered if they could do it again. They asked Manfred Mann what he thought.

He said, *"I'm glad I had the opportunity of hearing it more than once. In fact, Klaus [Voorman] had a copy soon after it was recorded and brought it round for me to hear.*

"The first time I heard Penny Lane *I thought it was fairly pleasant, but it left me rather cold. Then I would find myself waking up in the middle of the night with a tune on my mind and realise it was* Penny Lane.

"It's an excellent record. It has an obvious, more immediate appeal than the other side. It must be a success. Must be number one. The lyrics are good.

"Strawberry Fields struck me at first as being manufactured and over-clever. Initially, I thought here are four guys trying to show they are not being left behind. On second hearing the song seems to hang together a bit more. It's very good. Basically a good melody. The way they record is brilliant. Everything here is so well thought out."

February 18, 1967 – *Disc and Music Echo*, Ray Coleman announced that the Beatles had won two more awards from *Disc* readers, Best Group and, for *Revolver*, Best LP. Coleman spoke with Paul McCartney and Ringo Starr.

Paul joked, *"I'm still getting over the surprise that Dave Clark hasn't knocked us off the top yet!*

"But it's good to have won."

Even though the Beatles had not toured the UK the previous year, they were still revered and secure in their position in the pop world.

Said Paul, *"I disagree with those people who say we are doing the wrong thing by not touring. It's difficult for people who don't realise how difficult it is for us to tour.*

"Nowadays, live TV is nearly the same as a concert, anyway, and the biggest problem for us now is that it's difficult for us to get in control of what we are going to do. We tend to get controlled!

"It doesn't mean we will never perform live again. At the moment, we haven't an act to suit the ordinary type of tour that goes on. If we can think of a way of getting four flying saucers landing on the top of the Albert Hall, it would be possible. But at the moment, there isn't much happening in that direction."

Ringo said, *"We find things restricting as far as moving about is concerned. I mean, if we want to freak out, the whole world knows, the papers print pictures, and all that. I've got used to it now. A couple of years ago, I was scared of growing old, and I said so. But not now.*

"I used to sit and think about where all this was leading, and what would all four of us be doing in nine years. But I suppose we've all grown up and learned to live with everything. What I'm doing now is what I'm doing now, who knows what's going to happen?"

March 11, 1967 – *Disc and Music Echo* reported that *Penny Lane / Strawberry Fields Forever* failed to hit number one as expected. Englebert Humperdinck's *Release Me* was sitting at number one. This was the first time since the Beatles had their first number one hit that they had been held off the top of the chart for two weeks in a row. *Please Please Me*, the Beatles' second single, had been their first number one hit.

A footnote mentioned that the Beatles had won two Grammy awards in the U.S. *Eleanor Rigby* was voted the best contemporary solo vocal performance and *Michelle* was voted song of the year. Also, Klaus Voorman, guitarist with Manfred Mann, won the best album cover award for *Revolver*.

March 18, 1967 – *Melody Maker* said with *Penny Lane / Strawberry Fields Forever* at the top of the charts, the Beatles had recorded six new tracks toward their next album, due out in May. One of the songs was backed by a forty-one-piece orchestra. They were presently working on four more songs, including one by George. And they were hoping to have to more recordings to fill out the album. Press officer Tony Barrow said the album would contain only twelve songs.

"After the LP is completed, the Beatles will probably carry on recording for a summer single," Barrow said.

Penny Lane had sold more than 1,500,000 in the U.S. where it was number one.

April 1, 1967 – *Record Mirror*, Jeremy Walsh wondered if the *Penny Lane / Strawberry Fields Forever* failure to hit number one in the charts was a world-shattering event, or if it even mattered. Was it inevitable that the Beatles would one day fail to reach number one? Even the group had expected it to happen eventually. So this record failed. So what?

According to Walsh, their first number one hit was *From Me to You* and their most recent one was *Eleanor Rigby*. In between were: *I Want to Hold Your Hand*, *I Feel Fine*, *She Loves You*, *Yellow Submarine*, *Day Tripper*, *Help*, *We Can Work It Out*, and others, brilliant songs all.

Walsh said it was not Englebert Humperdinck's *Release Me* that beat the Beatles for number one, it was the Beatles themselves. They were surging so far ahead of public taste, setting public taste, as it were, that no one quite understood what they were doing. The most recent single was just too uncommercial. It was ridiculous that the band who had recorded and released such an incredible body of work would choose to put out such an non-commercial effort as *Penny Lane / Strawberry Fields Forever*.

Some people thought the popularity of the Monkees had something to do with the Beatles being kept from the throne. But that was wrong. In spite of a hit TV show, the Beatles had so much more to offer than the American put-together, Hollywood-invented band. When the Monkees wrote something to rival *Yesterday* or *Eleanor Rigby*, Walsh would be tempted to rethink his position. Until that time, the Monkees were pretty much irrelevant.

He suggested part of the reason for the drop in Beatles sales was simply their age and their lack of youthful enthusiasm. The original excitement, the initial exhilaration, had faded from their work. Still creative, still inventive, still fresh… but the youth was missing, the youth that communicated itself so clearly to a youthful audience. Their records were clever, polished, professional, but they were also subtle and intricate, creatively brilliant, but perhaps ahead of their audience. They had lost that initial raw appeal that had been present in those initial raw recordings… and their fans had not caught up with them.

Walsh hoped the fans and the papers would not treat the group harshly over this first failure to hit number one. Even Elvis, at the height of his career, had records that failed to make it to the top. No one was invincible.

Another reason, perhaps, for any drop in the Beatles' popularity, related to the way they were ignoring their fans, not touring, not catering. The fans were seeking more attentive heroes.

Walsh closed by inviting readers to write and express their theories about why the Beatles failed to reach the top of the charts with *Penny Lane / Strawberry Fields Forever*.

April 1, 1967 – *Disc and Music Echo* mentioned simply that Paul McCartney liked Pink Floyd and thought they would go a long way.

April 8, 1967 – *Disc and Music Echo* announced that each individual Beatle would be featured independently on the group's new LP, *Sergeant Pepper's Lonely Heart's Club Band*, due to be released in May.

George Martin said, "*The boys have been working very long and very hard on it. I shall be glad to get it finished myself. Really, we have worked every night, right through the night. This time, there will be items by all four Beatles, Ringo, George, John and Paul.*"

Martin added that the album title was also the title track. There would be twelve tracks in all, rather than the usual fourteen, because some of the tunes were quite long.

"*Even with twelve tracks,*" Martin explained, "*the album will have a longer running time than* Revolver."

A footnote mentioned that Paul McCartney flew secretly to the States that week to visit Jane Asher for her 21st birthday.

April 22, 1967 – *Disc and Music Echo*, Derek Taylor reported from Hollywood. Paul McCartney had sneaked into L.A. on Frank Sinatra's Lear Jet and was gone again before most people had even noticed him. There were rumours of his presence but nothing concrete. Rumour also had it that Ringo was in town, with George planning to show up just behind Ravi Shankar. But the reality was much simpler. Paul and Malcolm Evans were in town for thirty-six hours, during which time Paul made his way to a Beach Boys recording session, a cheerful event for all concerned. He also hooked up with John and Michelle of the Mamas and the Papas, and David Crosby and Roger McGuinn of the Byrds, then again with Brian Wilson.

Taylor said McCartney was relaxed and happy the whole time he was in town. And he spoke enthusiastically about the Beatles new album, *Sergeant Pepper's Lonely Heart's Club Band*.

April 29, 1967 – *Disc and Music Echo* announced that Ringo's wife, Maureen, was pregnant again.

Said Ringo, "*We wouldn't mind another boy, but it doesn't really matter so much this time. We'd made up our minds that we wanted a boy before.*"

Their first kid, Zak, was now eighteen months old.

More Beatles news: Madame Tussaud's Wax Museum gave their Beatles a face-lift, trying to make the group appear more modern, more in keeping with their current look.

A footnote mentioned that Barry Gibb of the Bee Gees was denying, ferociously, that their new single, *New York Mining Disaster 1941*, had been written by Lennon and McCartney. He said, "*Complete rubbish. We've always written our own songs. I've been writing since I was ten, before Lennon and McCartney were even on stage. People can say what they like. If they don't believe us, they can ask The Beatles themselves.*"

The rumours started because Lennon and McCartney had been known to write under pen names (a song for Peter and Gordon had been written under the name Bernard Gibb); and because the Bee Gees had been signed by the Beatles' management firm.

May 6, 1967 – *Record Mirror* announced that the Beatles' disc sales had topped 200,000,000 singles (an album counted as six singles, an EP four).

They went on to say that the group's newest album, *Sergeant Pepper's Lonely Heart's Club Band*, was due to be released on the 1st of June. The LP had thirteen tracks, a dozen by Lennon and McCartney and one by George Harrison.

The tracks were:
Sergeant Pepper's Lonely Heart's Club Band, Paul singing lead.
With a Little Help From My Friends, Ringo with the lead vocals.
Lucy in the Sky With Diamonds, featuring John as the lead singer.
Getting Better, Paul doing the lead.
Fixing a Hole, Paul again.
Being for the Benefit of Mr. Kite, featuring John as the lead vocalist.
Within You Without You, with George singing, backed by an assortment of Indian musicians.

When I'm 64, featuring Paul.
Lovely Rita, Paul again.
Good Morning Good Morning, John singing.
Sergeant Pepper's Lonely Heart's Club Band Reprise, Paul yet again.
And finally:
A Day in the Life, featuring both John and Paul.

May 6, 1967 – *Disc and Music Echo* reported that Beatles record sales had passed the two hundred million mark. Also, the new album, *Sergeant Pepper's Lonely Heart's Club Band,* would be out on June 1st. They reviewed the songs in order, then mentioned that all the Beatles fan club members in the UK would be receiving a twenty inch by thirty inch poster that tied in with the album.

The group was probably going to do a cameo appearance later that year in a film directed by their former official photographer, Bob Whittaker. They were to spend two or three days working on their part. The working title for the movie was *The Inner Circle*.

Also, the release date for John Lennon's first solo film, *How I Won the War,* was tentatively set for July 16th.

A spokesman for the Rank Organisation said, *"We haven't even seen the film yet, but should any day now. The London release date is likely to be July 16th."*

How I Won the War also starred Michael Crawford and Roy Kinnear, directed by Dick Lester, who also directed *A Hard Day's Night* and *Help!*

How I Won the War was expected to premiere in London a fortnight before the general release.

May 6, 1967 – *Disc and Music Echo* said one of the tracks from the Beatles' new album, *Sergeant Pepper's Lonely Heart's Club Band,* had been banned by some Los Angeles radio stations. *A Day in the Life* was apparently a drug song, therefore unsuitable for airing in L.A. *A Day in the Life* was one of four tracks from the album that had been playing in the U.S. markets. The other three tracks were *She's Leaving Home, When I'm 64* and the title song.

Since some of the radio stations had jumped the gun by playing the songs without permission, EMI was considering changing the release date to May 19th. Said music publisher, Dick James, *"Nobody knows for sure how the Americans got hold of these tracks. Certainly any one would be worth five hundred dollars to them. My American office has been getting on to the station directors, about one hundred in all, to stop these airings, and generally we are getting all possible cooperation. Of course, the album should not be broadcast until we give permission; it is restricted until the release date.*

"I cannot understand how anyone could take exception to A Day in the Life. *Certainly this is an unusual song. There is reference to a man smoking, but it is quite innocuous. How anyone could object to it, especially in the Lost Angeles area, of all places, is beyond me. I know there have been objections, but I have not heard of its being banned. But the same*

thing was said about Yellow Submarine. *That anyone could connect such a song as that with drugs is unbelievable. But it has happened."*

Derek Taylor reported from Hollywood that the people banning *A Day in the Life* were offended by the line that made reference to *"forty thousand holes in my arm."* They had, of course, gotten the lyrics wrong. The holes were in Blackburn, Lancashire. It was quite a stretch to connect this to drugs.

May 20, 1967 – *Disc and Music Echo* reviewed *Sergeant Pepper's Lonely Heart's Club Band,* the Beatles' ninth album, calling it another masterpiece, musical genius, brilliant. The first hearing left you perplexed. Subsequent hearings revealed the multi-layered sounds, the incredible intricacies, and made it obvious that no one had ever done anything quite like this album. Parlophone would be releasing the album in June. *Disc* received a review copy and worked through it track by track, concluding that this record would flatten the rest of the pop world. A beautiful and potent record, unique, clever and stunning.

May 27, 1967 – *Record Mirror*, spoke with George Martin about *Sergeant Pepper's Lonely Heart's Club Band.*

Said Martin, *"It's like painting the Forth Bridge: after spending seven hundred hours in the studio since November working on* Sergeant Pepper's Lonely Heart's Club Band, *I've been starting all over again to record more material for future Beatles' releases. We've already completed three new tracks.*

"Sergeant Pepper was certainly the most ambitious Beatles album yet. It took a long time because they're perfectionists and wanted to get the LP exactly the way they had it in their minds. They've always wanted to be one step ahead, a policy that is courageous, dangerous but inevitable, too, if they wanted to survive. Relying on a well-trusted, can't-fail formula would be ineffective as well as contrary to the Beatles' temperaments.

"Obviously, the pressure is there. When you have succeeded so tremendously you wonder if you will continue to be successful. It was almost a relief when Penny Lane did not hit number one. They'd had such a long string of consecutive number ones and they knew that sooner or later the chain would be broken. Ironically, Penny Lane has sold more copies than the previous Yellow Submarine / Eleanor Rigby single, which did get to the top place.

"The aim of Sergeant Pepper is to sound like a complete programme, ostensibly by the club band. The title song gives you the feeling of being in a hall. There are sounds of applause and laughter from the audience. Then comes a solo from Billy Shears – Ringo. Each number follows hard on the heels of the previous one and though you lose the audience sound effects during the LP we return to it at the end of side two, which concludes with animals sounds, including a hunt in full cry. A chicken clucking blends into a guitar note for the ending.

"Fortunately for me, I'd had experience of building up sound pictures, which is what the Beatles were after, through recording Peter Sellers, Spike Milligan, Michael Bentine, Peter Ustinov, and the Beyond the Fringe *team. In fact, it was those old Peter Sellers' comedy LPs that first enabled me to hit it off with the Beatles.*

"When the boys realised I'd recorded the Sellers, whom they much admired, a little of the glory rubbed off on me. But, in many ways, the Beatles and I have different ways of life. They're night people and they don't like working in the mornings. Usually we start recording at seven in the evening and work through till three. Working on Sergeant Pepper, I several times had to carry on until seven a.m. That was the most arduous part of the LP for me.

"I certainly think the result has justified the effort we put into it. On George's track, Within You Without You, we used Indian musicians, and on John's Being for the Benefit of Mr. Kite we had an organ effect like a fairground noise. I played Hammond organ, the Beatles' road managers, Mal Evans and Neil Aspinall, played mouth organs, and I added a variety of electronic effects. On other tracks, we also used string players, as many as forty-one musicians for one track.

"Whenever the Beatles put out a bunch of new compositions, there are always plenty of artists waiting to hear them and record their own versions. I discussed this with John and Paul and they liked the idea of singers we record in the AIR London stable doing covers, so I've recorded David and Jonathan on She's Leaving Home and Bernard Cribbins on When I'm Sixty-Four. They'll be released on the first of June."

May 27, 1967 – Record Mirror, Peter Jones reviewed Sergeant Pepper's Lonely Heart's Club Band track by track. He had been invited to Brian Epstein's home for a listen, along with the Beatles, and was invited to ask questions. Regarding the banning of A Day in the Life, John Lennon said, "The banners have got it all wrong. We got the idea from a newspaper headline. It's nothing to do with drugs."

All-in-all, Jones was impressed with the album. Musically, lyrically, it was clever and brilliant, from raucous to poignant and back again. The production values were advanced, the arrangements original, a truly fine album.

May 27, 1967 – Disc and Music Echo, Ray Coleman interviewed all four Beatles. He began by saying their new album was great, as relevant to 1967 as She Loves You was to 1963. They had changed somewhat over the years, grown and matured, like their music. They were no longer the four mop tops. They were maturing creative artists.

Smoking American Lark cigarettes, Ringo said, "I used to go to all the 'in clubs' round town, but life's different. Then was then, now's now. 'The Changing Beatles' and all that, course we've changed.

"I've stopped being a regular at the clubs. You know, I used to get up, have corn flakes, then eat at the clubs at night. Now, I get fed quite regularly at home.

"I dunno. People seem to think that because we're not out raving round the continent, or doing a tour here, that we're sitting at home not working. Well, we spent five nights a week, sometimes from seven o'clock till two o'clock in the morning, making this LP.

"If that's not working, man, what is? It's as hard work as a miner's. We're doing what we can do best, making records. You just can't please everybody. How can we do a tour if we think we are not going to be pleased with ourselves? People aren't soft. We've found our best work comes in making records.

"Zak's two in September, great! You can see something happening now. Well, I mean, up to six months old, it's all 'Come on, coochy-coo' and all that. But now he's growing. Maureen's fine, our second baby's due in August.

"I just enjoy staying at home. We all still see plenty of each other, we used to be forced together, and I suppose that was the difference. It was okay, but we were forced together. Then, after the American tour, John went off to make his film, George went to India and all that, and when we came back to making an LP it was so nice and fresh.

"The thing is that now we can choose when we're together instead of being forced together. Nice. I mean, it was never a drag or anything.

"And you need to break up a bit to relax, man. Revolver, that was all we could do at that time. Sergeant Pepper is all we could do this time. We could spend our whole lives making one record, but what good would it be? It'd never come out!

"Yeah, I've heard some of the American groups' records. I like some of the tracks by the Doors, but not all. I like the Buffalo Springfield and the Jefferson Airplane. Some of the Monkees' TV shows are good, we've met Mike Nesmith and Mickey Dolenz and they seem nice.

"Nice people, man, as long as they're nice people, what does anything matter? They're doing their best, same as us. That all you can do. Your best at any one time."

Arms flying, Dickensian spectacles flashing, John said, "Yeah, we should go into the Common Market. We should get right in there with the rest of them. Europe's the only place for us, unless we want to go in with the States, and we don't, because we know where they're going. The competition would be good for some of the fuddy-duddy, hamstrung, tied-up industries here. Too many of them are asleep.

"We don't want anyone thrown out of work and all that, but really, man, we've got so much to sell. Swinging Britain and that, think how we could get it across on the Continent! Some parts of the Continent haven't even got over Bill Haley yet.

"We could sell Swinging Britain so cool. They'd dig it if we did it properly. We could stand the pace if we got in there, and anyone who couldn't would have to do something else. Yeah, we should join, the faster the better.

"Nobody knows what Harold Wilson's doing now, and nobody will know until he's done it. Well, I'd rather have him than Ted Heath. I'd sooner have Labour than the Tories, but I don't like any of 'em really. None of them seems to me to be doing as much as they could for the real benefit of the people. We want a party of truth, whether it's Communist, Catholic, Tory or anything.

"God help us if the pirates go. Something else would happen, local stations, they're mumbling about, or something. Liverpool half-hour! Terrible, local radio, all run by little councils. It'd probably choke itself to death fighting over who's going to say what.

The charts?

"I read them all. I don't mind them, there's room for everything. I don't mind Humperbert Engeldinck. They're the cats. It's their scene. Pictures of Lily – yeah! It's rude, though. It's rude. They say so, you know. They do. Who are these people who think it's pornography? I'd like to meet them all and shake it out of their tiny minds, man."

The Monkees?

"Great, man, let 'em dig the Monkees. Let 'em all dig their cuddly mop-tops till they change their minds. The Monkees are up there to be screamed at. We're busy, man, just living. And we're in such a groove."

Will the Beatles tour?

"How can we tour like we used to? We can't. Touring is for them. If we toured, we'd have to take the Alexandra Palace with us, or something. We could send out four waxwork dummies of ourselves and let them stand on stage and probably make another million quid, but we don't want it.

"How can we tour when we're making the stuff like we are doing like on the new album? We can only do what we're doing. We've toured. That was then. If we do another tour, we'll probably hire London for one big happening, and we'd have us and the Stones and the Who and everybody else on it.

"Unless that happens, forget it, man. I don't want to be a mop top. For those who want mop tops, the Monkees are right up there, man.

"We didn't make any images for ourselves. You did the image-making, the papers, TV, and all that. I've never cared a toss about images. There's this big scoop about the new-look Lennon being photographed at the airport or somewhere. Who cares, man? I don't. If some photographer wants to take pictures of me and say I've changed, let him. I'm there. I only answer to myself, man, nobody else.

"Everything we do is anti-war. Everything we've ever dreamed of is anti-war. We're not joining this movement or that movement because they are condemned before they start. War is nowhere. It never was the answer to anything, and never will be. But joining societies or anything doesn't help anybody. We've got our own subtle way of getting our beliefs over. The message is there all right, man.

"I'd like to meet the man who banned this song of ours. I'd like to turn him on to what's happening. Why don't they charge the Electricity Board with spreading drugs because to get electricity, you have to 'switch on?' Hidden meanings, man. Everything depends on the way you read a thing. If they want to read drugs into our stuff, they will. But it's them that's reading it. Them!"

Ex-moptop Paul McCartney said, "If they want to ban A Day in the Life, that's their business. Drugs must have been in their minds, not ours. And the point is, banning doesn't help. It just draws attention to the subject when all the time their aim is to force attention away from it. Banning never did any good. It's just beyond me what they mean.

"The Lady Dartmouth thing over Ulysses, how many people had really got that much in their minds before the whole thing blew up? Banning forces the issue of what they're trying to cover up. It's their interpretations of it that bans it.

"To say A Day in the Life is about drugs is just rubbish. We were just trying to reflect a day in anybody's life, and John read a newspaper story about somebody digging up a road in Blackburn, Lancashire. It was like images in a dream, that was what were after. Going upstairs on a bus and having a smoke. Does that have to be about drugs? Well, the BBC thinks it might be. As a matter of fact, we meant Park Drive.

"'Every morning, I went to school; woke up, fell out of bed, dragged the comb across my hair; found my coat and hat.' The song's just about anything. It goes into a story, and it forms a dream on the top of a bus. Nobody knows what you're talking about in a song, sometimes. If they'd wanted to, they could have found plenty of double meaning. There's double meaning in anything everyone says, if you search for it.

"Still, I don't care if they ban it. There are plenty of other tracks they'll play. It's exciting, actually, reading all this, and seeing where the album ends up and the different reactions different people have to the stuff on it.

"Music's always been fun to us and it still is. We've learned lots of things and we'll still learning. We've been through an incredible scene, and because we know what it's all about, we've come out of it good.

"So much has happened nicely for us, so many things, like say, meeting the Queen, being known by a lot of influential people in the world. This could have got a big hold on us in our heads if we hadn't properly realised what was going on.

"I think the big thing was that we were never ruthless. Being ruthless is a big mistake. Being ruthless is to learn to make a quick buck or struggle in the Bronx. That was never us, and the attitude was right. I'm sure of it.

"We've put a lot into this album. But we took a lot out of it, too, in kicks. You can get down to things in the studio.

"Yeah, I've still got Martha [his pet sheep dog]. Great. When am I getting married? I dunno. Stick around."

Said serious George, "People have been asking where do the Beatles go from here ever since it all started happening for us. But everything's relative. There's always plenty to be done. Please Please Me was relative to Penny Lane, we're different people now. We've had more experience of life, environment. As long as we want to carry on doing things, it will be different. The more we live, the better we ought to be, musically, technically, as people, just everything.

"You just have to keep striving for perfection. This LP, I think it's the best we've done, but only the best we could do at the time. The next one ought to be better. That's always got to be the goal.

"We were all born as musicians. That's our gig in life, whatever your gig is in life, you have to keep trying to improve. And you should improve if you're just soaking up life, and everything that's going on. We know what we're up to at the moment, and we realise we've got to keep progressing. So, on with the show!

"We're not trying to outwit the public. The whole idea is to try a little bit to lead people into different tastes. Then, the people with enough intelligence to understand what we're trying to do will get some pleasure.

"The charts are in a terrible state in some respects but not in others. I think it's really harder for new people to come up right now, musically. The people who came up with us, the Stones and others, they're grown up, musically, and we're all branching out. But to start out, you've got to have something underneath besides just the hope that you'll be famous. I think any talk about lucky breaks is a lot of rubbish. If you're going to make it, you'll make it."

What about Hendrix?

"Yes, I like Jimi Hendrix. He's such a great fellow. At first, I thought the playing-guitar-with-my-teeth bit was a gimmick, but even when the guitar's stuck in his mouth, he's in control. He's very good and he stands out because there's just something about him, when he's standing there.

"I've got the Indian thing more in perspective now. My trip to India was so good for me. I don't fancy myself the next Ravi Shankar! I met so many sitar students and players over there, well, it sort of made me realise when I got home that I probably wouldn't ever be a star sitar player.

"But I still prefer Indian music to any other form of music. It has taken over one hundred per cent of my musical life. I'm learning all the time and it knocks me out. Ravi has taught me a lot. He's been

great. Every time I see him, it makes me want to go home and play more and get better. Just learning the sitar has inspired me.

"You know how God is a sort of untouchable thing? Well, that's how it is with Indian music. It's a very spiritual thing, so subtle and related to philosophy and life. I still love rock, pop and electronic music. But there's more to get immersed in for me in Indian. I shall try to write more songs, and I think it can all be integrated into the Beatles quite nicely if I can keep improving.

"It's not easy to understand the music at first, but it's beautiful when you get it. You can't deny Indian music. It will win out in the end."

Footnotes mentioned that the Beatles had attended a Rolling Stones recording session. Said Paul, "They did some great stuff."

The title for Sergeant Pepper's Lonely Heart's Club Band came from Paul and Mal Evans.

Lennon had been losing weight. He said, "I just didn't fancy eating so much."

Neil Aspinall played an Indian instrument on Within You Without You.

A Day In The Life had a seemingly silent moment. In fact, though, there was a harmonium sound which could be heard by dogs.

Even the Beatles would have to wait for a table at London's West End nightclub, The Bag o' Nails. During the recording of Sergeant Pepper's Lonely Heart's Club Band, John and Paul would often drop by for a drink, but no one at the Bag o' Nails received preferential treatment. All stars were created equal. And no one who went to the club was bothered by photographers, reporters or the public.

May 27, 1967 – Disc and Music Echo said the Beatles were about to make history yet again. They were to star in a two-hour special for BBC-TV, a show that would be broadcast on Sunday, June 25th from five satellites to five hundred million people in thirty-one countries.

The Beatles were to be shown recording a song at the Abbey Road studios, a special composition by John and Paul.

The show was to be called Our World. The Beatles segment would be screened approximately half-way through the production.

Sergeant Pepper's Lonely Heart's Club Band was to be rush-released the following day rather than on June 1st, as originally planned. It had already run into trouble with the BBC. A Day in the Life had been banned because, said a BBC spokesman, "It might encourage a permissive attitude to drug-taking."

A footnote mentioned that the Beatles were planning a full-colour TV special based on Sergeant Pepper's Lonely Heart's Club Band. No details were available.

Also, a twenty by thirty inch poster had been sent out to all the British members of the Beatles Fan

Club. The picture featured the group in the bandsmen uniforms that they wore on *Sergeant Pepper's Lonely Heart's Club Band* album cover.

May 27, 1967 – *Melody Maker*, Jack Hutton attended the "listen-in" at Brian Epstein's home to hear *Sergeant Pepper's Lonely Heart's Club Band*. Food was served by waiters. Champagne flowed freely. And all the Beatles were in attendance.

Regarding *A Day in the Life* being banned, Paul said, "*John woke up one morning and read the* Daily Mail. *The news stories gave him ideas for the song. The man goes upstairs on a bus for a smoke. Everybody does that kind of thing. But what does the BBC say? Smoking? SMOKING? S-M-O-K-I-N-G? Well, BBC, he was actually smoking Park Drive! Even people at the BBC do these things. So, let's face it, BBC! You can read a double meaning into anything, if you want to. But we don't care if they ban our songs. It might help the LP. They'll play the other tracks.*

"*It's exciting to see the way an LP goes. To see how many different things can be taken from it.*"

When it was suggested that *Sergeant Pepper's Lonely Heart's Club Band* might be the Beatles' last album, both John and Paul laughed.

"*Rubbish,*" said Lennon. "*No more tours, no more mop tops. We could never hear ourselves playing properly. Anyway, what more could we do after playing to fifty-six thousand people? What next? More fame? More money?*

"*We were traveling all over the world and couldn't move outside our hotel.*"

Now, they wanted to give to their fans through their albums, without all the fuss.

Paul said, "*I even went on a bus from Liverpool to Chester the other day without much trouble. There was just a mustache involved. And nearly every morning, I take my dog for a walk in Regents Park.*"

Hutton said Lennon and McCartney were constantly expanding the scope of their musical ideas, ideas that embrace a whole new world of sound.

Said John, "*I don't practise. I only played guitar to accompany myself singing. You could study all your life and become the best bassoonist in Israel. So what? I like producing records. I want to do it all. I want a machine that produces all sounds. Studying music was like learning French. If there was a new method of learning music, yeah. But the present method is archaic.*"

"*We were never musicians,*" Paul said. "*In Hamburg, we got a lot of practice. But reading music for us is unnecessary.*"

For *A Day in the Life,* Paul had conducted a forty-one piece orchestra. At first, he was slightly embarrassed. He said, "*So I decided to treat them like human beings and not professional musicians. I tried to give myself to them. We chatted and drank champagne.*"

John added, "*Classical players are best on records. They can play anything. Jazzmen are the*

worst. *They can only play from there to there...*" He spread his hands two inches apart. "*And they all want to sound like Ronnie Scott or somebody else.*"

Regarding Dixieland and mainstream jazz, Lennon said, "*It's dying, man, like Black and White Minstrels. I like John Coltrane but I don't get to the clubs much because it's embarrassing. The so-called experts laugh at you – 'there's a Beatle in the audience, folks.' It's probably my blame, but that's what I feel.*"

June 3, 1967 – *Melody Maker* wondered who were the Beatles' greatest influences. Strauss, perhaps? Ravi Shankar? George Formby? Lonnie Donegan? Some ancient schoolteacher stranded in their childhood memories?

The Beatles liked to tell stories with their music, most especially stories about odd women. *Eleanor Rigby* was the one featured on *Revolver.* And on the new album, *Sergeant Pepper's Lonely Hearts Club Band,* it was *Lovely Rita* the meter maid.

Whatever their influences, whatever their inspiration, the Beatles had yet again launched a masterpiece of creativity and achievement. A number of the tracks were already being covered by other artists, Bernard Cribbins, David and Jonathan, and others.

Some people were suggesting this was to be the Beatles last album. The writer hoped that was not the case.

This new album was an extraordinary, valuable and meaningful contribution to the world's music.

June 10, 1967 – *Disc and Music Echo*, David Hughes wondered who Sergeant Pepper really was, that mysterious gent who managed to convince the four most expensive rock and rollers in the world to play in his Lonely Heart's Club Band.

The hunt began.

First, Hughes called the Chelsea Barracks in London, asking the switchboard girl if he could speak with Sergeant Pepper.

She said, *"Sergeant Pepper? Never heard of him. Which company is he in?"*

Hughes said he was not sure but he was pretty sure the sergeant was in the band.

The switchboard girl asked, *"But we have five bands here, you know. Hang on a minute, please."*

A new voice came on the line. *"Coldstream band. Who? No, we've no one of that name. Sure you don't want Sergeant Perkins, one of our trumpeters?"*

Perhaps the good sergeant was from the North. Hughes called up to Yorkshire and spoke with an orderly of the Royal Army Corps in Catterick.

Said the orderly, *"Pepper? Well, he's not in the Signals' Band, sir, but I'll give you the extensions of the others. We've got the Tanks Band, the Lancashire Band, the Alamein Band, and the Royal Irish Fusiliers Band."*

On to the next orderly. *"Who? How do you spell that?"*

And the next. *"That's not an Irish name, is it now?"*

Was there a band up there known a the Lonely Hearts Club Band?

"Do you mind, sir? None of our bands have nicknames."

Hopeless. Where on earth was Sergeant Pepper?

Maybe the Southeast, the garden of England, the Queen's Regiments at Canterbury.

Said the orderly, *"Sorry, no Sergeant Peppers here, sir. Oh, in the band you say. Hang on a minute. No, sorry, sir. All the junior soldiers are out on the playing field. Can you ring back later?"*

Maybe out West, the Somerset and Cornwall Light Infantry.

New orderly, *"Sorry, you did say Piper, didn't you? Oh, Pepper... no, I'm afraid not. You might like to talk to Sergeant Chapman, though, if it's about Aden."*

Okay, the last stop: Whitehall.

But the press officer at Whitehall caught on immediately, saying, *"We don't usually encourage stunts of this kind. We deal in hard news, you know. And if I may say so, sir, we have a rather more important matter on our hands at the moment – a possible war, for example."*

Click.

And down to defeat. There was no Sergeant Pepper to be found. The mystery man would remain a mystery.

June 10, 1967 – *Melody Maker*, Bob Dawbarn quoted the *Times* headline that proclaimed, "The Beatles revive hopes of progress in pop music."

Top People were reading serious stories about Pop People.

A TV discussion had Paul Jones and George Martin attempting to answer the question, "Is pop music art?"

Dawbarn said that at least a portion of today's pop music could not be dismissed as junk produced for adolescents. Pop musicians were beginning to create serious work, led by the Beatles.

July 1, 1967 – *Disc and Music Echo* announced that the Beatles' new single, *All You Need is Love*, was to be rush-released around the world. It was the song Paul and John had written for the Beatles' segment of the BBC show, Our World.

The B side was another Lennon / McCartney tune, *Baby You're a Rich Man,* a song that was originally written for the group's animated film *Yellow Submarine.* They were hard a work writing a new song for the film.

Paul, John and George all sang on the A and B sides of the new record with John taking the lead on both. *All You Need is Love* was the first song John and Paul had written for a specific special occasion. Thirteen session musicians accompanied them at EMI's St. John's Wood Studios.

The group's last single, *Penny Lane / Strawberry Fields Forever,* had been released four months ago. Within that space of time, the band had produced two singles and one entire album. The previous year during the same time period, they had managed only one single. This was their most prolific output since 1963.

Production of an hour-long TV special based on *Sergeant Pepper's Lonely Hearts Club Band* had been suspended while the Beatles created new material for the animated film, *Yellow Submarine*. The special was now planned to be shot sometime before the end of August, nothing definite. It would be produced and written by the Beatles themselves. Lennon and McCartney had a new song around which the show would be constructed. The backgrounds had already been recorded, vocals were pending. Originally, the song was intended as a single but would now likely be on their next album, which was to be released in the fall.

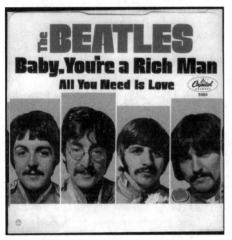

July 1, 1967 – *Disc and Music Echo,* **Penny Valentine wrote** *All You Need is Love* proves the Beatles are well into the flower era. Sung by John, it was a brilliant example of how the Beatles can take a simple set of lyrics and a simple composition and magically turn it into something glorious.

Singing along with the Beatles at the recording session were: Mick Jagger, Marianne Faithful, Keith Richards, Keith Moon, Mike McGear, Eric Clapton, Jane Asher, Graham Nash, Rose Nash and Gary Leeds.

July 1, 1967 – *Melody Maker* **announced** *All You Need is Love* was a surprise new single from the Beatles, the song John and Paul wrote for the Our World TV special.

Tapes of the song were rushed to New York, and Parlophone was planning to have the record in British shops within two weeks.

The flip side was *Baby You're a Rich Man,* also a Lennon / McCartney creation, originally slotted for the sound track of their new animated movie *Yellow Submarine.*

Thirteen session men backed the band for *All You Need is Love,* and the final vocal tracks were added live during the television showing.

The Beatles' last single, *Penny Lane,* had been released four months previously. A Beatles' spokesman said, *"By this time last year, the Beatles had only released one single. In 1967,*

they have released two singles and an LP in four months. It's the most prolific output rate since the early days in 1963."

Originally, the group had planned to make a TV special based on their album *Sergeant Pepper's Lonely Hearts Club Band.* Now, they would work on new material for the special. The show would be written and produced by the Beatles and would feature guests. They were also planning a new album for release in the autumn.

July 1, 1967 – *Melody Maker* **ran a poll** to get a general public opinion of Paul McCartney's unrepentant announcement to the world that he had tried LSD. They wondered about the wisdom of that decision and interviewed one hundred teenagers throughout Britain. They asked four questions: Was it a mistake for Paul to announce he had taken LSD? Would the fact that Paul had tried it inspire you to try it? Should LSD be legal or illegal? Do any of your friends or acquaintances take LSD?

Question One: Fifty-seven people said Paul was wrong to confess he had taken acid. Thirty-seven thought he was right to tell the world. Three were not sure. And three thought he was lying, that it was all just a publicity stunt.

Question Two: Ninety-six claimed that McCartney could not influence them to try the drug. Two were unsure. And two thought they might give it a try because Paul had.

Question Three: Seventy-six thought acid should be illegal. Eighteen thought it should be legal. Six were uncertain.

Question Four: Eighty-nine said they did not know anyone who had tried LSD. Four were unsure. And seven said they did know some acid users.

In summation, *Melody Maker* said the majority of British teenagers believed acid to be evil, believed McCartney wrong to have announced taking it. And they would not be trying it themselves.

July 8, 1967 – *Melody Maker* **ran** a photograph of John, Paul and George playing trumpets while Brian Epstein looked on. They said the Beatles were "having a blow."

July 8, 1967 – Nick Jones wrote for *Melody Maker…* The Beatles' *All You Need is Love* was a calculated catchy singsong recorded live in front of an audience of four million during the BBC's satellite-broadcast special *Our World.* It was a straight forward commercial song, beautiful, and much easier to hear than *Strawberry Fields.* The message was love and Jones hoped the world was listening.

The B side, *Baby You're a Rich Man,* was pleasing and was sure to be played a lot.

July 16, 1967 – *Melody Maker* **announced** that the Beatles new single, *All You Need is Love,* had hit the charts at number three, three days after its release. A spokesman for EMI said, *"The record has sold almost three hundred thousand copies already."*

A spokesman for NEMS said, *"There is no news for the Beatles at present. There is nothing on the TV spectacular or their third film."*

July 22, 1967 – Disc and Music Echo said the Beatles were back! But their new direction, their new musical style, was creating serious problems for the producer of Top of the Pops, Johnnie Stewart. He did not know how to present them these days. They could not go on the show to play live since all the new stuff was studio work.

There was of course the BBC film of *All You Need is Love…* *"But,"* Stewart explained, *"Once is enough for that. People soon tire of seeing the same film over and over again."*

The Beatles were likely to hold the top of the charts for the next few weeks and Stewart needed to present them to his audience. He said, *"It's the same every time the Beatles have a new release. Previously, we've got by, using their film, but there doesn't seem to be any available this time; and I'm desperately hoping Eppy will relent and we can have them actually on the show."*

The group's last appearance on Top of the Pops had been a year ago when they were promoting *Paperback Writer.*

July 22, 1967 – Bob Farmer wrote for Disc and Music Echo… about *How I Won the War* and how John Lennon had been branded a fascist, a thief, a scrounger… for the movie.

Said director Dick Lester, *"John Lennon has to be a real louse. But he does have his moment of glory by showing some courage when the crunch comes in the film."*

The film was the story of a World War Two platoon commanded by Michael Crawford. John Lennon, as Gripweed, was his batman.

Lester continued, *"There is no real story, as such. It's a series of flashbacks between 1939 and the 1960s, recounting the platoon's vivid memories of the war, in the desert and crossing the Rhine, and their attitudes as to what the war accomplished twenty-five years afterwards.*

"It's a bit involved to explain, but I think it will appeal to a wide audience. Really, it's a comic film, but the comedy is for a serious purpose.

"Well, it's easy to imply that we used John as a box office gimmick, but to avoid these accusations, we've shunned publicity about the picture, which is why there are still no sneak showings for the press. We didn't want hordes of Beatle fans about when we were on location in Spain and Germany, because we wanted to give John a fair chance to act without distraction."

Was he any good?

"As an actor, he's very good. Actually, his is a relatively minor role. He has about the sixth largest part in the script. But although he really set about proving to himself that he could act, I don't say he has any great ambitions towards acting."

If John was not simply a ploy for the box office, why did he get the role?

"The part fitted John better than any of the other Beatles. And I chose him because I wanted actors who were completely different in terms of their acting technique, but who had an appeal to the audience. A group, in fact, who were interesting in their own right, rather than a platoon of straight actors. And John fitted in just fine.

"There is no definite release date, other than to say it'll be the early autumn."

Would there be another Beatles film?

"Another Beatles film? Will there be one? One's been due for two years. Still, there's no point in making a film for the sake of it."

July 22, 1967 – Melody Maker again ran the photograph of George, John and Paul playing trumpets while Epstein watched. The caption, though, announced that the Beatles were back on top. *All You Need is Love* had hit number one, bumping the Monkees from the top spot.

A spokesman for NEMS said, *"Apart from the record's success, there is absolutely no fresh news about the group at the moment."*

Said George Harrison, *"Fab. Gear. It's great, you know, because we never really expect these things to happen."*

Added Ringo, *"We've got love."*

Another article on the front page talked about a super session, an experimental session, arranged by Paul McCartney and Graham Nash in London the previous week. None of the musicians involved would comment on it; all of them had contracts with different recording companies.

Attending the recording session were: McCartney and Nash, of course; Spencer Davis; Dave Mason of Traffic; Gary Leeds; Barry Fantoni and the Scaffold, including Mike McGear.

The chance of any sort of release from this effort was quite remote.

July 22, 1967 – Melody Maker, Mike Hennessey spoke with Brian Epstein about the Beatles' new music in general, *All You Need is Love* in particular.

Epstein said this had been a particularly good week. *"It began last weekend when all the Beatles stayed at my house in Sussex. Then I went to Knokke to see the NEMS team score top marks in the European Cup. And now* All You Need is Love *is in the top three."*

The Beatles' ability to continually create super-hits was astonishing.

Said Epstein, *"I've never had a moment's worry that they wouldn't come up with something marvelous. The commitment for the TV programme was arranged some months ago. The time got nearer and nearer and they still hadn't written anything. Then about three weeks before the programme, they sat down to write. The record was completed in ten days.*

"For me, All You Need is Love *is the best thing they've done, at the moment. But I'm not surprised that it is such a huge success because I have such great faith in the Beatles.*

"This is an inspired song because they wrote it for a worldwide programme and they really wanted to give the world a message. It could hardly have been a better message. It is a wonderful, beautiful, spine-chilling record."

Hennessey said it was almost a distillation of the group's entire musical output from *She Loves You* to *Sergeant Pepper's Lonely Hearts Club Band.*

Brian agreed, saying, *"The nice thing about the record, too, is that it cannot be misinterpreted. It is a clear message saying that love is everything. When you say* All You Need is Love *you are saying everything."*

Regarding the Beatles' control over what they recorded, Epstein said, *"I would say they are even more involved now than before. I think the new single is a bit more John than Paul, but, of course, they worked very closely together. There were thirteen other musicians on the record including violins, cellos and trumpets, and Ringo played drums throughout. There was no other percussion. The record is exactly the same as the TV performance, except for a re-mix when John's voice was put on again.*

"I think it is certain to be a number one in Britain and America. I've just heard today that it is being played to death in the States. And the Sergeant Pepper *LP has sold more than four hundred thousand in Britain and well over a million in America, it's really fantastic."*

Would the group be doing any more concerts?

"No, not in the usual form. What they are doing now is working towards a TV programme for worldwide distribution, and they also want to make a film, but they want complete freedom to do it their way. They want to create all of it, with a little help from their friends.

"They feel they can manage the sound, so why not the visual side as well? We all know about visual things and there are good people in NEMS capable of helping with this."

July 22, 1967 – *Melody Maker***'s Mail Bag published** a letter from a reader saying the Beatles should not be called unmusical conmen. Another letter on the same subject wondered what the Beatles newest musical efforts would sound like without the competent backing of professional session men.

August 5, 1967 – *Disc and Music Echo* **quoted** Paul McCartney as being *"pleased"* that Mick Jagger and Keith Richards were not jailed over drug charges. *"I'm always pleased about the idea of people not going to jail,"* said Paul.

Paul and Jane Asher, along with John and Cynthia Lennon, had just returned from a holiday in Greece.

August 5, 1967 – *Melody Maker***, Mike Hennessey interviewed Brian Epstein. Part One:**

Hennessey said that Epstein's announcement about taking LSD was being attacked as irresponsible because it might influence people to try the drug. He wished to know Brian's reaction to that.

Said Epstein, *"Let me tell you the background to this. Paul rang me one Saturday to tell me that he had admitted to the press that he had taken LSD. At that time, I was very worried. I don't think I slept that night, and I thought about it all the following day. Then I came up to London on the Monday knowing I was going to be asked to comment on Paul's admission. I finally decided to admit that I had taken LSD as well.*

"There were several reasons for this. One was certainly to make things easier for Paul. People don't particularly enjoy being lone wolves; and I didn't feel like being dishonest and covering up, especially as I believe that an awful lot of good has come from hallucinatory drugs.

"People tend to think of San Francisco hippies as dirty and unhappy, but, in fact, they are doing rather better things than the people who lead our nation. Coupled with my admission was a warning that neither Paul nor I advocated the general use of LSD by all and sundry. We issued a statement to this effect. So my intention was, to a certain extent, to warn as well as to own up. There is also another factor in this. We wanted to help the cause of the Rolling Stones. It is particularly unfortunate that they should have been scapegoats."

Why try LSD?

"I'd heard a lot of good about it and I had sufficient understanding of it to know what I was doing. I had also read a lot about it."

Did the Beatles take it *after* Epstein?

"No. But we are a closely knit circle and we influence each other. All five of us come from Liverpool and lived within a few hundred yards of each other. In fact, the circle is even wider because Neil, Mal, Alistair Taylor and Peter Brown are also from the same background."

Had he done it often?

"About five times in the last fourteen months."

Had he quit taking it?

"I don't know."

Did he feel a need to take drugs?

"No, it was an experiment."

Had he smoke pot?

"Yes, from time to time. I really believe that pot, marijuana or hash, whatever you like to call it, is less harmful without question, than say, alcohol. I think there is a terrific misunderstanding about marijuana and its effects. So many people have said it must be bad that this verdict is accepted without question and, of course, there is the malicious association between

drugs and pop music. I think society's whole attitude to soft drugs must eventually change. There is a parallel with homosexuality when that was a cardinal sin. Isn't it silly that we have had to wait all this time for reforming legislation to go through?"

Did he support the new law that made homosexuality legal?

"Of course! In fact, the majority of people do, I'm certain. You hear of very few prosecutions for homosexual offenses these days."

Back to soft drugs, did he think there was a danger that the marijuana pushers would try to hook their customers on harder drugs?

"The laws governing soft drugs principally create the danger. But the danger exists already with alcoholics who turn on to hard drugs. I think, however, that the danger is remote in the present context. None of the people I know who smoke pot are interested in harder drugs. They are certainly aware of the dangers involved."

Was he not worried when he smoked marijuana and took LSD that he would become an addict?

"I did have some apprehension, but I took that risk. But then, I am in no way addicted to alcohol and seldom smoke cigarettes."

Did he know that LSD could be very harmful with, sometimes, deadly effects?

"It is true that LSD affects different people in different ways. Some people are supposed to have bad experiences. There was a terrible programme on television the other night when a panel of so-called experts talked a lot of nonsense about the drug. People who have had a bad experience are really few and far between, certainly not as numerous as the people who have died from overdoses of alcohol. And in any case, we don't know the details of these cases. They may have mixed alcohol with LSD. I certainly didn't feel I wanted to fly or jump off a ledge."

Could he explain what he felt?

"The feeling is too impressive and personal to convey in words. I know that I have sometimes had too much to drink and felt awful and unpleasant the morning after. But I have never had a hangover from smoking pot or taking LSD. I think LSD helped me to know myself better and I think it helped me to become less bad-tempered."

Was he often bad-tempered?

"Yes."

What were some of his other failings?

"Well, I reproach myself most often for being bad-tempered and for being mean from time to time. When I'm rude or mean to somebody, it takes me days to get over it."

What traits did he dislike the most in other people?

"I dislike ignorance, pettiness and prejudice. On the other hand, egomaniacs don't put me off. I think I, myself, have overcome a very large ego, so I'm very forgiving and tolerant or egomaniacs. There

are a lot them about and some of them are very brilliant and clever. I think this is the one failing one must be tolerant of.

"I also dislike dictatorship and I've never tried to dictate to my artists, although I'm aware that I command quite a bit of respect. The manager-artist relationship is one of mutual dependence, and one of the most perfect relationships there has ever been, in my experience, is that which exists between the Beatles and myself. If I'd been domineering or dictatorial, they would never have accepted me and it would all have gone wrong. You have to allow for freedom. You can easily be cut down to size in certain situations and you realise that humility is very important. When you waffle a great deal and it has no effect, you realise that you have to modify your attitude."

Had the Beatles re-sized his ego for him?

"Yes, they influenced me, and I think I influenced them. They are, after all, the Beatles. I also think that LSD had probably lessened my ego."

Years ago Epstein had said he needed to find a creative outlet. Did that still frustrate him?

"Whatever may have happened in the intervening time, I have learned to live with the idea that I'm the Beatles' manager. I'm a creative person to a degree, but the biggest thing that has ever happened to me is the Beatles. I have overcome the feelings of frustration, but the Beatles always make an effort to involve me in what they are doing. And they do involve me. They wanted me to sit in on the TV thing, but I wanted to watch it come over on TV so I wasn't there. And I'm still very nervous of cameras."

What did he fear most?

"Loneliness. I hope I'll never be lonely. Although, actually, one inflicts loneliness on oneself, to a certain extent."

August 12, 1967 – Melody Maker, Mike Hennessey interviewed Brian Epstein. Part Two:

Epstein had said loneliness was the thing he most feared. Had he considered getting married?

"Yes. Very often. I'd like it to happen, if it could happen. Apart from the companionship it represents, I would welcome it because I get very put out having to run two homes on my own."

Did he think he would get married anytime soon?

"No."

Why? Because of his attitude? Lack of prospects?

"I think because of me."

What traits did he want to find in a woman?

"Simplicity, understanding, and a loveliness that appeals to me."

Had he met one with those qualities?

"Of course I have, I've been introduced to many whom I would have liked to get to know better, but it just hasn't happened."

Did he like the company of women?

"Sometimes."

But he was certain he would not be getting married any time soon?

"I think the wish is slightly idealistic and unlikely to be fulfilled. But it is one of the biggest disappointments to me because I must be missing out somewhere, not having a wife and children. I would love to have children."

Had he encountered any anti-Jewish sentiments?

"I've been very lucky. But I think a lot of anti-Jewish prejudice is occasioned not by people who are anti-Semitic but by those who are affected by it. In other words, Jewish people sometimes have a defensive attitude because they expect *a hostile reception.*

"Funnily enough, I was with a man the other evening who commented on the fact that I was staying at a hotel run by Jews. 'But I am a Jew,' I told him. He was very embarrassed and said quickly, 'Yes, but the owners of that hotel are not very nice Jews.' Well, they may not have been very nice, I didn't meet them. But if they were not nice it was not because they were Jews. There are unpleasant Jews, Catholics, Protestants, and so on."

Hennessey had heard Epstein was asked to help with the Israeli cause and said no. Why was that?

"I refused to help because I'm as sorry for a wounded Arab as I am for a wounded Israeli. People fundamentally are all the same and I can't discriminate between Israelis and Arabs."

Were his Jewish friends upset that he refused?

"I think Bernard Delfont and Cyril Shane, who were among many who particularly asked me to help, were somewhat surprised at my negative reaction! But I can't help it. I feel that people should have no greater concern for the suffering of one race than they have for any other. I believe in and want to help, as far as I can do, to understand mankind whatever colour, creed, religion or nationality. And I think this sort of philosophy, however broad and general it sounds, is the only basic one the leaders of the world car work from to attain world peace."

Was being Jewish an important thing for him?

"Yes, naturally it figures necessarily in my thought. There are many beautiful and good things written in the scriptures and prayers, which I believe to be good and true. However, I find it difficult to accept religion of any kind in a ritualistic form. I find myself uneasy and unable to comprehend so much within the precincts of a Jewish house of worship. Indeed, the same would apply to any house of worship. But, because I'm of Jewish parentage, I find myself respectful and tolerant. I love my family dearly."

Had he prayed?

"Yes, I prayed as a child. I loosely studied Judaism and other religions. At school, I found myself interested in Roman Catholicism. I think that belief in life and God that ever prevails is better than ritualistic and religious praying."

Was there any reason to associate Jews with being cheap?

"No, I don't think so. Everybody is a bit mean. I'm mean because, although I know I've got enough money, I'll suddenly put the brake on and think, 'I can't carry on like this forever.'"

He had received a lot from life. What had he given back?

"I have done what I can and will continue to do so. People who criticise me may have a point and may be sincere, but it doesn't matter what they say. I know I have done my best. People get too wound up and serious. I've been rude to people in my life, too, but one discovers that it is quite unnecessary. During the very, very active period of Beatles management, I maintained as much calm and gave them as much of a boost to their morale as I could. I would agree that I was particularly lucky to have found them in the first place, but maybe it was destined to happen. That, to a certain extent, is what I believe."

Was he political?

"I am becoming more and more politically minded. I feel strongly about some issues and the main problem, not only in Vietnam but throughout the world, is that politicians are not single-minded in their beliefs. I think so many politicians allow so many other pressures to bear on them, restricting truthful and honest thought."

Did his politics lean to the left or to the right?

"I suppose I'm left, really, and I think I always have been."

What would he like to see in the way of social reform?

"I would like to see more tolerance all round, more understanding and less ignorance by those who consider themselves the leaders of the country."

Was the Rolling Stones' trial an example of misunderstanding and intolerance?

"I think it was an appalling mess which should never have reached the stage it did. On the other hand, maybe we will be grateful in the future that they were scapegoats. I really think the press interest in the Rolling Stones and drugs is in excess of the public interest."

Had he ever felt despair?

"There have been many instances throughout my successful, semi-successful and failure periods."

Had he ever considered suicide?

"Yes. But I think I've got over that period now."

Aside from managing the Beatles and running NEMS, what interested him?

"I have a natural curiosity about everything. And, at present, I am very keen on Spanish things. Also, I'm now very involved with my Sussex home which I bought five months ago."

How much was it?

"About thirty thousand pounds. I moved in with just the hangings and the carpets and now I'm enjoying installing bits and pieces of furniture and pictures."

When he was not working, where did he like to spend his time?

"Either in Sussex or New York. I'm greatly attracted to New York and feel great in that environment. It is a beautiful city. Fortunately, I'm also able to work from either place."

What did he think of the Flower Power scene?

"Flower power is becoming a tiny bit of a drag. It's becoming a cliché and a fashionable cult. I'm currently wondering whether the cult is not slightly akin to rock and roll, Merseybeat, Swinging London and so on. Basically, there's a lot to be said for the general attitude and, if the move is in this direction, which is toward love and things, could grow throughout the world, we might find this planet a better place to be living on. There is certainly nothing wrong with the attitudes expressed by the flower children. I think I've been a flower child all my life, but I hope the mood will progress and not become a commercial businessman's paradise, because then it defeats its purpose. There are some signs of this but the attitude is so good, sincere and lovely that one cannot but help be happy to be in its midst. It's an international feeling so I cannot differentiate."

August 19, 1967 – *Record Mirror,* **Peter Jones reviewed** *How I Won the War,* which featured John Lennon as Private Gripweed.

After a special showing of the film, an unidentified someone said, *"Any resemblance between this film and any other war film is extremely unlikely."*

Jones went on to say the movie was brilliant, funny, strange, a bit warped and somewhat sickening. He thought it was realistic, hilarious and frightening, as well as true to Patrick Ryan's book. As an afterthought, he mentioned that Lennon was good in the part of Gripweed.

August 19, 1967 – *Disc and Music Echo* **mentioned** that Ringo was about to be a father again. Maureen was due to give birth to their second child very soon.

August 19, 1967 – *Disc and Music Echo,* **Penny Valentine reviewed** *How I Won the War.* She started by saying that John Lennon was blown up towards the end of the film. She described him attempting to hold his stomach together just before he died. She used that to explain why she believed Lennon could actually play serious roles. Gripweed was a working-class man from Liverpool, insolent and witty, funny and clever, truly well-acted by Lennon.

How I Won the War was a very good, anti-war film, dedicated to the folly of man. But if fans were going to see a Beatle, if fans were going to indulge their lust for Beatlemania, they would be sadly disappointed. This was not about Beatles, this was about the stupidity and the misery of war.

August 19, 1967 – Derek Taylor wrote from Los Angeles for *Disc and Music Echo…* about George and Patti Harrison's trip to L.A. to attend a Ravi Shankar concert. A huge crowd was on hand at the airport as they arrived and, though they managed to dodge the crowd, there was no getting away from the journalists and their barrage of questions: What are you trying to say about marijuana… How come you do not tour any more… How old is your wife… What are you here for… Do you still like cheese slices and small blondes…

Eventually, they escaped the airport to stay at a private house on a street called Blue Jay Way. The following morning, George joined Ravi Shankar for a press conference, which happened in two phases.

Phase one was with the Establishment people. George was wearing a string of beads around his neck and a reporter wanted to know what he was wearing.

Said George, *"It's a necklace."* After a pause, he added, *"I got them in Greece and they've got magic eyes in the beads."*

What magic?

"My magic," replied George.

They asked about marijuana, LSD, et cetera. It was all very pleasant and relaxed.

"Will you be performing with Mr. Shankar, George?"

"No."

"What do you think of the Beatles, Mr. Shankar?"

"I like them. Although it is pop music, I like them very much. I hear good things in their music. They are unusually advanced. They are exceptional."

They talked about the forthcoming concert, about whether or not George was a good pupil, and was the sitar a gimmick…

"No."

As the regular press began to leave, the underground press began to arrive. Ravi Shankar also left and George confronted them alone. They sat at his feet, amazed that he was there, that he was real, they he could talk and smile and laugh just like any other human being.

Quite seriously, George said that drugs were not the answer to anything. *"I mean, we all know it isn't, don't we? So it's better to try and do without, isn't it?"*

Harrison spent the rest of the day shopping. The concert was the following day, at the Hollywood Bowl. It was suggested that George's presence did give ticket sales a boost. Eighteen thousand people attended the show.

Afterwards, they wandered around the city. On Monday, they flew to San Francisco for a visit to Haight-Ashbury to view the *Great Happening* first hand. But there was no evidence that the *good* people there were providing a serious alternative to the *bad* people of Madison Avenue.

After San Francisco, they went on to Monterey and the warm sands of Carmel.

Taylor concluded by saying that, singly or together, the Beatles were truly one of the world's great treasures.

August 19, 1967 – *Melody Maker*, Harry Pules reported from San Francisco…

Harrison was leading a pied piper march through Haight-Ashbury when someone, embracing him, said, *"You are our leader, George."*

"No. Wrong," said George.

"Oh yes, man," said the *hippie*, trotting to keep up with the crowd that was marching eight abreast up Haight Street, a thousand or more. *"You know where it's at, man."*

"It's you who should be leading yourself," explained George. *"You don't want to be following leaders, me or anyone else."*

"Too much!"

The crowd surged and danced around them and someone shouted, *"Hey, man, I gotta turn George on. Let me through. I got to lay some STP on him, man. Let me get to him, man."*

Later, George said, *"I heard him the first time, five minutes before he actually got to me. But I tried to ignore it, hoping it wasn't going to happen."*

"I got the STP, man," he insisted.

Others demanded, *"Give us some, man. Us too, man. Lay it on us. Let's do our thing all together with George."*

A purple pill was thrust towards George, the voice behind the hand saying, *"Here, George. I got the stuff to lay on you, man. STP, man. Blow your mind."*

Harrison said, *"No. Take it away. That's bullshit, man. Karma Yoga, remember? It isn't the answer. The answer's in your own head. Isn't it? I don't want that. Get away and thanks anyway."*

The kid with the pill faded away for just a moment, appearing again as Harrison and company were back in the car and attempting to leave.

Running along beside the car, hurt and angry, he shouted, *"Hey, George, I tried to give you a gift that would turn you on, man, and you put me down, man. I don't like that, man. That was wrong, man."*

"No, it wasn't. You don't need it," George said.

"You put me down!"

Later, George said, *"It's soft. He'll have to help himself. He has a choice."*

The trip through Haight-Ashbury had been exhilarating, interesting, fascinating. But, talking about the Indian music and philosophy, George said, *"This is still it. Ravi and all them are still right. This is where it is."*

What had George expected from his visit to Haight-Ashbury?

He was not sure. Perhaps kindred spirits, perhaps people who believed, as he did, in the liberation of the human soul… people who weren't chained the accepted standards of society.

He found kindness, generosity… He found pot and acid and STP… He found laughter and fun. And he found magic in the moment.

August 19, 1967 – *Melody Maker*, Mike Hennessey interviewed Brian Epstein. Part Three:

When his contract ran out with the Beatles later that year, did he have any doubts that they would sign again with him?

"No, I don't. I don't think they mind how long I sign them for. A contract doesn't mean much unless you can work and be happy together. And I am certain that they would not agree to be managed by anyone else. Obviously, I wouldn't, and couldn't, make them do anything they didn't want because of any legal rights I hold. Most of the time, we think in the same direction anyway. And so we just groove along. In fact, the principal value of a contract between us is really for the benefit of the lawyers, accountants and all that scene, because those people always think these things should be proved on paper."

When did he sign them up?

"In December, 1961, after hearing them at the Cavern in November."

The myth said he went to see them after so many people requested their record at his record store. Was that right?

"More or less. At the time, I was getting very bored with what I was doing. I'd been selling records in my families' stores for about five years and had attained just about as much success in that sphere as possible. I'd tried window dressing, selling furniture, soldiering, selling books in Charing Cross Road with varying degrees of success, and, just about that time, I was looking for something challenging and exciting."

He must be asked all the time if he had been aware of how big the Beatles would be when he signed them.

"I never had any doubts that they would be huge. But I couldn't have seen the turn of events. I saw the potential of the Beatles without knowing how it would evolve. The timing was right as well."

Would he still have become a manager had he not met the Beatles?

"I don't know. At sixteen, I wanted to be a dress designer, but it didn't happen. At twenty-two, I wanted to be an actor so I went to RADA, but I didn't like it. And then I started selling records and, after that, I met the Beatles."

Had he contributed much to their success?

"Well, they are certainly not where they are today because of me, if that is what you are suggesting. But our good relationship has been a contributing factor. When people ask why the Beatles have been so tremendously successful, they always expect one short answer. But there isn't one. There are hundreds of contributory factors."

Could someone else have managed them to such success?

"They may have been as successful, but I don't think they would have been as happy. I do know that I have always been straightforward and honest with them, and they appreciate this."

Did he claim twenty-five percent of whatever they earned?

"I certainly did at the beginning when I had more expense in promoting them. But now it works out roughly at a twenty percent share for all five of us."

Paul and John, as composers, had the biggest incomes?

"Yes, I imagine that, too."

Did he use the Beatles to promote other entertainers?

"In spite of everything that may have been said, this is absolutely untrue. I have never used them to promote other artists. I have always been perfectly single-minded about this, and I must say, in fairness, that the Beatles have been easy to manage. If they had decided on someone else to manage them, I am sure they would maintain the same faith and ideals. Faith and belief has existed mutually between us since the beginning."

Had his talents as a manger been overrated because of the incredible success of the Beatles?

"I think this used to happen more than it does now. I was simply showered with talent. But I am not looking for it any more. I have delegated all my responsibilities as agent and I think people have stopped overrating me."

People were saying the Monkees were the biggest thing since the Beatles. What did he think of that?

"I think the Monkees have been a great boost to the music industry but I don't think they can seriously compare with the Beatles."

Could something like the Beatles ever happen again?

"I think it unlikely in the same form or magnitude. When people refer to a group as being

the new Beatles, it doesn't worry me. It is the same as Bardot. She doesn't mind that there are forty-eight girls all being hailed as the new Bardot. But if another Beatles phenomenon does occur, I know that I'll be watching it rather than handling it.*

"I've been through all the phases of management with the Beatles and that is sufficient for me. I'd like to go on with the Beatles and with Cilla, and I'd like to see Gerry happen. Naturally, I am also proud to be associated through NEMS Enterprises with other artists. Especially the Cream, the Bee Gees, the Who, Matt Monro, Donovan and so on. But I obviously could not deal with all the NEMS activities personally, so I've given these responsibilities to the people who I think are right for the job."

Along with all the success, he had also had a number of failures as a manager.

"I feel very sorry for the artists who didn't make it under my management."

In those cases was it his judgment at fault, or was it the fans'?

"I think mostly, in the past, I was at fault. Then there are other factors of young people growing up and not maturing and progressing as one would have liked."

Since he first met them, had the Beatles changed?

"Yes, a lot."

People said the Beatles had lost touch with the fans who made them famous. What do he think?

"This is quite untrue. I don't think it is a good idea for them to talk to the press every minute. On the other hand, they have been quite open about a lot of things. Paul talked quite freely to the press recently. But there has to be somewhere that you stop. There are a hundred thousand reporters who want to interview them.

"When we launched the Sergeant Pepper LP, we considered for a long time the best way to do it. Finally, we decided to have a party at my pad. It was difficult to decide who to invite, we wanted people who were close to us and people who would spread the word. I suppose we had about fifteen journalists there. It proved a good idea because the story went round the world."

Would the Beatles be performing any more concerts?

"Not in the usual form. But it is difficult to predict future developments. For instance, I couldn't have said twelve months ago that the Beatles were going to appear to the whole world to tell everybody All You Need is Love. As you know, the Beatles are working towards a TV programme for distribution throughout the world. They are also keen to develop ideas for a film. Sergeant Pepper's Lonely Hearts Club Band has been a fantastic success. To date, it has sold five hundred and twenty-one thousand and forty-three copies in Britain, nearly two million in American, and huge sales figures have been received from many other countries.

"I think they would like to make a sort of Sergeant Pepper film. They have proved that they can do the

sound part and now, they feel they can tackle the visual part as well. They would like the film to come from within our orbit and there are plenty of good people in NEMS who can help them with this. They want complete freedom to make it and create it in their own way."

Were the Beatles less personally involved in their own recordings these days?

"No, they're not. Quite the reverse. They are move involved in the making of their records than they have ever been. I cannot emphasise the truth of that statement too much. Of course George Martin and others play their part. But the Beatles are still the creators. They go to many of the mixing sessions and have maintained control over everything. As far as I am concerned, I believe in them more than ever."

August 27, 1967 – The BBC announced that the Beatles' manager, Brian Epstein, had been found dead at his Belgravia home in London. He had been planning to join the rest of the Beatles the following day in Bangor, Wales at a meeting of the International Meditation Society.

From Wales, John Lennon said, *"Our meditations have given us confidence to stand such a shock."*

George Harrison said, *"There is no such thing as death, only in the physical sense. We know he is OK now. He will return because he was striving for happiness and desired bliss so much."*

A business colleague, Don Black, said his death was *"a terrible and stupid accident."*

A friend said: *"He has been unwell for some months. The reason for his death is at present unknown, but there were no untoward circumstances associated with it."*

September 2, 1967 – *Disc and Music Echo* wondered who would replace Brian Epstein.

Tony Barrow, the Beatles' press officer, said, *"No board meeting has been scheduled. If there is one, it won't be until after the funeral, which will probably be on Thursday."*

The funeral was to be a family affair, held in Liverpool.

Possible candidates for assuming control of NEMS were Robert Stigwood, joint managing director ever since his own company, The Robert Stigwood Organisation (which managed Cream and the Bee Gees) merged with NEMS; Clive Epstein, Brian's brother and the administrative director of NEMS; and Vic Lewis, of the Vic Lewis Agency (responsible for bringing the Monkees to the UK) which had also merged with NEMS.

It was possible that Epstein had left no will. That being the case, his estate would go to his widowed mother, Queenie, giving her roughly seventy per cent and controlling interest in NEMS.

It was reasonably certain that the Beatles would continue working with NEMS.

Assorted stars and public personalities paid tribute to Brian Epstein…

Barry Cameron, organist for Sounds Incorporated: *"Eppy was more than a manager, he was a great friend as well. He did a great deal to help us during the time we were with him, and we are all deeply shocked and unhappy. He is a great loss to the music business."*

Cliff Bennett: *"Although I was with NEMS for about three and a half years, I never really knew Brian. In fact, I suppose we only talked five times at all. He was terribly shy. He'd say 'hello' and then clam up. But everybody liked him and this news is tragic."*

Billy J. Kramer: *"It's going to be a great loss to me personally, to the public, and to many people in show business. There will never be anyone like him again. He was just too much."*

Disc jockey Alan Freeman: *"He's irreplaceable and one of the nicest persons I ever met. It's amazing that he remained as nice a person as he did right from the start, because so many of us, if we were at such a high level as he was, could so easily lose our sense of balance. But he didn't. I still can't believe it's happened."*

Jimmy Savile: *"Brian Epstein was one of the real beautiful people. I never had to say a wrong word about him, nor ever heard one. Still, that's life."*

DJ Simon Dee: *"He was an essential part of the emergence of all that is pop music today. Almost the whole of British pop music today is owed to Brian Epstein and Liverpool. I shall miss him a great deal, and he will be remembered."*

Record producer Denny Cordell: *"To me, Brian was a hero of our age. Everything he stood for was good and he brought humour, wit and distinction into what had become a very dreary industry. He opened a completely new approach through his integral belief in his artists, rather than using them as a piece of merchandise. I shall greatly miss him."*

Television producer Mike Mansfield: *"I still can't get over the shock. I can't stop thinking of the last time I saw him, at his Sussex house three weeks ago, and before I left, he personally picked a huge bunch of roses and gave them to me. That's how I remember him, a man of tremendous kindness and generosity. This is the end of an era, it's like cutting the top off a mountain."*

Denny Laine: *"This is a great tragedy. I feel it very personally because I knew Brian well. He was a very real person. I think his greatest asset was his realism, he wasn't the fake that so many people are in this business. Brian was a unique figure in contemporary show business."*

Music publisher, Dick James: *"Brian and I first met in October 1962 when we discussed the publication of John and Paul's* Please Please Me. *Our business association resulted in the now legendary success which achieved the world breakthrough for British pop songs. His integrity has never been exceeded by anyone else I have ever met in the entertainment industry, and his flair for making the right decision on behalf of his artists was quite incredible. He was shy yet tenacious, unassuming yet extravagant. Brian was a fine young man. I shall miss him. We all will."*

Producer / director Dick Lester: *"I knew and worked with Brian for four years, during which time he was always an absolute gentleman. He was a man who was always very, very kind, and extraordinarily decent, a rare quality indeed."*

George Martin: *"I am profoundly shocked and deeply grieved to hear of this awful tragedy. Brian has been a marvelous fellow to work with and an exceptionally good friend. His loss is something which will take us a long time to get over. We will certainly try to carry on with the work he started."*

Ken East, managing director of NEMS: *"My association with Brian was brief. I suppose I met him four or five times. I found him to be a very, very good person indeed to deal with. Always straight and to his word."*

Close friend Vicky Wickham: *"Brian's death will directly affect every single person in any way involved with pop music. He was the most progressive influence on the music scene and had the unique ability to translate teeny-bopper trends into practical developments."*

Top of the Pops producer, Johnnie Stewart: *"The news of Brian's sudden death came as a great shock to all of us. Many people on all sides of the business will miss an extremely popular and likable figure."*

Kit Lambert and Chris Stamp, co-managers of the Who: *"Brian Epstein was always extremely modest and kind to us; modesty and kindness will doubtless continue. But who, now, one wonders, will there be to have that marvelous snobbery and sense of grandeur that turned the Saville Theatre into the Court of Versailles and the drawing-room at Chapel Street into some ante-room of the Vatican? The emperor is gone from Nemperor."*

Cilla Black: *"The news of Brian's death is so awful, I scarcely know what to say. How can you put feelings like this into words? Of course, he was much more than a manager to me. He was a close friend and adviser in whom I had complete trust and faith. Brian has guided every step of my career since 1963. At the same time, my sympathies are with the rest of the Epstein family, whom I know very well."*

September 2, 1967 – Disc and Music Echo, Ray Coleman said the world was stunned by the death of Brian Epstein last Sunday. Epstein was volatile and colourful, sensitive and passionate. He cared about everything that involved his artists. He was enthusiastic and real, with an ego that was tempered by his awareness of it.

In 1962, in Liverpool, Epstein said to Coleman, *"The Beatles will be the biggest thing entertainment has ever known."*

How true that was.

He did business by heart and intuition, not by being a hard-nosed businessman. He was one of the people responsible to the Swinging Sixties.

Ray Coleman, and the world, would miss him.

While the Beatles were listening to transcendental meditation lectures by Maharishi Yogi in Bangor, Wales, Brian Epstein died. He had planned to join the group on Monday.

Instead, the Beatles were at home on Monday. Coleman spoke with Ringo and John at Lennon's home in Weybridge.

Said Ringo, *"It was lucky, in a funny way, that we got the news when we were in Bangor with the Maharishi. We asked him what to do and he told us we mustn't let it get us down.*

"If we got really brought down about it, Brian would know this because he would be able to feel our feelings in his spiritual state, and depression is no good for anybody.

"If we try to spread happiness, then Brian will be happy, too, because even though he is dead, his spirit is still here.

"Of course, it's a big personal loss. The thing is not to get too selfish about it, if you get depressed, it is a form of self-pity, because you are only sympathising with your own loss. Brian's spirit is still here, and it will always be here.

"I go a lot on transcendental meditation, I wish we'd heard about it before we ever went on those tours. They were such a drag and a strain that we just needed something like it.

"We got little sleep and some form of mental relaxation is what we missed. Now we know this form of meditation could have helped a lot.

"This meditation can be used by everyone. It isn't just because we have the freedom that we can do it, people in nine to five jobs can use it, because it can be done any time, and it can help people unwind and do their jobs properly.

"This is a very upsetting time for us, but we've got it under control I hope. People say, 'Why aren't you wearing a black tie?' It isn't disrespectful just because we don't wear black ties. It's what's in your mind that counts. You can be wearing a flowered shirt or a black tie, but neither governs what you're thinking."

Said John, *"We all feel very sad but it's a controlled grief and controlled emotion. As soon as I find myself feeling depressed, I think of something nice about him. But you can't hide the hurt, you know, I went to the phone book and saw his name and it hit me a few minutes ago. The memory must be kept nice, but of course there's something inside us that tells us that Brian's death is sad.*

"It hurts when someone close dies, and Brian was very close. You know, we've all been through that feeling of wanting a good cry. But it wouldn't get us anywhere, would it?

"We all feel it, but these talks on transcendental meditation have helped us to stand up to it so much better. You don't get upset, do you, when a young kid becomes a teenager, or a teenager becomes an adult or when an adult gets old? Well, Brian is just passing into the next phase.

"His spirit is still around, and always will be. It's a physical memory we have of him, and as men, we will build on that memory. It's a loss of genius, but other genius' bodies have died, as well, and the world stills gains from their spirits.

"It is up to us, now, to sort out the way we, and Brian, wanted things to go. He might be dead physically, but that's a negative way of thinking. He helped to give us the strength to do what we did, and the same urge is still alive.

"He was due to come up to Bangor and join us in these transcendental meditations with the Maharishi. It's a drag he didn't make it...

"Would the Beatles be where they are today if it weren't for Brian Epstein? Not the same as we know it, no. But the question doesn't apply, because we met him and what happened, happened. If he hadn't come along, we would all, the four of us and Brian, have been working towards the same thing, even though it might have been with different aims.

"We all knew what we wanted to get over, and he helped us and we helped him.

"We're all going to India soon for a couple of months, to study transcendental meditation properly. The only plans we had, before Brian died, were to make a record, do a TV show and make a film. But meeting the Maharishi has changed our thoughts a bit, and Brian's death has changed it a lot. It makes it more worthwhile now, somehow, going over to India.

"We want to learn the meditation thing properly, so we can propagate it and sell the whole idea to everyone. This is how we plan to use our power now, they've always called us leaders of youth, and we believe that this is a good way to give a lead.

"We want to try to set up an Academy in London and use all the power we have got to get it moving.

"The whole world will know what we mean, and all the people who are worried about youth and drugs and that scene, all these people with the short back and sides, they can all come along and dig it, too.

"It's no gospel, Bible-thumping, sing-along thing, and it needn't be a religion if people don't want to connect it with religion. It's all in the mind. It strengthens understanding and makes people relaxed.

"The whole place wants to relax more, and the people who get to know a bit about it will see it's not just a fad or a gimmick, but the way to calm down tensions.

"You learn about thoughts, about the way to trace your thoughts, you learn a bit about the meaning of life, and it's much better than acid.

"No, we have no idea of whether we'll get a new manager. We've always been in control of what we're doing, and we'll have to do what we have to,

now. We know what we should do and what we shouldn't do. Brian was a natural guide and we'll certainly miss him.

"If Brian had been in on the lectures in meditation, he would have understood. This is the biggest thing in our lives at the moment, and it's come at a time when we need it. We'll use everything we've got to get people to understand it. It's not a religion; there's no mysticism about it, either. It's just understanding.

"Brian has died only in body and his spirit will always be working with us. His power and force were everything, and his power and force will linger on. When we were on the right track, he knew it, and when we were on the wrong track, he told us so and he was usually right. But anyway, he isn't really dead."

September 2, 1967 – *Melody Maker* **talked** about the death of Brian Epstein. The beginning of his incredible pop career was in November 1961 when he first heard the Beatles at the Cavern Club in Liverpool. The end was sudden, on Sunday, August 27th, 1967.

In six years, he had earned roughly a million pounds while building a powerful entertainment empire. The writer wondered what would happen to that empire now.

As *Melody Maker* went to press, there was still no clear answer to that question. Control of NEMS Enterprises could fall to joint managing director, Robert Stigwood, or Vic Lewis, or David Shaw, or even Epstein's younger brother, Clive.

No will had, as yet, been found. If one did not exist, Brian Epstein's seventy per cent shares in NEMS would go to his mother, Queenie.

The only certainty was that the Beatles themselves would have total control of their own future; perhaps they would even manage themselves. Their NEMS contract was due to expire in October.

Press officer Tony Barrow, said, *"The Beatles are too numbed by Brian's death to make any plans at the moment, and, until there has been a full board meeting, nothing can be finalised."*

At the request of Epstein's family, not the Beatles, nor any other stars, would not be at the funeral.

Cilla Black abandoned her holiday in Portugal. She said, *"The news of Brian's death is so awful that I scarcely know what to say. That any great man, so young and so talented, should lose his life is tragic. But it means more when the man is someone so close. He was a close friend and adviser who has guided every step of my career. At the same time, my sympathies are with the rest of the Epstein family, whom I knew very well."*

September 2, 1967 – *Melody Maker* **printed** their eulogy for Brian Epstein. World show business had lost its most amazing and successful manager. In his short career, he had handled the Beatles, Cilla Black, Gerry and the Pacemakers, Billy J. Kramer and many others, some to incredible heights, some to not-so-incredible heights, all of them overshadowed by achievements of the Beatles.

As a manager, his career corresponded to theirs as stars. In management circles, what he accomplished was quite similar to what the Beatles had accomplished in music. He had tried, and abandoned, acting, window dressing, furniture sales, book sales and record sales. People often wondered if he made the Beatles or if the Beatles made him. Brian Epstein always said the group would have been just as big without him; he had believed in their inevitability the first moment he heard them.

He told anyone who would listen that the Beatles would eclipse Elvis. People laughed. For a while. Then the Beatles did what they did and the last laugh could have been Epstein's… but he was too much the gentleman to take it.

In August, *Melody Maker* had run a series of interviews with Brian Epstein. They had been conducted by Mike Hennessey in Knokke, Belgium after some of Epstein's singers had won the European Song Contest. *Melody Maker* asked Hennessey to comment.

He said, "*It may seem lunatic to talk of failure in connection with a millionaire. Yet the impression I formed of Brian Epstein was of a man desperately wanting to be creative, to express himself artistically, but knowing in his heart that he was destined for second hand fame, the reflected glory of the Beatles for whom his devotion and admiration were absolute. He wanted so much to be known as the fifth Beatle but I'm sure he was only too aware that he could not match their wit, their creative genius, their inexhaustible inventiveness. 'The Beatles,' he said to me revealingly in our last interview, 'always make an effort to involve me in what they're doing.' This significant remark is made more poignant by his further admission that his greatest fear was loneliness. Brian Epstein, a basically kind, sometimes petulant, always scrupulously honest man, had come to terms with the fact that the Beatles could have succeeded without him. And, although he had no inclination to put it to the test, he must also have wondered, 'Could I succeed without them?'*"

September 2, 1967 – Alan Walsh interviewed George Harrison for *Melody Maker*. Part One:

Seated at a table in the Mayfair offices of NEMS Enterprise, George began by saying, "*You may think this interview is of no importance to me, but you'd be wrong. It's very important. We have realised it's up to everyone, including the Beatles, to spread love and understanding and to communicate this in any way we can.*"

Walsh began by asking George what his impressions were of Haight-Ashbury in San Francisco.

Said George, "*Well, we were only in Haight-Ashbury for about thirty minutes but I did see quite a bit. We parked our limousine a block away and walked along the street for about a hundred yards, half like a tourist and half like a hippie. We were trying to have a look in a few shops.*"

Who accompanied him?

"*Pattie, her sister Jenny, a friend of Jenny's, Derek Taylor, Neil Aspinall, our road manager, and Magic Alex, who's a friend. We walked along and it was nice. At first they were just saying, 'Hello' and 'Can I shake your hand'… things like that. Then more and more people arrived and it got bigger and bigger. We walked into the park and it just became a bit of a joke. All these people were just following us along.*"

Someone offered him STP?

"*They were trying to give me everything. This is a thing that I want to try and get over to people. Although we've been identified a lot with hippies, especially since all this thing about pot and LSD's come out, we don't want to tell anyone else to have it because it's something that is up to the person himself. Although it was like a key that opened the door and showed a lot of things on the other side, it's still up to people themselves what they do with it.*

"*LSD isn't a real answer. It can't give you anything but it enables you to see a lot of possibilities that you might never have noticed before. But it isn't the answer. You don't just take LSD and that's it for ever, you're done.*

"*A hippie is supposed to be someone who becomes hip, you're hip if you know what's going on. But if you're really hip, you don't get involved with LSD and things like that. You see the potential that it has and the good that can come from it, but you also see that you don't really need it.*

"*I needed it the first time I ever had it. Actually, I didn't know that I'd had it, I'd never even heard of it then. This is something that just hasn't been told. Everybody now knows that we've had it but the circumstances were that somebody just shoved it in our coffee before we had ever heard of the stuff, so we happened to have it quite unaware of the fact.*

"*I don't mind telling people I've had it. I'm not embarrassed. It makes no difference because I know that I didn't actually go out and try to get some.*"

He had never purposely taken LSD?

"*No, not really. For me, it was a good thing but it showed me that LSD isn't really the answer to everything. It can help you to go from A to B, but when you get to B, you see C. And you see that to get really high, you have to do it straight. There are special ways of getting high without drugs, with yoga, meditation and all those things, so this was the disappointing thing about LSD.*

"*In this physical world we live in, there's always duality, good and bad, black and white, yes and no. Whatever there is, there's always the opposite. There's always something equal and opposite to everything and this is why you can't say LSD is good or it's bad because it's good and it's bad. It's both of* them and it's neither of them, all together. People don't consider that.

"Haight-Ashbury was a bit of a shock because, although there were so many great people, really nice people who only wanted to be friends and didn't want to impose anything or be anything, there was still the black bit, the opposite. There was the bit where people were so out of their minds trying to shove STP on me, and acid... Every step I took, there was somebody trying to give me something... But I didn't want to know about that. I want to get high and you can't get high on LSD. You can take it and take it as many times as you like, but you get to a point that you can't get any further unless you stop taking it.

"Haight-Ashbury reminded me a bit of the Bowery. There were these people just sitting round the pavement begging, saying, 'give us some money for a blanket.' These are hypocrites. They are making fun of tourists and all that, and, at the same time, they are holding their hands out, begging off them. That's what I don't like.

"I don't mind anybody dropping out of anything, but it's the imposition on somebody else I don't like. The moment you start dropping out and then begging off somebody else to help you, then it's no good. I've just realised through a lot of things that it doesn't matter what you are, as long as you work. It doesn't matter if you chop wood, as long as you chop and keep chopping. Then you get what's coming to you. You don't have to drop out. If fact, if you drop out, you put yourself further away from the goal of life than if you were to keep working."

What was his goal in life?

"We've all got the same goal whether we realise it or not. We're all striving for something which is called God. For a reunion, complete. Everybody has realised at some time or other that, no matter how happy they are, there's still always the unhappiness that comes with it.

"Everyone is a potential Jesus Christ, really. We are all trying to get where Jesus Christ got. And we're going to be on this world until we get there. We're all different people and we are all doing different things in life, but that doesn't matter, because the whole point of life is to harmonise with everything, every aspect in creation. That means down to not killing the flies, eating the meat, killing people or chopping the trees down."

Was it possible to attain that?

"You can only do it if you believe in it. Everybody is potentially divine. It's just a matter of self-realisation before it will all happen. The hippies are a good idea, love, flowers and that is great, but when you see the other half of it, it's like anything. I love all these people, too, those who are honest and trying to find a bit of truth and to straighten out the untruths. I'm with them one hundred per cent, but when I see the bad side of it, I'm not so happy."

Did a person have to be a hippie to achieve what he was talking about?

"Anybody can do it. I doubt if anyone who is a hippie or flower person feels that he is. It's only you, the press, who call us that. They've always got to have some tag. If you like, I'm a hippie or a flower person. I know I'm not. I'm George Harrison, a person. Just like everybody else, but different to everybody else at the same time. You get to a point where you realise that it doesn't matter what people think you are, it's what you think you are yourself that matters. Or what you know you are. Anyone can make it. You don't have to put a flowery shirt on."

A bank clerk?

"Anyone can, but they've got to have the desire. The Beatles got all the material wealth that we needed and that was enough to show us that this thing wasn't material. We are all in the physical world, yet what we are striving for isn't physical. We all get so hung up with material things like cars and televisions and houses, yet what they can give you is only there for a little bit and then it's gone."

Had he considered disposing of all his material wealth?

"Yes, but now that I've got the material thing in perspective, it's okay. The whole reason I've got material things is because they were given to me as a gift, so it's not really bad that I've got it because I didn't ask for it. It was just mine. All I did was be me.

"All we ever had to do was just be ourselves and it all happened. It was there, given to us. All this. But then, it was given to us to enable us to see that that wasn't it. There was more to it."

How did these ideas and beliefs blend with his music, with the music of the Beatles?

"I'm a musician. I don't know why. This is a thing that I've looked back on since my birth. Many people think life is predestined. I think it is vaguely, but it's still up to you which way your life's going to go. All I've ever done is keep being me and it's just all worked out. It just did it all... magic... it just did it. We never planned anything, so it's obvious, because I'm a musician now, that's what I was destined to be. It's my gig."

September 9, 1967 – *Record Mirror* ran their tribute to Brian Epstein. Brian was dead, but his creation, the modern pop scene, would live on. The lover of classical music who had once so desperately desired to be a successful actor had passed with a stunning suddenness. But the pop world would go on... remembering.

The writer reflected on the day Epstein brought the Beatles into his office. Awkwardly, he stared at them. They stared right back in silence. It was one of the group's first interviews and the writer had never heard of them. Epstein charmed the situation. He talked about first seeing the Beatles in the dismal Cavern Club in Liverpool, about how he had disliked the way they looked...

Said Epstein, *"They appeared rather unkempt."*
The Beatles shuffled in their seats. The writer examined them again. They were well-dressed and well-scrubbed, clearly under the influence of their manager, a man who spoke earnestly and honestly, without bravado, without boasting. Simply, he had worked hard with the group. They were here, and they had a recording contract.

The writer felt, at that point, that all he had to do was watch and wait for the inevitable. And it happened. It happened so fast and so hard that the Beatles and Epstein dragged the dying British pop scene, kicking and screaming, into a new era, an era created in their own image, precisely the way Brian Epstein had planned it.

Then he got down to the hard part. He repeated his success, on a somewhat smaller scale but huge nonetheless, with Gerry and the Pacemakers, with Cilla Black, with Billy J. Kramer and the Dakotas.

Epstein became the Nemperor of Pop, the voice of the music business, crossing the Atlantic to conquer America, beating the Americans at the game they invented.

He was the fifth Beatle, sharing in the glory, working night and day for artists he considered friends, earning serious respect in a cut and slash business, honest in an industry of lies and hype, tough when bargaining, gentle with friends.

Once upon a time, Colonel Tom Parker was the only legendary rock and roll manager. Brian Epstein caught up with him, met him, and surpassed him. In five years, he built an empire with no equals, a rock and roll empire of a sort the world had never seen before.

And now, the rock scene, the group scene, was his memorial. Everyone involved in music benefited from the success of the Beatles… and the success of Brian Epstein.

Had Brian not wandered into the Cavern on that miserable November day, would it all have happened? Would the Beatles have happened? Perhaps. But Epstein certainly speeded up the process.
He would be missed.

September 9, 1967 – *Disc and Music Echo* announced that the Beatles were planning a four-day mini-tour. Next week, they would be traveling by coach around southwest England, shooting a full-colour TV spectacular, *Magical Mystery Tour.*

Also, they planned to visit India in October for a holiday / meditation study with Maharishi Yogi. They would return to England before Christmas.

The title song, *Magical Mystery Tour,* by John and Paul, was already written. There were plans to write at least four more songs along with a soundtrack score for the show.

All of the exterior shooting was to be completed on the coach trip, with the group choosing the day's locations as they found them. Following the road trip would be a few weeks of studio work.

At least one guest star would be joining the Beatles but no names had been announced. Also, several non-pop acts would be involved.

The show was to be offered worldwide. The Beatles were hoping to screen it on British TV at Christmas time.

Initially, the group had planned to do a TV special around the *Sergeant Pepper* album, but that idea had been shelved when they were invited to participate in the global satellite program *Our World. Magical Mystery Tour* was to replace the *Pepper* project, though some of the music from the *Pepper* LP might be used.

September 9, 1967 – *Disc and Music Echo* reported that Clive Epstein had been unanimously elected to take over his brother Brian's duties at NEMS Enterprises. Robert Stigwood was to be the managing director, while the other directors would maintain their positions.

The company would carry on business as usual, although no one would be taking over as personal manager to the Beatles.

Brian Epstein's funeral had taken place Wednesday last at Long Lane Cemetery in Liverpool. A memorial service was being planned in London but no date had been announced.

September 9, 1967 – *Disc and Music Echo* published Derek Taylor's tribute to Brian Epstein. Taylor had been the Beatles' press officer and had worked with Epstein before moving to the U.S. to work with the Byrds, the Beach Boys, and others.

He said he first heard about Epstein's death from Ivor Davis of the *Daily Express.* Davis said, *"Well, I don't know whether you've heard anything from London, the news, you know, have you?"*

Taylor asked him what he wanted.
Davis said, *"Well, Brian Epstein's dead."*
Davis had no details but he wanted a quote. In shock, Taylor said, *"Naturally, I'm shocked. I'm shattered. I'm stunned. It is a terrible blow. It is an*

irreplaceable loss. This is awful news. I am too upset now to speak."

He told Davis he did not have much to say except that Brian was loved.

Reluctantly, Davis asked, *"Can you expand it?"*

"Yes. He was easy to love, but he wasn't easy to understand. I don't know anyone who understood him except the Beatles, who understand everything."

The next caller was Jack Beverly, another reporter. Beverly said there was a rumour going round that the Beatles were trying to get Derek Taylor to manage them, that the Beatles were ready to dump Brian Epstein.

Taylor explained that the Beatles would never have left Brian. He said he was considering a return to England to work for the Beatles again, but not as a manager. Never as a manager.

After talking to a neighbour about the news, Taylor called London and spoke briefly with Epstein's secretary, Joanne. She was too upset for conversation and Peter Brown, an old pal of Brian's, took the phone.

Taylor asked about Brian's mother and about the Beatles, who were still in Wales, though returning soon. Brown said the street outside was jammed with reporters.

The radio stations in L.A. were reporting hourly... *"Brian Epstein, the man who masterminded the Beatles to top the pop charts, dead at thirty-two in his London home..."*

On the same page, *Disc and Music Echo* quoted ex-Cavern DJ Bob Wooler: *"He was a fascinating enigma. Capricious, shy, easily embarrassed, slightly sardonic and very charming. One of his most valuable assets was his ability to make it virtually impossible to say no to his wish.*

"It has been said Brian Epstein would have been nothing but for the Beatles, that they were the explosion and he was merely the echo. But it was Brian who ignited the explosion and caused the supersonic pop boom that was heard around the world. I am convinced that if Brian had not happened along when he did, the Beatles would have split up before the end of 1961.

"To me, Brian was the gentleman genius of pop. I once said of the Beatles that I didn't think anything like them would ever happen again. That goes for Brian, too."

And Gerry Marsden, *"Brian was not just a manager. After a while, he became a close friend and inspiration for us. We never had the feeling that he was a manager in the business sense.*

"If it hadn't been for Brian, I would still be working on the railways or something like that. I want to show him that what he did for us was not wasted.

"I am very happy that Clive Epstein has taken over from him. He is also a close friend of mine and it is wonderful to know he will be carrying on where Brian left off."

September 9, 1967 – *Melody Maker* **announced** that the Beatles were going on the road for a four-day tour to shoot the location footage for their new TV special, *Magical Mystery Tour.* Lennon and McCartney had already written the title song and were planning at least four more compositions as well as the instrumental sound track.

No decision had been made about how the music would be released on disc, whether as an EP or an LP.

Following the road trip, the group planned to spend a fortnight recording and filming in studios.

An as yet unnamed pop star would also be joining them along with an assortment of non-pop acts. The film was to be shot in colour and distributed worldwide. Christmas was the target for the British release.

After filming, the Beatles intended to join the Maharishi Mahesh Yogi in India for meditation and a holiday. They hoped to be back in England for Christmas.

September 9, 1967 – Alan Walsh interviewed George Harrison for *Melody Maker.* **Part Two:**

What were the Beatles trying to do musically, now?

"Nothing. We're not trying to do anything. This is the big joke. It's all Cosmic Joke Forty Three. Everyone gets our records and says, 'Wonder how they thought of that?' or 'Wonder what they're planning next?' or whatever they say. But we don't plan anything. We don't do anything. All we do is just keep on being ourselves. It just comes out. It's the Beatles.

"All any of us are trying to do now is get as much peace and love as possible. Love will never be played out because you can't play out the truth. Whatever I say can be taken a million different ways, depending on how screwed up the reader is.

"But the Beatles is just a hobby, really, it's just doing it on its own. We don't even have to think about it. The songs write themselves. It just all works out. Everything that we're taking into our minds and trying to learn or find out, and I feel personally it's such a lot, there's so much to get in, and yet the output coming out the back end is still so much smaller than what you're putting in.

"Everything is relative to everything else. We know that now, so we've got to a point where, when people say, 'There's nothing else you can do,' we know that's only from where they are. They look up and think we can't do any more, but when you're up there, you see you haven't started.

"Take Ravi Shankar, who is so brilliant. With pop music, the more you listen to it, the more you get to know it, the more you see through it and the less satisfaction it gives you, whereas Indian music and Ravi Shankar as a person... it's exactly the opposite because, the more you're able to understand the music, the more you see there is to appreciate. The more you get back out of it. You can have just one record of Indian music and play it for the rest of your life and you'd probably still never see all the

subtleties in it. It's the same with Ravi Shankar. He feels as though he hasn't started, and yet, he's doing so much, teaching so many people, writing film music, everything."

Did he know what the Beatles would do the next time they were in a recording studio?

"No idea. We won't know until we do it. We're naturally influenced by everything that's going on around us. If you weren't influenced, you wouldn't be able to do anything. That's all anything is, an influence from one person to another. We'll write songs and go into the studios and record them, and we'll try and make them good. We'll make a better LP than Sergeant Pepper. But I don't know what it's going to be."

If he had a kid, how would he be as a father?

"I haven't, and I can't really know what I'd do. But I do know I wouldn't let it go to school. I'm not letting Fascist teachers put things into the child's head. I'd get an Indian guru to teach him... and me, too."

It was said that the Beatles were planning to make a film, and planning to write the script and the music.

"Yes. We've got to the point now where we've found out that if you rely on other people, things never work out. This may sound conceited but it's not. It's just what happens. The things that we've decided ourselves, and that we've gone ahead and done ourselves, have always worked out right, or at least satisfactorily, whereas the moment you get involved with other people, it goes wrong.

"It's like a record company. You hand them the whole LP and the sleeve and everything there on a plate. All they've got to do is print it. Then all the crap starts: 'You can't have that' and 'You don't do this' and we get so involved with trivial little things that it all starts deteriorating around us.

"And it's the same with a film. The more involved we get with film people, the less of a Beatles film it's going to be. Take that Our World television show. We were trying to make it into a recording session and a good time, and the BBC were trying to make it into a television show. It's a constant struggle to get ourselves across through all these other people, all hassling.

"In the end, it'll be best if we write the music, write the visual and the script, film it, edit it, do everything ourselves. But then, it's such a hell of a job that you have to get involved and that means you couldn't do other things.

"But we'll have to get other people to do things because we can't give that much time to just a film, because it's only a film and there are more important things in life."

Would the film happen soon?

"Yes. I think it'll probably all happen next year sometime."

September 23, 1967 – Disc and Music Echo spoke with Freda Kelly of Liverpool, national secretary of the Beatles Fan Club. Freda, along with Jeni Crowley, London area fan club secretary, Sylvia

Nightingale of Sussex, and Barbara King of Essex, were personally chosen by the Beatles to join their Magical Mystery Tour.

Said Freda, "We've had a great time. Everyone really enjoyed it all. It was quite a surprise for me when I had a phone call asking me to come to London ready to go filming with the boys."

The girls had no specific roles to play, they were simply among the coach party.

Freda said, "Everything's very spontaneous. I fell asleep once and awoke to find the cameras trained on me.

"The party split into two the other day. Paul and Ringo directed one lot of us in and out of the coach, while George and John worked on beach scenes and around a swimming pool with girls in bikinis."

Filming even went on during lunch, Freda explained, adding, "It worked out perfectly. Apparently, the Beatles were in the ballroom the night before having a drink and got chatting to this band leader chap. Paul asked him what he was doing for lunch the next day, and when he said, 'Nothing,' he was recruited to play while we ate."

How did they plan the day's shoot?

"There's no prepared script as such. They just put their heads together the night before and prepared some ideas. That business when the coach couldn't get over a bridge, for instance. It was a completely genuine incident and was filmed as it happened."

Even the spectators were filmed. Spencer Davis was holidaying with his wife and kids and the Beatles drafted him as well.

Said Freda, "There was a crowd of between two and three hundred mums and dads and kiddies outside our hotel, too, and they were all filmed."

During the trip, she was able to chat with the group on a number of occasions. She said, "They're still much the same. I've known them for six whole years now, so I feel almost one of the family. They're still the same old John, Paul, George and Ritchie deep down.

"I loved every minute of it. A nice, all-expenses-paid holiday!"

September 23, 1967 – Disc and Music Echo said the Beatles' next single was likely to be the title song from the film on which they had been working, Magical Mystery Tour. It was also possible that an EP of the four numbers featured in the TV movie would be released. Three of the songs were by Lennon and McCartney, the fourth by George Harrison.

The Beatles had been touring Devon and Cornwall the previous week, shooting on location. This week was spent mostly in film studios. On Monday, though, Paul McCartney was at Raymond's Revuebar in Soho to shoot some scenes featuring the Bonzo Dog Do Dah Band.

Filming was to end that week. Another two weeks would be devoted to the musical sound track.

And the finished full-colour film was to be shown on TV at Christmas time.

When the studio work was completed, the group was heading for India, back in time for Christmas.

How I Won the War was to be premiered at the London Pavilion on October 18th. A United Artists spokesman said, *"Invitations are being sent out to show business personalities, the trade and the press. John Lennon has been invited, of course, and seems likely to attend, but it is not sure whether the other Beatles will be there."*

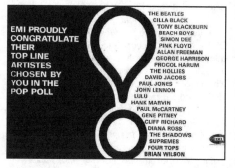

EMI PROUDLY CONGRATULATE THEIR TOP LINE ARTISTES CHOSEN BY YOU IN THE POP POLL

THE BEATLES
CILLA BLACK
TONY BLACKBURN
BEACH BOYS
SIMON DEE
PINK FLOYD
ALLAN FREEMAN
GEORGE HARRISON
PROCOL HARUM
THE HOLLIES
DAVID JACOBS
PAUL JONES
JOHN LENNON
LULU
HANK MARVIN
PAUL McCARTNEY
GENE PITNEY
CLIFF RICHARD
DIANA ROSS
THE SHADOWS
SUPREMES
FOUR TOPS
BRIAN WILSON

September 23, 1967 *– Melody Maker* **announced** that the Beatles had, once again, been voted the top group in Britain. The group also took the best album award for *Sergeant Pepper's Lonely Hearts Club Band.*

September 23, 1967 *– Melody Maker* **sent** writer Chris Welch and photographer Barrie Wentzell to Cornwall to track down the Beatles on their *Magical Mystery Tour.* They spent a couple of hapless, hopeless days chasing the magic coach around the countryside in an ailing, failing, beat-up Ford Consul, finally catching up with them at the Atlantic Hotel near Newquay.

They found John and George directing a gang of bikini-clad girls around the swimming pool. The day was cold, John and George wearing jackets while blue girls jumped in and out of the pool, pretending to have a warm, happy holiday.

The following morning, the Beatles were off again. Welch and Wentzell were trapped behind a gang of fans in the roadway, unable to keep up… and unable to rejoin the *Mystery Tour.* After hopelessly cruising the countryside, they gave up and returned to London.

Later, Spencer Davis said, *"The Beatles want to know what happened to Chris Welch. There was a wild theory somebody has pushed him into the swimming pool and he had drowned. Later, his ghost was seen in a car peering through the coach windscreen. The Beatles are having buttons made with* Where is Chris Welch? *written on them."*

September 30, 1967 *– Melody Maker* **reported** that the Beatles were leaving England for two months at the end of October. They were going to Swargshram, India, where they planned to attend the Academy of Transcendental Meditation on the Ganges with Maharishi Mahesh Yogi.

A spokesman for NEMS said, *"This is all the news that will be announced about the trip because they are going as private individuals. There will be no press facilities either during their trip to and from India or while they are in India."*

They would be back in Britain for Christmas.

The filming of their self-directed TV movie, *Magical Mystery Tour,* was finished. Time would now be devoted to editing and recording.

Said NEMS, *"Reports that the film will be shown on BBC-2 are speculative. The Beatles will finish the film before it is decided who will show it."*

The *Melody Maker* album chart showed *Sergeant Pepper's Lonely Hearts Club Band* still holding the number one position.

October 7, 1967 *– Disc and Music Echo* **said** the Beatles were releasing an instrumental track on their forthcoming EP, *Magical Mystery Tour.* This was the first time since the beginning of their recording careers in 1962 that the group had featured an instrumental tune.

Four or six compositions by John and Paul were being made for *Magical Mystery Tour,* along with *Blue Jay Way* by George Harrison. George had written it in Hollywood in August; the title was from the place he rented while he was there.

All week the group had been in the recording studio, working on *Magical Mystery Tour.* The fifth anniversary of their first recording, *Love Me Do on* October 4th, 1962 – came and went without celebration. They were too busy working.

Speaking for NEMS, Tony Barrow said, *"Apart from these, there is also the music for the soundtrack to be written and recorded. And this can't be done until the TV film has been edited and is ready for viewing by the boys. It should be ready with the next fortnight."*

Talking about John and George's appearance on the David Frost TV show, Barrow said, *"Apart from Juke Box Jury, which one doesn't really count, this is the first time the Beatles have ever taken part in a TV discussion programme."*

The Frost program was made during a recording session break. Frost wanted to know about the Indian mystic, Maharishi Mahesh Yogi.

October 7, 1967 *– Mike Ledgerwood wrote for Disc and Music Echo*… The Beatles had set many trends over the years, high-heeled boots, collarless jackets, long hair… and, of course, the music, spawning scores of imitators, scores of bands who just tried to keep up. When Lennon sported a new hat, people went mad trying to find their own version. When he had his Rolls repainted as a psychedelic testament, the world was awed and shocked. When the group grew facial hair, so did everyone else.

Virtually everything the Beatles did was copied by their followers.

Even since John, Paul, George, Mick Jagger and Marianne Faithful attended a London lecture, the crowds were flocking to transcendental meditation.

Said Matthew West, International Meditation Society press officer, "*More than fifteen people a week are becoming meditators. The Beatles helped the organisation enormously by coming along to the lecture. And they're helping to spread the message.*

"*It's generally young people who are taking an interest, too. Art students, actors and actresses. All sorts actually. People are eager to learn and attend lectures even more now.*"

Shortly after the death of Brian Epstein, John Lennon spoke with *Disc*, saying, "*We want to learn the meditation thing properly, so we can propagate it and sell the whole idea to everyone.*

"*This is how we plan to use our power now. They've always called us leaders of youth. We believe this is a good way to give a lead.*

"*We want to try to set up an Academy in London and use all the power we have to get it moving. The whole world will know what we mean.*"

Ledgerwood said anyone could learn transcendental meditation. No qualifications were required. And the course was free.

Explained Matthew West, "*It's purely a charity organisation. The whole thing is run on donations. There are no fees whatsoever. Anyone is welcome to join. Initially, there's an introductory lecture that explains the principles on which it is based and the results which may be expected. Then, if you wish to learn the method, it will be taught individually and privately.*

"*We usually have a collection at lecture meetings, and people who wish to take up meditation are asked to give a week's wages in place of a fee.*

"*Obviously, the fact that the Beatles would give a week's earnings, which would be quite formidable, has made a lot of people take notice. The Beatles haven't given anything yet. But after going to India, I think they will realise their potential all right.*"

Ledgerwood wondered what other rockers thought about the Beatles being involved with transcendental meditation.

Pete Townsend, of the Who, said, "*I'm sure the Beatles are very, very genuine in their belief. I have not gone very deeply into this, but I'm aware of a definite feeling throughout the whole section of the teenage public.*

"*Everything is down to something. It goes a lot deeper than working, living and dying. A couple of years ago, I didn't believe in this life-after-death bit, or God. Now I do! If we don't reach a state of understanding, of how we can escape the world*

situations, we'll just fade away.

"*The only real escape is via meditation. To be able to meditate yourself to another level. If everyone throughout the world was aware of the purpose of life, we could all further ourselves.*

"*You don't have to be intelligent, to have experienced LSD, been turned-on or freaked out, just have faith in something big. People are becoming stagnant. They only believe in what they're actually seeing. The whole world's becoming stagnant.*"

October 7, 1967 – *Melody Maker* **said** the new Beatles single and EP might be released while the band was visiting India. This week, they were recording the music for *Magical Mystery Tour* at EMI's St. John's Wood studio. They were doing the title song, along with four or six other tunes, including one by George Harrison, *Blue Jay Way*, which George had written during his August visit to Hollywood. Also included would be an instrumental song, the first ever recorded by the band.

Said press officer Tony Barrow, "*No final decision has been made, but the tracks will probably be released as a single and an EP. There is no definite release date because the final number of tracks has not been decided by the boys.*"

The Beatles were also working on the editing of the film. When that phase was complete, they would write and record the incidental music.

October 14, 1967 – *Record Mirror* **reprinted a review** by critic Z.M. from *The Times of India*. The critic had just heard the *Sergeant Pepper* album.

He said, "*The Beatles have changed their dress, their music. They now sport droopy French mustaches and colourful costumes, practise mysticism, and their sounds have begun to explore farther reaches in the musical firmament.*

"*Their latest LP is an excellent example of their experiments with change. The title song begins with Presley-like screams. The Beatles sing in rock tempo to the accompaniment of a big brass band.*

"*From their early recordings which featured only three guitars and drums, the Beatles have progressed to an astonishing array of unlikely instruments. Their lyrics are now more intelligible. Hippie flower power pervades.*

"*The lyrics are as beautiful as the melody on* Lucy in the Sky*. Amid great pathos, the Beatles lament* She's Leaving Home*. It's difficult to believe that the Beatles can manage without their explosive guitars. A regular string orchestra accompanies their singing.*

"*Memorable is George Harrison's* Within You Without You*. It sounds quite Indian with sitar and table accompanying his philosophic thought.*

"*The coda,* A Day in the Life*, is fascinating. Its electronic crescendo really turns you on. Composed by Lennon and McCartney; arranged and produced by George Martin. Splendid hearing is guaranteed for all.*"

October 14, 1967 – Disc and Music Echo announced that Ringo Starr had been invited to participate, along with Marlon Brando and Richard Burton, in the film *Candy*, to be directed by Christian Marquand.

The novel, originally published as by Maxwell Kenton but actually written by Terry Southern and Mason Hoffenberg, had been banned in a number of places in the States.

Ringo would be the second Beatle to have a project marked with the X certificate. John Lennon's *How I Won the War* had also been given the restricted label by the British Board of Film Censors.

Ringo would be playing a Mexican gardener.

Said NEMS press officer Tony Barrow, *"No exact date has been fixed for filming Ringo, but it will probably be around December, on location in either Italy or Spain. This would mean that Ringo may cut short his trip to India with the other Beatles.*

"I've no idea what certificate the film will get, but, in view of the book being banned, I suppose there is a possibility of an X."

October 14, 1967 – Disc and Music Echo said John Lennon, along with Paul McCartney, George Harrison and Ringo Starr, would be attending the world premiere of *How I Won the War* at the London Pavilion, Piccadilly, on October 18th. Other celebrities expected to attend included: the Rolling Stones, Procol Harum, Cilla Black, Marianne Faithful, Sandie Shaw, Anita Harris, Paul and Barry Ryan, the Who, Adam Faith, Warren Mitchell, Spike Milligan, Albert Finney, Charlie Drake and Lance Percival.

October 14, 1967 – Disc and Music Echo said an excerpt from the soundtrack of *How I Won the War*, featuring the voice of John Lennon, was to be released the following day by United Artists. The record was called *How I Won the War* by Musketeer Gripweed and the Third Troop.

The single, written by Ken Thorne, was not featured in the film. Thorne explained, *"It is just a novelty to put a synopsis of the film on a forty-five record. I took some of the soundtrack and some of the dialogue and sound effects and built them up to a big climax. John Lennon is heard saying, 'I did. I let the bloody water out, make it lighter.'"*

Said Tony Barrow, *"As so many fans know that John Lennon plays Private Gripweed in the film, we want to make it clear that John's contribution to the record is only five or ten seconds of soundtrack; he doesn't sing or play on either side. But we are not objecting to the record in any way."*

October 21, 1967 – Disc and Music Echo reported that a minimum of one million dollars – more than three hundred thousand pounds – would be paid for the Beatles' *Magical Mystery Tour* TV movie.

Worldwide, companies were bidding for the television rights, including the three major American networks and an assortment of independent U.S.

stations. More than forty offers had been received so far, including bids from Germany, Japan, Australia, South Africa and Mexico.

The show would also be viewed on British television, of course, but where had not, as yet, been settled.

Said Tony Barrow, *"The Beatles will not show the production to TV executives until the film editing and sound recording is completed. They are now working on this, and may have to postpone their pending trip to India until the New Year."*

The Beatles were intending to fly to India to be with Maharishi Mahesh Yogi for three months, starting in November.

Magical Mystery Tour would likely be finished by the end of October and ready for TV sales at the beginning of November. It was likely to be shown on British TV either Christmas Eve or Christmas Day, with simultaneous broadcasts around the world.

A footnote mentioned that Ringo would be flying to Rome at the end of November to shoot his part as Emmanuel the Gardener in the film *Candy*.

October 21, 1967 – Melody Maker reported the possibility of a Beatles / Rolling Stones merger. The news had been announced over the weekend by Jonathan King on his *Good Evening* television show.

Explained NEMS press officer, Tony Barrow, *"It's highly possible that the two groups will get together for fresh business ventures, but there is no chance of any sort of co-operation on a record, as the two groups are contracted to rival record companies.*

"One idea that they are discussing is obtaining a recording studio where they can each make their own records and possibly record other artists.

"And there is a possibility of future intriguing schemes. These could include a talent school."

Discussions were in the early stages. Paul McCartney and Mick Jagger had kicked around a few ideas for business ventures.

A spokesman for the Rolling Stones said, *"The conversations between Mick and Paul were of a purely exploratory nature. They discussed the possibility or advisability of opening a recording studio. But these conversations have not been resolved."*

The article finished by saying a new Beatles single, probably from *Magical Mystery Tour*, was likely to be released at the end of November. Nothing had been decided regarding the *Mystery Tour* EP.

November 4, 1967 – Record Mirror, Alan Stinton wrote a history of the Beatles' recordings in facts and figures. Five years ago October, a more-or-less unknown rock group from Liverpool made its first appearance in a national British pop chart. It was *Record Mirror*'s Top Fifty. The song was *Love Me Do*. And it debuted at number forty-nine. The highest position it reached was number seventeen.

During the five years since October, 1962, the

Beatles' recognition had become legendary. Their incredible success was clearly documented in the four main charts published weekly by *Record Mirror*: UK Singles; US Singles; UK EPs; and UK LPs.

Celebrating the fifth anniversary of the Beatles' chart debut, Stinton was presenting a Beatles discography. The group had stunned the pop world. The lists of their recordings were a record of chart busting that would never be seen again.

November 11, 1967 – Disc and Music Echo celebrated the history of the Beatles with a series of articles entitled *Five Years of Beatles*. They began with quotes from other stars.

Ray Davies: *"It's funny we should be celebrating the fifth anniversary of the Beatles at the same times as the fiftieth anniversary of the Russian Revolution. For the Beatles changed people's images. Before them, art and films had been changing, but they brought a change to pop. Previously, it had been all glossy, with people like Cliff Richard, so they did, in a way, start a revolution. If only they'd had the Beatles in Russia, they wouldn't have needed guns!"*

Alan Price: *"Sergeant Pepper opened up a new field for a lot of groups. They can now make adventurous singles that previously might not have been accepted. The Beatles started with the teen scene, made a lot of bread, but then, instead of resting, used their position to be even more creative. They were naturals, and I don't think they would ever break up."*

Tom Jones: *"The Beatles are on their own. I don't think of them as a performing group that goes on stage; if they were still doing that, I wouldn't rate them so much because generally I don't rate groups. But they've written some fantastic songs, Yesterday, for instance, and I'd love Lennon and McCartney to write a song for me."*

Spencer Davis: *"It's ironic that the fifth anniversary of the Beatles should coincide with the Russian Revolution of 1917. Ray Davies said the same thing? Then it's one Davis thinking like another! The Beatles really caused a social revolution. Musically and lyrically, the Beatles have broken through many conservative ideas, and opened up a whole new field for the groups. If one can look at the Beatles impartially, I regard them on par with the storm and stress poetry movement in*

BEATLE'S UK SINGLES

Title	Weeks on Chart	Highest Position	Weeks No. 1
Love Me Do	18	17	
Please Please Me	18	2	
From Me to You	21	1	7
My Bonnie	1	48	
She Loves You	33	1	6
I Want to Hold Your Hand	22	1	5
Can't Buy Me Love	15	1	3
Ain't She Sweet	6	29	
A Hard Day's Night	13	1	3
I Feel Fine	13	1	5
Ticket to Ride	12	1	3
Help	14	1	3
Day Tripper / We Can Work It Out	12	1	5
Paperback Writer	11	1	2
Yellow Submarine / Eleanor Rigby	13	1	4
Penny Lane / Strawberry Fields Forever	11	2	
All You Need is Love	13	1	3

BEATLE'S UK EPs

Title	Weeks on Chart	Highest Position	Weeks No. 1
Twist and Shout	64	1	21
The Beatles' Hits	44	1	3
The Beatles No. 1	29	2	
All My Loving	44	1	8
Long Tall Sally	37	1	7
A Hard Day's Night	29	1	6
A Hard Day's Night 2	16	7	
Beatles For Sale	47	1	5
Beatles For Sale 2	24	5	
Beatles' Million Sellers	26	1	4
Yesterday	13	1	8
Nowhere Man	18	4	

BEATLE'S UK LPs

Title	Weeks on Chart	Highest Position	Weeks No. 1
Please Please Me	70	1	30
With The Beatles	50	1	21
A Hard Day's Night	38	1	21
Beatles For Sale	46	1	11
Help!	36	1	9
Rubber Soul	42	1	8
Revolver	27	1	7
A Collection of Beatles' Oldies	18	7	
Sergeant Pepper	20	1	19

Germany at the turn of the eighteenth century."

Flowerpot Man Tony Burrows: *"They're definitely the most imaginative and original group ever to come out of Britain. They've always set the trend. I was with a group, the Kestrels, who toured with them on their first stage show. It was with Helen Shapiro. I remember they were at the bottom of the bill, but they generated such excitement even in those days, they ended by closing the first half. They asked us how they should take their bow. They did, like a little regiment. And this also set the style for other groups."*

Dave Dee: *"They're still tops as far as groups go. I don't think any group will ever emulate the Beatles again. I can't see anyone coming along with the song writing talent of Lennon and McCartney. Lots of people write songs, then just seem to dry up. But John and Paul just pour them out. And there must be a hell of a lot of talent still there. I suppose they're happy. I don't know. I like to think so. But sometimes I have my doubts, due to the fact that, at twenty-six or twenty-seven, they've made so much money, seen everything, done everything. I often wonder if that isn't the one sad thing about being a Beatle."*

Mike Pinder of the Moody Blues: *"For five years, their great success has been rewarded by money and material things, for which they now have no need. Yet, it's now that they're getting the reward they deserve."*

George Martin: *"They're four very different people who get together to form a unit that is virtually impregnable. If, for instance, someone should find fault with anything one of them has done, the others rush to his defense. They close their ranks. They're very close indeed. A lot closer than people think."*

Denny Laine, former Moody Blue: *"The biggest thing I learned from them has been teamwork. They had their own leaders; this is what kept them going. But in a sense, they were really always their own leaders. So involved in everything. I've appreciated them and learned a lot from them."*

Cilla Black: *"I know I'm a bit biased, because I knew them in Liverpool. But honestly, nobody can top them. They're the best thing that ever happened to the entertainment world. Everything they do is new and different. The difference between the*

BEATLE'S US SINGLES

Title	Weeks on Chart	Highest Position	Weeks No. 1
I Want to Hold Your Hand	16	1	8
She Loves You	15	1	2
Please Please Me	12	3	
My Bonnie	5	29	
Twist and Shout	11	1	1
Can't Buy Me Love	10	1	5
Roll Over Beethoven	4	30	
From Me to You	3	41	
Do You Want to Know a Secret	11	3	
All My Loving	5	31	
Love Me Do	14	1	1
Thank You Girl	2	38	
P.S. I Love You	8	10	
A Hard Day's Night	12	1	3
Ain't She Sweet	7	14	
I'll Cry Instead	7	22	
And I Love Her	7	14	
I Should Have Known Better	2	43	
Matchbox	7	17	
Slow Down	4	34	
I Feel Fine	11	1	4
She's a Woman	8	8	
Eight Days a Week	10	1	3
Ticket to Ride	11	1	1
Help	13	1	1
Yesterday	11	1	3
Act Naturally	6	28	
We Can Work It Out	11	1	4
Day Tripper	9	10	
Nowhere Man	9	2	
Paperback Writer	10	1	2
Rain	3	31	
Yellow Submarine	10	1	1
Eleanor Rigby	7	12	
Penny Lane	10	1	2
Strawberry Fields Forever	9	10	
All You Need Is Love	9	1	2

Beatles and any other big pop name is that the Beatles will go on being tops for as long as they want to be."

Scott Walker: *"You just have to regard the Beatles highly. They've always put down what they thought was true. And they must be the show business phenomenon of all time. But actually, I don't have any Beatles albums, because I just don't listen to that kind of music. If I wanted to hear a Beatles song, I'd buy a jazz instrumental version of one of their titles. This, though, doesn't mean I'm not a great admirer. You have to admire them for all they've achieved."*

November 11, 1967 – *Disc and Music Echo* **talked** about the machine behind the Beatles, the people who made it all work.

First, there were the fans, the people of the world who paid to see them, the ones who bought their records and contributed to the group's phenomenal success.

More specifically, though, there were the magnificent seven, starting with Brian Epstein, Eppy, the one closest to the group, their manager, their spirit guide and, without doubt, one of their biggest fans. About the Beatles, he said, *"They are quite magnificent human beings, utterly honest, often irritating, but splendid citizens shining in a fairly ordinary, not very pleasing world."*

And then there was George Martin, the one behind them musically, their musical spirit guide, as it were. Said Martin, *"I'm there to realise what they want. I effect the transition of their ideas."*

Press officer Tony Barrow handled the never-ending requests for information. Almost hourly, someone wanted to know what the Beatles were doing. It was his job to let them know.

Whenever the group was working, on the road or in the studio, or even just relaxing somewhere away from the constant scrutiny, it was the job of Malcolm Evans and Neil Aspinall to make sure things went well for them. They were called road managers, but they were more than that. They were friends, companions, organisers, arrangers, gophers…

And Freda Kelly, the national secretary of their fan club…

And Dick James, the publisher of their music. Before the Beatles, he operated a small music publishing business in London. After the Beatles, he became a music publisher without equal. Every composition by John Lennon and Paul McCartney went through his company, a fortune in royalties.

November 11, 1967 – *Disc and Music Echo*, **Ray Coleman wrote** about the Beatles themselves, the individual personalities that combined to create a unique force.

John Lennon was likely a genius. Clever, motivated, an inventive, hard-edged poet and song writer. He was the fastest thinker of the four, with an unquenchable thirst for knowledge, a barbed wit that bordered on rudeness and cruelty, and a certain originality that had helped lift the Beatles to their incredible heights.

Paul McCartney was the romantic one with the face that made girls swoon. He wrote beautiful, melodic, lyrical songs and never rested on what he had done but constantly strived to be better. In his own way, he was as inventive and original as Lennon. And he was adventurous, leading the group into the electronic age, exploring the sound potential in the recording studios. His thought processes were fast, his plans were deliberate, his attention to detail considerable. He was organised and thoughtful, fast-talking and fast-thinking.

George was the shrewd one, but natural and unaffected. He thought before he spoke. He was intense. Once subdued by the force of Lennon and McCartney, he was coming into his own as both a songwriter and a person. And he had the respect of the others as he studied music and brought fresh sounds to the band. In the early days, his lead guitar rang out and helped the Beatles achieve that sound, that indescribable sound that enchanted the world.

And Ringo was the comedian with the nicest sense of humour. More self-contained than the other three, he was less complicated and less changed by success. Coleman had once asked him how he would like to be remembered by the world when he was gone. Said Ringo, *"With a smile."*

November 11, 1967 – *Disc and Music Echo* **continuing** their series of articles subtitled *Five Years of Beatles,* ran a series of quotes from the Beatles gathered over the years…

John: *"At art school, I maintained that abstract art painting was easy and chucked paint everywhere. They said it was rubbish and I said 'prove it.' They did."*

Paul: *"When you don't have to earn a living, a job takes on new meaning."*

George: *"All of us are trying to get as much love and peace as possible."*

Ringo: *"I've come to terms with my nose. It's the talking point when people discuss me, it goes up one nostril and down the other."*

Paul: *"I even went on a bus from Liverpool to Chester the other day without much trouble. There was a mustache involved."*

John, after the Duke of Edinburgh said the Beatles were on the wane: *"That bloke's getting no money from me for his playing fields."*

John: *"Sometimes I wish I could paint a smile on my face."*

George, when asked by a lady in New York what he called his haircut: *"Arthur."*

George: *"Everyone is a potential Jesus Christ."*

John: *"My auntie said, 'Ah, this music is all very well, but you'll never earn a living at it.'"*

John, talking about the group's bad reception in the Philippines: *"I thought I was going to get hurt so I just headed for three nuns and two monks."*

John: *"The first time I saw Donovan on TV I nearly fell off my chair. I thought, 'Good God, Dylan's back in Britain.' I couldn't believe it."*

John, talking about the marriage of Ringo and Maureen: *"The first thing I thought was, what a sneaky thing to do before I'm back from holiday."*

Paul, after Lennon's so-called anti-Christ comments: *"If they'd wanted to shoot us, it would have been easy for them, at one of those concerts with thousands of people milling around."*

John: *"Whether we look our age or not, very often we feel a lot older than we really are."*

Ringo, to a reporter who asked him what time it

was: *"Time you were in bed."*

Paul, about a Japanese massage: *"I was waiting for the knee-in-your-back bit. When the girl pressed her thumbs into the back of my neck, it was like pushing stuffing into a broken teddy bear."*

George: *"I think Ray Davies and the Beatles have plenty in common."*

John: *"There's something wrong with the present way of governing the country. What we need to change things is a bloody revolution."*

November 11, 1967 – Disc and Music Echo talked about two hundred million record sales. In Britain, the group had had fifteen singles, nine LPs and ten EPs, a remarkable output in just five years. For their British recordings, they had received nineteen Silver Discs, six Gold Discs, and had scored thirteen number one singles.

Their first single, *Love Me Do,* hit the charts five years ago at number twenty-eight, reached number twenty-four and dropped out before Christmas. But their next single, *Please Please Me,* entered the charts at number nine and hit number one three weeks later. *I Want To Hold Your Hand* was their first record to enter the charts at number one. And, until *We Can Work It Out / Day Tripper,* all their subsequent singles automatically started at number one.

After *Love Me Do, Penny Lane / Strawberry Fields Forever* was their first song that failed to reach number one. It came in at number three and only moved up to number two.

Their most recent single, *All You Need is Love,* started at number six and reached number one the following week.

Their fifteen British singles were: *Love Me Do, Please Please Me, From Me to You, She Loves You, I Want to Hold Your Hand, Can't Buy Me Love, A Hard Day's Night, I Feel Fine, Ticket to Ride, Help!, We Can Work It Out / Day Tripper, Paperback Writer / Rain, Yellow Submarine / Eleanor Rigby, Penny Lane / Strawberry Fields Forever* and *All You Need is Love.*

Their nine British albums were: *Please Please Me, With the Beatles, A Hard Day's Night, Beatles For Sale, Help!, Rubber Soul, Revolver, A Collection of Beatles Oldie,* and *Sergeant Pepper's Lonely Hearts Club Band.*

Their ten British EPs were: *Beatles Hits, Twist and Shout, Beatles No. 1, All My Loving, Long Tall Sally, A Hard Day's Night – 1, A Hard Day's Night – 2, Beatles For Sale – 1, Beatles For Sale – 2, Beatles Million Sellers, Yesterday* and *Nowhere Man.*

Their thirteen number one British singles were: *Please Please Me* – February 23, 1963; *From Me to You* – May 4, 1963; *She Loves You* – September 7, 1963; *I Want to Hold Your Hand* – December 7, 1963; *Can't Buy Me Love* – March 28, 1964; *A Hard Day's Night* – July 18, 1964; *I Feel Fine* – December 6, 1964; *Ticket to Ride* – April 17, 1965; *Help!* – July 31, 1965; *We Can Work It Out / Day*

Tripper – December 11, 1965; *Paperback Writer / Rain* – June 18, 1966; *Yellow Submarine / Eleanor Rigby* – August 13, 1966; and *All You Need is Love* – July 15, 1967.

Their nineteen Silver Discs were: *Please Please Me, I Want to Hold Your Hand, Can't Buy Me Love, The Beatles Hits* – EP, *She Loves You, Twist and Shout* – EP, *From Me to You, A Hard Day's Night, The Beatles No. 1* – EP, *All My Loving* – EP, *Long Tall Sally* – EP, *I Feel Fine, We Can Work It Out / Day Tripper, Paperback Writer / Rain, Help!, Ticket to Ride, Yellow Submarine / Eleanor Rigby, Penny Lane / Strawberry Fields Forever* and *All You Need is Love.*

Their six British Gold Discs were: *She Loves You, I Want to Hold Your Hand, Can't Buy Me Love, I Feel Fine, We Can Work It Out / Day Tripper* and *With the Beatles* – LP.

November 11, 1967 – Disc and Music Echo, Penny Valentine added her contribution to *Five Years of Beatles.* She said, to truly enjoy Beatles' music these days you had to *"turn off your mind and float downstream."* A simplification, perhaps, but they had certainly come a long way from the days when you could just crank the volume on your teenage record player and relax in the tub.

In twenty months, the Beatles had evolved from a social phenomena to the undisputed musical leaders of an entire generation.

At first, though original, their music was merely fresh and new. It was energetic. It was sounds for the screamers to scream about. Then came *Rubber Soul* in August, 1965, and *Eleanor Rigby* in August, 1966. Musically, they leapt out in front of the rest of the world, way out in front. And they never looked back.

When Ella Fitzgerald recorded her cover of *Can't Buy Me Love,* backed by Count Basie, the world began to notice that the Beatles were actually songwriters of note. But when they recorded *Rubber Soul,* and, most particularly, *Norwegian Wood,* with its sitar, they began to influence just about everyone. Production values, instruments, rhythms and chords, scoring… Their music grew up, and the rest of the world attempted to follow.

Almost every track on *Rubber Soul* was covered by other entertainers, a guaranteed appearance in the pop charts.

And in America, where the Beatles had eclipsed all the current groups and solo acts, people were following their lead, experimenting with new sounds, creating a new form for pop music.

And just when they all thought they had caught up with the Beatles, *Sergeant Pepper's Lonely Hearts Club Band* hit the airwaves and left them all in the dust again. *Pepper* was the most significant Beatles' record to date, perhaps the most significant *record* to date by anyone anytime anywhere. And it was the end of the just-four-Beatles days. From that moment on, they became a creative force with no boundaries, going ever onwards, leagues ahead of everyone else in the world of music.

November 11, 1967 – *Disc and Music Echo*, **Derek Taylor said t**he Beatles were the best people to be around. Even if they were not the Beatles, that would likely be true.

They were unlike any other group in the history of the world. There were dozens of groups these days, many of them rich, creative and special. But none of them were like the Beatles, none of them had the influence and the originality of the Beatles.

And none of them evoked the same powerful reactions that the Beatles evoked. The joy, the pleasure, the anger, the distaste for the constantly successful, the jealousy, the respect, the disrespect, the criticism, the warmth, the hero worship, the love…

But the Beatles were the best of the best.

The Beatles were too much.

November 11, 1967 – Disc and Music Echo, finally, Laurie Henshaw closed Five Years of Beatles… They spanned all social circles, paupers to princes, presidents to prime ministers, ranged in age from two to ninety, and had one certain thing in common: they were devoted to four young men from Liverpool, four young men who revolutionised the world of music and added a new word to the dictionary: *Beatlemania.*

He talked briefly about the group's early days, the near-anonymous tours, the visits to Hamburg, the Cavern Club… all leading up to the eruption of *Beatlemania*, October 13th, 1963, when the group appeared on TV – *Sunday Night at the London Palladium.*

Said Tony Barrow, *"Great Marlborough Street and Argyll Street, in the vicinity of the London Palladium, were jam-packed with wildly enthusiastic fans. They blocked the traffic and the police had to be called out to clear the streets and get the cars moving.*

"Beatlemania is just as uninhibited in all countries; it just seems wilder in America because of the vaster crowds involved. For instance, you'll get a crowd of three thousand at a venue in Britain, as many as eleven thousand in Japan, where it's the thing to wave handkerchiefs rather than banners, and sixty thousand in the States.

"A Beatles appearance at New York's Shea Stadium is not a concert, it's an experience. At these big baseball parks the fans will somehow break through. At one place, the concert was stopped for forty-five minutes when things almost got out of hand.

"At San Francisco's Cow Palace people were pressed tight against the stage. They were fainting all over the place and were passed behind the stage to a girl who was doing a real Florence Nightingale act reviving them. Joan Baez was her name."

Beatle fans crossed the Atlantic to see their heroes. They camped out overnight to get tickets. They traveled great distances, on foot, by bike and limousine, a pilgrimage to Beatle homes. They remembered Beatle birthdays at least as well as their own. They sent presents and cards and letters. They bought and sold Beatle autographs for outrageous amounts of money. And they all dreamed of the day when they might meet one or two or three or four, live, in person, in the street, in a bar, or, best of all, backstage at a concert, to bask for a moment in the glory, to get an autograph, perhaps, or just a word or two… from John, Paul, George or Ringo Beatle.

November 11, 1967 – *Melody Maker* **announced** that the new Beatles single, *Hello Goodbye*, would be released on November 24th. The A side was written by John Lennon and Paul McCartney to be released as the single. The B side, also by Lennon and McCartney, was *I Am the Walrus*, from *Magical Mystery Tour.*

Paul sang the lead vocals on the A side, John on the B side, with George and Ringo singing back-up on both.

The group was planning to make a short film of *Hello Goodbye*. It was to be shown on television to promote the release.

At press time, the group was still working on the final edit and the final recordings for *Magical Mystery Tour*, which was expected to shown on British television at Christmas.

November 18, 1967 – *Melody Maker* **announced** the release of a new Beatles single, *Hello Goodbye*, backed by *I am the Walrus*, a cut from *Magical Mystery Tour*. Of course, it would be another hit. Musically simpler, gentler, than their recent recordings, but brilliant nonetheless.

November 18, 1967 – *Melody Maker* **said** the recordings from *Magical Mystery Tour* were due to be released in a special book, one week after their new single, *Hello Goodbye*.

The book would include two seven-inch, 45 rpm discs and thirty-two pages of illustrations, priced at

19s 6d. The records would be available in both mono and stereo.

The songs were: Disc One, Side One: *Magical Mystery Tour, Your Mother Should Know*. Side Two: *I am the Walrus*. Disc Two, Side One: *The Fool on the Hill, Flying*. Side Two: *Blue Jay Way*.

Flying was the first song that all four members of the group had written together; it was also the first instrumental released on the Parlophone label.

The book was to have one record inside the front cover, the other inside the back. Shots from the TV film would be printed in both colour and black and white; there would also be half-a-dozen pages of cartoons, illustrating the story, art by Bob Wilson, text by Tony Barrow. Also included would be a lyric sheet.

Said press officer Tony Barrow, *"The Beatles were anxious to keep the cost of the whole production under one pound, and EMI cooperated with this."*

The U.S. version would be an LP with the *Magical Mystery Tour* songs on Side One. Side Two would have: *Hello Goodbye, Penny Lane, Strawberry Fields Forever, All You Need is Love* and *Baby You're a Rich Man*. The book would be released separately.

November 25, 1967 – Disc and Music Echo announced that the Beatles were to appear on Top of the Pops that night (Thursday). It was their first TV appearance since they launched *All You Need is Love* on Our World back in June.

Three short films, directed by the Beatles themselves, had been made for their new single, *Hello Goodbye*. They were to be shown simultaneously in a dozen countries around the world.

A preview of the songs from *Magical Mystery Tour* was to be broadcast on BBC-1 on Saturday at 2 p.m. Kenny Everett would be interviewing John Lennon.

John, Paul, George and Ringo, along with NEMS Enterprises, Subafilms Ltd. And Northern Songs Ltd., had been named in a High Court action in connection with *Yellow Submarine,* the animated film which was now in production in England.

The action had been brought by Thomas Weber, director of Peacock Productions Ltd. The aim was to stop the release of the film.

Said press officer Tony Barrow, *"The action has been put back for a while. We have nothing to say."*

November 25, 1967 – Penny Valentine reviewed the music from *Magical Mystery Tour* for *Disc and Music Echo*... The world would soon be singing yet another Lennon and McCartney composition.

Fool on the Hill featured Paul sadly singing the new Yesterday, complete with penny whistles and a piano.

Magical Mystery Tour had John doing the lead vocals with the rest of the group chanting in the background.

Your Mother Should Know was a nice little tune and the least effective of them all.

Flying was the first Beatles instrumental. It was written by the entire group and featured distant monkish voices chanting in the background.

Blue Jay Way was penned by George Harrison, a strange monotone number.

I am the Walrus explained why John Lennon was dressed in animal fur on the cover.

November 25, 1967 – Melody Maker said *Magical Mystery Tour* would be shown on British television on Christmas Day, but it had yet to be determined whether BBC or ITV would have the broadcast rights. Both apparently wanted it. A spokesman for the BBC said, *"We'd be interested to see it and then take things from there."*

The film directed by the Beatles for *Hello Goodbye* was to be shown on Top of the Pops that day (Thursday). And the music from Magical

Mystery Tour would be previewed on Radio One's Where It's At on Saturday. John Lennon would be on hand to be interviewed by Kenny Everett.

In 1968, the Beatles intended to visit the Maharishi Mahesh Yogi in India. Also planned were a new album by summer and a feature film which they would write, produce and direct themselves.

The *Melody Maker* music chart showed *Sergeant Pepper's Lonely Hearts Club Band* still hanging on the album list at number two.

November 25, 1967 – Melody Maker, Bob Dawbarn said the single should be released in stereo. To illustrate his point, he suggested listening first to the single disc version of *I am the Walrus* in mono, then listening to the stereo version on the *Magical Mystery Tour* EP.

Melody Maker had received the preview package of the new EP that week. Dawbarn said the group had done it yet again. They had released six new songs so inventive, so original, that no other group in the world could hope to equal them. He went on to review the songs individually and finished by saying the stereo effects increased the dynamics of the harmonies and the arrangements.

In a separate article on the same page, Dawbarn said stereo recording had first been revealed at the Audio Fair in 1958. He spoke with Les Cocks, general manager of Pye Records, who said, "*I think eventually everything will be released in stereo only, although this is naturally looking quite a long way ahead.*

"*At the moment, the problem is simply that there is not enough equipment available, not enough players have been adapted from stereo. It's just like the early days of LPs. Lots of people were reluctant to part with their old players, and we had to go on producing seventy-eight rpm discs long after they were outdated.*"

December 2, 1967 – Record Mirror, in a footnote, mentioned that the Beatles' *Magical Mystery Tour* Booklet listed the names and address of all the Beatles Fan Clubs, along with the words, "Hurry now! Don't Delay! Amaze Your Friends and Write Today!"

December 2, 1967 – Disc and Music Echo announced that the Beatles' short film of *Hello Goodbye* had been banned from Top of the Pops. Instead, scenes from *A Hard Day's Night* had been shown along with the song.

Said BBC-TV producer Johnnie Stewart, "*I went to see the three films in Wardour Street on Tuesday night of last week. I realised, because of the Musicians' Union ban on miming, we would run into problems right away.*

"*The first two films were absolutely out of the question. They were mimed from start to finish. The third featured part miming, and I thought there might be a chance of using it. But when I looked at it later, I realised we could have to make so many cuts, it would spoil the production.*

"*I had taken a chap along for some shots of the Beatles while they were editing* Magical Mystery Tour *in Soho. But there wasn't time to prepare this for the show on Thursday. However, we may be able to use this film at a later date.*

"*Frankly, I am surprised the Beatles should have made such miming films for TV. They must know about the MU ban. Everybody else does.*"

Press officer Tony Barrow said, "*The Beatles were disappointed rather than amazed that the film was not shown on* Top of the Pops."

The film was also due to be shown later on that same evening on *Late Night Line-up*. This was also prevented by Musicians' Union ban. Instead, the Condon Jazz Four played an assortment of Beatles' songs.

Said Tony Barrow, "*A coast-to-coast American audience saw the Beatles' film on Ed Sullivan's show on Sunday night.*"

Regarding the rumour that the Beatles planned to open a nightclub in New York named after their *Pepper* album, Barrow said, "*One of the Beatles' companies is discussing the project, but I have nothing to say beyond this.*"

Hello Goodbye had already sold over 300,000 copies, earning it a Silver Disc.

Ringo was due to fly to Rome to start filming *Candy* very soon.

December 2, 1967 – Melody Maker reported advance sales of *Hello Goodbye* had topped 250,000. The day after the record's release, sales were over 300,000. It entered the music charts at number three and was certain to hit number one.

The Beatles' short film that was to be shown on Top of the Pops had been dropped by the BBC; their agreement with the Musicians' Union did not allow miming [lip-syncing].

Said NEMS press officer, Tony Barrow, *"It was a surprise to the Beatles that it was dropped because they had made themselves available to the BBC a couple of days earlier for extra filming to replace the bits of the clip which contravened the miming regulations. But executives at the BBC ruled that it could not be shown."*

The BBC said, quite clearly, that they had no plans to ever run the clip.

Tony Barrow confirmed that a Beatles' company was negotiating to open a night club in New York, possibly to be called *Sergeant Pepper's Lonely Hearts Club Band.* Barrow said it was *"feasible but undecided,"* adding that there were no plans to open a comparable club in England.

Ringo Starr was due to fly to Rome soon to begin filming his role as the Mexican gardener in *Candy.*

December 2, 1967 – *Melody Maker,* **Jack Hutton interviewed Ringo Starr** during a break from editing *Magical Mystery Tour* in the cutting room in Old Compton Street. Hutton said Ringo was likely the most unquoted Beatle…

He said pop music and drugs were being linked together these days and he asked if drugs had made a difference to the music.

Said Ringo, *"It's made a lot of difference to the type of music and the words. It gave everyone more scope and more things to talk about. The words were more relevant and a lot of people don't get it, but others do. It's been a good experience for everybody because it brought out new styles. A lot of people who weren't getting anywhere came out and said it and then got somewhere."*

According to the law, drugs were illegal. Did he condone them?

"It used to be legal until a couple of fellas got around a table and said we're going to make it illegal. Even in hospitals now, they can't get it as they're not allowed to have it for research. This is silly. You can't say to someone 'don't take pot, it's no good.' Or you can't say, 'take it 'cause it is good.' It's up to the person. It's not a harmful thing and I don't see why the law says you can't have it."

Were people influenced by what the Beatles did?

"I hope not, but, by all reports, some of them are. Sometimes it worries me but if people are going to do what you say anyway… If someone says it, they'll do it. They're just a sillier sort of person."

Did he think young musicians should take drugs?

"Oh no, you don't have to. The Troggs haven't, so they tell me, and they're doing all right. It's not 'without it you can't make it.'"

Did he wish the Beatles would do live shows?

"No. That was the scene and that's what we were doing. It's changed now. I'm not against going out, just going out as we were. I was never worried about violence because I've never been hurt. We were always well protected."*

After a show like Shea Stadium, there was little they could do to top it. True?

"No, but there's something. We don't know what it is yet. We keep topping our last LP all the time."

What was his life like these days?

"Very quiet. I get up at nine and come up to town every day. It's like an office job, really. It's a change. I get home about half past seven, have my dinner, chat, do whatever you do and then go to bed. I drive in with John and see Paul and George in town."

Did they ever get together to play?

"No, the only time we ever play is when we're recording. We don't set up in each other's house and say 'Whoopee! Off we go!'"

Did he practice?

"No."

Did he play along with records?

"No."

Did he have a drum kit at home?

"No, haven't got a kit at home, folks. The other week I thought, 'I'll have a kit up here.' Maybe I'll get to it, maybe not. When we don't record, I don't play. The first week, it's like starting again. My style changes on every LP. After a week or so, I find my style."

Did he go out to hear other drummers?

"No. Perhaps it's soft playing drums, because I've never been interested in watching drummers or listening to solos. I've never done a solo because it bores me."

People criticised his playing, and the playing of the rest of the Beatles.

"Yes. People think I can't play. I don't consider myself a great player. I do a rock and roll offbeat and I'm quite happy with that. I don't want to get progressive. When people knock me, I sometimes think I should do something. But that would be catering to them.

"There are a lot of good drummers around. I'd last two lessons and give it up. John and Paul, because they write songs, know how they want it to be done and, in some small way, I complement it. They've usually got a rough idea of how the drum goes as well as the guitar, and the organ, and the piano, and the forty piece orchestra. They say I'd like that bit to do that. They more or less direct me in the style I can play."

Did he want to write music himself?

"I try. I have a guitar and piano and play a few chords, but they're all just chinga-lingas. There's no great tune comes out as far as I'm concerned."

Had he any current musical favourites?

"No, I don't really have favourites. I buy Jimi Hendrix's LP and then I buy someone else's LP. One sort of takes over from the other."

Pop music standards were a lot higher than when the Beatles started.

"Yeah. What we used to play is like Those Were the Days. *It's harder for young fellas now. When I started, I couldn't play anything and none of us could. Now, to get into a group, you've got to have been playing a couple of years and you have to be pretty good."*

Did he think instant success and a lot of money was good?

"They don't get it very fast. A couple of number ones and then out eighteen months later won't make you rich. You'll be back on the buses."

Was the Maharishi important to him?

"Yes. I got to a point where I wondered what I was and what it all was. This looks like answering those questions like nothing else can. I think they'll be the right answers."

Was he ready to spend a lot of time in India to find out?

"Yes. It's the only way. It would be nice if you could sit around and the answers were brought to you, but you've got to find them. Seek and ye shall find, as George keeps saying."

Some people thought the Maharishi asking for a week's wages was questionable.

"Yes, my uncle said that. 'He's after yer money, lads.' But a week's wages is only a lot when they talk about people like us because they think we make a million a day. But for an ordinary man, it's twenty quid, fifteen quid. And that's a fair bargain, one week of your working life you give, and the Maharishi gives you something for the rest of your life."

What would he get out of it?

"A lot of peace and answers. It's not going to come in a week, you know. One fella came to get initiated – a terrible word but that's the word – and he said, 'I've seen him! I've seen him!' Maybe he has, but…"

Was he preparing?

"You meditate every day in a quiet room. You close your eyes anyway so you don't have to decorate a room! Or go into pitch blackness. I do it before I go to work or when I get home from work."

Had Beatles publicity got a lot of people onto the band wagon?

"I suppose some people have followed us. If so, it's a good thing."

Had young people's morals relaxed in Britain?

"I think it's always been the same. Now, there is more publicity and people are talking about these things. Before, if you lived in a little village and one of the girls who wasn't married happened to have a baby, the news would stay in the village. Now, it's different. Newspapers love to build you up. The Beatles or the hippies or any movement. But when you get big, they can only knock you down. They only print the crap, then. They don't print the nice things."

Was the flower movement over?

"It's finished in Britain because we can't afford to keep those lightweight clothes on. You'd freeze to death. So flower people are putting on overcoats again. But people are still feeling nice towards each other, even though they're back into suits.

"One of the reasons it happened was because of all the troubles in the world. We all feel we didn't cause this trouble. It was all these old fellas who run the country. You know, give me a war, I need a war!"

What about conscription, like the Americans for Vietnam?

"No, but the American situation is their situation. The point I'd make about Vietnam is the killing of each other. There's no good reason to take anyone else's life."

In Britain, judges were getting severe with pop musicians.

"Yes, that's because they are the old men again. Judges are old men. And I'm not saying all old people are bad. But some judges think it's a great joke. They're trying to kill the pop people.

"But as soon as they grab one of them, the news is all over everywhere so they've been spreading it. They haven't caught on to that yet. They think it's great, you know, if the police raid a place. But fifty million people have read about it again and a couple of thousand say 'I'll try drugs,' so they're building the case for it, more than against it, because of their silly attitude."

What was next for the Beatles?

"Well, we don't really know. We'll have to see. It's maybe the magical boat ride. We'll go on as we are. I may break out and do a film part. Because of the last two films, they sort of stuck on me as Ringo the film star, because I don't write or anything like that."

From the background, Paul McCartney shouted, *"Naw, but yer great in films, Ring. You make the grooviest films!"*

December 9, 1967 – Ray Coleman interviewed John Lennon and Paul McCartney for *Disc and Music Echo*. Part One: It was lunch time in Soho. John and Paul were walking slowly along the street. No one mobbed them. The cops did not order them off the street for their own protection. They were free and un-hassled. In a shop window, there was a calendar featuring scantily clad girls.

Said John, *"Bet you daren't go in and buy it."*

Replied Paul, *"Okay."* He went into the shop, returning moments later with a plain brown envelope. He said, *"Discretion always. As you can see, I asked them to give it to me under plain wrapper…"*

Such freedom had not always been possible for the Beatles. But times were changing.

They went to lunch at the Trattoria Terraza…

Said Paul, *"Oh yes, the swinging Beatles have to eat at the in-place!"*

He addressed their new freedom… *"We never did really like being surrounded by a big team of bodyguards and all that, although it was necessary* at times. *Now, it's much more like the old Cavern days, it's lovely to be able to be friends with fans.*

"If people come and stand at the end of my road, I try to go and talk to them, and the relationship is so normal. They get autographs, if they want them, and I enjoy finding out what they've got to say. It's great.

"This pop-glamour bit, nobody is really like that. People who behave as great big stars are kidding themselves and nobody else.

"The thing is, we never believed in Beatlemania. If you're the Beatles, who people everywhere talk about and write about, you've got to be a Beatle for twenty-four hours a day. And you believe in it for the twenty-four hours.

"But we never really believed in it, never took the whole thing that seriously, I suppose. That way, we managed to stay sane."

Said John, *"That's right. The Beatles are sane."*

Coleman asked if they were unaware of what was going on during their tours and during the height of Beatlemania.

Answered Paul, *"Oh, we knew a bit of it, but things moved so fast it was hard to take it all in. We didn't have time to sit back and consider it. But we knew a lot was going on, and when we had a few months off, we started thinking about it a bit more. It had gone round in a circle. Today, we're still doing roughly what we were always doing, only now it's in other directions. It's like a zig-zag. And it doesn't only apply to records. It applies to everything."*

Added John, *"We think we're only just starting. As far as I'm concerned, we're starting afresh every day. Who wants to rest on what's gone? That was then. It's history. It's all happened and finished. We've got to prove ourselves all the time."*

Paul explained they did not want to live their lives getting Beatlemania reactions. *"We'd like the recognition, of course, but without the scenes that go with it."*

John said, *"It's a groove, having different kinds of fans now. People who are just interested in what we are producing instead of just who we are."*

For lunch, Paul ordered chicken and John had pancakes.

"I occasionally eat meat," Paul said. *"John and George feel more like vegetarians than me, but I'm a sympathiser."*

"It happened way before the Maharishi," John explained. *"I just decided I didn't fancy the idea of eating meat any more. I occasionally eat meat, but I believe in vegetarianism."*

"If you've ever opened an egg," Paul said, *"and seen a little chicken in there, you'll know what the feeling behind this is. We've decided we don't need meat. There's no need at all to eat it, and a lot of people say it's no good for you. I like bacon and eggs and things like that but at least I'm aware of doing without it."*

John said, *"One day, I just decided that was it. George had been talking about it, and it had been going through my mind, anyway, for a long time. I just started looking at this meat on my plate and thought: Why?"*

Said Paul, *"Oh, let's stop talking about it. People already think the Beatles are cranks who get hung up on things. The thing is, we've got our beliefs, and we're not saying anybody should follow us. 'Cranky Beatles don't eat meat but they meditate' and all that."*

They talked about meditation and the suspicion regarding the methods of the Maharishi Mahesh Yogi, and the critics who said transcendental mediation was an irresponsible opting-out of society.

Said John, *"It's not opting out, it's opting in! You don't have to go to Wales and do it, or even cut yourself off from society or reality. And you don't have to get so hung up about it that you go round in a trance. I can't understand why people are so stubborn, and why they're not open-minded. I do my meditation in the car on the way back home from work."*

Paul said, *"People who put these things down, like meditation, don't listen to anything. They have closed minds. They always advance some argument against it, and that's easy to do. It's so stupid, you see, because they're not allowing anything fresh or different to get inside their heads. Even if they could possibly be right, or good.*

"They're the cranks, trying to force the issue. We're not trying to force any issues or say we're right, even. We're just trying, while other people fight against a natural enthusiasm for something."

John said, *"If the Maharishi was asking people to devote their lives to meditation, that would be different. But what possible harm can it do anyone to try for half-an-hour a day, something that could be good?"*

Paul added, *"We're just trying to find out about things instead of putting them down as a lot of rubbish. Instead of doing what a lot of others do, go naturally against things, all suspicious-like, we're giving the benefit of the doubt.*

"Meditation might be a big con. That doesn't matter, either. I don't think it is a con, but, if it is, I want to find out why. I don't believe the Maharishi is a con. I believe he's telling the truth."

December 9, 1967 – Disc and Music Echo, Penny Valentine wrote about the McCartney brothers. The article was mainly concerned with Mike McGear. But she compared the two, explaining how unalike they were. Paul was the musical visionary, a careful, tactful, diplomatic man who planned his moves carefully. Mike, on the other hand, was extroverted and more immediate. His life unfolded as if by accident, while Paul's life was as controlled as possible.

Valentine's article was mostly about McGear and his band, the Scaffold, who were making a name for themselves.

Said Mike, *"Dad was a pianist with the Jimmy Mack Jazz Band in Liverpool and he always wanted* us to get up and bash away. I just didn't want to know about it, but he bought me a drum kit and Paul a lovely guitar. I managed to break my arm so the drum kit was useless, but Paul just went mad about his guitar. He wouldn't put it down, took it everywhere with him, even to the bathroom."

The McCartney family had been ecstatic over the success of the Beatles. Now, with the Scaffold's growing success, two LPs to date, they were even happier.

Mike said, "You know, they were just saying the other day how they felt exactly as they did with when the Beatles started to happen. Me Auntie Jean sits in front of the telly having kittens in case we make a mistake or something, just as she did when Paul started. Odd, really."

December 9, 1967 – *Melody Maker* **announced** that *Hello Goodbye* had hit number one in the charts that week but *Magical Mystery Tour*, even with advance orders of 250,000, had not made it into the top thirty, a mystery in itself.

EMI press officer, Sid Gillingham, cleared up the mystery: *Magical Mystery Tour* had not reached the music stores yet. "We never announced a firm release date for it. All we said was that it would be released in the first week of December, and, in fact, it is going out to dealers today."

Press officer, Tony Barrow, said, "I think dealers are not sure how to deal with the record, because it isn't a conventional single or album. But it should be treated as a single record."

The Beatles were also releasing another Christmas record for their fans. It would not be available to the public.

In the U.S., *Hello Goodbye* had already sold 900,000 copies and was expected to earn a Gold Disc by the weekend.

December 16, 1967 – *Record Mirror*, **in their Pop Shorts section**, said the Beatles film, *Magical Mystery Tour*, had been banned by the BBC but was now scheduled to be shown on Boxing Day by BBC-1 and would be shown again within two weeks on BBC-2.

December 16, 1967 – Ray Coleman interviewed John Lennon and Paul McCartney for *Disc and Music Echo*. **Part Two:**

Said Paul, "If there is any message at all in Hello Goodbye, it is that the answer to everything is so simple. It's a song about everything... and nothing. Stop – go. Yes – no. If you have black, you also have white. That's the amazing thing about life, all the time. Realisation and awareness of views, different things..."

For years, Beatle students had been analysing Beatle lyrics, digging out hidden messages. John and Paul tended to shrug it off.

Paul said, "Our songs are about people and things, love playing a big role, if you like, because it's a nice subject, and anyway, it's always been sort of traditional to have love as a theme for songs. But with Hello Goodbye, the song's about blacks and whites in the world, something like the Bee Gees' thing, 'Today I found out the world is round and it doesn't rain every day.'"

Lennon and McCartney did not believe the new realism in their songs was particularly significant.

John said, "It will be back round to love songs very soon. We haven't stopped writing love songs. Lucy In the Sky was a love song. We all started writing easy love songs, and at the moment, it's all down to writing about anything, like Hello Goodbye. It's not a pointer, particularly."

Paul said, "I personally love good love songs, although I went through a spell of finding myself embarrassed by them. You go through periods, sometimes you fancy doing a solid, manly song about life without love in it, then you do an easy love song."

John added, "Walrus is just saying a dream, the words don't mean a lot. People draw so many conclusions, and it's ridiculous."

Coleman wanted to know if the Beatles would ever tour again, or if they would concentrate on making albums, brilliant albums like *Pepper*.

"At the moment, tours are out," Paul said.

John explained, "You never know, but they are such big things to plan, and a bit of a drag to do. At least, a drag organised in the normal way as most people know them. If we could find some different way of doing a tour, it could be that we'd do it, but it'd just have to be in a different way. There's no point in repeating what we've done before. We wouldn't be putting up anything different."

Don't they think they have a responsibility to the fans who would like to see them on stage?

John answered, "No, I don't think we have a responsibility to fans. You give them the choice of liking what you're doing, or not liking it. If they don't like it, they let you know... fast.

"If you allow everything to be dictated by fans, you're just running your life for other people. All we do is try to give fans an even deal. We try to behave politely, sometimes in the face of some very impolite people, and we try to treat people with respect because they're human beings."

Paul said, "People who say, 'I have a big responsibility to my public' are the biggest rogues out. You can tell they're lying, anyway, you can see through them. They're not kidding me, nor anybody else who knows the scene. The only people they're kidding are themselves.

"We're probably nicer to people because we don't have this big thing about feeling a big responsibility to the world. The people who talk about responsibilities include politicians, and they show their great sense of responsibility by starting wars and putting people in prison. They're the ones who say things like, 'The younger generation don't know what they're talking about. We've had experience.'

"Well, all I can say is, they've not used their experiences very well, some of 'em."

Said John, *"They're just playing the political game. 'We know what's best' and all that. Quintin Hogg reckons we're leading the youth of Britain astray. Quintin Hogg!"*

They talked about age, and John said, *"It's a groove, growing older. I'm looking forward to it, when I'm say, sixty-seven, and they'll have me on the Eamonn Andrews show. 'And here he is, ladies and gentlemen, carrying the very guitar he played on stage at the world famous Cavern in Liverpool: John Lennon.'"*

Paul said, *"And then you'll play* She Loves You."

"Yeah, what a groove," John told him.

December 16, 1967 – *Disc and Music Echo* **said** that the Beatles were playing Santa Claus to forty thousand fans. They were sending out their fifth Christmas album, free to Beatle fans. This year, it was to be played at LP speed and was titled: *Christmas Time is Here Again.* It was a six-minute EP in a colour sleeve, the cover a montage of photographs put together by John and Ringo. Copies had been sent out to radio stations but the record would not be for sale in shops.

December 16, 1967 – *Disc and Music Echo,* **Penny Valentine wrote** about the new Apple, the Beatles' shop at 94 Baker Street, London. In a riot of lights and TV cameras, clowns and champagne… and apples, the shop had opened the previous week.

The outside walls had been painted in vibrant psychedelic colours, shocking the neighbourhood.

On December 5th, the lights went on and "buy Beatles, buy best" was just about ready.

Apple was to showcase everything the Beatles liked best, everything they believed in. In the Apple bazaar, you could find almost anything: clothes, books, records, furniture, jewelry, candles, bangles, joss sticks, purses, shoes… There were one hundred and fifty designs in five hundred colours, something for just about everybody.

All the designs were by The Fool – the Beatles, the Hollies and Stones' friends Josie and Barry and Simon and Marjike.

Apple was not simply a new boutique. It was a way of life.

More shops were planned for Birmingham, Manchester and Liverpool.

December 16, 1967 – *Melody Maker,* **Nick Jones interviewed George Harrison. Part One:**

The Maharishi and the Beatles were already being criticised with regards to transcendental meditation.

Said George, *"It's easier to criticise somebody than to see yourself. We had got to the point where we were looking for somebody like the Maharishi, and then there he was. Most other people had never thought about this before and suddenly, there he is being thrust down their necks."*

This did not just happen all of a sudden?

"No, it's been about three years' thinking, looking for why we're here, the purpose of what we're doing here on this world, getting born and dying. Normally, people don't think about it, and then they just die, and then they've gone and missed it, because we do come here for some purpose.

"And I've found out that the reason we come here is to get back to that thing God had, whatever you might call God, you know, that scene. The thing is, everybody is potentially divine, every human being is potentially a Christ."

So the Beatles were into this before the Maharishi and the publicity?

"Yeah. When you're young, you get taken to church by your parents and you get pushed into religion in school. They're trying to put something into your mind. But it's wrong, you know. Obviously, because nobody goes to church and nobody believes in God. Why? Because religious teachers don't know what they're teaching. They haven't interpreted the Bible as it was intended.

"This is the thing that led me into the Indian scene, that I didn't really believe in God as I'd been taught it. It was just like something out of a science fiction novel.

"I think it was really after acid, because acid was the big sort of psychological reaction. It's really only after acid that it pushes home to you that you're only little, really. And there's all that infinity out there and there's something doing it, you know.

"It's not just that it's us doing it or the Queen doing it, but that it's some great power that's doing it.

"Then the music, Indian music, just seemed to have something very spiritual for me, and it became a stepping stone for me to find out about a whole lot of other things. Finding out all about Hinduism and all those sort of religions made me realise that Christianity is that as well, every religion is just the same scene, really.

"For Christianity, it's the people who profess to be the religious teachers who screw the whole thing up. They're the people who create the sectarianism, the prejudices and the hate that goes on. You know, those people who are supposed to be propagating the Lord's word, they're screwing it all up.

"You're taught to just have faith, you have to worry about it, just believe what we're telling you. And this is what makes the Indian one such a groove for me, and I'm sure a lot of other people, because over there, they say 'don't believe in anything… if there's a God, we must see him, if there's a soul, we must perceive it,' and so on.

"It's better to be an outspoken atheist than a hypocrite, so their whole teaching is, don't believe in nothing until you've witnessed it for yourself. I really feel and believe very much in this whole sort of scene, you know, God. You know when you said the

word 'god' people are going to curl up and cringe, they all interpret it in a different way.

"The Maharishi is a monk and he hasn't got a penny and he doesn't want to have any. He doesn't have any money and, obviously, you get the press saying he's staying at the Hilton and he does this or he does that, but in actual fact, he didn't stay in the Hilton but in a meditator's suite.

"And he's been here for nine years and, for eight of those years, he never had a word written about him, and then the Beatles got interested in him and then here he gets all this. And we all know where the press is at and all those people are putting him down, because they're only writing about him because of us."

How does this all fit into his day-to-day life? Was he saying that everything was predestined?

"Well, yes. This is what the Maharishi says. The more you meditate, the more you harmonise with life in general and the more nature supports you. Nature has supported you since you were born, if you like to think about it.

"I mean, why did I go that school at that time and this fella, who met this fell, and we did this, you know, why?

"Why did I meet Ravi Shankar? And the difference between the thing of me meeting Ravi Shankar is that people will see this from their point of view, but actually it's much different. When I met him and got to know him, it was like I'd known him for a thousand years, and the same response back from him.

"The more I've got into it, the more you find out about the truth, then the more you can see this thing we call reality isn't reality at all, this is all an illusion.

"And this is the big drag because everybody lives their lives thinking this is reality and then say to people like us, 'oh, you're just escaping from reality.'

"They seriously term this scene of waking up, going out to work, going home again, going to sleep, dreaming, waking up again and all that, reality! But in actual fact, you're into illusion, it's nothing to do with reality because reality is God alone. Everything else is illusion.

"Those people in the Himalayas, the Yogi who are very advanced spiritually, and all the ones on other planets, well, it's just a joke to them, all this that we do and call reality. I mean, it's even a joke if you just take yourself out of it and watch all the things going on.

"It's a joke. And the joke's on all the people who take it seriously. There's so much more to it. You see, every so often, somebody comes to Earth, like Jesus did, and they've been coming every so often, these people, divine incarnations, like Buddha, Jesus, and all that. There's always these people coming, and they are the truth, like God, this great force, whatever it is, manifesting itself into a physical form.

"And there are quite a few people walking around on Earth this minute who have attained all that, all over the world, in the Himalayas, in America,

everywhere, and they just look like funny little old men. I mean, like Maharishi, they look like that.

"People, of course, don't take much notice of them or put 'em down, when all these people are doing is telling the truth, they're always there.

"I read somewhere that the next fella like that, the next Messiah like, he'll come and he'll just be too much. Anybody who doesn't believe that he's the one then, he'll just show 'em, you know. He's just gonna come down and zap them all.

"Miracles, like. That's why this whole thing is getting better and better. It's building up to a great peak. It's the cycle moving on. The majority of people are going to believe and they'll be digging everything and he'll come and say, 'yeah, baby, that's right,' and all those other people who are bastards, they're gonna get something else. Instead, when they die, they won't reincarnate on this Earth, they'll get put down on another planet that's still got to come through the evolutionary thousands of years that we've just been through. It's just fantastic, you know.

"Really, it's all too much, because everybody who's becoming involved realises it is part of the plot.

"I don't like to use the word 'religious' but when you get into whatever that is, that scene, when you go through yoga and meditation, it's just… self realisation.

"And the next world that's coming along is going to bring us into this age that's known as the Golden Age.

"You know that scene about the Iron Age, the Stone Age, the Ice Age, and that's this thing of evolution, the cycles that it goes through, and the Golden Age is when everything is really nice.

"A pleasure to be here."

December 23, 1967 – *Disc and Music Echo* **said** that the Beatles were hosting two Christmas parties that year. The first one had been for the fan club secretaries, at the Hanover Grand Film and Art Theatre, London, the previous Sunday. Fans were entertained by George and John, and were giving screenings of *Magical Mystery Tour* and *The Beatles at Shea Stadium*.

Ringo had missed the first party; it was held as he returned from Rome. Paul McCartney was missing both parties. He and Jane Asher were staying at Paul's farm house in the Scottish Highlands.

The second party, to be held that day at a secret location, was for the cast and crew of *Magical Mystery Tour* and the staff of NEMS, along with a few close friends. It was to be a fancy dress affair.

Hello Goodbye was still holding the number one position in the charts with sales of over half a million. The *Magical Mystery Tour* EP had sold almost half a million and had qualified for a Silver Disc award.

Magical Mystery Tour was still to be shown by BBC-1 the day after Christmas.

December 30, 1967 – *Record Mirror* **announced** that the sales of the American LP, *Magical Mystery Tour,* had hit 1,600,000 copies in the three weeks since its release, making a total of eight million dollars. *Hello Goodbye* was still number one in the U.S. music charts.

December 30, 1967 – *Melody Maker***, Nick Jones interviewed George Harrison. Part Two:**

Jones began by saying they had been talking about how meditation and yoga could lead to self-realisation.

Said George, *"Yes, that's the whole thing, why people have missed God. They haven't been able to see God because he is hidden in themselves. All the time, people concentrated their energies and actions outwards of this surface that we live on.*

"But it's only by turning your concentration and directing it inwards into a form of meditation, that you can see your own god there. When you realise a lot of things about this surface, because you're now looking at it from a more subtle point of view.

"I mean really, there's people on every planet going on different planes. Not necessarily in a form as we know it, but in a different form.

"Like Venus. They've gone to Venus and they come back and say, 'Oh, very sorry, it's too hot to live there' and all that scene, but they're looking for people as we know them, people like us. Really, what they're saying is, you can't live on Venus in the physical body as we know it. As we understand people to be the same as us, then they couldn't possibly live there, but in actual fact, you won't see anybody if you go there unless you're on their frequency."

Did he think music was important in this evolutionary cycle?

"Yeah, very important. I think there is a need for spiritual music. This is why I got so hung up on Indian music and from the day I got into it till the day I die, I still believe it's the greatest music ever on our level of existence. It's really so, so subtle, that's the whole thing about this level of consciousness that we're on, the opposite of the subtle level.

"Everything those Indian musicians do, it's just indescribable, an inner feeling, yeah, and it's like saying, 'It's this, man!' You know, all the music that's going on, just the first thing people get into, the soul kick, but when you really get into the soul, that's God.

"But the music is very important because of the mass media point of view. I think music is the main interest of the younger people. It doesn't really matter about the older people now, because they're finished anyway. There's still going to be years and years of having these old fools who are governing us and who are bombing us and doing all that because, you know, it's always there.

"But it's no good getting hung up about them because the main thing is to get the kids. You know, this is the Catholic trip, they nail you when you're young and brainwash you, and then they've got you for the rest of your life.

"In actual fact, do this sort of thing, but brainwash people with the truth, turn them all onto music and books at that age, then they'll live a better life. Then it's the next generation that does it more, and after that… so it doesn't really matter if we see the perfection of the Golden Age or not. I don't expect to see the world in a perfect state of bliss, you know, like one hundred per cent, but it doesn't matter, it's on the way now, so, really, with the Maharishi, we've gone into all these things and scenes, and I've learned a hell of a lot about Hinduism from being in India, things I've read, and from Ravi Shankar, who's really too much, so great, not only in his music but in him as well.

"This is the thing. He is the music, and the music is him. The whole culture of the Indian philosophy, the background and all that. Mainly, it's this thing of discipline. Discipline is something that we don't like, especially young people, where they have to go through school, and they put you in the army, and all that discipline. But in a different way, I've found out it's very important, because the only way those musicians are great is because they've been disciplined by their guru or teacher, and they've surrendered themselves to the person they want to be.

"It's only by complete surrender and doing what that bloke tells you that you're going to get there, too, so with their music, they do just that. You must practice twelve hours a day for years and years and years, and Shankar has really studied every part of the music until he just improvises the music until it is just him, he is the music."

Was that the point they were attempting to make in the ads that said *"Sergeant Pepper IS the Beatles?"*

"I feel this is something we've been trying to do all the time. Keep that identification with people. It gets harder and harder the more famous you get. People see you, they put you up on that pedestal and they really believe you're different from them. With Sergeant Pepper, we've always tried to keep this identification and tried to do things for those people, to please those people, because, in actual fact, they're us, too, really.

"It's no good us doing it all for ourselves, it's for them. With Pepper, it's just that anybody who wants to be in Pepper's band is in it. Anybody who feels any identification. And this all gets back again to God. But at the same time, we're all responsible, in a way, because a lot of people are following us, we're influencing a lot of people, so really, it's to influence them in the right way."

Did people realise what he was giving them?

"Well, lots of people do, but then there's always the other ones who write in saying, 'Why the fuck do you think you are doing that?' There's always that,

you see, and it all gets back to the thing of the Maharishi and God.

"The Maharishi says this level that we're on is like the surface of the ocean, which is always changing, chopping and changing, and we're living on the surface with these waves crashing about. But unless we're anchored on the bottom, we're at the mercy of whatever goes on on the surface, so you go into meditation and your thoughts get smaller all the time, finer and finer, until you get right down there until that's just pure consciousness and you anchor yourself to that, and once you've established that anchor, then it doesn't matter what goes on up on the surface.

"The more people who do it, the more they'll realise. You can't tell somebody what it's like until they try it for themselves. If you can contact that absolute state, you can just tap that amazing source of energy and intelligence. It's there, anyway, you've just got to contact it and then it will make whatever you do easier and better. Everything in life works out better because everybody is happier with themselves."

— Chapter Eight: 1968 —

January 27, 1968 – *Disc and Music Echo* **ran a brief article** about Cilla Black's new single, *Come Inside Luv,* written for her by Paul McCartney and meant to be the opening and closing number of her new TV show, starting January 30th on BBC-1.

It was the third Beatles composition to be released by Black as a single. The first two were *Love of the Loved* and *It's For You.*

Ringo Starr would be a guest on Cilla's February 6th show.

January 27, 1968 – *Disc and Music Echo* **announced** the launching of Grapefruit, the first group signed to the Beatles' Apple music publishing company. Their debut record was *Dear Delilah.* On hand for the launch party were Brian Jones, Donovan, Cilla Black, John Lennon, Ringo Starr and Paul McCartney.

Twiggy had approached the Beatles about producing her first film. Nothing had been finalised, but the group was interested.

Paul McCartney played drums to back up Paul Jones, ex-Manfred Mann singer, on his new single, produced by Peter Asher.

March 9, 1968 – *Disc and Music Echo,* **Bob Farmer wrote** that the Beatles were intending to release a record for charity, *Across the Universe.* The song had been written and sung by John Lennon.

The charity to receive the royalties was likely to be associated with the Maharishi Mahesh Yogi.

Another Beatles song, *All Together Now,* was due to be released in May. It had been written for the animated film *Yellow Submarine.*

It was thought that the Beatles were going to make a film about their studies of transcendental meditation under the Maharishi.

A footnote mentioned that *Sergeant Pepper's Lonely Hearts Club Band* had won four U.S. Grammy awards. Album of the Year; Best Technically Engineered Album; Best Contemporary LP of the Year; and Best Album Cover. Recording manager, George Martin, had been to New York last week to collect the awards.

Another footnote mentioned that Ringo and his wife, Maureen, were home from India after only ten days of study at the Maharishi's meditation centre. The rest of the group was expected to remain in India for another six to eight weeks.

Said Ringo, *"We didn't come home early. We never planned to be away from the children for more than a couple of weeks. I thoroughly enjoyed the visit and so did Maureen. Some people have got the wrong idea about the Maharishi's place. It's comfortable and the food's okay. All is well and of the best holiday standard."*

March 9, 1968 – *Melody Maker,* **Don Short wrote** about being with the Beatles in India. He said the Beatles had the most loyal fans in the world, fans who followed them through every new chapter of their story. He could not help wondering if the fans would also follow their heroes into the meditation thing.

At first, Short thought the group had finally lost it, they were crazy. But he realised quite quickly that they were serious about transcendental meditation as a possible solution to the problems of the world.

Said George Harrison, *"Its ultimate message is love for one another."*

Meditation, practiced seriously, would mean an end to all the bad things in life, each one dropping away until a state of bliss was attained.

The group was quite sincere about it, hence their pilgrimage to the Himalayas and the Maharishi's ashram, which was set in the forested foothills overlooking India's holy river, the Ganges. The circular camp, one hundred and forty miles from New Delhi, was composed of white chalets for the pupils, a meditation hall, an open-air amphitheatre, a laundry, a post office and a dining hall. Just across the river was Rishikesh, a town of twelve thousand people, ten thousand of whom were monks.

When the Beatles, their three wives and Jane Asher arrived, there were already sixty converts present. Since their arrival, they had been having private sessions with the Maharishi, a sort of crash course to help them catch up to the other meditators.

The Maharishi was predicting that when the Beatles left his Academy, *"They will become the practical philosophers of their age."*

An argument could be made that they had already achieved that status.

There were no iron-clad rules at the Academy. Scheduling was tight, time well used.

There were morning and afternoon sessions at the amphitheatre, guided by either the Maharishi or one of his top disciples. The sessions lasted for six hours but, with each passing day, the hours of study were shortened, the hours for meditation, lengthened.

Said the Maharishi, *"Soon, the students will reach thirty-hour sessions of meditation without eating, drinking or sleeping."*

Short was endlessly asked if the Maharishi was *"taking them all for a ride?"*

He still did not know. But he liked the Maharishi, liked his sense of humour and the depth of his sincerity. People often accused the Maharishi of being in it for the money, but Short saw no evidence of that. The man spent most of his time meditating. The money he received went towards expanding the movement and the construction of new meditation centres throughout the world.

As for the Beatles, they, along with the Beach Boys, had promised to help garner donations. For the Beatles, there was no turning back.

Said John Lennon, *"They had to kill Jesus Christ first, before they proved he was Jesus Christ. And even if the Maharishi vanished now, we would still say that how far we had gone with him was worthwhile."*

George added, *"The Maharishi is the kind of person the knockers are bound to knock. But one day, they will all wonder why they did."*

Ringo and Paul shared similar views.

Said Paul, *"We feel that, through our music, we will be shown the way we are really going. And others, we hope, will follow us."*

The Maharishi was certain that the Beatles would be able to influence vast numbers of people with his message.

Short wondered if the fans would *"still hesitate before they meditate."*

March 9, 1968 – *Melody Maker*, said Ringo Starr and his wife unexpectedly flew home after only ten days with the Maharishi in India.

Ringo said, *"The Maharishi didn't really want us to leave and kept asking us if everything was all right. He suggested that perhaps we should go off somewhere and take a holiday and then go back to the meditation centre, but we wanted to come home.*

"Really, his meditation centre is a bit like a Butlin's holiday camp. We'd been sent lists of what to take with us, like blankets and camping things, but we didn't need any of them. It's all very luxurious.

"It wasn't what you'd call a hard life. We all lived in chalets and we used to get up in the morning, not particularly early, then all go down to the canteen for breakfast, then perhaps walk about a bit and meditate or bathe.

"Of course, there were lectures or things all the time, but it was very much like a holiday. The Maharishi did everything he could to make us comfortable. I suppose there is a possibility we may go to his other centre in Kashmir, but I don't know yet."

March 16, 1968 – *Disc and Music Echo*, Ray Coleman spoke with Ringo Starr in Tony Barrow's London office.

It was four in the afternoon and Ringo had not eaten lunch; he asked Barrow's secretary if it would be possible to get a sandwich.

"Prawn, cheese or ham?" she asked.

"Is that all you've got?"

"Well, yes."

"I'll skip it then," Ringo said. *"I don't eat any of that stuff any more. A cup of coffee'll do."*

He explained to Coleman why he did not eat meat.

"It's nothing to do with what the Maharishi told us," Ringo said. *"The Maharishi is vegetarian more because of his religion than anything. We simply all decided to try it because we knew there wouldn't be* any meat over in India. On the way over, we decided we'd go the whole way, well, nearly the whole way. I still eat eggs, but that's about all in that line.

"I suppose it would be better to call us fruitatarians than anything else. We all think it's a lot healthier than eating meat, anyway."

Ringo returned from India early, after a mere ten days of meditation. But he still believed in meditation. He came home because he and his wife missed their children and had learned as much as they wanted.

"I didn't leave India because I've had enough of meditation, or anything like that. I still think the whole thing is good. The Maharishi is interested in helping people enjoy life two hundred per cent instead of one hundred per cent. He doesn't say you mustn't drink, smoke, or eat meat or anything like that. He just shows you that, through meditation, you achieve a sort of inner peace.

"I've found it works, anyway. So have the others. We all feel such a lot better for it."

Precisely how did he do it?

"At the moment, I meditate every day, well, I might skip the odd day, if I get up late, or arrive in town late, or something. Meditation consists of just sitting down, closing your eyes, and letting your mind free. It takes about an hour a day, usually. You are given a word on which to meditate, this is called your mantra.

"It's important to meditate on the word, but also important not to let your concentration on it take over completely, or else your mind goes too far down into your being.

"No, I can't tell anyone else what my mantra is. The Maharishi gives you a personal mantra on which to meditate and it should only be used by the person he gives it to.

"If, for instance, my mantra was bootlace, it might be completely wrong for anyone else to use it because it wouldn't suit them. They have to be given their own personal mantra, which is only for them and not for anyone else.

"All the words used as a mantra are very old and tried for generations in India, they've tried them out for hundreds of thousands of years, and they know exactly what they do to you, what effect they have.

"There are household mantras and monk's mantras. Household mantras mean that you can carry on with a normal life, not changing your basic ideas at all if you don't want to. But a monk's mantra would involve him in removing himself completely from society, maybe."

Ringo was certain that meditation was helping him enjoy life to the fullest, but had not changed him in any significant way.

He said, *"I'm still likely to get angry, you know, and I can still get worked up about things, just like anyone else. But now there's definitely a change of reason why, and at least I know why I'm worked up* to the state I'm in. If I do get angry now, I realise it's something I must get over. Of course, it's natural to get angry, get worked up now and then. But somehow, I feel I can control it more now.

"It's over a period of time that you notice you feel better."

A lot of people believed the Beatles were wasting their time, that meditation was a joke. P.J. Proby was one of the more vocal people saying it was all a hoax.

Ringo said, "I'm not trying to convert them all. All I'll say is that we'll do what we want to do and they can do what they want to do. Who wants to have an argument about it? Not us.

"I notice that the people who have been having a go at meditation and the Maharishi, most of them haven't even tried it. I'd like them to just try it, at least, before they shoot their mouths off and call it rubbish."

Ringo and Maureen were teaching their children about meditation and its benefits. Said Ringo, "If we, that's the older teenagers, can encourage the younger generation to take an interest in it, the Maharishi says we'd have a happier world. People would have better things to think about than going out shooting each other."

March 16, 1968 – *Melody Maker* **spoke with Alan Freeman about** the Beatles new single, *Lady Madonna*. Said Freeman, "Oh God! You would ask me about this. I think the moment you know you are hearing the Beatles, you listen more intently than to any other records. After *Sergeant Pepper*, I don't feel they could have progressed any further and still made contact with their fans, and I do believe that, above all else, keeping contact with the fans is what they want to do. I don't hear this as rock and roll at all, just up-tempo Beatles, and anything of theirs is surrounded by an aura of magic."

March 16, 1968 – *Melody Maker*, **Alan Walsh interviewed Ringo Starr**.

"Just because the others are in India, I get all the interviews," joked Ringo.

They were in NEMS' new Mayfair offices. Walsh said *Lady Madonna* seemed to almost be a return to rock and roll.

Said Ringo, "Yes, that what it is, almost a return to rock and roll."

What were they trying to accomplish with the record?

"The thing is, we've been trying to make a rock and roll record for five years. Because rock and roll has suddenly hit the headlines, the great revival, because this one is a rocker – a slight one anyway – people are saying it's a rock and roll record."

When did they first think about this song?

"Paul thought of it, originally. He did it like Fats Waller first. I only heard it in the studio. Paul plays piano on it. What he's doing on piano is a sort of Bad Penny Blues. We said to George Martin, 'How did they do it on Bad Penny Blues?' And he said they used brushes, so I used brushes and we did a

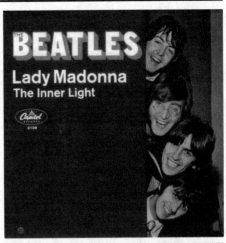

track with just brushes and the piano, and then we decided we needed an off-beat, so we put an off-beat on it, and then Paul decided to sing it in his sort-of Elvis voice."

A lot of people thought he was doing the singing.

"Yes, a lot of people did. It didn't sound like me to me."

Was this the closest they had gotten to a rock song in five years?

"Ever since rock and roll, rock and roll records have been made, but people forgot to say rock and roll. All through the years, there have been people who have come out with rock and roll records but now, suddenly, everyone wants rock and roll to come back so they're saying this is a rock record and that's a rock record.

"They've picked out records that have an off-beat, or a saxy thing, or a Duane Eddy thing. They're calling ours rock and roll, and the Move's Fire Brigade, and Elvis's record. I don't think anyone will ever go back to rock and roll as it was years ago, the reissues will be the only ones because there's so much more musical influence now from all the years that have gone before.

"Rock originally was influenced by country and western and the blues mainly, but now we've had ten or fifteen different types, so all the new rock and roll records will have a bit of that in as well. They'll be technically a bit more advanced and have a lot more musicians in them, so I don't think it's really your old rock and roll. It's just a title."

Lady Madonna is different from the sort of thing found on the Sergeant Pepper album.

"We always try to be different. If people hadn't been saying 'the great rock and roll revival' we most probably still would have done this record, and it would have been just the new Beatles single. It would have been rock and roll Beatles."

Did he like the early days of rock and roll?

"They were the greatest days for me. I was just at the right age, but I don't even think the re-releases of the old rock and roll records will sell. It's nostalgia for us, you and me... the people who went through that. The twenty-fives and over."

Would that nostalgia ever make him want to play it again?

"No, I don't think I ever would. I don't want to play again on stage. Not at the moment, anyway."

Did this record indicate any specific direction for the Beatles?

"It's not a backwards step, as some people have said. Because it doesn't freak out, people think you're going backwards. It's just another step, that's what they all are. Just because we do certain things on some records, it's called progression. This one is just us doing a record, it's just a record. It's not a step back or a step forward or sideways. It's just another step. It's just another type of song from the Beatles."

He was only in India for ten days. When he returned, was there any confusion about why he returned?

"I wasn't confused. The newspapers were confused. I came back because I just felt like coming back. That's the whole simple thing to it. I just thought, well, I'll go home. We got there and it was great and the sun was shining. Nice place."

Did disappointment or regret influence his decision to return home?

"No, it was just that we felt like coming back. We still meditate. The whole point of going there was because we were away from everything and Maharishi would like you to graduate to as many hours as you can do, and while you're there, you can. But it's impossible at home to do ten or twelve hours, because you have a lot to do. But you can do it there because everything's provided, and you've got your room. You don't have any worries about all the work you have to do. We weren't disenchanted. It was just a feeling. I think everyone must get it sometimes, wherever you go."

Homesickness?

"Yes, it can be described as a lot of things. I think Maureen was missing the kids. That was only one thing. I mean, we didn't say suddenly, 'Oh, we've got to see the kids.' It was like a hundred reasons which formed into one thing: you feel like coming home; so we came home."

People said the Maharishi was disappointed by his departure.

"We went to see him and he wanted us to stay because he's helping us. If you're going to learn something, you might as well learn it from the boss man, and he's the guv'nor."

Were the other members of the group disappointed?

"No, we just said we're going home, and they said all right, see you when we get back. Not one of us holds the other."

Since his return, what had he been doing?

"This is the first day's work. Apart from that, I've been at home doing whatever you do at home. I've just taken up enlarging and developing films. I've been doing that the past few days. That's all, really."

Back in December, he said it seemed the Maharishi would be answering a lot of questions for him.

"He still does. Somebody said that I looked at him and said, 'There I am.' But he's a long way ahead from where I am. He's so great. There's something about him. I can't tell you what it is, really. You just know, there's a great man."

Did he think the Maharishi could lead him where he wanted to go?

"He's put me on the road. Now it's up to me whether I follow or get off."

Would he continue with meditation?

"At the moment, yes. I've never, with anything, said, 'In five years, I'll still be doing what I'm doing now,' because I don't know."

Had it been helping him?

"It's calmed me and made me more relaxed, although, I still have the same emotions as anyone else. But I feel more relaxed."

How did he meditate when he was at home?

"Half an hour meditation in the morning and half an hour at night. The rest of the time, you just do what you normally do.

"It's meditation because we're householders, that's the word for people who have to get up and do jobs and who can't be monks and sit in a cave and not do anything, so we do the householder's meditation, half an hour in the morning and half an hour at night, and this eases your mind in the morning before you're out doing your job.

"Then, when you're finished, everyone's mind's a bit tight, and meditation relaxes you. You're a better person.

"All the worries, troubles and tribulations of the day, if they are there, they build up, and that's when you get all the aggression, because everyone is so tied up that they are not thinking straight, and they *are out shooting and fighting before they know what's happening, so, that way, you relax yourself and relax your brain, and no problem seems to be as big as you make it out to be."*

The Maharishi had received a lot of publicity thanks to the Beatles.

"The publicity we've tried to give has been good publicity, but all the people who think it's something else have just been saying a lot of rubbish, really. This has been bad publicity. But you are going to get this, you get good and bad with everything, and it's just a pity that all the people who have never tried it are giving it a lot of bad publicity, like the press and a few pop stars."

Had it helped their music?

"I don't think it's helped me musically, no. Our songs will be influenced by it because of John and Paul. It's another influence so it'll influence our songs. But I don't think I'll be a cosmic drummer."

Did he have any desire to get deeper into the music?

"No. I have the phases where I want to play guitar or I want to play piano, or anything I can play a tune on, because I get sick of bang bang all the time, though some drummers can make them talk and can play tunes on drums. But I haven't done any of that, really."

Did he write songs?

"No, I have the odd go, but it's a joke. It's tunes I find the hardest thing to do. I don't think the words are very hard. Usually, I write a song and then I sing it to someone and they say, 'Oh, aye, Blue Moon,' and it is. The first ones I used to write used to be pinches from Jerry Lee Lewis, all his B sides."

Since they are away from touring, and just working in the studio, did he find he appreciated any other kinds of music?

"Not really. I still appreciate the same music that I used to, which is country, rock and roll, pop and the odd classics."

Jazz?

"I've been through it all, you know? I've been through trad jazz and that got boring, and I went through modern jazz, and I still like some modern jazz. I like small combos, Chico Hamilton, Yusef Lateef, people like that, small groups more than big bands. But there's no great urge in any of them. I just play the odd LP and I have to be in that mood to play that sort of record."

What did he mostly listen to?

"I don't think I listen to anything more than anything else. I stick LPs on from Tamla to country. I put them all on."

Aside from Beatles' work, how did he spend his time?

"Photography, playing with the kids, answering the telephone, just being a normal person who lives in a house."

Did he miss touring?

"No. When we toured, it was such a frenzy and so exciting that I'd had enough at the end of it, five

years of it at the pace we did it was enough for me. I don't feel at this moment that I want to do a tour."

Did his age effect him?

"Yes, that as well. It's like when I first moved down to London, I used to go out to the clubs every night and I had great times. But if I go now, I sort of expect it to be like it used to be, but it never is. Although you blame the club and the people, it's you yourself as well, because you've got older and you've changed yourself."

Did he ever miss the early days and Beatlemania?

"Not yet. Maybe I will in a few more years. We haven't been away from it that long, really. Maybe in ten years, like I'm still nostalgic for rock and roll now."

Did he miss Liverpool?

"No, because now I have my own family and my own life. I still go up and see them, and I still enjoy going to Liverpool. If this all finished and I was back to not being Ringo, back to normal, I suppose I might move up there again, but I don't know, really."

Back to normal was an interesting choice of words. What did he mean by it?

"Well, it is. But it's one of the phrases you use. I consider myself as Richard Starkey and Ringo Starr; they are really like two different people. But they're not. It's just I think Ritchie Starkey has got his life to lead, and he doesn't want it in all the papers or the whole world shouting about it.

"And there's Ringo, where I'm quite willing to put up with it. This is a Ringo interview. It's no interest if you write Richard Starkey, if it wasn't me. I still make two different scenes altogether. I try to keep them separate, but you can't."

March 23, 1968 – Derek Boltwood interviewed Ringo Starr for *Record Mirror*. Part One:

A lot of people were speculating about why Ringo chose to leave India so suddenly. They wondered if it was all a hoax, if Ringo was the only one to see through it, if he was really into mediation…

Said Ringo, *"No, it is not a gigantic hoax or con trip. Yes, meditation is my cup of tea.*

"My decision to leave India was very sudden. I didn't decide to return to England for any particular reason, except that I felt I should return. It was nothing to do with not enjoying it out there, or being fed up with the whole thing, I just thought to myself, 'I think I'll go home now,' and so we came home. We didn't discuss it or anything, we just jumped on a plane and left.

"A lot of people are going to say that I left because I was disillusioned by it all. But that just isn't so. The Academy is a great place, and I enjoyed it a lot. I still meditate every day for half an hour in the morning and half an hour every evening, and I think I'm a much better person for it. I'm far more relaxed now than I ever have been.

"You know, if you're working very hard, and things are a bit chaotic, you get all tensed up, and

screwed up inside. You feel as if you have to break something, or hit someone. But if you spend a short while in the mornings and evenings meditating, it completely relaxes you, and it's easier to see your way through problems.

"If everyone in the world started meditating, then the world would be a much happier place, and there would be less wars and things. And I seriously believe this could happen in a few years' time, not in our generation even, but eventually. It only needs the younger generation at the present moment, all over the world, to follow the Maharishi's teachings, for us all to become a bit more civilised.

"It could happen, but it would be very difficult to get things started. At the moment, everybody seems to think the Maharishi is a con man or something. But he isn't, he's a very sincere person, and really believes in what he's doing. Contrary to what people think, he doesn't make a fortune out of his business. All the money paid to him by his students is paid in to the organisation in their own countries, and is used to keep that particular branch going, so, if fact, most of the money that comes in is plowed back into the business. What the Maharishi wants to do, eventually, is have an Academy in the capital of every country.

"When we were out at the Academy in India, a lot of people said that we were getting preferential treatment just because we're the Beatles. But this wasn't so, the only reason the Maharishi was spending more time with us than the others was because we joined the course late, and we had to catch up on all the studies we'd missed, so he had to give us some individual coaching. You're left on your own a lot on the course, and there is a library for reference, and then the students get together with their guru every day so that they can ask questions and be put straight on the points they don't understand.

"I'd really like to see meditation become a popular thing, and I'm pleased that the Maharishi has had a lot of publicity through the Beatles. Now at least, everyone has heard of the Maharishi, whether they think he's genuine or not. But I assure you, he is genuine. I suppose people mistrust a thing they don't know a lot about. If people took the trouble to learn about meditation, then they'd discover that it can do nothing but good. I'd like to see the Maharishi's teachings become a sort of pop meditation, because then it would appeal to the kids, and it could bring about a much better understanding between the younger generation in all the various countries.

"But it's a matter of breaking down a barrier of mistrust first, and that isn't an easy thing to do. Especially when a lot of newspapers write stories saying things like, 'Is the Maharishi a big con man?' and so on, generally knocking him, and putting meditation down. Because people believe what they read in the papers, you know; it must be true, it said

so in the newspapers. It's only when you're personally involved in something where you come into contact with the way papers work, that you realise that everything you read in print isn't necessarily the exact truth.

"When I decided to leave the Academy and return to England, a lot of people started to read things into it. But, as I said, it was a spur-of-the-moment decision, and nothing to do with being bored with meditation and the teachings of the Maharishi.

"I always like to let things happen rather than plan things out for myself. And if I decide to do something, then, within reason, I do it. I believe there is a greater plan, with a pattern and a reason for everything you do. Therefore, there must have been a reason for me to suddenly decide to return home.

"Personally, I think that when you're born, there is a very complex pattern that is planned out for your whole life. It's like a network of paths, and you decide which path you want to take, and everything that happens to you along that path is planned to the minutest detail. The major decisions are yours, if you decided to do one thing, then everything that happens to you because of that decision has been planned out in advance. Whichever direction you take at the crossroads, your life has been planned out for you, so I never worry about what's going to happen in the future, and I never plan too far ahead, because I know that things are planned to happen, whatever I do.

"Anyway, I'm quite happy to sit back and wait for whatever's coming next. I haven't found out the answer to the question, 'What's life all about?' and I don't suppose I ever shall. It would take millions of philosophers millions of years to sort that out. As I said, I have my own ideas, and I do know that meditation is an important part of being a relaxed and sane human being."

March 23, 1968 – *Disc and Music Echo***, Ray Coleman spoke with Ringo Starr.**

Ringo lamented the death of pirate radio. Radio Caroline was the most recent casualty. Said Ringo, "The pirates helped to keep the scene alive and lively, it's been duller since they've been gone.

"We're now left with the monopoly of the BBC, and what seems like half a dozen terrible bands playing for most of the day. Twelve to one's the best time, at least you get some up-to-date records then. But, sometimes, I put the radio on about eleven thirty and you get all that stuff like, 'Hello, this is Mrs. Smith from Barnsley and I'm a housewife.' Really, Mrs. Smith, isn't that wonderful. Well, what's the weather like up there in Barnsley? Ah yes, nice day for hanging out the washing then...' Then, from two to five, it's Pete Brady and the usual bands, then Roundabout, and that's it. It's not really very exciting, is it?

"It's not good for the scene, because it's a fact that we've got to have some action on the radio, and competition. There was so much more variety with the pirates, and if they were still around legally, the BBC would have to fight harder to catch up. But what happened was that they got rid of the pirates by law and told us, 'You'll have this or nothing.'

"If the BBC isn't worried about competition, they ought to set up a commercial radio on land. It could easily be done properly."

Coleman said that, if pirate radio still existed, they would be featuring the rock and roll revival.

Said Ringo, "I can't really believe a lot about the return of rock, well, not rock as we all know it, anyway. Rock and roll happened about 1956, and what we're getting now is something similar but not the same. It's just called rock and roll because people want to call it something, and rock sounds okay. But the thing is, a rock scene doesn't happen overnight. It takes months, maybe a year, to creep up and get any strength. It's too early to say yet whether there's a big rock revival.

"Anyway, the only records I can think of that are anything like rock are Fire Brigade and Elvis's Guitar Man and ours. Still, it would be nice, for a few months, to have rock and roll. I think it all started with Bonnie and Clyde, the violent bit sort of fits the music, doesn't it?

"But we can never get rock the same as it used to be. Music changes all the time, and the people who play the music today can't do it like it was played by, say, Bill Haley. It'll be a new kind of rock and roll, because new people will be doing it."

Talking about Lady Madonna, Ringo said, "We've been trying to make a rock and roll record ever since we started, and, as far as I know, we haven't done a decent one yet. This is another bash. It's pretty near it. But, you see, it must be a combination of all the things we've been through, like straight beat, country, twist, psychedelic and other labels. You can't just go into a recording studio and say, 'Right, let's make a rock record' because you automatically put every bit of your experience into everything you ever play."

There were rumours that the Beatles would not release any more singles but would only concentrate on albums.

"Not true, rubbish. We still like making singles, and, like anybody in this business, we like getting single hits. We've never had more than four out in one year, because we don't like being rushed. It always takes us quite a time to make anything, it takes us so long to make an album these days, but they're the best we can do at the time, and we wouldn't put out anything we didn't like."

The Beatles would spend as long as it took in studio until they were happy with their sound. The hours were irrelevant. And they smoked a lot. Both John and Ringo had tried to quit.

Ringo said, "It's just a habit, but so hard to break. I find that after a day of cutting them out, I'm back

smoking. I say to myself, 'That's good, I've given up smoking,' then a few minutes later, I find a fag in my hand, and I can't even remember lighting up.

"I've just about packed up drinking. I just decided that I didn't like it any more. I have just the odd bourbon or bottle of beer, but nothing like I used to. I've found there's more to do in life than think about smoking or drinking.

"I've got a new hobby, developing films. There's a lot you can do with a negative, and I'm interested a lot in colour photography, well, I've always been quite keen on the camera, but now I've bought the equipment, and it's good to develop all my own films."

Ringo was planning to get rid of his Facel Vega and replace it with a Mercedes-Benz… "The Facel Vega's been a good car, and it's only done six or eight thousand miles. But I've been thinking about it, and I reckon it was a good car to have when I was single. You know, it looked nice and flash. I just don't need to buy a car now for the sake of it looking nice and flash. We just fancy a nice new car that's comfortable."

March 30, 1968 – Derek Boltwood interviewed Ringo Starr for *Record Mirror*. Part Two:

"What do you think of rock and roll?" Ringo asked.

Boltwood said he thought it was on the way back. The Beatles had released a rock and roll record – Lady Madonna. If the Beatles were doing rock and roll, then there was absolutely no doubt about it: rock and roll was on the rise.

Said Ringo, "I don't think Lady Madonna is strictly rock and roll, though. But it has a lot of rock clichés in it. We've always been basically a rock group, you know, if we get together for a jam session or something, between recording, we invariably start playing the basic rock chords and rhythms as soon as we pick up our instruments.

"If we'd brought this record out at a different time, a few months ago or something, no one would have called it rock and roll. But now, everyone's giving it that tag because it's an in thing.

"All things being equal, we'd have released this disc whether rock and roll was in or not. What we do is record a few numbers and then listen to them all afterwards to decide which is the most commercial. Then we release that as our next single. In this case, it was Lady Madonna, regardless of its rock content. I must admit, though, that we must have had the thought at the back of our minds that rock and roll is on the way back, or it wouldn't be quite so rock influenced. It has a lot swing in it as well, from the era just before rock and roll started in a big way with Bill Haley and Elvis, you know, that sound of the swinging saxes in the background.

"When we recorded it, as in most of our records now, we did the backing track first, and then built up on top of that. But there's a lovely sound in it that's like sort of muted trumpets, or a kazoo or something.

But in actual fact, it's just John and Paul sort of humming through their hands into the mike.

"It was purely by accident that we discovered that sound. We'd just finished taping a bit of the record, and John and Paul started to hum into the mike with their hands cupped around their mouths. When we played back the piece of tape with this bit tagged on to the end, it sounded great, so we decided to use it.

"Paul plays piano and sings on the record, but it doesn't sound a bit like his voice. It's funny, because a lot of people have said that it sounds like me singing on Lady Madonna, but I didn't notice that at all. I don't think it does sound a lot like me, and I'd never thought of it until Cynthia, I think it was, pointed it out to me. And, since then, quite a few people have said it. It's a good voice for the song, though, it gives that rock sound even greater emphasis. But it wasn't planned or anything. Sometimes, when we've just been messing about, Paul's used that voice, but we never thought anything of it. And then, when we started recording Lady Madonna, Paul started singing with this voice. It all just happened, and ended up sounding great.

"In fact, you could say that about the whole record. It wasn't planned to sound like rock. It just ended up that way.

"But we've again put ourselves in the position where people are going to say rock and roll must be coming back, even the new Beatles single is rock and roll. And they're going to say that we've started a new trend. But people always latch on to us as trendsetters, some to copy us, and others not to copy us. For example, when we started wearing those mustaches, hundreds of people started growing them. But equally, a lot said, 'You wouldn't catch me wearing a mustache just because the Beatles have got them.' The thing is that people are going to latch onto whatever we do as being a new trend so that they can either follow it or knock it. But it's a thing we've got to accept.

"Anyway, there were signs of a rock revival, and obviously, this influenced Lady Madonna to a certain extent. But I still maintain that, had we brought the record out a few months ago, no one would have called it rock and roll, but they do now, because they want to believe that we're spearheading a rock revival. And the copyists will copy, and the knockers will knock… regardless."

March 30, 1968 – *Disc and Music Echo*, Hugh Nolan interviewed Geoffrey Emerick, the Beatles' recording engineer…

A huge amount of work went into recording a Beatles record. *Sergeant Pepper's Lonely Hearts Club Band* had been started in November, 1966, and took seven hundred hours of studio work before it was deemed ready.

Said Geoffrey Emerick, *"All our social life went for a Burton. We were just living for the record. We'd all*

leave the studio exhausted, and then be back the next day. Finally, to finish it, we were working weekends as well. But it was well worth it, in the end…"

Nolan agreed, mentioning that the album had just picked up four Grammy Awards in the States.

Emerick had been working in silence with George Martin and the Beatles since the days of *Paperback Writer*. Winning an award for *Best Technically Engineered Album* moved him from the shadow.

He said, *"I've never heard of an engineer on the pop scene in this country winning this award before. But it seems more of an achievement to me to have taken it away from the Americans!"*

Essentially, the making of a Beatle record involves the four band members asking Martin and Emerick for the unattainable, the impossible, the unheard of… and then attaining it.

Emerick said, *"We were all working as a team, one unit, and we all wanted something really good. They kept asking George and me for fantastic things which just seemed impossible at the time."*

John and Paul would arrive at the studio with an idea, voice it on the piano, and the others would take it from there, all four band members adding ideas.

Both Martin and Emerick liked *A Day in the Life* more than anything else on the *Pepper* album. Said Emerick, *"Towards the end of doing the album, we were getting a bit overwhelmed, I mean, we weren't losing our tempers or anything, it was just that we couldn't see it ever coming to an end, so, whenever things started slowing up, we'd play* A Day in the Life *to cheer us up."*

Emerick's favourite Beatle song, though, was *Strawberry Fields Forever*. He said, "Strawberry Fields *was made up of two different sessions. We started it and John didn't much like what we were doing, so we redid it the following week. One particular bit, though, turned out to be better on the original, so John wanted to use that with the rest of the song from the second session.*

"*We thought it was impossible at the time, because both bits were in different keys. It meant sliding down the scale and all sorts of things. But John wanted to do it, so we did it.*"

Emerick started with the Beatles when their previous engineer, Norman Smith, quit EMI. Emerick had been hired by EMI right out of school.

He said, *"The Beatles needed another engineer, and George Martin picked me. I suppose he had his own reasons; he said I was adventurous. George is the producer, and that's it. He's a great person to work with, he understands everything. He's always ready to help out musically on Beatle records when they get stuck."*

May 25, 1968 – *Record Mirror* **said** John Lennon and Paul McCartney were in New York City to promote their new company, Apple Corps. They appeared on the Tonight Show, being guest-hosted that evening by Joe Garigiola. Also on hand when Lennon and

McCartney took the stage were Johnny Carson's sidekick, Ed McMahon and guest, Tallulah Bankhead.

There were screams from the audience as Garigiola introduced them. After some idle chatter, Tallulah Bankhead asked them, *"May I ask you, a big favourite all over the world, a question? Are the other two gentlemen… of the four of you… are they still in India?"*

John replied, *"No, they're in England."*

Bankhead: *"I want to ask you something, because I wish I'd learned to meditate, and I can't… I don't know how you do it. I would love to."*

John: *"Well, you gotta go and find out, haven't you."*

Bankhead: *"Well, I'm not going that far."*

John: *"Oh, well."*

Paul: *"Forget it."*

Bankhead: *"If it's taken me this long, and couldn't do it, I couldn't learn there."*

John: *"Well, you can't learn to swim if you keep inland, can you? Unless you've got a good pool around you."*

Bankhead: *"Oh honey, I can float sitting up. Don't be silly."*

After more chatter, Garigiola asked if all four Beatles were socially close.

Said Paul, *"Yeah."*

Lennon added, *"We're close friends, you know."*

Garigiola suggested that, sometimes, people who work together go their separate ways when the job is done. He wanted to know if they lived close to each other.

John replied, *"Within twenty miles, all together."*

If you hadn't made it in the music business, what do you think you would do?

John: *"Uh, I don't know. Films for me."*

Paul: *"So, what would I have like to have been?"*

John: *"A policeman."*

Paul: *"No, not a policeman. Uh, I don't know, you know. I was nearly gonna be a teacher, but that fell through, luckily."*

Music started up for a commercial break and Paul hummed along with it. Girls in the audience screamed and Garigiola suggested John read a cue card to see how the audience reacted.

Misreading on purpose, John said, *"And now a word from your local stallion."*

Garigiola quickly corrected that to *"station."*

After the break, Garigiola asked Paul about being in Central Park, unrecognised.

Said Paul, *"Yes, that's true. Yes."*

John: *"We were very pleased, you know."*

You just wandered around unescorted?

John: *"No, we just walked out, you know. We often do it. If people don't know, expect us, what are they gonna do but see a bit of long hair walking around like all the other long hair."*

Have you been in New York long?

Paul: *"Three days."*

John: *"Is it three, now?"*

Paul: *"Three days."*

John: *"And we still haven't got a tan."*

Paul: *"And it's been enough, you know, actually."*

Did you ever see much of a city when you were on tour?

John: *"You just pick up the vibrations. We never saw it, you know."*

Paul: *"The room."*

John: *"A castle full of rooms all over the place."*

Tell us about Apple.

John: *"Oh yeah, well, you see, our accountant came up and said, 'We got this amount of money. Do you want to give it to the government or do something with it?' So we thought…"*

Which government?

John: *"Oh, any old government. So we decided to play businessmen for a bit, because, uh, we've got to run our own affairs now, so we've got this thing called Apple, which is going to be records, films, and electronics, which all tie up. And to make a sort of umbrella so people who want to make films about… grass… don't have to go on their knees in an office, you know, begging for a break. We'll try to do it like that. That's the idea. I mean, we'll find out what happens, but that's what we're trying to do."*

Paul: *"If you want to do something, normally, you've got to go to big business and you've gotta go to 'them,' the big people, you know."*

John: *"You don't even get there, because you can't get through the door 'cause of the colour of your shoes."*

Paul: *"But, you know, people are normally… Big companies are so big that if you're little and good, it takes you sixty years to make it. And so people miss out on these little good people."*

John: *"It just takes 'em longer."*

Paul: *"So we're trying to find a few."*

Are you doing this because you come from a poor background?

John: *"No, it's no sort of… it's just a common thing."*

Paul: *"There's a little bit of that."*

Was it tough to get started?

John: *"Well, no tougher than anybody else, you see, but George said, 'I'm sick of being told to keep out of the park.' That's what it's about, you know. We're trying to make a park for people to come in and do what they want."*

Paul: *"Symbolically speaking."*

John, is Paul the spokesman?

John: *"Well, if his spokes are working, he is. And if mine are…"*

Do you have privacy these days?

John: *"We have enough to keep us sane, you know. If we are sane… we have enough. But it's not like touring. Our life isn't like a tour, or A Hard Day's Night or any of those things. That's only what we're doing now. We create that, or that is created. But when we're just living, it's calm."*

Is that so, Paul?

Paul: "*Yeah. Not at the moment, you know. It's hectic, New York. Very hectic place. 'Cause we came over from England and it's a very sort of quiet place, you know.*"

Bankhead asked, "*Are you nervous on a show like this?*"

Paul: "*Always nervous.*"

John: "*Yeah, sure, sure.*"

Garigiola wanted to know why they would be nervous.

John: "*Because, uh, it's not natural. I mean, this situation isn't natural.*"

Paul: "*If we meet you and talk at your house, then that's all right, you know, because we can actually talk naturally. It's a bit difficult when you know you're going out to a million homes. You know that old show biz thing, everybody says, 'Well, you know, you always get nervous before you go on the stage.' When you go on stage, it's just one of those things.*"

Garigiola explained that he had something in common with them. He had met the Maharishi, he said. Then he mentioned that the Maharishi had gone out on tour with the Beach Boys and the tour folded.

Said John, "*Yeah, right.*"

What do you think of the Maharishi as a stage act?

John: "*Yeah, well, we found out that we made a mistake there.*"

Paul: "*We tried to persuade him against that, you know. I thought it was a terrible idea.*"

John: "*We believe in meditation, but not the Maharishi and his scene. But that's a personal mistake we made in public.*"

When did you realise it was a mistake?

John: "*Well, uh, I can't remember the date, you know, but it was in India. And meditation is good, and does what they say. It's like exercise or cleaning your teeth, you know. It works, but uh, we've finished with that bit.*"

Ed McMahon asked if the Maharishi had changed.

John: "*Well, no, I think it's just that we're seeing him a bit more in perspective, you know, 'cause we're as naive as the next person about a lot of things.*"

Paul: "*We get carried away with things like that, though. I mean, we thought he was, uh, magic, you know, just floating around and everything. Flying.*"

Have kids in America rejected him?

John: "*Well, it could be something to do with it. But I wouldn't say, 'Don't meditate' to them, because a lot of them would get a great deal from it.*"

Paul: "*You know, the system is more important than all those things.*"

John: "*He's surrounded with, it seems like, the old Establishment that we know so well.*"

Are you telling people to meditate but not with the Maharishi?

Paul: "*Yeah, I mean, he's good. There's nothing wrong with him. But we think the system is more important than all the two-bit personality bit. You know, he gets sort of treated like a big star. He's on*

the road with the Beach Boys, and it's all that scene. And also, it folds, you know. That's the silly thing.*"

Bankhead: "*Does he giggle as much as…*"

John: "*Yes, it's his natural asset. Well, you see, it depends on what way you're looking at the time. If it's not getting on your nerves, it's 'Oh, what a happy fellow.' It depends how you feel when you look at him.*"

Garigiola explained he had had the Maharishi on the show and the man had giggled the entire time. He asked who amongst the Beatles first met him.

John: "*We met him at the same time.*"

What were the circumstances?

John: "*Well, he was just doing a lecture in London at the Hilton, so we all went and we thought, 'What a nice man.' And we were looking for that. You know, everybody's looking for it, but we were looking for it that day, as well. And then we met him and he was good, you know. He's got a good thing in him. And we went along with it.*"

But not now. You've left the ride?

John: "*Right, nice trip, thank you very much.*"

Has your career changed? Your audience?

John: "*See, everything changes, so we change as well. And our audience changes, too, all the time. We don't sort of put our finger on what age group or why, but we know, everything changes, and us too.*"

Paul: "*When we first started, we had leather jackets on, you know. Little caps and big cowboy boots. But then we change to suits, you know.*"

John: "*We thought, that'll get 'em.*"

Paul: "*And we lost a whole lot of fans. They all said, 'You've gone ponced.' They didn't like it, you know, because we were all clean, so we lost that crowd, but we gained all the ones that liked suits. It happens like that. That's what keeps happening. And we lost a lot of people with Sergeant Pepper, but I think we gained more.*"

Can you do better than *Sergeant Pepper*?

John: "*Well, you know, it's the next move and I can't say yes or no, but I think so. Why not? 'Cause it's only another LP, really, it's not that important.*"

Do you and Paul work together on your songs?

John: "*It's all those combinations you can think of. Every combination of two people writing a song, inasmuch as we can both write them completely separately, and together, and not together. But we obviously influence each other, like groups and people do.*"

My favourite is *Yesterday*. How did you write it?

Paul: "*You know, I just started playing it and this tune came, 'cause that's what happens. They just sort of, they come, you know. It just came and I couldn't think of any words to it, so, originally, it was just* Scrambled Egg. *It was called Scrambled Egg for a couple of months until I thought of* Yesterday. *And that's it.*"

You're kidding me. You wrote a song called *Scrambled Egg*.

Paul: "*No, that's true.*"

John: *"Didn't do so well, that title, you know."*

Before you go, what is the one question that bugs you the most. About your hair?

John: *"No, we're past being bugged by questions, unless they're very personal. I mean, you just get normal human reactions to a question. You know, but there used to be one about 'What are you going to do when the bubble bursts?' and we thought we'd have hysterics because somebody always asked it."*

What are you going to do when the bubble bursts?

John: *"I haven't a clue, you know. I'm still looking for the bubble."*

Even though they were in New York to promote Apple, their rejection of the Maharishi made the most news.

June 15, 1968 – *Disc and Music Echo* quoted Davy Jones talking about the Monkees' movies. He said, *"It's hard to write a movie about the Monkees. Hard Day's Night was okay for the Beatles. It was about them and anybody could have played their roles. But the Beatles couldn't play our parts in the film we've made."*

July 13, 1968 – *Disc and Music Echo*, Hugh Nolan wrote about *Yellow Submarine*. He said regardless of reports to the contrary, psychedelia was not over. *Yellow Submarine* would soon be opening in Britain and it was more psychedelic than anything that had happened during the flower power days.

The Beatles had done it again. They had explored new territory, set new standards. Animation had limitless possibilities and the Beatles had set about examining them. True, they had little to do with the actual film. But their original ideas were the inspiration.

Said Paul, *"I haven't seen the whole film yet, although I liked what I saw. We're not really involved with it at all. It's just got our music in it, that's all."*

It was all about an attack on happy, joyful Pepperland by a gang of thugs known as The Blue Meanies, with John, Paul, George and Ringo to the rescue... in their Yellow Submarine.

There were four new songs by the Beatles: *Hey Bulldog*, *All Too Much*, *Altogether Now*, and *Northern Song*. Also included in the film were: *Eleanor Rigby*, *Nowhere Man* and *Lucy in the Sky*. The animation that went with these classic songs introduced a new perspective and gave the song new life.

Technically, the film was brilliant.

July 20, 1968 – *Disc and Music Echo* announced that the Beatles helped launch a new discotheque, *Yellow Submarine*. The club was in the Royal Lancaster Hotel on Bayswater Road. It was decorated to look like the interior of the submarine used in the film. The Beatles did not own the club but were agreeable to having the name used.

Paul McCartney and Jane Asher were now officially engaged. Said Tony Barrow, *"Their engagement has been one of those things. If anybody specifically asked me, I'd say they got engaged last Christmas. It's just that they didn't make any fuss about it. They wanted it that way."*

Revolution was likely to be the Beatles next single, its release to coincide with all the other releases on their new Apple label: *Those Were the Days* by Mary Hopkin, produced by Paul McCartney; *Thingumybob* backed by *Yellow Submarine*, by the Black Dyke Mills Band, produced by Paul; and the *Wonderwall* soundtrack album by George Harrison. Two weeks after those releases, Apple would release *Sour Milk Sea* by Jackie Lomax, produced by George Harrison.

The Beatles were unhappy with the first version of *Revolution* and re-recorded it.

Their next album would likely be released in late September or early October. *Sergeant Pepper* had been their last album.

July 20, 1968 – *Melody Maker* talked about *Yellow Submarine*.

"What a boring waste of time," snapped a reporter at Paul McCartney after the press viewing of *Yellow Submarine*.

Paul, along with George and Ringo, stayed friendly and polite, pretending to be at a gathering of intelligent human beings.

The Beatles provided the music and the inspiration for *Yellow Submarine*, and were somewhat involved with the promotion. That was where there involvement ended.

After talking about the film, other subjects were brought up. The interviewer asked if their new album would be as heavily produced as *Sergeant Pepper*, or was it likely to be somewhat simpler.

Said Paul, *"Well, we started all our music simply. The point is, some of the songs will be simple, if they are phenomenal songs. If they aren't, they will need production. John Wesley Harding was simple and didn't have big productions."*

How did he like the film, *Yellow Submarine*?

"I like what I've seen about it. But I hate premieres. I just go to make sure it's a picture I've seen. The point is, we haven't made this film. It's not us. I won't take the credit, even if it's a big smash. It's like saying Bambi made Walt Disney."

While McCartney spoke, a crowd was gathering around George Harrison.

Said Paul, *"George is being very significant."*

A reporter suggested to George that the Beatles were in a position to do anything they wanted.

"This is only in other people's eyes," George explained. *"It's not a case of just us being able to do anything we like. Everybody can do anything like that.*

"A car mechanic, when he mends a car, has just done something he likes. People don't have to curse and hate their employer. They just create bad vibrations from the way they do things. Even if a bloke can't get a job and has got eight kids, at least he's still got that! There is no such thing as good or

bad luck. There is the reaction you are getting from life. You create the world you want to live in."

How did he feel about the Maharishi and his trip to India?

"I didn't hope for anything. I got a lot of good things out of it and a lot of disappointments. I'm still meditating and I'm still a vegetarian. No, I'm not in touch with the Maharishi."

Paul said, *"He's still a nice fella, but we don't go out with him anymore."*

Are the Beatles still happy together?

"We've been together now for forty years, and it don't seem a day too much."

July 27, 1968 – Record Mirror, David Griffiths focused on George Harrison, after the press showing of *Yellow Submarine*. Harrison had shaved off his mustache and reporters were saying he looked younger.

Said George, *"Yes, well, if I cut my hair as well, I'll look even younger. Might be able to join the Small Faces."*

Was he still into meditation?

"Yes."

Did he still speak with the Maharishi?

"No."

Did he still like India and things Indian?

"Yes, very much so. There's a lot of suffering and poverty, but there's so much beauty and the people are very pleasant."

Had he considered trying to do something for the country?

"Well, what? I'd be very interested if you could tell me how it could be done. It's a huge country, full of political problems, and, as far as I can see, the Indians will have to straighten it out for themselves."

Griffith mentioned that the Beatles had already done a lot for India by making the West more aware of the art and the culture. Perhaps they had even given people a sense of pride in the fact that one of the world's most popular entertainers liked and emulated Indian music, specifically, *Within You Without You* from the *Pepper* album.

Said George, *"Yes, I felt that was well worth doing. There are so many people who don't understand the sentiments of* Within You Without You. *They can't see outside themselves, they're too self-important and can't see how small we all are."*

Someone asked if the Beatles were still working.

"Oh, we still work, only it's a different kind of work. We used to travel about getting in and out of transport, hanging around airports. Now, it's office work."

Office hours?

"Not ten to six, exactly, but we spend a lot of our time behind desks. It's a pity, in a way. I'd just as soon concentrate on being a musician, but we have to take care of business. And I do things because I like doing them. There's a satisfaction to be had from trying to do a job as well as you can. That's the trouble today, too few workers get any pleasure from

their work. But, say you're a car mechanic, you can really dig that work if you want to."

Griffith suggested it was easy to take that point of view when you are rich. Harrison did not think money mattered all that much. Another reporter pointed out that, for most people, there were no options, they had to work… for money… at jobs they did not like. Obviously, money did make a difference. After a few moments, Harrison quietly agreed.

When the subject of luck was mentioned, Harrison said, *"There's no such thing as luck, it's all cause and effect."*

Griffith wandered off at that point, to where Paul McCartney was holding court. McCartney was explaining that pop music, like animated films, was not treated seriously by critics.

Said Paul, *"But that's all changing and I have no doubt that, in fifty years' time, they'll be talking about those Nineteenth – or is it Twentieth – Century composers, Lennon and McCartney. They'll be analysing our work. It's inevitable."*

August 3, 1968 – Disc and Music Echo wondered about the new girl in Paul McCartney's life. He was seen holding hands with a dark-haired girl in a London nightclub shortly after Jane Asher had announced the end of their engagement.

McCartney was at the *Revolution* discotheque, accompanied by an American girl whom he introduced as Fran.

Said a friend, *"They arrived around one a.m. and stayed till almost four. They had a meal and drinks together and held hands a lot. She seemed very nice, but didn't talk much. She danced, but not with Paul."*

When questioned about her at the Beatles' office, Derek Taylor said, *"I don't know anything about the boys' personal affairs."*

And Tony Barrow said, *"We don't wish to comment."*

Jane Asher had announced to the world, on the *Dee Time* TV show, on Saturday, June 20th, that her engagement to McCartney was over. She said she had not broken it.

Asher and McCartney had known each other for more than five years, before the serious *Beatlemania* erupted, and had been together ever since. They had become officially engaged on Christmas Day last.

Revolution was still expected to be the Beatles' next single release. It would be on their new Apple label.

To date, they had eleven new songs recorded and their next album, the follow-up to *Sergeant Pepper's Lonely Hearts Club Band,* was due out in September. Lennon and McCartney were spending time together, writing more material.

Over the weekend, the group had left London for a photo session with Don McCullin.

An Apple spokesman said, *"It's important for them to have some up-to-date pictures. They've changed over the last few months."*

The new shots would be used to promote their new single and album.

August 10, 1968 – *Disc and Music Echo*, **Ray Coleman wrote** about the closing of the Apple boutique in London. The Beatles had decided that shopkeeping was not their cup of tea. Instead of just locking the doors, they threw them wide open and invited people to take away all the stock... for free. Critics saw this as just another disaster in a long chain of disasters that the Beatles had been experiencing of late.

It started when McCartney publicly confessed to taking LSD, moved through the terrible reception for *Magical Mystery Tour*, on into the embarrassing time with the Maharishi Mahesh Yogi and their joining the flower power thing (in the past, the Beatles had *set* trends, they had not followed them); then came the awkwardly announced break-up of Paul and Jane; and the discovery of John and Yoko Ono; and the bizarre spectre of Lennon talking about vibrations and wearing and button that read, *"You are here"*; *Yellow Submarine* had not been well received; and now, the Apple boutique was going out of business. The critics were descending like vultures on a rotting corpse.

Virginia Ironside of the *Daily Mail* declared, *'One boob too many.'* She criticised George Harrison for his pretentious songs; she lamented the expiration of John Lennon's cynicism; and she said Paul McCartney was the only Beatle left unsullied by the new Beatles' world. She said, *"They had the world on its knees to them and boobed... It's sad."*

Others were saying, *"The only thing they have left for them now is their music. As people, they're just millionaire drags, it's a good job they make good records."*

Their achievements as musicians had no equal. As for the rest of their lives... Coleman wondered if they cared at all what people thought of them, cared at all about the criticism.

He spoke with George Harrison in the Apple offices, trying to find out what the Beatles were thinking these days. He said he was met with an anti-press, anti-journalist attitude as Harrison declared that reporters spend too much time writing about rubbish. He said the Beatles were not making mistakes. It was simply, *"experience, like life."*

Said George, *"It's the press that calls them mistakes, they are all just sitting there, waiting to knock us down and see us do things wrong, wrong, that is, according to them."*

Coleman thought George was using the press a scapegoat because things were not going as planned. It was impossible for George, and the Beatles, to dismiss the criticism by ranting about the unfair press – the problems were deeper than that. He said, however, that the anti-press attitude was Harrison's main point of view as he answered the questions.

Coleman asked why the Apple boutique had closed.

Said George, *"Because we didn't enjoy it, it just wasn't our scene, that's all. The original idea didn't work out and it became something else, so, rather than continue with something that wasn't natural to us, we shut the shop. It's rather like us doing a trad record, just not right. There's plenty of other things going for us, so we'll concentrate on the music side. The reason we've been so successful as Beatles is that we've specialised in being Beatles, so we'll just concentrate on the music side, with Apple Records and Apple Electronics."*

If the shop was not going the way they wanted, why did they not change things instead of simply shutting it down?

"Because our course just isn't shopkeeping. It's not really a mistake, the only mistake anyone ever made was getting born. All the rest is life. You can only measure good against bad and mistakes against things that are not mistakes. It just so happens that we're perpetually on show to the world and the press needs things to write about. All we're doing is being. There are certain things we've got to do, and whether people think we are making mistakes or not, we are going to do them. We'll do what we like, and, if it's wrong, we'll find out by experience."

Did they regret starting up the shop?

"No, we don't regret the shop at all. People obviously want to enjoy writing and saying, 'Ahhh, the Beatles lost a hundred thousand pounds,' but you see, it doesn't matter like that to us. It started off by not making much money but, in the end, it was making a good profit. The average owner would have been satisfied with it, but we didn't like the whole thing, so we decided to give it away. It seemed better than having a final sale and, this way, we were not mistaken for little Jewish businessmen, getting five thousand pounds out of closing down. We're just not interested in owning shops, so why have them? We don't like things that just make money, they've got to please us. No, the shop wasn't a mistake, just part of life."

Closing the shop, though, had been part of a number of recent disasters. *Magical Mystery Tour*, the Maharishi, drugs... A number of their admirers have been upset with them lately.

"Yes, all the criticism started, I suppose, when Paul admitted taking LSD. But what's wrong with that? I disagree with Paul when he says the Maharishi was a mistake. I don't agree. Nor Magical Mystery. *They were no more mistakes than* I Want to Hold Your Hand *was a mistake. We all benefited. It's how other people see it that decides whether it's a mistake. On the outside looking in, people don't know all the circumstances, so it's easy for them so sit back and write 'Mistake! Boobed again!'"*

The Beatles were four public personalities and people were always going to talk and write about everything they did. Were other people's opinions of no importance?

"Critics must see my point of view as well. If I want to go out and buy that building over there with a hundred thousand pounds of my money and turn it

into a junk shop, then what I'm doing is nothing to do with anyone else. It's my business. The thing is, are people like Virginia Ironside doing whatever they're doing as best they can? We are. Is she?"

Did the Beatles care what people thought?

"Look, the press made us out to be superhuman, so, instead of making an ordinary mistake, we are supposed to have made a superhuman mistake. Nothing's a mistake! You benefit from all life and experience. All we want to do is carry on being ourselves. The only people who create images of us are press people, and anyway, by the time their image of us gets across, it's out of date because we've changed again."

Back to Apple and opening shops, it was understood that they wanted to open a chain of them. John had made a joke about rivaling Woolworths.

"No, we never did envisage a chain of shops. I've never been mad about that. We just want to concern ourselves with music – publishing, recording and producing. And, in this field, we want to do things we think are good, even if the records we put out, for instance, never reach the hit parade.

"I wouldn't mind if we turned out something like Sue Records, they didn't often reach the hit parade with their records, but all the stuff they issued was great. We don't want to be associated with anything we don't like, and that's why the shop closed."

Some people were saying that John Lennon's recent exploits with Yoko Ono, and that Paul McCartney's break-up with Jane Asher, were tarnishing the Beatles' image. Did this worry him?

"The press has always gone after the rubbish, and if people are that interested in the Beatles' private lives, they'll always find something to write about. We are four young people who have normal things happening to us. The press loves that sort of thing, you know, kicking people's doors down and getting down underneath people's private lives. They're doing what they consider to be a public service, but, if I was to spend my life worrying about it and reading about it, I'd be stupid."

It did not matter what people said about him?

"I care more that people tend to read something in the papers and believe it to be true, without question. A lot of innocent people really believe what they see in the papers has just got to be true. People only hear about the bits of rubbish written about the Beatles. If the public knew the whole story all the time, they might get a different impression. Too many people take things at first sight. They should try finding out sometimes."

Did he resent his public image?

"It's the press who inflicted this image on us, an image of four young men who never made a mistake. But, who's to say what's a mistake or not? Who's to say that doing the Royal Command Performance wasn't a mistake, seen now? Or Sergeant Pepper, that might have been a mistake. It depends on what side of the fence you try to sit on. We just do what's in our minds at any one time.

"We are four young people and we're playing the game of life, which goes up and down, up and down. We are not trying to say we're anything special, or any better, or worse, than anything or anyone else. We are just being, and doing our jobs.

"The thing that bugs our critics is that we have had a lot of success and, consequently, we have had the opportunity to do things, and we're now doing things, and some of the money is going. But these other people would probably count their hundred thousand pounds every night and keep it under the carpet.

"We can either become successful show biz personalities, and lie back in our millionaire mansions, or carry on doing things.

"The old concept of success for anyone in music is that he makes a pile and sits back, but to me, and the Beatles, that's just not making it. You don't make it till you die, and who knows whether you make it then or not, so people have an easy choice, either be interested in us... or not. If you are interested in us, you ought to be a pop fan, I suppose, in which case, you should know by now we're not perfect. And, if you're not a pop fan, you are probably only interested in us because we've got money.

"The whole point is, we are just people. There are going to be a whole lot more Apple Shops – Magical Mysteries – LSD – type stories that will be easily written if people want to go on thinking that way. But we won't be steered any way. We'll please ourselves, what we do and what we think. We are not asking anyone to love us or hate us. I want to concentrate on positives rather than negatives, and I don't want to be answerable to anyone, the Queen, the public, nobody except myself.

"Bob Dylan said, 'It's only people's games you've got to dodge.' Well, they'll continue playing their games, and I'll continue dodging them.

"The pop music scene is the nearest thing to salvation we're going to get. It should be a balance for all the other rubbish going on in the world. The music scene's much more important than a boutique that's just closed down. I wish people would concentrate on the credit side as well as the other. If we have things that deserve criticising, we also have things that deserve credit. Who was it said we were the goody-goody fab four moptops? Not us. We're not. We're four young people going through life just like everybody else, learning all the time, and parts of us are lousy and rotten and we are pricks sometimes as well.

"If we can live with ourselves, that's all that matters. I know I can. Can all the people who say and write such shit live with themselves, even though they're writing such shit?"

August 17, 1968 – *Record Mirror*, David Griffiths wrote that the attempt to be objective about the Beatles was quite difficult and made even more difficult by George Harrison criticising the press for criticising the group. He said George's attitude was understandable, even justified, but not nearly as calm as you would expect from someone who practices meditation and yoga.

George had said all journalists were *"just sitting there, waiting to knock us down and see us do things wrong."*

Griffiths wanted to go on record saying he was *not* one of those journalists. He had no interest in joining the fashionable attacks on the Beatles, nor was he interested in stroking their egos with false praise. He wanted to examine the issues, discover the truth, and reach a conclusion or two.

During a brief conversation with Harrison after the *Yellow Submarine* press showing, he had asked how *Magical Mystery Tour* had fared in the States. Had the American press been as critical as the British press? Had the film actually been shown on American network television? Harrison did not know. He called a business associate to his side. This man explained that *Magical Mystery Tour* had not been shown on U.S. TV but, instead, had been screened at colleges and other semi-private venues. Griffiths said this sounded as if the American TV people had been put off by the unfavourable reception in Britain.

Said George, *"Well, it wasn't as bad as was made out, especially not if seen in colour."*

Griffiths had enjoyed the film and agreed with Harrison. He had not gone out expecting to see some glossy professional film; he had seen what he had expected, a more-or-less amateur film that provided a colourful back-drop for some great music. Why had the critics been so savage in their criticism? Surely, for no other reason than that they had felt it was time to cut down the Beatles. James Thomas of the *Daily Express*, for one, had confessed he believed the Beatles were overrated.

After the death of Brian Epstein, the Beatles had so obviously been vulnerable. They were on their own and expanding their ambitions, trying new things, things in which they were completely inexperienced. Griffiths thought encouragement and praise for their courage and for their adventurous natures, rather than criticism for their screw-ups, might have been a more justifiable – not-to-mention decent – approach.

Yellow Submarine had been enjoyed and admired by every critic he knew, and still, people were knocking it. Not all the theatres were sold out for every showing, so the film was dropped from a few of them. For some reason, this translated as the Beatles' fault. Thin audiences in midsummer cinemas – how could that possibly be considered unusual? The Beatles had nothing of which to be ashamed, particularly since their connection to the film was tenuous at best.

As for the closing of the Apple boutique, well, if the Beatles were tired of being shop-keepers and nice

enough to give everything away rather than trying to squeeze ever last shilling out of the stock, well, that was their business, was it not? And quite generous, to say the least.

With regards to their private lives, well, the Beatles were public figures. Their exploits just naturally came under scrutiny from the scandal-mongers. If the group happened to lead somewhat more wild and messy lives than people wanted, well, it was their business, no one else's. Given the fame / notoriety, the cash, and the opportunity, who would not be tempted to live it up a bit?

Griffiths admired their search for spirituality, for meaning, though he was somewhat disenchanted with the way they were a bit bitchy about the Maharishi after they realised his game was not their own. It might have been better if the group had not talked about their experiences with transcendental meditation and the Maharishi. It might have been better had they simply let the whole thing fade away. He thought that, as the Beatles publicly condemned the Maharishi, what they were really doing was condemning their own gullibility.

And then there was LSD. Once again, it was their business. A reporter had tried to get Paul McCartney to admit that taking LSD was probably a bad influence on the fans. McCartney said he had simply told the truth when he was asked if had taken it; he wondered if it would have been better had he lied. Regardless, though, publicising this was not up to the Beatles but the press. Said Paul, *"If you'll shut up about it, I'll shut up."*

Griffiths said, despite the right or wrong of taking acid, when something as brilliant as the *Pepper* album can grow out of it, it cannot be all bad.

And finally, it all came down to the music. After six stunningly creative years, the Beatles were still in business, still coming up with incredible and haunting sounds. For that, they deserved to be thanked. A new album would be out soon. It might be disappointing but there was no chance it would be dull. He suspected it would be their best so far, something that might just shut up the knockers.

August 31, 1968 – *Disc and Music Echo,* **Caroline Boucher wrote** about Paul McCartney and Mary Hopkin.

Mary was a schoolgirl, just eighteen, when she appeared on Opportunity Knocks, an ITV program hosted by Hughie Green. Twiggy was watching the show, rang up Paul McCartney and, shortly after that, McCartney called Mary and asked her to come to London. He signed her to Apple.

She said, *"I've met all the Beatles, and they've been so kind to me. I've met Paul more often than the others, and I don't think he's spoilt. I didn't know him before, but I don't think he is. George gave me a fabulous Spanish guitar."*

With regards to *Those Were the Days,* she said, *"Paul chose it. We listened to a couple of others, but he liked that one and said it would be good. I heard the demo and I liked it, but I didn't think I could do it. I kept saying I couldn't, and he kept saying I could, just to be natural and not to try too hard."*

August 31, 1968 – *Disc and Music Echo* **said** Jackie Lomax was about to be Apple's first male solo performer. He was starting with a song by George Harrison called *Sour Milk Sea.*

Lomax said, *"I'm not really a friend of the Beatles, I just know them. The thing about the Beatles' business plans is that they want a business, but an amicable business. They want to get away from the old idea of the man with the big cigar and office talking down to his staff. You always used to find that agents treated artists as children. The Beatles are changing all this. Artists will become more personally involved with what they are doing, instead of being told what to do all the time. Surely, this can only be a good development?"*

He agreed that he was lucky to have this chance. Lomax had first met the Beatles through Brian Epstein, who had intended to manage him. He was not worried about being, *"Beatles-backed. Even though people are putting the Beatles down, there's a great interest in the things they do, which can only be good for me."*

August 31, 1968 – *Disc and Music Echo*, **Penny Valentine reviewed** the new Beatles record, *Hey Jude,* to be released by Apple the following day. She said people would soon be singing it. It was the best Beatles' record since four discs back. It was brilliant, a slow, deliberate song that crawled straight into your head. Sung by Paul, at first quite sweetly, and then growing loud and hard as he went into his Little Richard sound. Perhaps it could have been slightly shorter, but she was not too worried about that.

September 14, 1968 – *Disc and Music Echo* **announced** that David Frost had managed to get both the Beatles and Mary Hopkin on his TV show. It was the first time the Beatles had been seen together in public since the BBC's Our World TV show last July, when they were filmed recording *All You Need is Love.*

After *Hey Jude* entered the pop charts at number one, the group decided to make some promotional films for it, and for the B side, *Revolver.* Their own Apple company made the short films, under the direction of Michael Lindsay-Hogg.

Hey Jude had already sole over 300,000 copies in Britain, earning the band their twenty-first Silver Disc. In the U.S., the record immediately hit the top ten and had sold over a million copies.

One of the *Hey Jude* promotional films would be shown on Top of the Pops that night, and it was possible that the *Revolution* film would be screened the following week.

September 14, 1968 – *Disc and Music Echo*, **Richard Robinson reported from New York about** a book being planned by an American publisher. It was to be called *The Beatles Book.* Chapters were to be written by William F. Buckley, Ralph Gleason, Nat Hentoff, Timothy Leary, Richard Goldstein, and others. The work was intended to analyse, dissect and explain the Beatles' impact on fashion, films, art, thought, and, of course, music.

September 14, 1968 – *Melody Maker*, **Bob Dawbarn spoke** with Paul McCartney.

Said Paul, *"There seems to be a big cloud of anti-Beatle matter hanging around at the moment. But it usually works itself out. And the fact that the record has gone to number one proves it."*

Regardless of how well *Hey Jude* was doing in the charts, critics were saying the song was too long and claiming that it was a step backwards for the Beatles. Dawbarn asked Paul if he thought those were valid criticisms.

"Steps back are fine. If we can make a record as good as, say Great Balls of Fire, *we will be delighted. It's only phony intellectuals who want to step forward all the time. We felt it was time to step back because that was what we wanted to do. You can still make good music without going forward. Some people want us to go on until we vanish up our own B sides.*

"As far as the ending is concerned, we were faced with the choice of fading out early, which was the obvious thing to do. I know people think we are a bit thick, but we do know that if you are to make a record commercial, you must make it nice and short. But we liked the end. We liked it going on. The deejays can always fade it down, if they want to, like a TV program. If you get fed up with it, you can always it turn over. You don't have to sit through it, although a lot of people enjoy every second of the end, and there isn't really much repetition in it."

How was the new LP going?

"We should finish it next month. A lot of the tracks are done, and we always speed up towards the end, doing tracks in a day or so."

Was there anything unusual on it?

"There will be a couple that people will talk about. People seem to think that everything we say and do and sing is like a political statement, but it isn't. In the end, it is always only a song.

"One or two of the tracks will make some people wonder what we are doing. But what we are doing is just singing songs.

"This business of people taking everything we say as an important pronouncement sometimes gets me down. Then I realise it doesn't really matter at all, and I don't really mind.

"The knockers don't really upset us. Once you've got to number one, you can't go any higher. You are only faced with the possibility of coming down. That sort of thing doesn't worry me, though I suppose it could.

"I remember Brian Matthew reviewed She Loves You *and said it was utter drivel and the worst record we had ever made. He said it would never be a hit. It was a fantastically anti review and we were all worried about it. Of course, it turned out to be one of the biggest ever. The reviewers have been proved wrong so often, we don't worry any more."*

Paul said that the Beatles were not, as yet, planning a third movie. When he was asked about Apple, he said, *"Things are going a lot better now than they have done. And we have got two hits. Ours, and Mary Hopkin's."*

Dawbarn wondered if Paul had any interest in the American music scene, if he planned to see either the Doors or the Jefferson Airplane while they were in England.

"I might. I don't plan these things, really. I like that scene and I saw Jefferson Airplane in San Francisco. They are nice people.

"But, really, I'd rather see Elvis. I've never seen him and that would be nice. I saw a great TV show he did, with lots of rock things in it. You know what I'd love to do? I'd love to produce an album for Elvis. His albums haven't been produced very well and, as I am a fan of his, I think I'd be able to produce him well. I'd try to get the same feel as the first couple of his albums had. It would be great!"

September 14, 1968 – *Melody Maker* **spoke with** Paul McCartney about signing Mary Hopkin.

Said Paul, *"I heard of Mary first in Liverpool. Justin and Twiggy had come up in their new car, showing off again, you know how it is. Well, we were eating our pudding later that evening and we talked about* Opportunity Knocks *and discovery shows generally, and I wondered whether anyone ever got discovered, I mean really discovered, on discovery shows.*

"Then Twiggy said she had seen a great girl singer on Opportunity Knocks *and, luckily as it turned out, this was the time we were looking around for singers for Apple Records.*

"When I got back to London the next day, several other people mentioned her, so it began to look as if Mary really was something. Twiggy's not soft. So I got her phone number from the television company and rang her at her home in Pontardawe, somewhere in Wales, and this beautiful little Welsh voice came on the phone and I said, 'This Is Apple Records here. Would you be interested in coming down here to record for us?' She said, 'Well, would you like to speak to my mother?' And then her mother came on the line and we had a chat and two further telephone conversations and, later that week, Mary and her mum came to London.

"We had a nice lunch and went to Dick James's studios in Oxford Street, and I thought she was great. But, at the same time, I thought she was very Joan Baez, a lot of Joan's influence showed. However, Mary said she could do other things and I agreed that there was no limit to her possibilities. There couldn't be a limit because she was very together.

"Well, a long time earlier, maybe a couple of years ago, I'd first heard Those Were the Days *when Gene and Francesca, American singers, sang it in the Blue Angel in London, and I'd always remembered it. I'd tried to get someone to record it because it was so good. I'd hoped the Moody Blues might do it, but it didn't really work out and, later, in India, I played it to Donovan who loved it but didn't get around to doing it.*

"We rang Essex Music, the publishers of the song, but they didn't know anything about it, other than that they owned the song. They had no lead-sheets, no demos. But David Platz of Essex, nice man, sent to America and we got the demo and everything.

"I showed Mary how I thought the song should be done and she picked it up very easily, as if she'd known it for years. At first though, she was singing it as if she didn't mean it, which was strange for Mary, very strange.

"But it was her first time in the studio and it can be frightening. After a few tapes, I kept showing her the way she should sing it, and generally worked on it, and suddenly she got it and we just put a tambourine on it and went home.

"She really is like the girl next door, the real thing, kind and quiet and she blushes and smiles shyly. It's like when she says, 'Yes, I go out with boys but it's just kissing.' Great. It's due to her background. Normal. Her parents are good solid Welsh parents, her father works for the local council, and her mother is a very intelligent woman, so we are going to look after Mary and make sure no harm comes to her.

"Work starts on her album soon, and we are going in all kinds of directions as she's capable of singing anything. I'd like to hear her shout. That would be good. To hear her really shout. I know she can. Everyone can."

September 21, 1968 – *Disc and Music Echo* **said** the Beatles wanted to do a concert for television. The film would be made by Apple and sold to TV stations around the world.

Said press officer, Tony Barrow, *"They were very happy with the way the promotion films for* Hey Jude *and* Revolution *worked out. And they think that the next logical step would be to do a sort of TV concert. In fact, a forty-five to sixty minute show is a distinct possibility."*

The previous Friday, deejay Kenny Everett had played *Hey Bulldog* and *All Together Now* on his radio show. These were two of the four new songs from *Yellow Submarine*, an, as yet, unreleased record.

Said Barrow, *"The four new songs from the film will probably go out on a EP here around Christmas time. But in America, they will be part of a full album, the new tracks and eight other songs already out."*

The *Revolution* film was to be shown on Top of the Pops that night. And the Beatles next album was expected to be finished by the end of the month and in the record shops by November.

September 28, 1968 – *Melody Maker* **announced** that the Beatles' new LP, their first since *Sergeant Pepper's Lonely Hearts Club Band,* would be a double album, with twenty-four tracks, all different. As yet, the record was untitled. Decisions were being made this week about the price, the marketing and the cover.

Derek Taylor, of Apple, said, *"This is the first time the Beatles have put out a double album in Britain."*

He went on to say the material on the LP was, *"very varied, right down the middle of the road."*

The sound ranged from simple ballads with light guitar, to the full orchestral sound that had accompanied *Hey Jude.* Said Taylor, *"There is also hard rock and roll, hard and light numbers, and some standards. John and Paul have written most of the material, and Paul seems to be writing a song a week, at the moment. There are also a couple of numbers by George and one by Ringo, although he also sings on a couple of others."*

The band was still doing studio work on the album.

September 28, 1968 – *Melody Maker,* **Tony Wilson spoke** with George Harrison and Jackie Lomax. Lomax's song, *Sour Milk Sea,* was one of the first four singles on the Apple label. It had been produced by George, who also played acoustic guitar on the record. Also on the record were Ringo Starr, Nicky Hopkins and Eddie Clayton.

George and Jackie had known each other back in Liverpool. They re-met when Lomax was visiting Apple.

Said Harrison, *"I walked in and said 'Hi Jackie, I'm off to India.' Now I'm back and here we are."*

Talking about *Sour Milk Sea,* George said, *"It's a glorified jam session, like the Stones' record. It's a pity that everybody hasn't got into it. I was pleased*

with the way it came out, although it's not everybody's cup of meat.

"There's no hang-up about recording his own stuff. Whether you want a hit or not, good things don't have to be commercial. But it definitely is a good record."

This was the simple aim of Apple: to make good records whether they sold or not. George was presently dividing his time between making the Beatles' new albums and producing Lomax's first album. He said, *"By the time the album is finished, there'll be a band and then it'll be hit the road, Jackie."*

Said Lomax, *"When people heard that I was on the Apple label, they said, 'You've got it made.' But I'm not really connected with the Beatles, just with George as an individual."*

Harrison said, *"The thing is, Jackie is with me, I am in the Beatles, and Apple is owned by the Beatles. There's a whole big myth about the Beatles. We have to be connected with people. You get the good side and the bad side, really, just as in any normal relationship with people.*

"But, you know, when we started Apple, we thought that even if we don't have a hit, as long as every record is good, that's all that matters. We never think of anything as A or B sides. We juts try to make them all very good with what's around us, with the musicians and the studios."

Producing records was, lately, one of Harrison's main activities. He said, *"I'm getting more and more into it, now. It's another side to the music. It's the idea of getting it all together, trying to get everybody to do their best.*

"It's psychologically trying to get people to do their best without imposing on them, and without letting them freak out. I've learnt a lot from it. Also, it makes you aware of the musicians around the scene. You get to know who is best in their field, whether it's guitar, organ, bass or drums. Like Nicky Hopkins, who plays as if he is not a session musician."

Rumour had it that the Beatles were going to do live performances. What did George think about being on tour again?

"The idea of coming out is appealing. On the other hand, some people wouldn't like what we'd play and other people would. I'd like to be resident in a club, with the amps there all the time so you could just walk on stage and plug in."

October 5, 1968 – *Disc and Music Echo* **said** Graham Nash was going to ask Paul McCartney if he would host a charity concert for the *Invalid Children's Aid Association* that was being organised by the Hollies. Said Nash, *"I'm going to try and get Paul interested. If we can get the Beatles involved in any way, it means we can make an extra several thousand pounds for the charity. I'd really like Apple to film the concert. That way, we can sell the show around the world and made extra money…"*

A footnote mentioned that Mary Hopkin had withdrawn from a concert date because Apple said she was not ready for major public appearances.

The American Top Twenty Chart for that week showed *Hey Jude* in the number one position.

October 5, 1968 – *Disc and Music Echo*, David Hughes reviewed the Hunter Davies authorised biography of the Beatles. He said the entire feeling of the book gave the impression that the Beatles were done, that it was all over for them, that a future did not exist. Aside from that, though, Hughes did, at least, manage to make the story interesting, even though it had been told many times.

October 5, 1968 – *Disc and Music Echo*, John Kercher spoke with Yoko Ono. Face to face with her, he said, you feel as if you are looking at a piece of delicate porcelain. She had child-like quality and seemed, at first, faultless.

She said, *"I'm full of holes and the air passes through me and doesn't worry me."*

It was only recently that her name became widely known. Her friendship with John Lennon placed a spotlight on her. But she had been known in the underground art circles and as one of the leading avant-garde artists as well as the founder of concept art.

She said, *"After a supposed two-week visit to the auto-destruction symposium, I was invited to hold an exhibition of my work and ideas at the Indica Gallery, and it was there that I met John. I didn't know it was him, at the time, but I sensed an immediate communication between us when he asked me if he could bang an imaginary nail into one of my paintings."*

Regarding John, she said she was certain she had not influenced him at all, adding, *"We communicate with each other. He comes from an art school background, so it has always been there with him. My early life was very academic, although I hated it and have always been aware of the more beautiful things in natural life. For instance, John comes to me with ideas of holding the* You are Here *exhibition with fifty charity boxes as models. I was tremendously enthused, but he went on from there and released three hundred and sixty-five gas-filled balloons with address tags from the gallery, inviting people to write to him."*

It was possible that some of those letters would end up in a new book Lennon was putting together.

Whether or not she had any influence, Lennon was becoming very interested in making art films. She had made a forty-five minute film of John still and smiling. She explained, *"In fact, it was shot with a high speed camera in three minutes and then slowed down to its present length. It's a technique I have been developing of late. But we don't know whether or not this film will be released…"*

She believed that art could be found in everything and found herself with so many ideas that she could barely handle them all. She said, *"So now I find myself starting a project and letting someone else finish it. I like doing half things."*

Regarding the Apple boutique, Yoko Ono said, *"There was also a great deal of artistry in the closing of the Apple boutique in Baker Street. I mean, what a wonderful idea, to just give away clothes to people. The Beatles had letters asking them why they didn't sell the stock and donate the money to charity, but things like that, they can do individually any time. But to give away the contents of an entire shop may be the only opportunity. If I had done it, it would have been declared a happening, and so it should be with them. A thing like that in New York would make modern history."*

Would there be future Lennon and Ono projects?

"Well, we've just completed a sound LP called Two Virgins*, and even the process of distribution will, in its own way, be artistic and tactful. But the major thing is a film that John and I are making. There is no deadline, and we are just going out weekends and shooting when and what we fancy. But the idea's secret. We only release that after completion on any project. And it won't be one of these 'directed by Yoko, produced by John' things. Just a joint production."*

Marriage?

"Just a piece of paper."

Love?

"You try and define love."

October 12, 1968 – *Disc and Music Echo* announced that the Beatles would have two new albums out for Christmas, their as-yet-untitled follow-up to *Sergeant Pepper's Lonely Hearts Club Band,* and the *Yellow Submarine* album, which would feature the four new songs that they'd written for the animated film. Side One would have: *Hey Bulldog, All Together Now, All Too Much* and *Northern Song*, along with *All You Need is Love* and *Yellow Submarine.* Side Two would feature six tracks from the movie's incidental music, re-recorded by George Martin and his orchestra.

The follow-up to *Pepper* was to be, definitely, a double album. Both albums were expected to be released in December.

Rumour had it that London's Royal Albert Hall had booked Paul McCartney for a special Beatles concert in December. The rumour was false.

Said press officer, Tony Barrow, *"It is an unlikely venue anyway. And, if the boys do decide to do a show, it would be in a studio on the lines of the appearances they made to promote* Hey Jude.*"*

Derek Taylor, of Apple, said, *"The Beatles will appear live, but not before the New Year. It will be on the lines of their* Hey Jude *TV film, with a proper audience, but it will be a much longer performance."*

Another rumour said John Lennon and Yoko Ono might appear nude on the cover of their *Two Virgins* album. Tony Barrow confirmed that they had done a photo session for the album. Said Barrow, *"No final decision has been made. And the LP hasn't even been scheduled yet."*

Lennon's first idea was to show himself and Yoko nude on both sides of the album.

A footnote mentioned that new Apple releases, due in November, were by American James Taylor, discovered and produced by Peter Asher, and the soundtrack from the film *Wonderwall* by George Harrison.

In a footnote, she mentioned going to a Ravi Shankar concert, which was also attended by George and Patti Harrison…

October 12, 1968 – *Disc and Music Echo* said *Sergeant Pepper's Lonely Hearts Club Band* started it all, started the revolution in the appearance of album sleeves. After *Pepper*, album covers developed into an art form.

October 12, 1968 – *Melody Maker* said there was a mystery developing over the Beatles' possible live concert appearances. It was certain that the group wanted to play again to a live audience. A TV special was the most likely form for the concert. Last week, though, a rumour said the Beatles were booked to play at the Royal Albert Hall. Press officer, Tony Barrow, denied this, but Apple executive, Jeremy Banks, did not.

Said Tony Barrow, *"The Royal Albert Hall has definitely not been booked. The Beatles want to do some sort of live show, but it is almost certain to be before a special audience of perhaps five hundred. The show would be filmed for TV and would require a more intimate venue than the Albert Hall. The group would probably prefer somewhere with theatrical stage facilities."*

Jeremy Banks said, *"It's possible they'll do a concert there, and it's possible they won't."*

Still no decision had been made regarding the title for the new album. But the John Lennon and Yoko Ono album, *Two Virgins,* was to be released as soon as possible. No decision had been made about the cover but it was rumoured that Lennon and Ono would appear naked.

Also, the *Yellow Submarine* album was to be released in December.

October 12, 1968 – *Disc and Music Echo*, Judy Sims reported from London instead of Hollywood this week. She had attended a Beatles' recording session. The group was working on a song by John called *Happiness is a Warm Gun.* George explained that the song had been inspired by an ad in a gun magazine.

November 2, 1968 – *Disc and Music Echo*, Judy Sims reported from Hollywood that George Harrison was in Los Angeles with Mal Evans and Jackie Lomax, producing music for Lomax with Hollywood studio musicians.

November 9, 1968 – *Disc and Music Echo*, **Penny Valentine reviewed** the Beatles' new album. It was titled, simply, *The Beatles*. It had thirty tracks and ran for an hour and a half. Hearing it left her breathless. The song writing was better than every before. The thought behind each recording surpassed all they had ever done. And it proved, finally, that the Beatles were a very good group. *This* was the Beatles, the pure Beatles. Of the thirty songs, she thought twenty-seven of them were absolutely brilliant. She reviewed the album track by track.

Side One:

Back in the U.S.S.R.: Paul sang the lead and it was a song Americans would hate. She thought it was a send-up of the Beach Boys.

Dear Prudence: John sang the lead, a song about a man living for the smile of his girlfriend. A gentle, lovely love song.

Glass Onion: Sung by John, a mockery of the people who seek significance in Beatle songs.

Ob-La-Di Ob-La-Da: Said quickly enough, the first word of the title became *Oh Bloody*, which, of course, was insignificant. The band had a West Indian / Jamaican sound, with Paul singing the lead.

Honey Pie – Part One: Hysterical voices with Indian sounds, bordering on madness, in the background.

The Continuing Story of Bungalow Bill: Sung by John, a humorous flashback to Saturday morning pictures, complete with Captain Marvel.

While My Guitar Gently Weeps: This was a George Harrison song with some fine guitar work.

Happiness is a Warm Gun: Valentine said the dividing line between Lennon songs and McCartney songs was always obvious. This was most definitely a Lennon song, lyrically fascinating, musically penetrating.

Side Two:

Martha My Dear: Apparently, this was a song Paul wrote about his sheep dog, but he sang it as if Martha was the love of his life. She predicted a lot of bands would cover this tune.

I'm So Tired: Another Lennon song, sad, edgy, doubled tracked.

Blackbird: This was Paul unaccompanied, singing, playing the guitar and tapping his foot. A beautiful song, sure to be covered by a lot of artists.

Piggies: George Harrison again, a nasty little song about piggy people with piggy habits.

Rocky Raccoon: Paul telling a sad barroom tale.

Don't Pass Me By: This was the first song ever written by Ringo Starr, sung by Ringo himself. Nice enough but too long.

Why Don't We Do It in the Road: A hard rhythm and blues number. Do what? she wondered.

I Will: A pure pop song.

Julia: A warmer than usual song by John, destined to be covered by someone.

Side Three:

Birthday: Hard rock with Paul doing his Little Richard thing.

Yer Blues: A hard-driving home-grown blues number.

Mother Nature's Son: This is Paul with a small, pretty song sung so sweetly it hurts.

Everybody's Got Something to Hide Except Me and My Monkey: Another hard rocker by John. People were wondering who his monkey actually was.

Sexie Sadie: Nice enough; sung nicely by Paul.

Helter Skelter: The biggest, loudest track on the entire album. Powerful.

Long Long Long: George's third song on the LP, very pretty, not very mysterious, unusual for George.

Side Four:

Revolution: A different version than the one on the flip side of *Hey Jude,* slower and somehow more insistent.

Honey Pie: Paul doing a Hollywood-sounding thing quite nicely.

Savoy Truffle: George's final song.

Cry Baby Cry: John singing.

Revolution 9: Many minutes of distorted tapes. The listeners would either love it or hate it.

Good Night: The final song on an exhausting album. It was sung by Ringo and Valentine predicted it would be taken seriously, but she considered it the final send-up.

November 9, 1968 – *Melody Maker*, Alan Walsh reviewed the Beatles' new album, *The Beatles*. He said the new record was in no way at all like the *Sergeant Pepper* LP. It had more variety. It had a distinct range of moods. It presented hard rock tempered by McCartney's lyrical charm and Harrison's virtuoso guitar.

The differences between the writing of Lennon and that of McCartney had never been more obvious. Paul was charming and melodic, gentle; Lennon was aggressive and angry.

The *Pepper* album showed the Beatles' subtlety. Well, *The Beatles* also had a healthy dose of subtlety… but in the lyrics, rather than the music. The album clearly illustrated each of the four Beatles was going his own way creatively. People would say the band was moving backwards. Walsh disagreed. Sideways was a more apt description.

He then reviewed the album track by track. For the most part, he agreed with Penny Valentine. He did state, though, that *Revolution 9* was, *"noisy, boring and meaningless."*

November 16, 1968 – *Disc and Music Echo* **started a four-part series** by Derek Taylor called *So You Think You Know the Beatles*. Part One: Ringo.

Ringo was glamorous. Ringo was dash and élan, panache and charm. No home should be without a Ringo. All the best homes had one, the salt of the earth. You could lean on him. You could borrow from him and not repay him. And he would remain… kind.

Once, he was the newest Beatle. By existing, he made that irrelevant. Also, he was the Chosen Beatle. The rest just fell together, but Ringo was… chosen. Pete Best was un-Beatled, a fate, as it turned out, that was almost worse than death. Ringo was Beatled, and fate was still turning that out but it seemed quite clear that John, Paul and George had been wise to select him. Ringo Starr had been equal to the stardom, equal to the drumming tasks, probably the most perfect drummer for the Beatles.

And Ringo Beatle had slid through the years all but unscathed, all but untouched by the viciousness of the press, unlike John, Paul and George Beatle.

Ringo's key to survival was simple: He was a good man. It was impossible to be near Ringo without being glad to be alive.

John was the brain; Paul was the vision; George was the soul; and Ringo was the heart of the group.

When it was clear that *Hey Jude* and Mary Hopkin were runaway triumphs for the Beatles, Taylor suggested it would be a good thing to telephone some U.S. disc jockeys, just to chat…

Said Ringo, *"I wouldn't mind doing that. I like talking to America. I'll do it. You fix the calls and be with me and I'll do it."*

And he did. With each call, he varied his chatter, changed his jokes, responded to each deejay as if the man were actually human rather than merely a voice.

Ringo was happy. Happy with marriage, happy with a home, happy with children… and happy to be a Beatle.

November 16, 1968 – *Disc and Music Echo* announced that three thousand people would be seeing the Beatles live. They were planning to work at the Chalk Farm Roadhouse in London, from the 14th to the 21st of December, producing a new TV special based and their newest album.

They would rehearse, do a dress rehearsal and then the actual show, playing live. One thousand people would attend each section of the show.

Said Derek Taylor, *"We haven't decided yet how to allocate the tickets."*

It was rumoured that Lord Beeching, the former chief of British Railways, would be hired by the Beatles to help them run Apple. After talking with Paul and John, Lord Beeching said, *"I would like to help the Beatles, as I greatly admire their talent, but it is not an appointment to which I could give total involvement as I see it now."*

The mystery man behind *The Urban Spaceman* by the Bonzo Dog Doo-Dah Band was none other than Paul McCartney. He helped with the production, using the alias Apollo C. Vermouth. Said Roger Ruskin Spear of the Bonzos, *"Apollo C. Vermouth is a chap who is virtually us. Nobody produces our records, it's a battle as to who can*

shout the loudest. We suddenly decided we needed someone to have the last word, and in walked Paul. Actually, I thought he'd come to mend the heating or something but, it turned out Vivian had invited him along. Paul twiddled a few knobs in the studio, added a few ideas, and left."

Someone from Apple said, "Urban Spaceman *wasn't a Paul McCartney production in the sense that Mary Hopkin's record was. It was just a friendly gesture on Paul's part."*

November 23, 1968 – *Disc and Music Echo* continued with the four-part series by Derek Taylor called *So You Think You Know the Beatles*. Part Two: George.

George was wonderful. George was the Beatle who shed his skin, the Beatle who went through a metamorphosis right there in public, all but unnoticed until the change was complete. He was the un-examined, un-studied, un-heralded Beatle. He was quiet, modest. He hated flying. He was ordinary. His dad was a bus driver. And he was rich, truly rich.

They said he was the business Beatle. But he was not.

For a long time, he had lived in the shadow of John and Paul. Now he did not.

David Crosby of the Byrds had discovered Ravi Shankar. He told George about the sitar player. *Rubber Soul* was born. George dropped acid, smoked pot and became the darling of the hip folk, the semi-Indian mystic, definite, determined, fluent, lucid.

For Taylor, it was a joy to spend time with George and Pattie. George was funny, serious, honest, in fact, so honest at times that it seemed brutal, rude, out-Lennoning John Lennon.

Said George, *"You reap what you sow and you sow what you reap. It's all karma. Action, reaction."*

It was all there in his songs, those anguished passionate songs. He wished his lyrics would flow better, but he was proud of his own music, proud to create it and offer it to the world.

He was very together and, more than the other three, had a serious distaste for the press. He believed the press never ever wrote about anyone with good will in mind, but always looked for the nasty and made it up when they couldn't find it.

After a bad day at Apple, shortly after the flight from the Maharishi, sad from that, forlorn in the lobby, he said, *"The great thing about life, maybe the only thing, is that you've got to die."*

November 23, 1968 – *Disc and Music Echo*, Bob Farmer said Linda Eastman was the new girl in Paul McCartney's life. She had traveled with him to his farm in Argyllshire the previous week. She said, *"He's fantastic, one of the nicest people in the world."*

Eastman was not a star-struck fan but a New York socialite, described by a friend as being blasé, *"the type of person that affects to be bored with everything."* Until she met Paul.

Linda was a pop photographer who had done sessions with the Beatles. She was the daughter of a rich New York lawyer. She was twenty-seven years old, divorced, and had a five year old daughter named Heather. Linda first got friendly with Paul earlier that year when he was in New York on business. They renewed their friendship a few weeks ago when Linda showed up in London. When she returned to New York, Paul followed on a later flight, then brought her back to Britain for a holiday on his farm.

A footnote mentioned that Ringo Starr might be hosting a two-hour show on Radio Luxembourg that night, a show entirely devoted to the new Beatles album.

November 30, 1968 – Disc and Music Echo continued with the four-part series by Derek Taylor called *So You Think You Know the Beatles*. Part Three: John.

Taylor said this piece was to those who love John Lennon and to those who did not. It was for those who loved the way he spoke his mind, the way he dropped his walls and allowed the world to see his true self. It was for those who did not love the way his pain was there for all to see, for John Lennon was alive and well, vibrant and brilliant.

There he was in public, a confessed atheist and anarchist, committing adultery, more popular than Jesus, dropping acid, getting arrested for pot, getting divorced, even posing naked, front and back, for a record album. Lennon, constantly on trial with no need to defend. Taylor called him good and brave and clever and dangerous and real, the greatest show on Earth, no ordinary man, imperfect yet bold, his pain and the attendant creative genius right there in front of everyone.

He said to Taylor, *"I saw you said George 'out-Lennoned' me for rudeness, why don't you say I out-Lennon Lennon, because it's mostly myself I amaze, you know?"*

December 7, 1968 – Disc and Music Echo finished with the four-part series by Derek Taylor called *So You Think You Know the Beatles*. Part Four: Paul.

Taylor said Paul was the fastest Beatle ever. He agonised over writing about him. John, George and Ringo had not been easy. Paul was nearly impossible. Paul was too complicated, too human, too clever, too simple, too strong, too humble, too vain, too provincial, too elegant. He defied a simple analysis.

He was a great man, a crusader who believed in fairness and equality, peace and freedom. He was a teen-idol, a leader who could follow, a drop-out who could join. The facts of his life were simple, his background, his family. The rest was not so simple.

But Apple had been Paul's idea. The others liked it, but Paul had envisioned it. Paul was the star of a movie that no one would make, no one could make. Only now was he beginning to truly fly. The Beatles were just a warm-up for what came next.

December 7, 1968 – Disc and Music Echo, Richard Robinson wrote about the scene in New York City, the continuous stream of parties, the writers and musicians, photographers, producers, attending each event; and he wrote about how Linda Eastman was one of that crowd. She was a photographer whose work had been printed in the *New York Times*, in *Rolling Stone*, in big glossy hard cover books, recognised, appreciated, not exactly a full-time photographer but not an amateur, either.

She had started out by working for free. When the quality of her work was recognised, she began to receive paying jobs, some non-rock things, some rock things, her work increasing in demand until she became one of the top rock and roll photographers in New York.

She was charming, witty, and able to converse intelligently. She was blonde and attractive and dressed somewhat conservatively. And she had known the Beatles for some time, even sitting in the front row at the press conference given by John and Paul to promote Apple.

The rumours about her and Paul started not long after that.

As he was writing the article, Robinson tried to contact Linda in New York. He was told she was in London.

Perhaps the rumours were more than merely rumours.

December 7, 1968 – Disc and Music Echo announced that John Lennon was writing a new book, had designed a calendar for 1969, and had filled a gift box for a New York charity. The book was being written around the replies he received to the balloons launched by he and Yoko, released at Robert Fraser Gallery during the summer. Each balloon had a note attached that read, *"You are here. Write to the Robert Fraser Gallery."*

Said Derek Taylor, *"John was amazed at the energy of people in replying so plentifully. The farthest distant reply came from Hungary, and the various answers were amusing, abusive and intelligent. Some asked why he had changed in appearance, some said bluntly and nicely what they thought of him, others asked why he had betrayed the middle classes."*

The calendar was illustrated by Lennon, a picture for each main Beatle event in each month of 1968. It would be distributed in the UK and the States.

The gift box was filled with an assortment of things selected by Lennon and meant to be sold to raise money for the charity.

Forthcoming Lennon projects included a possible film showing at the London Cinema of Contemporary Arts, and more records with Yoko Ono, including one about her recent miscarriage and the time she and John spent in the hospital.

December 7, 1968 – *Melody Maker* said that the Beatles' live show was changing again. It would now take place on January 18th but the venue was still unsettled.

Said press officer, Derek Taylor, *"It does not look as though it will be the Round House and reports that it will take place in Liverpool are also unlikely."*

It would most likely be shot in London because the Beatles wanted it to be in colour and all the colour equipment was in London. The taping was set for the 18th, but the group would also have an audience for a run-through and a rehearsal on the 16th or 17th.

A footnote mentioned that the Spectrum had just recorded Ob-La-Di Ob-La-Da from the Beatles' newest album.

Another footnote mentioned that George Harrison and his wife Pattie had met Frank Sinatra in Los Angeles. They had been at a Sinatra recording session and had been invited to spend a few days with him in Palm Springs, which they accepted, whiling the hours away in long conversations. They were expected back in England at the end of the week, traveling home by ship.

December 14, 1968 – *Disc and Music Echo*, **Mike Ledgerwood said** the Beatles may be doing a live show at the Cavern Club in Liverpool sometime in 1969.

Paul McCartney had visited Liverpool just recently and, supposedly, said he would like to play there again with the rest of the Beatles. The group's last show at the Cavern had been in August, 1963.

Club owner, Alf Geoghan, said, *"He didn't definitely state that they would come. But he did express a desire to play again. He seemed quite delighted to find the place comparatively unchanged. He said he expected padded walls and Japanese waitresses."*

Paul had spent two hours at the Cavern, renewing acquaintances with the doorman, Pat Delaney, and local disc jockey, Billy Butler. Said Geoghan, *"He greeted Pat like a real long-lost friend. Pat remembers the Beatles from way back. He virtually nursed them along in those days.*

"Paul said, 'We're on tomorrow night, Paddy. And it won't be for all the Coke we can drink. We're in the big time now. We'll want fifteen pounds.'"

Hanging outside the Cavern on Mathew Street was a sign that read, *"The Beatles Played Here 292 Times."*

"It would be nice to change that. Make it two hundred and ninety-three," Geoghan said.

Said press officer, Derek Taylor, *"The idea of the Beatles playing the Cavern isn't as bizarre as it sounds. We won't say possibly or probably, but it's very attractive."*

December 21, 1968 – *Disc and Music Echo*, **Bob Farmer wrote** about Ringo and John deserting the Surrey stockbroker belt. They had their homes up for sale, Ringo asking fifty thousand pounds, John asking forty thousand, both homes to be sold by estate agents Knight Frank and Rutley in conjunction with Mann and Company.

George Harrison was also thinking about selling his Surrey house. Only Paul was content with his home, a large place in St. John's Wood, London.

Press officer, Derek Taylor, said, *"People just get tired of the place they live in. It's nice to keep moving. Otherwise, you get a stupid attachment for the bits of earth and the walls which happen to be yours.*

"Ringo's already on the way to finding a new house. He's planning to move into a house at Elstead in Surrey which used to be Peter Sellers' place, so he's another who moves a lot. Big difference with Ringo's present estate is that it has lakes and trees and his Weybridge one didn't. I expect, after a time, he'll want a place with a large park; then later he'll want the Duke of Wellington's place; then the Queen's."

Note, on Wednesday December 18th, John and Yoko attended the underground art movement's Christmas Party, the *Alchemical Wedding* at the Royal Albert Hall. They appeared on stage in a large white bag, writhing inside. Yoko called it *bagism*. She explained that, by staying out of sight, the force of their message would not be contaminated by their physical appearance.

— Chapter Nine: 1969 —

January 4, 1969 – *Disc and Music Echo* **announced** that the Beatles were planning to make their first live album, along with four other LPs, each one filled with songs chosen by each individual Beatle. They were all meeting at Apple this week to select the new Lennon / McCartney compositions that would be recorded for the live album during their TV special.

Press officer, Derek Taylor, said, *"It will be their first-ever live album. All the songs will be new and fresh. There'll be no hangover numbers from a year ago or anything like that."*

It was expected they would record the new LP and the TV show later in the month, although just the right venue for the show had not been found.

The four-album set had been proposed by Capitol Records in the States. They would each be invited to select their favourite Beatles songs. Said Taylor, *"This multi-album will be done mainly for America, but, like everything, there is a strong possibility it will come out in Britain also."*

No tracks had been chosen yet.

Their double album was nearing four million in world sales and *Hey Jude* had sold nearly six million.

January 4, 1969 – *Melody Maker* **said** that the Beatles were planning to record their first-ever live album, to be made during the taping of their TV show.

Said press officer, Derek Taylor, *"The group started writing and rehearsing a number of songs this weekend. There is no shortage of material. Paul has eight or nine songs finished, John has a few, and George also has some material. They are writing all the time. It's a question of selecting the right material for the show."*

This would be the Beatles' first live appearance in over two years. They would do a run-through, a rehearsal and then the live show, each with a different audience. January 18th had been the date set but Taylor explained this was now doubtful, and the venue itself was undetermined.

He said, *"The date that we originally stated for the spectacular, which was to be recorded for television, was our own date. Because of that, we are not fixed by it. If we can't do it then, it doesn't matter. The best thing I can say at this moment is that we hope the shows will happen before the end of the winter."*

The Beatles would do twelve to fourteen songs for the album.

It would be their first live album to be released. Their Hollywood Bowl concert had been recorded but no record had been issued. The only other live recordings of the group were made in Hamburg with Tony Sheridan.

January 11, 1969 – *Disc and Music Echo* **said** George Harrison, along with press officer and friend Derek Taylor, was planning to write a musical for the stage. It was to be based on daily life at Apple.

Said Taylor, *"George has already written an outline and some of the music. I'm in charge of ideas and lyrics. We started last Wednesday after Mike Connor, who is charge of Apple offices in Los Angeles, suggested we get together on a musical."*

By basing the show around events at Apple, the co-authors hoped to escape the foolishness of people on stage bursting into song for no apparent reason.

Taylor explained, *"For everyone, life is a mixture of fact and fiction. Often, this office is like* Alice in Wonderland. *And since Apple is constantly surrounded and involved in music, it seemed a natural subject to base a musical around."*

This would be George's first major venture into anything musical since scoring the film *Wonderwall* the previous year.

The Beatles were rehearsing their TV show at Twickenham studios this week. The show would be the first time that the Beatles had played publicly in six months, since they had taped *Hey Jude*. They were intending to perform fourteen new songs which would be later released as an album.

Taylor said, *"They aren't going to do anything revolutionary on stage. They just want to get in front of an audience and play and sing, nothing adventurous."*

According to Judy Garland, when she appeared at the National Film Theatre in London a few days previously, Paul McCartney was writing a song for her.

Said Derek Taylor, *"She's a great singer and her advisers have been in touch with Apple, so this is probably what it was all about."*

January 11, 1969 – *Melody Maker* **said** four new Beatle albums, in addition to the live album, were likely to be released by Apple sometime soon. It would be special four-LP package or reissued material. Each member of the group was to choose his own favourites and each one's choices would make up an album.

It was also possible that each of the Beatles would record special introductions to the albums. Said an Apple spokesman, *"There could, of course, be some duplication. But the idea came from Capitol in America and is primarily intended for the U.S. market, although they would also be available here, probably at a reasonable price."*

The Beatles' live album was still tentative. The date and the venue had yet to be chosen.

January 18, 1969 – *Record Mirror* **reviewed** the Beatles' new *Yellow Submarine* album. The LP included four new songs: *Only a Northern Song, All Together Now, Hey Bulldog* and *It's All Too Much*; the film's incidental music included : *Pepperland; Sea of Holes; Sea of Monsters; March of the Meanies; Pepperland Laid Waste; and Yellow Submarine in Pepperland*; along with *Yellow Submarine* and *All You Need is Love*.

Only a Northern Song: By George Harrison, this seemed to be an experiment in how many off-key variations of a single background could actually be blended into a song and still sound good, which this did.

All Together Now: A bouncy happy song.

Hey Bulldog: Big beat with a pounding bass line.

It's All Too Much: Another George Harrison song and perhaps the finest sound on the record, a rock song built around a single background note.

George Martin's orchestration for the B side was also worth a mention. This album was well worth the price.

January 18, 1969 – *Disc and Music Echo***, Ray Coleman interviewed John Lennon**.

Said John, *"People think I'm a perverted crank now, just because of the nude bit. They think Yoko and I are ravers, only interested in sex and causing a stir. But really, we're the quietest pair of spinsters around. I'm looking for a small farm where I can grown my own macro-biotic food. I'd like it to be within two hours of London, have eight acres, a lake or a stream, and I'll get a few chickens. I've got twelve cats. I reckon if I can keep them, I can keep hens. I quite fancy it…"*

At twenty-eight, Lennon was no longer the moptop belting out his songs on stage. People thought he was weird, writhing around in a sack at the Albert Hall, hanging out with that strange Japanese girl.

Coleman said people believed the Beatles, and especially John, had changed from four fresh kids into very strange people. He wondered what Lennon thought of that.

Said John, *"I'd say people are as entitled to think what they like as we are entitled to be what we are and do what we do. We never were moptops except in other people's minds, and I don't remember us ever being thought of as nice. So what's the difference between then and now?"*

They think he was out of step with society. Where had the cynical wit of John Lennon gone?

"I'm still quite cynical, but I'm more relaxed. I'm happier now than I've ever been. I don't know what made me cynical before, but, somehow, I got this reputation for saying things that people thought were staggering. They weren't staggering things, just staggering things coming from a moptop."

Now that he had achieved so much and had so much money, what did he still hope to do?

"Having money's okay, but it doesn't matter that much, there's nothing rewarding about material

gain. *I'd be content with a roof, somewhere to work and somewhere to sleep."*

He would not miss what he had?

"No, there's nothing I can think of I couldn't do without."

Was he glad to be free of Beatlemania? The screaming mobs? Living from hotel room to hotel room?

"I'm very pleased to have got that over, yes."

Did he still enjoy it when the autograph seekers found him? Does it satisfy his ego?

"Sure, I have an ego. I've always been like this about autograph hunters and fans: If kids want my signature and I'm in the right mood and it's the right person, they can have it. Depends on the person who asks. I think I'd rather have a following that didn't need autographs."

Would he miss the glory?

"Probably for a while but I'd get over it pretty quickly."

Was he happy with Apple?

"No, not really. I think it's a bit messy and it wants tightening up. We haven't got half the money people think we have. We have enough to live on but we can't let Apple go on like it is. We started off with loads of ideas of what we wanted to do, an umbrella for different activities. But, like one or two Beatle things, it didn't work because we aren't practical and we weren't quick enough to realise that we need a businessman's brain to run the whole thing.

"You can't offer facilities to poets and charities and film-makers unless you have money definitely coming in. It's been pie-in-the-sky from the start. Apple's losing money every week because it needs closely running by a big businessman. We did it all wrong, you know, Paul and me running to New York saying we'll do this and encourage this and that. It's got be a business first, we realise that now.

"It needs a new broom and a lot of people will have to go. It needs streamlining. It doesn't need to make vast profits but, if it carries on like this, all of us will be broke in the next six months."

He missed the business sense of Brian Epstein?

"Sure we miss him. His death was a loss. That's probably what's the matter with Apple or the Beatles at the moment. Brian's death has left us on our own. He handled the business and we find it hard to do."

Would he have tried to stop them from going so far-out?

"No, rubbish. He would never have attempted anything like that. He knew us and realised that what would happen would have to happen. We could only ever be us."

Did he and Yoko regret doing the nude cover?

"Why should we regret it? That was what we wanted to do at that time, and we did it."

Would he do it again? Would he show up nude in public?

"If the occasion arose and there was a reason for appearing nude in public, we'd be nude. There's no

shame in appearing as you were born. We believe it was right for what we were trying to say. Other people's minds were wrong, not ours. We get all sorts of letters now from people who think we're ravers. We never wanted that scene."

Should nudism be accepted?

"If civilisation is going to progress at all, it must be accepted. If people can't look at a nude body without all that fuss and bitter hatred, it's going to be pretty bad."

Did he care what people thought about him?

"I care, yes. I have an ego and I don't want to be thought ill of. But I also want to be understood."

He was a vegetarian?

"Yes, well, a macro-biotic. It works like Zen Buddhism or meditation, you eat what you think's best for you, and it's commonsense to me that you shouldn't eat most of the chemically-treated rubbish most people seem to stuff themselves with."

What did he eat?

"Most vegetarians don't get enough protein. They're trying to get it from cheese and milk but they get more fat than protein. Macro-biotics like me have soya beans for protein. It's based on the Yin Yang principle of positive and negative, to make sure... The diet's based on meal, bread which Yoko makes, rice and no sugar. We have honey if anything needs sweetening."

No meat?

"No."

Were his shoes made of leather?

"I'm always wearing sneakers. I still wear the shoes I wore before I changed my views, I don't see the point in not using them. I won't buy any more leather ones, though. I don't think animals were meant to be eaten or worn and we have enough resources to do without them. It's big business again, see."

Were the other Beatles vegetarians?

"Paul and Ringo aren't. George goes on and off it, I think."

Did eating this way make him feel better?

"Yes. Well, a car might last a long time on the wrong petrol but, one day, it packs up. I feel better, but maybe it's not right for everybody. It just suits me."

Beatles' music would sell simply because it was Beatles' music. Knowing that, how much did he care about trying to improve and progress?

"We can't afford not to care. Our sales vary, you know. If the record's no good, it doesn't sell so many, whether it's by the Beatles or anyone. Look at Presley, he's as good as he ever was, but if he makes a bum record, he flops, same with us."

How did he view the Beatles' future?

"I can visualise us appealing to a smaller group of people, in time, as Beatles. It depends on what we're capable of. Who knows? We're going along with whatever's going along. I think now, people are beginning to realise we don't set any of these trends, and never did. We're just part of the whole thing."

Did he listen to the new music? Did he listen to Radio One?

"John Peel's the only thing worth listening to. The charts are boring. 1968 was one of those years. They used to say the Monkees were a drag, but I'd rather have another thing like the Monkees come up than have the stuff we've been getting, Lily the Pink and Englebert. I even listened to Luxembourg the other night and that seemed quite swinging. At least, it wasn't packed with hit parade stuff every minute."

What new groups did he like?

"I don't get time to listen to much. I like that Fleetwood Mac instrumental. I like The Band, very good. Bits of Canned Heat, Taj Mahal, they're on the Stones' Rock 'n' Roll Circus and they've got a great guitarist. It's like listening to classical, you can take in too much. I keep my feelers out to find out what's happening and leave it at that."

The Beatles were in the forefront of pop music. Did he worry about that?

"No, we just do what we do as well as we can. We've no preconceived ideas of who we are or what's expected of us. Other people decide that. We just write a few little ditties, record them, hope they're liked."

There were critics who put them higher than classical composers.

"I think they're right, we're better than most of 'em. Most classical music's a load of crap. It's 'then' music. The more I listen to classical, the less I want to hear of it."

Did he have any idea how Beatlemania would affect him?

"We didn't know what we'd become. We knew what we wouldn't become."

Is there a generation gap?

"I suppose there is. I don't concern myself with it a great deal. There are a lot of gaps in the world, and they all need closing."

Did he care about politics?

"Politics? No, that's just as bad as ever. Wilson and Heath, they're all the same. Running it all in their own interests. Their only concern is themselves; anything else is a by-product."

Was he still into meditation?

"Yes, now and then. I believe in it as much as I ever did."

How did he feel about death?

"Oh, I'm quite looking forward to it. We ought to enjoy death just like we do life."

Did the Maharishi help with his attitudes towards it?

"In a way. He was good for me, just like anybody who has something to tell you that you don't know enough about."

Something to fill in for religion?

"I don't need a substitute for religion, religion's something else. There's a lot of good in Christianity, but you've got to learn the basics of that, and the basics from the East, and work them together for yourself. Christianity in this country used to be quite good until it turned into a business."

Had he come across any good books recently?

"No, there isn't time. Reading's a bit like classical music, it's all right, but it's 'then.'"

But there were some great books…

"Yeah, but you can spend your whole life reading and listening to bits of music just because other people regard them as the things to be read and heard. There isn't much place for classical music and reading for me, because I'm more interested in what's happening now and in the future. The only thing I want to read is pornographic books but they're hard to get hold of."

Any belief in God?

"I believe in something. I believe there's a lot of force at work that you can't physically account for."

The Bonzo Dog Band made a mockery of people they considered normal, the nine to five suit and tie set. Did he think of people that way, too?

"The Bonzos are good. I like some of their stuff. Normals? There are a lot of normals who aren't normals. A man went to court in a rainbow suit, on a steam roller. He was just an ordinary bloke who did that, a normal. Society's full of normal people who aren't normal.

"It's wrong to think of people as normal because it's the same as judging us as hippies just because we happen to have long hair. It's more what a man's scene is, in his mind, than how he looks and what he wears. You can be a pretty cool coal-bin man…"

The Beatles had a lot of power. How did he use it?

"I'm using my power all the time, by doing things like putting out Two Virgins, trying to open people's minds. People said the Rolling Stones and Elvis and long hair were obscene, but they accepted them in the end. I hope it's the same with my scene. Lots of narrow minds need expanding. It might surprise some Disc readers, and Jonathan King, that people do understand what we're trying to do, people all over the world. And there are a lot of us."

He wanted people to approve of what he said and did?

"Well, Yoko and I are fighting a bit of a fight to spread understanding and a kind of freedom. I don't expect everybody to understand us, but I just wish they'd try to be a little more open-minded, that's all."

Would he win?

"It's the goodies and the baddies, the Blue Meanies and the rest. I think I'll win, because I believe in what Jesus said."

A footnote mentioned that John and Yoko would be appearing in the Rolling Stones' Rock 'n' Roll Circus TV show.

January 18, 1969 – Disc and Music Echo, Gavin Petrie said Ringo Starr's first solo film, Candy, was almost ready for release. Ringo played Emmanuel, a Mexican gardener who was training to be a priest… until he met Candy, played by Ewa Aulin, and got it on with her on a pool table.

Said Ringo, "I was going to get my first screen kiss, just like Hayley Mills. But the script kept me too busy."

Candy was due to premiere in London at the end of February and would be released throughout Britain in the early spring. With Candy out of the way, Ringo was set to start working on his next film, Magic Christian, with Peter Sellers.

January 18, 1969 – Disc and Music Echo reviewed the Beatles' Yellow Submarine album, saying the group charmed with everything it did. Even All Together Now, a nothing song, was charming. The LP was Beatles entertainment at its best. And George Harrison's song writing skills were improving all the time. It's All Too Much was brilliant; and Only a Northern Song was catchy, while George Martin's orchestration for Side Two was clever, with an air of fantasy.

January 18, 1969 – Melody Maker announced that an hour-long documentary of the Beatles at work was in the process of being shot at Twickenham Studios in London. They were rehearsing the songs for their forthcoming live concert.

Dennis O'Dell was producing the film for Apple, shooting footage of the Beatles immersed in song writing, rehearsing, recording, even chatting.

"It has never been done before," said press officer, Derek Taylor. "There's never been a film of the Beatles actually at work. It'll all be there, the work, the breaks, everything. When the shooting is finished and the thing's been edited, it will be offered for sale to world TV companies."

Eight songs were already completed.

Taylor said the concert would not take place as originally planned. "The only thing I can say now is that it will take place, perhaps abroad."

One rumour suggested the concert would be held at a Roman amphitheatre in North Africa. Said Taylor, "There may now be some truth in this. It's an idea around at the moment, to do the shows abroad and take the fans along. It would certainly be *expensive, but an idea is to run some form of competition and take the winners."*

Apple's plan was to release an album and a documentary film. Taylor also mentioned that intentions to release an EP of *Yellow Submarine* had been canceled.

February 8, 1969 – *Disc and Music Echo*, Mike Ledgerwood suggested that Paul McCartney might be wed before the end of the month. Rumour had it that he was to secretly marry his American girlfriend, Linda Eastman.

American friends of Linda, who had met Paul nearly two years ago while she was working as a photographer, claimed Paul and Linda had decided to get married up to seven months ago.

The news of their romance had been revealed exclusively by *Disc* last October.

The wedding was to be a civil ceremony at a register office in London.

A spokesman for Apple said, *"We have no confirmation of this report. There were rumours about Paul and Jane. There will be stories about Paul and Linda."*

Linda was staying with Paul at his home in St. John's Wood. Linda's father, a wealthy American lawyer, said to friends, *"Linda hasn't told me anything about getting married. I've met Paul when she brought him to the house."*

John Eastman, Linda's brother, also a lawyer, was supposed to be receiving a legal appointment with Apple sometime soon.

Another rumour had Olivia Hussey, star of *Romeo and Juliet,* in love with Paul McCartney. She explained, *"Someone has made a big mistake. My steady boyfriend is Paul Ryan, and I think the world of him. I have only met Paul McCartney once."*

A footnote mentioned that the Beatles next single might be called *Get Back.* Recording with the group on that track was Billy Preston, an American piano player.

Get Back was among the songs the group was rehearsing in their Apple basement studio. Preston had been playing along. It was expected that the song would be included on their forthcoming live album, to be recorded as their TV show was filmed.

Preston, who had known the Beatles in the early days while he was touring with Little Richard, had dropped by the Apple offices and been invited to jam with the band. He said, *"They had some good things going. Paul was on piano and invited me to join in. I started playing and we all just fell on into it. The track was called* Get Back *and I played solo piano on it. They said then that it was good enough to become their next single."*

Said press officer, Derek Taylor, *"I don't think there is a new single yet. But I have heard them talking about this particular song."*

Said Preston's agent, Larry Kurzon, *"Billy is signing with Apple. They want to record him for a*

single. He has a number of compositions of his own, and George Harrison is involved in a deal with him."

Allen Klein, the business manager for the Rolling Stones, had been hired by the Beatles to investigate their Apple affairs, most particularly, their financial woes. This followed John Lennon's comment to Ray Coleman, *"Apple is losing money. If it carries on like this, we'll be broke in six months."*

Klein would look into everything. As well as working for the Stones, he was also record producer Mickie Most's business manager. Most handled Lulu, Herman's Hermits, Donovan, Jeff Beck and Terry Reid.

Back in 1966, it had been rumoured that Klein was to take over the Beatles, even while Brian Epstein was alive. Epstein had dismissed the rumours as outright lies.

February 8, 1969 – *Disc and Music Echo*, Bob Farmer said John Lennon's remarks about Radio Luxembourg in a recent interview were quite encouraging to the station as an indication that they were on the right track and heading in the right direction. Lennon had said that he, *"listened to Luxembourg the other night and that seemed quite swinging. At least it wasn't packed with hit parade stuff every minute."*

February 8, 1969 – *Disc and Music Echo* said that the Beatles' newest Apple band was called Trash, formerly known as White Trash, from Glasgow. While doing some session work in London, they were taped by Tony Meehan, who played the tape for George Harrison and Paul McCartney. They heard Trash's new song, *Road to Nowhere,* liked it, and that was that. The band was signed.

March 15, 1969 – *Disc and Music Echo* said that Paul McCartney was intending to marry Linda Eastman at the Marylebone Register Office the previous day, ending weeks of speculation since *Disc*'s exclusive initial announcement back in February.

Linda was the daughter of Lee Eastman, a rich American lawyer and a member of Kodak / Eastman family. She had met Paul two years ago. She was divorced and had a six-year-old daughter.

Disc had also provided the first information about their romance the previous October when McCartney and Eastman went for a holiday at Paul's farm in Scotland, just a few short months after Paul's engagement to Jane Asher was ended.

Paul was the last unmarried Beatle. He had met Linda at Brian Epstein's London home in 1967, at a launch party for *Sergeant Pepper's Lonely Hearts Club Band.* That same year, on Christmas day, Paul and Jane were engaged, but the engagement was broken off the following summer.

The McCartney / Eastman wedding was supposed to happen in February, according to some of Linda's friends.

At the time, McCartney refused to comment, but a spokesman for Apple said, *"There were rumours about Paul and Jane. There will be stories about Paul and Linda."*

Supposedly, they decided quite suddenly this week to get married. Official notice was given at the register office on Tuesday.

Derek Taylor, on Tuesday, said the ceremony would happen the following morning. No friends, no Beatles and no family would attend.

March 22, 1969 – *Disc and Music Echo*, **Caroline Boucher wrote** that Wednesday, March 12th was rainy and dark, somehow appropriate for the wedding of the last unmarried Beatle. The night before, it was announced that the wedding was set for 11 a.m. Said Paul, *"You'll have to be up early if you want to catch us."*

By 9:20 a.m. Wednesday, it was said that Paul and Linda were on their way to register office in Marylebone. Photographers and reporters flocked the office, waiting in the cold wet street at the front of the office. At 9:50, Paul and Linda arrived at the back of the office, along with Linda's daughter, Heather.

Linda was clad in a bright yellow coat, a beige dress beneath, and heavy brown shoes, with barely a trace of makeup on her face, all in total disregard for current fashion dictates, displaying her individuality. Paul wore a black suit.

Quickly, before the flock of reporters, photographers and fans had time to realise they were there, they were gone, into the register office through an alleyway door.

Police began to arrive. Paul's brother, Mike McGear, arrived in a rush, bearing parcels, late.

Fans chanted, *"We love you, Paul."*

Rain fell.

And then the McCartneys, Mr. and Mrs., were there, Paul with an arm around Linda and holding hands with Heather while the crowd surged forward in flashback to Beatlemania, screams cutting the moist air, tears flowing with the rain. Linda, obviously frightened, tossed her bridal bouquet to the crowd. Like sharks on a blood trail, the fans dove for the flowers as the McCartneys escaped in their car, more fans chasing the car.

Almost a non-event, it was over. The car with the newlyweds was gone. Girls wept in the roadway. And the dark cold ordinary day resumed.

March 22, 1969 – *Disc and Music Echo* said that while the madness in the streets was happening at Marylebone, the Beatles' Liverpool fan club was gearing up for the fall-out.

Said national secretary, Freda Kelly, *"We knew about the wedding on Tuesday, because Peter Brown rang and told us from Apple, so we were prepared for the phone calls. And we certainly got them, the phone didn't stop ringing all day.*

"Seventy-five percent of them realised, and wished Paul and Linda the best of luck, but the other twenty-five percent were very upset and there were a few tears over the phone. I think it dawned on them that it was for good, so they were suffering from shock. But I explained to them, I haven't met her but, by all accounts, she seems a very nice girl.

"We haven't had the mail in yet, that will come in by the sackful, especially the American letters, they're worse than anywhere else. But it might be all right, and they won't be too upset because Linda is American, so they might think it's good that one Beatle has got an American.

"But the questions the fans ask now have changed, anyway. They ask about records, and who's playing what. Before, it was always who's Paul going out with; they know all that now."

One of Kelly's assistants, Elfa Breden, said, *"I think they were working their way up to liking Linda, they had Jane Asher for a good few years, that was the main shock because Linda hasn't been around for so long."*

March 22, 1969 – *Disc and Music Echo*, **Bob Farmer wrote** the marriage of James Paul McCartney and Linda Eastman would forever be a landmark in the record book the Marylebone Register Office, not so much because it was Paul McCartney getting married… but because the signatures were nearly covered by a large smudge of ink. Explained the registrar, E.R. Sanders, *"But it wasn't their fault. Paul was using the superintendent registrar's pen, which seemed to be leaking."*

That was not the only government screw-up on the day. Paul's brother Mike was to be the best man. He was traveling down from Birmingham by train and the train broke down, delaying McGear's arrival by an hour, holding up the ceremony.

Wednesday, March 12th, Ash Wednesday for McCartney fans. They started to gather at 6 a.m. outside the register office, the fans to mourn, the photographers to prepare for any early arrivals.

But Paul and Linda kept to their schedule, arriving just before 10 a.m. The best man was absent. Apple executive, Peter Brown, contacted British Railways and learned that the train from Birmingham had broken down.

Said Paul, *"Good old British Railways."*

An hour late, McGear rushed into the reception room.

"Ah, here you are, Mike," said Paul.

"Forgive me, it wasn't my fault. Have you been done?"

"No," Paul told him. *"We've been waiting for you."*

The ceremony lasted all of ten minutes. Downstairs and through the front doors, the McCartneys confronted the crowd and the questions.

"How do you feel, Paul?"

"Fantastic."

"Are you going on a honeymoon?"

"No, not till later."

WE 954355

CERTIFIED COPY of an ENTRY OF MARRIAGE
Pursuant to the Marriage Act, 1949

[Printed by authority of the Regi] M. R.B

The statutory fee for this certificate is 3s. 9d. Where a search is necessary to find the entry, a search fee is payable in addition.

Registration District	St. Marylebone.						
1969 Marriage solemnized at	the Register Office						in the
District of St. Marylebone.	in the	CITY OF WESTMINSTER					in the

No.	When married	Name and surname	Age	Condition	Rank or profession	Residence at the time of marriage	Father's name and surname	Rank or profession of father
37	Twelfth March 1969	James Paul Mc.CARTNEY	26 years	Bachelor	Musician M.B.E.	7 Cavendish Avenue N. W. 8.	James Mc.Cartney	Cotton Salesman (retired)
		Linda EASTMAN otherwise Linda Eastman SEE	27 years	Previous marriage dissolved	Photographer	7 Cavendish Avenue N. W. 8.	Lee Eastman	Lawyer

Married in the Register Office   by Licence before   by me,

This marriage was solemnized between us,	Paul Mc. Cartney	in the presence of us,	Michael Mc.Cartney	J. L. Jevans Superintendent Registrar
	Linda Eastman		M. F. Evans	E. R. Sanders Registrar

I, ERNEST R. SANDERS Registrar for the District of St. Marylebone. , in the CITY OF WESTMINSTER do hereby certify that this is a true copy of the entry number 37 in the Register Book of Marriages for the said District, and that such Register Book is now legally in my custody. WITNESS MY HAND this 12th day of March , 19 69 Z. R. Sanders. Registrar.

CAUTION—Any person who (1) falsifies any of the particulars on this certificate, or (2) uses a falsified certificate as true, knowing it to be false, is liable to prosecution.

Linda's daughter Heather got lost in the crowd and was rescued by a cop. And then the McCartneys were on their way home, to face another onslaught of photographers and reporters.

Paul explained how he had first met Linda at a New York press conference, how they had re-met by accident in London, and how she had always been in the back of his mind. *"But,"* he said, *"we didn't get to know each other until we went out for a night on a bit of a thrash."*

Later, Paul and Linda went to St. John's Wood Parish Church for a short service and blessing by the Reverend Noel Perry-Gore.

Still later, Paul went to work, supervising a recording session.

March 22, 1969 – *Disc and Music Echo* **spoke** with the wet and windblown fans who had gathered outside the Apple building on Paul's wedding day.

Sobbing, leaning against the railing outside the Apple building, waiting and waiting in vain for a quick peek at her idol because someone from Apple had said he would be there, Mary Morton said, *"He shouldn't have done it. I've always loved Paul the best. What will I do now? All I wanted was one glimpse of him. They told us he'd come to Apple sometime during the day. I've been a Beatles fan from the start. But I've never seen Paul. I can't believe he'd do this to us. It's just not fair."*

Another fan, Sandra Dobson, said, *"I missed school so I could see him. I spent most of my pocket money getting up to town. Then I missed them both by a few minutes."*

They may not have seen Paul and Linda, but John and Yoko arrived at Apple.

Diane Robbins said, *"He arrived with Yoko and was singing* I'm Getting Married in the Morning. *We love John and Yoko. He always speaks to us. She's awfully nice, too. Very sweet. I think they'll be getting married soon, also."* Diane, too, had waited

through the day. *"It's all over now. It's the end, in a way, isn't it?"*

Said Donna Ross, *"He hardly knows her. I do hope he knows what he's doing. We're not against him marrying. It's just that we want him to be happy. I think everyone hoped it would be Jane Asher."*

March 22, 1969 – *Disc and Music Echo* **spoke** with Mike McGear.

Said Mike, *"The wedding was arranged for nine forty-five a.m. and my train was due in to Euston at nine-oh-five a.m. except, of course, that it broke down and British Railways had to put on a new engine, so, by the time I arrived at Euston, about ten-thirty a.m., I had given up. On the train, I knew I couldn't possibly make it and I thought there would be no point in even bothering to go to the register office, as I knew he had somebody else there who could stand in for me as one of his two witnesses.*

"I'd had to come down from Birmingham, where the Scaffold were appearing in a cabaret, in any case because we were filming a commercial, and I was being met at Euston by a bloke from the film company. On an impulse, I asked him if he'd mind if we just called by the register office to see if anyone was still around.

"I knew Paul and Linda were arriving by the back entrance so that's where we drove to. It was all deserted except for a policeman. 'Are they still here?' I asked him and, of course, he shouted, 'Yes, but you'll have to go in round the front way' so round I rushed, went in, and said, 'Forgive me, it wasn't my fault. Have you been done?' and Paul simply said, 'No, we've been waiting for you.'

"I've always had a reputation for being late all the time. I always try to be on time, but things always go wrong. I thought there might be a few tempers, but all Paul said was, 'Ah, you've come, Mike.' It made me feel very relieved.

"We went straight in then to get done, and I gave Paul the ring during the ceremony. Afterwards, we came out and had some of the champagne I had bought for them, together with a few other soft things, a couple of sparklers, a Kodak film for Linda. Heather always wants presents so she said, 'What did you bring for me?' I said, 'I brought your dad,' which, off the cuff, I thought quite good.

"I'm glad Paul and Linda got married. Actually, I found out by seeing it on a newspaper poster in Birmingham on Tuesday afternoon. Beatle Paul To Wed, so I rang him up and found out it was true. It surprised me since there was no real reason to get married. But it's good because it's a sign of proof to a woman that you love her. Men tend to think, 'Well, what's the bloody good of marriage?' so it's good that Paul decided to go ahead."

March 22, 1969 – *Disc and Music Echo*, Derek Taylor expressed his thoughts about the marriage. They had heard it before, rumours of Paul's impending marriage. But this time, it was not a rumour, it was true. Paul had told a writer from the *London Evening Standard*, at the Apple offices, *"I'm getting married tomorrow, Ray."*

And Ray Connolly announced it.

Thus, everyone heard that Paul and Linda were getting married. Paul getting married was the end of something. It was nice, and to a nice girl from Manhattan. He wished them well.

They were all married now – well, John did not really count – and the moptops were moptops no longer, no longer Brian Epstein's peter-panned boys. He truly wished them well.

March 22, 1969 – *Disc and Music Echo* recalled the sequence of the romance, beginning with the broken engagement between Paul and Jane. Fans were relieved. Paul was again available to their dreams and prayers… until October 18th, 1968, when Bob Farmer announced that Paul's *"current companion is blonde American photographer, Linda Eastman."*

A mere twenty weeks and four days later, Linda Eastman changed her name to McCartney.

At first, Paul was very quiet about Linda, he hardly knew her, she was just another girlfriend. Their first meeting at been at the home of Brian Epstein, an informal party to launch the *Pepper* album. A few journalists and photographers had been invited, Linda among them. She and Paul had talked a lot. The date was June 1st, 1967.

May 11th, 1968, Paul and Linda met again, this time at a press conference in New York, where they spent a lot of time together.

Next, Linda flew to England to visit with Paul and he followed her back to the States, then brought her back to London.

November 23rd, 1968, *Disc* printed the first-ever picture of Paul and Linda together, holidaying in Scotland.

On February 8th, Mike Ledgerwood said it seemed that Paul was about to be married.

Apple denied it.

February 14th, Paul and Linda were at a party to launch Mary Hopkin's first album, but they dodged the reporters' questions.

February 15th, sources in New York said the couple were already married.

March 9th, the plans were set.

March 10th, Linda filed notice at the register office.

March 12th, the deed was done and millions of hearts were broken.

March 22, 1969 – *Disc and Music Echo*, Richard Robinson wrote about Linda Eastman, who he had known for a long time. Her marriage to Paul McCartney was disappointing for a lot of Americans.

First, there were the millions of American girls who had pined forever for Paul, knowing he was single, knowing he was possible, knowing he was their sacred symbol. No one had the right to marry Paul, it was that simple. Linda was evil.

Then there were the hip night-clubbers all over the country who did not like marriage and did not like Linda and resented that the last cool Beatle was no longer cool.

And finally, there were the ones who disagreed with divorce and thought Linda had no right even to the divorce, never mind getting married again.

Robinson said Linda had done what she thought was right, it was that simple. She lived on her own terms and photography was how she communicated. She was real and she was honest. She was quiet, conservative, natural and more like a college girl than a well-recognised photographer moving amongst the rock elite.

He liked her.

The last time he had seen her had been at the New York press conference John and Paul had given to promote Apple. He had her voice on tape, saying to Paul, *"Hi, how are you?"*

Paul replied, *"Fine."*

She asked Paul when he was returning to England and Paul said he was not certain. And Robinson asked himself, *"Was that the beginning of it all?"*

March 22, 1969 – *Disc and Music Echo*, Bob Farmer said he thought the new surge of Beatle love surrounding the marriage of Paul McCartney would affect the value of Northern Songs shares on the stock market. But a stock broker told him, *"I wouldn't think there'll be any great buying. But, you could have made a real killing in the Beatles' shares had you bought them back in January, when they were only worth fifteen shillings each."*

They were now selling at thirty-five shillings each.

Back in January, Lennon had confessed that Apple was losing money. The shares had dropped to their lowest point ever, the perfect time to buy. People panicked, dumping their shares in Northern

Songs as fast as they could. That would have been the perfect time to buy.

As one shareholder said, *"How stupid. How could the Beatles be going bust?"*

He had started buying. Almost immediately, Northern Songs shares were back to thirty-five shillings. Smart money bought as much as possible at fifteen shillings.

March 22, 1969 – *Disc and Music Echo*, Cilla Black was asked to name her favourite records. Amongst them, she named *Julia*, saying, *"I suppose it's a bit cheating to choose this track from their latest LP, but it more or less counts as a single, doesn't it? It's so difficult to pick one Beatles' song, but this one is super. The lyrics are so good. Considering what people have been saying about the Beatles in the last months, if only they'd listened to this song, they'd see anyone who could conceive these lyrics must be beautiful."*

She went on to mention *Sergeant Pepper's Lonely Hearts Club Band*. *"That's the best thing that happened, there no question of ever considering any other LP as my favourite. Every track is brilliant."*

March 29, 1969 – *Disc and Music Echo* said John Lennon and Yoko Ono had been married in Gibraltar last Thursday and were holding a honeymoon love-in at the Hilton Hotel in Amsterdam this week.

All interested parties were invited to attend the honeymoon.

They had spent the first week of married life in Paris, whiling away the time with various social events, including a lunch with Salvador Dali, then moving on to Holland on the Monday night.

Rumour had it that John had been invited to play Jesus Christ in a lengthy television series for the BBC. The rumour was denied by Peter Graham Scott, managing director of the company that planned to finance the series. He said, *"John Lennon has the right sort of chemistry, but it might upset some people."*

April 5, 1969 – *Disc and Music Echo*, Jonathan King admitted he had, in the past, reprimanded John Lennon for some of the things he had said and done. Then he talked about an attack on Lennon made by John Gordon in the *Sunday Express*.

He explained that Gordon's column had high standards and strict ethics, but Gordon's most recent column about Lennon simply showed that Gordon feared and hated anything he could not understand. He despised what John and Yoko were doing, the bed-in in Holland, the naked pictures, despised the way they were carrying on, considered them stupid, therefore dangerous and criminal, not to mention wicked.

King explained that John and Yoko did not exactly conform to his own notions of logic, either, but they were doing no harm. And they were free and entitled to do whatever they liked, as long as

they continued to do no harm. King was on their side; whether he agreed with them or not was irrelevant.

April 5, 1969 – *Melody Maker* announced that the Beatles' next single would be *Get Back,* featuring Billy Preston on keyboards. No release date had been set, but they were hoping it would be out before the end of June.

Said an Apple spokesman, *"The group want to release it by then as they are planning to release their new album then."*

The B side song was still undecided.

At press time, John Lennon and Yoko Ono were still honeymooning at the Amsterdam Hilton. They were spending seven days in bed and were expected back in London before Easter.

The Beatles were not holding any more recording sessions for their new album until Ringo was back. He was presently filming *The Magic Christian* with Peter Sellers.

April 12, 1969 – *Disc and Music Echo*, Bob Farmer talked again about buying shares in Northern Songs. The value of the shares had risen steadily from thirty-five shillings to thirty-nine shillings, four and a half pence.

ATV, part of Sir Lew Grade's empire, was making a takeover bid for Northern. EMI was also attempting to buy it. And just recently, an unnamed American company was also joining the fray.

What all that meant was money.

John and Paul, both returning from their honeymoons, were against the takeover. Unfortunately for them, neither of them owned a large enough piece of Northern to do anything about it.

Said Sir Lew Grade, *"We are determined to buy Northern Songs. Music is an essential part of our business and there's no denying the brilliance of the Beatles as musicians."*

April 12, 1969 – *Melody Maker* said that the Beatles, as always, were in the news. Two companies, Nemperor Holdings (originally NEMS Enterprises) and Triumph Investment Trust, had attempted to freeze more than one million pounds in royalties on Beatle records. They were attempting to prevent American businessman Allen Klein from getting his hands on the money. A High Court judge refused to freeze the money.

Apparently, there had been a dispute about the royalties ever since the death of Brian Epstein. When the Beatles formed Apple, they had written to EMI, requesting that all royalties be paid directly to Apple. Nemperor Holdings and Triumph Investments insisted that EMI send the royalties to *them* until the dispute was settled.

John Lennon said his bank balance was *"scratching the deck."* But he confessed he could still come up with fifty thousand pounds in cash. Also, he owned more than a million pounds worth of shares in Northern Songs and had no intention of selling the shares to Sir Lew Grade.

Get Back was still to be the Beatles' next single. And their new LP was still expected to be released in June. Also, they had decided on a script for their next film but no details were forthcoming.

The *Melody Maker* Top Twenty Albums chart showed *The Beatles* double album [the White Album] at number fourteen after twelve weeks.

April 12, 1969 – *Melody Maker*, B.P. Fallon spoke with John Lennon. Part One of Three:

He began by calling John a Beatle and a poet, a movie maker and a revolutionary. Praised and damned, no matter what, he was likely the most famous man in the world.

Bearded, hair down to his shoulders, Lennon was relaxed as Fallon asked him if he felt cut off from the average person, the legendary man in the street.

Said John, *"I was always cut off from average people, even before I was a Beatle. I've never been normal, or so-called normal. I was never a lorry driver or a clerk, and I had no intention of being one as soon as I found out what they were, as a kid.*

"I don't socialise, except with very close friends, so I miss nothing. I don't miss communicating in the streets. I walk down the street whenever I like. We did it in Paris before the marriage, and nobody took a blind bit of notice. Just, 'Ah, le Beatle' and 'Oh, Yoko.'

"That's okay. I don't miss people. I never knew anybody. The people I knew were Beatles."

Certain people in the press were saying the Beatles were breaking up…

"They've tried to separate us from the word go. But it's just a natural reaction, a kind of jealousy. Some people spent their whole careers trying to split the Beatles and they're still trying. Every time we do something separate, they say, 'Ah ha! You're leaving, are you?' That's the way they live. Let them go around in circles, I refuse.

"Yeah, sure, we see less of each other. Two years ago, we were touring. We were together twelve hours a day like four married couples. Like being married to three people. And so, when we had less Beatle work to do, we saw each other less.

"Before we had a lot of gigs, in Liverpool, we didn't see each other every day, like lovers. Paul would come around maybe once a week, like you do with friends.

"Do you know anybody who sees their closest friends every day? How often do you see your closest friends? The Beatles are my closest friends. But I've got a busy life apart from them, and they have lives apart from me.

"All I can say is, 'Wait and see.' We'll be around, we'll be together when we're sixty. But we can't be following each other around like sheep dogs."

Fallon mentioned there was a forthcoming album by John and Yoko, as well as a new Beatles album, and a movie…

"We filmed the whole thing showing all the traumas we go through. Every time we make an album, we go through a hellish trip."

George had said everything that happened in the studio had been recorded, all the madness, all the joy. Would the group release an album like that?

"If we did, it would be about fifteen albums at once. I think we'll make a sort of straight album of the straight stuff and, maybe later, release a collection of the daft things like Rip It Up *and* Blue Suede Shoes.

"Working on my own with Yoko, I can go as far out as I like. Take Revolution No. 9. *I thought I imposed that on the Beatles for all the people who just want to hear the beat all the time, so George has brought out his own electronic album called* Electronic Sound *or something, and I'll freak out on my own, too. Let's have a finished-product Beatles. When I'm making pop music, I prefer that. I prefer doctoring it."*

They talked about love songs in general and, specifically, a song called *Fingertips* which was not very good but still managed to be exciting.

Said John, *"I'd do that, yeah, if I could sing as well as Stevie Wonder. I get hung up about my voice. I'd prefer to have a spade's voice. However, I can't do that, so I doctor them. I used to be very embarrassed about early records."*

In the recent biography by Hunter Davies, Lennon had put down the early Beatle records.

"I used to be hung up on different records but now, I accept them. Yeah, I've changed my opinion. Still, none of the records I make are what I want. A, because I'm not a good musician, and B, because I'm always writing soul music but I can't say it like I want. I've a terrible voice.

"Sure, people say to me, 'Your voice is all right, man.' But, when it's your own, you can't leave it alone, you're always doctoring or editing. Paul or George, and Yoko now, say, 'Leave it alone.' And I say, 'Well, I'll just put a little echo on here.' I don't doctor them enough. I allow the others some say."

John and Yoko did a live appearance in Cambridge. What was that?

"They were having a so-called avant-garde music session. Now, Yoko was from the so-called avant-garde world and I was from the so-called pop world. Intellectually, all musicians talk about no barriers between music and poetry. Yet more of them show it. We're doing it. Yoko will make pop records with me to show 'em.

"We went to Cambridge to do what they call avant-garde music. Yoko did her voice modulation, as she calls it, which would be screaming to the layman. And I turned me guitar on and played feedback. It's a pretty fantastic sound, and that's half of the next album.

"We didn't want to be rude and say, 'Don't play with us.' We didn't really want anyone else, just us

two. The musicians only came in at the end, as we were finishing, and we walked off. It was like a continuous show.

"Who were they? John Tchicai or somebody. He was with Ornette Coleman or somebody, I don't know. He's some big noise in Sweden. And there was..." Lennon broke off and turned to Yoko, then said, "Who were the guys from London? Yeah, John Stevens, who's got a little combo in London, playing jazz-cum-avant-garde, whatever that means.

"Jazz people are playing the same old crap over again. I don't want to bother with that. If I'm going to play other than rock and roll, I want to play it the way I like it.

"I don't mind community sessions, but I haven't played alone in that kind of field enough yet to want a group to play with Yoko and me. We played ten, twenty minutes together, but the bit I'm bringing out is just us two.

"There's all this intellectual crap in jazz. I went to show this in Cambridge, 'cause they were all being very serious about their doodle dooting, and that's what we did in Two Virgins, so John Cage, Stockenhausen, they're just in an intellectual bag and so are all of 'em. I enjoy some of their rock, but it's just intellectual crap. It's a joke.

"We've brought each other out of our bags, and that's what we've seen. Hell, we were in a bag too, you know."

Once there were some nice moptops from Liverpool, adored by one and all. Why has so much public love changed into so much public hate of late?

"It always varied, even with the Beatles. There was never a period where everyone was for us. Okay, so they all loved us and gave us an MBE, but there was a bloody outcry going on at the same time. There's always been both, you know. The public have always loved us and hated us.

"In Liverpool, before we left them, we had a public that loved us and a public that hated us. When we left Liverpool, they hated us for leaving. 'How dare our boys leave Liverpool?' Then we got down to London and we got ridiculed for having long hair and being from the North, so we conquered that, then we took over Britain and, okay, some were for us, some were against us.

"Soon, we went to America and they started knocking the shit out of us, 'cause we'd left Britain. 'How dare you leave Britain? You're only going to American for the money.' What else? So, it's been going on forever, and it doesn't mean a thing, and it'll be like that.

"The British press especially treat the Beatles like their child, and we don't mind that 'cause we've come to understand it, so, like any child, the parents aren't always wrong and neither is the child.

"We could pull some good publicity stunts anytime we want, in the middle of all that crap, but we compromised enough being Beatles, and we got

lost in it, and I, for one, and I know the others feel the same way to varying degrees, we got sick of compromising two or three years back.

"We compromised to get where we were, we went through a lot of crap. We thought the angle was to get famous and be rich, so we got famous and rich, and it's nowhere.

"We then gave up being moptops.

"We always thought there was some kind of goal, an end to it, because we were naive to think there was some end product in it.

"You think a number one record will do, then two number one records will do, conquer America will do, conquer the world will do, there was always something else, so it kept happening, so where were we?

"Rich and famous and sod all going on in our minds, so we said, 'We're stopping it.' And it took us two years to get our of the hole, and Brian died in the middle of it, and that threw us back another year, so we've had two years of finding out where we are. And now I know, so I'm here. Now's the time, we all know that intellectually.

"I'm not speculating on tomorrow, we might all be dead, earthquake, fall out of the window. Sod it. Now's the time. I've still plans for the future, but now's the time."

April 19, 1969 – Disc and Music Echo, Mike Ledgerwood spoke with Ringo and George, the other two Beatles, one half of the most incredible pop group ever. Ringo was on the set of The Magic Christian. George was holding the fort at Apple.

Ledgerwood asked George who he was.

"That's hard to define. I'm life, really. Spiritually and mystically. I'm life, and life is either up or down, in or out, left or right. It's like the North Pole; there has to be a South Pole. You can't have one without the other.

"Life is like waves on the ocean. Always chopping and changing. And we are at the mercy of the ocean unless we are anchored. We're all like little boats on the surface of life.

"Some people are securely anchored. Now, as each day goes by, I feel myself becoming more and more securely anchored. The real me is the real you and the real him."

And Ringo Starr... Who was he?

"I'm the family man. The marrying type. It's true, I am. I enjoy having kids. I live in a nice house. And I love my wife. I'm happy. And at the end of a day's filming, I like going home and seeing it all there. It's nice."

Had the Beatles image lost some of its glow lately?

Said Ringo, "Bad publicity always reflects on the other three. Sometimes it can be nice; sometimes it's a drag. Either way, though, it's life. Take John, for instance. Some people think he and Yoko are mad. But he's only being John and doing what people expect of him. What really worries people is when you're not doing what they want you to do. They want people, and us, I imagine, to stay as we are. John won't do that because he's John. I suppose it's a bit different with me. I'm Ringo and staying Ringo. It's what people expect of me."

And George, "*Publicity, exposure, and our image, depends really on what's said and how it's said. I wouldn't say our image was tarnished. If people write the truth, or as near to the truth as they see it, it's okay. But it really doesn't matter anymore.*

"*Even if they kicked me to death or nailed me to the wall, it doesn't get them anywhere. You know the saying, 'Sticks and stones may break my bones, but words will never hurt me...'*"

How much are you involved in Apple?

Said George, "*On the recording side, I'm almost totally immersed in it. But not so much with what goes on from day-to-day. Yes, we have been checking out and finding out recently. Without knowing what happened before, there's no hope of knowing what will happen in the future. Allen Klein is reporting all the time.*

"*Personally, I hope to get to a point where I can completely retire from the business side of things. Business is one thing, writing and creating, which we all want to do, is another thing entirely. But we want to retire knowing everything's really fine. The reason Apple wasn't in order before is that the Beatles weren't in order themselves.*

"*The Beatles have to be one. Four definite people contribute something each to make the Beatles. The trouble, as with many things today, starts when one tries to take over. It happens all the time. But we're now at a point where we can do something to each other's individual satisfaction.*

"*We're allowing each other to be what we want to be. In other words, by allowing each other to be each other, we can become Beatles again.*"

Ringo said, "*I'm only involved in Apple as much as I have to be. If there's a decision to blow up the building, I'll go along and raise my hand and say 'Aye.' Obviously, I'm interested in how it's being run, but that's about all. Recently, we have been assessing what's been going on with Apple. We just stopped everything, pulled everything in, and had a think.*"

Did they miss the Beatlemania days? Would they like doing live shows again?

Ringo said, "*I don't miss being a Beatle any more. Just like I don't miss being a teenager any more. You can't get those days back. Sometimes, I think I'd like to go back to Liverpool and have a good time, but it's no good living in the past.*

"*Nostalgia is great, but you only remember the good times anyway. And in those days, even the bad times were good.*

"*Personally, I don't want to play in public again. I just don't want to do it. And I don't think any of us want to do anything like an American tour.*

"*It would be nice to go into a little club somewhere and play like we used to play. But that* wouldn't be possible now. We'd have to do a show for everyone. We still do our old group act when we're recording. Play around in the studio, for our own personal entertainment.*"

George said, "*For a year before we stopped touring, I was fed up. I couldn't take it anymore. But I resigned myself to suffering it for another year. Today? I don't know. Maybe after the first show, I'd want to do it all again. Maybe go on tour, do the lot. I really don't know.*"

How did they feel about the fans these days?

Said George, "*I don't think of them as fans anymore. I think of them as people. Each one individually, almost. One is good, one is bad. I wouldn't like to put them in one box together. Some fans are fantastic and don't demand anything except to look at you. Others are just demanding. I don't mean that we're nothing without the fans. Their part in the play is equally important as ours. We're acting out our scene, and they are doing theirs. They're just as important as anyone.*"

Ringo said, "*Fans are both good and very annoying, at one time or another. Personally, I've usually found them very good. They're also very clever. They often know where we're going before we do ourselves. It's fantastic!*"

April 19, 1969 – *Melody Maker***, B.P. Fallon spoke with John Lennon. Part Two of Three:**

The last live performance by the Beatles had been in August, 1966, in San Francisco. It was the last time the Beatles had been the back-up band for massive host of wailing screamers. And then, last Christmas, it was announced that the Beatles would do a live show. And slowly, the idea withered, crumbled, fell apart. Would they play to the public again?

Said Ringo, "*No.*"

Said John, "*Yes. I'm saying we will do a live show, or live shows, so I'll have to work on Ringo or he'll work on me and may the best man win.*

"*It won't be anything fantastically different, it'll just be shows. We'll probably take a few tapes or electronic things with us, or maybe a few extra horns, depending on what we wanted. But all I need is me guitar, you know.*"

Will it be *Twist and Shout* all over again?

"*It might be. I'm still twistin' and shoutin', only now, we call it something else. It's still rock and roll.*

"*Who have I seen live recently? I haven't seen anybody for about a year or so. The last person I saw was Jimi Hendrix, when he was still playing the clubs, and I watched him make love to his amplifier and his guitar and I thought it was very effective. Oh, and Dylan, last time he was in Britain. I haven't seen anybody since then, I don't think.*"

What about writing with Paul? It was not always so easy to tell who wrote what, but it is easy now. Still, it was not obvious that Lennon wrote *Goodnight*.

"*When I wrote it, it was just like a child's lullaby. I just picked it on guitar, though it doesn't sound* anything like that now. If I'd recorded it, I would have done it straight, with just picking and singing and nothing else. But then, I thought it'd be good for Ringo. Ringo sings in that style when he sings a ballad, and hadn't recorded a ballad before, so I just said to George Martin, 'Arrange it just like Hollywood.' Yeah, corny. I just told him about two things to do in it, and George Martin's great at that, just whoosh, and that was it."

Even though John and Paul wrote separately, they still shared all the royalties from Lennon / McCartney songs.

"I copped money for Family Way, the film music that Paul wrote while I was out of the country making How I Won the War," said Lennon laughing. "I said to Paul, 'You'd better keep that,' and he said, 'Don't be soft.' It's the concept, we inspired each other so much in the early days. We write how we write now because of each other.

"Paul was there for five or ten years, and I wouldn't write like I write now if it weren't for Paul, and he wouldn't write like he does if it weren't for me."

Right now, John was happier than he had ever been before. But did he wonder sometimes if this was it, the top of the top and that the only direction possible was down?

"I thought that about everything. Like, a number one was a pinnacle, two number ones was a pinnacle, top of Britain was a pinnacle, top of America. It's infinite, you know. I believe in infinity and eternal whatever. The pinnacle is God, or whatever you like to call Him. There's the pinnacle, and that's a long way off yet.

"Sure, I believe implicitly in God, but my version of God mightn't be the same as yours. I think of God as a power, like electricity, that's neither good nor bad, you know. He just is.

"And what use we make of this electricity or nuclear power is up to us. That's what they mean when they say, 'God is within you, the Kingdom of Heaven is within you, et cetera, et cetera.'

"I think God is. People blame God for starvation and war, but they've no right to blame God. God is. He's neither one thing nor the other. He is everything, so how can they blame him? It's people's faults for what happens."

Would he send his kids to the sort of schools as they are now? And what about his son?

"I was trying not to, but now he's less in my control. I don't trust any of the schools. I wouldn't prevent him from learning the three Rs, 'cause he's going to need it anyway, before the whole systems changed. I had hopes of starting up a school, I might still do it, if I can get the bread together. 'A school is not economically viable.' That's what they keep telling me, so it just means giving it away. There must be some way to have a school that you can afford to run, like where people who can afford to pay, pay, and the one's who can't afford it, don't.

"I just don't trust 'em. I mean, they just fill their minds full of crap since they're born. Yeah, brainwashing.

"I can't do it for Julian but, maybe if Yoko and I have one, by the time that comes, maybe we might be able to get something together. But it's a hard scene, trying to change the educational system. You can't do it on your own. I even thought when they came home, I'd tell 'em, 'Forget it.' That's the best I could do.

"Rubbish, they teach 'em, about Napoleon and Wellington, and nothing about what's going on now." Macro-biotics?

"No, I'm not completely macro-biotic. I eat a lot of rubbish, then I start off again. You should try eating just brown rice for ten days. It clears your system, cleans your mind.

"Yeah, you do get kinda stoned, well, not stoned, but like after you've taken acid, you know? That's why the Viet Cong are winning, the Americans fill themselves up with ice creams and cakes and crap."

They continued with politics. Said Lennon, "The world is in a dangerous state because it's swinging to the Right. That's dangerous. It's getting too violent, too intellectual, too serious. Don't forget about peaceful protest, it's gone by the wind.

"Okay, All You Need is Love and all the acid heads, where have they all gone? It's all got back to 'Let's have the revolution now,' and, 'Let's smash the scene down.' Nobody bothers with the non-violent thing, and that's what I'm for.

"The Establishment know how to use violence, it's their game. They know it damn well. They've been playing it for years. And what good are we against violence? They've got all the power and all the money, so even to get the power and the money and the guns off them in a violent way, is going to cost more. Then it's going to take thousands of years building it all up, getting back on our feet again."

Did he believe violence was more powerful than peace?

"No, I don't, no. If it was, we mightn't all be here. There's enough goodness and peace around for us all to be still alive. Hitler didn't get us, and all the other ones didn't get us, so I believe that good will win out.

"But that doesn't mean you can sit back on your arse and wait for it. You've got to do something about it, anything. Like Yoko and I gave up one week of our holiday in Amsterdam. The Blue Meanies, or whoever they are, are promoting violence all the time in every newspaper, every TV show, and every magazine. The least Yoko and I can do is hog the headlines and make people laugh, anything. I'd sooner see our faces in a bed in a paper than another politician smiling at the people and shaking hands."

Was the Amsterdam protest done tongue-in-cheek?

"The sincerity of the peace thing, dedicating a week of our holidays, that was one hundred per cent serious. *But there were some good jokes in it, too, like the front page headline everywhere: 'There are two people in bed on their honeymoon.' That's a good joke.*

"And Yoko calls her work concept art. Take the 'cept' off and you've got con art and you're getting near the point. We're here to give people laughs as well."

April 19, 1969 – *Melody Maker*, **John Peel reviewed** the new Beatles single, *Get Back*, a very simple song with a Chuck Berry guitar riff. He said he always had the same reaction to a new Beatles song. First, disappointment, then, after a few plays, awe.

Beyond the record, he wanted to know what the Beatles were thinking, most particularly, John Lennon. He thought it was illogical for John and Yoko to spend a week in bed for peace at twenty pounds a night but then, it certainly had more people thinking about peace than war that week.

April 26, 1969 – *Disc and Music Echo* **said** the latest Apple release, *King of Fuh* by Brute Force, was banned by EMI. EMI distributed Apple records throughout Britain; they refused to handle *King of Fuh*.

Said press officer, Derek Taylor, *"We've been told that the record is classed as obscene. They claim we're trying to be sensational."*

George Harrison had come across *King of Fuh* during a visit to New York City. It had been written by Brute Force and was produced by the Tokens with George's guidance.

Said Taylor, *"Brute Force was signed to Apple for this one record only. The song is well sung and the message is good. And some fine people have already received it, played it, and enjoyed it."*

Ken East, managing director of EMI, said, *"EMI don't think it is suitable for us to distribute this record."*

King of Fuh would have been the ninth single release by Apple. During the past seven months, combined world LP and single sales by Apple artists had passed sixteen million, of which eight and a half million had been by the Beatles.

Get Back, their newest single, entered the charts at number two and sold over a quarter of a million copies in Britain almost immediately.

Mary Hopkin's latest, *Goodbye*, was at number three and quickly closing in on the same number of sales as *Get Back*.

An new song by Jackie Lomax, *New Day*, was due to be released on May 2nd.

Recording engineer Geoff Emerick, the winner of a Grammy Award for his work on the *Pepper* album, was leaving EMI to work for Apple on May 1st.

April 26, 1969 – *Disc and Music Echo*, **Caroline Boucher spoke with** Leslie Cavendish, the Beatles' hairdresser. Three years ago, one his clients wanted him to cut her boyfriend's hair. The client had been Jane Asher, the boyfriend, Paul McCartney, and Cavendish worked at Vidal Sassoon in London.

McCartney had wanted his hair cut on a Saturday afternoon.

Said Cavendish, *"I'd never cut anyone's hair on Saturday afternoon, so I went to watch Chelsea, and then went round to cut his hair afterwards."*

And he had been cutting Beatle hair ever since, getting to know them well along the way. He had been the only non-musical person to sit in on a Beatles recording session; and he had traveled on the bus with them for *Magical Mystery Tour*. Even though their hair had been the subject of many conversations right from the start, they were actually unconcerned with it.

Said Cavendish, *"As long as they can wash it and brush it and just leave it at that, they're happy.*

"People thought they purposely came on the scene with long hair, but it wasn't true. It was very short, at first. The record came out and they never had time to get to the hairdressers.

"It was round the time of Sergeant Pepper *that John started growing his hair, and they started growing mustaches. They realised what hair could do to you, and how much it can change you."*

Over the years, many people had tried to get clippings of Beatle hair from Cavendish. But Cavendish made certain it was tossed in the garbage along with all the other hair he cut.

About Paul, he said, *"I probably know him the best, since I've been doing his hair the longest. He has it cut every four weeks, and I go to his house in St. John's Wood to do it.*

"After the second time I cut his hair, I thought I'd never be doing it again. He was going on safari to Nairobi and didn't want to be recognised so, as a joke, I said, 'How about having it cut to a quarter of an inch all over?' And he said okay. After the first few snips, I thought, this is it, I've ruined it. It was very long at the time.

"But I carried on and, when I'd finished, there was nothing left, it was as if he'd just been called up to go to Vietnam. Paul couldn't believe it either. It was only after he'd gone and I read in the newspapers he wasn't recognised that I got any satisfaction.

"I went round to his house to cut all their hair last week. For the first time in three years, Paul turned round and asked Linda how she liked it, 'Do you want it any shorter here and there?'

"I've never heard him do that before. I thought, oh-oh. Then I cut her hair, and Heather's. She's an unbelievable little girl, she'll say, 'Hey Paul, that's a groovy record you've put on,' and she can't believe all the girls waiting outside the house.

"Paul's got good thick hair that he's wearing off his face at the moment. He's got a fascination for ears, he thinks ears should be shown."

Regarding John, Cavendish said, *"His last words to me, about a year ago, were, 'I'm going to let my hair grow down to my waist.' I haven't cut his hair since, and I don't think anyone else has either. But if* he lets his hair grow, it will get to a certain point and it'll just break off.

"He's got very thin hair anyway, and the way he carries on with it, if he doesn't have it cut, it'll break off at the ends and get very weak. Out of the four, he's the most likely to go bald, and he could, unless he's careful.

"I told Paul this and Paul just said, 'Oh, I expect he'll have it cut.'

"I was more nervous of John than anyone else, at first. But after a while, he was just very nice. He never interfered with me cutting his hair. As far as music in concerned, nobody interferes with him and, if he wants his hair done, he won't interfere with me.

"I know why he's growing his hair. He wants to see what happens if you let nature be nature. But he should be careful. If he goes out in the sun, it will dry up, and his hair's very dry anyway."

On to George, he said, "I didn't really meet George until last year. He's got the thickest head of hair I think I know, there's no danger of him going bald.

"He rang me up one day and said he'd found a bloke, Jackie Lomax, and he wanted me to go down to the studios and design a hair style for him. We tried all sorts of things, but, in the end, decided to leave it long. After all, that's Jackie, isn't it? And anything else wouldn't have been.

"I did George's hair when he was in hospital recently, and that's when we decided to have it off his face.

"He called into the shop the other day to have it cut again, but usually I go round to the Apple offices to do his hair. He asked me to take Pattie to a film a couple of weeks ago when he couldn't go."

And finally, Ringo, Cavendish said, "I haven't done his hair since he got married, because his wife, Maureen, is a hairdresser, I think. I got to know him on Magical Mystery Tour. One evening, we went to a pub owned by Spencer Davis' road manager, and, at about one o'clock we were all having a big singsong with Paul playing Knees Up Mother Brown on a piano, and Ringo plucking away at an old mandolin with only one string. After about two hours, he said, 'Hey, do you know, I think I've worn my thumb away,' and it was pouring blood.

"Ringo's hair is nearly gray, he's got a superb gray streak down one side. Funnily enough, I've got a small part in his film The Magic Christian as a mad hairdresser."

April 26, 1969 – *Melody Maker*, B.P. Fallon spoke with John Lennon. Part Three of Three:

John and Yoko, the two names sounding right, poetic all on their own. Real people with real emotions. Real people easily hurt by the mindless morons who condemned their every move. Once public lovers, now married. Why?

Said John, "*Everything, even the Establishment, has some good things, and marriage is one of them. Yeah, it's good.*"

How are they handling all the personal attacks?

Said Yoko, "*It hasn't been that bad, has it?*"

And John said, "*No, not that bad. Just a few nasty things in the Sunday papers that are meant to be funny. But they'll get over it. I get really puzzled how people can be upset with two people in love. Really puzzled... I mean, we're human, too. I do get hurt when they attack Yoko, or say she's ugly, or something.*"

Fallon had a magazine article that called Yoko bossy and pushy. He asked her if she was.

Replied Yoko, "*I don't know about being bossy. I am a pusher, in a way, I guess, because it's so easy to just fall back on my chair and say, 'Well, I'm over thirty and I did quite a lot.' By nature, I have to communicate, and there are many things we have to communicate right now. In that sense, I'm pushy.*"

Added John, "*The woman who wrote the article was pushy as, uh, anything, because she pushed her way into our lives by saying she was an old school friend of Yoko's, which she was, and she got in there and pasted Yoko. But we were kind to her. Yoko's pushy about her work and, who isn't?*"

Fallon suggested John sometimes seemed forgetful and asked Yoko if she pushed him to get his act together.

"*Both of us, it's like a blind man and a cripple, we help each other. He has a fantastically clear and articulate side, and he understands very practical things, too, and he has a very unpractical mind at the same time. In other words, he's full of paradox. Of course, I am, too, so we sort of support each other.*

"*I tell him, 'You'd better write your name, sign it' every time he does a drawing, because his drawing is good. But what he was doing, just like any impractical artist could do, is draw it and forget it. Now, he's keeping track of his drawing.*"

Even racial prejudice had hit their relationship.

Said John, "*Some people said, 'Why don't you get yourself an English woman? Why some foreigner, a Japanese woman?' Then, in a reply to a Japanese visitor, 'No, I don't know Japan well, I was only in Japan once... when I was a Beatle.*"

Without doubt, the naked album cover had caused the most public uproar.

John said, "*The reaction was typical of narrow-minded, compressed heads. A few people understand it. What was it? Just two people naked. It's not lewd or obscene, and there's nothing wrong with it. It's just two people without any clothes on. They think that once you get past babyhood, there's something sinful about it. It's time they woke up. We're all naked underneath.*

"*Our press office came up with the Genesis bit about Adam and Eve. 'Man and his wife were both naked and they were not ashamed.' You see, not ashamed, get it? See, from the Bible.*"

They had a new album ready for release.

"*There it is*," John said, pointing at the cover, which showed John sitting on the floor beside Yoko, who was in a hospital bed after a miscarriage. The flip side showed John and Yoko surrounded by cops after leaving court with a drug conviction. "*We finished it during the miscarriage. One side is things we recorded in the hospital, a thing we sing together, and there's the baby's heartbeat and two minute's silence, which we've copy-righted!*

"*The other side is Yoko and I playing in Cambridge to a group of nearly deaf students. No, they were deaf afterwards, we stunned them!*"

Said Yoko, "*We hope to do more of that.*"

Fallon mentioned that *Two Virgins* seemed very personal. Would the new album continue in that vein?

John said, "*Oh yeah, sure, it'll be Part Two. It took me a long time to realise the Beatles were doing a diary, too, on records. Everything anyone does is his own diary, but I became aware of it as a Beatle.*

"*I'm trying to get over as quickly as I can what exactly is happening to me at this given time, and so, we collect photos, tape it or make films of what's happening.*"

John had been filming the interview. He said, "*We've made five films now. Well, this'll be the fifth. They're all feature length, apart from* Two Virgins, *which is twenty minutes. Names? Number Five. Two Virgins. There you are. Rape and this one. We did that one while we were in hospital, see. As Yoko's word is concept art, we've concept films, really.*

"*We just think of the idea and send the guy out, you don't need to be there with the camera. On* Rape, *we finally found a cameraman we could connect with. The others were just always getting things wrong. It's hard to find the right person, but I think we've got one now that's pretty good.*"

Name?

Lennon laughed, "*Uh, I've forgotten. I just know where he is...*"

"*Nick,*" said Yoko.

"*Yeah, Nick. Nick Knowles.*"

Paul was working with Mary Hopkin, and George with Jackie Lomax. What was John doing?

"*I have Yoko. It's together, yeah, but I'm more of the producer because I know more about tapes, that's all. But she produces, too. She's a heavy girl. That's why that woman thought she was bossy. Yoko's like a man and the other woman couldn't stand it. She's just like a guy, her mind is. I mean, like a guy because that's the only thing I can think of.*

"*If I produced for other people, they'd have to be bloody good for me to waste me time, because I couldn't be bothered fiddlin' about with records.*

"*While we were in India, they were all making their plans and I was going to produce Yoko, and I would've been producing her, had we not fallen in love, anyway. She'd done shows in the Carnegie Hall and the Albert Hall with Ornette Coleman, and all those other heads, and I thought she was great

and I was going to produce her as an individual artist, so I wouldn't been doing that.*

"*But it didn't turn out like that, and now, we're together. Yes, it turned out much better. And it's getting better all the time...*"

May 3, 1969 – *Disc and Music Echo* announced that Yoko Ono was to record a song written for her by John Lennon. Said John, "*We messed around with a song together last night. It was supposed to be me singing a song about her, but all I have to do is change the name to John and she can record it.*"

Yoko is expected to make a single sometime in the next few weeks.

The Beatles were getting set to release a follow-up to *Get Back* called *The Ballad of John and Yoko*. George and Ringo would not be playing on it, just John and Paul.

John said, "*We'll probably release it soon after Get Back drops out of the chart. It's a nice, simple, oldie-type ballad about Yoko and I. Us getting married and that sort of thing.*

"*George was out of the country and Ringo was working on the film. Paul and I just got together in the studio and it turned out well. We didn't want to have to do it again, so we left it as it was.*"

Lennon and McCartney were hard at work, composing for a new album. Their TV movie was still being edited.

John said, "*I don't know how the TV thing will turn out. They're trying to bring it down to around five hours running time. Personally, I'd like to see the film made into a series and run like The Dales.*"

David Platz, boss of Essex Music, was joining the Apple music publishing company, in a supervisory and advisory capacity. Ron Kass, who formerly held the position, had, according to Allen Klein, "*decided he could do better in another working arrangement.*" Klein went on to say that the Kass departure did not mean the Apple executives were being cut.

Derek Taylor, press officer, said, "*People have left Apple over the past twelve months; and two or three in the past month. But that's all.*"

Allen Klein denied he was intending to become the Beatles' full-time manager. John Lennon said, "*Allen is simply doing a job for us. If he does something, he gets paid. If he doesn't, he isn't.*"

Klein said, "*I have no contract with the Beatles. It is simply a personal service agreement between us.*"

May 10, 1969 – *Disc and Music Echo* said that the Beatles' new album, recorded while they were filming their TV special, was being delayed. The released date had been switched from June to late summer. According to Apple, the group was running behind schedule.

John Lennon had said that he and McCartney were writing non-stop to meet the deadline but the final finishing touches were going to take longer than anticipated. Most of the songs had been recorded as they were happening, during the filming and the rehearsals, without any sound filters.

Said Mavis Smith of Apple, "*At the moment, all the recordings are unedited and the plan originally was to release the LP like this. But they may decide to make some changes.*"

Get Back was still at number one, total sales over two million.

Next week, Ringo was to fly to New York to shoot the final scenes for *The Magic Christian*.

This week, John Lennon spent one hundred and fifty thousand pounds on a seven-bedroom, Georgian mansion surrounded by seventy-two acres of land at Tittenhurst Park near Ascot. John and Yoko were to move in sometime in August.

May 17, 1969 – *Disc and Music Echo* **interviewed Beatles' biographer Hunter Davies.** Davies said when Paul needed to work out a new song, he would grab a guitar, lock himself in the lavatory, have a seat and start strumming. That was left out of Davies' book about the Beatles, which had, so far, earned him one hundred and fifty thousand pounds in royalties.

He said, "*It wasn't in the book simply because I completely forgot about it until Paul came to Portugal to stay with my family for a few days just before last Christmas. Paul decided to fly over with Linda Eastman and her daughter, Heather, on the spur of the moment, which is typical of him. He hired a plane at fantastic expense, as there were no other available flights, arrived in the middle of the night, shouting, 'Wake up, it's me,' and when we let him in, he headed straight for the loo with his guitar!*"

Paul was the one who worked to get official approval from Brian Epstein so Davies could write the book.

Davies said, "*I'd first met Paul through interviewing him for my Atticus column in the* Sunday Times, *and, when I came to do the screenplay of my book,* Round the Mulberry Bush, *I asked him if he'd write the music. He wouldn't; Traffic did instead, but, being involved in something outside journalism, I suppose, we became that much more friendly and, eventually, I asked him if there was any chance of my writing a biography of the Beatles.*

"*This was around the end of 1966 and they'd just stopped touring. It was the end of a huge phase in their lives and a good time to do such a book.*

"*Paul liked the idea and even took the trouble of helping me write a suitable letter to Brian Epstein, proposing the idea. 'Stress that you work for the* Sunday Times,' *he said, 'and mention all the snobbish sort of things you can think of.' It worked, of course, and I worked on the book for the next eighteen months, which takes their story up to shortly before they became disillusioned with meditation.*"

The Beatles' story had expanded considerably since the Davies book was published. John had split up with Cynthia and taken up with Yoko Ono; the

cops had started hassling the group about pot; Paul had started seeing Linda Eastman; the Apple boutique had opened, then died.

Davies said he if he could append and update his book, he had a story he would like to add. Regarding Yoko Ono , he said, "*I met her before John did. She phoned me at the* Sunday Times *to say she'd like to use my bottom in her film on the subject. I said I couldn't very well allow her to do that, but, as a compromise, I'd write a piece on her for Atticus.*

"*I suppose I was amazed when it all came to pass that John and Cyn had broken up. But then, none of the Beatles is really married in the accepted sense of the word. With them, it's equality in originalness. In fact, the Beatles are closer to each other than to their wives. They can communicate with each other without needing to speak. Jane Asher didn't want to be the fifth Beatle, she wanted to be married to Paul, not four blokes.*

"*John meeting Yoko was really meeting a piece of himself, because he's a freak-out bloke. She is very intelligent and funny, serious and genuine. He was always the raver and completely selfish and I thought their coming together might mean John moving away spiritually from the other Beatles. But it hasn't seemed to affect their relationship at all.*

Davies liked the idea of Apple. He said, "*I meet a lot of intelligent, progressive people in my job, but the Beatles are light years ahead of them all in goodness. They're conceited, but don't believe they're God's gift to us. They don't want to stash away their money. Their idea is to give back something from what they've got. They felt, 'Why can't we help others?' which is great, but really talented people don't want charity. They have the conceit and don't want help because they have the conviction that they'll make it anyway.*

"*Can it come off? I don't know. What matters is that they are trying.*"

For him, the most interesting recent thing was whether or not the Beatles would do a live show. He said, "*Paul and George are keen, Ringo and John against the idea.*"

What about Paul and Linda?

"*I like them both. But why Paul preferred to marry Linda is impossible to say, because you can't describe love. It was just smooth, they gelled, whereas with Jane, there were always deep discussions and arguments. Jane has this compulsion to work, to have a career, and be a person. Linda, too, but photography is not the most important thing in the world to her.*"

May 17, 1969 – *Disc and Music Echo* **reviewed** John and Yoko's new album *Unfinished Music No.2: Life With the Lions*.

Side One, Cambridge 1969, featured Yoko doing the vocals. For thirty-five minutes, she wailed and whined, sobbed and cried and screamed in agony. The result would have you ether praying for silence while cynically laughing… or it would have you wondering just what they were getting at.

Side Two, No Bed For John; Baby's Heartbeat; Two Minutes Silence; and Radio Play began with Yoko chanting about the controversy when *Two Virgins* was released and when John slept on the floor beside her in the hospital after her miscarriage.

The reviewer thought the album was sad. The reason for releasing it was simply to communicate but, unfortunately, most people would not get it.

Disc invited owners of the album to write in about it. They stipulated that the people who bought it had to have heard it before they made the purchase. *Disc* wanted to know why. The best letters would be used in the paper and the writers would be given an LP of their choice.

May 17, 1969 – Disc and Music Echo, Penny Valentine interviewed Mike d'Abo. He said, "*I have a tremendous admiration for Paul McCartney. I identify with him musically. Everything he does has my mind ticking over and I say, 'Yes, I understand that.' I envy his branching out from just being a Beatle to song-writing and producing. It's the ideal state I'd like to emulate.*"

May 24, 1969 – Disc and Music Echo announced that John Lennon, along with Mick Jagger, had been asked to write a play for children.

A spokesman for the Institute of Contemporary Arts said, "*Mick Jagger and John Lennon were chosen because they both have very creative minds.*"

Apparently, both were interested. The plays were to be performed by children at a special show called Play Orbit in November.

May 24, 1969 – Disc and Music Echo mentioned that the Beatles had lost their battle to maintain control of Northern Songs. Sir Lew Grade and company managed to put together a controlling interest in the company to win the fight.

The Northern Songs board would have six new members, including one appointed by the Beatles.

Said John Lennon, "*Nice of them to let us have one.*"

The group's new single, *The Ballad of John and Yoko*, was due to be released in June, before their new album.

George Harrison was working on a single and an album by Billy Preston, due to be released sometime during the summer.

And Paul McCartney confirmed the rumours that he and Linda were expecting a baby at Christmas, roughly ten months after their marriage.

May 24, 1969 – Disc and Music Echo spoke with actress / comedienne Judy Carne, who said meeting George Harrison was the greatest thrill of her past year. She went on to say, "*I think it's so sad that people are not behind the Beatles here like they are in the States. We should be proud of them. They've done so much for England, and so many don't seem to*

appreciate that. And, because of the way they've been treated in England, they may never be able to go to America, where they are so loved.*"

May 24, 1969 – Disc and Music Echo, Caroline Boucher visited John and Yoko's new home in Ascot. She said one hundred and fifty thousand pound homes were not uncommon in that neighbourhood. As John Lennon looked around the huge, thirty-room Georgian mansion, he said, "*Well, I suppose it's very functional.*"

The house was three hundred years old, set on seventy-two acres of parkland which included formal gardens, cottages, outhouses, a farm and a lodge.

It was one hundred and fifty thousand pounds worth of privacy. The house was situated deep in the property, invisible from the road at any angle. It was a two-story place with seven main bedrooms, three bathrooms, three reception rooms, some large kitchen areas… and staff quarters.

May 24, 1969 – Disc and Music Echo printed six letters that were written in response to their request to hear from fans who purchased, *after* hearing it, the new John and Yoko LP *Unfinished Music No.2: Life With the Lions*.

"*I bought it without hesitation,*" said Philip Higgs.

Said N.W. Laird-Clowes, "*I bought it because, in my way of thinking, there has never been an album like it. I play it every day before school and at night in bed. I do hope that in future, John and Yoko will release more LPs and one day, even a single.*"

J. Coleman said, "*John and Yoko's LP is by no means a masterpiece, but it is a valid art form. John and Yoko are sending out feelers to explore new areas of experimental music. Instead of taking tentative steps, like many groups, John and Yoko have gone in head first, and are courageous to have done this.*"

Said Russell Carey, "*To enjoy this LP you should ignore conventions and, most important of all, you should have no musical prejudices; thus you should be able to appreciate all types of musical entertainment, including John and Yoko's type… I enjoy this LP for its sound, its simplicity and its emotion…*"

David Stark said, "*Life With the Lions is not worth two quid, it's worth a hell of a lot more. I bought it after having listened to it a couple of times, and I have found it to be a haunting and intriguing experience. Its pure concept is so refreshing, and the sadness of the music…*"

And finally, Philip Harnes said, "*This album certainly has something to offer…*"

May 24, 1969 – Melody Maker reviewed *Unfinished Music No.2: Life With the Lions.* Yoko's extraordinary voice had the innocence of a wailing baby, the tortured grief of the damned and "*the stamina of an Alpine yodeler. Miss Ono has unleashed the most terrifying sound since the development of the jet engine…*"

Side One was her recorded performance at the Cambridge Natural Music Festival. It was a non-stop wail of agony, evoking in the reviewer: laughter, irritation, anger, boredom, bewilderment and satisfaction. Only a football match could create similar mood changes...

Side Two was John and Yoko chanting about themselves... "all the rhythmic excitement a tube train can sometimes provide..."

Clearly, the unnamed reviewer was un-enchanted with *Unfinished Music No.2: Life With the Lions.*

May 31, 1969 – *Disc and Music Echo* **reviewed** *The Ballad of John and Yoko*, which was due to be released the following day. It was okay, but it was merely John being self-indulgent and whining about being martyred along with Yoko. The lyrics were somewhat less than imaginative. It should not have been the new Beatles' record. Sub-standard, unexciting, empty and dated, uninspired, disappointing...

June 7, 1969 – *Disc and Music Echo* **printed** a round-up of brief Beatle news.

A film shot by John and Yoko to promote the Beatles' new single, *The Ballad of John and Yoko*, would be shown on Top of the Pops that night. The song opened at number fifteen on the Disc pop chart.

John and Yoko were in Montreal and had recorded a song for peace in their hotel room. Rabbi Abraham Feinberg of Toronto, once a New York radio singer, had joined them.

George Harrison and Richie Havens were seen chatting at the Speakeasy Club in London. Havens was in England for a series of concerts and had just recorded *Lady Madonna* as a new British single.

Frank Zappa of the Mothers of Invention was planning a rock concert in Canada in October. He wanted the Beatles to join in.

June 14, 1969 – *Disc and Music Echo*, **Richard Robinson wrote** from New York, saying the States had been exposed to two Beatles during the last two weeks. Their reception was less than wonderful.

Ringo, along with his family and Peter Sellers, were in New York to promote *The Magic Christian*. The music press were unaware that Ringo was arriving. The only reporters there for the interview were from the regular press. The questions harkened back to 1964, why Ringo wore funny clothes, etc. After a few days in New York, Ringo flew to Bermuda for a holiday.

John was next. Due to a drug bust, he was not allowed in the U.S. but he wanted to promote *The Ballad of John and Yoko*. From a hotel room in Toronto, he made phone calls to some of the major American radio stations to talk about the record and peace and himself and the Beatles. A number of the stations had no interest in talking to him. They would not be playing the song because of the word Christ and because of the line "peace in bed." Some of the stations that would play it had cut out the word

Christ; others had cut the word, reversed it to sound like Tsirhc, and looped it back in.

June 14, 1969 – *Melody Maker* **announced** that the Beatles' new album, likely to be called *Get Back*, was due to be released in July. It would include *Get Back*, *Don't Let Me Down*, and twelve other songs.

At present, *Get Back* was just the working title but an Apple spokesman said, "*This will probably remain the title.*"

The Beatles were thinking about making a film for TV to promote the LP.

John Lennon and Ringo Starr were back in England, Lennon from Montreal, Canada and Ringo from New York by way of Bermuda. Paul McCartney and George Harrison were expected to return soon.

Recording at the Apple studios was supposed to resume during the next week.

The newest Apple release was a single by Billy Preston, *That's the Way God Planned It*, produced by George Harrison.

And the Apple group White Trash was to begin touring with Marsha Hunt.

June 21, 1969 – *Disc and Music Echo*, **Mike Ledgerwood announced** that the Beatles new film was expected to be *The Lord of the Rings*, a fantasy thing based on a series of books by J.R.R. Tolkien.

The group said the script idea was, "*the best they've read so far.*"

Said press officer, Derek Taylor, "*All four have read the books and are very enthusiastic. After this, nothing else seems to be up to standard.*"

The Lord of the Rings, which was published in 1955 as a follow-up to Tolkien's children's book *The Hobbit*, recounted the adventures of Frodo and Sam, two Hobbits, who, with the help of the good wizard Gandalf, return an evil magic ring to its source. Other characters included Gollum, an evil Hobbit; Savron (sic) a bad wizard after the ring; and Avagorn (sic) the Prince.

Said Taylor, "*The story has quite a bit of relevance to the highly controversial TV version of* Alice in Wonderland, *produced by Jonathan Miller, which starred Malcolm Muggeridge and Peter Cook, where a lot of things make sense, as well as non-sense.*"

In a footnote, Penny Valentine thought *Lord of the Rings* seemed a likely vehicle for the Beatles. Much like *Yellow Submarine*, it was the story of good against evil, though the treatment would need to be less gimmicky.

She gave a synopsis of the story and suggested that Paul could play Frodo, the hero who conquers his own fear against horrific odds; John, based on his acting in *How I Won the War*, would do well as the whining, mewling and pathetic Gollum; Ringo could play the ever-faithful Sam; and George could be the wizard Gandalf.

June 21, 1969 – *Melody Maker* said *The Ballad of John and Yoko* had hit number one on their charts that week. At the same time, news leaked that John and Yoko had recorded a peace song, due to be released by Apple on July 4th.

The song was *Give Peace a Chance* by the Plastic Ono Band. The recording was made in a Toronto hotel room on equipment provided by Capitol Records. John and Yoko, along with "about forty other people" perform the song, a "hypnotic chant."

"*It's a fantastic song that will turn the world around*," said a spokesman for Apple. It furthered John and Yoko's crusade for world peace.

The Ballad of John and Yoko was about society trying to crucify John and his wife for wanting peace.

Worldwide sales were already near the million mark. A Gold Disc was expected soon. It hit number one while *Get Back* was still in the charts at number five.

A book of photographs and text would be included with the group's next LP, due to be released in early July. The album was likely to be titled *Get Back*.

July 19, 1969 – *Melody Maker*, **Laurie Henshaw spoke** with money man Allen Klein. Some people believed the Beatles were like four young innocents, naive and ripe to be plucked. Henshaw asked Klein if he was a ruthless operator, kicking and gouging his way to the top, the way some people were suggesting.

Replied Klein, "*How did that idea get around? If being one hundred per cent concerned with the people I represent is being ruthless, then I am ruthless.*"

Klein had no sympathy for the British-style businessman who hid behind a mask of manners and politeness. He said, "*They cut you up... and the blood comes out a lot later.*

"*As Paul McCartney once said, 'Some people feel this way about me because I negotiate very tough deals. And the people I negotiate with are bad losers.' Why will people underestimate the Beatles and refuse to take them seriously? They're not four little boys who don't know what they're doing; they're four grown men.*

"*If all this business happened to anyone else, no one would take any notice of it. But because it's the Beatles, everything they do is magnified. My prime function is to see that, other than paper equities, the Beatles have sterling pound equities after tax. That's the first thing. And that's what I'm working on now.*

"*And to do this, they had to free themselves from the NEMS / Triumph situation. Triumph bought from them their interest in NEMS. And for their ten per cent interest in NEMS, each one received one hundred and fifteen thousand pounds, subject to capital gains tax of thirty per cent.*"

Henshaw wondered if John Lennon's peace crusade had made him unaware of Beatle financial matters.

Said Klein, "*John is probably one of the most commercially minded of them all, but only because* he realises that there must be constant changes. He was the first to recognise this, now they all know it.

"*It's not an easy thing to break out into new directions, to have the courage of your convictions. But, don't forget, many people have died for their beliefs. John Lennon does what John Lennon believes is right. John made* Give Peace a Chance *because he wanted to get his message across in the simplest possible way. Would it have satisfied his critics more if he had called it* Give War a Chance? *Would that then have been all right?*"

Apple had recently been attacked for it extravagances.

Klein said, "*I intend to make it financially successful and tailored to the Beatles' own specifications.*"

More staff cuts?

"*That's not necessarily a requisite. But when you get a lot of energy wasted, it doesn't make for an efficient organisation.*"

Would Apple expand its activities?

"*The Beatles don't intend to make it another EMI. But they will continue to sign up artists they believe in, and concentrated on these. They had the foresight to sign up Billy Preston, you have to give George Harrison credit for that. And Paul recorded Mary Hopkin. But I leave this side of Apple's activities to them. They leave the business to me.*"

Is it possible that his work with the Rolling Stones could conflict with his work for the Beatles?

"*There's no conflict. It just means I do two jobs in one day.*"

Regarding his work with the Beatles, Klein said, "*You have no idea of the monumental task involved.*" His job was to see that the Beatles received their fair share of the money their work generated. Each pound was filtered through stockholders and a limited company, and by the time the tax department got through gouging out their chunk, there was very little left.

"*With everyone taking a little piece, there's really not much left for them*," Klein said.

July 26, 1969 – *Disc and Music Echo*, **Derek Taylor, of the Plastic Ono Band, wrote** *Give Peace a Chance* was a number one record and it was nice to be a member of a band that had a hit.

The Plastic Ono Band belonged to Apple. And it belonged to everyone. It represented freedom, the freedom for performers to perform as they wished. It could be anything.

A tour was planned. The British version would tour the UK. The American version would tour the U.S.

Give Peace a Chance had been born in Montreal on a Saturday night. John had written it for the Beatles. But it happened in Montreal, with John and Yoko and Derek Taylor and Timothy Leary and Tom Smothers and some journalists and friends and peace activists and maybe even a guy from the CIA in drag.

YOU are the Plastic Ono Band, Taylor declared. And YOU have a hit record, *Give Peace a Chance.*

August 2, 1969 – *Disc and Music Echo*, John Peel said he liked being a member of the Plastic Ono Band – he reminded readers that, according to Derek Taylor, they too were members – and what a good feeling it was to have a hit record.

He explained he had only met John and Yoko twice, briefly, and would likely never meet them again. Talking to the two of them was like talking to one person. It was a joy to know they were alive, somewhere, somehow.

Maybe *Give Peace a Chance* was just another song, and maybe Apple was just another group of businessmen, and maybe John Lennon and Yoko Ono were just two more people in a world full of people. But to Peel, it was all magic.

August 2, 1969 – *Disc and Music Echo*, Jonathan King said YOU are the Plastic Ono Band. Bad luck. He remembered when four darling moptops sang *She Loves You – Yeah Yeah Yeah.* He remembered how they sang it simply and truly, with a melody and with a certain freshness. It was obviously a pop song and obviously meant to be enjoyed. With the Plastic Ono Band, you had to wonder: was it monotonous tuneless garbage, or was it a great art form?

King talked about how Allen Klein was making Beatle information freely accessible to the press. He said one of Brian Epstein's greatest strengths had been his ability to keep things private, his ability to use the press.

That week, *Disc* showed *The Ballad of John and Yoko* sitting at number ten in the American charts.

August 16, 1969 – *Disc and Music Echo* said that John Lennon was the most popular Beatle. His crusade for peace, his bed-ins with Yoko, had brought him respect rather than ridicule.

Disc had polled its readers and discovered that young people were still cheering for the Beatles and were giving their total support to the much-harassed John Lennon. When asked if John and Yoko's behaviour could be considered a bit weird, half of the readers agreed that it was, but that it was sincere, which was what mattered most.

Votes for favourite Beatle were overwhelmingly for John. The Beatles were still number one in the world. Perhaps their popularity had peaked but most fans believed the best was yet to come.

August 23, 1969 – *Disc and Music Echo* said that the Beatles' movies, *A Hard Day's Night* and *Help!*, were to be featured at the Newcastle Tyneside Pop Festival in October. *All My Loving,* starring the Beatles, a TV documentary by Tony Palmer, would also be screened.

August 23, 1969 – *Disc and Music Echo*, Ray Coleman reviewed the book *Pop From the Beginning* by Nik Cohn. Cohn had said, *"Indirectly, the Beatles*

have brought pop to its knees." He went on to say he was sure pop music would be revived and he was equally sure it would not be the Beatles who revived it. Cohn did not care for their music and believed that, in thirty years, it will be shown that Elvis Presley meant far more to music than the Beatles.

Cohn's theory was that Bob Dylan and the Beatles were guilty of giving pop music meaning, taking it beyond bubble gum and Coca Cola into the realm of art. Following them, the new wave of groups were wallowing in bad poetry, regurgitated philosophies and pitifully weak perceptions. And the teenagers were the losers.

Coleman thought Cohn was being unfair to the Beatles. It was true, they had moved on from relatively simple pop songs into artier things. But the Beatles could hardly be blamed for the loss of direction on pop music. They had to forge ahead, they had to grow and improve. It was unfair to tear them apart for being so good, for being so much better than all that came before and after.

Coleman said, *"Nik Cohn's criticism of the Beatles is one of the most incomprehensible chapters in his book."*

Later, Cohn insisted it was the Rolling Stones, not the Beatles, who led the pop revolution. He said the Beatles were not committed; the Stones were. Coleman agreed that the Stones were committed. Committed to making hits and getting famous, which they did. Just as the Beatles did. To proclaim that the Rolling Stones contributed more to the pop revolution than the Beatles was ridiculous. Cohn's book was a sermon, not an objective view.

August 30, 1969 – *Record Mirror* announced the title of the new Beatles album was to be *Abbey Road.* The final mixing was being done and the LP would be released by the end of September.

Abbey Road was replacing the *Get Back* album; release for that one had been postponed until the end of the year.

One side of the new album featured a medley of new songs which, said Paul McCartney, *"Goes on long enough to have a bath by."*

George Martin produced the album. And Derek Taylor said it was a return to the style of *Rubber Soul.*

Taylor said, *"The Beatles have been working on* Abbey Road *for eight weeks."* He added that *The Ballad of John and Yoko* had sold 1,250,000 copies in the States. Sales of *Give Peace a Chance* had hit 19,000 in Britain, 700,000 in America.

August 30, 1969 – *Record Mirror*, David Skan said Apple was one year old that week. Apple was the Beatles trying to take control of their own business. And Skan reviewed the year, the Apple boutique disaster, the giveaway of all the goods, Paul McCartney saying, *"We should never have tried to beat Marks and Spencer at their own game."*

John was getting divorced.

Paul was not marrying Jane Asher.

Later, Paul married Linda Eastman.

Later, John married Yoko Ono.

And someone was talking about Allen Klein.

And the Beatles moved into 3 Saville Row and had desks and sat at them and worked just like they had real jobs.

And the Beatles were in business.

At first, they wanted to spend their time and money promoting dirt poor young people who needed cash to do their own thing. That gig started costing them twenty thousand pounds a week.

They stopped being quite so… un-business-like. Said Paul, *"We used to be too generous. But now, if a group asks us to buy them amplifiers, we'll tell them to get themselves together as a group first and then come and see us."*

Twenty-five people worked in the Apple building, which cost a quarter of a million dollars and had four floors. And Allen Klein had signed a one-year contract to manage Beatle business.

First things first, Klein made up a list of unnecessary people. Lennon agreed to their dismissal… as long as he did not have to give them the news. The people vanished. And the Beatles had finally done it, they had beaten the odds-makers and the prognosticators, they had gotten themselves together to make Apple succeed.

In one year, Apple had sold twelve million singles, some of those, of course, by the Beatles themselves. But Mary Hopkin and Billy Preston had been remarkably successful.

Other branches of Apple had been put on hold; no great loss.

And the Beatles, in Allen Klein, had found someone they could trust in a world on untrustworthy people.

A sidebar listed the singles and LPs released by Apple in England.

The singles:

Those Were the Days by Mary Hopkin, *Hey Jude* by the Beatles, *Sour Milk Sea* by Jackie Lomax, *Thingumybob* by the Black Dyke Mills Band, *Maybe Tomorrow* by the Joys, *Goodbye* by Mary Hopkin, *Road to Nowhere* by White Trash, *Get Back* by the Beatles, *That's the Way God Planned It* by Billy Preston, *The Ballad of John and Yoko* by the Beatles, *Give Peace a Chance* by the Plastic Ono Band, and *New Day Dawning* by Jackie Lomax.

The albums:

That's the Way God Planned It by Billy Preston, *Wonderwall* by George Harrison, *Two Virgins* by John and Yoko, *James Taylor* by James Taylor, *Under the Jasmine Tree* by (MJQ) the Modern Jazz Quartet, *Postcard* by Mary Hopkin, *Is This What You Want* by Jackie Lomax, *Unfinished Music No. 2* by John and Yoko, and *The Beatles' Electronic Music* by George Harrison.

September 20, 1969 – *Disc and Music Echo* **ran** a short note by Mike Ledgerwood. He said James Brown was bigger than the Beatles… in Tunisia.

On the same page, it was announced that the group had reserved a number from the *Abbey Road* album for White Trash, hoping to get a hit for them. Also, Paul McCartney had written a song for the Iveys, *Come and Get It,* which was to be featured in Ringo's new movie, *The Magic Christian.*

Said a spokesman for Apple, *"White Trash are a very good group. It's only a matter of time before they make it. We thought we may as well have our own Marmalade this time."* Marmalade had covered *Ob La Di Ob La Da* and had scored a number one hit with it. The title of the song White Trash would cover was being kept secret until the release date, September 26th.

Jackie Lomax, the George Harrison discovery, also hitless, was writing songs with Doris Troy, a new Apple signing.

The Plastic Ono Band's new single and album would be released in November.

A footnote said Radio Luxembourg was the Beatles' favourite station. Ringo was to make a one-hour appearance, at his own request, the following Thursday. And Lennon and McCartney were going to introduce the *Abbey Road* on the 24th of September.

Ringo had called up the station, asking to appear on Kid Jensen's show because, *"I think he's a really cool deejay and I'd like to do a show with him."*

Jensen was coming to England to record the show.

September 20, 1969 – *Disc and Music Echo* **spoke** with John Lennon about reports that he and Yoko had been booed off-stage during a rock festival in Canada, which also featured Bo Diddley, Jerry Lee Lewis and Chuck Berry.

Said John, *"It there was booing, I didn't hear it. But you expect a few not to like you in a crowd of twenty thousand."*

Beatles' assistant, Mal Evans, said, *"We were brought down by the reports of booing. I suppose eighty per cent of the audience enjoyed the two songs Yoko did at the end. And they were a very tough audience."*

The Lennons, along with Klaus Voorman, formerly of Manfred Mann, and Eric Clapton of Blind Faith, made a surprise appearance at the Rock Revival show.

Evans said, *"Yoko spent the first two numbers sitting in a bag at the side of the stage. They did a lot of old rock and roll numbers. For* Give Peace a Chance, *the audience was standing up swaying in time to the music. It was incredible."*

John said, *"It was the first gig I've played since the Beatles stopped doing live performances in 1966. I can't remember when I had such a good time. I don't care who I have to play with, I'm going back to playing rock on stage."*

September 20, 1969 – *Disc and Music Echo,* **Gavin Petrie, film critic, said** the audience filed in to the sounds of *Abbey Road* while hosts and hostesses handed out pictures and bits of literature and art by John and Yoko.

It was *An Evening With John and Yoko* at the New Cinema Club. There were three hundred people in the audience.

The first film shown was *Two Virgins*. During the showing, a large white bag was helped down the aisle to the stage. Also during the show, autographed pie plates and wooden spoons were handed out.

While the next film, *Smile*, was playing, sounds began to issue from the white bag, a tinkle of bells, then two voices chanting the *Hare Krishna Mantra*. As the film ran... and ran, the audience was encouraged to bang on the pie plates with the wooden spoons while the *Hare Krishna Mantra* droned on.

As the film ended, the white bag continued to chant. Eventually, it was helped off-stage.

There was an intermission.

Then the *John and Yoko Honeymoon* was screened. Next came the world premiere of *Self Portrait*, shown to the sounds of *Abbey Road*. The final film was *Rape*. *The Queen* was played and the theatre emptied.

In the final analysis, the five-hour evening had been boring. Petrie said Lennon was not crazy, that he was almost on to something, but the work went on too long, the work went on so long that the best thing about each one was when it ended.

He believed John and Yoko were onto something, but just were not quite good enough to get the message across.

"Realism," said John, "leaves a lot to the imagination."

In the end, though, Petrie wished they would make a more conventional film, one for a good laugh and a good cry, one that would be easily identified with, one that would clearly put the message across... whatever that message was.

September 20, 1969 – *Melody Maker*, Richard Williams said John Lennon had not received a royalty cheque in two years.

"The problem," John said, "is that two years ago our accountants made us sign over eighty per cent of all our royalties to Apple. We can't touch any of it, and it's a ridiculous situation. All the money comes into this little building and it never gets out.

"If I could get my money out of the company, I'd split away and start doing my own projects independently. I'd have much more freedom and we'd all be happier.

"I still feel part of Apple and the Beatles, and there's no animosity, but they tend to ignore Yoko and me.

"For instance, Kenny Everett recently made a promotional record for Apple which was played at the big yearly EMI meeting. It plugged James Taylor, the Ivies, and so on, but it didn't mention the things Yoko and I have been doing. And I think that what we're doing is a lot more important than James Taylor.

"Apple seems to be scared of us. They didn't want to have anything to do with our *Two Virgins* film, for instance.

"The Beatles wealth is all a myth. The only expensive things I've ever owned are my house and my cars, and I just haven't got anything else. I don't even break even on the films we make, and that worries me."

Williams asked Lennon why he felt it necessary to make films like *Self Portrait* when Andy Warhol had already done it.

"It's not like Warhol at all. He's negative and we're positive. I can't stand negative things, and our attitude is completely different. Self Portrait *has vibrations of love, and it has an immediate message of humanity. When Yoko showed me her* Bottoms *film, I thought it was ridiculous, but she explained it to me and I was convinced, I don't remember how. I think it was the humour of the film, and that's what we try to keep in our films.*

"If we're going to get these films shown, we've got to get into the scene. We'd like to make a film that wasn't so underground in concept, but we wouldn't do something like* Barbarella *or* 2001, *although that was lovely trip.*

"Films are moving ahead so fast, much faster than music or anything else. We're hoping to have talks with a big company which I shouldn't name, oh well, why not, it's United Artists, who seem to be interested. We'd like to get on at the West End."

Said Yoko, sitting beside John, "We don't know how to go about it. We're sussing it out at the moment."

John continued, "It's not like films, it's more like TV. Dylan was right, it should be less important. Our films, and the Beatles' and Stones' albums, shouldn't have so much noise made about them.

"The process of production is so slow. We'd like to speed the process up and get a new album and a new film out every month.

"For instance, we haven't been able to get our* Wedding *film out yet. And the trouble is that people will say we copied Jane Birkin on one track, but we didn't, it's just that we couldn't get it out fast enough.

"Most of our films are like portraits. For instance,* Smile *is simply a portrait of me sending out love vibrations to Yoko, who's on the other end of the camera. People say it's boring, but they'll look at a Van Gogh, which doesn't move at all, and they'll have it on their walls."

Perhaps he had shown it to the wrong audience?

"Yes, it would probably be best if people had the film at home and could show it on their walls and look at it when they felt like it. The ICA night was too long, but they asked for five hours of film and that's what I gave them."

Was their work an open diary? Were diaries not meant to be private?

"Yes, but who doesn't like to read other people's diaries. That's exactly what it is, but you must realise that the Beatles' albums, and Dylan's, for that matter, are all diaries. We're just bringing it out into the open and making it more honest."

Could this lead to disposable art?

"Yes, that's what we're aiming at. Yoko's having her book of poetry, Grapefruit, *reprinted, and at the end there's an instruction to the reader to eat the book."*

Said Yoko, *"When you keep things, they become tombstones. The world would be clogged up with useless objects."*

Any new ideas for the peace crusade?

"There's this Peace Ship plan," John said, *"which is very strange because recently I read a book which contained almost exactly the same idea. There was this bloke in the book who had a white ship from which he broadcast peace messages, and then when I'd read the book, a real guy came to me with the plan for actually doing it.*

"Someone's also given me some ideas for doing things in Nigeria and Biafra, but I can't talk about that at the moment."

Would he be more directly involved with war and peace?

"Not really, because I think that what we've done already, like staying in bed for peace, has been very direct. It wouldn't do any good, for instance, if I was to go to Vietnam and get shot. That proves nothing, but it's what people are always telling me to do.

"We're after people's minds. If we got to see Nixon, for instance, it wouldn't make him down tools, but we could find out what he thinks and tell other people. We'd know where he was at.

"You can't change anything by violence. You have to be aggressive, that's part of everyone and I'm aggressive, but we have the machinery to channel it. We don't have to get involved in other people's games, and I think that all the killers should be allowed to take their tanks into the desert and kill each other off.

"But I don't want any part of it, and we've got the power to do something about it."

With both *Abbey Road* and *Get Back* recorded, would the Beatles take a break from recording?

"The trouble is that we've got too much material. Now that George is writing a lot, we could put out a double album every month, but they're so difficult to produce.

"After Get Back *is released in January, we'll probably go back into the studios and record another one. It's just a shame that we can't get more albums out faster."*

September 27, 1969 – *Record Mirror*, Lon Goddard reviewed *Abbey Road*. He thought the Beatles grew more amazing by the minute. *Abbey Road* was at least as good as their last three albums. Four kids from Liverpool had turned into two bearded guys, an actor, and *"the barefoot boy."* The front of the album had them strolling across a zebra crossing on *Abbey Road*…

Come Together: John wailing out the lyrics in a powerful song.

Something: A new George Harrison song, sweet and beautiful, drifting through the scales with a heavy orchestral arrangement.

Maxwell's Silver Hammer: A happy little song about a serial killer…

Oh! Darling: A hard driving number with Paul belting out the lyrics.

Octopus's Garden: Ringo's sequel to *Yellow Submarine*.

I Want You – She's So Heavy: A heavy blues tune, John's voice following every note that Harrison played, ending with a surprise.

Here Comes the Sun: Western style melody with Beach Boys style harmonies.

Because: Symphonic and lyrical.

You Never Give Me Your Money: A frantic rock and roller.

Sun King: Nice.

Mean Mr. Mustard; Polyethylene Pam; She Came in Through the Bathroom Window: Fast changes with some confusion in the lyrics.

Golden Slumbers: Paul singing a lullaby.

Carry That Weight: Strong.

The End: Nice finish.

A sidebar mentioned that John and Yoko's next LP was to be their *Wedding Album*, a multi-media package that would sell for four pounds, their most expensive album yet. Included with the record was a sixteen-page box full of press clippings, a collage of photographs, a strip of film and a picture of a wedding cake.

September 27, 1969 – *Disc and Music Echo* announced that the next Beatles single would be a song by George Harrison, *Something*, the first Beatles A-side that was not sung by Lennon and/or McCartney. The B-side was *Come Together*. Both songs were from the *Abbey Road* album and were only for release in North America. The next British release was, as yet, undecided.

Prior to this, George's best song yet, he had only been used on the B-sides of records: *Inner Light* backing *Lady Madonna*; and *Old Brown Shoe* on the flip side of *The Ballad of John and Yoko*.

Said press officer, Derek Taylor, "Something *is being released in the States within the next couple of weeks. It has quite definitely emerged as the DJ's favourite track over there and is getting enormous air play."*

Something was also the first time that the Beatles had released an LP song as a single. Both *A Hard Day's Night* and *Help!* were issued as singles before they were put on an album.

White Trash was to release a single the next day, *Golden Slumbers / Carry That Weight*.

Orange Bicycle had already recorded a cover of *Carry That Weight / You Never Give Me Your Money*, due to be released the next day.

The La De Das were releasing *Come Together*, also the following day.

And *She Came in Through the Bathroom Window* had already been recorded by Joe Cocker, who had had a hit with another Lennon / McCartney song, *With a Little Help From My Friends*.

Ringo had been interviewed for Radio Luxembourg, the show to air that night.

And Mary Hopkin was to do a new Paul McCartney song.

October 4, 1969 – *Record Mirror*, David Skan spoke with John Lennon. Part One:

Said Lennon, "*Beatlemusic is when we all get together. You know, if I want to sound like* Come Together *and* I Want You *all the time, which I always did and always do, or whatever it is I want to be, and Paul wants it to be whatever he wants it to be and George, et cetera, et cetera, so, when the combination works, you come out with what we call Beatlemusic. Of course, we don't write songs together any more. We haven't written together for two years, not really, anyway, you know, occasional bits, a line or two. It doesn't make any odds. When the Beatles perform, that makes it into Beatlemusic.*

"*I mean, it's a long time since we've sat down and written, for many reasons. We used to write mainly on tours. We got bored, so we wrote. Today, the Beatles just go into a studio and it happens.*

"*We've never had a direction. I mean, it was just whoever was pushing the limits of the bag, you know. We often all pushed at the same point. It was never this is the way we are going. As far as we are concerned, this album is more Beatley than The Beatles double album, that was just us saying this is my song and we'll do it this way, this is your song, you do it your way.*

"*We've got a lot of songs, that's why we did the double album. It's hard to bring out double albums all the time. We let them out in other things, like through the Plastic Ono or something like that. It's like being constipated with all the material. That's the only way we can do it, really. We don't have conceptions of albums. No, I think Paul does. But I don't. All I am interested in is sound and I don't care about concept.*

"*I like it to be whatever happens.*

"*We like gags, you know, we always have. We like little jokes and surprises at the end of things. We've all got a bit of the stage act in us. Perhaps that's what it is... but we don't long for those days. We stopped doing it because it was a drag. I dug performing in Toronto, but I didn't have that Beatles mystique to live up to, which is the drag about performing as Beatles.*

"*Not going out as a Beatle, nothing is expected of John and Yoko, and yet, everything's expected of John and Yoko. They could be anybody or perform anything with that sort of freedom, there's no hang-ups.*

"*I am in love and that's the end of it. She is now fifty per cent of me. Every time I pick up a guitar, I sing about Yoko and that's the end of it. I am influenced by her ideas or wherever she came from... she came in through the bathroom window, actually.*"

Yoko said, "*It's not something in me which went into him. It was all there anyway. We wake each other up a bit.*"

Said John, "*I don't know how it affected the Beatles. Of course, all the things have affected them, me getting married to Yoko and Paul getting married to Linda and all that. When you get down to it, I'm only interested in Yoko and peace.*

"*It's like I'm going through my blue period as a painter, he's going to paint this cup for a year and really get into it, so maybe I'm doing that. I'll do it till I get tired of it. On Twenty-four Hours, they just sardonically read the lyrics of* I Want You. *They said all it says is 'I want you.' But to me, it's a damn sight better than* Walrus, *lyric-wise. It's a progression, to me.*

"*I want to write songs with one word or no words. Maybe that's Yoko's influence or whatever. In the early meetings with Dylan, he was always saying listen to the words, man, and I said I can't be bothered, I listen to the sound of it. Soon afterwards, I reversed it and listened to the words, but now I am only interested in pure sound.*

"*I'm interested in voice modulation as well.*

"*That was the thing that got me about* Heartbreak Hotel *in the early days. I couldn't hear what he was saying, it was just the experience of it, and of having my hair stand on end.*

"*If there must be words, they can be rubbish, what I call rubbing, which is just word play or 'I love you... I love you... You love me... and Let's get together,' because I don't want to sing about suburbia. I think one note is as complex as anything.*

"*I can't spend the rest of my life explaining that to musical critics who want complex musical harmonies and tonal cadences and all that crap. I'm a primitive, so I don't need it. I am not interested in that. Paul himself said that we'll end up with a one note pop song, and I believe it.*

"*I can groove to the sound of electricity in the house or the water pipes, and a lot of people do groove to that, but if I lay it down on record, we're going to get all that 'who do you think you are' scene.*

"*Why do I have to explain what sound is? We all sit by the sea and listen to it and nobody says, 'this sea is good because it's reminiscent of childhood experiences or it's like your mother's water.' People just lie in fields and listen to birds. If I record that, all I've got to say is 'This is birds.' You only grunt when you come.*

"*Most of the teenybopper fans didn't dig* Revolution Number Nine, *but what am I supposed to do? I probably won't impose it on a Beatles album again. I'll do it separately. I can't keep framing my thing within Beatlemusic.*

"Apple is right as Apple, as a company that makes records. All that other stuff has gone to the wind. It was a dream that didn't happen. All our money went into a box and never came out. Nobody got it. Apple itself, as what it is now, is running well and doing all right. Apple will keep changing.

"The other things I'd like to do would be films. I don't know if that would be related to Apple. That depends on what the businessmen can do for us with Apple now. We are not entirely in their hands, but they are expert, they are the only people who can tell us how to get our money out of the box and use it.

"You see, most of what I earn goes into Apple and never comes back. Nobody gets the benefit. If I could sort that out, it would be nice. That's what we all need. Other things like films and that, I am keeping separate at the moment. If Apple was more fluid, I'd channel some of my creative energy into Apple. I do it a lot now. We all use up energy on Apple.

"All I want to do is free my money to do what I want with it. I'd like whatever Apple is to run on its own without me so I can get on with... there's too much energy wasted on just running it... just to keep it ticking over.

"All I did was get in a bag and that was the end of the experience. If I painted myself blue, what can we do about it? There will always be people complaining because we left the Cavern and went away to Manchester. That's all it really is: how dare you leave the Cavern and jump into a white bag in the Albert Hall?

"You can't wait around for those people to decide they'd like me go and do tap dancing. If the Beatles had just gone into show biz, we would probably have ended up quite good and having nothing but praise.

"We're not looking for that, at least, I'm not, so I must do what I want."

October 11, 1969 – Record Mirror, David Skan spoke with John Lennon. Part Two:

Said John, "If I had something to say to the students, I suppose it would be, 'Don't shake your fist at the building.' The building itself isn't important. But I know how they feel. Christ, I get angry. I feel like jumping about sometimes. The Biafra thing, the oil companies... Shell!!! What they're doing is awful.

"And then people come up and say, 'Well, what are you doing about it, then?' And they say, 'John and Yoko, the hip aware people, have forgotten,' so we have to trip out again. But you get so hooked by television and radio that it becomes very difficult to find out what really is happening.

"You see, it's such a big fight we are in. On the peace thing, somebody said we ought to do something. We knew that anyway. But we spent three weeks thinking about the most effective way of doing something for us, for John and Yoko. Then we came up with the bed idea.

"It was a very thought out thing. Every time any of the media came up to us, there were great notices with the word 'peace' on them, and we spent hours of tape explaining all about it, and the point is that it did make all the papers and all the radio and television.

"You see, before I met Yoko, I was doing the All You Need is Love thing, and Yoko was doing it separately through her hammer and nail piece. It was hammering in the nail to get rid of the aggravation bit. But when we got together, we felt we had to do something more.

"You see, you either create something, or you destroy it.

"After the bed-in, we both went through a big depression. We wondered if people had got the point. Then we began to get letters from young people which showed that they knew, they understood what was happening. All revolution produces status quo, even including Cuba, the red tape just gets redder and longer. The people don't really have any control at all.

"I am trying to do something different. I am trying to change people's minds, to change their attitudes to things. We are the 'head' generation. And the game, the political game, is a lot more subtle than people think. You can't sell peace like soap. You have to infiltrate people's vocabulary, and the things people do.

"For instance, everywhere we go, the kids give us the V-sign. The kids do it everywhere, it's become the peace sign. Peaceniks do it. We get feedback through letters, as I've said. But a very nice reaction is that, at every garden party, the kids were dressing up as John and Yoko in bed for the fancy dress competitions... and they were winning!

"We know we were the joke of the summer.

"But that wasn't the point. If it's going to work, it's got to be small, to start with. You start with yourself. There's no man in the sky who's going to zap us all out. It's a process, not an event. But you need the events to make the process."

Yoko said, "We are in a much better position than the Prime Minister. And, anyway, the politicians are doing such a bad job."

John continued, "You see, the politicians need the people much more than the people need the politicians. They know this, obviously. But the great thing is that there are millions of people who feel that they are outside the political game completely. They are a really big force, now. And we are trying to muster them, to get them together.

"When Apple first started, we all got conned on the grossest level. We got all the bums. The vibes were getting insane. I was seeing everybody who came to the office, day in, day out. There were terrible scenes. I had to take it slower, and we had to agree more to be able to move forward together. I am very impetuous, and that scene taught me that I just had to slow down.

"I can afford to relax now. Yoko is like a mother to me. I could never relax before. Now, I am not hiding anything. When we were watching television in Montreal, a Harvard professor was on saying about these eleven- and twelve-year-olds who were divided into streams at random. But the teachers were told that they had been divided up on intelligence, so they gave all the As good marks. In fact, they conned the teachers completely. They all believe it.

"Who told us we weren't artists? Some guy comes in and says 'you're no good. You are this, son, and that's it.' It's nothing to do with kids' limits, it what other people think their limits are.

"For two years before I met Yoko, I went through a terrible depression. I was going through murder. I spent years trying to destroy my ego, then I went to the Maharishi and he said ego's fine as long as you can control it. Derek (Taylor) did a great job for my ego at his house one weekend, then Yoko came down and it was great. She opened the door. For her to love me was the answer, she couldn't have loved a dummy. She goes through the same thing. But together, we can make it. It's freedom. It's a relief. Some people never escape from the hell on Earth.

"I can't wait to get old and to get the slowness.

"I have fear and paranoia and joy and we all have them. I am not alone. If we go naked to the world, it helps.

"It worked, you see.

"It was ironic in Toronto. We have seen the film of it, and that's anything but peaceful. On the film, we are raving and shouting. It's very violent.

"Skinheads are a new thing to me. It's a thing you go through for identification, I suppose. They are bound to make a bit of bother. I am still, I mean, I have still a bit of the teddy boy in me. That was my scene, but it was only a club to belong to at the time. We've got a skinhead working at Apple. I think he beat somebody up to get the job. In the 30s, they wore flathats. It's back to the village fights and things. It's just a scene.

"The books? I suppose they were manifestations of hidden cruelties. They were very Alice in Wonderland and Winnie the Pooh. I was very hung-up then. I got rid of a lot of that. It was my version of what was happening then. It was the usual criticisms, as some critic put it."

Yoko said, "But, you see, we are not trying to be original. The reason I was doing the howling was that friends of mine were all doing electronic music and that. It was to bring back the human thing."

Said John, "Indians are so far ahead in modulation structure. I saw Yehudi Menhuin playing with Ravi Shankar. It's a joke. Yehudi Menhuin sounded like a joke.

"I am a primitive musician. Writing actual sheet music would be all right, if it was updated. On most of my songs, the sheet music is wrong. I think it's bluesy, the people that do it say it's a mistake.

"I wouldn't fight. Not for Queen and country and all that. Up to eighteen, there was still call-up. I

remember because I was always thinking I could go to Southern Ireland, if it came to it. I didn't know what I was going to do there, I hadn't thought that far. But fighting somebody who breaks into your house is different. I wouldn't have any qualms then. But I couldn't just kill somebody for the nation and thank-you-very-much here's your medal.

"If we don't keep shouting peace there could be war!"

October 11, 1969 – *Disc and Music Echo* **spoke** with George Harrison about Abbey Road.

He said, "To me, listening to Abbey Road is like listening to somebody else. It doesn't feel like the Beatles. But overall, I think it's a very good album.

"Come Together, the first track on side one, was one of the last tracks to be recorded. John wrote it just after his car accident. It's a twelve-bar type of tune, and one of the nicest things we've done musically. Ringo's drumming is great. It's an upbeat, rock-a-beat-a-boogie with some very Lennon lyrics.

"Something is a song of mine. I wrote it just as we were finishing that last album, the white one. But it was never finished. I could never think of the right words for it. Joe Cocker has done a version, too, and there's talk of it being the next Beatles' single. When I recorded it, I imagined somebody like Ray Charles doing it, that was the feel I thought it should have. But because I'm not Ray Charles, I'm much more limited in what I can do; we just did what we could. It's nice though, probably the nicest melody I've ever written.

"Maxwell's Silver Hammer is just something of Paul's. We spent a hell of a lot of time recording this one. It's one of those instant, whistle-along tunes which some people will hate and other will love. It's like Honey Pie, a fun sort of song, but probably sick as well because the guy keeps killing everybody. We used my Moog Synthesizer on this track, and I think it came out effectively.

"Oh Darling is another of Paul's songs, which is typical 1959-1960 sort of period in its chord structure. It's a typical 1955 song which thousands of groups used to make, the Moonglows, the Paragons, the Shells and so on.

"Octopus's Garden is Ringo's song, the second he's written. It's lovely. Ringo gets very bored playing the drums, so at home, he plays the piano. But he only knows about three chords, and he knows about the same on guitar. He mainly likes country music, so this a C and W feel. It's really a great song. On the surface, it's a daft kids' song, but I find the lyrics very meaningful. I find very deep meaning in the lyrics, which Ringo probably doesn't even know about. It makes me realise that when you get deep into your consciousness, it's very peaceful, so Ringo writes his cosmic songs without knowing it.

"I Want You – She's So Heavy is very heavy. It has John playing lead guitar and singing the same as he plays. This is good because the riff he sings is basically a blues. But it's a very original Lennon-like *song, even though people thought I'd written it. The middle bit is great... John has an amazing thing with his timing. He always comes across with different timing things, for example,* All You Need is Love, *which sort of skips beats out and changes from three-four to four-four all the time, in and out of each other, yet, when you question him about it, he doesn't know. He just does it naturally and you can't pin him down.*

"Here Comes the Sun, *the first cut on side two, is the other song I wrote for the album. It was written on a very nice, sunny day in Eric Clapton's garden. We'd been through real hell with business, and it was all very heavy. Being in Eric's garden felt like playing hooky from school. I found some sort of release and the song just came.*

"Because *is one of the most beautiful things we've ever done. It has a three-part harmony, John, Paul and George. John wrote the song, and the backing is a bit like Beethoven. It does resemble Paul's writing style, but only because of the sweetness it has. Paul usually writes the sweet things and John does the rave-ups and freaker things. But every now and then, John just wants to write a simple twelve-bar thing. I think this is my favourite track on the album, it's so simple, especially the lyrics. The harmony was very difficult to do, we had to really learn it.*

"You Never Give Me Your Money *is like two songs, the bridge of it is like a completely different song. You whip out of that and in* Sun King, *which John wrote. He originally called it* Los Paranois.

"Mean Mr. Mustard *and* Polythene Pam *are two short songs which John wrote in India eighteen months ago.*

"She Came in Through the Bathroom Window *is a very good song of Paul's with great lyrics.*

"Golden Slumbers *is another very melodic song by Paul which links up.*

"Carry That Weight *keeps coming in and out of the medley all the way through.*

"The End *is just that, a little sequence which ends it all."*

A footnote mentioned that Paul and Linda McCartney were cottage-hunting in Sussex.

In October 1969, a New York disc jockey received a story from an anonymous caller: Paul McCartney was dead; Paul McCartney had been decapitated in a car crash in 1966. The man everyone thought was Paul was actually a look-alike named William Campbell. The "Butcher" album was the proof, that was Paul's body parts, not just chunks of steak, draped over the band. When the album was recalled and covered up with a new photo, the one with Paul sitting in the coffin-like packing trunk, that supposedly proved the cover-up of his death. And then there were the song lyrics, all sorts of references to car crashes, to death and dying, all making it obvious that Paul was dead. The breakdown of the clues just went on and on.

The major points were a badge he had on his uniform on the *Pepper* album, the one that said O.P.D. (actually it said O.P.P. and stood for Ontario Provincial Police, it did not stand for Officially Pronounced Dead); and then there was the black flower he wore in *Magical Mystery Tour,* the barefoot picture on *Abbey Road* (supposedly people were buried barefoot in England). Then there was the Volkswagen with the LMW letters – Linda McCartney Weeps. And then there were all the backwards tapes... ad infinitum. Justifiably upset by the whole thing, the following was what Paul had to say about it all...

"It is all bloody stupid. I picked up that OPD badge in Canada. It was a police badge. Perhaps it means Ontario Police Department or something. I was wearing a black flower because they ran out of red ones. It is John, not me, dressed in black on the cover and inside of* Magical Mystery Tour. *On* Abbey Road *we were wearing our ordinary clothes. I was walking barefoot because it was a hot day. The Volkswagen just happened to be parked there.*

"Perhaps the rumour started because I haven't been much in the press lately. I have done enough press for a lifetime, and I don't have anything to say these days. I am happy to be with my family and I will work when I work. I was switched on for ten years and I never switched off. Now I am switching off whenever I can. I would rather be a little less famous these days.*

"I would rather do what I began by doing, which is making music. We make good music and we want to go on making good music. But the Beatle thing is over.* [Note: that was the first time the words were said; hardly anyone at the time picked up on it.] *It has been exploded, partly by what we have done, and partly by other people. We are individuals – all different. John married Yoko, I married Linda. We didn't marry the same girl.*

"The people who are making up these rumours should look to themselves a little more. There is not enough time in life. They should worry about themselves instead of worrying whether I am dead or not.*

"What I have to say is all in the music. If I want to say anything I write a song. Can you spread it around that I am just an ordinary person and want to live in peace? We have to go now. We have two children at home."*

To cash in on the "death," Polydor released an album of the Beatles' Hamburg recordings. A candle was snuffed out on the front...

October 25, 1969 – *Disc and Music Echo,* **Penny Valentine reviewed** the newest record from the Plastic Ono Band, *Cold Turkey,* due for release in a week. She found it disturbing, shocking, even frightening, proof that the Plastic Ono Band was not merely around to provide uplifting sing-alongs like *Give Peace a Chance.*

The sound was brilliant, Lennon's voice double-tracked, Eric Clapton's guitar work raw and nerve wracking. The recording was as tight as the best of the Beatles' music. It was about horror and agony of withdrawal from addictive drugs. She thought people would be shattered by it.

November 1, 1969 – Disc and Music Echo spoke with Klaus Voorman, ex-Manfred Mann, about the Plastic Ono Band. He had received a phone call from Terry Doran, George Harrison's personal assistant. Doran told him, *"John and Yoko are going to do a concert in Canada. There's a plane leaving in two hours. Be on it."*

Eventually, John and Yoko, Eric Clapton, drummer Alan Wright, and Voorman, met at the airport and went to Toronto.

Said Voorman, *"Apparently, John had met some people on his last visit when he did Give Peace a Chance who suddenly phoned and asked him to appear at the concert. He said he couldn't because he didn't have a band. They said, 'Of course you can, don't worry,' so he phoned round everyone he knew and liked working with to see if we were free."*

Clapton and Voorman had done some session work at Apple for Billy Preston and George Harrison.

"When John phoned, I was really quite excited and very pleased. It sounded like such a good idea, even though none of us had ever played together on a stage before. On the plane going over, we tried to vaguely rehearse. We picked out chords on the guitar, which you couldn't hear because we had nowhere to plug in, and, of course, Alan didn't have his drums on the plane with him, so, really, when we walked out on the stage, it was a glorified jam session. John had stood in the dressing room, which was admittedly rather tatty, beforehand saying, 'What am I doing here? I could have gone to Brighton.' After all, it was rather a long way to go for one concert. But the feeling when we all got out on stage and started playing together was truly fantastic."

Talking about the newest Plastic Ono recording, *Cold Turkey,* Voorman said, *"The first time we did it, it started with John playing very straight rhythm guitar. Then we did tracks with drums and bass. In the end, we had loads of incredible guitar pieces, and when we finally finished, we scrapped nearly all the original ideas and got back to a very hard, tight sound which everyone was pleased with."*

Regarding the future of the Plastic Ono Band, he said, *"John is really quite vague about it at the moment. So far, there hasn't been any trouble with recording sessions. Eric and I have always managed to be free when we're required for sessions, and it really is a matter of a last minute phone call from John. Nobody ever plans sessions months ahead.*

"You see, the great thing is we have no contract to say we are a group. We are just friends playing together. And that is such a marvelous way to work.

There's no pressure on us and, because of that, much better things get done. In fact, the first thing ever to come out as the Ono Band was very nearly a ridiculous jam session we all did at the studios one day when everyone was just fiddling about.

"I don't know whether John wants to make anything permanent out of it. He didn't set it up with the idea that this is a band. And the last thing anyone wants is to see something like this take on a such a steady fixed position that it might split the Beatles up. This way, John can do what he wants to within the confines of the Beatles, just as he can do his films and his peace thing, just as Paul can record Mary Hopkin and George can record Billy Preston or Jackie Lomax.

"As things are at the moment, each one of us, John, Eric, or myself, are free to do anything we want to."

November 5, 1969 – Record Mirror, David Skan spoke with Ringo Starr, who lived a bit more quietly than the others, Ringo, who liked his family and liked to play with his kids, and said, quite simply about the other Beatles, *"I'm sorry but I'm just not like them."*

He worked at Apple, usually, three days a week. And he spent a lot of time at home. And now, he was making an album, all old songs, dedicated to nostalgia.

Said Ringo, *"It started with my Dad. I wanted my Dad to do it but he had trouble with his throat.*

"I love the standards. I was brought up on them. They all have memories for me. You see, at home, everyone had to do a party piece. You'd get up and do your turn and everybody always did the same thing so these numbers have a special memory for me.

"Obviously, I couldn't do them with a rock group, nor us, so I decided to do them with a big band. Each track is being done by an incredible arranger, George Martin, Count Basie or Paul or somebody.

"They'd be sung just like they were, but the arrangements will be different. They all know what the tune is. You can't alter Stardust or Have I Told You Lately That I Love You or Sentimental Journey or Whispering Grass.

"Stardust was my dad's great number."

Talking about the naked Lennon / Ono cover, Ringo said, *"I was a bit embarrassed, at first. It was only a picture, though. We don't all have to do it. And anyway, everybody takes it in their stride now. I mean all that fuss about hair, now it's like Noddy Goes to Brighton.*

"I don't particularly dig what John and Yoko are doing. We all feel strongly about things. It's just a matter of how far you'll go. I mean, I just like to make my peace at home."

Did it matter to Ringo that he was being called the show biz Beatle?

"All right, so I get all the old ladies," he said. *"John gets all the freaks and George gets all the mystics.*

"You see, we all have our part to play. We are four completely different people. We have all stopped doing things together. We are only together for meetings and recordings now. We are not all squeezed into the same room now."

Ringo had just formed his own company, Startling Music, because, *"I prefer to own myself."*

November 8, 1969 – *Disc and Music Echo* **said** that Ringo was working on a solo album of old standards, with arrangements by Count Basie, Billy May and others, all produced by George Martin. It was the first of many solo projects planned by individual Beatles for the next year.

A spokesman for Apple said, *"Ringo wanted to do old standards, but songs that meant something to him. He solicited the opinion of his parents and family before deciding on the titles."*

Ringo's solo effort would be followed up almost immediately by an LP by George. Paul and John were both to make solo albums in 1970 as well.

Two new Beatle albums were planned for 1970, one was the *Get Back* LP, the other a collection of songs by Lennon and McCartney.

November 8, 1969 – *Disc and Music Echo***, Ray Coleman interviewed John and Yoko. Part One:**

He began by quoting an unnamed source, *"The Beatles? Oh, they've lost all credibility. They might not be drugged in the physical sense any more, but apart from Paul McCartney, they're all riding high on a cloud of total illusion. They seem to have completely lost touch with what the people want. And Lennon! He's still under the impression that he discovered nudity!"*

And the story continues, some people hating them, some loving them, hardly anyone anywhere indifferent to them. John and Yoko were the easy targets, mostly because John had been so self-indulgent lately. His Plastic Ono Band was almost anti-Beatles. Paul had never played with the Ono Band, nor even attended a recording session. It seemed as if Paul was the only real Beatle left. George had revolted against being a pop star and found solace of sorts in India. Ringo became a movie star because the Beatles were not working and he had the time, the inclination.

Only Paul remained a Beatle at heart. He was almost running Apple alone, and he still believed…

In 1969, the Beatles were a recording group with their own label. But were they the Beatles?

Still, Lennon had won the most recent *Disc* popularity poll.

Said John, *"I was so knocked out by the way they took it, I was always saying we'd never get through. But they, those readers, realised that what we're doing wasn't a con. It's like when a new Beatles single comes out, people have to stop and think, then they realise it might be good."*

Yoko said, *"That poll did us a load of good, because it proved that there is another generation coming up, and instead of belonging to a cult, like the Beatles generation a few years ago, this new generation of young people is more alive to the world and what is needed, a will to get peace. I had a very strong feeling all along that twelve-year-olds would understand our music, our thing."*

Were they aware of how hard people were laughing at them?

"Oh yes," John said, *"We were laughed at in the early stages. But you have to go through a sort of rebirth to get anything on the road. We knew what people said, yes. And anyway, I don't mind giving them a laugh if that's the way they see us."*

He explained that what he and Yoko were doing for peace, *"is all a Beatles thing, really. If George or I do a thing, it's a Beatles thing. If Ringo and I or Paul and I do a thing without the others, it's a Beatles thing. These peace things really are still Beatles things because people write about me as Beatle John Lennon, that's all."*

As for his relationship with Yoko, *"I just feel, well, just at peace with the world and in love."*

Were he and Yoko part of an underground movement, a guerrilla movement for peace?

"I don't think we're particularly loved by the underground. They go with whatever seems to be against the Establishment, and we're not really that. Do I like being loved by the underground? I like being loved by anyone who will be kind to us. We're not snobs. Whether it's Prince Charles or Tariq Ali, if they're extending the hand of love and joy to us, that's fine and we're grateful."

Said Yoko, *"I think the underground thought I sold out."*

And John, *"Yeah, she was in the underground, originally. Then we decided to get together and do our own thing, regardless of what the underground thought. You can't please all of them, either."*

And Yoko, *"I am very proud of John because of that. He could have risked a lot by joining with me and going on this, er, shall we say it is a mission? I don't trust most men because they are all just hypocrites. That's one of the reasons the whole world is messed up, because the wrong men are controlling everything. It is very sad, but the men have made a mess of so many things."*

John laughed, *"But women allowed it to happen."*

Yoko continued, *"Well, my John is not a hypocrite, and I think the* Disc *Poll proved that the readers who wrote in, they saw that he and I were sincere. It was really nice, surprisingly so."*

Said John, *"I was quite prepared for the world to say, 'Look, since* Magical Mystery*, you've gone mad and ruined the Beatles.' Christ, I was beginning to believe it myself and I said, 'Okay, it had to end someday and it was good while it lasted.' Suddenly, this* Disc *poll came out and I said to George, 'Hey,* look, the Beatles have still got some fans.' He seemed to be the only one who wasn't surprised."

Yoko said, "I thought I had wrecked John's position. Everyone around us was nervous."

And John, "I think what we all ignored was that they're very hip kids. They are terrific, idea-wise. And the letters we get, as well as the ones printed in Disc after the poll and the drawing, they really have great minds."

A sidebar mentioned that Doris Troy had signed with Apple. She said, "I met George the last time I was over. He and I sat in a club singing our heads off at two a.m. Then, in May this year, Madeline Bell rang me to do backing voices with her on the Billy Preston album. I walked into the studios and there was George. Well, a lot of hugging and kissing went on, and when he found I was free from contracts, we decided to work together."

She was planning to live in England during her three-year contract with Apple.

November 15, 1969 – *Disc and Music Echo*, **Ray Coleman interviewed John and Yoko. Part Two:**

Said John, "We'd like to be remembered as the Romeo and Juliet of the 1960s."

Added Yoko, "When people get cynical about love, they should look at us and see that it is possible."

Coleman asked about goals and about how they would like to be remembered after death.

John said, "I'd like everyone to remember us with a smile. But, if possible, as John and Yoko who created world peace forever in the year 1971. The whole life is a preparation for death. I'm not worried about dying. When we go, we'd like to leave behind a better place."

How would you do that? If you were Prime Minister, how would you, specifically, go about making the world more peaceful?

"I'd stop selling arms to Nigeria and all that. I'd get rid of the army and the air force and become a Sweden. I'm not a practical guy. I only know peace can exist, and the first thing is for the world to disarm. But would I have enough power, as Prime Minister, to do this? How much control does Wilson have? What chance would a peacenik Prime Minister have? I don't know. I just know things are not very good now, and it must be worth a try."

He and Yoko were living almost communally at their estate in Ascot. A number of members of the *Krishna Consciousness Society* were living there.

Said John, "You don't have to be poor to be a Communist. My money that I earned as a Beatle, it's almost a by-product. I'm not just going to give it all away to some people, just so that I can starve like a lot of others. What's that going to achieve?

"But the money doesn't give me any hang-ups. We're not sure we shouldn't have bought a cottage in the country instead of the place at Ascot. Both Yoko and I have this dream of living in a small cottage in

the country, eventually. But we ended up with this big Georgian house. Now, we're going through this big house scene before moving on."

Yoko added, "But for the moment, we enjoy it."

John said, "It means nothing to me. A little bit of ivory I bought in Japan, that's my grossest material possession, which I like as much as anything."

Yoko said, "Material pleasures are all right as long as they don't clog your mind."

"I wouldn't worry," John continued, "if I never had a thing. If it took too much to carry on living in this big house, I wouldn't want to stay and live there, but I'm hoping to farm some of the land. The Krishna people are helping me do this. We have between fifteen and thirty of them there, and they're happy to farm and get on with their own lives. Nothing binding. We're hoping to grow non-chemical food, maybe we can sell it to Harrods."

It all just seemed so far away from the Beatles. After playing live with the Plastic Ono Band in Canada, was it possible that the Beatles would re-take the stage?

"At the Isle of Wight thing, I saw Dylan on stage and I felt like going on. Next day, I didn't. The trouble is, you can't get the group's power across on a stage. I thought The Band was great at the Isle of Wight. But you'd have to be standing next to them, on the stage, to know what they were really all about.

"That was the trouble with the Beatles touring. As soon as we realised that our power on stage wasn't getting across, we had to pack it in. We might as well have sent out four waxwork dummies for all the people cared about the sound.

"If audiences could somehow come up on stage and the group could be integrated properly, that would be okay. But I couldn't stand any more one-nighters like we used to do. It's impossible for the Beatles to play clubs, but if something really off-beat could be fixed, I don't know. We wouldn't mind doing something, it's just getting it right, and we don't know how to do that, yet. Those old tours were okay at the time, but once we had taken over from Helen Shapiro, there was nothing else to do, except for us to go around and other people to see us standing there, doing the same songs and not hearing a note.

"The Stones seemed to get a good thing in Hyde Park, but it's different from us. We're not that type. Jagger is the Charlie Chaplin of rock and roll, it's okay for Mick because he's dancing around like a puppet and putting on a show. We don't. We couldn't stand the shell of unreality, standing there like four dolls in the middle of Shea Stadium. It killed our music.

"But when I see a group like The Band playing, I think we should have got going again before now."

Would the Plastic Ono Band last longer than the Beatles?

"I think it will survive, you know, my records with Yoko and the Plastic Ono have sold well. We sold twenty-five thousand copies of *Two Virgins* in the

States and sixty thousand copies of Life With the Lions. *That's good going in the States.*

"Our new album, John and Yoko's Wedding Album, *is going to sell as well. But in Britain, we only sold about five thousand each of those albums. I can understand that, though. See, Americans like our albums because, if you land in New York, it's like* Life With the Lions *anyway. If you play it in Britain, it doesn't have the same urgency, because of the environment and that. It'll be a few years before they turn on to that sort of thing properly here."*

"But we are patient," Yoko said, *"Because we are doing something worthwhile."*

Coleman wondered if Lennon was simply years ahead of his time, mentally and spiritually… and musically.

Said John, *"I am an artist and my art is peace and I happen to be a musician. My music is done with the Beatles, that's where I get my wages from. The peace thing isn't a gimmick. Other people call it a gimmick. Yoko and I are serious…"*

November 15, 1969 – *Melody Maker* **Richard Williams announced** that *John and Yoko's Wedding Album* was to be released soon by Apple. It was one of the most lavish pop productions ever. It included two albums, a collection of press clippings, a photograph of the wedding cake, a series of cartoons by John, a postcard, wedding photos, and a number of other photos.

Williams called it a continuation of the open diary of Mr. and Mrs. Lennon. He questioned its purpose, though suggested it might be an interesting time capsule.

He talked about the album sides, the electronic sounds, the repeated noises, the screams and shouts, the singing, the pleading, the heartbeat rhythms, the few actual songs, and he suggested it might make interesting listening in twenty years' time.

November 22, 1969 – *Disc and Music Echo* **called** *John and Yoko's Wedding Album* an expensive bore. It was a beautiful presentation, full of wonderful things. But, after the things was the album, the *music*.

Side One was John and Yoko saying it was wise to take apples on a honeymoon. They screamed and grunted each other's name.

Side Two began with Yoko singing about peace. Then there was a recorded interview of them talking with a reporter about peace, and later, some chats about their bed-ins.

Apart from the handsome packaging, and the interesting peace lecture, a terrible bore, the Lennons' idiosyncrasies.

December 6, 1969 – *Disc and Music Echo* **asked** an assortment of stars for their opinion about John Lennon's decision to return his MBE to the Queen in protest of Biafra and Vietnam. *Disc* suggested it was either a significant peace gesture, or a publicity gimmick.

Said Kenny Everett, *"I don't think it was of any importance in itself, but it was very funny the way John went about it. I fell about when I saw the news on TV. I'm sure John intended it to be funny, just as a giant send-up and a plug for his record. There aren't many young people who would take this sort of thing seriously these days, anyway. But perhaps a few middle-aged people think he did it as a protest for peace. I certainly didn't take it seriously."*

Steve Ellis said, *"I agree with John Lennon. After all, when he first got it, he said it was only a lump of metal. It would have meant something if he was a war hero, but he was only in a group. I agree with him, therefore, that it's a good way to protest about the Vietnam war, because he's got the status to make people listen. But I don't think he did it as a cheap publicity stunt. John Lennon doesn't need publicity; he's the biggest pop personality of all. If he wanted publicity, there are a dozen ways he could get it. He might be a con with all this peace bit, but he knocks me out every time, so it's 'stick up for Lenny' as far as I'm concerned."*

Said Pete Townsend, *"If he can't rescind the title, what's the point of the gesture? And what's it got to do with the Queen, anyway? It was a thorough waste of time. Lennon's a madman, but he's one of my favourite madmen. He knows that people think of him as a clown for some of the things he's done, but he's also aware that clowns have changed the world before."*

And Dave Dee, *"I think it's stupid. If it was me, I'd be honoured to have the award. Every time Lennon sees things go a little bit quiet for the Beatles these days, he seems to leap to the forefront and do something silly. I'm beginning to wonder if there isn't a big publicity gimmick behind it all. I don't doubt his sincerity for peace, mind. I'm in favour of it, too. But wars have been going on for such a long time now that one person giving back an MBE isn't going to make any difference. I think John's a very shrewd person, but I sometimes wonder what's the real reason behind some of his gestures. And, while I don't condone everything he does, he does do so many different things that it's a job to sort out fact from fiction."*

Carl Wayne said, *"I think he's got a perfect right to do whatever he wants with his MBE, providing he doesn't do anything with it or connected with it that might bring embarrassment to the Queen. I don't think he needs an MBE, to be honest. And I think it's a little out of context on the end of his name, at present. And I think perhaps he would like to look forward to the day, and so do I because I believe his motives are sincere, when he'll be presented with an MBE for his efforts to bring a little peace to the world."*

Alan Price said, *"I don't suppose he ever really accepted it, anyway. They never really took it seriously. Publicity gimmick? I don't think they need publicity that much. I know he's voicing his sentiments, but it won't do any good. Bigger men than him have been trying to stop war without success. I think John just does what he feels. MBEs are rather out of character, too. They should just be given to people who can run faster than anyone else. Or to people who run libraries the longest. Would I do the same? I don't supposed I'd ever get one. Anyway, it's bad enough trying to pass my driving test!"*

And finally, Ringo Starr, *"I don't mind John sending his MBE back. It wasn't done in an indignant and personal way, like some grumpy stockbroker who says 'I got mine for service to my country.' It was sent back as a wider gesture. In the old days, people thought their very own MBEs had been debased because someone they despised had got one. Anyone can insult a Beatle because they're young and rich. The MBE was awarded to John for peaceful efforts and it was returned as a peaceful effort. That seems to be the full circle. Good luck to John."*

December 6, 1969 – *Disc and Music Echo* ran a sort of news roundup about what the Beatles were doing. The Plastic Ono Band had planned to release a new single but that had been shelved. It was called *You Know My Name.* Said a spokesman for Apple, *"It was mutually decided by the Beatles that it sounded more like the Beatles themselves than the Plastic Ono Band. No other title has been substituted."*

Across the Universe, a Lennon / McCartney song, was to be released on the 12th of December.

Ringo Starr was making TV appearances to promote his new movie, *The Magic Christian.*

A film about John and Yoko as film makers was to be shown sometime soon on BBC.

Paul McCartney was to launch a new Beatles magazine.

And the Beatles fan club Christmas record was ready for mailing.

December 6, 1969 – *Melody Maker* announced that Apple was about to release *Live Peace From Toronto*, the first LP from the Plastic Ono Band, recorded at Varsity Stadium in Toronto the previous September. This was the first live show performed by the band, which was made up of John and Yoko, Eric Clapton, Klaus Voorman and Alan White. The reviewer thought, despite the fact that John was the only Beatle on the stage, the first few tracks on the album were like a memorial to how the Beatles must have sounded in their Cavern days.

Blue Suede Shoes, Money, Dizzy Miss Lizzie, Yer Blues and *Cold Turkey* kicked off the first side, unrehearsed, raw and sweaty and powerful, a nostalgic dream. With audience participation, they also did *Give Peace a Chance.* Yoko was featured on the second side, performing *Don't worry Kyoko – Mummy's Only Looking for Her Hand in the Snow* and *John John – Let's Hope For Peace.*

The reviewer thought Varsity Stadium in Toronto would have been a nice place to be that night.

December 6, 1969 – *Melody Maker*, **Richard Williams started a three-part interview with John and Yoko. Part One:**

The Beatles had clearly grown further and further apart over the years. The Fab Four Moptop fairy tale was being slowly being revealed as the myth that it was. The truth was coming out. Some thought it unnecessary to shatter the myth but, for John Lennon, having lived the legend, it was a must. He had no desire to live with it any longer, no desire to pretend it was something it was not, no desire to hide the truth.

Said John, *"In the beginning, it was a constant fight between Brian and Paul on one side, and me and George on the other. Brian put us in neat suits and shirts, and Paul was right behind him. I didn't dig that, and I used to try and get George to rebel with me. I'd say to him, 'Look, we don't need these fucking suits. Let's chuck them out the window.'*

"My little rebellion was to have my tie loose, with the top button of my shirt undone, but Paul'd always come up to me and put it straight.

"I saw the film the other night, the first television film we ever did. The Granada people came down to film us, and there we were in suits and everything, it just wasn't us, and watching that film, I knew that that was where we started to sell out.

"We had to do a lot of selling out then. Taking the MBE was a sell-out for me. You know, before you get an MBE, the Palace writes to you to ask if you're going to accept it, because you're not supposed to reject it publicly and they sound you out first. I chucked the letter in with all the fan-mail, until Brian asked me if I had it. He and a few other people persuaded me that it was in our interests to take it, and it was hypocritical of me to accept it.

"But I'm glad, really, that I did accept it, because it meant that four years later, I could use it to make a gesture.

"We did manage to refuse all sorts of things that people don't know about. For instance, we did the Royal Variety Show once, and we were asked discreetly to do it every year after that, but we always said, 'Stuff it,' so every year, there was always a story in the newspapers, saying, 'Why No Beatles for the Queen?' which was pretty funny, because they didn't know we'd refused it.

"That show's a bad gig anyway. Everybody's very nervous and uptight, and nobody performs well. The time we did do it, I cracked a joke on stage. I was fantastically nervous, but I wanted to say something, just to rebel a bit, and that was the best I could do."

Was there anything at all he enjoyed about Beatlemania?

"Oh, sure, I dug the fame, the power, the money, and playing to big crowds. Conquering America was the best thing. You see, we wanted to be bigger than Elvis, that was the main thing. At first, we wanted to be Goffin and King, then we wanted to be Eddie

Cochran, then we wanted to be Buddy Holly, and finally, we arrived at wanting to be bigger than the biggest, and that was Elvis. We reckoned we could make it because there were four of us. None of us would've made it alone, because Paul wasn't quite strong enough, I didn't have enough girl-appeal, George was too quiet, and Ringo was the drummer. But we thought that everyone would be able to dig at least one of us, and that's how it turned out."

When John had returned his MBE as a protest against Vietnam and Biafra, he had also added, "And against Cold Turkey slipping down the charts." Williams asked if that was because Cold Turkey really meant something to him.

"Yes, because it's my record. When I wrote it, I went to the other three Beatles and said, 'Hey lads, I think I've written a new single.' But they all said, 'Ummm, arrrrr, wellll,' because it was going to be my project, and so I thought, 'Bugger you, I'll put it out myself.'

"That had happened once before, when I was wanting to put Revolution out as a single but Hey Jude went out instead."

Is the Plastic Ono Band a sort of alternate Beatles for him?

"Yes, I suppose so. It's a way of getting my music out to the public. I don't bother so much about the others' songs. For instance, I don't give a damn about how Something is doing in the charts, I watch Come Together, because that's my song."

Did he think there would come a time when he did not want Paul's and George's music to share the same album as his?

"I can see it happening. The Beatles can go on appealing to a wide audience as long as they make albums like Abbey Road, which have nice little folk songs like Maxwell's Silver Hammer for the grannies to dig.

"About Maxwell's Hammer, well, all I can say is that I dig Engelbert Humperdinck as much as I dig John Cage, and I don't listen to either of them.

"I always wanted to have other people on our records, like the Stones and our other friends. But some of the others wanted to keep it tight, just the Beatles, you know? But you wait, it's starting to get looser, and there should be some fantastic sessions in the next few years. That's what I wanted all along."

Did he enjoy making A Hard Day's Night and Help?

"I dug Hard Day's Night, although Alun Owen was only with us for two days before he wrote the script. He invented that word 'grotty,' did you know that? We thought the word was really weird, and George curled up with embarrassment every time he had to say it. But it's part of the language now, you hear society people using it. Amazing.

"Help was a drag, because we didn't know what was happening. In fact, Lester was a bit ahead of his time with the Batman thing, but we were on pot by then and all the best stuff is on the cutting-room floor, with us breaking up and falling all over the place."

Has Allen Klein's presence at Apple been helpful?

"Oh, it's really marvelous. People were very scared of him to start with, and some still are, but that's probably good. He's swept out all the rubbish and the deadwood, and stopped it being a rest-house for the world's hippies. He won't let people order antique furniture for their offices and so forth, he's really tightened it up, and it's starting to work a lot better.

"He noticed that the Beatles had stopped selling records as they were doing around the world, and he found out that it was because the record company simply wasn't bothering to push them. They thought that our records would sell themselves, and they were wrong. They don't.

"If you can get to number one in Turkey, Greece, Switzerland, and a couple of other countries, then that's as good financially as getting a number one in Britain, they don't realise that.

"Klein's very good. He's going to make sure they stop sitting on the records and actually release them. He's even keeping tabs on me. I usually make mistakes about who to get to survey my house, and I can spend a fortune without getting anything done. He's making sure that I do it the right way."

December 13, 1969 – Disc and Music Echo, David Hughes reviewed Ringo's new movie, The Magic Christian, which was due to be released the following day at the Kensington Odeon in London. He said Ringo as Youngman Grand was a poor actor but very good at being himself, delivering his lines with some degree of competence, though a bit monotonously.

There were cameo appearances by all sorts of stars, including John and Yoko. And the main song was Come and Get It, written by Paul McCartney and played by the Ivies, now known as Badfinger.

The Magic Christian was a good film, well worth seeing on a Christmas visit to London.

December 13, 1969 – Melody Maker, Richard Williams continued his three-part interview with John and Yoko. Part Two:

John and Yoko's Peace Crusade had been evoking some serious emotions in people. Unfortunately, most of those emotions were negative. They were mocked and criticised and vilified. Through all the insults, the Lennons had maintained their position, which was, quite simply, how can peace be wrong?

The public was seeing them as leaders of the peace movement.

Said John, "I'm not falling for that one. Like Pete Seeger said, 'We don't have a leader but we have a song – Give Peace a Chance,' so I refuse to be leader, and I'll always show my genitals or do something which prevents me from being Martin Luther King or Ghandi and getting killed, because that's what happens to leaders. Our whole mistake is having leaders and people we can rely on or point a finger at."

Yoko said, *"For instance, many people say if you want to do that kind of thing, about peace, don't do anything that is misleading, like showing your genitals. Always keep a clean image so that people can believe in your peace movement.*

"But that's exactly what the Establishment is doing..."

John tossed in, *"And that's what the Beatles did, too."*

"...taking their children to church on Sundays. This is showing that 'I'm the President of the United States and I'm all right and I'm healthy and very moral, et cetera.' You don't get anywhere that way, you become just another hypocrite, and you're playing the Establishment game.

"We don't want to do that. We try to be honest and, the point is, if we are really honest, just to make it between us is a lifetime thing, and if we can't make it together and endure each other, the world is nowhere.

"If ordinary couples can make it together and make it with their children and so forth, love-wise...

Said John, *"She doesn't mean make it as in lay."*

"...then you can look after the world."

John said, *"One thing we've found out is that love is a great gift, like a precious flower or something. You have to feed it and look after it and it has storms to go through and snow, but you have to protect it.*

"It's like a pet cat. You know, people get a cat and they don't want to feed it, or they get a dog and they don't want to walk it. But love has to be nurtured like a very sensitive animal, because that's what it is. And you have to work at love, you don't just sit round with it and it doesn't just do it for you.

"You've got to be very careful with it. It's the most delicate thing you can be given. It's a very delicate situation."

What can you do about Vietnam and Biafra?

"We'll keep promoting peace in the way we do which, whichever way you look at it, is our way, because we're artists and not politicians.

"We don't organise; we do it the best way we know how, to make people aware that if they want war to stop, only they can do it. The politicians can't do it. I think our whole movement is successful, as shown by Nixon, who's having to wriggle around a bit now and make propaganda films about the moratorium, claiming that the silent majority is with him, with a highly polished Negro in an Italian suit saying how great it is to be American.

"Nixon has been moved by the peace movement, that included John and Yoko and all the people in the world who are doing it, and that's how we're going to change it. We're not going to Vietnam to die for it, or going to Biafra to die for it. We've considered everything, not dying, but going to the places. People prefer a dead saint to a living annoyance like John and Yoko. But we don't intend to be dead saints for people's convenience.

"They prefer Ghandi and Martin Luther King, since they died, but you should see them in India now, celebrating Ghandi Year, *anything less like Ghandi's principles going on in India, you've never seen. It's a hoax.*

"And so we don't intend to be dead saints, or living saints either. People don't like saints."

Their *Wedding Album* caused a lot of controversy. Why did they make it?

Yoko said, *"It's like a diary, it reflects our love and peace ideas."*

And John, *"When people get married, they usually make their own wedding albums. We're public personalities, and I'd enjoy reading Jackie and Onassis's album. Our wedding was public, so we're sharing our diaries and our feelings with the world, so one side shows our involvement with each other, and the other side shows what we do together outside of our involvement with each other, which is promote peace."*

Is there a danger of becoming too public?

"We have nothing to hide. 'Everybody's got something to hide except me and my monkey,' you know? We keep certain parts of our life private because we're not as wild as people think. I doubt if we'll ever make love in public, or invite the TV cameras into our bedroom, and I doubt if I'll ever go to the toilet in public.

"Just because I think some things, I don't want to show that side of me."

Said Yoko, *"We're from a certain generation, you can't deny that, and for people in our generation, it is so difficult, and maybe the next John and Yoko will..."*

"Show all," John said. *"Maybe we will before we die. People hide themselves from each other all the time, and everybody's frightened of saying something nice about somebody in case they don't say anything nice back or in case they get hurt, or of looking at somebody in case they say, 'what are you looking at?'*

"Everybody's so uptight and they're always building these walls around themselves. All you can do is try and break the walls down and show that there's nothing there but people. It's just like looking in a mirror, there's nothing to worry about, it's only people."

Yoko said, *"And even we are not relaxed enough as people. We have many complexities and tensions. We try hard to be honest and expose ourselves, but there are certain things that we just can't... maybe in the next generation, they can, good luck to them. We're trying hard as we are."*

John always seemed to approach everything with a sense of humour and fun. Some people were suggesting that he was just "taking the mickey."

"That's true, although we're not taking the mickey. Everybody's frightened of being conned, of being tricked. If you say something nice to somebody, they're not sure if you mean it, so that rather than respond to your loving movement, they'll reject you, and that's what the press do, because if

they're frightened of what we did with the MBE about the Biafra thing, they'll write about my Auntie Mimi's reaction to me giving the MBE back, because they don't want to fall for the con of 'is he joking?'

"Of course, we're joking as well. We mustn't take ourselves too seriously, otherwise it's the end. We think the mistake of everyone, Ghandi and Martin Luther King and the left wing and the students and all society, is taking it too seriously. If you take it seriously, it is serious. What we try to do is be non-serious about things, but we are very serious about being not serious."

Yoko said, "We may be too serious, even. We try to have a sense of humour and we try to smile at everyone, a really genuine smile from the bottom of our hearts. But it's very difficult for our generation to really genuinely smile, but we're trying."

Said John, "It's like when I sent the MBE back, and I wrote that it was against Britain's involvement in Biafra and Vietnam and against Cold Turkey slipping down the charts. When we thought of that, we were screaming with laughter, and so a few snobs and hypocrites got very upset about mentioning Cold Turkey with the problem of Biafra and Vietnam, but that saved it from being too serious and being another Colonel protesting.

"You have to try and do everything with humour, and keep smiling."

December 20, 1969 – *Disc and Music Echo* **spoke** with producer Jack Good, who was in England to record Sylvia McNeill. Said Good, *"Pop in the sixties came in with a squelch and is going out in a mess, the only good things to emerge being the Beatles, the resurgence in popularity of Elvis, the continuing success of Cliff and the arrival of just a few real showmen like Ian Anderson of Jethro Tull.*

"My views on the Beatles are really quite commonplace in that I think they're fantastic, and quite the best thing to come out of the sixties. At the beginning of their career, I didn't know about them until Marty Wilde phoned to say, 'I've just heard this terrific group you'd like.' Then Brian Epstein phoned to ask me to do a show with them.

"At the time, I'd just heard this folk singer called Bob Dylan, who I thought was going to be the biggest thing in the sixties, but I listened to early Beatles records and liked them because they were doing rock and roll, even though their version of the Isley's Twist And Shout *was too slow.*

"I like them because they've always done what they felt like and everything they've done has been absolutely great for the time they were doing it. I still think Cold Turkey *is possibly the best record I've ever heard, and, underneath all the peace thing, John Lennon is a really vicious rocker at heart.*

"I wouldn't be surprised if sometimes he doesn't slip away and put on good old hard rock records to listen to."

December 20, 1969 – *Melody Maker***, Richard Williams concluded his three-part interview with John and Yoko. Part Three:**

It was clear that during their two years together, the publicity, good and bad, desired and otherwise, had given John and Yoko very little time to have a private life together. They presented their lives together to the public as a good example. They were even helping to bring marriage back into fashion…

Said John, *"There's nothing I like more than to get home at the end of the day and sit next to Yoko and say, 'Well, we're together at last.' Although we may have been holding hands all day, it's not the same when we're working or talking to the press. We feel a hundred miles apart by comparison."*

Clearly, they had changed each other. John's earlier life had been thoroughly reported in the press and on television; his changes were obvious. Williams asked how John had changed Yoko.

Yoko replied, *"He's changed everything, in the sense that I was a very lonely person before I met him. Most people in the world are very lonely, that's the biggest problem, and because of their loneliness, they become suspicious. And the reason we're lonely is because we can't communicate enough from the various complexes we have and the various social habits we've created.*

"We become very inhibited, but when I met John, I started to open up a little, through love, you know, and that's the greatest thing that happened to me yet. There are various facets to my life and my personality, and I never met anybody else who could understand me. We understand each other so well, and I'm not lonely anymore, which is a shocking experience, really.

"Also, through loneliness or something, I was starting to become a very firm and strong ego, but that's melting away, and it's very nice."

And how did John see the way Yoko had changed him?

"Exactly the same, of course. I was lonely, and didn't have full communication with anybody, and it took a bit of adjusting. She rediscovered or cultivated the thing that existed in me before I left Liverpool, maybe, and recultivated the natural John Lennon that been lost in the Beatles thing and the worldwide thing.

"She encouraged me to be myself, because it was me that she fell in love with, not the Beatles or whatever I was.

"When you get sidetracked, you believe it, and when you're in the dark, you believe it. She came and reminded me that there was light, and when you remember there's light, you don't want to get back in the dark again. That's what she did for me."

Yoko said, *"But you know, I didn't do it intentionally or anything. It's the falling in love bit. You start to see all sorts of things that you don't see if you're not in love."*

"*I found that he has these qualities that he was hiding away. Even in a practical sense, music-wise, he was doing all sorts of freaky things at home, just recording it on a cassette or something, but not really showing it publicly. Publicly, he was doing the Beatles' things. But he showed me all these cassettes and things and I said, 'why don't you produce these as records?'*

"*I performed the role of a mirror, in a way. He was doing all those things anyway, I didn't suggest them. It was there, and that goes for his drawing, paintings, and poetry, too, especially his drawings.*

"*He's got a stack of beautiful drawings at home, and this one series he did is going to be produced as a sort of lithograph. They're not like his cartoons, they're another kind of drawing. I think they're better than Picasso.*"

"*She's biased,*" John said.

"*You'll see them next year. And those things were always there in John, they just came out, but artists do need encouragement.*

"*We're always together, like twenty-four hours of the day. At the beginning, when we were less sure and we were still the previous us, once in a while, when John was recording, I'd go shopping on the King's Road or something, now we couldn't conceive of that.*"

Added John, "*We're never apart by more than a hundred yards.*"

"*People say that if you're together twenty-four hours a day for two years,*" Yoko continued, "*You must get sick and tired of each other, but it's the contrary. We got so addicted to that situation that we miss each other more. It's a very strange scene.*"

Said John, "*Somebody said 'Won't you get so reliant on each other that you can't manage without each other?' And we said, 'Yes. The only thing that could split us is death, and we have to face that, and we don't even believe we'll be split then, if we work on it.*

"*Our only worry in the world is that we die together, otherwise even if it's only three minutes later, it's going to be hell. I couldn't bear three minutes of it.*

"*Most marriages have a little pretense going on, and we thought, are we going to pretend that we're happy together because we daren't say that we want to be apart? But that doesn't happen.*

"*When two of you are together, man and wife, there's nothing that can touch you. You have the power of two people, you have the protection, you don't need society or the room or the uniform or the gun because you have the power of two minds, which is a pretty powerful thing.*"

Were they planning children?

"*We're not even sure that we want children,*" John said. "*We're that jealous. But if God or whoever gives us a child, we'll accept it. Maybe we'd like two or three. But even then, we have to consider, is a child going to interfere between us? How can we look after a child and be together twenty-four hours a day?*"

Yoko added, "*It's not fair to the child, maybe, because we are so close. The child will be somebody that will be saying 'hello' once in a while.*"

And John, "*Obviously, it'll probably be different if we have one, because all the time she was pregnant, we considered it. We're full into it, wanting a child, but when you lose it and you get over the pain, then you consider whether you wanted the child. Now, maybe we had that in the back of our minds all along, and that's why she lost it.*

"*We don't really know whether we want one or not. If she gets pregnant, we'll want one, but I'd like her not to be pregnant for a bit, she's been pregnant since I met her!*

"*I'd like her to stay slim for a year, and then maybe have one. But we don't fancy birth pills, because I don't trust them, and anything else is out of the question, because it's inconvenient. We're not like that, we try to act naturally at all times. That's one of our problems, besides death. It's in God's hands.*"

December 27, 1969 – Disc and Music Echo spoke with Derek Taylor about the 1970 version of the Beatles.

Said Taylor, "*Well, Yoko's really one of them. Without Yoko there wouldn't be the Beatles.*"

1969 had not been a good year for the Beatles as a group. It had been a year of four individuals traveling under the same name.

"*And you can't speculate for the next year, either,*" said Taylor. "*But whatever happens in 1970, it has to be a compromise. John's been saying some very negative things lately, but they all lack one thing and that's Paul. About this time last year, after the double album had come out and was selling nicely and Apple was doing well, the Beatles had been dormant for a couple of months, very much as they are now.*

"*Last year, they allowed Paul to stimulate them by calling for a nine o'clock start on New Year's Day down at Twickenham studios, so they all turned up at nine o'clock and started to make the album with is now called* Get Back *and will be released in the New Year.*

"*Perhaps the same could happen this year, it only needs one of them to call up the other and say, 'how about making an album?' But, as it is, the four of them haven't been together since October when they met at Apple to give Allen Klein the go-ahead with the EMI deal.*

"*It's not as if they owe anyone anything, owe anyone an album, but idleness isn't good for them. It isn't good for anyone, particularly for the very rich, especially when they've got rid of their ego and are immensely successful and feeling fairly humble. John's coping well because he's got all these things going.*"

The Get Back *album, and the film that was made along with it, were definitely going to be released in early 1970.*

Said Taylor, *"All this happening will re-present the Beatles to the public. And the public will say, 'Hah, here they are again,' which will be good for the Beatles because then they'll start to feel more like Beatles. At the moment, I don't think they do. They feel like Lennon, McCartney, Starkey and Harrison.*

"Split? I think, as the time passes, and the longer the marriage goes on, the greater test it undergoes. The thing is, how strong are the Beatles? The demand is there. John's personal strength, in the sense of fulfillment, is the weakest link in the Beatles.

"Anyway, they're contracted together for a good five years more. But one mustn't forget, they're still each other's best friends, although they have, for a couple of years, looked on the Beatles as a distraction rather than themselves.

"Ringo's involved in films, George with Delaney and Bonnie, Doris Troy and Billy Preston, John is off on his own little tangent, so the big thing is, what's Paul McCartney going to do in 1970?

"Is he going to revitalise the four? He's the only one who doesn't seem to have an outlet for whatever he gets together, so I expect him to come back after his holiday in the Bahamas and after Christmas, we can expect a Beatle meeting to be called in January. At the beginning of last year, they were in India with no clear idea of what they were going to do, but they coped with 1969.

"Paul has this loyalty to the Beatles to the extent of not doing anything outside. He's very diligent, he enforces little disciplines on himself, like getting the train out to Twickenham and then a bus and walking the rest of the way to the studios."

Was it possible that the Beatles might go back on the road in 1970? Taylor was reasonably certain they would not tour, but the occasional concert together might be possible. But they had performed in public, from the rooftop of the Apple building. Taylor had not seen that coming, so anything was possible. Perhaps they would play with other musicians, something similar to the Plastic Ono Band. Who knows?

"George could fill an album now with what he's got," said Taylor. *"He's got great confidence now, and that's all that was needed, the music was always there. He's very popular with other musicians, and he's having a very happy time.*

"John hasn't damaged the Beatle image in the last year; he's done them a lot of good. He might look like a crank who takes up any cause that comes his way, but behind every single date and event in history, there's been a crank working and often dying for a cause.

"He's bright and very amusing, and he and Yoko capitalise on their moments of grief. And there are a lot of people who really love them, really straight people, and they see him as 'a young fighting man who'll have a go.'

"He and Yoko are fifty per cent of each other, so if John's a Beatle, that makes her a Beatle, too. They're just very complete in themselves."

The fun of 1970 would be waiting to see what the Beatles would do next. There would be more records, for sure, perhaps some live performances, a film. But they group would have to compromise to make things happen.

Said Taylor, *"The Beatles are written about and speculated on a great deal, which is a big obligation. But it's up to the four of them to launch the Beatles into 1970. They'll go on being Beatles, though. They'll be Beatles to death."*

December 27, 1969 – *Disc and Music Echo* **spoke** with George Martin about his predictions for the Beatles during 1970.

Said Martin, *"I'm not suggesting they'll split by talking about each one of them separately like this. They'll always be Beatles. They're very fond of each other and they do actually like being together. They've just grown apart and grown to love different women, which is a tremendous influence on any man. But they still have this tremendous affection for each other."*

Ringo?

"I'm working on an album with him at the moment, of old songs like Stardust, Night and Day, *old Sinatra favourites and Count Basie-type backings. His stepfather is very fond of this sort of music and Ringo shares this. He'll love singing these songs. He writes very simple songs, and doesn't rate himself as being a very great composer."*

George?

"I think it's possible that he'll emerge as a great musician and composer next year, it's up to him. He's got tremendous drive and imagination, and also the ability to show himself as a great composer on a parallel with Lennon and McCartney. He's already shown he's capable of writing really beautiful songs. Something *is one of the most lovely songs of this year."*

Paul?

"He will go his own particular way in 1970. He's got that incredible combination of knowing exactly what kind of music to write, with lovely melody, and the result is always bang up to date and commercial in the nicest aspect of the word. He can't go wrong."

And John?

"Well, John is John. Of course, I haven't seen so much of him lately because he produces his own albums. I helped him with some of the stuff when he needed advice, but it's not my style and he knows it. The things he's doing are hardly produced, anyway, they're things that happen. For 1970, who knows what he'll be up to? Sure, he's experimenting, and I'm sure he'll go on doing so, he's very inventive. But for him, yesterday is pretty dead as far as he's concerned."

— Chapter Ten: 1970 —

January 3, 1970 – *Record Mirror*, **Mike Hennessey** spoke with John Lennon. The Sixties had belonged to the Beatles. They had set new standards in music, made more people scream than Elvis, and had enough press coverage to rival anyone in history.

There would never be anything like it again.

The entire group grew up in full view of the world.

Hennessey said the Beatles had been elusive, or at least selective, when it came to interviews. These days, Lennon himself would talk to anyone.

Said John, *"The fact is, I've got a new group now and it's called Peace. When we were just Beatles, we didn't need the press after we'd made it, except when we had a new record out, because they only wrote a lot of drivel about us anyway. But now, I'm promoting peace..."*

Lennon, at twenty-nine, was an agnostic pacifist and a socialistic millionaire who wanted to make pot legal, end censorship, ban all weapons and put a stop to violence, and because he was a Beatle, the press covered his propaganda.

He said, *"If I hadn't had the power of being a Beatle, I could at least have got as much publicity as Tariq Ali. But I chose the best road to power, not consciously, because I wasn't thinking about it then. But in the Western world, you either have to be a politician or a pop star to get yourself heard. In India, you have to be a guru.*

"Look what has happened since we started. There has been the moratorium and Woodstock and now, even Nixon is moving toward peace. Of course, Nixon's peace effort is laughable and we know we can't influence him. But if we can influence enough ordinary people, they can influence the politicians. If the politicians suddenly realise that working for peace might keep them in power, they'll work for peace."

Yoko said, *"I don't know why some people talk as though John is daft. He certainly isn't. He is extremely realistic."*

Hennessey asked Lennon about his *Cold Turkey* remark when he was returning his MBE, wondering if that would make people question his sincerity.

Said John, *"We are sincere about peace. But we are also anti-serious. We like a bit of camp now and again. The trouble with Ghandi and Martin Luther King was that they were too serious. I don't want to be a dead saint."*

Hennessey thought Lennon was shrewd enough to know that the reporters would give him even more attention if they thought he was putting everyone on.

During the MBE affair, Lennon had called himself a nationalist.

John explained, *"I really love Britain, the rain, the mist, the atmosphere. That's why I live here. It would take a lot to make me leave. I'm always bragging about England and our achievements.*

"Of course, I'm ashamed about all the fascist stuff in our history, and I'm not a nationalist to the extent of sending immigrants back to the West Indies. But I love the country itself. I love driving around Scotland, for example, whatever the colour of the natives. I just love the romantic mysticism of the place, King Arthur, Merlin, and all that."

What would he like to see happen in Britain during the Seventies?

"First of all, I'd like to see an end of all violence, withdrawal of our troops from foreign countries and peace in Biafra and Vietnam. I'd love to see marijuana legalised and abolition of all kinds of censorship. Let's also get working on building up the tourist industry and stop pretending to be King Kong. I'm for the Common Market. Let's go in with Germany and run the thing.

"Let's also be like Denmark about pornography. We are hung up on sex because of bad education. People are twisted because they are jealous of the sexual freedom young people have today. Kids have more sexual freedom now than I had when I was a kid. Good luck to them, I say. Lay for peace!"

What about fidelity in a relationship?

"It's up to the people concerned. Yoko and I are faithful to each other because the alternative is not acceptable. We're too possessive. But, looking at it purely intellectually, sexual freedom is a good thing.

"But Yoko and I are in love and sexual adventures just don't match up to sex in love. We've decided to be voyeurs instead, so if you know of any good scenes going... We also plan to make some sexy films and we'll watch porny scenes."

Lennon was obviously joking. Hennessey asked him what bands he would like to see make it in the Seventies.

Still joking, John said, *"I'd like to see the Rolling Stones become famous. I'd really like to see Frank Zappa make it big, and the Great Awakening and Creedence Clearwater, Fleetwood Mac and Jethro Tull. And, of course,* Cold Turkey *and the Plastic Ono Band.*

"I can't think of any others because I don't have much time to listen to records. I just listen to everything, including Traffic, and I usually listen to what's coming out on record before making albums."

And the Beatles in the Seventies? Were they falling apart? Was the damage beyond repair?

"I suppose it is a lot more difficult for us to get together now because everyone is involved in different things. The four of us only meet now when we're working on a record, though once we pick up the instruments, we react together just as we always have.

"But I don't think there'll be any more Beatle films or stage performances in the immediate future. For the Beatles to come back now, people would expect Jesus and Buddha. And look at the way the press knocked Dylan when he made the Isle of Wight appearance.

"I might appear on stage with the Plastic Ono Band, but it won't be a planned thing. Just when I feel like it. I'll leave all the sexy hip shaking to Mick Jagger. I'm less interested in being the Brigitte Bardot of the stage than in producing films.

"We have about seventy-eight hours of the Montreal bed-in and the Amsterdam bed-in to edit, and we are planning some other films which will blow a few minds. We also have a couple of books coming out, Grapefruit *by Yoko, and* You Are Here *which I finished a year ago. And we have the Plastic Ono album and the 1970 calendar with photos, poetry and jokes, give that a plug."*

Agreeing that the John and Yoko albums had not exactly been well received, John said, *"People have the same trouble understanding our stuff as they did when abstract art first appeared. It took people a long time to tell good from bad abstract art.*

"We are further out than John Coltrane, whose music I admire. In the past, I've always knocked jazz because jazz, to me in those days, was Humphrey Lyttleton and the British trad bands that used to keep us out of the Cavern. I wasn't even allowed to play rock and roll records on the Students' Union record player when I was in college because they all wanted jazz.

"But if people can dig Ascension, *then they should be able to dig the* Wedding Album *and* Life With the Lions. *The trouble is, they are intellectual snobs and, because I'm identified with pop music, it's assumed I can't produce any worthwhile avant garde stuff."*

Talking about formal music training, John said, *"It's frustrating when I think of a tune in bed and can't write it down. But now I have an expert composer with me. Yoko has had about a hundred years of classical training and is well versed in classical music and the New York avant garde. I've also learned a lot from my own experience.*

"The trouble is, most of the avant garde take the music too seriously and intellectualise it, so it finishes up in the same bag as the conventional music they are rebelling against.

"I suppose it would have been useful to have had some musical training, but I think that training has ruined a lot of musicians. I can hum a tune to Yoko and she can write it down. I've just got to teach her how to play boogie now and we'll be away."

Apple in the Seventies?

"Apple is in great shape now. Allen Klein has earned the Beatles more money than we've ever earned in our lives. We've plugged a few holes in the dike and Apple is now in fine form."

Still, despite his other interests, most of what John was doing was in some way involved with peace.

He said, *"I still get a kick out of getting stories in the papers because every time they mention us, they also mention peace and love, instead of haircuts and corn flakes. I'm using the experience gained in ten years of dealing with the press, TV and radio. It's almost as important now for me to be on the Eamonn Andrews Show as it is to make a new LP. Peace is infiltrating everywhere. John and Yoko are the joke of everyone from Private Eye to Frankie Howard. But our names are becoming synonymous with peace. John and Yoko will outrun The Mousetrap.*

"So, my New Year Message will still be Give Peace A Chance... and buy Cold Turkey."

January 24, 1970 – *Disc and Music Echo***, Richard Robinson mentioned** that John Lennon had been responsible for reviving interest in American / Canadian rock and roller, Ronnie Hawkins. Lennon had said, *"On my last trip to Canada, I stayed at Ronnie Hawkins' house. His new album was playing and I was listening and suddenly this track came on,* Down in the Alley, *and it really buzzed me. It sounds like now and then. And I like that."*

The song had originally been written by Jerry Wexler, vice-president of Atlantic Records, for the Clovers.

February 7, 1970 – *Disc and Music Echo***, Judy Sims wrote from Hollywood.** She had been at the premiere of *The Magic Christian.* She pointed out that most British reviewers had hated the film, but that did not surprise her since they had also hated *Magical Mystery Tour,* and she loved them both. Perhaps Ringo was not handing in a serious acting performance, but he was still Ringo. That was more than enough.

At the press conference, few reporters wanted to know about the movie, they were more concerned with Ringo and what his wife thought about him working with Raquel Welch and how much money he was worth...

February 7, 1970 – *Disc and Music Echo* said Ringo Starr had been in Las Vegas the previous weekend renewing his friendship with Elvis Presley, their first meeting since 1965. He had been sneaked in through the kitchen of the International Hotel, then seated in the audience for Presley's cabaret show.

During the act, Elvis announced that Ringo was in the audience and had him stand up for a bow.

Later, Ringo and Maureen and Peter Brown, of Apple, got together with Elvis and Colonel Parker for a chat. Ringo told reporters later that he and Elvis had considered working together.

Said Ringo, *"Elvis was great. Really fantastic. He was everything he's cracked up to be, and more."*

This week, Ringo was back from the States, getting to work on the final tracks for his Ringo *Stardust* LP.

George Harrison and Billy Preston were both playing with John Lennon on the newest Plastic Ono record, *Instant Karma*, produced by Phil Spector and due to be released very soon. Also on the record were Klaus Voorman and Alan White. The B side featured *Who Has Seen the Wind* by Yoko.

February 14, 1970 – *Disc and Music Echo*, **Mike Ledgerwood wondered** if the Beatles had already split up. Had the greatest group ever to grace the world ceased to exist? Were Lennon, McCartney, Harrison and Starr still friends?

It was well known that all four had not spoken together since the previous summer. Also, it had been many, many months since Paul and John had gotten together.

Of late, Lennon had been hogging all the headlines along with Yoko Ono, the Plastic Ono Band and his plea for world peace.

McCartney was nearly a recluse, out of touch with the workings of Apple and Allen Klein and the rest of the Beatles. Isolated at home in London, he was being a husband and father. His song writing was limited to solo recordings in his home studio. The only contact with Apple had been through the group Badfinger, who he was producing.

Harrison was as busy as Lennon these days, always at Apple, supervising sessions by Billy Preston and Jackie Lomax and Doris Troy, as well as working on his own stuff. At Apple, they were saying that George was only a part-time Beatle, the rest of the time he was George Harrison, though he did appear with the Plastic Ono Band at the Lyceum in London for the Peace For Christmas show on December 15th, and he was playing on the band's new single, *Instant Karma*.

And Starr, whether he wanted it or not, would always be kept a Beatle by the fans… and happy to be one. His Beatle image would always remain intact.

And that left Lennon, the one, the only one, who could make it all happen again… if he chose to. At the Lyceum, he had announced that he was no longer a Beatle. He was in the Plastic Ono Band and thus it should always be.

Instant Karma would have been a fine Beatles record, but John was in a hurry, wanted it released, did not want to wait for the rest of the group to get together.

But Ledgerwood believed that, at heart, John was still a Beatle because he enjoyed being a Beatle. He knew they would get together again.

February 14, 1970 – *Disc and Music Echo*, **Richard Robinson spoke** with John Lennon about being an ex-mop-top.

Said John, "*I have the hardest time in Britain. They don't take anything we do or say seriously, it's a continual put down.*

"*It's always been like that, you know, they treated the Beatles like… well, as long as we behaved ourselves, we were The Fab Four, you know. But if*

we went away and earned too many dollars or were away too long, well, naughty boys, so Britain's the toughest. It's like trying to turn your parents on is the hardest one. You can go and talk to your uncle, but you try telling your dad where it's at."

John and Yoko would not stop, regardless of whether the country was listening or not. They had found favour in the States and Canada. That was enough for now.

Robinson thought what they were doing, and how they were doing it, was completely alien to his way of life. He found it depressing that their propaganda approach to peace was no different than any other politician's propaganda approach to war. It did not show anything better about the human condition, it merely sidestepped into another subject. John and Yoko just seemed to be politicians with a different platform and the same old tired tactics.

February 28, 1970 – *Record Mirror*, **Lon Goddard spoke** with John Peel, a well-known advocate for world peace and supporter of the Campaign for Nuclear Disarmament. Peel questioned the sincerity of John and Yoko. He said, "*They spend a lot of time flying around the world and spending weeks in big hotels. This week, they bought another big expensive car. Is that for peace, too? I could buy a new telly for peace. They don't appear to be really sincere in what they are doing.*"

The Campaign for Nuclear Disarmament had asked Lennon to support their Easter march but their letter was ignored.

"*We have tried for many weeks to get in touch with John Lennon, but Apple always says come back later or next week,*" said a spokesman for the CND. "*We have phoned and I have written a letter to Apple, but received no reply. John Peel has phoned twice for us and got the same answer. I have had two appointments with John arranged through his assistant, Tony Bramwell, but each time he was out or forgot.*

"*Apple say they can't do anything, and it is possible that John does not even know. We did have one interview with him some time ago where we discussed the aims of the CND and he told us he would do as much as possible. We know it is difficult to get in touch with these people, as they have so much to do, but we have not asked until now. We have our Easter march and festival coming up on Easter Sunday, so we would like to get in touch with them.*"

Said John Peel, "*If they can't get in touch with the CND, then I have my doubts about how serious they are about working for peace. The CND exists solely for the pursuit of peace, so I think they could spare the time to see them.*"

A spokesman for Apple said, "*John hasn't been available for the last two or three weeks because he is in the studio editing some films. He hasn't even been into the office for the last two weeks. Sometimes, it is* difficult to get information to John when he is involved with something. If they could ring Diane here, I'm sure she will pass on the message."

February 28, 1970 – Disc and Music Echo, Mike Ledgerwood wrote about a mix-up between the Beatles, Aretha Franklin, John Lennon, and a pair of single records.

The previous week, Franklin had announced she was due to release a McCartney song called Let It Be. It would be an instant hit, of course, a great Beatle song by Aretha Franklin. Rumour had it that McCartney himself had sent her the song.

Unfortunately for Franklin, the exact same song was about to be released simultaneously... by the Beatles themselves.

There had been many covers of Beatle songs, but only after the group had released the music themselves. No one had ever tried to go head-to-head with them in the charts with one of their own compositions.

Other American entertainers, Jose Feliciano, Buddy Greco and others, were also rumoured to have designs on recording Let It Be, all rushing into the studio with what they believed was a passport to instant money.

With regard to Franklin, a spokesman for Apple said, "Good luck to Aretha. She's a fantastic artist and free to do Beatles songs like everyone else."

Then Atlantic Records, Franklin's label, scrapped the project.

Ledgerwood thought they should have both fought it out in the charts. It could not have hurt either one of them. He wondered what went wrong.

At Apple, Let It Be had been put back a week to keep it closer to the release of the film Get Back, in which it was featured, although no date had been decided for the movie's release.

Ledgerwood wondered if the real reason for the delay was to leave the chart clear for Instant Karma by John Lennon and the Plastic Ono Band. Having Lennon and McCartney battling for number one just would not do.

A spokesman for Apple said, "There is an innocence and beauty implicit in the making of music which Apple does not wish to contaminate with comment, chit chat, or controversy."

At Atlantic, a spokesman said, "Aretha's Let It Be was scrapped for two reasons. The main one being that Call Me, a song she wrote herself, and the B side here, was selling extraordinarily well as the A side in the States. And it was logical to assume it could do the same here. Also, we decided that perhaps putting a Beatles' song out on the same date was a bit unwise."

Let It Be, another beautiful, soulful ballad by McCartney, had been written a year ago for the Get Back album. At that time, it had not been considered for single release by the Beatles. Pirate recordings of the album had reached the U.S. and deejays were plugging a number of the songs, including Let It Be.

According to Atlantic, though, "As far as we know, Paul wrote the song specially for Aretha, and sent it to her to record. She did, and it was put on her album This Girl's in Love With You. It was released as a single because it's a very good song, very strong for Aretha, and she needs a hit here."

Plans were on hold, though, to release Let It Be by Franklin. Call Me, backed by Son of a Preacher Man, was to be Franklin's next British single. Let It Be would be issued later in the year.

February 28, 1970 – Disc and Music Echo, Roy Shipston spoke with John Lennon in the Apple offices, Lennon's hair freshly cut short, Yoko at his side.

What is the message in Instant Karma?

"It's action and reaction. Whenever you do something, whatever it is, there is a reaction to it. Even if you cough, you cough germs out all over the place. If you cough love out, out goes love. That's all Instant Karma means to me, action and reaction."

Were the Beatles less important to him than the Plastic Ono Band?

"I don't think anything is more important than anything else. That sounds a bit mad, do you know what I mean? Overall, no one thing is more important than the other."

Who would he rather play with?

"It depends. It depends on whoever is around. Sometimes Plastic Ono sessions are great, sometimes they are a drag. Sessions with the Beatles can be a drag, and they can be great, too. Just yourself and a tape recorder can be good, and boring as well."

Had the Beatles split?

"We're going through changes. The thing is that we change in public, it's a menopause, or something like that."

When was the last time he and Paul saw each other?

"About two months ago. I keep meaning to go and see him. We write a lot, we're always sending postcards from all over the place. I'd like to see him this week. I see Ringo and George almost every other day because they are usually here at Apple, but Paul hasn't been here for ages."

Did he know why Paul had lost interest in Apple?

"That's what I want to ask him. We had a heavy scene last year as far as business was concerned, and Paul got a bit fed up with all the effort of business. I think that's all it is. I hope so."

When was he last in Liverpool?

"Last year, yes, it was six months ago. I took Yoko to show her round the streets of my youth and meet all my relatives. When will we go there again? I don't know, we'll probably go up to do something at the arts school."

Music was still important to him?

"Yes. It's about the best way to communicate. Instant Karma is a great step forward. It's my kind of music. I want to write now and record now. There's no time to intellectualise. The greatest artists always come round to simplicity. Picasso went through the *whole bit. It took him sixty years to learn to paint like a child. I hope to record like an adult child."*

Was he writing as much as ever?

"I'm not really sure. When we were in India, we wrote thousands of songs. I suppose I've got half a dozen, or ten maybe, at the moment. I don't actually try and write now. In those days, we used to sit down and purposefully write fourteen songs, we had to have them for an album. It's not quite the same now. George has taken a load of the weight off. He writes beautiful songs, he's always recording and writing. It's an intense school of music he's going through."

Had his writing changed a lot since *A Day in the Life*?

"Yes, it has. I still listen to A Day in the Life *but that was Beatles' poetry, that was then. There's no time for poetry and books, people have only got time to listen and watch. I still read occasionally, but not much."*

What did he like to listen to?

"We listen to the radio all the time. There's always a couple of numbers in the chart I like. I heard Taste for the first time the other day and that bloke is going places. Fleetwood Mac I like a lot, and Zeppelin seem to be doing some good things. That B.B. King record, The Thrill is Gone, *blew my mind the first time I heard it. I even think that Elvis is sounding nice again. I'm an Elvis fan from way back.*

"I like all music, but I only have time to listen to the radio. Musicians are too busy playing to be listening. Time is so important. We got Instant Karma *out so fast, you know, it was out in a week. We had a race between here and America to see who could get it out first. We won, we had the master tapes. Time is available space, that's one of Allen Klein's more memorable quotes. And if I've got something buzzing, it's got to be done now, it can't wait till tomorrow."*

How were things with Apple?

"Apple is going beautifully. Just listen to the radio and watch the charts in about three weeks time. There has never been a recording company so successful so fast."

And its future?

"I'll tell you something, it's going to be bigger than the Beatles. The Beatles relies on our four talents only, but Apple involves several talents working together."

Was he making much of a contribution to peace?

"Very little, when you look at it in the light of the universe, which is the only way I can see it. Compared to the size of the Earth, even, it's very small, but I'm doing as much as I can."

Were people taking him more seriously now?

"It takes time to be taken seriously. It took the Beatles time to be taken seriously, and then they were taken too seriously, sometimes. It just takes time, as the Edwin Hawkins Singers sing."

At that point in the interview, the B.B. King tune was on the radio. Said John, *"Turn it up, this is a great record, you know."*

Did it worry him, the amount of money he had spent on peace?

"No. I believe you reap what you sow. Whatever you do, you get something back for it, money or whatever. And I earn a lot, you know…"

A number of people accused him of being a crank. What was his opinion of them?

"I think they're cranks. But I think we can get over to them, although I don't know how long it will take. I judge reaction from lorry drivers and taxi men. They used to pull faces and laugh. But now, the people I consider as representative of the public smile and wave, they're quite reasonable."

Had he found the right ways to send out his message?

"We are gradually finding out. It takes time and you are bound to make mistakes, although I don't think I've made any. I know you were going to ask, 'What mistakes?' I read you. I don't suppose we'll get over properly until we have access to the media, an hour on television every day. I don't know whether we'll ever get that."

Why did he compare himself with Christ so much?

"I was brought up Christian, and Christians talk about being perfect. Buddha was supposed to be perfect, so was Christ, and I was taught that as a child. Christ is the one who most people in the West refer to. I refer to Christ and Hitler, one for one thing and one for the other. If I could do what Christ did, be as Christ was, that's what being a Christian is all about. I try to live as Christ lived, it's tough, I can tell you."

What was the number one thing he had received from Yoko?

"Yoko made me myself again. She made me more like I used to be. I was just mucking about in public, just messing around enjoying myself. She brought real joy into my life. Jonathan King and my auntie think I'm too serious now, they think I never smile. You can tell them that I'm happier than I've ever been."

Were his future peace plans a secret?

"No, it's not a secret. Tomorrow, we're going to edit the bed-in film from Montreal. It should be out just after the Beatles' Get Back film, so after a good bit of pop, the kids can enjoy a nice peace promoting film. Then we are going to do an album with Phil Spector."

Would other Beatles be involved in that?

"I don't know. It depends on who is around. It's rather like Delaney and Bonnie and Friends, except that they thought of the name first."

What would he like to see the kids doing for his beliefs?

"Tell them they can go to the Black House and see if there is anything they can do there to help. They can help themselves by helping others. There's whites as well as blacks working there, helping each other. You see, people in ghettos need to be taught how to live humanely. We'd like people to go and see the place and find out if there's anything they can do. We've got to get together, black and white is beautiful."

What did he think of the kids' demonstrations?

"*It depends on the motive. The Welsh did a good job in court the other day. I don't like it when violence gets in. Demonstrations are fine if there is no violence. One thing I'd like to say is that people ought to realise that, although we are not at war, we are providing arms to other countries. People understand the idea of push-button war, but they don't see that we are pushing the button. We are killing by selling arms to other people.*"

Would he keep his hair short?

"*I don't know. I have no plans for my hair, I never have.*"

February 28, 1970 – *Melody Maker* said it was possible there would soon be a solo disc by Ringo. Late night recording sessions at Apple had taken place the previous week, with Ringo accompanied by George Harrison, Klaus Voorman and Steven Stills. The song had been written by Ringo and polished up during the session by the musicians and George Martin.

Ringo was the featured singer and drummer.

Stills was in London to record his first solo album. He said, "*Ringo came in with this little song, that is, he sat down and played eight bars and said, 'That's it,' so we all made suggestions and it came along very nicely. George told me that the session was for Ringo's surprise single, and I guess that could be right.*"

Said Apple press officer, Derek Taylor, "*They were just making music, man, just making music. Seriously though, that's all I can say.*"

March 7, 1970 – *Record Mirror*, **John and Yoko** replied to John Peel's February 28th attack on them by writing, "Instant Karma Hits John Peel!

"Peace Peace Peace Peace Peace

"Peace Peace Peace Peace to John

"Peel and all our brothers and sisters.

"Black and white is beautiful!

"love from John and Yoko."

March 7, 1970 – *Disc and Music Echo* said John and Yoko, along with a host of other rock and roll celebrities, had been invited to attend the Sunrise Festival, a six-day event, from March 9th - 15th, featuring progressive music and living theatre at the Roundhouse, Chalk Farm, London. It would be filmed for TV.

March 7, 1970 – *Melody Maker* announced that *Let It Be* might be hit through the EMI Records boycott being staged by record sellers in the Northwest. Up to five hundred shops were involved in the boycott which was protesting EMI's new policy of disallowing the shops to unload back stocks of unsold singles.

EMI refused to comment.

A footnote mentioned that a clip from the Beatles' *Get Back* film was to be shown on Top of the Pops that night to promote the new single, *Let It Be*.

On the same page, a photograph of Ringo showed his new short hair style as he followed in the trend set by John Lennon.

March 14, 1970 – *Disc and Music Echo*, said Ringo Starr's first solo single, *It Don't Come Easy,* was in the process of being recorded. Ringo was singing and drumming, and George Harrison was playing guitar. The song had a country feel to it.

And Ringo's first album, originally *Ringo Stardust* but now called *Sentimental Journey,* was due to be released on the 3rd of April. The tracks were: *Sentimental Journey, Dreams, Stardust, Whispering Grass, Bye Bye Blackbird, Blue Turning Grey Over You, Let The Rest of the World Go By, Night and Day, You Always Hurt the One You Love, Love is a Many Splendoured Thing, Have I Told You Lately That I Love You* and *I'm A Fool to Care.*

Paul McCartney, Maurice Gibb and Klaus Voorman were also involved with the record, while arrangements were specially done for Ringo by some truly big names in the pop and jazz scenes.

George Harrison was on his way to Paris with members of the Radha Krishna sect to help with setting up a new temple and to help sell their single *Govinda.*

Doris Troy was teaming up with George in hopes of revolutionising the UK concert scene. She said, "*George and I are getting this band together to travel with me and Billy Preston and we're gonna have singers and dancers with us to make up an Apple Revue, a sort of soul package.*"

Troy's new album, featuring George Harrison, Delaney and Bonnie, Eric Clapton, Billy Preston and Ringo Starr, was due out in May.

March 21, 1970 – *Record Mirror* announced that the Beatles' new single, *Let It Be,* had only reached number two in the charts before being knocked down to third by Simon and Garfunkel's *Bridge Over Troubled Water.* Only two other singles in Beatle history had missed hitting number one, *Love Me Do* and *Something.*

March 21, 1970 – *Record Mirror* said that the Beatles would be on Radio One for a special show at Easter, possibly to include some of their live material. The special would be called *The Beatles Today.* George Harrison had been involved with the planning and it was quite possible that some live Beatles tapes would be provided for the program.

On March 31st, Ringo was to be on the Open House broadcast with regular host, Pete Murray.

It was understood that the Beatles were planning to be involved more with radio and TV during 1970. Rumours were also going about that they would do a live concert somewhere in London.

March 21, 1970 – *Disc and Music Echo* announced that George and Ringo would be doing some special appearances on Radio One over Easter. It was possible that there would be some exclusive excerpts from the *Get Back* album released for the show.

Ringo was set to do Pete Murray's Open House morning request show at the end of the month. And the previous day, on Easter Monday, Harrison would be doing a forty-five minute interview with Johnny Moran called *The Beatles Today*.

Said BBC producer, Ted Beston, *"George rang us and said he'd like to do something on* Scene And Heard, *so we invited him to our studio in Bond Street. He arrived alone and spent a long while chatting to Johnny and myself."*

Regarding Ringo on Radio One, a spokesman for Apple said, *"He said he'd like to do a show to tie up with the release of his solo LP* Sentimental Journey.*"*

The previous weekend, Ringo had done a solo show for Talk of the Town, filmed as a promotional piece for *Sentimental Journey*.

Also, Paul McCartney's as yet untitled solo LP was due to be released on April 17th.

March 28, 1970 – *Disc and Music Echo* mentioned that Ringo Starr had been in the Island recording studios, working with Stephen Stills on his new solo album.

March 28, 1970 – *Disc and Music Echo* announced that John and Yoko, along with two members from Soft Machine and musician Ron Geesin, would be starring on John Peel's Top Gear radio show. The plan was for them to sing a song that had been created by a pair of chimpanzees. Peel's producer, John Walters, had a recording of the chimpanzees' piano playing. He invited Lennon to improvise something live over the composition. It would be the first time a Beatle had been heard live on the radio in five years. John promised to play the jew's harp while Yoko would lend her vocals to the effort. Soft Machine drummer Robert Wyatt and organist Mike Ratledge would also be playing.

Said Walters, *"The whole idea is purely experimental, of course. And I don't doubt some people will see it as outrageous. But, on the other hand, it could be seen as a serious thing by people with the right attitude to modern music."*

The chimps, Bugsy and Rosie, were found by Walters. He said, *"We only wanted one, but apparently, they work better in pairs, rather like Ferrante and Teicher, I suppose. They encourage each other at the keyboard. There's some interesting four-hand, and occasionally four-foot, harmony. And I don't think anyone would complain if it was put on Radio Three as a serious experimental piece."*

The chimp's number, called *Blues For Desmond Morris*, in honour of the author of *The Naked Ape*, had been edited into a continuous loop. John, Yoko and company were to improvise in the studio.

Said Walters, *"We offered to send them the tape, but they've said they'd like to come along and do it live."*

A footnote mentioned that Ringo Starr's album, *Sentimental Journey,* was due to be released that week.

April 4, 1970 – *Disc and Music Echo* announced that Ringo Starr intended to follow up his *Sentimental Journey* LP with a selection of Country songs. This had been confirmed by an Apple spokesman, who said it would likely not be recorded until later in the year.

Also, Paul McCartney's solo album, *McCartney,* was still due to be released on April 17th.

John Lennon announced over Easter that Yoko was pregnant. He said the child was *"a baby for peace."*

April 4, 1970 – *Disc and Music Echo*, Mike Ledgerwood spoke with Tony Sheridan after Sheridan had dropped in on Paul McCartney for a short visit. To get in to the St. John's Wood mansion where Paul had been secluding himself, Sheridan wandered up a neighbouring driveway into the back garden, and leapt over the wall into Paul's yard.

Dressed in pajamas and wearing a bushy black beard, Paul himself answered the door, exclaiming, *"It's Tony Sheridan! Nice to see you. Come on in."*

That had been two months ago and Paul had been quite pleased to see Sheridan again, a ghost from all those years ago in Hamburg when the Beatles, still with Pete Best and Stuart Sutcliffe, had backed up Sheridan on their first professional recordings. Paul and Sheridan had once composed a song together, *Tell Me If You Can.*

Sheridan said, *"It was one of the first things he mentioned when we met. I didn't think he'd remember.*

"I couldn't believe how little Paul had changed over the years. Yes, Paul's the one who has changed the least. The only difference was that he didn't smoke at all in the time we were together. He did it like mad in the old days.

"He wasn't at all surprised that I'd climbed over the wall. I've always been mad like that. We spent about an hour-and-a-half reminiscing over the old times in Hamburg."

Ledgerwood wondered why he had decided to drop in on Paul.

Sheridan said, *"I wasn't out for any favours when I went round there. I'd just heard that he'd locked himself away and, since we'd always got on well, I thought I'd go round and have a chat.*

"He introduced me to Linda and they made a cup of weak tea for me. Paul wasn't smoking, which I found surprising. We talked for over an hour, mostly about the Hamburg days and his songs. He suddenly sat down at the piano and said, 'What do you think of this?' ...and played Let It Be *out of the blue.*

"He asked what I'd been doing and suggested that I do some of the old stuff again with fresh arrangements.

"The house was a lot less luxurious than you'd imagine. The main room, the lounge, I suppose, was

very large, but quite plain. It was more like a studio which had been built to live in. There was a huge piano and several tape recorders and mikes. Things like that. On the walls were blow-up photos of Paul, Linda and the baby.

"He was very friendly and obviously involved in his songs. My main impression? That he wasn't doing much except writing."

April 18, 1970 – Record Mirror, Brian Mulligan wrote that the Beatles' long-awaited, formerly *Get Back*, now *Let It Be* LP was finally to be released, simultaneously in Britain and the States, on May 13th. Their documentary film would premiere in New York the same day, and in London and Liverpool on the 20th. Recording and filming had started in January 1969. The film, of course, was about the recording of the album.

Allen Klein had made a deal for the film to be shown in one hundred cities around the world at roughly the same time.

Surprisingly, Phil Spector had produced the LP. An Apple press statement claimed, *"Let It Be* is a new-phase Beatles album essential to the context of the film, so that they perform live for many of the tracks. In comes the warmth, the freshness of live performance, as reproduced for disc by Phil Spector."

That simply meant that the U.S. producer remixed some of the songs, dubbed in some orchestrations here and there, and even added a choir.

When told by the press that Spector had produced the album, George Martin said he was surprised he had not been told by the Beatles or someone from Apple. He said he had not heard this new version of the LP.

The reporter wondered if he would be involved in future Beatle records. Martin said, *"In view of the fact that the Beatles don't exist as the four young men I once knew, I don't want to record them as a split group, but I would like to record them as they were."*

By contract with EMI, Martin was still the band's official producer. But he had never had a contract with the Beatles themselves. He had worked with George Harrison and Ringo Starr in the past year, but had not been in touch with the whole group since the final mix of *Abbey Road*.

Recently, Paul had said, *"Allen Klein does not represent me in any way."*

A statement from Apple addressed the status of the Beatles, saying the group had entered a ten-year partnership agreement in April 1967, between the Beatles as individuals and Apple Corps. Apple became the majority partner in Beatles and Company. With the exception of films and song writing, The Beatles / Apple partnership owned the services of the Beatles, as entertainers, throughout the world.

The statement mentioned that no individual Beatle could, "offer his services, appear alone and/or with any other person in any branch of the entertainment industry as to which the partnership

has special rights, without the consent of Apple Corps and the other Beatles.

"It is reiterated that no person, film or corporation can act or negotiate for the Beatles or for the Apple group of companies other than ABKCO Industries, 1700 Broadway, New York City."

April 18, 1970 – Record Mirror, Peter Jones reviewed Paul McCartney's new solo album, *McCartney.* He went through it track-by-track.

The Lovely Linda: A gentle song with a touch of falsetto. Too short, just a prelude to a song McCartney hoped to record sometime later.

That Would Be Something: Repetitive but effective, with an Elvis sort of mood.

Valentine Day: An ad-libbed instrumental recorded at home on a four-track Studer, based on a slightly weak riff with some decent drumming.

Every Night: Almost done in a country style, very nice song.

Hot As Sun: Another strong but simple instrumental. Said Paul, *"I wrote it about 1958 when it was one of those songs that you play now and then."*

Glasses: An experimental thing done with wine glasses and some overdubbed voices.

Junk: This was more like McCartney, written in India at the Maharishi's retreat. Nice acoustic guitar with Linda singing harmonies.

Man We Was Lonely: Instant impact, simple but magical, with some steel guitar and both McCartneys singing.

Oo You: This began as an instrumental, nicely tough, the lyrics added later in a sort of Lennon imitation.

Momma Miss America: Yet another ad-libbed instrumental recorded at home.

Teddy Boy: Pure McCartney lyrics with Linda singing harmonies again.

Singalong Junk: An instrumental version of Junk, with a strong piano and a nice melody.

Maybe I'm Amazed: Almost a rock and roll rave-up with some good piano and solo guitar.

Kreen-Akrore: A very successful instrumental about which Paul said, *"There was a TV film about the Kreen-Akrore Indians in the Brazilian jungle and how the white man is trying to change their way of life. So I went out and did some drumming."*

About the making of the album, McCartney said, *"It was an easy album to do, as the things that normally hang a project up, like lack of decision, weren't there.*

"Playing with myself, as they say, was also easy because I knew what I was thinking. The only trouble was that, in order to keep time, I had to do drums first, on their own, and that was sometimes a bit hard, but fun.

"That front cover is a picture of a bowl of cherries we got from the barman at a hotel we stayed at in

Antigua, and we laid them out on the wall in front of our cottage so that the birds of the area could drink the juice and eat the cherries."

April 18, 1970 – *Record Mirror* published an interview with Paul McCartney.

Why did you make a solo album?

Said Paul, "*Because I got a Studer four-track, practiced on it, playing all instruments, liked the result, and decided to make it into an album.*"

Did John and the Plastic Ono Band and Ringo making a solo album influence your decision?

"*Sort of, but not really.*"

Are you the only musician and writer on the album?

"*Yes, sir.*"

Did you enjoy doing it that way?

"*Very much. I only had me to ask for a decision, and I agreed with me. Remember Linda's on it too, so it's really a double act.*"

What did she do?

"*Strictly speaking, she harmonises, but of course it's more than that because she is a shoulder to lean on, a second opinion, and a photographer of renown. More than all this, she believes in me, constantly.*"

Where did you do the recording?

"*At home, at EMI and at Morgan Studios, Willesden.*"

Can you detail your home equipment?

"*Studer four-track machine. I only had, however, one mike, and as Mr. Pender, Mr. Sweatenham and others, only managed to take six months or so. I worked without V.U. meters or a mixer, which meant that everything had to be listened to first, then recorded, so, the answer: Studer, one mike, and nerve.*"

No one knew about the album until it was nearly finished. Did you keep quiet about it on purpose?

"*Yes, because normally, an album is old before it comes out. Witness Get Back.*"

Why?

"*I've always wanted to buy a Beatles' album like people do, and be surprised as they must be, so this was the next best thing. Linda and I are the only two who will be sick of it by the release date. We love it, really.*"

Can you describe the feel of it, briefly?

"*Home, family, love.*"

How long did it take?

"*From just before Christmas until now. The Lovely Linda was the first thing I recorded at home, and was originally to test the equipment. That was around Christmas.*"

When did you write the songs?

"*One was 1958, two from India* – Junk and Teddy Boy – *and the rest are pretty recent.* Valentine Day, Momma Miss America *and* Oo You *were ad-libbed on the spot.*"

What instruments did you use?

"*Bass, drums, acoustic guitar, lead guitar, piano and organ-mellotron, toy xylophone, bow and arrow.*"

Had you played them all before, on other recordings?

"*Yes, drums being the one that I wouldn't normally do.*"

Why did you play them all?

"*I think I'm pretty good.*"

Will Linda record with you again?

"*Could be. We love singing together and have plenty of opportunity for practice.*"

Paul and Linda will become a John and Yoko?

"*No, they will become Paul and Linda.*"

Are you happy with your music?

"*Yes.*"

What did you learn?

"*That to make your own decisions about what to do is easy, and playing with yourself is difficult but satisfying.*"

Who did the design?

"*Linda has taken all the photos, and she and I designed the package.*"

Will Allen Klein or ABKCO be involved in any way with this new LP?

"*Not if I can help it.*"

Did you miss George Martin or the rest of the group while you were working on this?

"*No.*"

If the album is a hit, will you do another?

"*Even if it isn't, I will continue to do what I want, when I want to.*"

Are you planning to make any more records with the Beatles?

"*No.*"

Is this just a break from the group, or the beginning of a new career?

"*Time will tell. Being a solo album means it's the start of a solo career, and not being done with the Beatles means its a rest, so it's both.*"

Are you planning any live shows?

"*No.*"

This split with the Beatles, is it because of personal or musical differences?

"*Personal differences, business differences, musical differences, but most of all, because I have a better time with my family. Temporary or permanent? I don't know.*"

Can you imagine writing songs with John Lennon again?

"*No.*"

How do you feel about all the things John is into, the Plastic Ono Band, the peace thing, returning the MBE, Yoko?

"*I love John and respect what he does. It doesn't give me any pleasure.*"

Were any of the album songs planned for the Beatles?

"*The older ones were. Junk was intended for* Abbey Road *but something happened.*"

Were you happy with *Abbey Road*?

"*It was a good album.*"

What is your relationship with Allen Klein?

"It isn't. I am not in contact with him, and he does not represent me in any way."

And Apple?

"It is the office of a company which I part own with the other Beatles. I don't go there because I don't like offices or businesses, especially when I'm on holiday."

Will you create an independent company?

"McCartney Productions."

What music influenced you on this album?

"Light and loose."

Are you writing more now?

"About the same. I have a queue waiting to be recorded."

Do you have any plans now?

"My only plan is to grow up."

April 18, 1970 – Record Mirror, Derek Taylor wrote about the break-up of the Beatles and what had happened. He said that on Tuesday of the previous week, Paul's lawyers, Eastman and Eastman, Linda's father and brother, announced that Paul had formed his own production company, McCartney Productions. They had two initial projects, Paul's album, *McCartney*, and a film about *Rupert the Bear*.

The following day, Don Short of the *Daily Mirror* heard about a statement that was planned for the Friday, the gist of which being that Paul was happy to be working without the Beatles at the moment and that he did not know whether or not the break would be temporary or permanent. Taking a bit of a gamble, Short broke the story first, saying, *"Paul is quitting the Beatles."*

Neither Apple or Paul denied it.

Taylor said it was no good asking him for the absolute truth because he was merely a press agent; the absolute truth was not his story to tell.

But, how could a Beatle not be a Beatle, even if he was not, at that particular moment, a Beatle? Paul had merely paused to look at himself.

April 18, 1970 – Disc and Music Echo said that Paul McCartney, on the previous Friday, had left London and the world in shock when he announced he was no longer a Beatle. Said a friend of Paul's, *"He's not giving any interviews at the moment. In fact, fans and other people have been making his life a bit of a misery lately by picketing his pad. I wish they'd leave him alone to live his own life now."*

With his new album, *McCartney*, finished and ready for release, 19,000 advance copies ordered, he was ready to move on to his next project, which was produce and compose the music for a theatre-length animated film of *Rupert the Bear*.

A spokesman for Apple said, *"At the moment, Paul and Rupert are still only in the planning stages. We have no further details."*

April 18, 1970 – Disc and Music Echo, David Hughes wondered if the Beatles were truly dead. Had Paul really killed them?

It was a confusing situation. When Paul came out of hibernation to do his interview and then leave town before it all hit the fan, he did not actually say the Beatles were permanently done, nor would he admit the break was only temporary.

He was unavailable for interviews, refusing to discuss anything, locked behind the walls of his home in St. John's Wood.

Paul's withdrawal from the others had been a slow process, starting round about the time Apple was hit with financial problems and Allen Klein was brought in to fix things. Paul had never wanted Klein involved but had wanted Linda's father to handle things. The other three Beatles voted against him. And Paul retreated into married life, visits to Apple growing fewer and fewer. He came out to write *Come and Get It* for Ringo's film, *The Magic Christian*, and that was it, no further involvement for almost a year.

And now, the *McCartney* album and the... interview.

Maybe the Beatles were done, maybe not.

But all things change, all good things end. If the Beatles were finished, four new musical forces would take their place.

April 18, 1970 – Disc and Music Echo, Mike Ledgerwood wrote that he believed the McCartney interview, the end of the Beatles thing, was no more than a beautifully planned and well executed publicity trick to stir up some controversy and make sure that Paul's solo album received maximum exposure.

He spoke with John Lennon and John said, *"I received a phone call from Paul on Thursday afternoon. He said, 'I'm going to leave the Beatles as well.' I was happy to hear from Paul. It was nice to find that he was still alive. Anyway, Paul hasn't left, I sacked him."*

The Apple offices were mayhem, of course, when the news was announced, and the Beatles made the headlines yet again. The streets were packed with fans and reporters and onlookers while inside, Derek Taylor and Mavis Smith tried to cope with the barrage of calls.

When reporters spoke with Allen Klein, he said he had not seen Paul's statement but did not see how the situation was any different from what it had been for the last six months.

Ledgerwood said Paul was the culprit here. He had made his statement and then refused to meet with the press, refused to clarify anything.

Said Klein, *"I like Paul. We've had many meetings, but it's never pleasant when someone appears not to like you. I think his reasons are his own personal problems. Unfortunately, he's obligated to Apple for a considerable number of years."*

Derek Taylor said, *"Until Klein came on the scene, the Beatles had always taken one another's* recommendations. *Paul went along with the Maharishi thing, for instance, but when he suggested Lee Eastman, Linda's lawyer father, for Apple, the others said, 'We'll stay with Klein.'"*

That was that.

April 18, 1970 – *Disc and Music Echo*, **Penny Valentine** reviewed *McCartney*. She believed that what a man did with his life was his own business. And she believed that what a man did with his music was also his own business. But the moment that music was put on a record and offered up for sale, it became everybody's business. Paul McCartney was not responsible for his public mystique. But he was responsible for his music.

McCartney was bitterly disappointing. She had always believed that Paul had far more to give musically than any of the other Beatles. She could not wait to hear what he could do on his own. She was certain it would be magnificent.

She expected greatness.

It did not materialise.

She reviewed each song track-by-track but the only one she actually liked was *Maybe I'm Amazed*, a powerful song performed with a lot of enthusiasm, the real Paul McCartney.

April 18, 1970 – *Melody Maker*, **Richard Williams** said the announcement that Paul McCartney was breaking up the Beatles was the non-event of the year. It came out of an interview arranged by Apple, the first McCartney interview in years, and was sent around to all the papers in the country.

Paul said he was setting up his own production company, had no plans to work with the other Beatles, and that he had personal, musical and business problems with the others.

Yeah, so? This was not news. The same problems were going on when the Beatles made *Abbey Road*. The problems did not stop that album from being made and why should they stop any future Beatle albums from being made? They were all busy with their own projects. They were waiting for the release of *Let It Be*. And they had some relatively recent extra material, already recorded, enough for a least another single.

The furore over this was contrived. When the group finally stopped working together, it would simply be something that happened, a situation that would simply drift into being, not a monumental event, not a now-you-see-them now-you-don't affair. One day, they would wake up and realise that Beatles were no more.

Williams did not understand why McCartney did not get along with Allen Klein. Klein had gotten rid of Apple's dead weight and was making tons of money for the Beatles. How could one resent that?

At least superficially, Paul's distrust of Klein was irrational. The only visible motive for it was the

bitterness caused by the others wanting to stay with Klein rather than go with Paul's new family.

Even with McCartney Productions, Apple would still represent him.

An interesting sidelight to all of this was that throughout their entire career as song writers, it had been Lennon / McCartney, until recently. *Cold Turkey* and *Instant Karma* were credited only to John. *McCartney* had been written and produced by Paul McCartney.

Williams thought it was about time. Why would John want his name on something like *Maxwell's Silver Hammer*?

He finished by saying family members often have their differences but they go through so much together, how do they stop being family? Lennon and McCartney were brothers. Perhaps they disagreed with each other from time to time, but they still had all the old good feelings for each other. Perhaps they would get together again, perhaps not. It was irrelevant. They would both still be making music.

April 18, 1970 – *Melody Maker* **reviewed** Paul McCartney's new solo album. While John was calling up his friends and getting them into the studio to jam, and while Ringo was finding the best music arrangers money could hire, Paul was home singing folk songs into a four-track recording machine.

With a few exceptions, it was not a polished and well-produced album, just a man by himself playing with an assortment of musical instruments and recording unfinished songs. This album made McCartney's, and the Beatles', debt to George Martin quite obvious. Martin's production was likely vital to the success of quite a number of Beatle songs.

Maybe I'm Amazed was the only song that truly stood out on the album, a song worthy of Paul McCartney and even the Beatles, a rock song with a stunning guitar and Paul's best rock voice. The rest of the songs on the album were barely worth a mention.

April 25, 1970 – *Disc and Music Echo* **wrote about** the new Beatles' album, *Let It Be*. All four members of the group wrote one of the songs on the LP, *Dig It*.

Said Derek Taylor, *"They probably won't share composing credits on the record, but this was definitely a track they all contributed to."*

Also included on the album were two songs by George Harrison, *For You Blue* and *I Me My* (sic). John Lennon's *Across the Universe*, originally released on a charity album, and an oldie called *Maggie May*, would also be on the album. Paul's solo contributions were *Let It Be* and *The Long and Winding Road*.

The list of tracks: *Two of Us, Dig a Pony, Across the Universe, I Me My* (sic), *Dig It, Let It Be, Maggie May, I've Got a Feeling, One After 909, The Long and Winding Road, For You Blue* and *Get Back*.

Let It Be, produced by Phil Spector, was described by Apple as a new-phase Beatles' album, locked in tight with their film of the same name.

The LP would be in a box with colour shots of each individual Beatle on the cover. It would also include a series of colour stills from the movie. The release date was to be May 8th.

The *Let It Be* film, called, "a bioscopic experience," a colour documentary that showed the group at work, was to be premiered in New York City on May 13th. After that, it would be shown in one hundred cities worldwide.

A footnote mentioned that Aretha Franklin was going to release a new single on May 1st, *Let It Be*.

George Harrison interview, New York City, April 25, 1970.

You arrived in New York on Tuesday?

George: *"Yeah, Tuesday afternoon."*

How long will you stay?

"Just 'til next Monday."

Then you go back to London?

"Yeah, right. Well, Home – which is just outside of London."

Why are you here?

"Well, a bit of business, really. I came to see our new office – 1700 Broadway – and just a few little things to do with business. Also to see a few friends, and to pick up my visa. It's the first time I've had a visa for eighteen months, so I had to use it, you know."

Will you be doing any recording here?

"No. I can't work, you know – not that sort of work. I'd need a different visa, and all that sort of thing. Anyway, there's not enough time to record. But I am going to be recording in about three weeks. I'm gonna start an album of my own, as Ringo and Paul... This is gonna be the George album, and I start that in three to four weeks time, and I hope to do it with Phil Spector."

London?

"Yeah."

Your songs?

"Yeah. I've had songs for a long time, and lots of new songs. I've got about... enough songs for about three or four albums, actually. But if I do one, that'll be good enough for me."

There are so few of your songs on Beatle albums, no one knew you were so prolific.

"Yeah, well, I wrote some songs – in fact some songs which I feel are quite nice which I'll use on this album – I wrote about four years ago. But, uh, it was more difficult for me then to, you know, get in there to do it. It was the way the Beatles took off with Paul and John's songs, and it made it very difficult for me get in, and also, I suppose at that time I didn't have as much confidence when it came down to pushing my own material as I have now, so it took a while. You know, I think the first... I did write one song on about the second album, and I left it and didn't write

any more. That was just an exercise to see if I could write. About two years later I recorded a couple more songs – I think* Rubber Soul. *And then I've had one or two songs on each album. Well, there are four songs of mine on the double* White Album. *But now, uh, the output of songs is too much to be able to just sit around, you know, waiting to put two songs on an album. I've got to get 'em out, you know."*

Who decided how many songs you would have on a Beatle album? Or was it just, whoever was the loudest?

"Yeah. It's always... it was whoever would be the heaviest would get the most songs done. So consequently, I couldn't be bothered pushing, like, that much. You know, even on Abbey Road *for instance, we'd record about eight tracks before I got 'round to doing one of mine. Because uh, you know, you say 'Well, I've got a song,' and then with Paul – 'Well I've got a song as well and mine goes like this – diddle-diddle-diddle-duh,' and away you go! You know, it was just difficult to get in there, and I wasn't gonna push and shout. But it was just over the last year or so we worked something out, which is still a joke really – three songs for me, three songs for Paul, three songs for John, and two for Ringo. But that is the main problem, you see, because, I mean..."*

Only two for Ringo?

"Well, 'cause that's fair, isn't it! That's what you call being fair. Even Ringo, you see, is writing more songs. We just cut a track in London of Ringo's song called, uh... It Don't Come Easy, it's called, and so he, maybe he'll put that out as a single. But Paul and John and myself have got just so many songs, I think this is a good way, you know, if we do our own albums. That way we don't have to compromise. I mean, we lose whatever we get from each other – we sacrifice that in order to do a total sort of thing, you know. Because in a way, Paul wants to do his songs his way. He doesn't want to do his songs my way. and I don't wanna do my songs their way, really. And uh, I'm sure that after we've all completed an album or even two albums each, then that novelty will have worn off."

Will the Beatles be together again?

"Uh... Well, I don't... I couldn't tell, you know, if they do or not. I'll certainly try my best to do something with them again, you know. I mean, it's only a matter of accepting that the situation is a compromise. In a way it's a compromise, and it's a sacrifice, you know, because we all have to sacrifice a little in order to gain something really big. and there is a big gain by recording together – I think musically, and financially, and also spiritually, and for the rest of the world, you know, I think that Beatle music is such a big sort of scene – that I think it's the least we could do is to sacrifice three months of the year at least, you know, just to do an album or two. I think it's very selfish if the Beatles don't record together."

Everything looks grim right now.

"It's not, really. You know, it's no more gloomy than it's been for the last ten years. It really isn't any worse. It's just that now over the last year – what with John, and lately with Paul – everything that they've thought or said has come out, you know, to the public. It's been printed. It's been there for everybody to read, or to comment about, or to join in on. Whereas before..."

The feelings are always there?

"No, I wouldn't say that. In different ways, you know. We're just like anybody else. Familiarity breeds contempt, they do say. and we've had slight problems. But it's only been recently, you know, because we didn't work together for such a long time in the Yoko and John situation and then Paul and Linda. But it's really... It's not as bad as it seems, you know. Like, we're all having a good time individually, and..."

So much animosity between Paul and...

"Yeah."

It sounded like he was saying it was all over.

"But it's more of a personal thing, you know. That's down to the management situation, you know, with Apple. Because Paul, really – It was his idea to do Apple, and once it started going Paul was very active in there, and then it got really chaotic and we had to do something about it. When we started doing something about it, obviously Paul didn't have as much say in the matter, and then he decided... you know, because he wanted Lee Eastman, his in-laws, to run it and we didn't. Then that's the only reason, you know. That's the whole basis. But that's only a personal problem that he'll have to get over because that's... The reality is that he's out-voted and we're a partnership. We've got these companies which we all own twenty-five percent of each, and if there's a decision to be made then, like in any other business or group you have a vote, you know, and he was out-voted three to one and if he doesn't like it, it's really a pity. You know, because we're trying to do what's best for the Beatles as a group, or best for Apple as a company. We're not trying to do what's best for Paul and his in-laws, you know."

That is what the fight is over?

"Yeah, because it's on such a personal level that it is a big problem, really. You know – You imagine that situation if you were married and you wanted your in-laws to handle certain things. You know, it's like – It's a difficult one to overcome because... well, you can think of the subtleties, you know. But he's really living with it like that, you see. When I go home at night I'm not living there with Allen Klein, whereas in a way, Paul's living with the Eastmans, you see, and so it's purely... it's not really between Paul and us. You know, it's between Paul's advisors who are the Eastmans and our business advisor, which is Allen Klein. But it's all right."

It is hard to be optimistic.

"Yeah, it's all right. All things pass... away... as they say."

There seemed to be animosity between Linda and Yoko.

"Ah, I don't know. I don't think about it, you know. I refuse to be a part of any hassles like that. You know, Hare Krishna, Hare Krishna. Krishna, Krishna, Hare, Hare, and it'll all be okay, you know. Just give 'em time because they do really love each other, you know. I mean, we all do. We've been so close and through so much together that it really... to talk about it like this, you know, we'll never get any nearer to it. But the main thing is, like in anybody's life, they have slight problems, and it's just that our problems are always blown up, and uh, you know, shown to everybody. But it's not really... it's not a problem. It's only a problem if you think about it."

No great anger between Paul and John?

"No, I think there may be what you'd term a little bitchiness. But, you know, that's all it is. It's just being bitchy to each other, you know. Childish. Childish. Well, I get on well with Ringo and John, and I try my best to get on well with Paul, and uh, there's nothing much more we can... it's just a matter of time, you know, just for everybody to work out their own problems and once they've done that I'm sure we'll get back 'round the cycle again. But if not, you know, it's still alright. Whatever happens, you know, it's gonna be okay. In fact, it's never looked better from my point of view. It's really – it's very good now – in very good shape, the companies are in great shape. Apple Films, Apple Records. My song company is in good shape because I've been more productive over the last year or so. It's really good we got back a lot of money that a lot of people had that was ours; a lot of percents that different people had, and it's really..."

Klein did that?

"Mmmm."

Were you truly broke?

"We weren't broke, we'd earned a lot of money but we didn't actually have the money that we'd earned, you know. It was floating around, because the contracts... The structure of everything, you know, right back – that's really the history – Since 1962 the way everything was structured was just freaky, you know. None of us knew anything about it. We just spent money when we wanted to spend money, but we didn't know where we were spending it from, or if we paid taxes on it, you know. We were really in bad shape as far as that was concerned, because none of us really could be bothered. We just felt as though we were rich, because really we were rich by what we sold and what we did. But, uh, it wasn't really the case because it was so un-together – the business side of it. But now it's very together and we know exactly where everything is, and there's daily reports on where it is and what it is, and how much it is, and it's really good."

Will you play all the instruments on your new album?

"No, no. I'd much rather play with other people, you know, because... united we stand, divided we fall. I think, musically it can sound much more together if you have a bass player, a drummer, and you know, a few friends. A little help from your friends. So the songs – it depends really on how I see the arrangements. Some songs maybe I'll do just one or two just with acoustic guitars or something, but it's really down to how I see the songs should be interpreted. But I really want to use as much instrumentation as I think the songs need. You know, some will have orchestras, and some will have rock and roll, and some will have trumpets. You know, whatever. It'll be a production album."

Have you and Phil Spector gone over the music?

"No, no. I sang him a couple of the songs... I sang him a lot of songs that I had, but umm, at that time I hadn't decided really that I was doing an album. You know, I knew I'd do one eventually but I hadn't decided to do it this soon, and it was only after that I decided that I'd do it straight away, so now I've got to meet with Phil and decide really which tunes, you know. I've got an idea which ones I'd like to use."

You have heard Paul's LP?

"Yeah."

Your opinion?

"That Would Be Something *and* Maybe I'm Amazed *I think are great and everything else I think is fair, you know – is quite good – but umm, a little disappointing. But I don't know. Maybe I shouldn't be disappointed, maybe... It's best not to expect anything and then everything's bonus, you know. I think those two tracks in particular are really very good, and the others, I mean, just don't do much for me. Because I can hear other people play better drums and guitars and things, and the arrangements of some of these songs like...* Teddy Boy, *and* Junk, *and stuff – with a little bit more arrangement they could've sounded better. I suppose it was the only thing he felt he could do at the time, you know, and he started off just testing his machine. Eddie Cochran did something like that, though, didn't he.* Summertime Blues *and* Come On Everybody *he played bass, guitar, drums."*

Can the Beatles really work together again. Can you work out all the problems?

"Well, it's easy. You know, it's really quite easy. It's just easy. We've done it for years. We all know that we're all separate individuals, and if all we have to do is accept that we're all individuals and that we all have as much potential as the other... It's like, if we were all perfected beings we wouldn't be here in the physical world. The fact that we're all here in these bodies means that we're not perfected. So having accepted we're not perfected, we can allow for each other's inadequacies or failings with a little, you know, with a little compassion. I'm certainly ready to be able to try and work things out with whoever I'm with. But if whoever I'm with is full of hassles then I'm not going to be with him, am I? I'm gonna go with somebody else. I mean, that's really how things happened for me when I got tired of being with the Beatles. Because musically it was like being in a bag and they wouldn't let me out the bag, which was mainly Paul at that time. The conflict musically for me was Paul and yet I could play with any other band or musician and have a reasonably good time."*

What was the problem with Paul?

"It's just a thing like, you know, he'd written all these songs for years and stuff, and Paul and I went to school together. I got the feeling that, you know, everybody changes and sometimes people don't want other people to change, or even if you do change they won't accept that you've changed, and they keep in their mind some other image of you, you know. Gandhi said, 'Create and preserve the image of your choice.' and so different people have different images of their friends or people they see."

How did Paul see you?

"Well, I got the impression it was like, he still acted as if he was the groovy Lennon / McCartney. Because there was a point in my life where I realized anybody can be Lennon / McCartney, you know. 'Cause being part of Lennon / McCartney really I could see, you know, I could appreciate them – how good they actually are, and at the same time I could see the infatuation that the public had, or the praise that was put on them, and I could see everybody's a Lennon / McCartney if that's what you wanna be. But the point is nobody's special. There's not many special people around, and somebody else... If Lennon / McCartney are special, then Harrison and Starkey are special, too. That's really – what I'm saying is that I can be Lennon / McCartney too, but I'd rather be Harrison, you know."

April 25, 1970 – *Disc and Music Echo,* **Derek Taylor wrote** about why the Beatles left Paul McCartney. He started by explaining how outraged he was that Penny Valentine had called *McCartney* a "bitter blow." Paul had sent her a copy of the album. And here was Paul, exploring himself, discovering himself and trying to find his own post-Beatles personal musical identity, here he was opening himself, his heart, his art, his love to the world. Who was she to be so harsh? Who was she to suggest how cruel it was that her idol Paul would release such an album?

Taylor had received one, too, and, while it was not his favourite album, while it did not rival *Sergeant Pepper* or even *Revolver,* he still liked it, he appreciated how deeply personal it was.

This was Paul, just starting out.

He could not be a Beatle anymore because what the world knew as Beatles no longer existed. And it could never be recaptured. It had faded into a soul prison for four artists who needed to be free.

The memories would remain.

But no one left the Beatles, The Beatles left them. Now they were Paul McCartney, John Lennon, George Harrison and Richard Starkey, all trying to make their own way through a harsh world that judged them as Beatles.

A series of letters from readers on the same page concluded that on April 10th, 1970, the people who invented pop music died. An era was ending. Please do not let it happen.

— A Brief Cavern Club History —

For forty years, there has been a Cavern Club at 10 Mathew Street in Liverpool. The club opened in 1957 and was closed from 1973 until 1984. The original club was taken down in 1982 and the site was excavated. The bricks were saved and used to rebuild the club as it stands today.

The original plans from the original club were used to reconstruct it. The arches, the dimensions and the floor space are almost exactly what was there in the original Cavern.

There were three major differences:

Today's club occupies seventy-five per cent of the original site.

Today's club is deeper than the original, thirty stairs leading down rather than eighteen.

And with the original club, when you entered, the stage was immediately in front of you, now it is on the left.

— Postscript —
1971 *Melody Maker* Interview
with Paul McCartney

November 1971, *Melody Maker* **ran** an interview with Paul McCartney.   Paul talked about John Lennon and the break-up of the Beatles.

Said Paul, *"There was a bit of hype on the back of the* Let It Be *sleeve for the first time ever on a Beatles album.   At the time, the Beatles were very strained with each other and it wasn't a happy time.   It said it was a new-phase Beatles album, and there was nothing further from the truth.   That was the last Beatles album and everybody knew it.   Klein had it re-produced because he said it didn't sound commercial enough.*

"I just want the four of us to get together somewhere and sign a piece of paper saying it's all over and we want to divide the money four ways.   No one else would be there, not even Linda or Yoko or Allen Klein.   We'd just sign the paper and hand it to the business people and let them sort it out.   That's all I want now, but John won't do it.   Everybody thinks I am the aggressor but I'm not, you know.   I just want out.

"John and Yoko are not cool in what they're doing.   I saw them on television the other night and thought that what they are saying about what they wanted to do together is basically the same as what Linda and I want to do.

"John's whole image is very honest and open.   He's alright, is John.   I like his Imagine *album, but I didn't like the others.*   Imagine *is what John is really like but there was too much political stuff on the other albums.   You know,"* Paul joked, *"I only really listen to them to see if there's something I can pinch.*

"How Do You Sleep? I think it's silly.   So what if I live with straights?   I like straights.   I have straight babies.   It doesn't affect him.   He says the only thing I did was Yesterday.   *He knows that's wrong.   He knows.   And I know it's not true.*

"John wanted to do a big thing in Toronto [1969 Toronto Rock and Roll Revival] *but I didn't dig that at all.   I hear that before he went on stage he was sick, and that's just what I didn't want.   Like anybody else, I have been nervous because of the Beatles thing.*

"I wanted to get a van and do an unadvertised concert at a Saturday night hop at Slough Town Hall or somewhere like that.   We'd call ourselves Rikki and the Red Streaks or something and just up and play.   There'd be no press and we'd tell nobody about it.   John thought it was a daft idea.

"Before John was leaving the Beatles, I was lying in bed at home one night and I thought we could get a band together, like his Plastic Ono Band.   I felt the urge because we had never played live for years.   We all wanted to appear on a stage but not with the Beatles.   We couldn't do it as the Beatles because it would be so big.   We'd have to find a million-seater hall or something."

1974, John Lennon said about *How Do You Sleep,* *"It's not about Paul, it's about me.   I'm really attacking myself.   But I regret the association... well... what's to regret?   He lived through it.   The only thing that matters is how he and I feel about these things, not what the writer or the commentator thinks about it.   Him and me are okay."*

— Afterword —
1971 *Melody Maker* Interview
with George Martin

Do you remember how you met the Beatles?

Said Martin, *"Oh yes, very easily. Brian Epstein brought them to me, not to EMI... well, he had already taken them to EMI and they'd turned him down. I didn't know that until afterwards."*

Do you know who turned them down?

"The story is that first of all he took them to a guy who was the marketing manager – I don't think I'd better mention his name – and he played the tapes to two producers. Now, there were four producers at EMI at the time: Norrie Paramour, Norman Newell, Walter Ridley, and myself. Two of those four heard the tapes, and I didn't, so one of the other three is innocent! They said they weren't any good, so Epstein went away and played them to Decca, who showed an interest in them and brought them down for a test. It was fairly favourable to begin with, then later on, Brian found out that he'd got to bring them down for a second test while Decca made up their minds, and he got rather shirty about it. He'd tried other companies as well, I think... Pye, and Phillips.

"In desperation, he took the tapes to HMV in Oxford Street to get some lacquers cut, because he wanted to place the songs with a publisher, and the engineer there, Ted Huntley, thought the tapes were great. He took them upstairs to Sid Coleman, who ran EMI Publishing, and Sid liked them too and said, have you played them to EMI? Brian said yes, but nobody wants to know, and Sid told him to play them to me, because I was looking for something. Brian brought them round to me and that was that."

What songs were on the tape? Have you forgotten?

"No, I can remember. Your Feets Too Big was one of them. There was a motley collection, I think possibly Love Me Do was on it but I'm not sure. Certainly, the songs didn't knock me out. If fact, I wasn't knocked out at all, in defense of all those people who turned it down, it was a pretty lousy tape, recorded in a back room, very badly balanced, not very good songs, and a rather raw group.

"But I wanted something, and I thought they were interesting enough to bring down for a test. I said, bring them down from Liverpool, I don't want to go up there, and I'll have a look at them in the studio. Obviously, Brian inwardly groaned, thinking he was going to go through the same thing as Decca, but they came to London and I spent an afternoon with them in Number Three studio in Abbey Road. I liked them, I liked them as people apart from anything else, and I was convinced that we had the makings of a hit group but I didn't know what to do with them in terms of material."

Pop was in a slump at the time. Were you aware of that?

"Very much so. I was very envious of Norrie Paramour who had Cliff Richard, the big star. I'd been making comedy records, Peter Sellers, Charlie Drake, Bernard Cribbens, and I'd done it because I enjoyed it anyway. It was a way of giving Parlophone something different, and it was successful, so I became the Comedy King.

"I envied Norrie his success with Cliff, because every comedy record you made was a oncer, you had to start from scratch the next time around. Whereas if you had an artist like Cliff, once you'd got him up there, all you had to do was find a reasonably good song and give it to him, and you'd got a second hit. This, to me, was much easier, at least I thought so, and I was always looking for something of that sort.

"When the Beatles came along, I thought, well, I didn't know where I was going to get the song from, but they seemed a pretty good group and they seemed to have that kind of raw sound that people hadn't heard about yet."

What did they have that was so different? That they were raw? That they were a group and not a solo act?

"Well, I didn't recognise that, because the tapes weren't like that. They were occasionally singing together, but mostly they were alternating: sometimes, it was John, sometimes Paul, and sometimes George. If fact, my first sessions with them were looking for the voice. I thought they're great people, but who am I going to make the lead voice? I spent an afternoon with each of them in turn. I chucked out George pretty quickly, so it was either Paul or John."

Were they sharing the singing duties when they you met them?

"They were doing all those rock standards, Chains and Anna and so on, and they were doing them the way they heard the records, imitating the records. So they were singing together, but occasionally one would burst out in a solo.

"Then it suddenly hit me that I was being stupid, I was looking for a solo voice when I didn't need to, I should just take them as they were. Then we got rid of Pete Best, and Brian brought Ringo along. I was rather suspicious of him."

Why didn't you like Pete Best?

"He was the best looking of the group, which was rather curious, but he never joined in with the others. He was always a bit quiet, almost surly. But the basic thing was that I didn't like his drumming, it wasn't solid and he didn't bind the group together.

"I said to Brian that I didn't want to use him on the records, although he could do what he liked with him outside the studio, as part of the group. But there was no reason why I couldn't use a session drummer. No one was going to know. This was obviously the trigger, because the boys had been thinking of getting rid of him anyway, but they wanted someone to do the dirty work for them."

Did you like Ringo's drumming?

"I didn't give him a chance, to begin with. He suddenly turned up at a session. I didn't know he was coming and I booked Andy White, and I said, well, Andy's here and he's paid for, so he's going to play. You can join in on the tambourine if you like."

This was for *Love Me Do*?

"Yes, we actually did it again with Ringo playing drums, because when I heard him he was much better than Pete Best, he gave it more solidarity, and in fact, he was more raucous than Andy White, and it fitted the group anyway. He was pretty rough in those days, but pretty good."

That was actually Ringo on the single?

"Oh yes, but we had two versions of Love Me Do *and, in all honesty, I can't remember which was which. I think maybe the one Andy played on was on the album."*

Did you think of them as musicians? Guitarists? Composers?

"As composers, they didn't rate. They hadn't shown me they could write anything at all. Love Me Do *I thought was pretty poor, but it was the best we could do, they hadn't got anything else, and I hadn't got anything else to offer them either.*

"As players, they were quite adequate, they could play guitar pretty well and they had an uninhibited sound. The question of them being deep minds or great new images didn't occur to me, or to anybody, or to them, I should think. It was after we made Love Me Do *that I was determined to find a hit song for them. I was scouring the publisher's office, looking for material for our group, which nobody wanted to know about. EMI heard the Beatles, which they thought was a silly name anyway, and they didn't attach too much importance to it. Comedy man tries to get into pop field, you know. We hit number seventeen in the chart, which raised eyebrows, but only just, so I found them this song by Mitch Murray which I thought was just ideal for them to learn for the next session. When they turned up on the session, they said they didn't like it."*

What was the song?

"How Do You Do It. They actually recorded it but said they'd rather do one of their own numbers. I said that I hadn't heard anything of theirs that was any good, so they did How Do You Do It. John sang the solo, quite well actually, but he came to me and pleaded with me. He said, look, I think we can do better than this. If we write something better, can we do it? I said, Yes, but you're turning down a hit.

"They quickly came back with Please Please Me, *and I must confess, it knocked me out. They'd worked out all the little harmonies and it was super. I said, that's great, you've got your first number one hit. I was so confident about it and I gave* How do You Do It *to Gerry, and that became a number one, too, so I was justified both ways. That was the beginning of them."*

Did you think they would come up with another good composition as a follow up to *Please Please Me*?

"It all happened so fast then, events moved so quickly. Brian was pressuring them all the time to write new material, and they were caught up in this success whirlwind, and they wanted to continue writing. They'd come to me and say, what do you think of this? And that's how From Me to You *happened. As soon as we'd made* Please Please Me *I decided to make an album very quickly, and I brought them down for just one day.*

"We started at ten o'clock in the morning and finished at eleven o'clock at night and made the first album. Brian was also caught up on this success thing, and he wanted to load me with a lot of other stuff then, it was a kind of partnership: I'll give you the raw material and you give me the goods and we'll sell it. It was a very happy year but it was terribly hard work. I was in the studio the whole time, and I've never worked so hard in my life."

When did the Beatles' attitude begin to change? And when did yours? Towards each other and the music, that is.

"Even though they'd written their own songs, they had them as songs rather than as records. They weren't thinking in terms of records, they were thinking of a chorus, a middle eight and an ending. When I started off with them, I'd organise their beginnings and endings and their solos.

"It seems terribly elementary now, but when they sang the song first, I'd time the chorus, and when it came to one minute twenty seconds, I'd say, right, it's not long enough, go back to the middle eight, or else we'd have a little guitar solo or a bit of piano. It was all dead simple, and gradually the collaboration grew. It was just the four of them and if there was any keyboard stuff, I'd put it in. It wasn't until Yesterday *that we started using other instruments."*

When did you notice the odd construction in some of their songs?

"I can't really remember. They never noticed at all."

You never tried to change what they were doing?

"Not a bit. I recognised that those aberrations, so to speak, were part of them. It would have been silly to change them, because that would have destroyed their spirit. I don't think I ever quarrelled with them musically at all. The only time I ever really came to blows with them was over something quite different, which was a record sleeve. It was one that was never issued over here. They were dressed

up as butchers, and it came out in America. It was their idea of a joke."

Did John and Paul actually write together?

"Yes, but they also wrote separately. Please Please Me and From Me to You and I Want to Hold Your Hand were undoubtedly collaborative efforts. They'd sit down and literally construct the songs together. I can't remember the first individual songs, although obviously even before I met them, they were writing individually, but if you go through them, you can hear which of them are John-oriented and which are Paul-oriented. Yesterday is obviously Paul, and that's an interesting point because it was the first time we ever used anyone other than Beatles on a record. There was no one on that record but Paul and a string quartet."

How much did you contribute to Yesterday?

"What happened was that he had this song which'd been kicking around for a long time. He'd play it to me on the piano, and it was called Scrambled Egg. He was looking for lyrics all the time, and we all thought it was a good tune.

"When he'd finished it and he wanted to record it, I said that I couldn't see what Ringo could do with a drumbeat on a song like this. I told him the best thing to do was go down to the studio and just sing it, so he just played the guitar and sang. I honestly couldn't think of what to do with it, except to put strings on it. Paul said, what, Norrie Paramour stuff? Mantovani? No! Then I had the idea of using a string quartet, a very classical thing, and Paul thought that was a great idea.

It seemed to be quite the innovation at the time.

"It was. I spent a day with him, getting his ideas on how the strings should sound, and I went and wrote the score for the string quartet and recorded it."

Were they growing apart at all?

"Paul and John had their own identifiable styles. Paul was the syrupy one and John was the hard one. But the rift wasn't there, then. They were really a unit."

They must have been isolated, with all that pressure around them and on them.

"Even Brian was outside that little castle. Brian and I were looking on."

Was Brian involved in the music? Did he get involved, make suggestions, anything?

"Nothing at all. He was quite right not to. The relationship was fine, Brian was very much the businessman, fixing up all the dates and so on, and he had that tremendous air of... a snooty air with people which sold the Beatles as being more important. He had a great manner, really. He liked to be considered a part of the music.

"In fact, he was very hurt one day in the studio. The boys were downstairs and I was talking to them through the intercom. Brian picked up the mike and said, why don't you do such-and-such, and John said, Brian, you look after your money, and we'll look after our music. Brian flushed to the roots of his hair and never said any more. He was obviously very hurt by that."

Rubber Soul always seemed their finest album, the most perfect of them all. It was the last one that wasn't all dressed up?

"Yes, the last of the non-fabricated albums. I heard it again for the first time in ages while I was on holiday last year, and it sounded pretty good."

Revolver took them into new realms, using studio resources. Did they do that on purpose?

"I think so. The boys were curious all the time about the music and the world around them, and they were constantly exploring. I was trying to tell them as much as I knew about it, I'd spend some time with John, playing him some classical music, Ravel and so on, and it didn't come through to him very much. But they were into all sorts of things like Stockhausen... they discovered him very quickly in those days, and Tomorrow Never Knows was obviously influenced by him. I'd been doing some electronic music before they came along, anyway. I issued a single called Time Beat – d'you remember that? It was put out under the name of Ray Cathode, and I'd done it with the Radiophonics Workshop."

But was it the Beatles' discovery?

"They discovered Stockhausen for themselves. I guess we talked a lot about things and it's very difficult to put your finger on who discovered what. Tomorrow Never Knows though, they'd bought themselves tape-recorders and they'd started playing with them in their homes. I think Paul discovered it first. They got into making little loops for themselves.

"On any tape recorder, if you cover the erase head and put on a loop of tape, you can put on a sound and if you switch it off after a few seconds, it keeps going round and round, overdubbing itself. You can build up a funny whirring kind of sound, and by playing that at various speeds, they got all these weird sounds. For Tomorrow Never Knows they all went away and made loops at various speeds, and brought them to me. I'd play them on a machine, keep some, discard others, and we eventually ended up with eight loops of different sounds.

"We'd already laid down a basic track of John's voice, and the drums, and bass, I think, and we'd already put John's voice through a Leslie speaker, because he'd said to me, I want my voice to sound as though it is coming from a hill top in Tibet. Obviously, he was hung up on The Tibetan Book of the Dead. He wanted a voice in which you could hear the words, but it had to have an ethereal effect, so I put it through the Leslie and he was knocked out with it.

"Then putting all these loops on, we got eight tape machines and put one loop on each, and I fed each of those machines into the control desk so that by raising any of the faders at any moment, you could bring up the sound of any one particular loop. We already had the rhythm track and the voice, so then we did a mix, and brought up any loop we fancied at any particular time. That's how we got that effect."

Did you see all these innovations as being good for music in general?

"Oh yes, because by this time, we were so established that we could afford to take risks, and we could experiment. It was only one track on the whole album, and if people didn't like it, hard luck. It was an experiment, an indulgence, if you like, and we thought it was worthwhile."

There is apparently some controversy over how Eleanor Rigby came about. Do you remember how it started?

"Not the song, but I do remember the recording taking place. I had assumed that it was all Paul, in fact, I do remember, actually at the recording, Paul was missing a few lyrics, and want them, and going around asking people, what can we put in here? And Neil and Mal and I were coming up with suggestions. Rather pretty, really... everyone contributed things occasionally."

Was the arrangement the same as Yesterday?

"It was rather more complicated, in that I took as my model some writing of an American film composer, he's got the same name as the guy who runs The Northern Dance Orchestra, Bernard Herrman."

The guy who did the soundtrack for Psycho.

"That's right. He'd written for a film called Fahrenheit 451, and the string writing in that was great. That was my model for Eleanor Rigby. I worked a bit with Paul, getting his ideas on harmonies and so on, and that's how it evolved. It was comparatively easy because Paul was able to play the tune on the piano, and I could translate it for the strings in the style of Bernard Herrman."

And Sergeant Pepper...

"That was an incredible thing, because it took on its own character, it grew despite us. It was a complete change of life, a very long and arduous series of recordings, and I suppose that, looking back on it, it wouldn't have happened if the boys hadn't got into the drug scene. But I can also say that it wouldn't have happened if I hadn't been **not** on the drug scene, because if I hadn't been a normal person, I don't think Pepper would ever have been formed in that way, I don't think it would have been coherent."

Did you push hard to get it all together?

"No, I just had to be patient. You can't do much with a guy when he's giggling all the time."

Did it start as a normal album?

"Yes. It started of with Strawberry Fields, and that wasn't all that hung up. It was quite straightforward, and I love that, I think it's one of the best things they've ever done, and it was very much John's song. This was when the two of them became very separated to my mind.

"Strawberry Fields and Penny Lane were done at the same time, but they were completely different. One was very much Paul and one was very much John. It was in November of that year, we started off with Strawberry Fields and then we did When I'm Sixty-Four and then we did Penny Lane and then we had a break for Christmas. So that was the beginning of Pepper. We needed a single out so we put those two songs out, otherwise, I guess, they would have gone on the album as did When I'm Sixty-Four."

Where do you see the influence of acid and other drugs on Pepper?

"It was the beginning of psychedelia, the imagery in their little minds. They were ready for it in the creative way, they wanted something to blossom anyway, and if they hadn't been on drugs, it's possible something like that would've happened, but not quite so flowery, maybe. Certainly all the attributes to drugs afterwards were totally misplaced. Lucy in the Sky with Diamonds was honestly a phrase that young Julian Lennon had come out with. The song itself, all that stuff about floating downstream with garlands in your hair, obviously. It's a good song."

But without drugs...

"I'd dispute this with you. Was Salvador Dali ever on drugs? It's the same kind of surrealism."

What about the electronic effects, the sound effects, Mr. Kite?

"John got the idea of that from an actual poster, he often pinched things like that for his songs, and I thought it was a great idea. When he came to record it, he said he wanted to convey the impression of sawdust in the ring, to give the idea of a fairground and a circus.

"So I started working out my electronic sounds to make it just that. I got lots and lots of steam organ sounds, genuine calliope noises, which are tapes of Liberty Bell, Sousa marches, that kind of thing. I spent the morning with an engineer, put them all on one tape, and asked him to cut them up into sections fifteen inches long, which is about a second in length.

"He did that and they were all in a row on the desk. I said, now throw them in the air and pick 'em up and join 'em together. Inevitably, some were backwards and some were forwards, and when we played it back, it was a terrible mish-mash of sounds. That was fine, and we used it as a background noise. It was overlaid throughout the whole piece and then, on top of that, we put Mal Evans playing bass harmonica, and both John and I playing organ, I was on a Hammond and he was on a Lowrey. He was playing the tune and I was playing the harmonies, and the runs, because he said he wanted kind of swooping noises on it.

"To get that, I played chromatic runs going up and down on the Hammond, at half speed. We slowed the tape down, and went down an octave. I was quite pleased with that, it was a sound-picture thing, and I was doing, really, what I'd been doing with Peter Sellers, building up a little picture. Most of John's writing at that time was coming from little observations, like seeing the poster.

"The Day in the Life thing, the controversial bit about holes in the road which a lot of American journalists thought were puncture marks in your skin, was an extract from the Daily Mail."

Legend has it that you were the one who made Day in the Life into a song… from spare Beatle parts.

"No, let's explain that. John had this song, which started off with his observation, and his part was the beginning and the end, and Paul's was the middle bit. We started recording it with Paul on piano and John on guitar, and we decided we needed another riff in it, and Paul said, well, I've got this song – got up, got out of bed – and he was going to make a separate song. He said, you can use it if you like, put it in your one. Will it fit? They thought about it for a bit and decided it would work, and they wanted something different in it but didn't know what.

"They decided that they were going to put a lot of just rhythm in it, and add something later. So I said, let's make it a definite number of bars, let's have twenty-four bars of just rhythm in two places, and we'll decide what to do with them later. They said, how are we going to know it's twenty-four bars, because it's a long time? So we had Mal standing by the piano counting, one, two, three, and in fact, he had an alarm clock, because he was timing the thing as well, and it actually went off. On the record, you can hear Mal saying twenty-one, twenty-two, if you listen.

"When we'd done it, I asked them what they were going to do with those bloody great gaps. Paul said he wanted a symphony orchestra, and I said, don't be silly, Paul, it's all right having ninety-eight men, but you can do it with a smaller amount. He said, I want a symphony orchestra to freak out. So I said, if you really want one, let me write something for it. He said, no, I don't want you to. If you write it, it'll be all you. Let's have just something freaking out. I said, let's be practical, you can't get an orchestra in there and say, freak out, fellers, because nothing would happen. They'd just look around embarrassed and make a few funny noises. So I booked a forty-one piece orchestra, half the normal symphony orchestra, and I spent some time with Paul and John. I wrote out the obvious underlying harmonies, and during the main twenty-four bar sections, John and Paul suggested that we should have a tremendous shriek, starting out quietly and finishing up with a tremendous noise.

"So I took each instrument in the orchestra and, at the beginning of the twenty-four bars, I wrote down their lowest note, whatever it was, so that the cello for instance had a bottom C, and at the end of the twenty-four bars, I gave them their highest note related to the chord of E. And throughout the twenty-

four bars, I just wrote 'poco-a-poco gliss' and when it came to the session, I told the musicians that they had to slide very gradually up and those people in the woodwind who need to take breaths should take them at random. It was just a gentle slither.

"But when we came to do it, the boys said they wanted to make a real event of it. So they got all their friends to come along and dress up and, at that time, Mick and Marianne Faithfull came along, and all their Apple Shop friends – the Dutch people – and there must have been about forty of them, all freaking out with joss-sticks. Paul said, we're going to be in our flowers but we don't expect you to do that because we know you're not that kind of person. I said, thank you very much. He said, but I want you to wear evening dress, and the orchestra too. So I booked the orchestra in evening dress, and when it came to the point, Paul had bought a lot carnival gear, funny hats and false noses, and I distributed them among the orchestra. I wore a Cyrano de Bergerac nose myself. Eric Gruneberg, who's a great fiddle-player, selected a gorilla's paw for his bow-hand, which was lovely. It was great fun."

What was life like in those days when you were working with the Beatles?

"I never knew when I'd be in the studio. As like as not, it'd be ten o'clock one morning and – we're recording at eight o'clock tonight! No question of, can you be there? It was, you will be there. So one was constantly in a state of preparedness, and this was unfortunate where other artists were concerned. Up to the point of Let It Be, there was only one orchestration that was ever done by anybody else apart from me.

"I had conceitedly thought it was because they liked my style of scoring. I thought I was better than anybody else, and I was very upset when Paul rang me up and said that he wanted to do a score on a song that we'd been working together on anyway. I knew the song pretty well. He said, come at two o'clock this afternoon, and I said, sorry, Paul, I can't. He said, why not? And I said, I've got something else on, I'm recording Cilla. I said I'd go round and see him the next day. Apparently, he got Mike Leander to turn up at two o'clock, that's the only time he worked with anybody else."

What was the song?

"She's Leaving Home. Mike gave me the score, I booked the musicians, I altered the rhythm a bit, but not very much. It was basically Mike's score. I was rather upset by the peremptory way in which it was done. But it wouldn't have happened like that in the early days."

Lennon said something a bit nasty about you just recently. Show me some of George Martin's music, I'd like to hear some. Something like that. How do you feel about that?

"That's silly, of course. I guess I feel sorry for him, because he's obviously schizophrenic, in that respect. He must have a split mind, either he doesn't mean it, or, if he does mean it, he can't be in a normal state of mind at the time.

"The contrary thing is that, in June of last year, I was in the States and I did the David Frost Show with Diahann Carroll. Obviously, we talked about the Beatles, and I ended up playing the piano with Diahann singing, one of those terrible American show-biz things.

"It appeared to be quite a happy show, and I didn't think any more about it. Then about six weeks after I got back, I had a postcard from the Beverly Hills Hotel, written by John in his own fair hand, saying that he caught the Frost show, thought it was great, and it was so nice of me to say such nice things about him, and how he hoped that my wife and children were well, and Love from John and Yoko. That was the last time I heard from him, and that's the other side of the coin. He'd probably hate people to know that he was that sentimental."

What did you think of the group being involved with the Maharishi? Did you feel it hurt their music? Took them off course?

"No, they tried to convince me that I should take it up, but what they couldn't appreciate was that they were going through most of the things that people go through when they're adolescents, anyway. They were suddenly discovering new things, religion, mathematic arguments, the universe, as though no one else had discovered it before. I said, it's all right for people who like that sort of thing, but it's not for me, I'd rather go down to my cottage in the country and look at my pigs. So they did their little thing. I didn't honestly think it would last, and it didn't."

The White Album was their next major event, but it was harshly criticised, though I think there's some good songs on it.

"I didn't like it because there was too much material. They'd written an awful lot of stuff while they were out in India, and they'd come back just wanting to put them down. I said, okay, let's put them down and issue the best.

"But when we'd got them all down, they didn't want to ditch any of them, they wanted to make it a double album. There was such a variety of styles, there were obviously John songs and Paul songs and George songs, and there was no unity to the thing.

"After the unity of Pepper – you know, Pepper only became a unit when we put it together. It wasn't designed that way. It wasn't until I started piecing it together and cutting in sound effects and so on, that it really became a whole. I thought this was a good thing, and I was rather sad when we did the White Album that we'd chucked that out the window.

"I still wanted to do coherent work, and I didn't really persuade them to get down to it until Abbey Road, and even then, John was very against that. It was only Paul who really wanted the unifying bit. Curiously enough, I like the last bit of the White

Album, Revolution No 9, but a lot of people slated us for that."

How was it made?

"It was just an extension of Tomorrow Never Knows, a similar kind of thing with various tapes, and I guess this was largely influenced by Yoko, because it was her kind of scene. But again, I was painting a picture in sound, and, if you sat in front of the speakers, you just lost yourself in stereo. All sorts of things are happening in there. You can see people running all over the place and fires burning, it was real imagery in sound. It was funny, in places, too, but I suppose it went on a bit long."

Happiness is a Warm Gun?

"That was a great one, tremendous."

How did you get that rough, sort of seventy-eight-rpm effect?

"That's dead easy, anyone can do it. You just literally put on a scratchy surface and speed up the voices slightly. That song started off with my quoting to them from around the time of the Kennedy thing, a magazine headline, a sporting magazine…"

Guns and Ammo?

"Something like that, and that was the headline over a picture of a man with a gun in his hands. I showed it to John, and he made a song of it."

It's also the album where George comes into his own as a composer.

"Yes, he'd been awfully poor up to then, actually, some of the stuff he'd written was dead boring. The impression sometimes given is that we put him down. I don't think we ever did that, but possibly we didn't encourage him enough."

Was he allotted two songs per album?

"Not really. He'd write, with difficulty, and he'd bring them and we'd say, okay, we'll put them on the album then. But it was that way; we wouldn't say, what've you got then, George? We'd say, oh, you've got some more, have you? I must say that, looking back, it was a bit hard on him, but it was natural because the others were so talented. It was always slightly condescending, and it was a similar thing with Ringo. He'd come along with Octopus's Garden or something, he always wanted to do something, because he was left out in the cold. It wasn't until recently that George has really come through. I suppose Something was his breakthrough."

What do you think of Phil Spector's production of Let It Be?

"It was an unhappy album from the beginning, because this really was the time of dissent. It was before Abbey Road and I really thought that Let It Be was going to be the last album any of us did. They were all fighting like mad. John insisted that it was going to be a natural album, and he didn't want any faking, any of the Pepper stuff, any production. He said to me, your job is to make sure that we get a good sound. I don't want editing or overdubs of voices or instruments. It's got to be like it is.

"So we made it like that, and it was very tedious because they kept repeating the same things over and over again, and it's very difficult when you get to the twenty-seventh take to work out whether number thirteen was better than number nineteen.

"None of it was ever very good, none of it was perfect. It would have been if you could have edited things together. It had this rawness, and I could quite see the advantage of it, so we made up this album, which was an honest album, and that was it. It was left lying, and we recorded Abbey Road, *which was back to square one because we were able to produce it. I was much happier then, and after that."*

Did you know at the time that *Abbey Road* was going to be the end of it all?

"No, I really didn't. They'd got back, they were much happier with themselves. It was very much more of a produced album. We used a Moog for the first time, on George's Here Comes the Sun. *Everybody seemed to be working hard, and we'd got things nicely organised. It wasn't until after that that things started happening badly. I knew that John was going in the studios, doing some work on* Let It Be, *but I understood that, as they were making a film of it, they were doing some film tracks. When the record finally came out, I got a hell of a shock."*

Did you know anything about what was going on with it?

"Nothing. Neither did Paul, and Paul wrote to me to say that he was pretty appalled, if you'll forgive the pun. All the lush, un-Beatle-like orchestrations with harps and choirs in the background. And it was so contrary to what John asked for in the first place."

What's your opinion of what they have been doing individually?

"I have great admiration for George. He's done tremendously because it's a sort of devotion of duty, as far as he's concerned. We forced him into being a loner, I guess. He could never collaborate with anybody in his writing and, therefore, when the split came, he had more strength because he was forced to be alone. He learned an awful lot about producing, studio techniques, and so on, so that he was able – obviously, any one of them had the power, because they had the money, to spend as much time in the recording studio as they liked, and I know that, when George made his album, he spent six months doing nothing but overdubbing his own voice sixteen times and producing his album. To have the tenacity to do that, in itself, is something of an achievement, but to go along and actually produce good sounds and good music and good lyrics with it, is tremendous. I'm full of admiration for that.

"I think the other two have suffered by comparison, because they've each indulged themselves in their own way. John's became more obvious, in a way. Power to the People *is a rehash of* Give Peace a Chance, *and it isn't really very good. It doesn't have the intensity that John's capable of.*

"Paul, similarly, with his first album, it was nice enough, but very much a home-made affair, and very much a little family affair. I don't think he ever really rated it as being as important as the stuff he'd done before.

"I don't think Linda is a substitute for John Lennon any more than Yoko is a substitute for Paul McCartney."

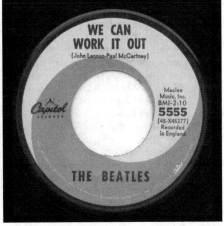

— Appendix One —
The Beatles' First Radio Interview

Recorded on October 28, 1962 at Hulme Hall in Port Sunlight, on the Wirral in England, this is the first radio interview with the Beatles. The interview was conducted by Monty Lister, with help from Malcolm Threadgill and Peter Smethurst.

Monty: It's a very great pleasure for us this evening to say hello to an up-and-coming Merseyside group, the Beatles. I know their names, and I'm going to try and put faces to them. Now, you're John Lennon, aren't you?

John: *Yes, that's right.*

Monty: What do you do in the group, John?

John: *I play harmonica, rhythm guitar, and vocal. That's what they call it.*

Monty: Then, there's Paul McCartney. That's you?

Paul: *Yeah, that's me. Yeah.*

Monty: And what do you do?

Paul: *Play bass guitar and uh, sing? ...I think! That's what they say.*

Monty: That's quite apart from being vocal?

Paul: *Well... yes, yes.*

Monty: Then there's George Harrison.

George: *How d'you do.*

Monty: How d'you do. What's your job?

George: *Uh, lead guitar and sort of singing.*

Monty: By playing lead guitar does that mean that you're sort of leader of the group or are you...?

George: *No, no. Just... Well you see, the other guitar is the rhythm. Ching, ching, ching, you see.*

Paul: *He's solo guitar, you see. John is in fact the leader of the group.*

Monty: And over in the background, here, and also in the background of the group making a lot of noise is Ringo Starr.

Ringo: *Hello.*

Monty: You're new to the group, aren't you Ringo?

Ringo: *Yes, umm, nine weeks now.*

Monty: Were you in on the act when the recording was made of *Love Me Do*?

Ringo: *Yes, I'm on the record. I'm on the disc. It's down on record, you know?*

Monty: Now, umm...

Ringo: *I'm the drummer!*

Monty: What's that offensive weapon you've got there? Those are your drumsticks?

Ringo: *Well, it's umm... just a pair of sticks I found. I just bought 'em, you know, 'cause we're going away.*

Monty: When you say you're going away, that leads us on to another question now. Where are you going?

Ringo: *Germany. Hamburg. For two weeks.*

Monty: You have standing and great engagements over there, haven't you?

Ringo: *Well, the boys have been there quite a lot, you know, and I've been there with other groups, but this is the first time I've been there with the Beatles.*

Monty: Paul, tell us. How do you get in on the act in Germany?

Paul: *Well, it was all through an old agent. We first went there for a fella who used to manage us, and Mr. Allan Williams of the Jacaranda Club in Liverpool, and he found the engagements so we sort of went there, and then went under our own...*

John: *Steam.*

Paul: *Steam...*

John: *...as they say.*

Paul: *As they say; afterwards, you know, and we've just been going backwards and forwards and backwards and forwards.*

Monty: You're not busy at all?

Paul: Well *yes, actually. Yes. It's been left-leg in all the war.*

Monty: George, were you brought up in Liverpool?

George: *Yes, so far, yes.*

Monty: Whereabouts?

George: *Well, born in Wavertree, and bred in Wavertree and Speke – where the airplanes are, you know.*

Monty: Are you all Liverpool types, then?

Ringo: *Yes.*

John: *Uh... types, yes.*

Paul: *Oh yeah.*

Ringo: *Liverpool-typed Paul, there.*

Monty: Now, I'm told that you were actually in the same form as young Ron Wycherley...

Ringo: *Ronald. Yes.*

Monty: Now Billy Fury.

Ringo: *In Saint Sylus.*

Monty: In which?

Ringo: *Saint Sylus.*

John: *Really?*

Ringo: *It wasn't Dingle Bay like you said in the Musical Express.*

Paul: *No, that was wrong. Saint Sylus school.*

Monty: Now I'd like to introduce a young disc jockey. His name is Malcolm Threadgill, he's 16 years old, and I'm sure he'd like to ask some questions from the teenage point of view.

Malcolm: I understand you've made other recordings before on a German label.

Paul: *Yeah.*

Malcolm: What ones were they?

Paul: *Well, we didn't make... First of all we made a recording with a fella called Tony Sheridan. We were working in a club called the Top Ten Club in Hamburg, and we made a recording with him called* My Bonnie, *which got to number five in the German Hit Parade.*

John: *Ach tung!*

Paul: *But it didn't do a thing over here, you know. It wasn't a very good record, but the Germans must've liked it a bit, and we did an instrumental which was released in France on an EP of Tony Sheridan's, which George and John wrote themselves. That wasn't released here. It got one copy. That's all, you know. It didn't do anything.*

Malcolm: You composed *P.S. I Love You* and *Love Me Do* yourself, didn't you? Who does the composing between you?

Paul: *Well, it's John and I. We write the songs between us. It's, you know... We've sort of signed contracts and things to say, that now if we...*

John: *It's equal shares.*

Paul: *Yeah, equal shares and royalties and things, so that really we just both write most of the stuff. George did write this instrumental, as we say. But mainly it's John and I. We've written over about a hundred songs but we don't use half of them, you know. We just happened to sort of rearrange* Love Me Do *and played it to the recording people, and* P.S. I Love You *and uh, they seemed to quite like it, so that's what we recorded.*

Malcolm: Is there anymore of your own compositions you intend to record?

John: *Well, we did record another song of our own when we were down there, but it wasn't finished enough, so, you know, we'll take it back next time and see how they like it then... Well... that's all from MY end!*

Monty: I would like to just ask you – and we're recording this at Hume Hall, Port Sunlight – Did any of you come over to this side before you became famous, as it were? Do you know this district?

Paul: *Well, we played here, uh... I don't know what you mean by famous, you know. If*

being famous is being in the Hit Parade, we've been over here – we were here about two months ago. Been here twice, haven't we?

John: *I've got relations here. Rockferry.*

Monty: Have you?

John: *Yes. Oh, all sides of the water, you know.*

Paul: *Yeah, I've got a relation in Clorton Village – Upton Road.*

Ringo: *I've got a friend in Birkenhead!*

Monty: I wish I had.

George: *I know a man in Chester!*

Monty: Now, that's a very dangerous thing to say. There's a mental home there, mate. Peter Smethurst is here as well, and he looks like he is bursting with a question.

Peter: There is just one question I'd like to ask. I'm sure it's the question everyone's asking. I'd like your impressions on your first appearance on television.

Paul: *Well, strangely enough, we thought we were gonna be dead nervous, and everyone said, 'You suddenly, when you see the cameras, you realize that there are two million people watching,' because there were two million watching that* People and Places *that we did... we heard afterwards. But, strangely enough, it didn't come to us. We didn't think at all about that, and it was much easier doing the television than it was doing the* [live performance] *radio. It's still nerve-wracking, but it was a bit easier than doing radio because there was a full audience for the radio broadcast.*

Monty: Do you find it nerve-wracking doing this now?

Paul: *Yeah, yeah.*

Monty: Over at Cleaver Hospital, a certain record on Parlophone – the top side has been requested, so perhaps the Beatles themselves would like to tell them what it's going to be.

Paul: *Yeah. Well, I think it's gonna be* Love Me Do.

John: *Parlophone R4949.*

Paul: *Love Me Do.*

Monty: And I'm sure, for them, the answer is P.S. I love you!

Paul: *Yeah.*

— Appendix Two —
Beatles Time Line

March 1957: John Lennon formed his first group, the Black Jacks. They later became the Quarrymen.

July 1957: Lennon met Paul McCartney.

July 1957: Paul joined the Quarrymen.

October 1957: Paul did his first live show with the Quarrymen at the New Clubmore Hall in Liverpool.

February 1958: George Harrison met the Quarrymen, and they liked his guitar playing so much they invited him to join the band.

March 1959: Richard Starkey joined Rory Storm and the Hurricanes.

August 1959: The Quarrymen, John Lennon, Paul McCartney, George Harrison, and Ken Brown, played at the Casbah Club which was owned by Pete Best's mother.

October 1959: Ken Brown left the group.

November 1959: John, Paul, and George continued to play together… as Johnny and the Moondogs. Even without a drummer, they passed an audition for TV Star Search at Liverpool's Empire Theatre.

January 1960: Lennon's friend from art college, Stuart Sutcliffe, joined the group when they talked him into buying a bass guitar after he sold one of his paintings.

May 1960: They changed their name to the Beatals.

May 1960: Tommy Moore signed on as the drummer and they changed their name to the Silver Beetles. With Moore, they auditioned for Larry Parnes; they also did a short tour of Scotland as a back-up band for singer Johnny Gentle.

July 1960: Norman Chapman joined up as their next drummer, but he was drafted and went up for National Service. At the time, the Silver Beetles had an assortment of gigs booked in Hamburg, Germany and around Britain. They changed their name yet again, this time to the Silver Beatles. They needed a drummer.

August 1960: Pete Best joined up to do the drumming. At that time, they became the Beatles and played their first gig in Hamburg.

December 1960: Back in Liverpool from Germany, the Beatles played at Litherland Town Hall. Their fans went a little crazy.

February 1961: The Beatles played their first gig at the Cavern Club, a lunch-hour show.

March 1961: The group played their first evening show at the Cavern Club.

Spring 1961: Stuart Sutcliffe quit the Beatles to stay in Germany and pursue his art studies.

June 1961: The Beatles were recorded for the first time, playing back-up for Tony Sheridan. Bert Kaempfert, the producer, also recorded them playing without Sheridan.

November 1961: Brian Epstein first saw the Beatles at the Cavern Club.

December 1961: The Beatles got together with Epstein for the first time. They accepted Epstein's offer to manage them.

January 1962: Brian Epstein arranged for an audition at Decca Records. Nothing came of it.

January 1962: The Beatles came in number one in the Mersey Beat poll of bands around Liverpool.

April 1962: Twenty-one year old Stuart Sutcliffe died in Germany of a brain haemorrhage.

June 1962: The Beatles auditioned for George Martin at EMI studios.

August 1962: At Martin's request, Pete Best was fired from the group. Ringo Starr joined the Beatles.

August 1962: John married Cynthia Powell.

October 1962: They released their first disc, *Love Me Do*, to modest sales.

January 1963: The Beatles did their first TV gig, Thank Your Lucky Stars. They played *Please Please Me*.

February 1963: The group recorded ten songs for their first album, *Please Please Me.*

April 1963: John Charles Julian Lennon was born.

August 1963: The Beatles played the Cavern Club for the final time.

September 1963: The Beatles received an award for Top Vocal Group of the Year at the Variety Club Awards.

November 1963: The term "Beatlemania" was coined by the *Daily Mirror*.

November 1963: Clark's Grammar School in Guildford, Surrey officially became the first school to suspend a kid for wearing a Beatle haircut.

January 1964: *Meet the Beatles* was released by Capitol Records in the United States. By February 15 it hit number one on the Billboard charts and stayed there for eleven weeks.

February 1964: The Beatles arrived in New York City where they performed on The Ed Sullivan Show. The estimated audience for their American debut was 73 million viewers. They performed *All My Loving, Till There Was You, She Loves You, I Saw Her Standing There* and *I Want to Hold Your Hand.*

February 1964: The Beatles did their first live American show at the Washington Coliseum, Washington, D.C.

February 1964: They did a gig at Carnegie Hall, New York City.

March 1964: Filming began on the Beatles' first movie. The name for the film was finalised when Ringo, after a late night studio session, made the comment, "*It's been a hard day's night, that was.*" Filming took eight weeks and cost half a million dollars.

July 1964: *A Hard Day's Night* premiered in London to good reviews from the papers and the fans.

August 1964: *A Hard Day's Night* opened in the States, also to a good reception.

February 1965: Ringo married Mary Maureen Cox.

February 1965: Filming began on the Beatles' second movie, *Help!*

June 1965: The Beatles were awarded MBEs (Members of the British Empire) by the Queen.

July 1965: *Help!* opened in London.

August 1965: *Help!* opened in the States.

August 1965: The Beatles played for 55,600 people at Shea Stadium in New York.

August 1965: The Beatles met Elvis Presley.

September 1965: Ringo and Maureen have their first child, Zak Starkey.

January 1966: George married Patricia Ann (Pattie) Boyd, whom he had met on the set of *A Hard Day's Night.*

March 1966: John Lennon caused an international uproar when he was misunderstood for saying the Beatles were more popular than Jesus.

May 1966: The Beatles gave their last real concert in England, at Empire Pool, Wembley.

August 1966: Brian Epstein held a press conference in New York to try to cool off the Americans with regards to the Jesus Incident.

August 1966: John apologised to the press and attempted to explain what he really meant by his comments about Jesus.

August 1966: The Beatles performed their last live concert, in San Francisco.

June 1967: *Sergeant Pepper's Lonely Hearts Club Band* was released in Britain. It made number one in the charts all over the world and received four Grammy Award, including Best Album of the Year.

June 1967: The first live, worldwide television satellite show, Our World, is aired, a two-hour event starring the Beatles. They played *All You Need is Love.*

August 1967: Ringo and Maureen have their second son, Jason Starkey.

August 1967: Brian Epstein died of a drug overdose; The Beatles missed the funeral.

October 1967: A memorial service was held for Brian Epstein in Abbey Road.

December 1967: *Magical Mystery Tour* was shown on TV in Britain. Roughly fourteen million people watched it; few of them liked it.

May 1968: John and Paul appeared together on *The Tonight Show starring Johnny Carson.*

July 1968: The animated film *Yellow Submarine* premiered in London.

July 1968: Jane Asher broke up with Paul McCartney.

August 1968: Cynthia Lennon filed for divorce on grounds of adultery.

August 1968: Ringo quit the band, walking out of a recording session for *The White Album.*

September 1968: Ringo relented.

January 1969: The Beatles gave their final performance together. They played live on the rooftop of the Apple headquarters in London. The event was filmed and the sequence used later in the movie *Let It Be.*

March 1969: Paul married photographer Linda Louise Eastman.

September 1969: John decided to leave the Beatles but he kept the news to himself to avoid interfering with the contract negotiations with EMI.

September 1969: The Beatles' final original album, *Abbey Road*, was released in Britain.

November 1969: John sent back his MBE award.

January 1970: The group's final recording session happened at EMI's Abbey Road studio. Paul, George and Ringo added a few finishing touches to George's song *I, Me, Mine* for the *Let It Be* LP.

April 1970: Paul announced the break-up of the Beatles. They would never play together again… although in 1995, George, Ringo and Paul completed a rough tape left by John, *Free as a Bird*. It was the first new Beatles hit in twenty-five years.